SYDNEY
BIOGRAPHY OF A CITY

SYDNEY
BIOGRAPHY OF A CITY

LUCY HUGHES TURNBULL

RANDOM HOUSE AUSTRALIA

Published by
Random House Australia Pty Ltd
20 Alfred Street, Milsons Point NSW 2061
Australia
http://www.randomhouse.com.au

Sydney   New York   Toronto
London   Auckland   Johannesburg
and agencies throughout the world

First published in 1999

National Library of Australia
Cataloguing-in-Publication data

Turnbull, Lucy, 1958–.
    Sydney : biography of a city.

    Bibliography.
    Includes index.
    ISBN 0 091 83905 X.

    1. Sydney (N.S.W.) – History. I. Title.

994.41

Internal design by Gayna Murphy, Greendot Design
Typeset in 11/15 pt Times New Roman
Typesetting and colour separation produced in Malaysia by The Color Gallery SDN BHD
Printed in Singapore by Tien Wah Press (PTE) LTD

Five Bells by Kenneth Slessor, reproduced with permission from Harper Collins

Page i: Beach in Middle Harbour, Port Jackson *(Wildlight Photo Agency)*
Pages ii–iii: View of Sydney Opera House and Circular Quay from Kirribilli *(Wildlight Photo Agency)*
Page iv: Bronte Beach with saltwater baths in foreground *(Wildlight Photo Agency)*

FOREWORD

EVEN SYDNEYSIDERS REFLECT with some wonder at the mystery by which Sydney grew from penal settlement to one of the world's most desirable, complex and glamorous cities. It is a matter for a kind of delight, for example, that some of the most famous early paintings of Sydney, which depict scenes in which the harbour remains the constant between past and present, were painted by transported convict artists such as Watling, Eyre and Lycett. These are some of the visions of Sydney which have shaped our sensibility. We are aware both of the quotient of exile apparent in the renderings of early European art in Sydney and the quotient of total at-home-ness in ourselves. We are stimulated by the contrast.

But there are other Sydneys of which even we, let alone the world, are ignorant; Sydneys which impinge upon our vision only marginally, through buildings or monuments scattered here and there throughout the streets. In delineating these, the city's less well known urban eras, as well as its more notorious or visible phases, Lucy Hughes Turnbull has provided an account which will be read and used with delight both by Australians and by those millions who will, in future, inevitably wish to visit and savour this great pleasure port of the South Seas.

She enquires, for example, into the geological formation of the Sydney Basin from the time it broke off from its mother, Gondwana, and answers the question as to why Botany Bay is gently shelving and shallow, and Sydney Harbour such a deep anchorage, with a folded, hilly and thus humanly refreshing terrain. She introduces us to the pre- and post-European lives of Sydney's plentiful Aboriginal people, who would be the first of their kind to be puzzled, disorientated and decimated by contact with energetic, blindly certain European culture.

Turnbull gives an appropriate weight to the splendid activities of the Sydney anti-transportationists, whose peaceable but eloquent rebellions were all to do with ending British convict transportation to Australia. Their activism introduced representative government of a sophisticated nature in Macquarie Street, Sydney, and thus to New South Wales. But we hear with equal appropriateness of Sydney's first great bust, the depression of the 1840s. It came close to obliterating a city where land prices had already taken on a pattern of reaching periodically fantastical levels and then falling with equal suddenness. For, as the author shows us, despite the town's reputation for rootless hedonism, real estate and the price of land would always be two of Sydney's compulsions, engaged in not only by the wealthy, but also by the humble cottager. Real estate was well established as a civic obsession by the time any suburban sprawl began.

One phase of Sydney's history other than convictism of which we were generally permitted to taste in the classrooms of our childhood was the gold rush. Lucy Hughes Turnbull vividly relates the story of how Sydney was transformed by gold and, in particular, she recaptures the manic exaltation of that high hour. Now the city took on an international lustre it would probably not reacquire until the 1980s, and the relentless spread to suburbs such as Woolloomooloo, Paddington, Surry Hills, Redfern, Glebe and Balmain began in earnest.

But again, as I implied above, what is particularly welcome in this book are the well-textured renderings of Sydneys which are not well known even by Sydneysiders. The Sydney of the late 1860s, for example; the city of the suburban building boom of the ten years from 1879; the Sydney which, despite that, was considered by one visitor to lack the 'metropolitan tone' of Melbourne; the Sydney of the centennial of European founding in 1888; the Sydney of the 1890s, riven by industrial conflict, by the social outfall of the partial failure of Australia as 'working man's Utopia', and the larrikin groups or 'pushes' of the poorer areas of the city. The pace and significance of the 1890s—the push towards a federal Australia in an era when grand public buildings absorbed some of the discontented populace in that favourite of Sydney industries, construction, and when Federation was succeeded by an outbreak of bubonic plague—are all grandly reproduced here by the author.

We begin, in fact, to see Sydney as a series of struggles: struggles of politics and sects; struggles between place and architecture; struggles between the free spirits and the wowsers; and struggles of ethos between respectability and larrikinism. And, appropriately for a city of immigrants, a city which had once seen convict grandees such as Simeon Lord, Turnbull's Sydney was, and would remain, despite any other pretensions it tried to maintain, the city *par excellence* of the *parvenu*. Through every transformation, she reminds us, the reputation of Sydney as 'a wild and lawless town' remained, sometimes unfairly, sometimes with obvious truth.

This life story of Sydney argues, amongst other interesting propositions, a line of descent from the Currency Lads of the 1820s, the diggers of the goldfields from whom Australian soldiers borrowed their name, and the Australian diggers of World War I, and is eloquent on the question of how, from these inputs, there emerged a consistent image of the Sydneysider or, at least, of New South Wales people. It was, of course, often a male figure who was depicted, crass in some eyes, forthright in others. 'He was fearlessly himself,' said one observer of World War I troops from New South Wales. 'He behaved in the Strand as he would have done on a Saturday night in Wagga Wagga.'

By 1931, a severe year in a Sydney struck hard by the Great Depression, the population had reached 1.25 million. The city now proved that it could be as harsh an environment for the unemployed worker as any place on earth, except for the undeniable boon of a milder climate than Europe's. And, in spite of hardship, like most New World cities in the twentieth century, Turnbull's Sydney took vigorously to the automobile—330 000 registrations in 1939, we are told—and to radio and the 'talkies'.

So we see, through Turnbull's eyes, the racy Sydney of World War II, and the postwar city transformed in character and enlarged in lifestyle by immigrants, themselves becoming its enthusiastic citizens. The impact of Menzies, a prime minister who, while urging us to honour our Imperial connections, made a number of decisions which guaranteed an increasing internationalism in Australian policy, is nicely canvassed; as is the impact of one of those decisions—participation in the Vietnam War. And so through further booms and busts, Turnbull brings us to the city of the present. This is the city of the Olympics, prodigious in extent and notable in its glories, self-confidence, international renown, unresolved questions.

IX

Having completed the general version, the author then has the generosity to descend into welcome detail on the regions of the city: the Quay, The Rocks, the Bridge, the eastern edge of the city, the major building and monuments, Darling Harbour; Sydney Harbour itself and its ferries and 18-footers and yachts; the islands, the sundry delightful bays and beaches; Kings Cross—ever the focus of raucousness and urban blues—and Potts Point; Darlinghurst, Surry Hills, the elegant eastern suburbs; the sedate northern ones, the northern beaches; half-gentrified, half-raw Redfern and South Sydney; the southeastern and southern suburbs; the vast and thickly populated western suburbs which dwindle away into semi-rural properties which, in time and almost inevitably, will themselves become suburbs.

Sydneysiders will be engrossed by the insights into their own suburbs, and by the shifting phases of local human occupation. But this is once more the touchstone of Turnbull's biography of our splendid town. In giving this tale to the world, in providing resounding history and splendid guidebook in one, Lucy Hughes Turnbull has done more than a local favour.

TOM KENEALLY
January 1999

ABOVE: An aerial view of Sydney Harbour at 16 000 feet taken in 1966 by photographer David Moore.

CONTENTS

PREFACE

OVER THE PAST FIFTEEN YEARS, it has become clear that Sydney was a very different place to the one I remember as a small child in the early 1960s. In my mind's eye, I can still conjure dim pools of early memory: the sensation of the sun as it streamed onto the city streets and through the large, timber windows of old buildings; the well-worn interiors that shone with the patina of age and the passage of thousands of feet; old theatres with grand stairways and rich architectural detail. The old images of Sydney seems to lie beyond the physical world, but they are not yet entirely erased in many people's minds. In a sense, they are like ghosts beneath the concrete and steel of the late twentieth century. These old ghosts are as much part of my childhood as the sinuous shape of Sydney Harbour and the sand and surf of Bondi Beach. Unlike the built environment, however, the harbour and its beaches have always been an elemental memory for generations of Sydneysiders both before and after 1788.

These persistent images which characterise Sydney up to the present day are a source of consolation when everything else, both physical and social, seems to be in a state of permanent flux. The city's growth over the past fifty years has transformed it into an energetic urban centre within our geopolitical sphere, the Asia–Pacific rim—a region that half a century ago, in the early post-colonial era, did not exist even as an idea.

Sydney is no longer so young. Its origins are firmly rooted in the eighteenth century. Like the sandstone upon which much of it lies, Sydney was built up, layer upon layer. It will always be a work in progress. There was no short-term frenzy of economic activity that uniquely marked Sydney, as has been the case with some other cities. No grand urban scheme has ever been executed here that has shaped or limited the city's growth. As the city has been built up, the suburbs have sprawled ever outwards, sometimes with apparent disregard to the economic, social or environmental costs.

In this book, I have tried to explore how Sydney has become the place it is and to chart the way the city has developed. Sydney has been created by the constant interplay of different forces—physical, historical, political, social and cultural. Sometimes, Sydney has been the principal stage upon which the events and ideas that have shaped it have been played out— the early years of the colony, the first contact with Aboriginal Austalians, and the first democratic urges of the nineteenth century. Then, as European settlement fanned across the continent, Sydney's growth was sometimes the result of events and ideas that were principally played out elsewhere in Australia or in other parts of the world. These events have been refracted onto Sydney like light through a prism, but are no less important because they are indirect.

I have often pondered the effects that growing up in different cities might have on people's perceptions of place or sense of belonging. To use two Australian examples, does growing up under the southerly light and the flat, wide and wisely laid-out streets of Melbourne create a different sense of space, light and urban correctness? Does growing up in steamy Brisbane in a house built one storey off the ground with mangos and avocados growing in the backyard create a different idea of what an urban environment is—and should be? As someone who has not spent any extended time in either Melbourne or Brisbane—or in any other urban part of Australia—I will never know the answer to these questions, but I have wondered to what extent growing up in Sydney has shaped my spatial consciousness and sense of belonging.

The first part of the book looks at Sydney through prehistory up to the present day. The latter half looks at the different physical components of Sydney by trying to put them in some historical and cultural context. This journey starts (where else?) at Sydney Cove, and moves through the city, then to the harbour and the suburbs. Each component of this vast, sprawling Sydney has its own stories to tell.

Any attempt to interpret such a great city can only be partial, so I apologise in advance for inevitable omissions and errors. Trying to bridge the distances between local, regional and national development has sometimes been a challenging task, but no exploration of the Sydney region would be complete without trying to provide some overall picture of greater Sydney, even if it can only really be a series of snapshots.

This book would never have been written without the love and support of my family. Malcolm, Alex and Daisy Turnbull—I can never thank you enough for helping me take the time to explore the many facets of the place we call home. Thank you also to Sandy Grant and Adrian Collette for your early support of the book, and to my publisher Deb Callaghan and editor Siobhan O'Connor for carrying the project through. To all those who helped me discover what I needed to know, thank you as well. As well as the many librarians and local experts, I would like to thank Tim Flannery and Val Attenbrow at the Australian Museum, who taught me about the geographic and Aboriginal pre-history of Sydney. Thank you to those who gave their time to tell me about their city. Thank you all for that most precious gift, your time.

I also owe a great debt to the late Kenneth Slessor, that acute and lyrical observer of Sydney in the mid-twentieth century. Like no other writer before or since, Slessor treated Sydney as the subject of much of his work. He had the capacity to breathe life into an otherwise static picture of the pre-war city I was too young to know.

CHAPTER ONE

A BIRD'S-EYE VIEW

Where's the steward?—Bar-room steward? Berth? O any Berth will do—
I have left a three-pound billet just to come along with you.
Brighter shines the Star of Rovers on a world that's growing wide
But I think I'd give a kingdom for a glimpse of Sydney-Side.

Run of rocky shelves at sunrise, with their base on ocean's bed;
Homes of Coogee, homes of Bondi, and the lighthouse on South Head
For in loneliness and hardship—and with just a touch of Pride—
Has my heart been taught to whisper, 'You belong to Sydney Side.'

O there never dawned a morning, in the long and lonely days,
But I thought I saw the ferries streaming out along the bays—
And as fresh and fair in fancy did the picture rise again
As the sunrise flushed the city from Woollahra to Balmain;

With the sunny water frothing round the liners black and red,
And the coastal schooners working on the loom of Bradley's Head;
With the whistles and the sirens that re-echo far and wide—
All the life and light and beauty that belongs to Sydney-Side.

And the dreary cloud line never veiled the end of one day more,
But the city set in jewels rose before me from 'The Shore'.
Round the sea-world shine the beacons of a thousand ports o' call
But the harbour-lights of Sydney are the grandest of them all!

Excerpt from 'Sydney-Side', HENRY LAWSON, 1898

THE BEAUTY OF SYDNEY HARBOUR has been etched into the souls of locals and visitors for thousands of years. No other city makes a more spectacular first impression. Approaching Sydney by air, the modern traveller flies down the rocky, honey-coloured coastline in the bright early morning sunshine and then across the ultramarine harbour fringed with green-grey bushland. The aeroplane banks over the city's shiny skyscrapers, often giving a fleeting glimpse of the great surfing beaches on the coast, then finally descends into Sydney Airport on the shores of Botany Bay, where Sydney's modern history began.

Sydney is one of the world's great maritime cities. There is no other city in the world of which it can more truthfully be said that the best things in life are free. Everyone has easy access to the things that make Sydney great—climate, harbour, beaches and parks. While it is true that the coastline and the harbour are some distance from the bulk of Sydney's population in the western half of Sydney, the roads and the railways all lead to the historical centre of the oldest and largest city in Australia, and that is on the harbour, close to the sea.

Sydney is home to almost 4 million people.[1] Most of Australia's population clings to the coast, as if thrown out to its maritime margins by some great centrifugal force. Australia's three biggest cities—Sydney, Melbourne and Brisbane—lie on the fertile crescent of land on the southeastern corner of the continent. This is also where most of the nation's food is produced. Sydney sits at the centre of this fertile sliver, almost halfway between Melbourne, the second-largest Australian city, and Brisbane, the third-largest.

Sydney is a city full of newcomers. In 1991, 30 per cent of the population were born overseas, and just over one in five Sydneysiders were born in a non–English-speaking country. Therefore, in a certain sense, Sydney is not just a city but a social laboratory. It has travelled a long way since 1788 when the First Fleet arrived. Back then, the region was occupied by a few thousand Aborigines who had lived their lives undisturbed for thousands of years. This soon changed. In the early days of European settlement—or invasion—colonial Sydney was no more than a camp, a struggling and hungry penal outpost perched precariously on the coast of a huge, largely unknown and relatively arid continent. How it has developed from these humble origins is the subject of this book.

In the past fifty years, Sydney has shrugged off the dull grey mantle of Anglo-Celtic provincialism to become a lively and vibrant city. The more sombre tones and ambience of British cities never suited the city's strong clear sunlight, the warm climate which lent itself so well to life out of doors, or the upbeat, optimistic personality of Sydneysiders.

Despite the huge impetus for urban growth fed by the wool boom of the 1830s, the gold rushes of the 1850s and the long boom of the nineteenth century, there was not a significant degree of racial or cultural diversity in Sydney until after 1945. It was only from the late 1940s that large numbers of non–English-speaking immigrants started to arrive, many of them seeking a new life far away from war-ravaged Europe. The traditionally homogeneous nature of Sydney's population was the result of carefully honed colonial, and later national, immigration policies, directed towards restricting high levels of immigration from Asian countries. The changes that followed this greater social and cultural diversity are now a central part of Sydney's urban fabric. One obvious change is the increasing popularity for outdoor dining in Mediterranean-style cafés. The changes to life in Sydney in the past fifty years have, however, extended far beyond eating habits.

High postwar population growth went hand in hand with economic and physical growth. Property speculation and development, since early colonial days a source of wealth creation close to the hearts of many Sydneysiders, became a major form of economic activity—with huge consequences upon the built environment of the city proper as well as the suburbs. It seems as if the city will always be a work in progress, never fixed architecturally in any particular point in time as many cities of the Old World are. On a sadder note, too many of the city's grand old architectural landmarks (and much of the city's social heritage) fell victim to the wrecker's hammer when they should not have. Some of the casualties were tragic.

The changes to Sydney in the latter half of the twentieth century have been more than just physical. The narrow, isolationist attitudes of the late nineteenth and early twentieth centuries have melted away and a confident and independent culture has emerged. Sydneysiders are no longer defensive about their city, and they no longer deferentially seek approval from foreign

3

BELOW: Easterly view of Pyrmont, Ultimo and Darling Harbour and the city centre beyond before the Anzac Bridge was built and the extensive redevelopment of the Pyrmont peninsula in the 1990s. Note the old Glebe Island Bridge in the centre of the picture and a portion of the Glebe Island Container Terminal to its left.

visitors. This is a big change from the 1950s and 1960s, when the standard approach to visitors—particularly well-known ones—was to ask them within minutes of their arrival what they thought of the place—and to demand a positive response.

Sydney is antipodean, which suggests inversion, compared to Europe anyway, and the British Isles in particular. In the early years of the colony, the manifestations of strangeness were often sought out, and even exaggerated. Not many British readers back home would ever take the journey out to the Antipodes to verify the claims against the reality. The climate was reversed—it was summertime in December, and winter in June. That was only to be expected. Another aspect of inversion was the landscape itself.

Usually, rivers rise in high country, which gradually flattens into coastal plains before running into the sea. The opposite happens in Sydney. Rivers that run through the Sydney Basin have their origins in the low, flat country of the Cumberland Plain, and further along that course cut their way along the rocky sandstone country before they reach the sea at Port Jackson and Broken Bay. For every inversion, there is a reason, but it was not until only quite recently, with the development of the theory of continental drift or tectonic plate movement, that the curious topography of Sydney could be explained.

About 470 million years ago, what is now the Australian continent was part of Gondwana, a mega-continent which included Antarctica, India, Africa, Arabia, South America, New Zealand and New Guinea.[2] Two hundred million years ago, large mountain ranges stood to the east, south and west of Sydney. A great, fast-flowing river sprang from these mountains and ran northward across where Sydney, and much of the eastern edge of Australia, lies. Over millions of years, the river laid down sediments as it flowed and these sediments were compressed to form Sydney's sandstone, out of which some of the city's finest architecture has been built. The sandstone is subtly layered in colours that range from white to yellow to grey, orange and red—depending on what particles the ancient river was carrying, and the speed at which the river was travelling at the time. The layering of the sandstone is most easily seen along the coastline, and at the heads of Sydney Harbour.

Over millions of years, the Gondwanan river system weakened. As the rivers slowed, finer particles of sediments were laid down. These materials were compressed to form the Wianamatta shale soils of Western Sydney. These soils are more fertile than sandstone— although that is not saying a great deal. It was on these shale-based soils that the earliest experiments in developing Australia's pastoral industry took place before the Blue Mountains were crossed successfully by the colonists and westward expansion of settlement began.

As Gondwana drifted northward the eastern sections sheared off. They formed the bedrock of New Zealand and of Norfolk and Lord Howe islands. Other sections, or landmasses, sank as they drifted east—and now lie beneath the Tasman Sea. This is why some parts of what was left behind, including the cliffs and headlands of Sydney's coastline, look so brutally severed. The separation between southeastern Australia and the eastern fringe of Gondwana occurred between 80 and 60 million years ago. A map of the Tasman Sea and the Australian continental shelf tells an interesting tale. The shallower depths of the eastern Tasman Sea reveal where the sunken ancient Gondwanan landmasses lie.

In the course of this geological activity, the area around Sydney became a 'hot spot'. The edges of its basin were uplifted and moulded like soft, warm putty. This was when the sometimes craggy, but always curvy, undulations on the harbour's foreshores and huge sandstone plateaux to the north and south were created. On the western side of Sydney, more mountain building, in the shape of today's Blue Mountains, was taking place. The course of the rivers in and around Sydney changed from a north–south direction and flowed east. The rivers had to cut through these 'new' mountains, or hilly plateaux as they ran towards the sea. The Hawkesbury and Parramatta rivers lie on or near geological fault lines created at the time of the mountain building.

The narrow gap between the heads of the harbour and its irregular course through the undulating landscape have had important consequences. Sand and other sediments have built up in irregular patterns on the drowned river valley floor, depending on the width of the harbour and the level of exposure to tidal and ocean currents. This is why there is a sometimes bewildering range of water depths in the harbour. For example, Sydney Harbour is 50 metres deep beneath the Harbour Bridge, one of the narrowest parts of the harbour, yet only 18 metres at the heads where ocean currents have created a huge sandbar. These effects are in stark contrast to the flatter, wider and more regular landscape around Botany Bay, less than 10 kilometres to the south, which was never a geological 'hot spot'. The sea floor there is shallower and more even, and this has encouraged the growth of sea grasses and therefore more fish (and better fishing) than there is in the harbour itself.

When the Ice Age ended between 6000 and 20 000 years ago, sea levels rose and land, including the coastal river valleys, was flooded. Port Hacking, Sydney Harbour, Pittwater and Broken Bay were formed. Sand from the ocean floor was washed up by the rising sea to form Sydney's beaches. Today, the city's thirty ocean beaches are spread discontinuously along 60 kilometres of coastline from Broken Bay in the north to Port Hacking in the south. The beaches around the harbour and further to the south have soft, fine, light golden sand. The northern beaches are made from redder and heavier Narrabeen sandstone, formed at an earlier time by the ancient Gondwanan river, when it was running faster.

Far beneath the sandstone and shale lie earlier coal deposits, created when the climate was warm and humid. A primitive forest of ferns and ancient conifers lay in a huge, swampy river basin that extended from Newcastle to Wollongong. Over millions of years, this forest decayed and became compressed and fossilised into the massive coal deposits that lie beneath the sandstone. Fortunately, these coal deposits lie so far beneath Sydney that they are not economic to mine—although this did not stop some people from trying to do so (without success) in the late nineteenth and early twentieth centuries. The coal seams at the rim of this huge coal deposit on the South Coast and along the Hunter River valley are extensively exploited and today coal is Australia's largest export earner and the source of Sydney's electrical power.

Through the Sydney area run two small, mostly tidal rivers: the Parramatta River which rises in the northwest and becomes Sydney Harbour, and the Georges River that flows into Botany Bay. For many years before the evolution of Gondwana was understood, it was hard to explain how Sydney's waterways were created by these two small rivers which had no great mountains to feed them.

The largest river in the Sydney area is the Hawkesbury–Nepean. It curves around the perimeter of the Sydney Basin, north around the fault line at the foothills of the Blue Mountains, skirts the edge of the Cumberland Plain in Sydney's west and the Hawkesbury Plateau to the north, turns eastward, cuts through the sandstone plateau to Sydney's north and flows into the sea at Broken Bay, 50 kilometres north of the city. On the other side of the Hawkesbury lies the Central Coast, which is undergoing rapid suburban transformation and has one of the fastest-growing populations in the greater Sydney metropolitan region.

Sydney Harbour is one of the finest deep-water harbours in the world. The grand sandstone cliffs of North and South Head protect it from strong wind and sea swells. Within it, the sandstone ridges and jagged headlands protect 250 kilometres of sandy and rocky foreshore. Much of the land on the northern side of the harbour is hillier and higher than that on the southern side, because the fault line, along which parts of the Parramatta River and Sydney Harbour lie, tilts northward to the Hawkesbury Plateau. As the harbour runs westward it becomes the Parramatta River, and the scenery becomes less topographically dramatic.

On the western section of Sydney lies the Cumberland Plain. Not much of this plain exists today in its native state. Unlike many of the harbour foreshores that were saved from residential settlement by enthusiastic political agitation early in the twentieth century, advocacy of the importance of the Cumberland Plain to the ecosystem of Sydney and the Hawkesbury River did not become a political issue until late in the twentieth century.

The antipodean strangeness of the flora and fauna was often commented on by European observers. Trees and bushes were not deciduous in the 'normal' sense—the bark of trees, rather than their leaves, shed seasonally. The early settler Louisa Meredith wrote:

> [I]nstead of the 'fall of the leaf' here we have the stripping of the bark, which peels off in certain seasons in long pendent ragged ribands, leaving the disrobed tree almost as white and as smooth as the paper I am now writing. At first I did not like this at all, but now the slim stems of a young handsome gum-tree seem a pleasing variety amidst the sombre hues of an Australian forest.[3]

The year-round shedding of evergreen trees is still a matter of some consternation to tidy suburban gardeners, who are happier tending trees and plants with less messy habits. As Surgeon John White, a keen amateur naturalist and member of the First Fleet, wrote in his journal in 1790:

LEFT: *Raper Drawing No. 67 Emu of Port Jackson, George Raper, 1791, ink and watercolour (The Natural History Museum, London)*

One of the strangest animals encountered at Port Jackson by the European colonists was the emu. This large bird compensated for its inability to fly by running at great speed to avoid being hunted and shot.

1

2

ABOVE: When a stuffed platypus was sent to London from the colony to exhibit an example of the native fauna, many people thought this strange creature was an elaborate hoax. Platypus, *C. A. Leseur (Image Library, State Library of NSW)*

ABOVE: The city skyline today, looking south from Taronga Zoo across to Farm Cove and the Royal Botanic Gardens, Fort Denison, in the foreground, was built in the mid-nineteenth century. *(Marcus Clinton)*

ABOVE: The fireworks display on Sydney Harbour on New Year's Eve is one of the most spectacular events in the city's calendar. (*Australian Tourist Commission*)

ABOVE: Sydney's annual Gay and Lesbian Mardi Gras Festival, which culminates in the colourful parade along Oxford Street, draws revellers and participants from around the globe. (*Australian Tourist Commission*)

ABOVE: An image by convict artist Joseph Lycett, showing Aborigines using fire to hunt or 'smoke out' kangaroos from densely wooded countryside. *Plate 17*, Aborigines using fire to hunt kangaroos, *c. 1775–1828, Joseph Lycett, in his* Drawings of the natives & scenery of Australia & Van Dieman's Island, 1830 *(National Library of Australia)*

BELOW: An Aboriginal funeral procession on the southern shores of Sydney Harbour, as depicted by Joseph Lycett. *Plate 20*, An Aboriginal Funeral, *c. 1830, Joseph Lycett, in his* Drawings of the natives & scenery of Australia & Van Dieman's Island, 1830 *(National Library of Australia)*

The trees of this country are immensely large, and clear of branches to an amazing height. While standing, many of them look fair and good to the eye, and appear sufficient to make a mast for the largest ship; but, when cut down, they are scarcely convertible to any use whatsoever. At the heart they are full of veins, through which an amazing quantity of an astringent red gum issues. This gum I have found very serviceable in an obstinate dysentery that raged at our first landing. When these trees are sawed, and any way exposed to the sun, the gum melts, or gets so very brittle, that the wood falls to pieces. How any houses, except those built of the cabbage tree, can be raised up, the timber being so exceedingly bad, is impossible to determine.[4]

Most of Sydney's (and Australia's) native flora—the eucalypts, melaleucas and acacias—is of the dry sclerophyll type. They have learnt to live with drought, bushfire and low soil fertility. Nature has even harnessed the heat of a bushfire, which is the trigger for seed propagation for some species. Regeneration of the Australian landscape after bushfire is an extraordinary phenomenon for eyes adjusted to other climes. The new growth from the charcoal-coloured tree trunks is a determined assertion of an ability to survive in an apparently hostile environment.

Bushfires still pose a real, and relatively frequent, threat to the vegetation of Sydney. Many of them are lit by lightning or are caused by spontaneous combustion in hot, dry weather. In some incidents, arsonists are also responsible. The most serious Sydney bushfires in fifty years raged around the periphery of the city in January 1994. Multiple fires ringed Sydney, and thick brown smoke made the air almost unbreathable tens of kilometres away from the fires. Smoke engulfed the entire city and ash fell in the central business district and the inner suburbs. Most of the Royal National Park to Sydney's south was burnt out, and several people lost their lives. Other areas to the north of Sydney, including the Lane Cove National Park and Frenchs Forest, were also seriously affected, as were many thousands of hectares of the Blue Mountains.

One of the trees which is most evocative of the Sydney sandstone landscape is the gnarled and tenacious *Angophora costata* (smooth-barked apple) which thrives on the wetter sandstone country around the harbour. It will grow anywhere it can, even out of sandstone rocks, cleaving them with its strong root system as it matures. The beautiful *Angophora* is so well adapted to infertile sandstone soils that it does not thrive anywhere else. There were tall stands of *Angophora* and blackbutt (*Eucalyptus piperata*) around Sydney Cove in 1788. Beneath these trees and along the shorelines grew banksia, acacias, wattle and cabbage palms (*Livistonia australis*).

The native Port Jackson fig is a strong presence in Sydney's parks and along the harbourside. It often stands near its larger, lusher and statelier cousin introduced from further north, the Moreton Bay fig. There are many fine old specimens of these trees in the Domain, Centennial Park, and in other parks around the harbour. For some Sydneysiders, the sight and sounds of bats flying over the Moreton Bay figs of the Domain are one of the most vivid images of summer in the city.

One of the saddest phenomena around the sandstone country on the harbour foreshores and the coastline is the demise of many trees which thrived before the advent of European colonisation. Some species such as *Angophora* had adapted over thousands of years to the infertility of the soil and, in doing so, became intolerant of new introduced nutrients, or fertilisers. This became problematic as settlement spread and the soil was 'improved' making the native flora less able to defend itself from new invasive weeds such as lantana.

On the more fertile Wianamatta shale soils to the north and west of the harbour, the great, tall blue gum forests grew where the soil was deep and the rainfall was high. The North Shore area of Sydney was once completely covered with this forest. Where the rainfall was lower and the soil shallower, blue gum gradually gave way to sparser turpentine and ironbark forests. The main home for these forests in Sydney was the land which lay between the southern edge of the city and Parramatta. West of Parramatta, the forest receded to drier woodlands of grey box and forest red gum. This is the land where Australia's pastoral industry was founded. John Macarthur and Samuel Marsden, both founders of the wool industry in Australia, wasted no time in taking advantage of this opportunity.

8

European settlers have also made a strong mark on Sydney's vegetation. One of the first exotic imports was the Norfolk Island pine, introduced by George Johnston, the military leader of the Rum Rebellion which deposed Governor William Bligh in 1808. At first, it was imagined that this tall (but brittle) tree would provide tall masts for the British navy; Johnston recognised its possible decorative uses. Tall, dark Norfolk Island pines can be seen along some of our beaches, such as Manly and Palm Beach, and in the older harbourside suburbs. Another nineteenth-century import is the jacaranda, a native of South America. In early November, its blaze of bright blue flowers is a harbinger of the hot weather of summer to come. The jacaranda season also heralds the onslaught of end of academic year exams at universities and schools, and, for many longer-term Sydneysiders, the blooms of this beautiful exotic tree are a reminder of the long and frantic days (and nights) at exam time.

For the Europeans, the most bizarre feature about the strange new continent was the fauna. As James O'Hara observed in 1817:

> Nature may be said to have in this country indulged in a whim. She sometimes mimics herself in giving to smaller animals, such as the native rat, the general form and characteristics of the kangaroo; she gives to a great variety of species, the false belly of that animal. The whole animal creation appeared to be different from that of every other region.[5]

The kangaroo, already observed by the naturalists and crew of the *Endeavour* on Cook's voyage to the South Seas in 1770, was an object of continued interest. Western naturalists had never observed the suckling of offspring in the pouch before. The kangaroo seemed to come in all sizes, from the large ones, which weighed up to 68 kilograms, to minuscule kangaroo rats. As Surgeon John White wrote:

ABOVE: Manly beach looking southwest to the city skyline—'seven miles from Sydney and a thousand miles from care'.
The natural bushland at Dobroyd Head (at centre), part of Sydney Harbour National Park, is just one of many such
pockets of native vegetation to be found throughout Sydney.

> Every animal in this country partakes, in a great measure, of the nature of the Kangaroo. We have the Kangaroo opossum, the Kangaroo Rat, etc. In fact every quadruped that we have seen, except for the flying squirrel, and a spotted creature, nearly the size of a Martin, resembles the Kangaroo.[6]

Members of the First Fleet were amazed by the muscular power of the kangaroo's hind legs which enabled it to jump in strides of up to 9 metres, and the heavy tail, which was used as a counterbalance and as a weapon in fights with rival kangaroos and other animals. In the early years of the colony, kangaroos and emus lived in the Governor's Domain on the eastern edge of the town. The Governor's Domain, now known simply as the Domain, was a haven of natural bushland for these indigenous animals until the middle of the nineteenth century. Later, its greatest claim was as the place where anyone could engage in free speech.

The variety of birds and animals fascinated many members of the First Fleet, and later visitors to Sydney. Among them were the cockatoos, both sulphur-crested and the rarer and bigger red-tailed black cockatoo, galahs, rainbow lorikeets, king parrots, crimson parrots (later named 'rosellas', an abbreviation of Rose Hill, where they were often found), sacred kingfishers, kookaburras and the blue wren (also known as the 'superb warbler')—all captivated observant European settlers. Some of these birds were and still are raucously loud; for some, this raucousness added to the sense of being in a strange new land. Most intriguing of all was the bird later known as the emu, which stood up to 2.1 metres tall and was unable to fly. It made up for this deficiency by being able to run at great speed. The emu, like the kangaroo, was also a source of food for Aborigines and the early colonists.

Other mammals, such as the brown and black cat-like marsupial quoll, have not survived European occupation and settlement. The destruction of their natural habitat, and predatory instincts of domesticated cats and dogs have claimed these poor creatures. The quoll was described as being about 24 inches (60 centimetres) long with 'the countenance [which] much resembles that of a fox, but [whose] manners approach more nearly to those of a squirrel'.[7] Other victims of the growth and prosperity of Sydney are the rabbit-sized marsupials called bandicoots, especially the long-nosed bandicoot.

Fish and shellfish were not as prolific as had been hoped by the First Fleeters. Their presence was seasonal and concentrated in the warmer months, as opposed to the ready year-round supply the colonists wished for. The most highly prized fish was what we now call the snapper, but which were called 'helmet fish' in the early years of the colony.[8] There were also sharks of 'enormous size'. Aborigines were understandably fearful of them. One of the Aborigines with whom the early settlers came into contact was a boy called Bondel, whose father had been killed in battle, and whose mother had been eaten by a shark.[9]

The abundant shellfish around Sydney's waterways were a staple form of food for Sydney's indigenous inhabitants. The discarded shells were built up over many years into shell middens, which were used by the colonists as the only available source of lime mortar for their earliest buildings. The famous Sydney rock oyster is cultivated on the Hawkesbury River.

Sydney is a subtropical city. It sits on the meteorological boundary between temperate winter-rainfall country to the south, and tropical summer-rainfall to the north. This means it can rain, often quite heavily, at any time of the year. The driest months are in the late winter and early spring months of August, September and October. Sydney's climate becomes drier to the west: the average rainfall on the coast is 1200 millimetres a year, but west of Parramatta it is a much lower 800 millimetres. Averages, however, can be misleading, and should never be heavily relied upon, especially in Australia. Sydney, like most of Australia, often experiences extremes in climate, 'from droughts to flooding rains', to quote Sydney poet Dorothea Mackellar.

Sydney's rainfall, and most of Australia's, is greatly affected by the El Niño Southern Oscillation (ENSO), a phenomenon which has only been understood in recent years. ENSO is responsible for the wide range in weather patterns, from humid and wet to either warm or cold, dry weather. When an ENSO event occurs, the constant east–west trade winds across the Pacific Ocean stop blowing. There is a massive transfer of a warm body of water from the east coast of Australia and other parts of the western Pacific Ocean towards the eastern Pacific, and the coastlines of South and Central America.

Colder water means less cloud formation on the Australian coastline, and therefore less rain. The converse is also true: when eastern Australia is exposed to drought, parts of the western coasts of South and Central America experience abnormally wet weather. The cycle of ENSO can be anywhere from two to ten years. In most parts of Australia, drought is not uncommon.

In Sydney, when it rains it often pours. Day after day of dreary light drizzle is unusual. The city does, however, have the highest rainfall records for one- and two-hour periods of all the cities and major towns in Australia, including those in the tropical north. These records are 118 millimetres in one hour and 194 millimetres in two hours.[10] This is quite an achievement!

Sydney's location between the colder temperate Melbourne and steamily subtropical Brisbane places it in the middle of the range, latitudinally speaking, of the climatic variations for Australia's biggest cities. Mild winters and warm, sometimes humid and thunderstorm-prone summers mean that Sydney's climate is usually equable with relatively few extremes of hot or cold. The average maximum temperature in January is 26°C, and in July it is 16°C. Hot summer afternoons on the coast are tempered by onshore cooling nor'-easters. These can become quite strong in the late afternoons before they peter out in the cool of the evening. A summer heatwave, which seldom lasts more than a couple of days, is usually relieved by the southerly buster which blows itself out in a few hours and brings with it a welcome cool change. January and February, however, can be torpid and humid. Long, steamy days and persistent heavy summer rainfall can be enervating.

In winter, the harshest winds are the westerlies and southerlies. The winter equivalent of the southerly buster are southerly gales. They are stronger, can last for more than a week, and can be wild and dangerous. Winter southerlies travel from the Antarctic, across the cold and formidable Southern Ocean to Melbourne, then over the Snowy Mountains and Great Dividing Range to Sydney. Most of the shipwrecks along the Sydney coastline have happened during these gales. Dry westerlies and northwesterlies can be cold in late winter, when they start to blow. They warm up during spring and summer. Sometimes they seem to be drying everything in their wake as they carry waves of dust from the hot continental interior.

Everyone is entitled to his or her preferences, but many agree that Sydney is at her most beautiful in the sharper, clearer and less hazy light of autumn, winter and early spring. This is when the breezes and humidity of summer have died away and the sky is at its bluest. The sun hangs lower in the sky, casting shadows over the landscape and architecture, giving a sense of greater clarity and definition.

People who are used to living in a less congenial climate might say that life is too easy. Sydney, some might argue, lacks the dignity and gravity of purpose that big cities (such as Melbourne) with more temperate climates claim for themselves. On the other hand, people living further north suggest that Sydney's winters are unendurably cold. Some days are cold, but not many, and these are easier to bear than month after month of tropical torpor, when heat and humidity force one as far indoors as freezing temperatures on a cold winter's day.

12

The Aborigines, unlike European colonists, lived almost symbiotically with the landscape as semi-nomadic hunter–gatherers. Survival on this infertile continent was sometimes precarious, and ensuring an adequate food supply played a central role in the Aboriginal way of life. They adapted the landscape by the skilful use of fire. Some parts of Sydney's landscape were fashioned by the Aborigines to attract the marsupials they hunted. The understorey of scrubby woodland was burnt so that new grass could be encouraged to grow, and game would come to graze upon it.

Despite the delicate balance between humans and nature that had existed for thousands of years, the first European settlers (the more observant of whom had noticed the park-like appearance of the Sydney area) wasted no time in fashioning the environment to their own uses, without any appreciation of the consequences. This was done in an insensitive manner, and in ignorance of the subtleties of the landscape and the climate. Within a few years, the bushland around Sydney was facing a challenge greater than any bushfire or flood it had ever experienced.

The well-spaced, park-like nature of the forests in the Sydney region at the time of European colonisation was commented upon by the early explorers and colonists. Sydney Parkinson, who travelled with James Cook on the *Endeavour*, wrote that 'The country looked very pleasant and fertile; and the trees, quite free from underwood, appeared like plantations in a gentleman's park.'[11] This Arcadian view was confirmed by Arthur Bowes Smyth when he sailed into Port Jackson with the First Fleet on 26 January 1788:

[D]istinct plantations of the tallest and most stately trees I ever saw in any nobleman's grounds in England, cannot excel in beauty those [which] nature now presented to our view. The singing of the various birds amongst the trees, and the flight of the numerous parakeets, lorikeets, cockatoos, and macaws, made all around appear like an enchantment; the stupendous rocks from the summit of the hills and down to the very water's edge hanging over in a most awful manner from above, and forming the most commodious quays by the water, beggared all description.[12]

Appearances were deceiving, however, and it did not take long for the promise of the early days of the colony to fade. The first successful attempts at establishing European agriculture were made, not along the coast or the harbour, but inland on better soils, in places such as Parramatta, Liverpool and along the Hawkesbury.

Land clearance was the most urgent practical priority from January 1788. It was not an easy task. The tools the First Fleeters had brought with them were designed to be worked on European softwoods, not the hardwoods that stood around Sydney Cove and throughout the rest of the countryside. The sandstone soil was some of the most infertile in the world. As agricultural activities moved west, trees were felled on the banks of the Hawkesbury–Nepean. This created large-scale erosion and the disappearance of much fertile alluvial soil during floods. In 1803, Governor King, one of the colony's early administrators, tried to arrest this problem by forbidding the clearing of trees and shrubs within 10 yards (9 metres) of the river bank. Like so many others in those days, this governmental edict was ignored.

Civilising the land became synonymous with razing all the vegetation, as the perceptive author and artist Louisa Meredith observed in 1839:

> The system of 'clearing' here, by the total destruction of every native tree and shrub, gives a most bare, raw, and ugly appearance to a new place. In England we plant groves and woods, and think our country residences unfinished and incomplete without them; but here the exact contrary is the case, and unless a settler can see an expanse of bare, naked, unvaried, shadeless, dry, dusty land spread all about him, he fancies his dwelling 'wild and uncivilised'.[13]

The nature of the growth and transformation of Sydney has not always been perfect. A statement made in 1879 still has some resonance today, although there has been some improvement in recent decades:

> The fairy godmothers of Sydney gifted her with a noble site, magnificent surroundings, and the finest building material in the world; but a combination of disorder, narrow mindedness, impecuniosity, greed, jealousy, venality, have retarded her progress, and done their best to destroy her fair frame, and bring reproach upon her. But she is a handsome, and a progressive city in spite of it all, and if she maintains her present rate of progress, and finds capable and patriotic men to preside over her councils, she may yet sit among the nations, one of the proud cities of the universe, and claim with justice her boasted titles of the pearl of Australia and metropolis of the Antipodes.[14]

13

It is only in the past twenty-five years that there has been a significant communal interest in the nature and quality of the built environment, and this is still too sporadic. The administration of the city has been splintered into the hands of many bureaucracies with different responsibilities and values, both at the local council and state government levels, and the decision-making processes and their outcomes are sometimes hard to comprehend. Although things have been improving, a city such as Sydney deserves much more than just a few flashes of outstanding architecture and planning; however, like an unusually attractive person, the city still manages to stand out for its beauty, no matter how unflatteringly and drearily dressed it can sometimes be.

By the early years of this century, most of the tall forests of the Sydney region had disappeared, particularly in the more accessible areas to provide materials for the building industry, and wherever else the course of the railways and tramlines brought new suburban development. This expansion was just a dress rehearsal, however, for the transformation brought about by the advent of the motor vehicle and the postwar economic boom. New garden suburbs were hungry for fresh land and subdivision of grasslands and woodlands proceeded as fast as land could be released from private or government ownership. It seemed only geography could limit the growth of Sydney, and sometimes even this was not enough. Many homes were built on the rocky and precipitous land around the upper reaches of the harbour in areas such as Killarney Heights and on the rocky plateaux above the northern beaches, destroying much native bushland in the process. Further south, the scenic country around the lower reaches of the Georges River was gobbled up by suburban subdivisions. The limits to the physical growth of the metropolis are still not discernible.

The total area of Sydney is almost 2000 square kilometres. Its footprint on the earth's surface is as big as London's, which has more than twice the population, and that of Beijing's, which has a population of 19 million.[15] Most of the growth in the population is occurring on the outskirts of the city.

The main reason that Sydneysiders are so spread out is that home ownership has long been an important part of Sydney's—and Australia's—way of life. Home ownership is a critical ingredient in the idea of Australia as a worker's paradise, accessible to members of all social classes. It is often seen as more of a right than a privilege, and one which politicians ignore at their peril. Nearly 70 per cent of Sydney's population live in owner-occupied homes.[16] The standard block of land in the suburbs is large—a quarter of an acre, or 1000 square metres, typically 20 metres wide and 50 metres deep—so Sydney has a huge, apparently insatiable appetite for land.

Until recent times, the back yards of these suburban homes were often bleak, treeless, bare patches of land strewn with bits of old rubbish and the home of the clothesline and later the Hills hoist—that once ubiquitous rotary clothesline which came onto the market in 1945. In the past twenty years, many of these back yards have become landscaped, even terraced, patios with built-in barbecues and swimming pools. Home improvement, gardening and landscaping are big businesses now.

Although the early settlers may not have agreed, it is extremely fortunate for contemporary Sydneysiders that so much land proved unsuitable for agricultural development, because today Sydney is virtually ringed by national parks. There is the Royal National Park to the south, Ku-ring-gai Chase National Park to the north, the Blue Mountains, Wollemi, Yengo and Dharug National Parks to the west and northwest, and the Sydney Harbour National Park.

Sydney has, since the early colonial period, been home to the 'larrikin' and his predecessor, the 'currency lad'. These expressions refer to young *men* only, an important phenomenon in shaping the culture of Australian society. Of the 1030 members of the First Fleet, there were only 188 women, and the consequences of the imbalance in the population have only been erased in recent decades.

The 'currency lad' was a term coined to refer to Australian-born boys of European descent. The implication of the expression was that they were, like the colonial currency of the day, worth less than their British, or 'sterling', equivalent. As Surgeon Peter Cunningham described them in 1827,[17] these new Sydneysiders were energetic, courageous and quick-tempered, with an independent mind. They were also very proud of their country and tended towards clannishness. This clannishness led to a willingness to settle disputes physically, often in a street fight. Their sisters, the 'currency lasses', on the other hand, were mild-tempered, modest, credulous 'children of nature', who loved swimming and the outdoor life, and did not rank chastity as the highest of virtues. Many of Sydney's early colonial women had to struggle to survive in a male-dominated and masculine world by forming attachments to men who could protect them—such as members of the Marine Corps, and prosperous emancipist traders. Other women took matters into their own hands and established their own businesses. Some, like Mary Reiby, did both.

In the mid-1850s, the clannishness of Australian society adapted to, and further evolved in the goldfields of New South Wales and Victoria. It then filtered back in the later decades of the nineteenth century as Australia became more and more urbanised, and its population concentrated in the large capital cities. The legend of the 'digger'—a term still used for Australian soldiers at war—was most famously expressed at the populist and democratic Eureka Stockade led by Peter Lalor. The democratic spirit of the goldfields also seeped into Australian popular culture. The less palatable side of the legend of the digger became evident in the emergence of that late–nineteenth-century creature of Sydney, the larrikin.

Larrikins in Sydney formed gangs, or 'pushes', that roamed their own particular patch of the inner city—Woolloomooloo, Millers Point, The Rocks (which had various pushes divided along sectarian lines) and Surry Hills to name just a few. Larrikins intimidated people who were not members of their push, and generally got up to various degrees of mischief. The outsiders larrikins preyed upon could be members of other pushes, unwary passers-by or people from different racial backgrounds, such as the Chinese. But there were various strains of larrikins and larrikinism, and some were more menacing than others. Mark Twain, for

ABOVE: Pillow fight demonstrating athletic prowess at Bondi Surf Carnival in the mid-twentieth century. The sun-bronzed lifesaver became an Australian cultural icon and was once a dominant feature of the ideal of masculinity.

16

example, thought the Sydney larrikin was less of a threat than he was imagined to be, and that Sydney was a relatively safe place at night.[18] Some of Sydney's more colourful people have possessed a beguiling form of the larrikin streak. Hallmarks of this streak are irreverence and disrespect for authority and social or intellectual pretension. It will be interesting to see whether this predominantly Anglo-Celtic trait persists in the twenty-first century, with rapid growth of the proportion of the population of non–English-speaking background since 1945.

Unable to match the clannishness of the currency lad and the larrikin, women for many years played a subservient role in Sydney's life, as they did elsewhere around the world. This subservience was even more marked in a society where physicality and bravery were more important attributes than intellectual endeavour, and where the main locus of social activity was the pub, which was never female territory. In recent years, the relative status of women has risen and they have become active in fields that were previously the exclusive domain of men. Despite this rebalancing, strong-minded women who manifest the female variant of the larrikin streak are subject to the ambivalent comment: 'She's a bit of a character, isn't she?' This is often accompanied by non-verbal expressions that suggest confusion and even bewilderment rather than approbation. In the past it has been hard, even for women who inhabit the upper reaches of society, to assert themselves and play roles of influence as they could do more easily in England and Western Europe, where the ability to converse and discuss ideas was better developed.

Another consequence of the long years when Sydney was dominated by a heavy cloak of traditionally masculine values (even if it was leavened with larrikin irreverence) is the high profile of the gay and lesbian community today. This community makes a significant and noticeable contribution to Sydney's culture, most conspicuously during the month leading to the Gay and Lesbian Mardi Gras Parade, and in everyday life in many inner-city suburbs, such as Darlinghurst, Surry Hills and Newtown. This is something that Sydney and San Francisco have in common, as well as their physical beauty. It could be that the open presence of gay culture in these cities today is a reaction to the cities' strongly masculinist, frontier-like origins, and, at least in Sydney's case, an ongoing idealisation of masculine culture. For example, early–twentieth-century images of perfectly formed, bronzed lifesavers have a certain homo-erotic quality simmering beneath the surface. In the second half of the twentieth century, this undertone percolated to the forefront of public consciousness with the emergence of social liberalism and tolerance from the mid-1960s onwards.

In the past fifty years, there has been much scholarly and popular discussion of the strengths and the weaknesses of Australian culture and the Australian personality.[19] The egalitarian and noble qualities that are part of the currency lads, diggers and larrikin tradition have a darker side. The soft underside of egalitarianism is mediocrity, and the desire to cut down 'tall poppies'. The negative aspect of group solidarity, or 'mateship', is a sneaking disrespect for individualism, diversity and outspokenness, and the desire to make all things as close to 'normal' as possible. Sometimes this cynical mistrust of outspokenness and individualism means that the motives and *bona fides* of any person who tries to achieve something out of the ordinary are automatically questioned. Politicians are frequent victims of this attitude.

The levelling urge in Australian society was probably imported here from Britain in 1788, but its effects were magnified in the new colony, where the English class system was not well established. It is usually wise to sound a caveat before expounding on any collective phenomenon—stereotypes, good or bad, are often misleading, even though they might sometimes strike a chord. In Sydney, however, these tendencies are sometimes thrown into sharper relief. Being the biggest and brightest Australian city, it has a higher concentration of tall poppies—and Sydney is sometimes considered a bit of a tall poppy itself. These tall poppies may be artists, politicians, business people or anyone else in the public spotlight. There is no cult of celebrity here, at least not in the same form as exists in the United States. If a Sydneysider does bump into someone famous, they may approach him or her in the friendly and familiar manner of a long-lost friend. This can be disconcerting for a visitor accustomed to more remote formality and respect. The outsider's ability to recover from this familiarity is sometimes the basis on which his or her personality or character is judged.

The dangers of the darker side of the seductive, lotus-like lifestyle Sydney has to offer have been well articulated by leading Sydney-born Australian artist John Olsen, who has lived outside Sydney for nearly thirty years:

17

I really love the light and atmosphere and the *laissez-faire* lifestyle. But I am also very aware that it is a blue bitch. I know its destructive force and think it can destroy people by seducing them. It's basically a very undisciplined city and underneath, for all its brilliance, it doesn't love. It's careless with its people. At a certain point after I had become well known I could see myself becoming sucked into this vacuum, this bluey ooze, and it was a terrifying feeling.[20]

The harsh and mostly infertile physical environment and the drought-prone climate that makes the supply of water and feed for grazing stock often so precarious mean that survival is more of a challenge than it is in other parts of the New World such as the United States and Canada. Not only has the general economy been strongly affected by drought at various times, but it has also been driven by the prices of commodities such as wool, wheat, beef, coal, gold and other minerals. Both these factors have worked to create strong 'boom and bust' cycles in the economy. The busts have made life tough, not only for people on the land, but also for people in cities such as Sydney that have depended on high volumes of trade and associated business activity to fuel prosperity.

The democratic ideal in Australia—and Sydney—is often expressed as the right to a 'fair go', rather than the right to be protected by some formal declaration of the Rights of Man. This Australian reliance on a more implied and less intellectualised right to be treated fairly may be, in part, an outcome of the realities of the struggle for survival in a hostile environment, where 'fair' outcomes are more important than the democratic processes and ideals that underpin them. Another outcome of the survival mentality is a sometime slap-dash approach, that near enough is good enough. This is well expressed in the optimistic expression 'She'll be right, mate.' This attitude has sometimes prevailed where it should not have.

Sydney has undergone a major change in the patterns of employment and economic activity since the early 1970s. There has been a sharp and, for many, a painful decline in the number of jobs in the manufacturing industry caused by declining levels of tariff and other forms of protection to certain industries, which has been only partially offset by growth in the finance and services sectors. The relatively harmonious shift in employment patterns is one of the more remarkable features of Sydney's (and Australia's) recent history. Between 1972 and 1991, the number of people in Sydney employed in manufacturing shrank from 385 000 to 219 000 or by 43 per cent, while the population of Sydney has grown by over a third.[21] Now, just 14 per cent of the population are employed in factories, while over 15 per cent of Sydney's population work in the financial and property services sectors.

Just as in any city, Sydney's affluence is concentrated. Most of the more expensive suburbs lie around the harbour and along Sydney's eastern fringe, close to the beaches. The affluent areas run north–south from the leafy North Shore to Cronulla. The less affluent suburbs lie to the west and southwest, and, to a declining degree, the inner city.

There is a perceptible annual rhythm to life in Sydney. New Year begins with a massive fireworks display from the Sydney Harbour Bridge, Darling Harbour and the tallest building

ABOVE: An engraving of Circular Quay in 1874, taken from the *Illustrated Sydney News*. Sydney Cove, site of the first settlement by European colonists, is still a focal point for Sydneysiders and visitors.

in the city, AMP Tower. The fireworks are accompanied by street parties around The Rocks. A couple of days after that the Festival of Sydney, a program of cultural events begins. It runs until the end of the summer holidays on Australia Day on 26 January. Highlights of the festival are Symphony Under the Stars, Jazz in the Domain, and Opera in the Park (the latter performed by Opera Australia)—all of which are held in the Domain. Another major summer event for those who prefer pop and rock music is the Big Day Out held at Homebush Bay. The many attractions of the Sydney Festival are so considerable that many Sydneysiders have begun to think twice before leaving town for the summer. For those less culturally inclined during the summer holidays, there are always the harbour, the beaches and the surf, cricket Test matches and the Colonial Classic at Homebush. The main Australia Day focus is around the harbour and at Sydney Cove, the site of the first settlement. There is a Great Ferry Race, a Tall Ships Race heralded by the spectacular display of the fireboat spraying water to clear the path of the tall ships. In another event on the harbour, a prize is awarded to the best-dressed boat (and its crew) just before the start of the Australia Day evening fireworks.

Chinese New Year, which falls either in late January or early February, has recently become another important summer date in the Sydney calendar. Chinese performers and the public celebrate the New Year in Chinatown, at the southern end of the central business district.

February is an important month in the gay Sydney calendar. A series of events leads up to the Mardi Gras, held in either late February or early March. Mardi Gras is the greatest source of tourist income in Australia—even including sporting events. Thousands of people from Sydney and all over the world come to watch the spectacle of the gay and lesbian parade that proceeds through the city, down Oxford and Flinders streets. Tickets to the party afterwards are keenly sought. A relatively new and very popular event in February is Tropfest, a festival of short films held in the Domain. Shortly after this, the Royal Easter Show and the Easter Racing Carnival at Randwick are held. The Royal Easter Show brings many people who live in rural New South Wales to the city. Since 1998, the Easter Show has moved from the former RAS Showground at Moore Park to Homebush.

March is the month when the Archibald Prize for portraiture, the Wynne Prize for landscape painting and the Sulman Prize for genre painting are awarded by the Trustees of the Art Gallery of New South Wales. The selection of the Archibald Prize is observed with great interest by Sydneysiders, who sometimes disagree with the work selected by the judges. As a concession to popular taste, there is another prize given for the people's choice of the best portrait entered in the Archibald.

June, when the nights are at their longest, is the month of the Sydney Film Festival, held in the grand Art Deco–style State Theatre in Market Street. Both short and longer films from around the world are screened there continuously over two weeks. Two months later, in August, the Sydney Boat Show takes place in the Exhibition Centre at Darling Harbour. The same month, just as the days are beginning to lengthen, the City to Surf Race is held. Competitors start in Park Street opposite the Australian Museum, proceed down William Street and along New South Head Road, and up 'heartbreak hill' to Vaucluse. The course then turns southeast to finish at Bondi Beach. Hundreds of thousands of people join in this 14-kilometre run (or walk) every year.

Springtime is heralded in the city by the David Jones Flower Show, held on the ground floor of the Elizabeth Street store in the first half of September. In the second half of the month, the focus moves to the Botanic Gardens Spring Festival. The major sporting event in September is the National Rugby League Grand Final. The Festival of the Winds takes place at Bondi in early September, the best time of year for kites, when the strong westerly winds are blowing. Exotically decorated kites and a wide variety of music remind everyone what a socially and ethnically diverse city Sydney is.

In December, the school summer holidays begin again, and everyone gets ready for Christmas. For visitors from the northern hemisphere, Christmas shopping in the December summer heat is incongruous; for Sydneysiders, Christmas shopping in an early summer heatwave is plain unpleasant. Australians have only recently started to adapt traditional Christmas fare to the antipodean seasons, preferring to postpone the full hot Christmas dinner to the middle of the year. Carols in the Domain on the Saturday before Christmas are a popular family event. Then, when everyone has woken up on Boxing Day, 26 December, they can look forward to watching the start of the Sydney–Hobart 900-kilometre yacht race before starting their annual summer holidays in earnest.

The cycle of life in Sydney begins again.

CHAPTER TWO

THE KOORIS

From what I have said of the Natives of New Holland they may appear to some to be the most wretched people on Earth, but in reality they are far more happier [sic] than we Europeans; being wholly unacquainted not only with the superfluous but the necessary Conveniences so much sought after in Europe, they are happy in not knowing the use of them. They live in tranquillity which is not disturb'd by the Inequality of Condition: The Earth and the sea of their own accord furnishes them with all things necessary for in life, they covet not … they live in a warm and fine Climate and live in wholesome Air, so that they have very little need [of] Clothing … In short they seem'd to set no Value upon anything we gave them.

Captain James Cook[1]

Warra warra!
Translation: Go away!

THE LIFESTYLE COOK described did not survive for many years after the white invasion. The process of change was swift and severe. The Aborigines of Sydney were the first to be exposed to this dangerous, and often lethal, threat to their existence. The fate of the Australian Aborigines since 1788 is an issue about which many non-Aboriginal Australians feel a great deal of collective responsibility, even if, as individuals, they played no direct role in the action or inaction that led to the near destruction of the indigenous population and culture. Others deny the less heroic elements of Australian history and ignore the extent to which the past intrudes upon the present. Aborigines today are, on any test, much worse off than other Australians: they die younger, they are poorer, they are more likely to turn to crime, alcohol or drugs, and they are disproportionately represented in the prison population.

There are almost 300 000 Aborigines in Australia. About 34 500 of them live in Sydney.

They are concentrated in the inner suburbs of Sydney, at Redfern, Waterloo, Marrickville, Leichhardt; at Matraville and La Perouse on the northern shore of Botany Bay; and further west and southwest at Mount Druitt and Campbelltown. Many Aborigines living in the west of Sydney live in public housing, in areas such as Tregear, Mount Druitt and Dharruk. There are Aboriginal housing companies scattered throughout Sydney.

The precise origin of the Aborigines is uncertain. Aborigines do not have any legends, or dreaming stories, of migration. Their traditional belief is that they have always lived on the Australian continent, and did not arrive as part of a southerly migration from Papua New Guinea and the Indonesian archipelago, which is the generally accepted view of archaeologists and palaeontologists.

There is considerable ongoing debate about when Aborigines first migrated to Australia, but there is evidence of occupation about 50 000 to 60 000 years ago. Migration south onto the Australian continent would have been much easier in prehistoric times during the period of the last Ice Age. Sea levels were lower and island hopping short distances was easier. The most likely entry points are in the Kimberley region of northwestern Australia or Arnhem Land in the Northern Territory. The pattern of occupation was southward, but the point of entry, pattern and manner—by canoe or on foot—are unknown. There is little archaeological evidence of the way the Aborigines migrated across the Australian continent.

One of the many remarkable feats of Aboriginal culture was to live in such a hostile, infertile environment with irregular rainfall. Aborigines in the Sydney area, however, would have faced fewer challenges to survival. The climate was wetter and the land more fertile, with abundant fish and animal life. In other words, the terrain of southeastern Australia including the Sydney region may have been attractive to Aborigines for exactly the same reasons as it was to Europeans. The earliest archaeological evidence of Aboriginal occupation of the Sydney area is 15 000 years ago at Emu Plains in Sydney's west. Most of the evidence is much more recent—in the past 4000 years. This may be because the population increased significantly in this period, particularly about 2000 years ago.[2]

The question of how many Aborigines lived in Australia and the Sydney area before 1788 is controversial. Captain Cook guessed that the population for all Australia would have been in the order of 150 000. Recent and better-informed estimates are that the Aboriginal population was about 750 000 in 1788.[3] Governor Phillip estimated that there were no more than 1500 Aborigines living in the Sydney area, but his assessment was no more than guesswork. It could have been double this amount, or even more than that. Many Aborigines (quite understandably) spent their time trying to elude the new settlers, or invaders, so population estimates were susceptible to considerable margins of error. The first official census of Aborigines did not take place until 1971. The fact that Aborigines tried to evade the colonists may also explain the discrepancy between early observations of their lifestyle and the evidence in the archaeological record of the Sydney area.

The Aborigines were hunters and gatherers. In parts of the Sydney area and along the coast, as in other parts of Australia, they fashioned some of the landscape to suit their way of life by using fire to clear the understorey of woodlands. This made kangaroos, wallabies and other game more visible—they would be speared as they escaped from the fire—and encouraged the growth of new grass.

The burning-off of the forests and woodlands of Australia is often referred to as 'firestick' farming. There is evidence of regular burning in the Lane Cove River area and at Ku-ring-gai Chase National Park 3000 years ago.[4] The Aborigines lit fires by cutting a hole in a reed, inserting a stick into the hole and rubbing it until the friction produced a spark and flame. Firesticks were carried when moving from place to place.

The park-like scenery along the harbour and the coast, created by burning off, is why the foreshores of Sydney were described rather optimistically by Captain John Hunter in 1788 as 'tolerable land which may be cultivated without waiting for its being cleared of wood'.[5] Now that firestick agriculture is no longer practised, the more open forests around Sydney are scrubbier and denser than they were before 1788, although the changes to the landscape around Sydney due to the absence of Aboriginal land management techniques are much less dramatic than changes wrought in Sydney and elsewhere by clearing, overgrazing and decimation of the natural fauna.

Forty thousand years ago, the Sydney area looked vastly different from its appearance now, and megafauna—giant kangaroos, herbivorous rhinoceros-sized diprotodon and carnivorous animals such as the Tasmanian tiger and tree-dwelling possum-like animals—still roamed the bush. Sydney Harbour, Botany Bay and Broken Bay were all still river valleys and the climate was colder and windier than it is today. Many early indicators of Aboriginal presence in the Sydney area were probably consumed as the sea level rose and the river valleys were drowned. Around Sydney Harbour, the sites that indicate prehistoric occupation are located in the bushy public reserves at Balls Head and Berry Island, at Balmoral Beach and along the undeveloped upper reaches of the Lane Cove River and Middle Harbour. Most of the evidence is in the form of shell middens, and stencils and rock carvings.[6]

In 1788, the Aborigines of the Sydney area consisted of larger language groups. The first to come into contact with the new colonists was the group which we call the Eora, or coastal members of the larger Dharruk group. The word 'Eora' is derived from *yura*, an Aboriginal word for person. The Aborigines probably never used the word 'Eora' to describe themselves. It is possible that they saw themselves as part of the large Dharruk language group. The term 'Eora' was adopted by the judge advocate of the First Fleet, David Collins, in his account of the settlement and later by Captain John Hunter, also of the First Fleet. Other Dharruk people lived further inland westward of Petersham, the Hawkesbury River and on the Cumberland Plain as far west as the Blue Mountains. These people hunted for game and picked the wild yams, or *dharruk*, after which they were named.[7] Another language group, the Dharawal, lived south of Botany Bay. Another large language group was the Ku-ring-gai, a word which is the possessive noun for *koori*.

23

Portrait of Bennilong a native of New Holland, who after experiencing for two years the Luxuries of England, returned to his own Country and resumed all his former Habits.

LEFT: An image (c. 1800) of Bennelong in all his British finery. Bennelong was forcibly brought to live in the colony at Sydney Cove in November 1789, on the orders of the then governor, Captain Arthur Phillip. Bennelong fled the colony a few months later, but later returned voluntarily, soon after Phillip was speared in the shoulder at Manly Cove in 1790.

Aboriginal people throughout the Sydney area identified themselves more strongly as members of smaller clans, or bands. There were an estimated twenty-nine different bands living in the Sydney area,[8] and between seven and eleven based near the shores of Sydney Harbour and the nearby coast. Each band had approximately fifty members. Like the Native Americans, the initial inability of the Aborigines of the Sydney region to bind together to form a united front against the European threat to their existence made them more vulnerable to the unwelcome European visitors.

Because of the semi-nomadic way of life, communication between the different language groups was fluid. Dialects would be at least familiar to bands or clans occupying neighbouring areas. Moreover, many bands would join together at large ceremonies held in the summer months around Port Jackson when fish were more plentiful.[9]

Each clan was connected to a particular area. For example, Bennelong (who was one of the first Aborigines to come into contact with the white colonists) claimed to be of the Wangal clan that lived along the southern side of the Parramatta River between Darling Harbour and Parramatta, and that he owned Goat Island.[10] The Wallumedegal tribe lived opposite the Wangal on the northern shore of the Parramatta River.[11]

Wives were exchanged between clans, and each man and child in the clans claimed a common ancestor, although the wife became a full member of the clan into which she married, as well as maintaining links with the clan of her birth.[12] The clans foraged on land which lay within the territory of other clans, but the rules for resource sharing were settled, and had been ongoing for many centuries. Some clans combined with others to form bands for foraging. When disputes did occasionally break out, they were usually settled on sites set aside for fighting. The European settlers learned that the Gweagals, who were members of the Dharawal group, settled disputes in an area between where Goulburn Street and Central Station stand today at the southern end of the city, although that was traditionally Gadigal land.[13]

The Gadigal, who lived on the southern shores of the harbour from South Head to as far west as Darling Harbour, were the first to be exposed to the invaders of the First Fleet. The Kameraigal, the most numerous and powerful of the clans living around Sydney, lived on the northern side of the harbour. The suburb of Cammeray is named after them. The source of their power, according to Watkin Tench, may have been their access to some of the best fishing in the harbour.

People had the right to use items which came from their area, and to exchange them with members of other clans. The Booberonagal living on the banks of the Hawkesbury River had rights over the basalt pebbles on the river bed which were used to make hatchets. Another clan had the rights to use and exchange red silcrete rocks which could be broken into flakes to make spearheads.[14]

25

Corroborees were the main means of social contact between different clans. Different forms of corroborees were held to celebrate different events: marriage, adult initiation or a gathering of a larger group. Men and women painted themselves in bold patterns with white clay, ochre and charcoal. It was at certain corroborees that exchange of goods between clans took place. Gifts were important tokens of kinship. While differences between, and attachment to, individual clans might have been strong, the regular intercourse at corroborees meant that each tribe did not consider itself as completely isolated and independent.

Every aspect of the lives of the Aborigines was regulated by religious beliefs, which sometimes varied from tribe to tribe. The general collection of beliefs, known as 'the Dreaming', not only explains the past and how the present came to be, but also prescribes codes of conduct for important events. When a person died, the ritual of the funeral ceremony had to be observed so that the deceased person could be reunited with his or her Dreaming and ancestors.

The Dreaming guided social relations and behaviour, and formed a core of traditions and lore which have been followed over thousands of years. There were Aboriginal Dreaming tracks that crisscrossed the continent, to and from valuable resources (such as particular foods and materials, like ochre) and to sites of spiritual significance to local clans and tribes.

One of the most important and powerful spirits of the Dreaming is the large and god-like Rainbow Serpent. It is the original magnificent and god-like being, and creator/destroyer of the universe. According to Aboriginal legend, the land was flat at the time of its arrival, and as the giant serpent slid and writhed from place to place, the gorges, rivers, valleys and mountains were formed.[15]

Intriguingly, there is a temporal connection with the creation of the legend of the Rainbow Serpent and the end of the last Ice Age, when sea levels were consuming between 25 and 45 metres of coastal land per year, at the same time as the climate was warmer and wetter than it had been during the Ice Age.[16] Creatures upon which the image of the Rainbow Serpent seem to have been based—the pipefish, seahorse and, to a lesser degree, snakes[17]—were seen in great numbers as the coastline invaded the land. The Aborigines appear to have developed the myth and composite image of the Rainbow Serpent at a time of great climatic, cultural and geographic change, as a way of explaining how the world came to be.

There is little evidence of Dreaming tracks within the Sydney region, but that does not mean they never existed. Rather, our lack of knowledge about them is a sad reminder of the consequences of European settlement and the indifference of the early colonists to the traditional Aboriginal way of life. This indifference has not abated. Ian Bandeluk ('Rosella') Watson, a descendant of the Booberonagal clan, objected to the construction of the M2 Motorway (which links the lower North Shore with the Baulkham Hills district) because an Aboriginal site which was more than 6500 years old was destroyed.

One local example of a Dreaming story is the Dharawal legend of how the waratah, the official emblem of New South Wales, became red. The waratah was created many, many years ago, when all waratahs were white. During this time, a pigeon came to camp in the bush with her mate, who went searching for food but did not return. The pigeon searched the bushland but could not see her mate, so she decided to fly above the trees to get a better look, thereby risking attack by a hawk. She spotted her mate, caught in some bushes, but while flying to him, the pigeon was swooped upon by a hawk, who tore open her breast with his claws. The pigeon managed to escape. She could only fly short distances, however, and each time she landed she rested on a bed of white waratah blossoms, which her blood stained red. After that, as a testament to her love and loyalty, all waratahs were red.

The main rites in the lives of Aboriginal peoples were adult initiation, marriage and death. Marriage matches were usually arranged by the grandparents of the people involved. Accounts written by the members of the First Fleet give some indication of the appearance and lifestyle of Sydney's Aborigines. One aspect of their culture which made quite an impact on those early observers was the treatment of women. The disposition of the women with whom any contact was made was far less friendly than that of the men, and Governor Phillip noted that they were under 'great subjection'. Women were treated with 'savage barbarity', had the task of carrying children and 'all other burthens',[18] and were often kicked and brutalised. The women Marine Captain Watkin Tench saw were marked with contusions and scars. On the other hand, the horror expressed by Aborigines at some European customs—such as flogging convicts and leaving the corpses of hanged criminals to rot as a discouragement to others— was observed, but seldom commented upon.

Many colonists were intrigued to learn why several women had the last two joints of their left-hand little finger removed. This practice, known as *mal-gun*, was not confined to the Sydney area, but extended as far north as Port Stephens on the Central Coast. Some European observers thought it must have been part of the marriage ceremony ritual, but the phenomenon was not limited to married women. Other explanations were given and the settlers were informed that it was to enable the women to catch more fish, because the removal of this part of the finger made wrapping fishing line around the hands easier. This explanation can be partially reconciled with the account of an Aboriginal woman who lived at Port Stephens in the middle of the nineteenth century. Her little finger had been tied tightly so that the top of it eventually fell off. This part of her finger was then ceremoniously dropped in the water so that the fish would develop a taste for the sweetness of her flesh and always be attracted to her fishing hand.[19]

Just as women sacrificed the top of their little fingers to ensure a bountiful fish supply, so the men around Port Jackson had their right front tooth removed at the ceremony which initiated them into adulthood. The dominant band around Sydney Harbour were the Kameraigal, and it was this clan that extracted the tooth from other males from nearby bands as a gesture of fealty to the strongest group. In the Sydney area, two male initiation ceremonies, called *yoo-lahng erah-ba-daihng*, were held after 1788—one in 1791 and one in 1795—the last performed in the Sydney area as far as the colonists were aware. Judge Advocate David Collins attended the ceremony in 1795.

In 1791, a day in the life of an Aboriginal family living on the coast was recorded by Watkin Tench, who spent four years in the colony.[20] In the morning, the wife set out with the firestick to do the morning's fishing in her canoe, taking any suckling baby with her. The baby was fed at the same time as the woman fished, all the while maintaining the balance of the canoe by kneeling on it and pressing the side of the boat with her knees—a considerable feat. Fish caught would be cooked immediately in the clay base at the bottom of the canoe. At the end of the fishing lines were fish hooks made from tarban shells. The fish hook was a technological innovation introduced to the Sydney area about 900 years ago. Canoes were made of the bark of casuarina trees, bent into shape, tied at each end, and sealed with resin from a local plant. The canoes served their purpose well and, when the band moved on, the canoes were left behind and new ones built quickly when they were needed again.[21]

The husband, in the meantime, moved from rock to rock looking for fish to spear. A cockle was used for bait, as on the boat. He chewed up and threw it in the water to attract fish. If there were no fish close to shore, he would go out in a canoe and use his fish gig, and spear fish with great dexterity. The men considered it degrading to use a fishing line.

The men used a three- or four-pronged spear which had a sharpened sliver of bone attached to each prong. The cunning and skill of the men in using this technique—lying down across the canoe, with his face under the water for a better view—was recognised by the colonists, but they were less impressed by the canoes they used, as they could not see the use of such primitive, temporary craft. Tench's observations, as acute as they were, may have overlooked other more technologically complex ways of fishing in the waters of Sydney Harbour and elsewhere.[22] The Aborigines in the Sydney area may have, like their neighbours to the north and south, used brush and stone weirs, and fish traps and small scoop nets. Fish remains excavated at a rock shelter at Mount Trefle near Neilsen Park in the outer harbour indicate that a wider range of fishing techniques was used by the Aborigines in the open waters of the outer harbour. The small size of the fish remains indicated that they were probably caught by the use of small nets or artificial tidal fish traps, caught near creeks or tidal rock pools. As this sort of fishing activity would have been engaged in in smaller, more sheltered estuarine bays and coves, it is not surprising that it was unobserved—but the gap between observation and the archaeological record is a telling example of the weaknesses of relying on early historical accounts alone for a good understanding of Aboriginal culture before 1788.

Life away from the coast was heavily dependent upon the hunting of game such as kangaroos and wallabies. Another important source of game was the swamps around Sydney's waterways where wild duck and waterbirds were hunted. Like spearing fish, hunting was an exclusively male activity, done with spears and axes. The edge-ground axe was developed about 4000 years ago (about 24 000 years later than in northwestern Australia), possibly when kangaroos and wallabies had become scarcer and more difficult to catch. It was used to cut holes in trees for hunters to run up so they could pursue possums. Tench observed Gomberee, who lived near the Hawkesbury River, climbing a tree in the following manner:

> With his tool, he cut a small notch in the tree he intended to climb, about two and a half feet above the ground, in which he fixed the great toe of his left foot, and sprung upwards, at the same time embracing the tree with his left arm: in an instant he had cut a second notch for his right toe on the other side of the tree, into which he sprung; and thus alternately cutting on each side, he mounted to the height of twenty feet, in nearly as short a space as if he had ascended by a ladder … To us it was a matter of astonishment but to him it was sport.[23]

Tench was a close observer of the way of life of these hunter–gatherers. Some lived in rock shelters and others lived in huts which were 'nothing more than a large piece of bark, bent in the middle, and open at both ends, resembling two cards, set up to form an acute angle'. He also saw 'squirrel traps' and decoys for ensnaring birds, which were 'formed of underwood and reeds, long and narrow, shaped like a mound raised over a grave; with a small aperture at one end for the admission of the prey; and a grate made of sticks at the other …. Most of the decoys were full of feathers.'[24]

The women spent most of their time searching for edible roots and gathering berries. Along the Hawkesbury and Nepean rivers yams were a vital, and abundant, food source, as were the roots of native orchids and ferns. There were also fruit and vegetables available to the gatherers. Most important was the burrawang, a plant which produced clusters of extremely poisonous seeds. To remove the toxins, the women pounded the seeds and placed them in running water for about two weeks, after which time they would pound them again to make a flour which was then baked into flat cakes. Fruit from the Port Jackson figs were eaten. The nectar of banksias, grevilleas, waratahs and melaleucas was another food source. Women used multipurpose carriers called *coolamons* which were made out of hollowed tree roots as containers for carrying water, food and small children. Baskets were woven from the leaves of gymea lilies and the reeds of cabbage tree palms. The inner bark of native hibiscus was used to make string bags and fishing nets.

In the colder months, Aborigines living in the area now covered by Western Sydney kept themselves warm with the furs of possums, wallabies and kangaroos. Cloaks were made by sewing together pelts with the sinews from kangaroo tails. Aborigines prized the front teeth of kangaroos as a form of adornment, but also used shells, bones and feathers.[25]

For the Aborigines of coastal Sydney, the sea was a collective resource to be shared by everyone, and Aboriginal customs about access to traditional fishing and hunting grounds essential to everyone's survival were to be observed. That is why the newly arrived fishermen of the First Fleet so gravely offended the local Aborigines when they refused to share their bountiful catch with them.

When Arthur Phillip was given his instructions from the British government before the First Fleet sailed, he was not instructed to negotiate or enter into treaties with the Aborigines for the use or purchase of land. To Europeans, possession or title to land depended on working or cultivating it. Cook had observed on his journey on the *Endeavour* Aborigines did not work or improve the land, so that it was *terra nullius*, and therefore able to be claimed by the British government.

This doctrine of international law was strongly biased in favour of European colonisation, without regard to compensating the indigenous peoples for the annexation of their land. (It should be pointed out that it is unlikely that the terms of any treaty would have been observed. New Zealand's Treaty of Waitangi was not, nor were the many treaties made with native Americans in the early years of the settlement of North America.)[26]

Despite this large cultural blind spot in official policy about the pre-existing rights of the Aborigines, Phillip was enjoined, in his official instructions from the King, to:

> endeavour by every possible means to open an intercourse with the natives, and to conciliate their affections ... And if any of our subjects shall wantonly destroy them, or give them any *unnecessary interruption* in the exercise of their several occupations, it is our will and pleasure that you do cause such offenders to be brought to punishment *according to the degree of the offence.* [emphasis added] You will endeavour to procure an account of the numbers inhabiting the neighbourhood of the intended settlement, and report your opinion to one of our Secretaries of State in what manner our intercourse with these people may be turned to the advantage of this colony.[27]

At the time of the First Fleet's arrival in Sydney, Phillip was well intentioned towards the Aborigines. The ideal of the 'noble savage' expounded by French philosopher Jean-Jacques Rousseau had influenced some of the more enlightened sections of European society. Aborigines were to be treated in a conciliatory fashion. Any wrongdoing towards them was to be punished.

Despite Phillip's good intentions, he was well aware that the real problems would lie not in official attitudes towards the Aborigines, but in those of the lesser military personnel and the convicts. His desire to prevent interaction by these groups with the Aborigines for as long as possible was impossible to fulfil.

The high-minded principles espoused by Phillip and the British government were often conveniently ignored when the interests of the colony were at stake. Throughout the nineteenth century, the dichotomy between policy and reality remained. In the early years of the colony, the official policy fluctuated uneasily between trying to 'civilise' the Aborigines and indiscriminately violating their property and personal rights whenever their interests clashed with the colony's—and that was nearly all the time.

The first mistake the British colonists made was not to understand and appreciate the religious and traditional spiritual significance of the land to the Aborigines, as well as its importance as a source of food and survival. This was particularly ironic in the circumstances of the First Fleet. Most of the offenders had committed property crimes, which were dealt with very seriously by the penal system of Georgian England, yet the system of government had not developed any process for dealing with traditional land usage and possession by less 'civilised' societies.

The critical difference between European and Aboriginal notions of land possession and ownership was that, for the Aborigines, there was no conception of the right of an individual to hold private property to the exclusion of everyone else. For the colonists, there was no conception of anything else. Aborigines were closely connected to the land, but in a wider and more collective sense, not in the personal legalistic manner land was possessed in European society. From the outset, the stage was set for a fundamental and irreconcilable clash between cultures, which would soon impoverish the lives of Australia's indigenous people.

Phillip's initial contact with the Aborigines was at Botany Bay. When he approached a group of armed Aborigines, they readily laid down their arms when Phillip indicated that they should. But they were not happy about the new arrivals and as the ships of the First Fleet sailed around to Port Jackson Aborigines stood along the shores of the coast and harbour shouting '*Warra warra*' ('Go away'). The Aborigines of Port Jackson were not only more vocal than their compatriots at Botany Bay, they were also more heavily armed. However, they too were willing to lay down their arms as soon as they were persuaded that there was no danger. The preparedness of these people to put down their arms may have been because they believed these newcomers would not stay for long. After all, Captain Cook and his crew on the *Endeavour* had soon moved on. Another possible explanation is that they thought that these European people were ghosts, who were, in the tradition of the Dreaming, white. The local Aboriginal word for ghost was '*man*'.

Though the Aborigines were not aggressive, Phillip was impressed by their lack of fear, and named Manly Cove on the north side of Port Jackson in honour of 'their confidence and manly behaviour'.[28] The Aborigines were happy to accept the gifts laid down before them by Phillip, and showed great curiosity about the boats and the trinkets.

Despite this manliness, a recurring theme throughout the various descriptions of the Aborigines in the first three months of European settlement was their acquiescence and willingness to do as they were told. On one occasion, Phillip and a group of men were dining on one of the harbour beaches when they were approached by a group of Aborigines armed with lances, shields and wooden swords. Rather than attacking, they grew so curious that they began to irritate the officers so much that Phillip got up from his meal and drew a circle in the sand, indicating to the Aborigines that they were not to step inside it. This order was obeyed and the Aborigines 'sat down very quiet [sic]'.[29]

However, relations cooled very quickly. Within three days of the First Fleet's arrival at Sydney Cove, the Aborigines showed displeasure at the clearing of the land around the freshwater stream that would become known as the Tank Stream as the area had, up until then, been one of the most bountiful sources of game and fresh water in the Sydney area.

By May, it was becoming clear that the 'ghosts' were here to stay, and the Aborigines were avoiding the settlement completely. In the short term, their withdrawal was a good thing in that antagonistic contacts between Aborigines and convicts could be avoided—as more land was cleared, however, incidents began to occur on the margins of white settlement that indicated the Aborigines were not going to melt away into the bushland forever.

The strength of Aboriginal resistance to the European invasion of their lands was, however, fragmented and sporadic, more in the nature of low-key guerrilla warfare than a mass uprising. By the middle of 1788, there was clear evidence that the delicate balance of nature in the area of Sydney around the harbour and Botany Bay had been upset by the arrival of the First Fleet. Some Aborigines 'stole' fish which had been netted in an effort to allay death by starvation, and others begged the newcomers for food.[30] This shortage of food would have weakened many Aborigines, and made them less able to withstand the epidemic of disease that broke out in April 1789.

The first reported incident of violence between Aborigines and Europeans was in July 1788. A convict who was searching for bushes which were used to make tea wandered some distance away from his camp and returned badly wounded by a spear. He said that he had seen another man being dragged away by a group of Aborigines. The man's clothing was subsequently discovered and it was assumed that he had been murdered. His body was found later.

There were other instances of violence by Aborigines towards the convicts, but there is no record of whether this violence was provoked by the Europeans' behaviour. Threatening traditional food supplies and land were, of themselves, provocative acts. There is, of course, no complete record of the incidence of violence towards Aborigines, just as there was no official census of the Aboriginal population.

Incidents of violence and threatened violence convinced Phillip that he should capture some Aborigines and retain them so that they could be better understood. No Aboriginal person would 'come among' the European settlement voluntarily, so Phillip ordered the capture of one, Arabanoo, in December 1788 at Manly Cove.

The terrified Arabanoo was dragged onto the boat which brought him to the small settlement. When taken to the governor's dining room, he believed he was about to be sacrificed and eaten. He was soon placated, however, and lived with Phillip for two months,

31

during which time he was clothed and fed in the European manner—and shackled. After two months he was freed of all restraints, having, it was agreed, become sufficiently accustomed to his position in the governor's 'set' for there to be little risk of his disappearance. Some information was gleaned regarding the customs and habits of his people, but Arabanoo's role as a mediator was limited as he was shunned by his own people. Arabanoo succumbed to the deadly epidemic that claimed so many Aborigines of the Sydney region (of which more later), and was buried in the grounds of Government House. There is a lookout named after him on the high land above Middle Head.

In late 1790, antagonism between the First Fleeters and the Aborigines escalated. The seventeenth white person to be wounded (in this case, fatally) by the Aborigines was John McEntire, Phillip's gamekeeper. He was speared at Botany Bay by Pemulwy, a famous Aboriginal warrior of the Bidegal tribe. Bennelong, another Aboriginal person whom Phillip befriended, and many other Aborigines in the Sydney area loathed McEntire. This may have been because he was a good hunter, and therefore a big threat to food supplies, or because McEntire had a very wide definition of what 'game' was. Certainly, Watkin Tench and others suspected McEntire of having shot or injured Aborigines while out hunting, although no one was able to extract a deathbed confession from him of any such atrocities.[31]

It was Tench who was later sent out by Phillip on two separate missions to track down Pemulwy. Both these expeditions were failures, although in the light of Tench's misgivings about McEntire's hostile relationship with the Aborigines, perhaps this was more than fortuitous. Phillip's nerve was sorely tested by McEntire's death and he ordered reprisals which, according to Tench, were to 'infuse an universal terror, which might operate to prevent further mischief'. Lieutenant Dawes, another marine who was in charge of the observatory on the west side of Sydney Cove, was a keen student of the Aboriginal language, had to struggle with his conscience and seek the advice of the chaplain before setting off with Tench on this expedition.[32] When Dawes refused to apologise for saying he regretted joining the expedition of reprisal, he was sent home with the rest of the marines in 1791, instead of being permitted to stay in the colony as he wished.

Pemulwy was a constant irritant to the white settlement and, over the next ten years, he led many other attacks around the Georges River, Parramatta and Seven Hills. Finally, in 1802, he was shot at Toongabbie while leading an attack. His severed head was sent in a jar to Sir Joseph Banks, Cook's botanist on the *Endeavour*. Pemulwy's son Tedbury continued the family tradition of resistance and sporadic warfare between 1800 and 1810.

From about April 1789, disease ravaged the Aborigines. It is not known how the disease spread. The nature and source of the disease remain a mystery, and will always be one, but there are various schools of thought about what it was and how it was introduced. There were no reported incidences of smallpox within the colony, nor were there any reported during the long voyage out to Botany Bay. The incubation period for the smallpox virus is up to two weeks, so it is hard to reconcile the lack of smallpox among the members of the First Fleet with the sudden appearance of it so long after its arrival. Not one European was afflicted during the outbreak, even those who were not old enough to have been inoculated against smallpox before the Fleet left England. Another explanation was that specimens of smallpox variola which came out as part of the medical supplies (smallpox inoculation was at a very early stage of development) somehow passed into the hands of Aborigines and, by accident or, even more malevolently, by design, spread when opened. However, it is not certain that the potency of the variola would have persisted so long after the departure of the First Fleet from Portsmouth. Another possibility is that by some extraordinary (yet conceivable) coincidence, smallpox initially brought to the Australian continent by Macassan fishermen seeking trepang in the waters off Arnhem Land spread across the Australian continent and arrived in the Sydney area soon after the arrival of the First Fleet. This theory does not explain the complete immunity of the Europeans to the disease. Another theory is that the disease was chickenpox or some other disease which was not remarkable enough to have been observed among the European population, but which took a calamitous toll on the indigenous people of the Sydney area whose immune systems were unprepared for it.[33]

Disease soon spread far beyond the Sydney region. This was because the first instinct of the Aborigines who witnessed the effects of the disease was to move further away. A stark indication of the magnitude of the epidemic was given by the Gadigal clan, whose numbers were reduced from around fifty down to three in 1791. The death rate around Sydney was so high that traditional Aboriginal burials, so central to their Dreaming, were abandoned, and people were left to rot in the caves where they died.

After Arabanoo died, Phillip issued a standing order to capture another native. In the meantime, Surgeon General John White and the Reverend Richard Johnson adopted two Aboriginal children, a nine-year-old boy called Nanbaree and a twelve-year-old girl called Boorong, both of whom had been orphaned in the epidemic. Phillip was concerned that these two children were not mature enough to act as spokespeople between the Aborigines and the colonists. They did, however, act as interpreters for the next two people, Bennelong and Colbee, who forcibly came to live within the small settlement in November 1789. Their captor, Lieutenant William Bradley, found the task of obeying Phillip's orders most distasteful, but he lured the two men away from their canoes by holding up two large fish as an inducement to come closer. As Bradley wrote:

> [T]he two poor devils were seized then landed into the boat in an instant. The noise of the men, the crying and screaming of the women and children together with the situation of the two miserable wretches in our possession was really a most distressing scene.[34]

Nanbaree recognised the men by name and they were presented to the governor scrubbed, clothed and shackled. Colbee, who had earned a reputation in the colony as a great warrior, shrugged off his chains and escaped after a few days. Bennelong started to adjust to his new surroundings and became quite cheerful. Quick to learn the English language, he was an enthusiastic dancer and great mimic. But after a few months he tired of life in the settlement and fled into the bush, much to Phillip's disappointment.

Colbee and Bennelong were sighted again by Captain Nepean at Manly Cove in September 1790, among a group of about 200 Aborigines. The Aborigines tried to exchange whale meat for metal hatchets. Bennelong asked to see Phillip, who was quickly sent for. He tried to persuade Bennelong to return. Phillip greeted Bennelong warmly, but the peaceful atmosphere soured quickly when Phillip approached another Aboriginal person who, fearful and apprehensive (with some justification) of the governor's intentions towards him, picked up a spear and threw it at Phillip. Phillip was struck on the shoulder and withdrew with his men back onto the boat. Phillip soon recovered and, understanding that the event was a result of a failure to communicate, did not seek retaliation for the attack upon him.

The event at Manly Cove proved to be a watershed in Aboriginal–European relations. Soon afterwards, Bennelong came to live in a house on Bennelong Point that had been built on Phillip's orders. The area around the house became a meeting place for Aborigines. Bennelong's move into the town in September 1790 was the first time that an Aboriginal person came to live voluntarily in the settlement, but others soon followed, often in search of bread and meat.

Gradually, from this time on, the Aborigines around Sydney became less independent and self-reliant as their traditional supplies of food dwindled. As hunters and gatherers, the Aborigines were forced to accept that the best and most accessible source of food lay within the town itself. In the eyes of the colonists, they became beggars and a significant drain on resources. The destruction of the traditional, well-watered hunting grounds around Sydney Cove and elsewhere was not considered a cause of the increasing dependence.

Bennelong visited Phillip several times while Phillip was recovering from his wound, and the relationship between the men was restored. Government House became another centre for communication between the Aborigines and the colonists, and some Aborigines voluntarily stayed there and became working members of the household.[35]

Some members of the First Fleet could not understand why Phillip was being so generous with the Aborigines, nor did they have much confidence in Bennelong's ability to open the channels of communication between the Aborigines and the colonists. They were exasperated by Bennelong's attitude to the house that had so generously been given to him—he and his family did not even sit or sleep inside it. This was not the only time the Aborigines' indifference to traditional European ideas of domesticity would be a matter of consternation to the colonists and, later, to generations of European Australians.

Phillip's critics could not see why it was so important that channels of communication between the colonists and the indigenous people be kept open. Communication was already going on at a different level. As was inevitable in a small European settlement where men outnumbered women by a huge margin, half-caste children were born to Aboriginal women, some of whom had been taken forcibly by convicts and marines. Venereal disease, brought with the Europeans, soon spread through the Aboriginal population.

Judge Advocate David Collins related one story of an Aboriginal woman who gave birth to a half-caste child and, unable to account for the baby's unusual appearance:

endeavoured to supply by art what she found deficient in nature, and actually held the poor babe, repeatedly, over the smoke of her fire, and rubbed its little body with ashes and dirt, to restore to it the hue with which her other children had been born. Her husband appeared as fond of it as if it had borne the undoubted sign of being his own …[36]

By the middle of 1791, there was regular trade between Aborigines and colonists at the settlement of Parramatta. The colonists bought fish and sold the Aborigines bread, rice and vegetables. One of the best fishermen on the Parramatta River was Balloderee. The Aborigines had an increasing appetite for bread, which they had at first disdained as inedible. Some colonists became tired of the Aborigines' growing reliance on the colony, even if it was clear indication that they were being 'civilised'. They were seen as a demanding nuisance. When his fishing canoe was destroyed by convicts, Balloderee speared another convict he came across in the bush. An order was given to seize Balloderee, who fled and no longer traded fish for meat and bread.

In 1792, Bennelong was sent off to London with Governor Phillip, whose commission was at an end. Bennelong had a companion, sixteen-year-old Yemmurrawannie, and the two men were paraded around London as curiosities until their novelty value subsided. At first they lived in Mayfair, but they were later retired to Kent where they were looked after by caretakers. Yemmurrawannie did not survive, but a homesick Bennelong travelled back to Sydney on the same ship as Governor Hunter. Surgeon George Bass was also on board and learned the Aboriginal language, which was of great assistance later in his exploration of the New South Wales coastline.

After Bennelong returned to Sydney in September 1795, he moved uneasily between European and Aboriginal cultures, and neither considered him to be part of their group. While he was away, he lost the affections of his wife to a younger man. She was not sufficiently overwhelmed by the gifts of English clothing Bennelong offered her as an inducement to stay with him. Nor was she persuaded to return to him after he won a duel against his young rival. Despite (or because of) his new-found 'sophistication', he could not persuade any other women of the extent of his charms and so was lonely for the rest of his life.

Bennelong paid a high price for his openness and curiosity. He died at Rydalmere on the Parramatta River in 1813. The editor of the *Sydney Gazette* scathingly observed:

> Of this veteran champion of the native tribe little can be said. His voyage to and benevolent treatment in Britain produced no change whatever in his manners and inclinations, which were naturally barbarous and ferocious.

Colbee, on the other hand, who had remained more aloof from the settlement, was better able to travel between the Aboriginal and European cultures. Years later, Macquarie granted him land at South Creek and Bathurst as a reward for his good behaviour.

By the time Bennelong returned to Sydney, the relationship between the Aborigines and the colonists had deteriorated sharply. As the colony grew around Parramatta and Prospect Hill, the Field of Mars (Ryde) and along the Hawkesbury River, more and more land was consumed by the settlement, thus reducing traditional Aboriginal land and hunting grounds. The sad cycle of dependence and resentment was set.

From the middle of the 1790s, Aborigines started to hold corroborees and duels within the town, near Sydney Cove, around the brick pits to the south, and the military barracks in George Street, Woolloomooloo and Botany Bay, in the full view of any of the convicts or marines who cared to watch. These duelling spectacles became more and more demeaning, as Jacques Arago described years later, in 1819, as we shall see below.

By the time Hunter arrived in 1795 there was still no official policy on how to deal with issues of land possession, or with Aborigines who resisted the destruction of their traditional hunting grounds. In the early to mid-1790s, crops were being plundered and burned regularly, and several 'accidents' had followed, resulting in the death, overall, of five Aborigines. In 1796, settlers in the Hawkesbury were encouraged by the government to bear arms to defend themselves from attack. While the ability to grow food along the Hawkesbury was essential to the colony becoming self-sufficient, Aboriginal dependence on the land as a source of food was not considered a significant issue for concern.

The antagonism between Aborigines and settlers in the Hawkesbury frightened Lieutenant Governor Paterson in 1798. Worried that the white settlers would choose to leave what was turning out to be the most fertile land in the colony, he sent in a detachment of the New South Wales Corps to keep guard in the area and drive the Aborigines off the land under cultivation. Many Aborigines were killed and five were taken captive. Paterson expressed concern over these harsh measures, but, like Phillip, showed more concern for what was in the greater interest of the white colony.

In 1799, again in the Hawkesbury River area, two Aboriginal boys were brutally murdered by a group of settlers who had accused them of theft and arson. Governor Hunter was shocked and the settlers were charged with murder. They unsuccessfully defended themselves on the novel legal ground that the murder was justified because the Aborigines were treacherous, evil-minded and bloodthirsty. This was not to be the only time such a defence was used. The death sentence was later remitted by order of the British Colonial Office.

These outbreaks were tempered with attempts at conciliation. The Colonial Secretary was at great pains to point out to Governor King when he assumed his commission in 1800 that this was his greatest duty:

> [T]he difficulty of restoring confidence with the Aborigines, alarmed and exasperated by the unjustifiable injuries they have too often experienced, will require all the attention which your active vigilance and humanity can bestow upon a subject so important …[37]

King subsequently issued a proclamation outlining his policy along these lines, and the level of violence decreased.

By 1805, the relationship between Aborigines and the colonists had deteriorated again. A military party was sent to the Hawkesbury with an order to drive the Aborigines back by whatever means necessary. The harsh nature of the policy was reflected in the remark of the usually sensitive Governor King to the Colonial Secretary: 'I am sorry to say that until some of them are killed their [sic] is no hope of their being quiet.'[38] One area along the Hawkesbury, Portland Head, became a flashpoint in the conflict, shortly after land grants were issued to free settlers there in the opening years of the nineteenth century.[39] Upon taking up the reins as governor in January 1810, Lachlan Macquarie did not change the policy towards the Aborigines that had applied since 1788, although the colony was better governed in many other ways. The policy adopted was still that every effort would be made to conciliate and appease them as long as the whites were allowed to do as they wished, and were not threatened economically or physically by Aborigines.

Meanwhile, the administrators and legal experts in the colony were trying to formulate legal guidelines for dealing with the Aboriginal people. They were troubled by the dilemma of how to bring an Aboriginal person to trial and get him or her to enter a plea to an indictment, under oath. How could such a people understand the charges against them, and how could they swear an oath? The solution to this was a practical one: if they did not under-stand the key ingredients of the legal system, they could not be subjected to, or protected by it. Judge Advocate Atkins advised King that it was, for the time being at least, impossible to try Aborigines for any crimes in a British criminal court because of their ignorance of Christian values. The only solution lay in a continuation of the policy already laid: arbitrary punishment usually at the discretion of the military commander in that particular situation.

The appropriation of more land for settlement resulted in increasing bursts of violence between settlers and Aborigines, and government policy concentrated on containing these outbursts rather than developing a way to avoid them. The policy of conflict containment lasted throughout the nineteenth and even into the early twentieth century in other parts of Australia. While the Hawkesbury was the largest theatre of war between Aborigines and colonists, other conflicts also occurred along the Georges River and the Illawarra. By 1806, all the land in the Sydney area on the Cumberland Plain as far west as the foot of the Blue Mountains had effectively been annexed by the colonists, but there was still sporadic fighting in the Hawkesbury area until 1815. In June of that year, settlers were attacked and the conflict was resolved (if that is the right expression) by Macquarie's decision to send a military party to the district on a punitive expedition. In the course of this action, fourteen Aborigines were shot and five were taken prisoner. An exasperated Macquarie thought military force was the only means left of controlling this 'rude and unenlightened' race.

By 1816, the lands to the west and southwest of Sydney were clearly in the hands of the settlers. Clans of Aborigines lived in camps on the properties now owned by people such as William Cox at Mulgoa, or Charles Marsden at South Creek.[40]

Other Aborigines came to live near the township of Sydney. White man's drugs and diseases also took a heavy toll on the Aboriginal population. Jacques Arago, the official artist on Louis de Freycinet's journey of discovery in the Pacific on board *L'Uranie*, was appalled by what he saw in 1819:

> Yesterday I went to the house of one of the richest and most respectable servants here, to spend the evening.[41] What was my astonishment, on entering the court, to see girls from fifteen to eighteen years old encouraging in their savage sports, men and women absolutely naked, and exhibiting all the appearance of the most disgusting wretchedness. These persons, covered with old scars, and armed with spears and clubs, had already received as rewards for their capers and grimaces, some pieces of bread, and a few glasses of wine, the active effect on them which was already perceptible by a boisterous mirth and frightful dancing. When these poor people had finished the prelude of their bacchanals, they began to brandish their clubs with greater force and dexterity against the adjacent fence, as if they were practising to strike more securely; afterwards these unfortunate men, whose gaiety at first appeared so peaceable, struck each other repeated blows; two of them were stretched on the ground dangerously wounded, and a third received a mortal blow. Their companions, who had taken hitherto no part in the action, but by encouraging the combatants then rose, quietly carried off the victims, and disappeared with their burdens. This scene took place in the midst of a civilised city; the spectators were respectable merchants, and elegant accomplished young ladies.[42]

In an effort to improve relations, Macquarie established the Native Institution at Parramatta in 1814. Both Macquarie and William Shelley, the missionary who ran this institution, thought that social intercourse with whites and conversion to Christianity would alleviate the Aborigines' disaffection. The idea behind the institution was to separate Aboriginal children from their parents at an early age so that the connections with their traditional culture could be severed. This was the earliest prototype of the assimilation policy of the latter part of the nineteenth and the twentieth centuries that led to the officially sanctioned and organised removal of Aboriginal children from their parents.

At the Native Institution, the children were taught Christian religion and educated in British ways. Their training was focused on how to make them well-trained, useful members of white society. The girls were taught needlework and the boys were given rudimentary lessons about agriculture in the large field attached to the school.

The institution started out with only twelve children. Parents justifiably viewed the institution with great suspicion; however, by 1817, seventeen students were enrolled, most of whom were able to read the Bible. In 1819, twenty children from the Native Institution competed against about a hundred children educated in European schools in the Anniversary School Examinations; a fourteen-year-old Aboriginal girl who had been at the Institution for three years took the main prize. The institution closed down in the late 1820s. Commissioner Bigge, who inquired into the state of the colony in 1819, criticised the Native Institution. He was concerned that, although Macquarie's experiment demonstrated the natural learning

ABOVE: Canoe fishing—diving under for the catch, with a fire burning in the canoe, ready to cook the fish as soon as it is landed. Fishing No. 1, Field Sports of the Native Inabitants of NSW *(Image Library, State Library of NSW)*

RIGHT: An early colonial artist's depiction of an Aboriginal corroboree. 'The dance', Field Sports of the Native Inhabitants of NSW *(Image Library, State Library of NSW)*

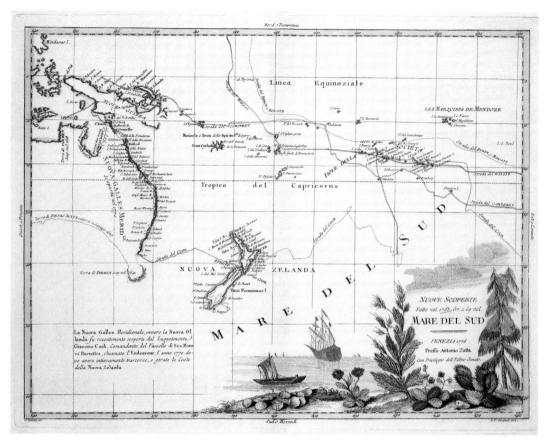

ABOVE: A Venetian map showing the Lieutenant James Cook's 1770 journey, aboard the *Endeavour*, when he claimed New South Wales for the British sovereign. Mare del Sud, *1776, published by Antonio Zatta (National Library of Australia)*
BELOW: View from the east side of Sydney Cove, c. 1811–12. *Artist unknown (Image Library, State Library of NSW)*

ABOVE: Mary Reiby, a former convict, became one of the most successful early business people and biggest landowners in the colony. (*Image Library, State Library of NSW*)

BELOW: Depiction of Hyde Park Barracks soon after completion. Convict Barracks, *c. 1820, watercolour attrib. to Joseph Lycett* (*Image Library, State Library of NSW*)

ABOVE: Commissioner John Thomas Bigge was sent out to conudct an inquiry into transportation and the colony's administration during Macquarie's term in office. *Portrait of John Thomas Bigge, 1819, Thomas Uwins* (*Image Library, State Library of NSW*)

ABOVE: Eastward view of the town from The Rocks, c. 1808. East View of Sydney in New South Wales, *c. 1808, John Eyre (Image Library, State Library of NSW)*
RIGHT: Portrait of Elizabeth Macarthur, wife of John Macarthur, both of whom helped found the wool industry in Australia. *(Image Library, State Library of NSW)*

abilities of the Aboriginal children, it was far from proven that any change that their education had provided would be permanent. There was apparent confirmation of Bigge's warning later on, when the director of the institution, Mrs Shelley, remarked that a number of its ex-pupils had resumed their former habits.

From 1816, Macquarie also tried to improve communication by holding annual feasts at Parramatta. The tone of the events was predictably patronising. Aborigines from the Sydney area, the Illawarra, Jervis Bay and beyond the Blue Mountains attended. There they could see the educational achievements of the inmates of the Native Institution who were 'paraded in the presence of their Parents, read before them, and produce[d] Specimens of their Progress in Education'.[43]

As well as feasting, cooperative behaviour was rewarded by the granting of tokens of appreciation. Land grants were also made,[44] such as ones over land at Black's Town (later Blacktown), where the Native Institution was moved in 1823. By 1835, the feasts were abandoned by Governor Bourke. The size of the audience had by that time greatly declined, and their utility as a forum for communication (and indoctrination) had passed.

As well as the Native Institution, Governor Macquarie tried to shepherd all the remaining Aborigines of the Sydney area into new 'tribes' without any consideration being given to their traditional kinship groupings, or their traditional areas of occupation. 'King' Bungaree was the person Macquarie nominated as the head of the 'Broken Bay tribe', an amalgam of tribal groups, many of which had succumbed to a variety of introduced diseases. The home Macquarie selected for this tribe was located at Georges Head in Sydney Harbour.

About seventy people lived at Georges Head and Bungaree was given a copper plate and chain declaiming his elevated status. It was one of the earliest 'King plates' to be awarded as a sign of appreciation for good behaviour. 'King' Bungaree was a brave mariner and explorer who circumnavigated Australia with Flinders in 1802–1803 and later voyaged with Lieutenant Phillip Parker King to the North West Cape in 1818. He was also a colourful local identity and figure of fun to the Europeans.

Bungaree would wear cast-off military uniforms as a further indication of his elevated status and amuse recently arrived visitors, whom he would seek out as soon as their ships entered the harbour, plying them for treats such as alcohol, sugar and tobacco. In 1820, a group of Russian visitors to the colony expressed dismay at the spectacle of Bungaree and his wife and children, who came aboard their ship and, having had large amounts to drink, behaved apparently with a great degree of vulgarity.[45] Bungaree died in 1830 and is buried at Rose Bay next to his wife, Gooseberry.

The idea of regrouping and resettling Aborigines of the Sydney area did not work any better than the Native Institution, and the settlement at Georges Head was abandoned by the 1830s. The Aborigines of Sydney, as elsewhere, showed little enthusiasm for tilling the soil, an activity which they remained disinterested in. It was totally foreign to them. They were much better suited to activities which more closely approximated their traditional hunter–gatherer way of life, such as fishing and whaling.

Little 'progress' was made in the 1820s towards 'civilising' and converting the Aborigines to European ways. Governor Darling, who took office in 1825, was instructed by the Colonial Office to give conciliation a more evangelical flavour, and officially encouraged conversion to Christianity. Many thought the money spent on the effort was wasted. It became clear that the Aborigines were not simply going to throw off long-held beliefs and embrace Christianity, so some colonists decided that attention should be concentrated on Aboriginal children, who could more easily be re-educated to Christian ways.

By 1834, the House of Commons felt concerned enough about indigenous people within the expanding British Empire to hold a Select Committee of Inquiry on Aborigines in British Settlements. The committee recognised that the Aborigines had been cruelly treated; their rights over territory had been completely disregarded; and that little care had been taken to protect them from violence and the contamination of mixing with the 'lower orders' of the colony. If matters were allowed to progress in the same fashion, the Australian Aborigines could become extinct.

Archdeacon (later Bishop) William Broughton was one of those who gave evidence at the inquiry into the state of Aborigines in New South Wales. Broughton, who had arrived in Sydney in 1829, said the Aborigines in Sydney were:

> ... in a state of which I consider one of extreme degradation and ignorance; they are, in fact in a situation much inferior to what I supposed them to have been before they had any communication with Europe ... they appear to lead an idle and vagrant life, subsisting on casual donations and fishing ... and beg, probably steal ... generally speaking you cannot induce them to work regularly. They are not of a dull disposition; they are quick, intelligent people, but they have, I may say, no wants; you find it impossible to excite any want in them which you can gratify, and therefore they have no inducement to remain under a state of restraint, nor are they willing to leave their children ... it was found [by Governor Macquarie] impossible to attach them to the soil.

As to the consequences of British colonisation, Broughton said:

> The effect of our settlement is to drive the kangaroo away, which is their principal means of subsistence. They still hunt and continue in their natural places, portions belonging to other tribes; they certainly return to it, and they seem to linger about it; but they have no settled place, a property so called. I am afraid they do not so much retire [from civilisation] but decay ... wherever Europeans meet with them, they appear to wear out, and gradually decay; they diminish in numbers ... it leads me to apprehend, that within a very limited period, those who are very much in contact with Europeans will be utterly extinct; I will not say exterminated, but they will be extinct.[46]

Broughton thought the moral character of the Aborigines had decayed as well and that those in the greatest contact with the European settlement were the most depraved due to the shortage of food from traditional sources and access to alcohol. Whenever Broughton asked the Aborigines whether they would like to live in houses and work the land, their universal reply was:

> that they like the bush best, if they have sufficiency of food only, they have no deficiency … the gratification that they seem to enjoy most is that of wandering over the country, and hunting wherever they have the opportunity.

Broughton was not examined on, and he did not volunteer any evidence about, the antipathy shown towards the Aborigines by many of the colonists, especially settlers near the fringes of settlement. At the time Broughton gave evidence, the frontier of settlement had moved beyond Sydney to cover the eastern half of present-day New South Wales and the southeastern corner of Queensland. The South Creek tribe still lived on Marsden property in 1835, but, in 1838, there were only 300 Aborigines left in the Sydney region. At Camden, which is now on the outskirts of Sydney, corroborees were still being held in the late 1830s.[47] By 1850, many of the Aborigines living around Sydney were based in camps and reserves on the Hawkesbury River and the Cumberland Plain.[48]

One of the main recommendations of the select committee of 1838 was that a protectorate scheme should be established to advocate and defend Aboriginal interests. In the period between the select committee's report and the implementation of the protectorate scheme, one of the worst atrocities against Aborigines took place at Myall Creek, outside Inverell, in the fertile, prime hunting (and cattle-grazing) country of the Liverpool Plains, 560 kilometres northwest of Sydney. Thirty Aborigines were captured and executed by a group of white settlers. Eleven men, all ex-convicts, were captured, brought to trial and acquitted. Certain sections of the community were outraged by this. The attorney-general intervened and applied to have seven of them detained on a further charge of murdering the women and children, and the accused were found guilty and sentenced to death. One of those who agitated to bring the perpetrators to trial was Francis O'Brien, the publisher of the *Monitor* and one of the earliest European residents of Bondi.

Other sections of the community were horrified that the accused should be executed for killing blacks. Following the massacre, Governor George Gipps, on account of his highly principled pursuit of the wrongdoers, fell out with many influential squatters (large pastoral landholders). In the *Sydney Gazette* of December 1838, there was a verbatim account of a conversation between a Sydneysider and a man from the bush. The bushman regretted the recent hanging of the Myall Creek murderers and advocated the systematic eradication of Aborigines by poisoning their damper, or bread.

In 1840, Gipps followed the recommendations of the House of Commons committee and appointed a chief protector of Aborigines. Stations were set up to which Aborigines could come if they wanted this protection, and be encouraged to make a living. The land within 5 miles (8 kilometres) of each of the stations was prohibited to settlers, so that contact could be reduced. The protectorate system was neither popular nor successful. Many settlers resented such expenditure on Aborigines at a time when the whole colony was feeling the

41

strain of a tight economy during the depression of the 1840s. People began to wonder whether the Aborigines could be 'civilised' at all.

By 1843, the British government had passed legislation which authorised some of its colonies to admit unsworn testimony in certain civil and criminal proceedings. This afforded Aborigines access to the court system, albeit on a limited basis; however, the Legislative Council, then firmly controlled by the squatters' interests, resisted the introduction of this legislation. Notable colonists such as William Charles Wentworth argued that the notion of accepting testimony from such debased creatures was impossible and the British government should keep its nose out of the colony's affairs. The issue of who had the right to determine policy affecting the Aborigines was one of the earliest flashpoints in the relationship between the British government, on the one hand, and the colonial administration, newly hungry for power, responsibility and independence on certain matters, on the other.

In 1849, a report of the select committee of the Legislative Council recommended that the protectorate system be brought to an end and that Aboriginal children should be the objects of attempts at assimilation. This was the seed of official policy for many generations, that 'the total separation of the parents from the children seems to be essential to the success of any plan, and your Committee believe[s] that to effect this object compulsory measures would be required'.[49]

The following year the Aborigines' legal position was a little more clearly defined: they were British subjects in terms of the rules they must follow and the sanctions imposed for failure to cooperate, but they were constantly and systematically denied any of the rights that usually correspond with the notion of citizenship. They were not granted the right to give unsworn testimony when standing criminal trial until 1876.

In the meantime, the condition of Aborigines around Sydney had been declining to the extent that the social consciences of some of its citizens were being pricked into action. In June 1844, a meeting was held at the Royal Hotel in George Street, Sydney, to discuss the condition of Sydney's Aborigines, and what sort of relief should be given to them. The meeting was provoked by the death, on the Hyde Park racecourse, of an Aboriginal man from exposure and intoxication. The *Sydney Dispatch* noted that the man, William Manen, had died in the park after being removed by two members of the police force from the steps of a nearby hotel and deposited where he died.[50] It was resolved that the 'Sydney tribe' be given enough money to buy a boat and fishing tackle so they could leave the township and subsist elsewhere.

By 1850, the decline in numbers of Aborigines in New South Wales had a huge effect on the social structure of the Aboriginal community: as well as often forcing tribal regrouping, the complex kinship and marriage systems began to break down and had to be reworked. Not surprisingly, Aboriginal tradition began to be 'supplemented with the folklore of persecution' from the 1850s.[51]

There was a significant measure of intermarriage between members of the Dharruk tribe and convicts.[52] Many of the Dharruks living in Sydney today can trace their ancestry to a marriage between Maria, a student at the Native Institution and daughter of a Dharruk leader, Yarramundi, and Robert Lock, who was transported to Australia in 1821. When Maria Lock, who had ten children, died in 1878, she was referred to in the church records as the 'last of the Black Town blacks'.[53]

By the 1860s, spear fishing and initiation ceremonies had died out in the Sydney region. At the same time, more and more Aborigines from rural New South Wales, unable to live the life of the hunter and gatherer because of closer settlement throughout the colony, started to move and settle in Sydney.

The European population continued to predict the decline of the race. In their view, it was an unfortunate fact of life that they were simply not fit to survive in the new, white Australia. All that could be done by governments and missionaries was to 'smooth the dying pillow'.[54] Others thought that there may still be a chance for the survival of the race, but only if they assimilated to the white man's ways. This could be achieved by separating children from their parents. Not a lot of weight was placed on the strength of parent–child relations, or the traditional inseparability of children from their parents. Those who supported assimilation through separation argued that Aboriginal parents did not have the same emotional capacity as their European counterparts, and would not feel the same hardship when separated from their children: 'In most cases, they would be induced to give up their children for a few figs of tobacco,' wrote one legislative councillor.[55]

Some missionaries, such as Englishman Daniel Matthews, tried to protect the Aborigines from the discrimination and harsh attitude of non-Aboriginal people. Travelling widely to collect Aborigines and resettle them at a reserve, he would have unwittingly played a part in breaking up family groups by persuading people to come with him and abandon their traditional tribal habits. Matthews lobbied the government successfully for the establishment of a second attempt at a protectorate system. In 1883, the Aboriginal Protection Board was established to carry out this task. It had authority over the Aboriginal population in New South Wales, then estimated to be about 9000.[56]

The policy of resettling Aborigines in reserves worked in tandem with the social and physical effects of alcohol. Traditional social structures were destroyed and tribal rituals and customs were threatened and often lost forever. The Protection Board had full jurisdiction over all Aborigines, and their power to order the removal of Aboriginal camps to any site they chose was sometimes enthusiastically exercised on their behalf by local policemen. By 1891, almost two-thirds of the Aboriginal population of New South Wales were living on reserves and most of the rest were camped on the fringes of towns.

Another task of the protectorate was to remove as many children from the influence of their parents, especially those of mixed descent who, because of their partly European blood, were considered to be the most likely targets for successful assimilation. They were taken great distances, given new names and sent to grow up with white families, often as unpaid domestics.

By the late 1880s, most Aborigines living near Sydney were eking out a meagre existence, which became even tougher in the economic depression of the 1890s. Long since exiled from

43

ABOVE: Children flocking around members of the Aboriginal Protection Board during a visit to the Aboriginal settlement at La Perouse in 1962.

44

their traditional way of life, they did not have any alternative but to do the best they could in the city.[57]

The main areas where Aborigines lived around Sydney were at Blacktown, the Field of Mars near Ryde, La Perouse, which was classified as a reserve by the Protection Board, and at Dolls Point. In 1898, the Sackville Reserve on the Hawkesbury River was sold and in 1920, the land at Blacktown which had been granted by Governor Macquarie to members of the Dharruk tribe was compulsorily taken by the Protection Board. The Aborigines living there were forcibly removed. The Blacktown Shire Council resisted a move by the Protection Board to have the Aborigines of La Perouse relocated there. Many years later, it was decided that the descendants of the original Dharruk grantees had abandoned their rights by moving (under duress) off the land.[58]

From the time of the federation of the Australian colonies in 1901, Australia was moving towards the establishment of a social welfare state. The old-age pension was introduced in 1909 and maternity allowances were granted in 1912. While these forms of social progress were proceeding, the policy of the Protection Board was becoming more systematically organised and assimilationist. Aborigines had no entitlement to any social welfare. To obtain the protection of the Protection Board people had to be full- or half-blood Aborigines. Those who did not pass this test were not classified as Aborigines, and therefore not allowed to live in the missions or reserves with their families. Denied rations, some of these Aborigines settled in towns or came to find work in Sydney.

By 1910, the foundations had been laid for a system of stringent control over the lives of Aboriginal children. The Protection Board was given the power to assume full custody and control over any Aboriginal child who was found to be neglected. In 1915, there was no longer any need to prove neglect—not that this was a hard task in a community where poverty was almost endemic. The board was also given the power to apprentice children to tradesmen, albeit with their parents' consent. In 1914, the Protection Board decided that all boys more than fourteen years of age were to be forced to leave the Aboriginal reserves and find work. All Aboriginal girls of more than fourteen years of age who were in reserves were sent to be trained at the Cootamundra Training Home until they found a job. The home did not close until 1969. Many of these girls later became pregnant and their children, in turn, were taken from them, thus creating two or three generations of children who were separated from their families. Any parent who wanted to appeal against a decision about their child had the burden of establishing why the child should remain in their custody.

As a result of these harsh policies, many Aborigines left the reserves to try to escape from the long arm of the Protection Board. The board also had the power to order the removal of Aboriginal men from reserves to find work. This meant that fathers and husbands were absent for most of the year, either voluntarily or involuntarily, travelling the countryside from town to town or trying their luck in the city in pursuit of seasonal employment. When work could not be found, especially during the drought of the 1920s and in the Depression years of the late 1920s and early 1930s, they were forced back onto the reserves for refuge.

45

BELOW: The settlement at La Perouse in the 1960s.

It was not until 1943 that the New South Wales government made it possible for Aborigines to be exempted from the restrictive *Aboriginal Protection Act* by being issued with a certificate commonly called a 'dog tag'. A dog tag was necessary to be able to drink in a hotel but could be taken away if any offences were committed, and was sometimes revoked arbitrarily by police. To get a dog tag, the applicant had to demonstrate that he or she was living a sober life and providing acceptable living standards for his or her family.

In 1937, the Commonwealth–State Native Welfare Conference resolved that the destiny of indigenous people of mixed descent lay in their 'ultimate absorption by the people of the Commonwealth'.[59] There was never any intention or belief on the part of the policy shapers that any of the 'assimilated' Aborigines would rise above the lowest levels of the working class. In 1938, the Public Service Board inquired into the state of the Aboriginal population and recommended that Aborigines be trained and educated in public schools so that they could be assimilated into the wider community. There was local hostility towards allowing Aboriginal children to attend public schools, and sometimes the local education boards succumbed to the pressure to exclude them. In 1949, however, the minister for education expressly stated that the recommendations of the Public Service Board should be observed.

In 1938, the sesquicentenary of the establishment of the colony in January 1788 saw the first concerted and public attempt by Aborigines to express their grievances. At Australia Hall, now the Mandolin cinema in Elizabeth Street, they proclaimed 26 January as the Day of Mourning. The grievances of the Kooris of New South Wales were forcefully put:

> You came here only recently, and you took our land away from us by force. You have almost exterminated our people, but there are enough of us remaining to expose the humbug of your claim, as white Australians, to be a civilised, progressive, kindly and humane nation. By your cruelty and callousness towards the Aborigines you stand condemned .... You hypocritically claim that you are trying to 'protect' us; but your modern policy of 'protection' is killing us off just as surely as the pioneer policy of giving us poisoned damper and shooting us down like dingoes! ... We do not ask for your charity, we do not ask you to study us as scientific freaks. We ask only for justice, decency and fair play.[60]

In 1998, the cinema was bought by the Koori community because of its significance to the development of the Aboriginal political movement.

The detrimental effects of the removal of children and the assimilationist training policies on the lives of generations of Aboriginal people cannot be overestimated. As one Aboriginal woman who was removed in the 1960s and placed in the Parramatta Girls' Home, a state correctional institution, stated:

> The biggest hurt, I think, was having my mum chase the welfare car—I'll always remember it—we were looking out the window and Mum was running behind us and

46

singing out for us. They locked us in the police cell up here and Mum was walking up and down outside the police station and crying and screaming out for us. There were ten of us.[61]

Urban Aborigines were not spared the attentions of the Protection Board, as one Aboriginal mother with five children learned in 1940. The family lived at inner-city Redfern and the local police, reporting on Redfern's unsavoury reputation to the Protection Board, advised that the children be taken away. One of the children later remembered:

My mother ... was looking after us and she was doing a bloody good job when they broke into our house at Redfern. There was a heap of coppers and they just dragged us out of bed at four o'clock in the morning. We were a big family and very close. It broke our family up. There was no need for it.[62]

There was often a labyrinth of transfers of children which made reunion difficult, if not impossible. Sometimes there were no records at all, so the children disappeared from their families forever. From the 1950s, fostering and adopting Aboriginal children became more common. This did not require expenditure on institutions which were not really working as instruments of assimilation and becoming an ineffectual drain on public funds.

Added to the social chaos of separation was the terrible mental conflict suffered by the children themselves, who were taught to want to be European and to regard the adult Aborigines who remained on the reserves or in Aboriginal family units as ugly, dirty and frightening. They were taught not to respect their own people while simultaneously being shown that they themselves would never be regarded by whites as any better than those they were told to discard.

The policy of assimilation continued for a number of decades, strongly supported and constantly justified despite clear evidence that it was in fact not working. Far from wanting to be just like the rest of society, many Aborigines wanted to maintain links to their traditional culture and identity rather than severing and ignoring them. By the 1950s there was growing concern among many members of the community about the treatment of Aborigines. Australia's often asserted reputation as a protector of human rights did not sit well with our record of systematically denying them to indigenous people. In 1957, the federal and state governments decided to direct future policies towards granting Aborigines the rights and privileges of full citizenship.

In 1967, a referendum finally gave Aborigines full citizenship and the right to be counted in the national census with the rest of the population for the first time. The referendum, which had the highest percentage of 'yes' votes ever in favour of amending the Constitution, also gave the federal government power to legislate in the area of Aboriginal welfare. In 1972, the federal Labor Party promised that Aborigines would be granted land rights in certain circumstances. A ministry of Aboriginal affairs was created. In Sydney, welfare services run by

47

Aborigines in Redfern were funded by the federal government. By the time the Labor government lost office in 1975, the budget for the Department of Aboriginal Affairs had risen to $141 million.

The new Liberal coalition government recognised in 1976 that the days of the old assimilation policy were over and that Aborigines had the right to maintain their identity and culture. As part of a policy of self-determination for Aborigines, the administration of Aboriginal affairs is in the hands of the Aboriginal and Torres Strait Islander Commission (ATSIC), which was established in 1990.

The policy of separating children from their families, however, was not abandoned until 1969, when the state Aboriginal Welfare Board was finally abolished. At the time, there were over a thousand children in institutional or family care. It is estimated by the state government that about 8000 children were taken from their parents in New South Wales alone.[63] The records indicate the number is closer to 6000, but, in a telling illustration of how little weight was put on the survival of Aboriginal family units, the records are incomplete.[64] From 1980, the family tracing agency Link Up (New South Wales) Aboriginal Corporation was established. It was not until the mid-1980s, however, that a policy in favour of placing Aboriginal children in need of adoption with other Aboriginal families was put into practice.

In 1994–95, $1.34 billion was spent by the federal government on funding ATSIC and Aboriginal welfare programs such as housing, employment and health. Many Australians are baffled, frustrated and incensed by the inability of large sums of money to improve the health, social and economic welfare of Aborigines.

While the federal government was flexing its new power over Aboriginal issues from 1972 onwards, the New South Wales government was also taking steps to introduce new policies. The Aboriginal Lands Trust was set up in 1973 and land that was formerly used for Aboriginal reserves was transferred into it. Five years later, the New South Wales Department of Aboriginal Affairs was created.

Then, in 1983, the *Aboriginal Land Rights Act* established the New South Wales Land Council and smaller regional and local councils, such as the La Perouse and Metropolitan land councils. Each council was given title to the land in their area which had been held by the Aboriginal Lands Trust.

It was not until the landmark High Court Mabo decision of 1992 that the doctrine of *terra nullius* throughout the Australian continent was rejected. In the judgment, Justice Brennan stated that there was an Aboriginal system of control of the land which varied from place to place but nevertheless existed. The continuation of native title depended on a continued connection to the land, for hunting or fishing, or as permanent or temporary accommodation. As a response to the High Court's decision in the Mabo case, the federal government under then prime minister Paul Keating passed the *Native Title Act* to put in place a process for making and adjudicating native title claims. The Native Title Tribunal has the task of hearing claims. The largest claim to date in New South Wales is for 2000 hectares near Queanbeyan by the Ngunnawal tribe.

In the Wik decision of the High Court in 1996, the question of native title on pastoral leasehold land was considered. The court said that Aboriginal land claims could exist alongside European occupation of Crown land which was being used for pastoral purposes or mining leases. While land claims over pastoral leasehold land do not directly affect the Aborigines living in Sydney today, resolving the issues of land ownership and the respective rights of various occupants of the land are an important ingredient in any attempt at reconciliation between Aborigines and people of non-Aboriginal descent. It is also an important barometer of the willingness of non-Aboriginal Australians to confront in a mature and responsible manner the less glorious achievements of the past. The Howard government, after a period of much political negotiation in the federal senate, has created a legislative framework to deal with the consequences of the Wik judgment.

By looking at any statistic, it is clear that Aborigines are far worse off than the rest of the population. Aborigines represent 12 per cent of the total prison population, but only 1.6 per cent of the Australian population. They are much less likely to have any tertiary education, and slightly less than half leave school before the age of sixteen. The infant

49

RIGHT: A demonstration march through the streets of Redfern in the 1980s, protesting against Aboriginal deaths in custody and championing the cause of Aboriginal land rights.

mortality rate is three times the national average, and life expectancy is fifteen years shorter. In New South Wales, there is a 35 per cent unemployment rate compared with an average of around 8 per cent for the community as a whole.

One of the saddest and most emotive issues in both Aboriginal and non-Aboriginal communities is the level of Aboriginal deaths in custody. Between 1980 and 1989, ninety-nine Aborigines died while in detention throughout Australia. Half of those who had died had been arrested for drunkenness. The average age was thirty-two, and only two people had completed high school. Half of them had been taken from their families as children, and eighty-three of them were unemployed. The deaths continue.

An important recommendation of the Royal Commission into Deaths in Custody, presided over by Justice Marcus Einfeld, was that administrative duplication of funding Aboriginal communities between state and federal government agencies be eliminated and that, while the management and accountability of funds should be centralised, regional communities should have more say in where the priorities lie. The New South Wales Land Council, for example, was concerned that ATSIC was spending too much money on land acquisition in the Northern Territory and went to court to have this policy decision reversed. The recommended coordination between federal and state bodies, however, still has not occurred. Other failures have included the five-year experiment with a dedicated Aboriginal health service, abandoned in 1995 and returned to the Department of Health. The Aboriginal Legal Service, established in 1970 and based at Redfern, came under heavy pressure because it did not comply with the conditions of grants from ATSIC. It has been reopened.

The Keating government's term of office from 1992 to 1996 was the high-water mark for the policy of reconciliation between Aboriginal and non-Aboriginal Australians. In December 1992, Prime Minister Paul Keating gave his 'Redfern speech' to launch the International Year of the World's Indigenous People. This was the strongest statement ever made by a prime minister on the history of Aboriginal and non-Aboriginal relations. The Prime Minister said, in part:

> We took the traditional lands and smashed the traditional way of life. We brought the diseases and the alcohol. We committed the murders. We took the children from their mothers. We practised discrimination and exclusion. It was our ignorance and our prejudice—and our failure to imagine these things being done to us.

The Liberal–National Party coalition government, elected in March 1996, has advocated and insisted on greater accountability for ATSIC. There has also been a governmental move to de-emphasise the importance of a national reconciliation between Aboriginal and non-Aboriginal Australia. Prime Minister John Howard has repeatedly refused to apologise, on behalf of non-Aboriginal Australians, for past injustices to the Aboriginal people.

The main Aboriginal communities in Sydney today are at La Perouse and Redfern. La Perouse, on the northern side of Botany Bay, has a community that has been based there from the 1880s.[65] Fifty Dharawal Aborigines who had been dispossessed from their lands further south settled at La Perouse after being moved on from Circular Quay. They sold shell trinkets to visiting day tourists and hired out boats. By 1895, the 7-acre (3-hectare) Aboriginal settlement at 'La Per' was proclaimed an official Aboriginal reserve by the protectorate. In the late nineteenth century, La Perouse and Botany Bay were popular day trips for Sydneysiders. There are also records of Aborigines living at nearby Dolls Point in the 1870s, and Aborigines were receiving rations from the Aboriginal Protectorate at Kogarah in 1887.

A Methodist mission house was established at La Perouse in 1894, and this became the headquarters of the United Aborigines Mission throughout Australia. Despite official attempts to discourage Aboriginal immigration to La Perouse, people continued to drift there from other areas, such as around Lake Burragorang, Sackville Reserve and Salt Pan Creek, a reserve on the Georges River.[66]

In the Depression of the 1930s, the Aboriginal communities based at La Perouse lived close to non-Aboriginal people who also had to live in makeshift camps at Happy Valley and Frog Hollow near Little Bay. After World War II, Randwick Council became increasingly concerned to move the Aboriginal communities on, so that the rateable value of the nearby land could be increased. To help lure home buyers, fibro cottages were built by the state government in the late 1950s, but many Aborigines at La Perouse still did not have electricity or a supply of running water. Racial tensions were highlighted when the new white residents successfully petitioned Randwick Council to change the name of the street bordering the reserve from Aborigines Avenue to Endeavour Avenue.

The Aborigines of La Perouse today have the longest continuous history of urban contact, having lived for over a century at the margins of a metropolitan centre. Nearly all of them are descended, at least in part, from the original inhabitants of the 1880s.[67] One of the better-known families from La Perouse is the Ella family, which includes famous rugby union players Mark, Gary and Glen. Gary Ella is the senior manager for Aboriginal relations for the Sydney Olympic Games.

By 1930, many urban Aborigines who were descended from rural communities to the west of the state lived in working-class inner-city suburbs such as Redfern, Balmain, Glebe, Surry Hills and Rozelle.[68] Some of the rural areas these Aborigines came from included Moree, Dubbo, the north coast and Queensland. People came to the city looking for work, better education and more freedom and opportunities than Aborigines living in country towns enjoyed. The drift into Sydney was accelerated during the optimistic years after the referendum of 1967, and the emerging liberation politics of African Americans from the mid-1960s, when the demand for self-determination became a political crusade. Many of the early Aboriginal activists of those years lived around Redfern—among them Sol, Bob and Kaye Bellear, Billy and Lyn Craigie, Paul Coe, Gary Foley and Garry Williams. Today, Redfern is the main meeting place for Kooris in Sydney.

By 1965, Redfern had an Aboriginal population of 12 000,[69] many of whom were employed in the local factories, which were far more numerous then than they are today. Nurses trained at inner-city hospitals such as the Royal Alexandra Hospital for Children, Camperdown.

51

ABOVE: Aboriginal boys in one of Redfern's narrow laneways (*Reproduced with permission of Mark Tedeschi/Image Library, State Library of New South Wales*)

52

The area where most of the Aboriginal community settled and now live in Redfern is known as 'The Block', between Eveleigh, Vine, Caroline and Hugo streets. Most of the housing on the Block has been owned by the Aboriginal Housing Commission (AHC) since 1973. The utopian vision of creating a self-governing oasis for members of Sydney's Koori community sadly has not come to pass. Due to a lack of maintenance, the houses are in a dilapidated state, and many are uninhabitable.

Some members of the Koori community there estimate that about 30 per cent of the residents on the Block are heroin users, and the Health Department drops off thousands of syringes a week to ensure that dirty needles do not spread HIV, hepatitis and other diseases. The scrupulousness of the AHC's administration has been questioned by some. The AHC sees the only way out of the problems within the Aboriginal community in Redfern as moving the residents out to new houses in other suburbs, which will be funded by ATSIC and the state government. As usual with such grand schemes, there is disagreement about who should pay. Some residents of the Block would be happy to move out: they see it as the only way of breaking out of the cycle of poverty and drug addiction.[70] A breakdown in the relationship between the New South Wales police service and the Aboriginal community at Redfern has not helped the situation.

There have been many instances of violence and excessive use of force by the police towards the Kooris of Redfern and neighbouring suburbs. The police have been accused of overzealousness in executing their duties. One instance was in 1989, when David Gundy was killed in a dawn raid at his home in Marrickville. Gundy was not a criminal suspect at the time he was shot by a member of the elite Special Weapons and Operations Squad—the suspect was a flatmate who was absent at the time of the raid.

In 1990, a report was commissioned by the National Inquiry into Racist Violence (the Cuneen Report), prompted by concern over the excessive use of police force against Aborigines in Redfern. The event which was the immediate reason for the inquiry was a dramatic dawn raid in February 1990 by 135 members of the elite police corps called the Tactical Response Group. Ten homes were stormed by police carrying iron bars and sledgehammers. Eight people were arrested for property crimes. The report found that the force used in the raid was excessive. It traced the history of Aboriginal relations with the police back to the 1960s, when relations with the police broke down in the Redfern area, and it told a sorry tale of aggression, distrust and overreaction.

In 1992, a year after the publication of the Cuneen Report, the Australian Broadcasting Commission aired a documentary about police conduct in Redfern called 'Cop it Sweet'. Remarkably, considering the racist and obscene language used by police, they were aware they were being filmed. It was clear to anyone who watched that the police had learnt little from what was said in the Cuneen Report and the vitriolic nature of the conflict in Redfern was brought directly into the homes of non-Aboriginal Sydneysiders. The police who were filmed were singled out for discipline, but little else was done to change the system as a whole, or police attitudes towards Aborigines. Few people accepted assurances from the police that the conduct filmed was atypical. With the stronger spotlight on police conduct, morals and methods as a consequence of the Wood Police Royal Commission into police conduct and corruption, it can only be hoped that the relationship between police and policed at Redfern will get better. There is plenty of room for improvement.

Heroin and other hard drugs have taken their toll on the Aboriginal community, as alcohol has for more than 200 years. Drug use has lifted the level of assaults and aggravated property crimes. The Redfern area has the highest crime rate in Sydney.[71] With the rise in inner-city property prices through the 1990s, popular sentiment appears to swing from ill-feeling towards the police force because of their treatment of Aborigines, to concern about police inaction and the increase in crime, especially in the inner-city suburbs.

From early 1997, there has been a police clampdown on illegal activity in Redfern. At first there was a flare-up in anti-police violence that led to a warning to taxi drivers not to enter the area; however, greater police surveillance and vigilance led to a decline in the crime rate in 1997. The Aboriginal Housing Commission decided to have several derelict houses in the Block demolished in early 1997, as these houses were often used as safe havens for trouble makers.

Some non-Aboriginal people have expressed doubt that the urban Aborigines are not 'real' Aborigines, that the genuine Aborigines have to be a certain colour and live a traditional way of life out of the city, ideally in the remote interior. This is a harsh and flawed view. Many Aborigines, just like non-Aboriginal Australians, were forced from rural areas to seek employment opportunities. Many of Sydney's Aborigines are descended from people who moved into the city generations ago in search of a better way of life. The fallacy of the need to have a certain skin colour or lead a particular lifestyle is a tattered fragment of the dark ages of assimilationist policy when children were taken from their families if they were not full-blooded or half-caste Aborigines so that they could be re-created as well-behaved and useful members of European society. This wrong-headed policy caused emotional and social trauma on a widespread scale which has been transmitted far beyond the immediate victims.

It is also wrong to believe that all the Aborigines of the Sydney region were killed or died out, although that does seem to be sadly true of those living on the coast. There are descendants of the Dharruk and the Dharawhal living here today. Many of Sydney's Kooris can trace their ancestors back to the early colonial days.

ABOVE: Easterly view of Sydney in 1821 taken from The Rocks, where the southern approach to the Harbour Bridge lies today. On the left, quarry men are busy working the sandstone that gave The Rocks its name. Note the obelisk in Macquarie Place, which is still standing, and prosperous emancipist Simeon Lord's house to the right. *Panoramic view of the town of Sydney, 1821, Major James Taylor (Image Library, State Library of NSW)*

BELOW: View of Woolloomooloo and the eastern side of the town in 1849, just before the gold rushes of the 1850s. *Sydney from Woolloomooloo, G. E. Peacock (Image Library, State Library of NSW)*

LEFT: William Charles Wentworth in 1872. *Portrait of W. C. Wentworth, James Anderson (Image Library, State Library of NSW)*

ABOVE: Portrait of a young Sir Henry Parkes, c. 1850. *(Image Library, State Library of NSW)*

RIGHT: Aerial illustration of Sydney produced in the city's centenary year, 1888. *Sydney in 1888, M. S. Hill (Image Library, State Library of NSW)*

ABOVE: World War I enlistment poster. (*Image Library, State Library of NSW*)

ABOVE: Opera House under construction—1996. (*David Moore*)
BELOW: Opera House at night. (*Marcus Clinton*)

CHAPTER THREE

THE CAMP: 1788–1820

The spot chosen for this purpose was at the head of the cove, near the run of fresh water, which stole silently along through a very thick wood, the stillness of which had then, for the first time since creation, been interrupted for the round sound of the labourer's axe and the downfall of its ancient inhabitants; a stillness and tranquillity which from that day were to give place to the voice of labour, the confusion of camps and towns, and the 'busy hum of its new possessors'.

Judge Advocate David Collins, 1798[1]

CAPTAIN JAMES COOK, Sir Joseph Banks and the crew of the *Endeavour* were the first recorded European visitors to the Sydney area. They arrived at Botany Bay in April 1770, in the process of navigating the east coast of Australia from Port Hicks in the south to the tip of Cape York Peninsula in the north. The voyage of the *Endeavour* was sponsored by the Royal Society, an institution dedicated to the promotion and study of science, and scientific observation. The voyage of the *Endeavour* was the first British government-sponsored voyage of discovery, inspired by the quest to obtain a greater scientific understanding of the natural world.

The principal purpose of the voyage was to observe the transit of Venus at Tahiti, and thus help determine the best means of measuring longitude. After leaving Tahiti, Cook sailed westward to New Zealand and the east coast of Australia. Upon the return of the *Endeavour* to England, both Cook and Banks optimistically advised the British government that Botany Bay would be a suitable site for a settlement:

Making an excursion about the country, we found it agreeably variegated with wood and lawn, the trees being strait [sic] and tall without any underwood. The country might be cultivated without cutting down one of them. The grass grows in large tufts, almost close to each other, and there is a great plenty of it … [Dr Solander, who was Banks's assistant and another person] went up the country, where they found the soil to be a deep black mould, which appeared to be calculated for the production of any kind of grain. They saw some of the finest meadows they ever beheld, and met with a few rocky places, the stone of which is sandy, and seemed to be admirably adapted to building …[2]

Joseph Banks, a gentleman scientist and a person of some political influence, continued his role as a leading advocate and expert on antipodean matters until his death in 1820, although he never returned to Australia.

In the intervening seventeen years between 1770 and 1787, the issue of what to do with the increasing number of convicts became critical, particularly after the American War of Independence in 1776. The newly independent American colonies, already well supplied with forced labour in the form of negro slaves, no longer wished to be the dumping ground for Britain's criminal classes; by the early 1780s, the prisons of Britain were overflowing with people who had often been forced, through circumstances, to resort to crime.

The industrial and agrarian revolutions were creating a new pool of unemployed people who left their small villages to find work in the steadily growing cities of Britain. Inventions such as the reaper and the mechanical seed planter forced many agricultural labourers out of paid work. The enclosure movement of the late eighteenth century was putting into the exclusive hands of local squires and landowners land which had, since medieval times, been shared communally.

With the invention of the flying shuttle and the spinning jenny, the textile industry became industrialised from the middle of the eighteenth century. A later but very important invention after 1800 was the machine loom. Added to all these changes in the traditional, pre-industrial ways of life, there was, from 1750, a boom in the population which further augmented the pool of unemployed workers.

The penal code of late–eighteenth-century Britain was notoriously harsh. Transportation for seven years was the minimum sentence imposed for minor property crimes. Other crimes attracted the death penalty. A fourteen-year sentence was imposed on those who had won a reprieve from the death sentence.

Some practical solution to the rising prison population had to be found. Decommissioned and dismasted warships, known as hulks, were used to accommodate prisoners, but they could not resolve the problem indefinitely. In the three years from the conclusion of the American War of Independence, the number of prisoners contained in the hulks had risen from 200 to 1240.[3] The idea of transportation had certain advantages: the further away the convicts, or exiles, were sent, the less likely it was they could return. Britain may be able to rid herself of many of them forever. Convicts were not given return passages after they had served their term of sentence, and the price of the journey home was beyond the financial capacity of most of them.

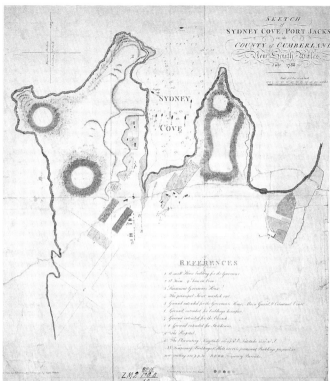

ABOVE: An engraved portrait of the colony's first governor, Captain Arthur Phillip. RIGHT: One of the earliest published sketches of Sydney Cove. The sketch was dated July 1788, and published the following year. The coastline was sketched by Lieutenant William Dawes and the depth soundings taken by Captain John Hunter.

57

At the same time as the transportation issue was under discussion, some politicians and opportunists of the day pressed the advantages of New South Wales and Norfolk Island as having some strategic importance. The French had a presence in the Pacific region with its colonies in the south Pacific, and any further territorial expansion to this newly charted part of the world by Britain's long-term adversary needed to be checked. With the American colonies gone, and the South American continent already taken by the Spaniards and the Portuguese, Britain's imperial ambitions were limited to Asia, the African continent, the Pacific and the Antipodes.

Empire building depended on strong ships with timber masts and flax for sail making. Cook, in his later, 1774 voyage to the South Seas, noticed the strong, straight stands of Norfolk Island pine trees. A form of the flax plant also grew on that island. Politician and lobbyist Joseph Matra was one of the people who advocated the strategic advantages of New South Wales as a source of timber and flax. Sniffing the political wind, he also noted the area's remoteness as a suitable place for containing felons.

Assured by, and heavily relying upon, Joseph Banks's opinion of Botany Bay's suitability, a committee led by Lord Beauchamp decided to establish a penal colony in New South Wales. The first choice of the committee had been in west Africa, but this site was rejected after due inquiry and an investigative journey there: despite its location on the trade route to southern Africa and Asia, the terrain was too arid. New South Wales was too far away for there to be time to conduct any further surveys, so the destination was chosen without any further examination. The accounts given by Cook and Banks seemed so promising that a survey seemed unnecessary.

The man chosen to lead the expedition was Captain Arthur Phillip of the Royal Navy, a man of forty-nine with an uninspiring but honourable record as a naval officer. Fortunately for the infant colony, Phillip had spent time farming, so he was at least somewhat acquainted with the science and practice of agriculture, although traditional British farming techniques would be of questionable utility in this strange, 'new' land. Phillip was a man whose views were quite enlightened by the standards of those days: he proposed to treat the Aborigines fairly and to try to encourage the convicts to reform themselves. As was indicated in the previous chapter, his good intentions regarding the Aborigines were not entirely fulfilled.

The First Fleet consisted of 1030 people, of whom 778 were convicts. Most of the convicts had been sentenced to seven years' transportation for minor theft. Many were second offenders. Some were guilty of more serious property crimes—slightly more than one hundred of the convicts had used violence. There were no political prisoners, although some of these came later. The youngest convict on the First Fleet was a nine-year-old chimney sweep.[4] Members of the First Fleet were not chosen according to whether they possessed suitable trades and this proved to be a problem for the young colony. There were no overseers, and only two brickmakers and six carpenters. The conditions on board the ships of the First Fleet were rudimentary. The voyage of the First Fleet was, however, a reasonably well-managed affair. Although the convicts were housed in overcrowded conditions—there was no light, little air and everyone below decks had to stoop—only twenty-three convicts died on the journey out. The explanation provided by Watkin Tench, a captain of the marines and recorder of the expedition to Botany Bay, was that the provisioning was adequate and well planned.[5]

The importance attached to religious observance was not high in the early years of the colony, as evidenced by the fact that the only chaplain of the First Fleet, Richard Johnson, was sent out as an afterthought at the urging of an English humanitarian and politician, William Wilberforce.[6]

The journey to Botany Bay took eight months. Finally, by 20 January 1788, all seven ships had dropped anchor at the chosen destination. Phillip and other officers were soon disappointed by what they saw: sandy soil and swampy land quite unsuitable for growing crops and grazing cattle. There was no abundance of fresh water either. Phillip, concerned that the convicts needed to disembark after the long journey out to Botany Bay, decided to keep exploring the coast to the north up to Broken Bay for more promising country.

On the afternoon of 21 January, Phillip sailed in to what he then called, and which can still be called today, the 'finest harbour in the world'. Phillip explored the coves in the harbour, and chose Sydney Cove for settlement. It was sheltered and cooled by a pleasant onshore breeze, had deep water suitable for shipping, no mangroves (which would have made disembarking difficult) and plentiful fresh water.

By an astounding coincidence, two French ships commanded by le Comte de la Pérouse arrived in Botany Bay within days of the First Fleet. Once everyone had got over their mutual surprise, the French and the English cast aside the issue of their nations' competing territorial ambitions and welcomed each other in the accommodating manner of stranded, homesick travellers. The French badly needed to regroup and repair after being attacked by Samoans in the Pacific Ocean. After building new longboats, they left Botany Bay, and were never seen again.

On the evening of 25 January, Phillip and some of his men disembarked at Sydney Cove and started to clear enough land for the officers and some of the convicts to camp. The area was densely timbered with very tall trees such as *Angophora costata*, forest red gums (*Eucalyptus tetricornis*) and blackbutt (*Eucalyptus pilularis*). These tall trees provided a canopy of shade and shelter from Sydney's typically heavy summer storms. Closer to the water's edge were cabbage palms (*Livistonia australis*). There were also stately Port Jackson figs (*Ficus rubignosa*) and, in the rocky outcrops along the shore, scrubby-looking wattle trees (*Acacia suaveolens*).

By 26 January, all the ships in the First Fleet had arrived in Sydney Cove. That evening, the Union Jack was raised and the King was toasted. By the next day, the rest of the male convicts had disembarked. The following days were a time of frenzied activity; more encampments were cleared, tents were erected and stores brought on shore. The temporary Government House, prefabricated in England from canvas, was erected on the eastern side of the cove. The marines were placed right in the middle at the head of the Tank Stream as a buffer zone between Phillip's domain and the convicts camped on the western side of the cove.

The effect of this early allocation of land is still apparent. The seat of government and many government offices lie on the eastern side of the Tank Stream. The early location of the convicts at The Rocks between the cove and the rocky escarpment after which the area was named explains why the area was so densely settled and built up.

In the first days after landing in the new colony, dysentery and scurvy broke out for the first time since the Fleet had left Portsmouth. The lack of antiscorbutics had been a contentious issue between Phillip and his superiors when the fleet had been commissioned. Scurvy was treated with wild celery, spinach and parsley, or what passed for them. These remedies might have helped alleviate vitamin deficiencies in the short term, but the problem of ensuring an adequate food supply dogged the colony for several years. Phillip predicted that the colony would be dependent on imported food for at least four years. Soil improvement was impossible without large supplies of animal manure, and there were precious few cattle and sheep available to provide this fertiliser.

Hardly any of the convicts were skilled agricultural labourers and the marines, in a strong assertion of the pecking order they sought to establish, did not want to perform the same tasks as the convicts. Nor did they want to oversee the convicts, build shelters or undertake hard work, or anything else other than keep the peace. This often meant 'dealing' with the Aborigines, especially when they were a 'problem'. Phillip was not authorised under the terms of his commission to induce better productivity by granting soldiers or marines land, so he had the difficult task of building the penal settlement without any willing labour.

Soon pilfering from the government stores broke out, although the only difference between the rations for the convicts and the rest was that the convicts had no alcohol. Undeterred by sentences such as 150 lashes, and exile to nearby Pinchgut Island (Fort Denison) on rations of bread and water, convicts continued to steal. Eventually, the first man was hanged in the colony for this offence in February 1788 on Gallows Hill[7] near the present-day corner of Harrington and Essex streets.[8] However, it was not only the convicts who posed the threat to security of the food supply. Six marines Tench called 'the flower of our battalion' were executed publicly in March 1789 for robbing the public stores.

In the middle of 1788, Watkin Tench dispatched his *Narrative of the Expedition to Botany Bay* to England by ship, and had the following to say about the state of progress:[9]

> The male convicts have been divided into gangs, over each of which a person, selected from among themselves, is placed. It is to be regretted that Government did not take this matter into consideration before we left England, and appoint proper persons [as overseers] … the behaviour of all classes of these people [the convicts] since our arrival in the settlement has been better than could, I think, have been expected of them. Temporary wooden storehouses covered with thatch or shingles[10] in which the cargoes of the ships have been lodged, are completed; and an hospital is erected … the encampments of the convicts and marines are still kept up; and to secure their owners from the coldness of the nights, are covered with bushes. Only houses of stone are yet begun, which are intended for the Governor and Lieutenant Governor.

In late 1788, the cattle herd of two bulls and four cows strayed from where they had been offloaded near Bennelong Point. They were found seven years later, at a place suitably called 'The Cowpastures', now Camden. Phillip soon realised that the infertile, stony and sandy soil at Farm Cove to the east of Sydney Cove—where the Royal Botanic Gardens are today— would not provide satisfactory conditions for growing crops so, in November, another settlement was established at Rose Hill. Rose Hill was renamed Parramatta in May 1791. By November 1791, there were more than 1600 people living there. At the end of 1790, Tench noted that 'our principal efforts [are] wisely being made at Rose Hill. Except building, sawing and brick-making, nothing of consequence is now carried on here [at Sydney Cove].'[11]

In November 1789, the precariousness of the food supply was a looming problem. Rations were reduced to two-thirds. In February 1790, the *Sirius* set off for the Cape of Good Hope to get more provisions, but the ship was wrecked at Norfolk Island, fortunately without any loss of life. The morale of the colony sank further: in April, the food ration was cut to half of what it had been in January 1788. Hours of work were reduced to take account of the weakened state of the convicts.

Construction would not have been an easy task, even on full rations. The members of the First Fleet, like all Europeans, were used to working with softwoods, not tough hardwood

60

eucalypts. The only useful timbers that could be easily worked were the cabbage tree palms used for making hats (among other things) and the casuarinas used to make shingles. The paltry supply of tools the First Fleet had arrived with was easily blunted on the hardwoods and soon the 'possession of a spade, a wheelbarrow or a dunghill was more coveted than the most refulgent arms in which heroism ever dazzled'.[12]

Bricks were made to the south of the camp near where Central Station is today. Convict gangs of twelve men had to haul five loads of 350 bricks every day:[13] there were no beasts of burden to do this heavy work. The job was tough—the road, better known as George Street, was much steeper then before it was levelled in the 1830s. Some of the buildings made of these bricks can still be seen, at St James' Church, the old courthouse and Hyde Park Barracks.

A lack of lime, essential to mortar the bricks together, was another problem for Sydney's early builders. Aboriginal shell middens on Bennelong Point were the first to be dug up and used as a substitute for lime, then, as they were depleted, other nearby middens around Cockle Bay (Darling Harbour) and Iron Cove were used.

A dry spell set in from 1790. This greatly reduced the first harvest at Parramatta which, in turn, put more pressure on food supplies. Early that year, there was enough salt beef to last another five months; the rice and flour would be finished by October. All the officers, struck by the precarious situation, volunteered to go fishing for food on boats in the harbour every evening, and the best marksmen were selected to hunt kangaroos and other animals. The collective depression, despair and feeling of abandonment and isolation can hardly be imagined, while, as Tench said, 'Famine was approaching with gigantic strides.'

The spirits of the new colony lifted with news from South Head that a ship was entering the harbour on 3 June 1790. Unfortunately, the *Lady Juliana* was not a store ship, but a transport with 221 female convicts and eleven children aboard. At least it brought news from home, and what news it was. The colony heard for the first time of the French Revolution of 1789 and of the damage done to the store ship *Guardian* destined for Sydney Cove which was forced to limp back to the Cape of Good Hope after hitting an iceberg. Best of all, there was news of the imminent arrival of the Second Fleet, bringing desperately needed supplies of food.

The first ship of the Second Fleet arrived seventeen days after the *Lady Juliana*. Full rations were restored in the colony the next day. Then, a few days later, the rest of the Second Fleet arrived with convicts in such a shocking state of health that, for the first time since leaving Portsmouth, members of the First Fleet had someone other than themselves to pity. Of the 1017 convicts who left England in the Second Fleet, only 626 survived the voyage and the period shortly after landing. The contractors responsible for provisioning and transporting the convicts were blamed.[14] The remuneration of the contractors had been assessed without any regard to the treatment or wellbeing of the convicts.

Two men who would play an important role in the colony arrived with the Second Fleet— John Macarthur and D'Arcy Wentworth. Macarthur was a lieutenant in the newly created New South Wales Corps and Wentworth was a distant relation of the Fitzwilliams, a family of Anglo-Irish aristrocats. His life had taken a wayward turn—he had been charged more than

LEFT: One-time Lieutenant and Paymaster in the New South Wales Corps, later pastoralist and businessman John Macarthur. Macarthur was one of the leaders of the group of 'exclusives' who led the Rum Rebellion in 1808.

62

once with highway robbery, but had not been convicted. Wentworth worked his way out as an assistant surgeon after having been persuaded by his friends to seek his fortune in the colony rather than risk transportation (or worse) if he were tried, once again, for highway robbery or some other serious crime. Both these men arrived in the colony at a fortuitous time for men of ambition. A proclamation was made shortly after the Second Fleet arrived which allowed grants of land to be made to marines—both officers and privates—to promote free settlement in New South Wales.

As a result of the dry spell and a disappointing harvest in 1790, a reduced food ration was reintroduced in April 1791. Water supplies were also threatened, so water-storage tanks were built into the stream of water flowing into Sydney Cove, hence the Tank Stream's name.

It was after the second imposition of reduced rations that the usually level-headed Watkin Tench seemed to be at his most exasperated. The members of the Second Fleet had not been given time to recover from their horrendous journey before privation set in again:

> I every day see wretches pale with disease and wasted with famine, struggle against the horrors of their situation. How striking is the effect of subordination; how dreadful is the fear of punishment!—the allotted task is still performed, even on the present subsistence:—the blacksmith sweats at the sultry forge; the sawyer labours pent up in his pit; the husbandman turns up the sterile glebe.—Shall I again hear arguments multiplied

to violate truth, and insult humanity!—Shall I again be told that the sufferings of the wretched Africans are indispensable for the culture of our sugar colonies: that white men are incapable of sustaining the heat of the climate![15]

By late 1791, the Third Fleet arrived, with 1800 convicts aboard. It took only half as long to reach Sydney as the First Fleet had. Members of the Fleet who would go on to play significant roles in the life of the colony (as we shall see) were convicts Simeon Lord, James Underwood, Isaac Nichols and Marine Lieutenant Colonel William Paterson. Another arrival was the well-known London pickpocket George Barrington, who had been transported for seven years for stealing a gold watch. His conduct in the colony was beyond reproach and he was subsequently appointed night watchman at Parramatta. He was later given land grants and settled on the Hawkesbury. In 1802, he published *Barrington's New South Wales*, a history of the colony extravagantly dedicated to King George III, his former gaoler.

From the early 1790s, the British government began to focus on making transportation more systematic and organised. There were to be two embarkations a year, and stores would be sent out with each new fleet of arrivals. The colonists were also told to expect grain from India and livestock from America.[16] By December 1792, when Phillip set sail back to England, the colony had almost doubled in size. There were about 1260 people at Sydney, and 1600 at Parramatta. Two-thirds of the population were convicts.

63

The new official government seal for New South Wales arrived in 1791. It was designed as an image of hope and aspiration. On the reverse side of the silver seal was an impression of convicts landing at Botany Bay, received by Industry, who 'surrounded by her attributes, a bale of merchandise, a bee-hive, a pick-axe, and a shovel, is releasing them from their fetters, and pointing to oxen ploughing, and a town rising on the summit of a hill, with a fort for its protection. The masts of a ship are seen in the bay.'[17]

The motto for the colony was also provided on the seal: '*Sic fortis Etruria crevit*', or 'Thus Etruria grew strong'. The words were a reference to Etruria, the geographical precursor to the Roman civilisation, founded by Romulus and Remus, children of Mars who were exiles from Greece and orphaned after their mother had been condemned to death. The history of Etruria demonstrated that colonies of exiles could achieve greatness. This motto was later adopted by the Bank of New South Wales (later renamed Westpac). Charles Darwin's grandfather Erasmus wrote a poem to commemorate the new seal and what it represented, which was, in the circumstances of the colony in 1791, a starry-eyed, futuristic fantasy. It appeared in the front pages of Governor Phillip's journal:

Where Sydney Cove her lucid bosom swells;
Courts her young navies, and the storm repels;
High on a rock amid the troubled air

HOPE stood sublime, and wav'd her golden hair;
And with sweet accents charm'd the winds to sleep;
To each wild plain she stretch'd her snowy hand,
High waving wood, and sea encircled strand.
'Hear me', she cried, 'ye rising Realms! record
Time's opening schemes, and Truth's unerring word—
There shall broad streets their stately walls extend,
The circus widen, and the crescent bend;
There, ray'd from cities o'er the cultured land,
Shall bright canals, and solid roads expand—
There the proud Arch, Colossus like, bestride
You glittering streams, and bound the chafing tide …'

There was, fortunately, something more for the convicts under sentence than simply a new seal. A government edict was promulgated making it possible for convicts to be pardoned for good behaviour, either absolutely or conditionally. After being pardoned, they could, if they were unable to pay their way home, receive land grants. This meant the convicts had a motive to behave well. Despite these inducements, some of the convicts chose to work their way home as sailors, but others took up the offer of land grants with eighteen months' supply of provisions from the government's commissariat stores. These new, emancipated settlers were to become significant agents in the transformation of the early penal colony and were to form the nucleus of Sydney's early middle class before the growth of free immigration from the 1830s onwards.[18]

Female convicts often did not fare well in the new colony. Their labour was less highly prized than the men's. They were not physically strong enough to cart bricks, chop wood or work the soil, and there was little demand for regular domestic duties in the crude accommodations of early Sydney. Often the only alternative for these women was to seek the protection of their gaolers. But things were not all bad: many successful and productive early colonial unions, although often never formally legitimised by marriage ceremony, were between convicts or between convicts and soldiers, sailors or marines. It was from these unions that many members of the first Australian-born generation of colonists sprang.

These children were known colloquially as 'currency lads and lasses'. If, on the other hand, female convicts had not found conjugal bliss in the colony, or what passed for it, by the time they served their terms or were pardoned, often their only choice was to work their passage home as a prostitute on board ship.

The threat of starvation had faded by late 1791, and never returned. Ships laden with speculative cargo, often liquor, or 'rum', were arriving regularly. Fortunately, Phillip never had to contend with the issue of how to deal with the convicts' thirst for liquor, as the first trading ship bearing a cargo of rum arrived two months after his departure. Phillip went back home to England as a man who was enthusiastic about the future of the colony he had started, despite the adverse conditions he had faced. He was convinced, however, that its future depended on the industriousness of free settlers, none of whom had arrived by the time he left Sydney. It was to be some time before free settlers were to be able to make a significant contribution to colonial life. The officers of the New South Wales Corps, typified by men such as John Macarthur, and some of the more astute and ambitious emancipated convicts, would be the first ones to prosper in the new colony, and to contribute to the development and growth of the town from the 1790s until the 1830s.

Although most of the early convicts were transported for crimes against property rather than political crimes, there were some interesting exceptions. In 1794, the Scottish Jacobins or 'Martyrs' arrived in Sydney. Their leader was Thomas Muir, head of a political discussion group in Glasgow that advocated the extension of the franchise and disseminated Thomas Paine's then revolutionary work *The Rights of Man*. Muir was tried for sedition by a jury hand-picked by the prosecution and sentenced to transportation for fourteen years. More political dissenters including Maurice Margarot and Joseph Gerrald were arrested in Edinburgh, where the National Convention of British Reformers was meeting. They arrived in Sydney and were given preferential treatment: they were not forced to work and two of them were given land grants. Gerrald was given a land grant in the Domain, where he died. He was buried in what is now the stream of the Royal Botanic Gardens. Another of them, Thomas Palmer, was active in the rum trade. Thomas Muir escaped from Sydney on a seal trading ship and died in France in 1799. Maurice Margarot had recanted his Jacobinism on his journey out to Sydney and lived there until 1810, where he played an uneasy role as agent of influence and possibly even *agent provocateur* between the administration and the convicts, including the Irish.[19]

It was not only these Scottish 'martyrs' who were sent to New South Wales for political crimes. The English penal system was hard on Irish Jacobins and other dissidents from the late 1790s. Some of these people were transported without trial. Catholics in Ireland (which by 1801 was completely colonised by England) were discriminated against at every turn. They could not vote, sit in parliament, teach, join the army, or use the rules of primogeniture to keep their estates or businesses intact. Any Irish person who acted in defiance of these laws was branded a political rebel. The first convict ships with a high component of Irish political prisoners arrived in 1798. By 1800 there were hundreds of Irish rebels in the colony. Added to the Irish who had been transported for simple property crimes, this amounted to a volatile mix in the eyes of the colonial administrators. The Irish prisoners were treated as an underclass within an underclass.

The expectations of an Irish uprising were not fulfilled until 1804, at Vinegar (Castle) Hill. It was crushed quickly and its leaders were hanged. Political prisoners continued to arrive, but they were better dispersed. Like the Aborigines, many Irish convicts developed their own folklore of political and religious persecution and oppression that was passed down the generations. As many of these Irish convicts were Catholics, this folklore fed the sectarian mood that prevailed in Sydney until the middle of the twentieth century.

There were fewer English political prisoners. About 1600 political dissidents arrived in New South Wales between 1788 and 1838, although classification of what constituted political or social crime is never perfect.[20]

Whales were sighted in the harbour in the early years of the colony. In July 1790, a few days after some people had ineptly tried to harpoon it, there was a tragic incident off Watsons Bay near South Head when a midshipman and two marines drowned after their small boat was attacked by a whale. The whale lifted the boat several metres out of the water on its back. As it dived under the water again, the men were sucked into the vortex. According to Judge Advocate Collins, the whale stayed in the harbour, but was beached at Manly Cove. It was being feasted upon by Aborigines at the time Governor Phillip was speared in the shoulder.[21]

One of the ships that arrived in Sydney as a convict transport with the Third Fleet was refitted and, in late 1791, went on to explore the southern seas for fish and whales. Watkin Tench, who left Sydney at the end of 1791, added a postscript to his narrative on the prospects of whaling in the waters off New South Wales. He reported that one of the captains of the transports of the Third Fleet saw 'more spermaceti whales that in all his former life' on the edge of the continental shelf off the south coast of New South Wales. He advised potential whalers not to be deterred by reports of bad weather. Duties on the importation of colonial whale oil, however, meant that it would not be until the 1830s that whaling on the New South Wales coast would become a major industry. The new colony would have to look elsewhere for an export staple to underpin its economy.

From the early 1790s, there were the first stirrings of commercial activity. The first men of commerce in the colony were the shrewder officers of the New South Wales Corps, later colloquially renamed the 'Rum Corps'. Phillip's successor, Acting Governor Francis Grose, had been a partner in chartering a ship laden with speculative cargo.[22] Grose was acting governor until late 1795. It was during his term in office that the moral and administrative rot in the colony really set in. Officer members of the New South Wales Corps were very adept at granting preferment to themselves, and many profited from the lack of wise and scrupulous government administration. To be fair, however, there was a boom in commercial activity associated with the Rum Corps activity that otherwise may not have occurred so soon, despite the corps's dubious motives and methods.

Many officers of the Rum Corps were given large, productive land grants. For example, in 1794, Macarthur had 400 acres of good farming land at Parramatta. These grants were conveniently and necessarily accompanied with access to assigned convict labour—the only labour pool there was.

Grose also tolerated the collusive tendering by officer members of the New South Wales Corps for newly arrived cargoes of goods, particularly alcohol. Members of the corps

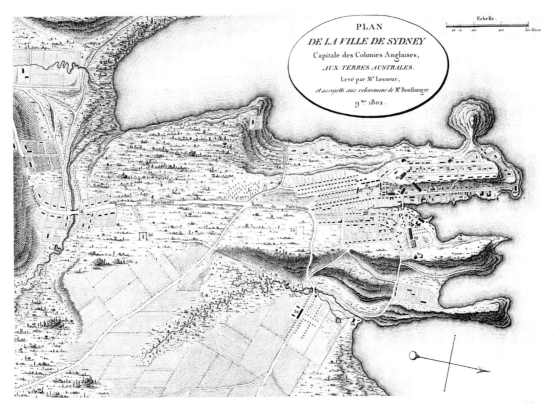

ABOVE: One of the early maps of Sydney, drawn in 1802 by Leseur, an illustrator on a voyage of discovery commissioned by the French government during the Napoleonic era. The natural waterline which existed before the land reclamation of the nineteenth and twentieth centuries can easily be seen, as can the early layout of the town, then just a small village.

67

purchased inbound cargoes, and sometimes even chartered entire ships. Leading lights of the corps were Macarthur, Grose, Paterson, Johnston, Foveaux, Rowley and Nepean. John Macarthur was also the paymaster for the colony. This gave the Rum Corps a huge advantage, as it had the power to issue bills that were the main form of currency. This meant that they not only controlled the flow of imports, but the money supply as well.

Convicts were assigned to work in the construction of farms and buildings in Sydney and Parramatta. By 1799, convicts amounted to 37 per cent of the population. The balance consisted of soldiers and emancipists who had served their terms or been pardoned. Sydney, Parramatta and Toongabbie were small townships. The main problem facing the colony in 1800 was no longer the food supply, but finding enough skilled labour to make growth possible.

The level of commercial activity meant that from about 1800 onwards, the town of Sydney started to assume a more permanent demeanour. Agricultural output rose sharply once the officers were granted large portions of land. One of the reasons for the Rum Corps's success was that its leaders, in particular John Macarthur, were very effective lobbyists for their own cause in London. This political effectiveness, and the real power and authority they had in the colony, made controlling them impossible. The financial profit made by the corps was enormous. One assertion by an observer of the day was that rum bought for 10 shillings a gallon was sold for thirty times that amount; tea bought for 10 shillings was sold for 5 guineas a pound.[23] There was a petition from the settlers in 1800 complaining that the officers of the Rum Corps had imported rum for 8 shillings a gallon, and sold it for between 20 and 60 shillings a gallon.[24]

But the monopoly of the officers of the Rum Corps was inherently unstable. It depended on there being no one else in the colony with access to capital or credit. Shrewder emancipists like Simeon Lord, postmaster Isaac Nichols, Henry Kable, James Underwood and Mary Reiby learnt quickly from their officer-masters. These emancipists acted as the middlemen in the trade of goods in the colony. Soon their wealth and influence eclipsed that of many members of the Rum Corps, whose position was further threatened by others such as D'Arcy Wentworth and junior officers who were not part of the inner Rum Corps.

The evolving relationship between emancipists and marine officer-masters was an interesting one. For example, Simeon Lord was transported for seven years in 1790 for theft. He was assigned to Captain Thomas Rowley, one of the more active members of the Rum Corps and one of its bigger traders. Rowley set Lord up as a baker and licensed victualler.[25] Lord soon prospered and, for forty years, he was one of Sydney's most successful businessmen. He acted as a commission agent, wholesaler and auctioneer, and had other diverse trading interests, as well as being active in the whale oil and sandalwood trades. He was one of the first manufacturers in Sydney, having set up a woollen mill on the northern shores of Botany Bay, near where Kingsford Smith (Sydney) Airport is today.

Another threat to the survival of the Rum Corps's trading activities was the arrival in 1800 of Robert Campbell, a Scottish merchant who had been trading in Calcutta before his arrival in Sydney. This new rival with capital, connections and mercantile expertise would not have been welcomed by many members of the corps. Campbell was the first free immigrant merchant who took the side of the free settlers and emancipists against the Rum Corps. He offered the settlers reasonable terms of credit and set up his trading activities in the area known as Campbells Cove. He also pioneered the shipbuilding and sealing industries. Campbell and other immigrant merchants who followed him to Sydney were responsible for the remarkable growth in the size of the livestock herd. Between 1800 and 1817, the total livestock numbers in the colony grew from 1000 to 45 000 head of cattle, and from 6000 to 170 000 head of sheep.[26] Until the herd of stock became large enough, much of the meat eaten in the colony was Tahitian pork.[27]

In the three years of Grose's term the Rum Corps commercial activities had become so entrenched that Governor Hunter, upon his arrival in 1795 until his departure in 1799, found the situation impossible to control, as did his successor, Philip Gidley King, who served from 1800–1806. King tried to restrain Macarthur's increasing dominance in the economic and political life of the colony by sending him back to England in 1801 to be court-martialled for duelling with another officer. Macarthur outsmarted King, and returned to Sydney in 1805 triumphantly holding a land grant for 5000 acres (2000 hectares) of prime grazing land at The Cowpastures (Camden). This grant was a strong reminder of Macarthur's political skills. The Cowpastures was the engine room of the Macarthur family's economic prosperity for many generations to come.

William Bligh succeeded Governor King in 1806. The Colonial Office expected that this authoritarian and autocratic naval officer, whose harsh and unforgiving conduct (especially towards incompetence) led to the mutiny of members of the crew of the *Bounty* in the Pacific Ocean in 1789, would be strong enough to bring the Rum Corps under control. It would, with the benefit of hindsight, have been a good idea to replace the Rum Corps as well.

Bligh did not arrive at an easy point in the life of Sydney and New South Wales. Severe flooding in the Hawkesbury in 1806 reduced the crop for the year. The Napoleonic Wars then raging in Europe reduced the amount of inbound shipping and, with it, the amount of imported goods and fresh labour. The enmity between Bligh and the Rum Corps soon escalated. Bligh's attempts to control the corps often depended on the legal advice of emancipist advocates such as George Crossley, a solicitor transported for forgery. The 'exclusive' officers of the Rum Corps thought these former felons were unfit to advocate anyone's cause in a court of law.

By 1806, Sydney had become a litigious place. Some observers noted the paradox of this resort to the law in a penal colony. John Turnbull, a merchant sea captain who went on a four-year voyage in the Pacific Ocean, commented colourfully on this tendency to resort quickly to legal process:

> Strange as it may appear, the multitude of law-suits and litigations in this colony exceed all proportion to its population. There were not less than three hundred capiases, summonses and executions [of judgment] to be brought forward at the next sitting of the civil court, and the fees of office to the provost marshal were said to amount to nearly three hundred pounds. Indeed the lawyers and the publicans are the most profitable trades in the colony. One of these kinds of gentlemen of the quill [lawyers] had the modesty to charge me £4 6s for writing half a sheet of paper and, in answer to my remonstrance, replied that he lost money by me. This fellow was a convict.[28]

From the early 1800s, the voice of the free settlers was heard for the first time. These people with small land grants were strongly opposed to the greed and high-handed attitude of the Rum Corps. The settlers told Bligh forcefully that Macarthur and his allies were not, and never would be, their spokesmen. Bligh believed that these small-scale yeoman farmers along the Hawkesbury were the key to the economic future of the colony, and that their agricultural activities should be encouraged in preference to the avaricious goals of Macarthur and others who wanted to create wealth from large-scale pastoral activities, such as sheep and cattle grazing.

The immediate cause of the Rum Rebellion was the demand by Bligh that John Macarthur, by then the wealthiest man in the colony, appear before Judge Advocate Richard Atkins, on 25 January 1808. Macarthur loathed Atkins. The two men were sworn enemies and, like so many others, were locked in litigation. Macarthur claimed Atkins owed him money and that he could not judge him because of his bias.

Macarthur was to be prosecuted for several offences: importing stills for the production of alcohol illegally on a ship in which he was part-owner; inducing the sailors on another ship he owned to come ashore to get rations without the governor's permission, and for 'deceitfully, wickedly and maliciously contriving and abetting against William Bligh'.[29]

Macarthur gave a strong and emotional speech in response to the charges against him in the courtroom the next day, hastily convened at the Orphan School on the corner of George and Bridge streets. He condemned Atkins and the injustices he, Macarthur, was being subjected to. He argued that it was grossly unfair to be prosecuted by the emancipist forger and former solicitor George Crossley, who Macarthur referred to as 'that well-known dismembered limb of the law'.[30] The military officers led by Lieutenant Governor George Johnston sided with Macarthur, and asked Bligh to surrender his commission. Bligh responded to this by instructing them to gaol Macarthur for his outburst in court the previous day.

Macarthur, well-organised politician that he was, had in the meantime arranged for a petition, signed by him and one hundred others—many of them by then important figures in the colony, including the Blaxland brothers, who were early free settlers of means, and Simeon Lord. The petition was presented to Lieutenant Governor George Johnston, imploring him to seize control of the colony. When it was put before him, Johnston quickly obliged. On 26 January, the date of the twentieth anniversary of European settlement in Sydney, the New South Wales Corps marched from their barracks in George Street at Wynyard up Bridge Street to Government House. Bligh and Atkins were arrested. The newly appointed Acting Judge Advocate Grimes and the six officers of the Rum Corps who were hearing the case unanimously moved to acquit Macarthur of all the charges against him.

The Rum Rebellion lasted for two years until the swearing in of Lachlan Macquarie on 1 January 1810. Responsibility passed from Johnston to Foveaux, then to Lieutenant Governor Paterson. Foveaux was a charming but, in the possibly unfair opinion of some, a cruel man who had spent time on Norfolk Island. His detractors have accused him of indifference to the plight of convicts being flogged, and of condoning the sale of attractive female convicts to free settlers.[31] Foveaux did, however, make some attempt to improve Sydney: he built new military barracks on the present site of Wynyard Square and built the Commissariat Stores on the present-day site of First Fleet Park and the Museum of Contemporary Art.[32]

The Rum Corps's favourites were well rewarded for their support with grants during the rebellion. Alexander Riley was granted 3000 acres (1200 hectares), and 40 000 gallons (182 000 litres) of spirits were given away to the civil and military officers who supported the rebels. The rebellion was reported back to London at a time when the new colony was a long way down the government's list of priorities. The Napoleonic Wars were still raging, and the strategic and economic value of the colony was insignificant. This insignificance was reflected in the fact that, in 1817, Bligh's successor, Lachlan Macquarie was paid as much as the governor of Sierra Leone. (Sierra Leone is a west African nation whose original purpose was to be a refuge for liberated slaves and, like New South Wales, was of little or no importance.[33])

Nevertheless, however unimportant the colony was in the overall scheme of the Empire (such as it then was), Viscount Castlereagh, the Colonial Secretary at the time, was not a man who would tolerate rebellion wherever it occurred. He had helped to crush the insurrection in his native Ireland in the lead-up to the enactment of the Act of Union in 1801 between Britain and Ireland.

Macquarie, a soldier born on the Isle of Mull with a distinguished service record, was chosen as the man to turn back the tide of mutiny. His first proclamation as governor was one that threw down the gauntlet to those who had been allied with, or benefited from the supporters of the rebellion. He declared illegal all the post-rebellion acts of the Rum Corps. To soften this administratively alarming blow to the validity of every governmental act for the previous two years, he gave an indemnity from prosecution to all magistrates, constables and gaolers who had acted at the time of the rebellion. He also confirmed the validity of all land grants made during the period.

The ambivalent attitude by the British government and Macquarie towards the Rum Corps was soon apparent. Although the 102nd Regiment was relieved by the 73rd, members of the Rum Corps were welcome at Government House and, in fact, Lieutenant Colonel William Paterson resided there with the Macquaries. Macquarie recommended the promotion of Foveaux, who became one of Macquarie's closest mentors. So the Rum Rebellion was a rebellion which went largely unpunished, except for the discharge of Major George Johnston from the army and the 'exile' of John Macarthur in England until 1817. The discharge of Major Johnston did not prevent him from returning to the colony in 1813. His journey back was paid for by the Colonial Office, which also provided an instruction to Macquarie that he be treated like any other settler. Johnston continued his preferred pursuit of grazing cattle. His home was at Annandale, a suburb named after Johnston's birthplace in Scotland. Johnston received land grants from 1793 to 1817 totalling 4200 acres (1700 hectares) in and around Sydney. Moreover, the Rum Corps itself was never punished or exiled as a whole: it was folded (as to almost half of it) neatly into the new 73rd Regiment which arrived with Macquarie: 377 of its 697 men stayed on.[34]

In 1810, the population of Sydney had grown to 6200. The town was closely built around the western side of Sydney Cove and along George Street. People usually lived in cottages with their own gardens. Some successful emancipists such as Simeon Lord had grand houses, as

ABOVE: The early settlement at Sydney Cove, as depicted by French illustrator Leseur in 1803 and published in his *Voyages de decouvertes aux Terres Australes* in 1811.

did those officers of the Rum Corps who had gone on to establish their own private empires. Lord's house was the biggest in Sydney. It stood in Macquarie Place until 1904. He operated a granary, storehouse, blacksmith's shop, foundry and dye works there.

Sydney had developed from the camp-like early years into a town with many of the comforts of home. There was a strong demand for luxury goods, possibly heightened by the distance from Britain. There were four breweries, small-scale cottage industries such as pottery making and leather production from kangaroo hides, as well as flour-milling and salt-making businesses. Henry Kable and James Underwood based their shipbuilding and sealing activities on the Tank Stream and employed about sixty men.

From the earliest days of the colony, gambling had been a popular pastime. People used to bet on cockfights and prizefights held in and around pubs on the western side of Sydney Cove and at Brickfield Hill. From the 1820s, prizefights, then often bloody and brutal affairs that were not yet governed by the civilising effects of the Marquess of Queensberry's rules, were moved to the periphery of the town on the North Shore and along the Georges and Cooks rivers to the south.[35] Cricket and football were played, although there were no official clubs or teams, and the rules of football were undeveloped.

Lachlan Macquarie's first priority was to develop a spirit of community and civic pride, and he did this with admirable and sometimes breathtaking speed. In May 1810 he proclaimed a sports week and in October a race week was held in the newly proclaimed Hyde Park. The promoters of the first racing carnival were the soldiers of the 73rd Regiment. The race was accompanied by a ball and dinner at Government House. Hyde Park was officially set aside and proclaimed because the brickmakers from Brickfield Hill were starting to encroach upon it. George Street was named in honour of the sovereign, and Macquarie Place was proclaimed. The market was relocated further down George Street to Market Square, on the corner of George and Market streets where the Queen Victoria Building now stands, and a new wharf was built at Cockle Bay down the road from the market, so that goods could easily be transported to and from market along the Parramatta River and along the Hawkesbury via Broken Bay. The first public schools were opened in Sydney and Parramatta. In 1811 the Macquarie towns of Windsor, Richmond, Wilberforce, Pitt Town, Castlereagh and Liverpool were established, and the Sydney Common (on the site of Moore Park, the Cricket Ground and the former RAS Showground) was proclaimed.

Macquarie then tackled the problem of how to fund and build a hospital. He struck a deal with Garnham Blaxcell, Alexander Riley and D'Arcy Wentworth. In return for a licence to import 60 000 gallons (272 000 litres) of rum upon which import duty was to be paid, the men would build a hospital—the 'Rum Hospital' in Macquarie Street. The transaction to build the Rum Hospital made good economic sense: in return for granting a profitable rum-importing licence, the government earned £9000 in duty, and the people of Sydney had a new hospital worth £40 000. But it was still the sign of a young colony in the frontier stage of its development that Wentworth, one of the people who were given the rum-import licence, was also the superintendent of police. Perhaps Macquarie was wise enough to know that those who wished to drink excessively would do so despite his efforts, and that in the circumstances the end (of building a new hospital) justified the means of paying for it.

Macquarie accelerated the rate of land grants to ex-convicts, encouraged further exploration of the countryside and became deeply involved in town planning and the construction of public works. More than 450 kilometres of roads were built, including one across the Blue Mountains to Bathurst. He also regularised the currency in the colony by importing £10 000 worth of Spanish dollars and cutting a hole in them, thus making them distinctive and less likely to be traded in other parts of the world. Before this occurred, there was little standardised currency in the colony. What little had been brought in was often taken back to Britain.

Macquarie's public building program was greatly enhanced by the arrival of the convict Francis Greenway in 1816. Greenway had been transported for forging part of a building contract. Up until his conviction, he had been an architect of some note in the west of England. Greenway's first job was to build a lighthouse at South Head. For his efforts, he was pardoned. Many other public works owe their construction to Macquarie and Greenway: the Hyde Park Barracks, St James' Church and parts of the courthouse nearby, and many bridges and other public works further from the city, particularly at Windsor.

Macquarie urged the Colonial Secretary to adopt the word 'Australia' for the island continent, a name which was used and promoted by navigator Matthew Flinders who circumnavigated the continent with 'King' Bungaree in 1802–1803. Before this, Australia was known as New Holland, a name used by the Dutch explorers of the seventeenth century. Macquarie's support of trial by jury, the construction of a liquor distillery and the deregulation of trade and shipping did not occur before he concluded his term in office, but they did eventually come to pass. Most significantly for the shape of Sydney today, Macquarie planned the streets of the central business district with the surveyor general's assistance. Little of this work has been undone.

Macquarie had to deal with the disorganised mess the transportation 'system' still was in the 1820s. The British government was sending convicts without any planning or notification to Macquarie of how many new arrivals he should expect. The convicts, although put to productive use as soon as possible, were at first a drain on the economy—after all, they had to be fed, clothed and housed. This stretched the scant resources of the colony and severely tested Macquarie's administrative skills.

The Macquarie era was one of the greatest for Sydney's development and improvement. When he arrived, Sydney lacked infrastructure such as roads and bridges and there were few notable public architectural works apart from the commissariat stores at Sydney Cove and the army barracks at Wynyard. There was little community morale. Macquarie left Sydney with its greatest public Colonial Georgian architecture, as well as Hyde Park itself, and a greater sense of community. During Macquarie's years, the population of New South Wales trebled. Free settlers, though minuscule in number compared with the number of inbound convicts, were for the first time encouraged to come here by the good economic prospects and low tax rate.

74

Macquarie's detractors soon made fun of his penchant for naming things after himself. One of them was Presbyterian Minister John Dunmore Lang, who arrived in Sydney just as Macquarie was leaving:

> 'Macquarie' for a name is all *the* go;
> The old Scotch Governor was fond of fame,
> Macquarie Street, Place, Fort, Town, Lake, River;
> 'Lachlan Macquarie, Esquire, Governor.' for ever![36]

Self-aggrandisement and a wish for immortality aside, Sydney would look vastly different, if the pre-Macquarie miserly and mean-spirited approach to the town's development had not been interrupted. Sydney owes as much, if not more, to Lachlan Macquarie than it does to any other political leader since 1788.

Macquarie was less successful at bridging the widening rift between the 'exclusives', who were free settlers of birth or means, often retired members of the Rum Corps, on the one hand, and the emancipist convicts on the other, than he was at improving morale. He sided with the emancipists and helped them to find their voice as the emerging middle class of the colony. Macquarie believed that pardoned or emancipated felons should be allowed to return to society with the same rights as everyone else, including, in the New South Wales context, the valuable right to governmental preferment if they so deserved. He appointed emancipists as magistrates, and he allowed them to practise as barristers. The exclusives (who were aptly named as they represented only 10 per cent of the colony's population in 1821) became most concerned about Macquarie's levelling instincts. The bogeyman of civil insurrection could be easily aroused in the decades after the French Revolution. Predictably, it could be said, the minority status of the exclusives added to their belief that they were better than anyone else. This made them even more strident.

Relations between exclusives and emancipists deteriorated from 1813 onwards. Exclusives even refused to dine with emancipists at Government House. This was a direct snub to Macquarie, and a challenge to his authority. It is more usual for such people to be extremely compliant and docile towards viceroys. In 1815, the newly appointed first Supreme Court judge, an effete and arrogant man called Jeffery Hart Bent, refused to hear cases in which emancipists were appearing as advocates. The intolerance by the exclusives towards the emancipists (and Macquarie) and their lobbying in London resulted in the arrival of Thomas Bigge. Bigge was sent by the British government to inquire into the state of the colony.

An inquiry may have happened anyway—from 1811, the rate of transportation had been rising, especially after war in Europe came to an end after the Battle of Waterloo in 1815. Postwar economic hardship was stalking England and a recently established police force meant that more people were being caught and charged with crimes. In the decade from 1811 to 1820, 17 500 convicts were sent out from England to New South Wales. The effectiveness of the transportation system had to be assessed to see whether there was scope for further growth in the number of convicts who could be transported.

Bigge's main task was to consider how effective the transportation system was as a crime deterrent. This was a case, if ever there was one, of the terms of inquiry themselves suggesting what the final recommendations should be. Any course of action which tended to make Sydney (and the rest of the colony) a better place to live could be subjected to harsh criticism on the grounds that all expenditure had to be directed towards entrenching the colony's primary function as a penal colony—or gaol. The other area Bigge explored was how the colony could become self-sustaining, rather than merely being a costly drain on the exchequer. To this end, he would try to identify future areas of economic activity that would earn the colony export revenue.

Macquarie's tolerance and support of emancipists was quickly criticised by Bigge. Bigge objected to the appointment of an emancipated naval surgeon, William Redfern, as a magistrate. Redfern had been transported in 1801 for inciting mutiny while serving in the British fleet in 1798. Macquarie stood his ground, Redfern was appointed and Bigge reported the incident to London.

Bigge's report to the House of Commons strongly favoured the exclusives. His vision of the new colony was for it to become a society based on the English model, where the exclusives would be the new entrenched landowning aristocracy, or plutocracy, emancipists would constitute the middle classes, and convicts would be the source of unpaid, forced labour. Emancipists should never, thought Bigge, be fully rehabilitated: they should not be able to practise law, sit on juries, nor should they be eligible for land grants.

Bigge recommended that expensive public works be curtailed. One of the grandest of these was Macquarie's plan for a large city square centred on George Street between Park and Liverpool streets, where St Andrew's Cathedral and the Town Hall stand today. It was with the square in mind that the cathedral was built to face away from George Street, towards the edge of the square. Bigge thought that all ornamental work should cease. Skilled convicts,

75

used to such effect by Macquarie in his public building program, should be assigned to private landowners in the country—especially to those pastoralists who produced fine wool which, he believed, would be the key to economic growth. In this way, the cost of the system would be reduced and the assigned convicts would be less tempted by the depravity of Sydney.[37]

Bigge had taken written and oral evidence from almost all the exclusives, fifty emancipists and hundreds of convicts.[38] His main recommendations on the convict system were that penal transportation should become more systematic and consistent. He advocated that those who had been transported for capital offences should be banished to the remote penal settlements of Moreton Bay (Brisbane) and Port Macquarie. Instead of flogging, convicts who misbehaved should be put to hard physical labour, on chain gangs building roads or clearing the countryside.

To promote the wool industry, Bigge also recommended that (exclusive) pastoralists should receive large land grants. Bigge's prediction that wool production would be an important ingredient in the colony's economic prosperity was taken seriously, and turned out to be correct. In 1821, the wool clip was worth £175 000. After Bigge's recommendation that import duties on colonial wool be eliminated was adopted, the export value of the wool clip increased to £1 million by 1829. The wool industry was the fuel that ignited the economic boom of the 1830s.

Macquarie left Australia in 1821 with a very warm send-off from Sydneysiders (exclusives excepted). One of his last governmental acts was to formalise the new regime of religious tolerance of Catholics and dissenters by laying the foundation stone of St Mary's Church (later Cathedral) at the eastern end of Hyde Park. Macquarie spent many of his later years trying to salvage the damage done to his reputation by Thomas Bigge and others whose interests he did not protect during his term of office. His lobbying had little effect and, to his disappointment, he was never given a knighthood.

Many of the images of Sydney that give us a glimpse of the town in its early years were created by convict artists, many of whom had been transported for turning their talents to forgery. In the late eighteenth century, this was a capital offence, but the death sentence was often commuted to fourteen years' transportation. Many were assigned to officers and administrators, rather than being put to more physically arduous labour. The value of these early convict artists in the colony was enhanced by the thirst for scientific knowledge and research heavily promoted by Sir Joseph Banks. Governors could advance their own political interests in London by providing Banks, who was influential in high political echelons there, with scientific information, often in the form of drawings and paintings.

As well as scientific observation, artists were also called upon by the local administration to provide visual records of the township so that the Colonial Office would have some appreciation of what Sydney looked like, and to indicate that it was more than an earthly hellhole peopled with the detritus of British society. These early works were intended to convey information about the topography of the place, rather than being executed as works of art in their own right—although sometimes the topography was ignored so that scenery could be made to look more picturesque.

Macquarie promoted artists and artistic endeavour in the same way as he promoted a sense of civic pride. Often drawings and paintings were used as the inspiration for lithographs, aquatints and engravings published and sold in London, which in turn fed a wider demand for information about the new town and colony. Some of these artists supplemented their incomes by teaching other people in the colony how to paint and draw. Thus they disseminated not only information abroad, but technique and expertise within Sydney and New South Wales.

The two earliest artists to arrive in the colony were not convicts. The unknown painter—or painters—attributed as the 'Port Jackson Painter', was (or were) probably a naval draughtsman.[39] He, or they, painted prolifically between 1788 and 1792. Much of the work is both vivid and descriptive, even if sometimes awkward. Aborigines were depicted less idealistically than by other artists and engravers of the day, many of whom were strongly imbued with the notion of the noble savage of classically heroic proportions. Later, when the relationship between the colonists and the Aborigines had deteriorated, caricature was often used to depict Aboriginal subjects. Most of the Port Jackson Painter's works are in the British Museum.

Another early artist who came to the colony voluntarily was John William Lewin, who arrived in 1800. His trip was sponsored by the Duke of Portsmouth and Alexander Macleay, two men living in England who were interested in natural science. Macleay later came to Sydney as the Colonial Secretary and was an influential member of the exclusives' social group. Lewin was the son of the author of *Birds of Great Britain* and took up his father's interest in ornithology, publishing *The Birds of New Holland with their Natural History* in 1813. Earlier he had published an entomology of local insects.

Lewin was the official artist on Macquarie's tour across the Blue Mountains. Many of his works are in the Mitchell Library, Sydney, and the Rex Nan Kivell Collection in the National Library of Australia, Canberra. From the early 1800s, there was a declining interest in the natural marvels in New South Wales, or in Lewin's depiction and account of them at any rate, and Lewin moved from his 100-acre land grant near Parramatta to Sydney, where he concentrated on topographical subjects.

The first convict artist to arrive in Sydney was Thomas Watling, a trained Scottish artist who was transported for fourteen years for forgery. He arrived in Sydney in 1792 when he was thirty, and was assigned to the surgeon and amateur natural scientist, John White. He was possibly assigned to Judge Advocate David Collins after that. Some of the plates in Collins's *Account of the English Colony in New South Wales* may have been adapted from Watling's work. Governor Hunter, who was a keen artist himself, gave Watling a conditional pardon in 1797, and Watling departed the colony. He did not enjoy his stay in Sydney. Most of Watling's works are in the British Museum, but some are in the Mitchell and Dixson libraries. Watling's major surviving work, *North–West View Taken from Rocks above Sydney*, is dated 1794 and inscribed to John White. It hangs in the Dixson Gallery of the State Library in Sydney.

John Eyre, who was born and raised in Coventry, was transported for seven years at the age of twenty-two for housebreaking. He arrived in Sydney in 1801 and was conditionally pardoned three years later. Eyre provided four pictures which were used in a publication, *The Present Picture of New South Wales* by D. D. Mann, in London in 1811. These drawings are in the Dixson Gallery. He also provided most of the drawings upon which the engravings in Absalom West's publication of *Twelve Views of Sydney, Parramatta, the Hawkesbury and Botany Bay* (1813) were based. With the money Eyre made from selling these works, he left the colony in 1812.

In 1811, Joseph Lycett was transported, like Watling, for forgery—a crime he did not forsake upon his arrival in the colony. In 1815, he forged five-shilling bills with an accomplice who worked in the post office. As punishment, he was sent to work at the Coal River (Newcastle). His talents were nurtured by the commandant there, Captain Wallis, a keen amateur artist. Later, when Lycett returned to Sydney, Governor Macquarie employed him to paint a view of Sydney to send to Lord Bathurst, then in charge of the Colonial Office. In 1824, back in London, he published a series of fifty aquatints representing views of New South Wales and Van Diemen's Land which were dedicated to Bathurst.

Michael Massey Robinson was one of the few people living in Sydney in the early colonial era with literary aspirations.[40] Oxford-educated, Robinson practised in London as a barrister. He was transported for blackmailing the victim of one of Robinson's defamatory verses which alleged he was a murderer: Robinson threatened to publish the verse unless the victim complied with this demand for money. Despite this lapse of judgment, legal talent was so keenly sought in the colony that Robinson was appointed as secretary to the new deputy judge advocate, then in ill health. Robinson was granted a conditional pardon and was made responsible for the registration of legal agreements. This put him in a position of considerable influence.

His extortionist urges were difficult to control and in 1802 he was convicted of forgery and transported to Norfolk Island. His supporters, including Simeon Lord, interceded on his behalf, and he remained in Sydney. Unable to heed the warning, his sentence was later enforced when he, together with one of the Scottish martyrs, Maurice Margarot, and heiress-abductor Henry Browne Hayes (the original owner of Vaucluse House) were charged with 'promoting discords' in the colony. Upon his return from Norfolk Island, Macquarie rehabilitated him and he was the unofficial poet laureate of the colony, although his formal title was 'Chief Clerk to the Governor's Secretary'.

Before Robinson, the only poetry written in the colony was the convict ballads and the anonymous political pipes that were usually anonymous, as they disparaged individuals or the colonial administration. The convict ballads and songs would be an important inspiration for the emergence of Australian poetry in the 1890s.

The first book of poetry published in Sydney was Barron Field's *First Fruits of Australian Poetry* (1819). The only newspaper in the early days of the colony was the *Sydney Gazette*, published by George Howe. This was where many of the colony's earliest poems and ballads were published. The most important prose of the early colonial period is the accounts given by members of the First Fleet. The journals and accounts of men such as Governor Arthur Phillip, Captain Watkin Tench, Judge Advocate David Collins, Captain (and later Governor) John Hunter, Surgeon John White and Lieutenant William Bradley are key historical sources for the colony's early years. The early history of Sydney would be impossible to explore without these works.

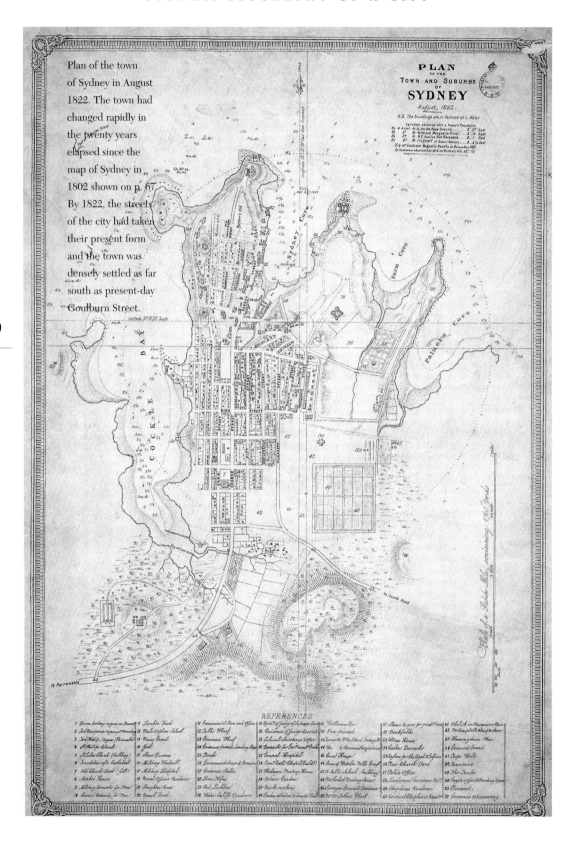

Plan of the town
of Sydney in August
1822. The town had
changed rapidly in
the twenty years
elapsed since the
map of Sydney in
1802 shown on p. 67
By 1822, the streets
of the city had taken
their present form
and the town was
densely settled as far
south as present-day
Goulburn Street.

80

CHAPTER FOUR

THE LAND, BOYS, WE LIVE IN: 1821-50

Australia! whilst met on this festive occasion
To yield thee our tribute of commemoration
We see with fond pride thy advancement to fame
And the pages of history honour thy name.

From whose art and that science thy bosom has nourished
Agriculture has prospered and commerce has flourished
Then to thee shall our heart purest homage be given
And the toast that succeeds be 'the land, boys, we live in'.

'The Land, Boys, We Live In',
Michael Massey Robinson, 1825

IN 1821, GOVERNOR THOMAS BRISBANE replaced Macquarie. His main task was to implement the recommendations in the Bigge Report. Despite the clear mandate in that report to give a high degree of economic and political latitude to the exclusives, Brisbane, like Macquarie, sided with the emancipists. Both these governors believed that the longer term viability of the new colony would depend on the emancipists' enterprise and their social and political rehabilitation, whatever their past transgressions or social origins.

Throughout the 1820s, the number of convicts transported to New South Wales continued to increase. The peak period for arrivals of the convict transports was from 1826 until the mid-1830s. There were several reasons for the surge in convict numbers. First, there was a doubling of the British population between 1805 and 1842. In the same period, with the assistance of a full-time police force, criminal prosecution rates in the British Isles rose by 600 per cent. A stirring of reaction against the harsh penal system meant that more people were transported instead of being hanged. The death penalty was abolished for over 200 offences.[1] This meant that a greater proportion of inbound convicts were convicted of serious and aggravated crimes.

Between 1821 and 1830, 33 000 convicts landed in New South Wales. In accordance with Thomas Bigge's recommendations, the transportation system became more orderly. Better behaved convicts were sent off to the remote interior where they worked as an unpaid labour force on farms and squatting runs. The less well behaved worked in chain gangs on the roads or cleared the countryside. The worst offenders were sent to harsher secondary penal outposts at Moreton Bay and Port Macquarie. By the 1820s, the word 'convict' was often replaced by the euphemistic expression 'government man'. This was an indication of the integral role these people played in a colony that no longer wanted to be constantly reminded of its penal status.

By 1820, the British government had come to see Australia as an appropriate place for free settlement. The growing perception of Australia as a destination for colonial pioneers was assisted by William Charles Wentworth's *Statistical Account of New South Wales,* published in London in 1824. One of the objectives of Wentworth's work was to repudiate Bigge's low opinion of the emancipists and non-exclusives, especially his father D'Arcy. Two years later, Peter Cunningham, a surgeon who worked on several convict transports, published a two-volume work, *Two Years in New South Wales*. He spoke warmly and enthusiastically of Sydney's physical charms and the peaceable nature of all her inhabitants, thus dispelling the awful spectre of New South Wales being a cess-pit full of desperate criminals:

> On the site of Sydney alone what change has been effected! Where, thirty-eight years ago, not a human hut was to be counted, nor the slightest hum of commerce heard, we now have a city occupying a mile square, crowded with industrious citizens, and teeming with vehicles wheeling along the varied productions of the soil …[2]

Cunningham noted there were twenty-two shipping agents, eleven auctioneers, a chamber of commerce, two banks (which paid dividends of 40 per cent on the value of their shares) and three newspapers. There were four Sydney-based whaling vessels and six sealing vessels; foreign ships were transporting cargo from India, Brazil and Canton. On the manufacturing side, woollen textiles were being produced by Simeon Lord's factory at Botany Bay and at the Female Factory in Parramatta, and rope was being manufactured from New Zealand flax.

The tide of free immigration, though slight to begin with, gathered momentum through the 1830s and 1840s. In the 1820s, approximately 8000 immigrants arrived in New South Wales. Between 1831 and 1840, there were about 40 000 and, in the 1840s, there were 76 000.[3] There was still a large social division between free settlers and emancipists through the 1820s. Possibly in an attempt to throw this division into higher relief, matters of etiquette were taken even more seriously by the exclusives than they were in England.[4]

There was another recognisable new class emerging during the 1820s: Australian-born people of European descent. They were considered by commentators of the time to be open, independent, hard-working and trustworthy. Bigge noted that these young Australians had little respect or time for the convicts, and they seldom married convicts who were serving terms. By the middle of the 1820s they called themselves 'currency lads' and 'currency lasses'. Many of them were fair-haired and blue-eyed. English-born people were 'sterling'. Cunningham wrote that the name was given to these new Australians by a paymaster of the 73rd Regiment—possibly John Macarthur—in an allusion to the fact that in those days £1 colonial currency was of a lesser value than the British pound sterling.[5]

Currency lads were also called 'cornstalks' because of their height. They preferred to become tradesmen or sailors, rather than work as farm hands or in more servile positions where they would have to pitch in with the convicts. They did not have a lot of respect for authority either, and a career in the army or police force was generally frowned upon. This independence and lack of deference would become a strong element in the development of Australian culture. Over time, this attitude soon set Australian colonial society apart from the British class system which had spawned it. Just as servility was discarded, so, at the opposite end of the spectrum, was its social corollary, *noblesse oblige*. And the more the 'exclusives' tried to distinguish themselves and rise above the lower classes of convicts without any commensurate sense of social responsibility, the less deference they were shown by convict, emancipist and currency lad and lass alike.

Very few members of the First Fleet could have imagined that in 1825 on the thirty-seventh anniversary of the founding of the colony, William Charles Wentworth, explorer and businessman whom we shall meet again below, William Redfern and eighty others would gather at Hill's Tavern on Hyde Park and sing proudly and heartily Michael Massey Robinson's 'The Land, Boys, We Live In', indicating that Sydney and Australia were becoming their real home.

The 1820s saw cultural advancement to match the new sense of belonging. The Subscription (later State) Library with one hundred volumes was founded in 1827, the same year as the establishment of the Colonial (later Australian) Museum. Musical concerts and plays were also held in a theatre built by successful emancipist and shipbuilder James Underwood.

By 1828, forty years after the arrival of the First Fleet, one-quarter (or almost 3500) of the colonial population were Australian-born people of European descent of more than twelve years of age. Already, many of the first generation of white Australians were fiercely proud of their land and its climate. Those who travelled beyond it often proclaimed the day of their return the happiest of their life. Like many an Australian tourist in any era, leaden European skies were not to their liking. To Cunningham's surprise, they even missed the sight of eucalypt trees.

In that same year, nearly all the 15 700 convicts were assigned to landholders living beyond the township. Sydney had a population of 11 000. It spread from Cockle Bay (Darling Harbour) on the west to the eastern edge of Hyde Park, and south to Brickfield Hill. The Rocks and Millers Point were the most densely settled areas. The better houses were detached,

ABOVE: An engraving by John Carmichael of George Street from Sydney Cove, looking towards Bridge Street, which appeared in his *Select Views of Sydney, New South Wales* (1829).

84

either single or double storey, built of sandstone or brick which was plastered and painted white, with front verandas. The streets were still unpaved and unlit.

Sydney Cove was becoming a hive of activity. Government boats were loaded and unloaded by convicts on the eastern side of the cove. Wharves and warehouses were also being built on the eastern side of Cockle Bay. On the southern corner of George and Bridge streets as far east as the Tank Stream (near where Pitt Street is today) stood the lumber yard, where skilled convict tradesmen performed their daily labours for the government.

The port area around Sydney Cove was bustling. Fishmongers and other vendors plied their trade, and the market on the corner of George and Market streets was like a village fair. Sydney was now large and diverse enough, and had sufficient infrastructure, to be the hub and trading centre for Australia's first economic boom that took off in the 1830s. By 1828, Sydney had travelled a considerable distance from its isolated prison-camp beginnings, and the time for loosening the shackles of absolute government was approaching. The only way of expressing the popular will or opinion at that time was by the signing of petitions that would be placed before the government and conveyed to the Colonial Office in London.

The hardest political struggle for most colonies is usually the struggle for self-government. In the early history of Sydney—and Australia—the precursor to this democratic aspiration was the surprising question of who should be eligible for jury duty. Nowadays, many people try to avoid this onerous task if they are able to, but from the 1820s the issue teased out the conflict inherent in a society that had started its existence as a gaol. It brought the exclusives into direct opposition with emancipists. The central ideal of the jury system is that people should be judged by one's peers. This begged the question of who, in a penal colony, your peers were. Emancipated or pardoned felons? Certainly not *our* peers, thought the exclusives. The position taken by the exclusives was part of a pattern of conduct directed towards establishing an elite ruling class which was closed to those who had been transported to the colony—and their descendants as well.

The adoption of the jury system in New South Wales was gradual. The first step was the *Constitution Act* of 1828 which provided for optional juries in civil trials where both parties agreed to a jury. The exclusives finally lost the battle in 1833 when Governor Richard Bourke exercised his casting vote in the Legislative Council, bringing the jury system in New South Wales into line with the English jury system. This legislative reform had strong popular support; a petition in favour of it was signed by 4000 people.

Until the arrival of Governor Ralph Darling, the governors of New South Wales had absolute power and discretion to administer the colony as they chose, subject to specific instructions from the British government. Darling was instructed to establish an advisory Executive Council. It was hardly representative or democratic but it was a first step: it met in secret, and consisted of the chief justice, the archdeacon, the Colonial Secretary and the lieutenant-governor. An embryonic form of a legislative council was also created. It had seven members and also met in secret.

In 1830, a petition was sent to the Colonial Secretary requesting taxation by representation. The petitioners, led by wealthy grazier Sir John Jamison (a man who, like so many others, did not comply with the strict social code of conduct imposed by the exclusives because he had a convict mistress), argued that, after forty years of the colony's existence, it was mature enough to cope with both jury trials and taxation by representation. The petition came to nothing in the short term. The British Colonial Office did not introduce representative government in New South Wales until 1842 when the transportation system had come to an end, despite popular entreaties and the support of Governor Richard Bourke, who replaced Darling in 1831.

Bourke was an Irish-born Whig and a distant relation of Edmund Burke, a leading Whig politician of the late eighteenth and early nineteenth centuries. Before his arrival in Sydney, Bourke had served as acting governor of the Cape Colony (South Africa). His sympathies lay with the emancipists and free (non-exclusive) settlers, and with the convicts who were often treated harshly by the court system. He took steps to reduce religious intolerance by resisting the establishment of the Church of England in New South Wales as the official church of the state. From 1836 onwards, the Church of England was treated like any other. Grants to it were based, like other churches, on the size of its congregation.

Methodism became popular in the urban working middle classes of England from the turn of the nineteenth century, and Sydney experienced a diluted wash of this new evangelism, which was cross-pollinated with Presbyterianism from Scotland. One of the greatest advocates of moral and social temperance was Presbyterian minister and fiery patriot and politician, John Dunmore Lang. The legacy of this moral crusading was considerable until well into the twentieth century in the form of 'wowserism'. In the 1830s, the campaign for temperance, sobriety and family values found many zealous supporters. Most of these enthusiasts came from the newly emerging middle class who migrated in the late 1820s and early 1830s. They had no familial connection with the colony's earlier penal era and they were proud of this difference.

One indication of the new mood was the creation of the Temperance Society in 1834. Public bathing was restricted to Woolloomooloo Bay, as this was more secluded than Sydney Cove and Cockle Bay. Sabbatarianism (the movement to deny any form of public recreation and entertainment on Sundays) also had its advocates. The remnants of the Sabbatarian reforms were not finally swept away until 1979, when Sunday trading in hotels was made legal. Evident as it was, the Sabbatarian movement was never as popular in Sydney as it was in Melbourne, and this accounts for a lot of the differences between the cities even today. In Melbourne, even the public art galleries and museums were closed on Sundays.

Bourke's term, which lasted from 1831 to 1838, was a period of rapidly rising prosperity in the colony, on the back of the wool boom. With this prosperity came greater demands for democratic reform. It was argued by some, including the leading nineteenth-century political figure Henry Parkes, that a lack of democracy in the colony would deter immigration. People should be able to enjoy the same rights in the colony as they enjoyed at home. Although Bourke had advised that the time was ripe for this to occur, representative government was strongly and effectively disapproved of by the exclusives, 398 of whom signed a petition against it in 1833. They argued that it was not a good idea for there to be any form of representative government until the free-born in the colony outnumbered convicts and emancipists.

Economic prosperity driven by the 1830s wool boom was assisted by the elimination of a ceiling on interest rates. This led to the establishment of several banks, including the Commercial Banking Company of Sydney, the corporate ancestor of the National Australia Bank, Australia's largest. A great deal of British capital was attracted to the colony. Most of the new banks were owned by British shareholders and lending was very profitable. Mortgage rates were 20 per cent and a 15 per cent return on capital was considered average.

The late 1830s saw the first of Sydney's many property booms. The first speculative terrace housing was built at Macquarie Street in 1837 by Samuel Terry, the emancipist 'Botany Bay Rothschild'. Soon Macquarie Street was the smartest address in town. Another early terrace development, and a model for much of the inner-city terrace housing up until 1900, was Lyons Terrace (1841) in Liverpool Street, facing onto Hyde Park on the site of today's Connaught Apartments. This, too, became one of Sydney's better addresses. There was, from the 1830s a movement by the affluent to the nearby areas such as Potts Point, Elizabeth Bay and, a little later, Darling Point and Double Bay, which was taken up by the middle and lower classes later in the nineteenth century.

Bourke quickly understood woolgrowing would need to be done on a large scale if it was to succeed in the dry Australian continent. To this end, he created a system of licensing wool runs. There were, of course, abuses of the licensing system by canny squatters who had already got in early during the opening decades of the nineteenth century, and occupied some of the best pastoral property. But whatever instances of unfairness there were, the economy prospered on the sheep's back. Until the Bourke's administration term, the Colonial Office had seen land usage as being agricultural along smaller-scale English lines. In Australia, the ideal of yeoman farmers being the pillars of economic life as they had been in pre-industrial Britain never came to pass, even in the fertile southeastern corner of Australia. The conomies of scale and concentration of rural production on large squatting runs, or stations, meant that the population was more concentrated in cities such as Sydney, and later Melbourne. A highly urbanised society was a paradoxical outcome for a huge island continent. Government-inspired attempts to promote agriculture and pastoral activities on a smaller scale have been doomed to fail. A vivid example of this failure is the soldier settlement schemes in South Australia and New South Wales of the twentieth century. Perhaps it was in the absence of the opportunity to become small yeoman farmers that Australians so heartily embraced the ideal of home ownership on large blocks of land in the suburbs. This ideal had an enormous effect on Sydney's size and shape.

During Bourke's time there was a great deal of expansion of the areas of settlement: Melbourne and Adelaide were founded, and the Riverina and northern Victoria were explored and surveyed by Surveyor General Thomas Mitchell. Bourke was a well-loved governor, and there was a huge farewell which 10 000 people attended when he left Sydney. The first statue erected in the colony was paid for by public subscription in 1842, to commemorate his term in office. The statue stands outside the Subscription (State) Library. In a less tangible but no less significant way, Bourke achieved just as much as Macquarie by promoting the introduction of the political freedoms needed for the Australian colonies to grow, even if his term expired too early for him to witness their introduction.

Charles Darwin visited Sydney as part of his voyage on the *Beagle* in January 1836. Although he did not take warmly to the natural environment, or to the social environment which was populated by convicts and emancipists, he was nevertheless impressed with the prosperity of the town and the outlook for the woolgrowing industry. The wool clip had grown from 175 000 pounds (80 tonnes) weight in 1822 to 2 million pounds (900 tonnes) in 1830 and 10 million pounds (4500 tonnes) in 1840. In the 1830s, the volume of exports grew more than eleven-fold, although there was still a trading deficit, as there had been since 1788.[6]

Sydney was growing bigger as well as more prosperous. The rate of growth took off most significantly from the middle of the 1830s when large numbers of immigrants started to arrive. The population had risen from 11 000 in 1828 to 30 000 in 1841 and then grew to 54 000 in 1851. The population of Sydney alone doubled in Bourke's term. People no longer easily recognised other people of similar social status in the street.

The first shipload of assisted immigrants left Britain for Australia in 1832. Under the 'Bounty Scheme' for immigrant employees devised by Governor Bourke, government policy was to increase the supply of free (as opposed to convict) labour. Bounties were paid to residents of

New South Wales who were prepared to sponsor and finance the migration of families, single women, male mechanics and farm labourers. These measures were designed to ease the labour shortage that followed the wool boom. In 1842, the process of setting aside money for assisted immigration became more orderly. Crown land was sold, and the proceeds of sale were used to pay the passage of immigrants. The price of the land was fixed at £1, irrespective of its quality or carrying capacity. However, whatever the faults of the scheme, the era of the free land grant, upon which many early squatting fortunes were based, was now over. From 1836 onwards, the purchase of land became a first-in, best-dressed affair.[7]

Between 1815 and 1840, a million people emigrated from the British Isles; however, because of the distance and costs involved, only 58 000 of these came to Australia.[8] Even though the number of immigrants who chose New South Wales was not great, by 1841 there were more free immigrants (53 000) than currency lads and lasses (30 000). In the census of 1841, there were still twice as many men as women in New South Wales. Single females were encouraged to migrate here to reduce the shortage of women in the colony. Despite the need to balance the population, the life of a recently arrived single female could be far from easy. She usually arrived without a job and without any accommodation. For some, working on the streets of Sydney was the only alternative. John Dunmore Lang thought that their arrival had rendered Sydney a 'sink of prostitution'.[9]

LEFT: The emigrants' friend, Caroline Chisholm, a leading humanitarian in the mid-nineteenth century.

Evangelical philanthropist Caroline Chisholm played an important role in finding work for many of these women, often in the remote interior of the continent. Chisholm was the English wife of an army officer. The family lived near Windsor. In 1841, Hyde Park Barracks, no longer required as a hostel for convicts on account of the dismantling of the transportation system, was provided as a home to recently arrived female immigrants. Next to the barracks was the only free employment registry in Sydney.[10] Chisholm relied on charity to keep the operations going, and travelled tirelessly around the countryside on horseback seeking employment for the immigrants. As she did so, she collected many accounts of immigrants, which told of their experience. These accounts were published in England as a guide for future settlers.

In 1849, Chisholm established the privately funded Family Colonisation Loan Society. This society provided loans to families wanting to emigrate to Australia. She also successfully advocated the improvement of conditions on the long and trying journey out to Australia. The *Passenger Act* of 1852 set minimum standards for accommodation in the lower decks. For all her good work, she became known as 'the emigrants' friend'.

89

The history of Sydney in the period between 1826 and the 1840s, and the story of the struggle for representative government, is impossible to tell without introducing William Charles Wentworth, a leading actor in the agitation for a democracy. Wentworth's life and career are an interesting barometer of the political and social mood of the colony from the 1820s to the 1850s. Wentworth was the son of two Second Fleeters, Assistant Surgeon D'Arcy Wentworth and Catherine Crowley, a woman convicted for stealing clothes. W. C. Wentworth was born shortly after the arrival of the Second Fleet, in August 1790.

The fact that his father had an (unproven) criminal background and his mother was a convict meant that he was never considered part of the coterie of exclusives, but that did not prevent either of them from prospering. He was brilliant, had a very sharp tongue, sharp wit and often a poisonous pen. He scorned exclusives such as Samuel Marsden and the Macarthurs, and mocked their social pretensions, calling them 'the yellow snakes of the colony'. However, he did for a time want to marry one of Macarthur's daughters—a marriage Macarthur did not sanction. Instead, Wentworth married the daughter of emancipists, and this was another nail in his social coffin, both in the narrow social circles of the exclusives and back in England where he lived most of his later years as well.

Wentworth was only twenty-two when, in 1813, with Gregory Blaxland and William Lawson, he made the first crossing of the Blue Mountains by Europeans. He went to England at the age of twenty-six and returned eight years later as an educated and brilliant barrister. Wentworth was one of the first and proudest native-born white Australians and a leading spokesman for the emancipists, who had, by the middle of the 1820s, become the most important force in the political life in the colony. It was not until the 1840s, that the old rivalry between emancipist and exclusive was replaced by the more traditional political struggle between capital and labour.

Wentworth championed trial by jury, freedom of the press, and the right of emancipists to be restored to an equal status after their liberty was restored. Wentworth also published, in partnership with emancipist Robert Wardell, the colony's second newspaper, *The Australian*.

Wentworth's publicly aired views led to a head-to-head political battle with the stern Governor Darling. By 1827, Darling had had enough of Wentworth's popular agitation in the press and decided that newspapers should be licensed. Fortunately, Chief Justice Francis Forbes vetoed this restriction of freedom of the press, on the grounds that it was repugnant to the laws of England. The chief justice was another avowed political enemy of the governor and sided with the convicts and emancipists.

Having achieved trial by jury by 1833 and freedom of the press, Wentworth and like-minded colonists started to turn their eye towards self-government. This coincided with the political agitation in Britain that led to the passing of the *Reform Act* in 1832. In 1833, the Australian Patriotic Association began to agitate for a written constitution. Wentworth wrote a draft of the constitution that was supported by Bourke and his successor, Gipps. The constitution was finally adopted in 1842. This provided for a partly elected Legislative Council of 50 members, of which only ten were nominated by the Executive Council. The voting qualification was owning land, or paying more than £20 rent annually. This was double the franchise qualification in England at the time—a reflection of the relatively high property and rental value in Sydney compared to London. The first elections were held in 1843, when Wentworth won the highest number of votes for the Legislative Council.

By the late 1840s, Wentworth's views were diverging from those of the free immigrants, who sought the complete abolition of the transportation system and full, not just partial representative government. Unlike the more recent arrivals, Wentworth stubbornly insisted that the upper house of the colonial parliament should be composed of members who were hereditarily entitled to sit there—so that it would become what orator and barrister Daniel Deniehy called a 'Bunyip Aristocracy'. Wentworth would, of course be an inaugural member. The voice of the free immigrants was better expressed by new public figures such as Robert Lowe, an albino barrister-politician and Henry Parkes, ivory turner, journalist and, later, politician.

Wentworth's increasingly conservative views were also reflected in his resistance to the reduction of the property franchise to those who owned land worth more than £100 and those who paid rent of more than £10 a year. This reduction was brought about by sleight of hand when the democratically minded colonists were able to convince the Colonial Office in London that property prices had fallen in the depression of the 1840s to such a degree that the franchise should be the same as in England.[11]

Wentworth was a lavish entertainer. His home at Vaucluse was on a large estate used for grand parties, the most extravagant being the partly to celebrate the departure of Wentworth's *bête noir*, Governor Darling. These festivities were attended by about 4000 people. The high point was the loud cheering that went up as Darling's ship sailed past Vaucluse Bay, towards the heads, removing the unpopular governor from Sydney forever. If Wentworth is Australia's

90

Thomas Jefferson, then Vaucluse House is the closest thing Sydney (and Australia) has to Monticello, the Virginian estate Jefferson created.

The quirkiness of the various extensions to Vaucluse House makes the building a metaphor for the way the colony developed during the early years. The grand staircase leads nowhere in particular, because the money ran out, as it so often did in Sydney, because of economic downturn caused by drought or a collapse in the price of wool. Wentworth's residence is a very different edifice from the finely proportioned and very grand Elizabeth Bay House, built by the influential exclusive Colonial Secretary Alexander Macleay, a good friend and strong ally of Darling's. The most significant common denominator shared by both houses is that neither was ever finished as the depression of the 1840s intervened.

Wentworth was never a man to do things by halves: he fell out badly with Governor Gipps when he, Wentworth, claimed to have bought about one-third of New Zealand from seven Maori chieftains. He strongly urged the chieftains not to treat with the British or acknowledge any right of the British Crown in New Zealand, and this did not endear him to the colonial administration. One of Wentworth's strongest beliefs was in the value of education, as it was for him the only way people could improve their social position. He played a leading role in establishing primary state schools and in founding the University of Sydney in 1852.

91

Wentworth chose to spend his last years in England where he died in 1872, although his body was brought back to Vaucluse House for burial. The funeral procession from St Andrew's Cathedral to Vaucluse House was the first state funeral in the colony. Wentworth has been referred to as a 'Gulliver in Lilliput'.

The fiftieth anniversary of the colony on 26 January 1838 was celebrated with a public holiday and a regatta on the harbour. The first annual rowing and sailing regatta had been held the previous year. It soon became one of the more lively sporting events in the Sydney calendar—and it is still held every year on what is now called Australia Day.

The economic mood in the late 1830s was optimistic. Two substantial public works had been commenced. The first was the new, grand, Gothic Revival Government House in the Botanic Gardens, designed by English architect Edward Blore. In 1845, this replaced the old government house in Bridge Street, where Governor Phillip Tower and the Museum of Sydney now stand.

The second major work was the reclamation of the swampy and rocky land around the eastern side of Sydney Cove as far as the Tank Stream. The reclamation and new sea wall were called Semi-Circular Quay. It was the last major public work to be built with convict labour. Both these works were clear indications of the colony's growing importance in the scheme of British empire building. Sydney was built mostly of sandstone and red brick. New exotic trees introduced since white settlement, such as Moreton Bay figs and Norfolk Island pines, were growing to maturity. The town had come a long way in two generations.

In 1838, Sam Terry died. Sent out to Sydney as a thief, he left a fortune estimated at £500 000. His funeral was well attended, and the band of the 50th Regiment played in the funeral procession. The sight of an army regiment sending Terry off must have been enough to make the intransigent old exclusives faint or turn in their graves. All their efforts to check the social progress of prosperous emancipists had failed. Samuel Terry's grand farewell was fitting in a town where making money had become a religion.

Until the 1830s, not many people disagreed with the proposition that transportation was an efficient and acceptable system for criminal punishment. Through the 1830s, however, newly emerging humanitarian and liberal views were gaining a foothold in British political life. As the British penal code became less harsh, it was, as a rule, only the more dangerous and hardened criminals who committed offences punishable by transportation. A deepening gulf between the newly arrived convicts and the rest of Sydney's population developed.

Crimes committed by escaped convicts roaming the countryside, such as the murder of Robert Wardell, the friend and business partner of W. C. Wentworth on the Cooks River, led many to believe that transportation was neither desirable nor necessary. Assigned convicts, it was argued, were lazy, unreliable and dangerous. There was also a readily available supply of voluntary immigrant labour. Newspapers wrote of a growing crime wave (not the only time this would happen), fed by disgruntled and desperate convicts, that threatened the fabric of colonial society.

One exception to the rule that the convicts who arrived in the 1830s were more hardened than those that had been transported earlier were political prisoners, such as the Swing Rioters. These people were part of a relatively widespread revolt by farm labourers opposed to the high price of grain in Britain. They took out their fury by burning the stores of grain they could not afford to buy. They also protested against the mechanisation of agriculture by vandalising their new enemy—the machines. It was considered a fitting punishment to remove these people from society. Canadian political prisoners were sent out in the late 1830s as well. Like the Swing Rioters, many of these were skilled tradesmen whose talents were quickly put to use at Victoria Barracks and elsewhere. The suburb of Canada Bay on the Parramatta River is named after these people.

Opposition to transportation grew through the 1830s. The main opponents to it were the urban-dwelling, immigrant middle and working classes. Those who most strongly favoured transportation were wealthy squatters and landowners who were heavily dependent on cheap convict labour. As the moral and humanitarian arguments against transportation gathered strength, even some of the scions of old exclusive families like James Macarthur swung around against it. In 1837, the Molesworth Committee was convened in England to report on transportation and its future.

Evidence about the lawlessness in the colony and the unpredictable nature of the system of assignment was well received by committee members, who were already well disposed to the idea of abolition. The committee's recommendations were that transportation should cease as soon as was practicable; that a punishment of hard labour be substituted for transportation; that any gaols established abroad be built far away from free settlement; that early release of convicts become more administratively orderly and consistent; and that once they have served their terms, convicts should be encouraged to go back home to enjoy the freedom they had temporarily forfeited.

Reaction to the recommendations of the Molesworth Report was quick. One of Governor Gipps's first administrative tasks when he took up his appointment in 1838 was to prohibit the assignment of convicts for domestic service in towns. They could only be assigned to work in remote areas. The last convicts were assigned in 1841. From 1840 to 1843, the number of assigned convicts shrank from 22 000 to slightly more than 4000.

In August 1840, an Order in Council prohibiting transportation to the east coast of Australia became effective. The last convict ship to arrive in Sydney as part of the old transportation system was the *Eden*, which arrived in late 1840. The idea of convict transportation was not, however, entirely dead. There were further attempts to revive it over the following ten years, but the existence of the system, as such, soon passed into history and Sydney started to work at erasing the legacy of her penal origins.

It is interesting to look at some statistics at the conclusion of the convict system. Almost 150 000 convicts were sent to eastern Australia. The vast majority of these were sent after 1815, most commonly for larceny which accounted for 80 per cent of convictions. More than two-thirds of convicts were tried in England, although this did not mean that they were all English. Many of the convicts came from urban, as opposed to rural, backgrounds. More than one-third of the English male convicts came from London and the northern English towns of Lancashire, and half the women came from these two areas. About half the convicts were second offenders. Most of the convicts were unmarried.[12]

The bogeyman of transportation lingered on, heavily promoted by W. C. Wentworth, among others. The Secretary of State for the Colonies (later Prime Minister) William Gladstone suggested in a letter to the governor of New South Wales that transportation could be resumed if the Legislative Council so wished. A committee of the Legislative Council, chaired by Wentworth, endorsed the reintroduction of assignment. He and other wealthy landowners wanted the supply of labour for the wool runs to be increased. After all, not many free immigrants wanted to start their new lives in New South Wales as shepherds on remote squatting runs. There was a popular backlash against the proposal, because of the effect this might have on both the price of labour (reduce it) and the crime rate (increase it). Despite the committee's recommendation, the Legislative Council recommended against the resumption of transportation, but only by a narrow majority. Although defeated in this instance, the squatting lobby still had political clout throughout the 1840s.

Another round of pressure was put on the Legislative Council two years later, and this time it relented. It agreed to the transportation of 236 'high-class' convicts. The broader population of Sydney greeted the news with a loud and resounding protest. Some people were fearful that such an unjust act so repugnant to the people might threaten their loyalty to the Crown. Eventually, another 1400 men were received unwillingly by the city and the colony, but the last convicts arrived in New South Wales in 1850. The anti-transportation movement

93

was one of the first and strongest political movements that bound the people of Sydney and New South Wales.

Henry Parkes cut his political teeth in the anti-transportation speeches of the late 1840s. On a wet day in 1849, between 7000 and 8000 Sydneysiders turned up to an anti-transportation rally held at Circular Quay to protest at the landing of the *Hashemy*, a convict transport. Forty-three years later, Parkes wrote:

> The proceedings of this new combination of men [anti-transportationists] surprised and produced something like consternation in the minds of the old colonial magnates, who hitherto had ruled with a peculiar order of absolutism representing the artificial feeling of domination on one hand and submission on the other which characterised old Virginian society.[13]

The transportation question still refused to go away after the rally. In 1851, at Barrack Square, Wynyard, there was another huge rally against transportation to defend those in Van Diemen's Land who sought its permanent abolition. A petition was signed by 16 000 people. Henry Parkes even invoked the threat of constitutional separation from the mother country as a means of resolving the issue once and for all.[14]

In 1840, Sydney was a thriving town with shops to match—although the architecture was somewhat irregular. Imposing four-storey buildings stood next to run-down cottages. Sydney's main economic activity was as a port and a commercial centre where the financing, handling and shipping of wool was based, and goods were bought and sold.

Just as the 1830s were the era of Sydney's first boom, the 1840s were the decade of the first bust. Sadly, this boom–bust cycle has been a feature of Australia's economy. The reason for this has been Australia's long-term dependence on commodities as the major source of export earnings. The prices of commodities rise and fall more sharply on world markets than do the prices of manufactured goods, and the sharper economic cycles reflect this. These peaks and troughs often coincide with big shifts in capital inflows and outflows, and have often been made even worse when the decline coincides with or is worsened by periods of drought.

Between 1837 and 1841, drought set in. The wool price held up until 1840, but when that collapsed, the economic picture worsened. The colony's balance of payments deteriorated and the continuing appetite for luxury goods made the trade imbalance even worse. Capital that only years before had been flowing into the country like rivers of gold flowed back out again, creating a credit squeeze. Seven banks failed, as did many other businesses—there were 600 insolvencies in 1842. It was not only professional speculators who were affected: the deputy sheriff committed suicide because of financial difficulties, and the registrar of the Supreme Court resigned for the same reason. The bounty system of immigration was suspended. Two of the city's first newspapers, the *Sydney Gazette* and the *Monitor*, folded, making the *Sydney Morning Herald*, founded by Charles Kemp and John Fairfax, more dominant. The recession took a toll on the construction of Fort Denison, where work was abandoned until 1855.

All this economic hardship took place in 1842, the same year as Sydney Council was incorporated. The city was incorporated—not because of any surge of civic pride on the part of Sydneysiders, but because the British Colonial Office was tired of funding Sydney's municipal services. Rates could be levied locally on property and this would reduce the financial burden on the British government. The first mayor was John Hosking, the son-in-law of Samuel Terry. The homes of many exclusives were closed to the mayor and his wife on the grounds that she was the daughter of a convict.[15] Some of Sydney's citizens quibbled that it was unfair that the British government insisted upon the council paying for the police force: the need for vigilance was a direct result of Sydney's continuing, although by this time increasingly vestigial, status as a penal colony. Eventually, the British colonial government yielded to the council and took financial responsibility for the police force from 1846.[16]

This dispute between the Colonial Office in London and the new council was the first of many jurisdictional battles the council would have in future years with the government of the day. There has often been an ongoing rivalry between the council and the colonial (later state) government about where the boundaries of their respective powers and obligations lie.

In 1848, Wynyard Barracks, one of the last remnants of the penal system remaining in the town, was relocated to Paddington, then on the fringe of the town. Victoria Barracks contains some of the most impressive early colonial architecture in Sydney. Within the town itself, the demolition of other buildings and workshops closely connected with Sydney's penal past had begun. By the end of the 1840s, neither the lumber yard nor the government dockyard was visible—the lumber yard was demolished and the dockyard covered when the land on the western side of Circular Quay was reclaimed. Nor were any convicts still quartered in the town. Even the Carters' Barracks on the southern edge of the town was closed and the remaining convicts were taken to Cockatoo Island in 1848. The convict 'stain' on the township was fading quickly.

Despite the economic downturn of the 1840s, there were some improvements to the town. Once Government House had been relocated further east, Macquarie Street was extended all the way to the eastern side of Sydney Cove. Smart terraces and mansions were built along it. Mortimer Lewis's Treasury Building on the corner of Bridge and Macquarie streets was also built. It is now the external shell of the lower levels of the Inter.Continental Sydney Hotel. The stature of Sydney as a town of serious public architecture was enhanced by the construction of the Mortimer Lewis–designed portion of the Australian Museum.

The Royal Botanic Gardens, opened to the public in 1831, and the Domain and Hyde Park were, and still are, the city's three most important open spaces. For many years, the Domain was the venue for Sydney's version of the European *passeggiata*. People gathered there in carriages, on horseback or on foot and listened to musical concerts on ground that had been the habitat of kangaroos and emus twenty years before. The trip by carriage to Mrs

Macquarie's Chair was very popular. The Domain swimming baths were the site of the first Australian swimming championships in 1846.

Theatre started to develop in Sydney from the 1830s, though there had been a few modest attempts before that. The first theatrical productions were organised by the colonial administration and the marines in an attempt to build morale in the early days of the colony. In 1790, the first theatrical production, *The Recruiting Officer*, was staged in Sydney. Later, in 1826 under Governor Darling's administration, theatrical performances were held within the old gaol in George Street, but they became too rowdy and were stopped in 1828.

Sydney's first major theatre was built by Barnett Levy within the walls of the original Royal Hotel in George Street, where the Dymock's Building is today. Barnett Levy was a versatile man: not only did he build theatres, he also wrote poems and performed on stage. One of his works was published in the *Sydney Gazette* in 1832, intended for performance in the Theatre Royal, with Levy dressed as a ticket-of-leave holder:[17]

> The Currency Lads may fill their glasses,
> And drink to the health of the Currency Lasses;
> But the girl I adore, the lass for me,
> Is the lass at the Female Factory.
>
> O! Molly's her name, and her name is Molly,
> Although she was tried by the name of Polly;
> She was tried and was cast for death at Newry,
> But the Judge was bribed and so were the Jury …
> The first time I saw this comely lass
> Was at Parramatta, going to mass;
> Says I 'I'll marry you now in an hour,'
> Says she, 'Well go and fetch Father P_____.'
>
> But *I got into trouble* that very same night!
> Being drunk in the street I got into a fight;
> A constable seized me—I gave him a box—
> And was put in the watch-house and then in the stocks.
>
> O! it's very unaisy as I may remember,
> To sit in the stocks in the month of December;
> With the north wind so hot and the hot sun right over,
> O! sure, and it's no place at all for a lover!
>
> But now I am out again, early and late
> I sigh and I cry at the Factory gate,
> 'O! Mrs R_____, late Mrs F_____n'
> 'O! won't you let Molly out very soon?'

'Is it Molly McGuigan?' says she to me,
'Is it not?' says I, for she know'd it was she.
'Is it her you mean that was put in the stocks
For beating her mistress, Mrs Cox?'

'O! yes and it is, madam, pray let me in,
'I have brought her a half-pint of Cooper's best gin,
'She likes it as well as she likes her own mother,
O! now let me in, for I am her brother.'

The theatre was dormant, however, by the late 1830s, and soon fell into the hands of one of the promoters of the Royal Victoria Theatre in Pitt Street which opened in 1838 with a capacity of 2000. The theatre was not only used for theatrical productions and operas, but as a meeting hall.

In 1844, *The Currency Lass* was performed. It was one of the first plays with an Australian subject, written from a colonial perspective. It was written by a former convict, Edward Geoghegan, to appeal directly to the Australian-born population. In the play, an English theatrical director, down on his luck in London, moves to Sydney where his son falls in love with a currency lass—although the plot is far more complicated than that. One of the heroes of the play had the following words to say:

I will not say but that I enjoyed my European tour exceedingly—but I will say that I return to my native land with redoubled zest. Many wonders have doubtless met my view and excited admiration, but my own country still possesses advantages surpassed by none. Let Italy boast her cloudless skies and beauteous dames—the skies of Australia are as pure, our native girls far more lovely. France may pride in her courtly airs and polished graces—to me the blunt sincerity and cordial frankness of a currency lad are far more grateful. And though 'tis the European mode to prefer other countries to one's own and find superior charms in other climes—oh never may that fashionable error reach my countrymen, but ever may they, like myself, prefer my native Australia to any other clime or nation under the sun![18]

On the topic of Sydney's attractions, eminent natural scientist Count Strzelecki was pleasantly surprised by the state of the town when he wrote:

Let the [English] authors of these [unflattering] epithets on New South Wales congratulate and applaud themselves; my mystification was complete … I found, however in the streets of Sydney a decency and a quiet which I have never witnessed in any other of the ports of the United Kingdom. No drunkenness, no sailors' quarrels, no appearances of prostitution. George Street, the Regent Street of Sydney, presented houses and shops modelled after those of London; but nowhere did its lamps and the numerous lights in its window, reflected upon the crowd, betray those signs of corrupt society common to the streets of other capitals.[19]

The leading visual artists in Sydney between the 1820s and 1850 were Augustus Earle, John Skinner Prout, Charles Rodius (a convict portraitist who did many drawings of the Aborigines of New South Wales as well as the local gentry), George Peacock, Conrad Martens and the artist–illustrator Joseph Fowles.

Earle was a painter who had trained and exhibited at the Royal Academy in London. A daring, seafaring gentleman-adventurer, he started his journeying in his early twenties around the Mediterranean, then spent time in Philadelphia, where he exhibited at the Academy of Fine Arts. Later he spent time in Chile and Brazil. He earned enough to survive by selling his portraits, landscapes or paintings of any other subject. Earle arrived in Sydney in 1825 in time to decorate a banquet hall for Governor Brisbane. He was commissioned to do many portraits, including those of Governors Brisbane and Darling, Captain John Piper and his wife, and other leading figures in Sydney society.

George Peacock was an attorney convicted of forgery and transported for life in 1836. He had an attractive and charming wife who arrived one year after Peacock with a letter of introduction from the Chancellor of the Exchequer, among others. It has been suggested that part of the reason for Peacock's impecuniousness and need to resort to crime was his wife's extravagant tastes.[20] Peacock was pardoned conditionally in 1846 and spent the next ten years working as a meteorologist at South Head. He painted views around the harbour and notable public buildings. Peacock's pictures were more atmospheric and less strictly topographical and conventional than were the descriptive works of the early colonial period.

Conrad Martens arrived in Sydney in 1835. Trained by Copley Fielding, a leading English romantic watercolourist of the day, he was heavily influenced by the Romantic movement. Despite his romantic style, Martens gained valuable experience as a topographical, or scientific, illustrator on board the *Beagle* with Charles Darwin, and the two men became friends. On the voyage of the *Beagle*, Martens became particularly interested in meteorological science and the atmospheric effects of clouds on light and on the landscape.[21] Martens lived in Cumberland Street, The Rocks, and as well as sketching, took in art students. His patrons included leading figures of the day such as governors, the Macleay family and Sir John Jamison. In the hard years of the 1840s, he supplemented his meagre income by selling lithographs including *Sydney from the North Shore* (where he later settled with his family) and *Sketches in the Environs of Sydney*. Martens found it hard to survive on private patronage alone in Sydney, so, in 1863, he sought and gained appointment as assistant parliamentary librarian.

John Skinner Prout lived and worked in Sydney in the same period as Conrad Martens. Like Martens and Peacock, he worked in a style that had been popular in the early colonial period. In the depression years of the 1840s when private commissions were hard to come by, he published views of the town of Sydney.

Horseracing attracted spectators from all levels of society. In the 1840s, it became more institutionalised. The races moved from Hyde Park to Grose Farm, Camperdown, where Sydney University stands today, then to the 'Sandy Course' at Randwick. Other races were held at Parramatta. W. C. Wentworth, with others, formed the Sydney Turf Club in the 1820s, but when Wentworth fell out with Darling, vice-regal patronage of the club was withdrawn. The club and a rival one had both failed by the early 1830s. In 1840, Wentworth, Captain John Piper and Sir John Jamison of Regentville, at Richmond, started the precursor of the Australian Jockey Club. A racecourse was built on Wentworth's land at Homebush and meetings were held there between 1842 and 1859.

Cricket became more organised with the growth of both gentlemen's and tradesmen's clubs from the 1820s. Unlike in England, teams from different social classes of society played against each other. The first football game which resembled rugby was played in the Military Barracks at Wynyard in 1829, but rugby would not become established in Sydney until 1870 when the first rugby club, the Wallaroo, was formed.[22] Further down the scale of social respectability, cockfights and prizefights were still held around Sydney until the 1850s. The respectable new middle class frowned upon these more primitive, unruly and violent sports, and their popularity gradually waned as Sydney became a less rowdy place. Many prizefighters and their fans left Sydney in the late 1840s for the gold rushes in California. Drinking was still a popular pastime, despite the efforts of the temperance movement.

As a concession to the town's increasing prosperity and the inhabitants' expectations, some new hotels were designed on more gracious lines. Not all of them were the simple bars and bloodhouses of the colony's early years. Some were good enough to become weekend destinations. Others held musical evenings called 'free and easys', where ballads, songs and sketches could be enjoyed, as in the emerging music halls in Britain and the United States. Some pubs had dancing rooms as well, where members of the opposite sex could mingle.[23]

On a more negative note, Sydney still had a chronic lack of drainage and sewerage, and very little in the way of a properly reticulated water supply. Only one in ten houses had access to plumbing, and only mansions and better hotels had water closets. The footpaths were in very bad condition, and very few streets were kerbed and guttered.

In 1848, the town of Sydney was well established in the Colonial Georgian style. Artist and illustrator Joseph Fowles published his work *Sydney in 1848* in an attempt to 'delineate Sydney as it really is, and not as some of our friends in England evidently imagine it to be'.[24] The image of Sydney as a wild and lawless town took much longer to erase in the eyes of those who never visited the colony—and it still lingers, mostly furtively but sometimes more openly in the febrile imagination of some British tabloid journalists.

There were almost 7500 houses in the township of Sydney proper by 1848, and suburbs such as Woolloomooloo, Paddington, Surry Hills, Redfern, Glebe and Balmain were also in an early stage of development. One incentive to moving further out of town was that residences beyond the town's municipal limits were not subject to paying rates until such time as a local council was incorporated.

There was a strong appetite in Sydney for education and self-improvement from the 1830s, and a growing amount of venues were provided for these purposes. Apart from the Subscription Library and the Museum, the first Mechanics School of Arts opened in Pitt Street in 1833, during Richard Bourke's term as governor. The building still stands there, next to the Hilton Hotel. Similar institutes proliferated in Sydney's suburbs during the nineteenth century. Their objective was to disseminate knowledge and instruct members of the working classes, especially in the theoretical, rather than just the practical, fields. The Society for the Promotion of Fine Arts and the Floral and Horticultural Society were also established in this period. State schools did not yet exist. The only available alternatives were private colleges, the domain of the better-off members of society, and twenty parochial religious schools run by various religious denominations.

By 1848, as the depression's grip was weakening, the Australian Mutual Provident Society (AMP), one of Australia's largest financial institutions, was founded. People would be able to buy life, fire and accident insurance and annuities, and an investment return would be made on the proceeds of the insurance premiums. The directors, who included leading businessmen Thomas Sutcliffe Mort and Thomas Holt, were disturbed by the ignorance and apathy of their target market. To remedy the situation, the AMP embarked on an extensive advertising campaign for customers which continues to this day.

In 1850, Sydney was in a self-congratulatory mood. The *Sydney Morning Herald*, by now wholly owned by the Fairfax family and published daily, editorialised that such progress was unprecedented in the history of British settlements. Sydney had emerged from the recession and was progressing steadily. Although some families who had made their fortunes in the colony and seen them disappear in the recession were living in reduced circumstances, wealth and prosperity seemed to be more widely distributed.

In 1850 New South Wales and Victoria were separated with the enactment of the *Australian Colonies Government Act*. Sydney was now only one of a number of young and growing Australian towns in an increasing number of colonies.

CHAPTER FIVE

THE LONG BOOM

We owe nothing to gold dust or precious stones. We have been the architects of our own fortunes. The enterprise and indomitable perseverance of our Anglo-Saxon blood have sufficed to make us what we are, and to lay a solid foundation of future greatness.

Editorial, *Sydney Morning Herald*, 1 January 1850

No words can describe the excitement occasioned in all classes of society. Those in whose hands the reins of government were held had no precedent to guide them in their new predicament. The most extravagant reports of the treasures discovered reached the capital day after day, and were of course diligently circulated by those who hoped to make a good market of such commodities as they had huddled together at the first flush of speculation.

Lieutenant Colonel Mundy describing
the gold rush in Sydney, May 1851

THE HISTORY OF SYDNEY and Australia took a very exciting turn in 1851 when Edward Hargraves discovered gold at Ophir, near Bathurst, soon after his return from an unsuccessful visit to the Californian goldfields. More gold discoveries were made at Sofala, a town that also lies to the west of Sydney. One of the nuggets weighed an astounding 1272 ounces (36 kilograms), bigger than anything found in California. It took a few months for the news to catch on, but by May, Sydney was abuzz with gold fever, which would ignite the long boom that lasted until the 1890s and changed the city forever. As a British army officer, Lieutenant Colonel Mundy, observed:

Sydney assumed an entirely new aspect. The shop fronts put on quite new faces. Wares suited to the wants and tastes of general purchasers were thrust ignominiously out of sight, and articles of outfit for goldmining only were displayed. Blue and red serge suits, Californian hats, leathern belts, 'real gold-digging gloves', mining boots, blankets, became show goods in fashionable streets. The pavements were lumbered with picks, pans, and pots, and the gold washing machine, or Virginian 'cradle', hitherto a stranger to our eyes, became in two days a familiar household utensil … In less than a week the diminution of street population of Sydney was very visible, while Parramatta, previously half deserted, became almost depopulated … Nothing can have a more levelling effect on society than the power of digging gold, for it can be done, for a time, at least, without any capital but that of health and strength.[1]

Later that same year gold was found in Victoria, and the diggings there proved to be even more fruitful. Hundreds of men abandoned their families and jobs and headed for the goldfields. The discoveries fuelled a flood of immigration to Australia, both assisted and unassisted, and a boom in capital creation. For Sydney, the gold rush dovetailed neatly with the end of transportation and the introduction of responsible government in New South Wales in 1856.

As the prospect of easy riches beckoned, employers in Sydney had to increase wages to keep people working. Money was not only made directly on the fields, but also in provisioning the 'diggers'. Speculators drove up the price of goods and there was a huge demand for tents, carts and all forms of mining tools and equipment. Prices were high and good servants were hard to get, as the ladylike English visitor Charlotte Godley found to her haughty displeasure:

> [T]his terrible gold fever, which, with one or other of its effects, meets you at every turn in Sydney now, and makes it a thoroughly uncomfortable place to live in. It has quite altered the state of society and put an end, comparatively, to all gaiety; made the rich in many cases poor, and the poor very rich … Domestic servants are, however, I believe the people who make the difference most felt to the dwellers of Sydney … you hear endless stories of ladies who have been used to large establishments, and giving parties, now obliged to give up all thoughts of appearance, and open the door even, themselves, or make their daughters do it, give up their carriage, etc. and thankfully receive the services of any dirty girl who will come and help.[2]

The gold rushes created a flood of inbound migrants. In the 1850s, 465 000 people arrived in Australia. Just under half of these were assisted.[3] Most took off for the goldfields as soon as they landed, but their presence had a marked effect on Sydney. The city was busier and more chaotic than it had been before. Between 1851 and 1861, the population of Sydney rose from 54 000 to 96 000. Small hamlet-suburbs were dotted outside the centre of the town, at Balmain, Glebe, Newtown, Paddington, Redfern and St Leonards. For the first time there were large numbers of 'foreigners' in the country, and the predominantly Anglo-Celtic composition of the population began to change. Migrants came from other European countries, and also increasingly from China, although there had been earlier Chinese migrants who had worked as coolie labour mostly on large sheep runs.[4]

Racist attitudes soon developed on the goldfields, particularly against the Chinese, who often kept to themselves and worked the diggings longer and harder than their European counterparts. These racist attitudes soon seeped into the Anglo-Celtic consciousness, and into the cities. In 1857, the colony of Victoria imposed restrictions on immigration by charging a substantial extra fee on the Chinese—£4 per year, which was a huge amount in those days. Many Chinese people responded to this tax by travelling north to New South Wales where the miners were no more tolerant. Anti-Chinese attitudes and riots on the goldfields of Lambing Flat near Young led to the imposition of the same levy in New South Wales in 1861. The anti-Chinese policy was effective. By 1891 there were only 14 000 Chinese and people of mixed Chinese descent in New South Wales out of a total population of 1.25 million.

The growth of Victoria's population was dramatic. In 1852, the population of Victoria almost doubled and, by 1855, it overtook New South Wales by a convincing margin: 347 000 compared to 266 000. Sydney's evolution in status continued. In 1859, when Queensland was carved from New South Wales's territory, the colony was only one-third of the size she had once been.

Manufacturing businesses in Sydney and other towns found it a struggle to compete against the flood of imported goods arriving to supply the steadily growing population, so the debate between free traders and protectionists was heard for the first time. In the early years of the debate, conservatives tended to be protectionist and less conservative people such as Henry Parkes tended to support free trade, as this meant a lower cost of living. Later, as we shall see, the debate divided along colonial lines. New South Wales developed a free-trade outlook and Victoria was to remain staunchly protectionist.

The spectacle of entering the harbour and seeing Sydney for the first time was commented upon by a visitor in 1857:

> Tiers of fine buildings seem to rise one above the other, like the seats in an amphitheatre, and towering above them all, is the tall spire of St James' Church.[5]

The growing maturity of Sydney as a colonial city was indicated by the establishment of the University of Sydney in 1852. The university boasted the motto 'Sidere mens eadem mutato' which means 'the same minds under different stars'. The implication of this motto was that the only difference there was to be between the new colonial society and that of Britain was geographical, rather than cultural. The architecture of the original buildings of the university reflects this notion of entire transplantation. The Edmund Blacket–designed main buildings and St Paul's College were constructed between 1854 and 1860 in the Gothic Revival style, with little regard to difference in climate. Nearby, the facade of the Physics Building (which was once the facade of the Commercial Banking Company of Sydney in George Street) was fashioned in the competing Classical Revival style.

In the Victorian period there was, throughout the British Empire, an ongoing discourse as to which architectural revival style was preferable: Gothic or Classical. Commercial and governmental enterprises preferred to evoke strength and solidity of great ancient empires by using Classical styles, while the more romantic and spiritual Gothic style was commonly employed for ecclesiastical and educational buildings. There are no finer examples of these two styles standing in Sydney today than those that can be seen at Sydney University. Beyond the university, houses were built in both styles, but it was the Classical style with its larger windows that would prove to be better suited to Sydney's climate.

By the mid-1850s, Sydney resembled a bustling English seaport. Steamships ran between Europe and Australia and mail arrived in 135 days rather than the 275 days that it had taken in the early nineteenth century.[6] Sydney had adopted a tone of Victorian sobriety and

BELOW: The Royal Exchange Building in Bridge Street in the late nineteenth century. This building housed the first stock exchange in Sydney and was a centre of Sydney's financial district for many decades. Sadly, it was demolished in the 1960s. Beyond it is the Lands Department Building, with its sculptures of famous explorers in the niches above street level.

spending time in Sydney was, in no sense of the word, '*roughing* it'. In the 1850s, it was Melbourne which had the ambience of a frontier town. Sydney's residents had museums and zoos to visit, and on Sunday horse-drawn omnibuses and ferries used to take them for trips to the countryside, such as to Botany, the Cooks River, down the Parramatta River, to Manly or to Watsons Bay. Promenading in late summer afternoons down Lovers Walk in Hyde Park was also popular. The walk ran from St James' Church to Liverpool Street. People enjoyed strolling in the park with the pleasant sea breezes and views down to the boats and villas on the harbour.[7] Gas lamps illuminated the streets of Sydney at night.

The main commercial streets in the city were (and still are) George and Pitt streets. In the 1850s, when Pitt Street was extended to Bridge Street, the Tank Stream was covered completely. The finest shops were in Pitt Street, between King and Market streets. There was still, however, a motley mix of single-storey and multi-storeyed buildings. The northern end of the city (north of the Post Office) was evolving into the financial centre. The opening of the Royal Exchange (stock exchange) in 1853 on the corner of Gresham, Pitt and Bridge streets promoted this, as did the construction of solemn banks built in the various revivalist architectural styles of the Victorian era.

In George Street, the 'bucks and Brummels of the Colony' visited the Café Francais. As well as good food, there were chess and billiard clubs there. Lunch time was taken seriously—the church bells would ring in the city at one o'clock each weekday afternoon, heralding the lunch hour. For one patron of the Café:

> Little marble tables, files of *Punch* and the *Times*, dominoes, sherry cobblers, strawberry ices, an entertaining hostess, and a big, bloused, lubberly, inoffensive host, are the noticeable points of the Café left on my recollection. They serve eight hundred dinners a day at this house.[8]

The Café Francais survived in Sydney until the middle of the twentieth century when it was knocked down to make way for Wynyard House.

As the city's commercial activity grew, the two main commercial east–west streets, Hunter and King streets, became the home of unusual and specialist shops and small businesses.

The finest town houses were in Macquarie Street. They were often grand and up to four storeys high. As one visitor in 1857 remarked:

> The best time to see this neighbourhood in all its glory is on a summer's evening, about an hour after sunset, when the drawing rooms are in a blaze of light. Then the rich tones of the piano, or some other musical instrument, are heard gushing forth from the open windows, accompanied by the sweet melody of female voices … Beautiful ladies, dressed in white, may be seen sitting upon the verandahs, or lounging in magnificent

couches, partially concealed by the folds of rich crimson curtains, in drawing rooms which display all the luxurious comforts and magnificence of the East, intermingled with the elegant utilities of the West.[9]

Another new residential area in the town was Wynyard Square, recently vacated by the army when it moved to Victoria Barracks at Paddington in 1848. Some of the residents of the area around Wynyard Square were Jewish merchants who lived in smart town houses. Most of the Jewish immigrants to Sydney before the post–World War II period came from the British Isles. Sydney's first synagogue (1844) was built nearby on the western side of York Street, in the Egyptian style.

In 1858, the same year that Sydney, Melbourne and Adelaide were linked by telegraph, an enthusiastic social observer, W. S. Jevons, engaged in a survey of Sydney housing. He noted that successful merchants, shopkeepers and professional men lived in mansions or villas, usually on elevated land just outside the city, such as Glenmore Road, Paddington, or Darlinghurst, Elizabeth Bay and Glebe, or in the middle of town in Macquarie Street or in Lower Fort Street. The middle classes (by which he meant skilled workers) lived in four-to-five roomed houses, clustered in districts such as Surry Hills, Strawberry Hill, Redfern, Glebe, Pyrmont, Balmain and the higher area of The Rocks around Millers Point. The worst housing was much older and located at The Rocks, the lower end of Sussex Street, and around Druitt and Goulburn streets.

In the late 1850s, the Riley Estate in Darlinghurst and Woolloomooloo was being subdivided into smaller areas of land upon which cheap housing was being built. Surry Hills was another busy construction zone. Houses and cottages were built in brick or weatherboard and were 'very wretched', according to the taste of Mr Jevons. Middle-class housing along what is now Oxford Street, Paddington, was also rising from the sandhills. Oxford Street between Victoria Street at Darlinghurst and present-day Whitlam Square was by then a busy thoroughfare 'of great pretentiousness'.

The western side of the city from George Street to Darling Harbour was occupied by the working classes and there were many businesses located close to the George Street markets. Goats roamed around the then mostly residential Sussex Street. Jevons must have spent considerable time scouring The Rocks, an area he found appalling. He could see the unplanned, haphazardly built remnants of Sydney's earliest architecture, and there was little sewerage and drainage. Houses were sometimes built just yards away from walls of rock over which spouts and drains projected effluent. Jevons was full of moral indignation about the state of the local residents:

Of the inhabitants I will not say much: in some cases misfortune may have led and may still keep them there; but in others the unhappy, debauched, wicked face, the slovenly, dirtily clothed person, tell too plain a tale. A young intoxicated woman with a black eye and bruised forehead, and a shrivelled old dame with a face of a yellow-brown colour, sitting in a poverty stricken room, enchained my attention—they were striking pictures of the first and last stages of vice … I am acquainted with most of the notorious parts of London … but in none of these places perhaps, would lower forms of vice and misery be seen than Sydney can produce. Nowhere too, is there a more complete abandonment of all the requirements of health and decency than in a few parts of Sydney. The evils are not of great extent here but they are intense.

By night, Jevons went hunting for more vice and dereliction (always in the interests of science, of course). He found Argyle Street cold, damp and disagreeable, but nevertheless quiet. People in the higher parts of The Rocks were busy doing their needlework or sitting around their dining tables talking among themselves. No vice was apparent around Kent, Sussex and Clarence streets either and he even heard the murmurs of good-humoured conversation.

All in all, Jevons seemed almost disappointed that the state of moral dissolution in the colony was not more widely spread.[10] The worst area for 'vice and dereliction' was the lanes and alleyways between George, Pitt, Goulburn and Campbell streets, adjacent to the Haymarket. He did not indicate exactly how much time he spent there.

In 1854, when Britain became involved in the Crimean War, Sydney took stock of her defence prospects for the first time. The town was defenceless against the British Empire's new enemy, Russia. The first defence vessel was launched, the command was finally given to complete the Martello Tower at Fort Denison, and gun batteries were constructed on Dawes Point, Kirribilli Point and Fort Macquarie (Bennelong Point). The war created a decline in inbound shipping, and the journey to Europe also became longer as ships sailed across the Pacific and Atlantic oceans.

In the 1850s and 1860s, the mechanisation of industry became well established, although the industrial revolution was less dramatic in Australia than it was in most other countries of the English-speaking world. The domestic Australian market was small and export markets were too far away for Australian products to be competitive; however, small factories sprang up on the western side of the city around Sussex, York and Kent streets, and later at Pyrmont. All these areas were close to Darling Harbour, the centre of the coal-shipping industry. The diggers returning from the goldfields in the 1860s formed the nucleus of the industrial labour force. The diggers worked with the new immigrants in factories producing machinery and iron. Zollner's Galvanising Iron Works in York Street was one example. In 1864, the Australian Steam Navigation Co. launched the first Australian-built iron steamship, *Leichhardt*, at Pyrmont. In the early 1860s there was a recession caused by the rising number of returned diggers seeking work in Sydney. Unemployment increased and assisted immigration was suspended between 1867 and 1873.

From the 1850s, there was a rise in the number of Irish immigrants to Australia. This immigration was considerably later than that provoked by the Irish potato famine of the

1840s, when most Irish emigrants settled in North America. The arrival of large numbers of Irish immigrants in Sydney promoted the growth of sectarianism. Sectarianism augmented the social and political unity of the Irish Catholic community. The Catholic Church was more unified than any one of the several various and diverse Protestant communities. Religious sectarianism was an important thread in social and political life for many years to come, not least in the issue of education.[11]

The first railway to be opened in Sydney was the line between Parramatta and Sydney. It would take many more years after this first step in 1855 before the railway network became a significant form of transport in either the rural areas or the Sydney area itself. Linking such a widely distributed population in such a vast continent was a gargantuan, and expensive, task. The railway was started by a private company, but soon fell into financial difficulties and ownership passed to the government. There were no railroad barons in New South Wales, nor indeed anywhere else in Australia, as there were in the United States, because the volume of trade was too low, and the distances which had to be covered were too high for railways to be profitable enough. Building a railway system in New South Wales was a greater challenge than it was for its geographically more compact colonial cousin, Victoria. Railway construction created a new form of employment, and the construction of the railways was an important component of the long boom—even if some of the features of the developing railway system were sometimes almost comical.

The early New South Wales railway network certainly had its weaknesses. The Hunter River railway (begun by another unsuccessful private consortium) terminated at Newcastle and the only form of transport between Sydney and Newcastle was by sea. It was only in 1889 with the opening of the railway bridge across the Hawkesbury River that Sydney was linked by rail to the north and northwest of the state.

The next obstacle was that the western and southern railway system terminated at Redfern, a considerable distance south of the harbour's port facilities. The site was selected because the land was cheap. This meant that a greater strain was put on George Street, the traffic artery between Redfern and the wharves. Goods were unloaded at Redfern and hauled to the port by carriage. The matter was only partially resolved when Central Station opened in 1906. There were trunk railway lines to Darling Harbour in the late nineteenth century, but these were of no use to many of the cargo ships which were berthed elsewhere. The fact that the railway did not link up with the port facilities was criticised strongly as far back as 1879:

> We leave the dingy looking overcrowded railway station and yard at Redfern—that melancholy evidence of narrow vision and utter lack of prescience and common forethought. It leaves the terminus of a national system of trunk lines and loop railways, the great arterial feeders of giant's life, cut off from the heart as it were, beached high and dry like a stranded hulk a short distance from the natural termination, the sea

shore … The accumulated wealth of natural produce of the continent … must be laboriously dragged through the crowded city's streets by the primitive traction of oxen and horses.[12]

Another big problem for developing an Australian railway network was the different railway gauges used by the various colonies. New South Wales used the standard English width, Victoria and South Australia used the wider Irish gauge. No one at the time that the railways were first being built thought sufficiently far ahead to imagine how big the problem would become. It was not until the second half of the twentieth century that a standard national railway gauge was established.

In the first twenty years of the railway age, far more time and money were spent by the New South Wales government extending country rail services than was spent developing a network within the Sydney region. There was an important and understandable reason for this: geographic extension of the railway in the direction of other colonies made it possible to annex, economically at least, another colony's economic hinterland. The greater the hinterland, the greater the economic activity, size and status of the colonial capital—and its role as a port. In 1864, Victoria effectively annexed the Riverina from New South Wales until 1878 when the New South Wales railway line reached Wagga Wagga.

Suburban railway networks in Sydney were not developed until after 1875. After that date, suburban railway systems to the west, south and north of Sydney were built. The pace of subdivision intensified, and new suburbs sprang up in the Inner West and along the North Shore line. The suburban railway system did not completely penetrate the city until 1932 with the opening of the Harbour Bridge and Wynyard, Town Hall and Museum stations.

Tramways, on the other hand, were easier and faster to build. The first tramway was built from Redfern Station to Hunter Street in 1879, just in time to be a showpiece for the opening of the Sydney International Exhibition at the Garden Palace in the Botanic Gardens. The tramway network soon crisscrossed Sydney. It spread in all directions to Randwick, Surry Hills, Woollahra, Paddington, Waverley, Coogee, Botany, Marrickville and Glebe Point. The growth of the tramways from the 1880s played a greater role in determining the pattern of growth and expanding the limits of Sydney than the railways did in the late nineteenth century.

The other form of public transport that became more popular was the ferry. Commuter ferries ran from Circular Quay to the lower North Shore, Manly and the lower reaches of the Parramatta River, and this also promoted the outward sprawl of the city. There was a six-fold increase in the number of ferries between 1880 and 1913. Long-established isolated villages around the harbour such as Hunters Hill, Mosman, Neutral Bay and Cremorne became commuter suburbs. Circular Quay bristled with commuters on their way to and from work, as well as being a busy seaport for cargo and long-distance travellers. As the facilities of Sydney Cove were stretched with new commuter traffic, many of Sydney's cargo wharves moved further west to Darling Harbour, Pyrmont and Rozelle.

It took a long time for Sydney's roads to become weatherproof. Local government, responsible for the roads in the city itself, did not perform with admirable competence:

[I]n wet weather, when the mud is churned up on the roads, by the throng of vehicles, quadrupeds, pedestrians, till the streets are covered a foot deep in places, with the sloppy deposit, would not favourably impress a stranger. Or again, let the observant foreigner encounter the full force of a 'southerly buster', in one of the principal streets of the New South Wales metropolis; his remarks, if heard at all amid the dust laden whirlwinds, will hardly be pleasant to hear ... in dry windy weather the dust whirls in eddying volumes through every thoroughfare, blinding the traveller, destroying clothes and any exposed merchandise and exacerbating the temper ... still, Sydney is not a whit inferior to other towns of equal pretensions ... Take, for instance Melbourne or even London. Sydney in its fiercest tornado, in its gustiest, dustiest, and bleakest day cannot for a moment vie with the whirlwinds of dust that completely blind the sun, on a windy day, in the Victorian capital. In her slushiest moments, her pavements are never so greasy, slimy and dangerous to pedestrians, as are the pavements of the Modern Babylon [London] during the continuance of a genuine November fog.[13]

110

Throughout the late 1870s and 1880s, wooden blocks were laid on Sydney's major streets. The asphalt available at the time could not withstand the heat of Sydney's summers. King Street was the first to get the blocks. By 1897, more than 100 acres (40 hectares) of wooden blocks had been laid. Gradually the dust level settled as the traffic noise of horses' hooves on wood increased. One of Sydney's lord mayors, Sir Allen Taylor, profited greatly from the introduction of wooden roadways. He had a monopoly on the supply of these blocks to the City Council over which he presided.[14]

The city's communication with the rest of Australia and the outside world sped up with the creation of the telegraph network during the late 1860s and 1870s. At the same time, the distance from the rest of the world was shrinking with the development of faster clippers and steamships. Sydney's first telephone exchange was opened in 1881 inside the Royal Exchange building. By the early 1890s, there were 2500 telephones in New South Wales.[15]

Sydneysiders witnessed many new technological breakthroughs in the 1890s. A packed audience in Sydney's Tivoli Theatre saw the first cinema film shown in Australia. They were shown images of London, military scenes of the Guards in London and locomotives moving across the screen. At the Engineering Exhibition of 1897 many innovations made possible with electricity were on display—electric lights, motors and other machinery such as electric bread-baking ovens, electric pans, refrigeration appliances, electrical alarm clocks and heaters. The phonograph was also becoming popular—large numbers were installed in New South Wales, bringing into homes the scratchy but audible voices of opera singers for the first time.

The gold rush had a levelling effect on Australian society that was noted with distaste by some English observers. The democratic undercurrent within the Australian colonies could be heard the loudest on the Victorian goldfields. While this was a long way from Sydney, its influence on the development of the collective national psyche was considerable. In 1854, the year before the Australian colonies were granted full representative government, diggers, represented by the Reform League, sought the same class of rights being sought by the Chartists in Britain. These were: full representation, manhood suffrage, payment of salaries for members of parliament, as well as, more particularly in the circumstances of the goldfields, the abolition of a gold-digger's licence fee. The diggers and the forces of the law skirmished and many diggers defiantly burnt their licences. The police came with bayonets, and the diggers, led by Peter Lalor, coalesced into a makeshift army. The Eureka flag with its southern cross was raised on the stockade diggers had built to protect themselves. The troops were sent in and quickly defeated the protesters. About forty people were killed.

The licence fee was abolished shortly afterwards, and democracy, in the form of representative government, although already in the process of being introduced, came about the following year. The democratic ideals of the diggers survived the stockade. A central theme of the protest was egalitarianism. Few diggers and other members of the working classes were prepared to allow pockets of privilege to become entrenched in an Australian society less than eighty years old.

The more egalitarian nature of Sydney society meant that social comportment did not always meet more exacting (and patronising) European standards. A German visitor to Sydney's Royal Victoria Theatre in 1851 thought that the audience was more interesting than the play, although the play was not very good:

111

> I really never found in any part of the world a more motley group in a theatre than was collected here. The first gallery contained the *haute volée*—the name already showed its destination—dress circle, and it is in fact the only decent place to go in the house. The second gallery is also visited by the good honest citizens and tradesmen of the town; but the pit is far more interesting. As if shaken out of a Noah's ark, grisettes and shopkeepers, tradesmen and water-men in the wildest mixture imaginable … During the play they amuse themselves with applauding, whistling, stamping, and clapping hands, all signs of the greatest satisfaction.[16]

A cacophony broke out at interval where pieces of fruit were hurled both from the pit and the galleries above.

Wealth and economic success were more widely distributed in Australia in the second half of the nineteenth century than they were in Britain, and there were not the same structural bars to social and economic advancement. This freeing-up of the social fabric had gathered momentum during the gold rush when rapid capital creation made economic and social advancement a real possibility, irrespective of education or background. This trend towards egalitarianism was enhanced by the smaller gap between wages for skilled and unskilled labour.

The Victorian era was one of enormous optimism throughout the British Empire, and Sydney was no exception. There was no greater way of expressing this optimism than by holding large public exhibitions of industrial, agricultural, scientific and technical achievements. The Crystal Palace Exhibition in London in 1856 was imitated through the Empire. Sydney had its first Easter Show in 1869, organised by the Agricultural Society. In 1870, there was an Intercolonial Exhibition at Prince Alfred Park to mark the centenary of Captain Cook's arrival in Botany Bay. At the time the exhibition was opened, many displayed fulsome pride at the progress of the colony in its short life. The world's second national park, the National Park (later Royal in 1954) on Sydney's southern fringe, was also dedicated in that year.

An observer noted the differences between life in Sydney and England at the time of the Sydney International Exhibition of 1879–80, held in the Garden Palace in The Domain (destroyed by fire in 1882).[17] In Sydney, less attention was paid to the fine arts and far more people were occupied with matters of commerce, but a taste for higher culture was emerging. Although there was little sign of a leisure class of wealthy people, the middle classes lived almost as comfortably as the upper classes in Sydney, and had more leisure time than their English counterparts.

112

Australia's reputation as a worker's paradise grew, and this in turn led to a rise in immigration. Working hours were shorter, wages were higher and living standards were better. It was also easier to use the leisure time in Sydney than it was in Britain as the climate was more congenial. Access to credit through building societies made home ownership an achievable goal.[18]

The prevalence of heavy industry was less marked in Sydney than it was in the British Isles, and therefore the workers seemed less oppressed by their circumstances. Many undertook piecework or worked seasonally. Though lacking a similar level of job security to the major industrial producers, workers had more time for themselves, and more public holidays:

> On these occasions everybody is early astir, and after an early breakfast crowds of people may be seen wending their way towards the steamer, the train, or other modes of transport to some favourite place of recreation … A pleasant trip on the harbour, or an excursion by rail or omnibus, brings them to the selected scene of the day's pleasure, and then free and unrestrained enjoyment is the order of the day. In the evening all the theatres and other places of amusement are thronged, and the festivities are kept up from beginning to end with unflagging zeal.[19]

In 1879, when there was more than a decade-long building boom to follow, the spread of Sydney in the previous decade was colourfully observed:

> The overflow of bricks and mortar has spread like a lava flood, over the adjacent slopes, heights and valleys, till the houses now lie, pile on pile, tier on tier, and succeed each other row after row, street after street, far into the surrounding country; and the eruption is still in active play … The sand drives are covered with cottages, the very marshes have

ABOVE: Bathers and bathing machines at Coogee Beach (c. 1880), before surf bathing in the daytime was legalised in Sydney. Many Sydneysiders took advantage of Sundays and public holidays to enjoy pastimes such as this.

113

a crop of dwellings that are springing up, like mushrooms; often, alas, like that very fragile and brittle and little calculated to withstand a lengthened wear and tear, nurtured in corruption and redolent of putridity and decay … suburban extension is proceeding with wonderful speed. Everywhere the sound of the workmen's tools is heard, all through the busy day. Brick-yards, iron foundries, saw-mills and joinery establishments are in full activity, and at present the building trades are in constant and vigorous employment.[20]

Writer Richard Twopeny, among others, remarked on the nature of Australian society. Compared to life in England the middle and upper classes mingled freely. Working-class people were too well paid, he thought, to provide a high level of service. Tradesmen were hard to find, and unreliable. The manner of the lower classes was so independent that 'one would wish they did not confound civility and servility as being equally degrading to the free and independent elector'.[21]

Melbourne was truly the metropolis of the southern hemisphere by the 1870s. Life in Sydney was not quite as fast as in Melbourne and it had an older, more picturesque flavour. Twopeny advised people to visit Sydney if they had to choose between the cities as it had greater natural beauty, the architecture was taller, loftier and more irregular, and its hilly topography enhanced its beauty. In his opinion, the people were less flashy and ostentatious than Melburnians.

Another writer, F. L. W. Adams, wrote that the relationship between Melbourne and Sydney was like that between Boston and New York, Melbourne being New York.[22] In 1886, Adams thought, Sydney lacked the 'metropolitan tone' of the great nineteenth-century cities. Sydneysiders took a keen interest in what was happening in Melbourne, whereas Melburnians thought little about the affairs of Sydney. That situation has now significantly reversed itself. The general attitude of Sydneysiders towards Melburnians today is like that of an older brother or sister, who, however fondly, looks down upon his or her younger siblings as plainer, less interesting and a lot more self-conscious. Today, it is the Sydneysiders who more frequently are accused by Melburnians of metropolitan brashness and haughtiness.

Sydney's growing civic pride and prosperity were reflected in its imposing new public architecture. The government architect of the middle and late nineteenth century was James Barnet. On account of his longevity, and the Victorians' urge to build great works, he left an indelible mark on Sydney. It is hard to imagine the city without his architectural legacy.

By the time of Sydney's first inter-colonial exhibition in 1870 Barnet had expanded the Australian Museum, started his greatest masterpiece, the General Post Office (GPO), and built the Redfern Mortuary Station. In the next twenty years, Barnet designed the Lands Department Building and the Chief Secretary's Building (both in Bridge Street), Customs House at Circular Quay, and numerous inner-city police stations, town halls and post offices. Many public works in the city and the suburbs were built in the 1880s, with a keen eye to completion before the centenary of European settlement in 1888.

Other architects working in the last quarter of the nineteenth century were Walter Liberty Vernon and William Wardell. Vernon formed a bridge between the Victorian Classical Revival and early twentieth-century styles of architecture. William Wardell, who worked in the Classical Academic and Classical Gothic styles designed St Mary's Cathedral and St John's College at Sydney University. In the later decades of the nineteenth century, the Gothic and Classical styles became freer and more eclectic, so that wealth and status could be more ostentatiously displayed. Many office buildings being built in the city were very highly decorated, especially after stuccoing with Portland cement became widespread. The 1880s were the era of 'wedding cake' architecture. Remnants of this style can be seen in the Pitt Street Mall between King and Market streets. Another great architectural work of the later nineteenth century was the Town Hall.

The late nineteenth century was also an era of impressive private-school building. John Hennessy designed St Patrick's Seminary at Manly and St Joseph's College, Hunters Hill, and many other works of ecclesiastical architecture. Horbury Hunt designed the main buildings and chapel of Kincoppal Rose Bay. Thomas Rowe designed the main block of Newington College at Stanmore in 1881.

In 1855, full representative government was introduced in New South Wales, Victoria and Tasmania. At the time, these new colonial constitutions were a radical and much more democratic departure from the British constitution. The first difference was that the constitution was written and the second was that men in the Australian colonies were to enjoy a wider suffrage than they would have enjoyed in Britain. Another point of departure was that the Upper House was not hereditary. An English supporter of this more democratic model of government was Liberal MP William Ewart Gladstone.[23]

The new written constitution created two houses of parliament, the Legislative Council, whose members were nominated by the governor, and the more democratically elected Legislative Assembly. The first elections for the Legislative Assembly in New South Wales were held early in 1856. The creation of parliamentary government had the effect of rebalancing power into the hands of the middle classes, miners and men of commerce. The long political reign of the squatters had passed its zenith. From the 1840s until the 1890s when the Labor Party was formed, politics in New South Wales was composed of loose and shifting alliances and coalitions of interests which often collapsed, leading to sudden changes in government.

Two years after the first parliamentary elections New South Wales adopted the practice, already followed in Victoria and South Australia, of the secret, or 'Australian', ballot. Universal manhood suffrage was also introduced, irrespective of property qualifications. This put the colonies even further ahead of Britain.

115

Just as William Charles Wentworth dominated political life from the 1820s to the 1850s, so Henry Parkes cast a long (and wide) shadow over politics in Sydney in the second half of the nineteenth century, and it is hard to explore this period without looking more closely at this giant of a man.[24] Henry Parkes was the son of a yeoman farmer who was forced off his rural holding into the city of Birmingham in England's newly industrialised Midlands when Henry was ten years old. Parkes was educated for only a few years, and later attended a mechanics' institute. His lack of formal education made his political, literary and oratorical skills all the more remarkable. In his teens, Parkes served an apprenticeship as an ivory turner and set up his own business when he was twenty-two. His business in Birmingham did not prosper, nor did he find London any better when he sought his fortune there. Before leaving Birmingham, however, he had observed, as a youth, the political agitation that led to the passing of the first Reform Bill in 1832. Parkes was greatly impressed and influenced by the quality of the oratory at these populist speeches, and even joined the Political Union, the alliance that strongly advocated the bill.[25]

Parkes, his first wife Clarinda and their newborn child reached Sydney in 1839 on an immigrant ship at a time when there were 1200 other immigrants on ships in the harbour waiting to land. Parkes and his wife did not know a soul in the colony, nor did they hold any letters of introduction. He must have felt as lost and as far from home as many of the others waiting on the water:

I was one of that floating crowd of adventurers ... Of necessity we had to remain on board some days. In those wearisome days of vague hope, fitful despondency, and youthful impatience, many hours of the early morning I spent hanging over the ship's side, looking out upon the monotonous, sullen and almost unbroken woods which then thickly clothed the north shore of the harbour.[26]

Parkes arrived in the colony too late to take advantage of the economic growth of the 1830s. The only work he could find was as an agricultural labourer on Sir John Jamison's estate, Regentville, near Richmond, 58 kilometres to the west of Sydney. He later worked at Thomas Burdekin's foundry and in a brass works. It was not until 1845 that he had saved enough money to set up an ivory-turning and importing business in Hunter Street. He and his family lived above the shop.

From the late 1840s, Parkes began to speak out in public on behalf of the free immigrant middle and working classes. He was in favour of an extension of the limited franchise granted in 1842 and against the resumption of transportation to the Australian colonies. His views, and the views of others of his political persuasion, offered a more or less middle course between liberalism and radicalism through much of the nineteenth century in New South Wales. However, throughout his long political career, he could never be accused of rigid consistency. One of the vehicles for the combination between radicals and liberals against the conservatives was Parkes's newspaper, the *Empire*, published between 1850 and 1858. Parkes strongly opposed Wentworth's outmoded eighteenth-century views on constitutional reform.

In 1854, Parkes won the seat of Sydney in parliament when Wentworth retired from politics and left for England. He won the election by a convincing two–one majority from his opponent Charles Kemp, one-time part-owner of the *Sydney Morning Herald*. His constituents were people like him: recently arrived free immigrants from working or middle-class backgrounds who did not care to be politically represented by conservatives. Parkes's political career was intermittent because of persistent financial problems and the vicissitudes of the electoral process, but spanned a period of forty years.

In 1860, one of Parkes's early public responsibilities was to chair a parliamentary select committee established to inquire into the condition of the working classes. The condition of housing was deplorable for many Sydneysiders. People lived in hovels; high rents led to overcrowding; and there were a thousand vagrant children roaming the streets. Many young girls were prostitutes. His contribution to that inquiry brought him to public attention and he was elevated to James Martin's ministry as Colonial Secretary in 1866.

Parkes, affected by what he had learned of the condition of young children while serving on the select committee, created a nautical school for male orphans on a hulk in Sydney Harbour. He also introduced professional nursing to New South Wales when he brought out Lucy Osburn, a nursing sister trained by Florence Nightingale, to teach local women professional nursing. Education was another important priority for him. He created a council to oversee both denominational and religious schools.

After a period in the political wilderness brought on by financial difficulties, he became premier (then called prime minister) in 1872. He put into place his free trade policies and embarked on an ambitious public works program. His first premiership came to an end in 1875 in a parliamentary battle over the right of the governor to stand by his agreement to remit notorious bushranger Frank Gardiner's long gaol sentence. Public opinion was against clemency. Both the governor and Parkes thought that Gardiner's exemplary conduct in the ten years between his escape from custody and his recapture in Queensland demonstrated a capacity to abide by the law. The general population, fired up by a law and order campaign stoked up by Parkes's political rivals, were furious that Parkes and the governor would not yield to public pressure. Parkes lost control of the Legislative Assembly and was thrown out of power for three years until 1878.

In his second term as premier, Parkes's major act was to reform education in New South Wales. Government-funded education became free, compulsory and secular, though truancy rates remained often high. State aid was withdrawn from religious schools. The abolition of state aid was an issue that festered within the Catholic community for another eighty-three years. That community believed it was being singled out for harsh treatment, as they saw themselves as the main victims of the change. Unwilling to lose control of their young flock to the state school system, Catholic parents were compelled to pay double for their children's education: first, they paid the fees to the parochial schools, and then they paid tax, some of which was used to pay for the elementary state school system.[27]

117

The state-aid issue was not resolved until 1963 when then prime minster, Robert Menzies, identifying a political opportunity to dislodge prosperous Catholics from the Labor Party's political grasp, offered a limited form of state aid to Catholic schools. State aid to private schools is now a bipartisan issue, and sectarianism within Sydney society has now virtually disappeared.

Another less controversial step was to provide for greater access to learning for the working classes. Free libraries had been established in the 1860s at a time when there were already thirty bookshops in Sydney.[28] In 1878, a university men's college was founded and, by 1892, there were 2000 enrolments.[29] Since then, this institution has evolved first into the Sydney Technical School and later it formed the nucleus of the University of New South Wales, Sydney's second-oldest university, established in 1949.

Henry Parkes's government lost office again in 1883; however, by that time he was referred in the London *Times* as 'the most commanding figure in Australian politics'.[30] He led another government, from 1887 until 1891, on the election platform of free trade and honest government, and was in charge of the police and military during the maritime strike of 1890.

From the late 1880s, Parkes's attention moved from parliamentary matters to the issue of Australian federation. He was the driving force for federation in New South Wales, which was the largest colony at the time of the final federation referenda, but the least convinced of its benefits. After Parkes's death in 1896, at Kenilworth in Johnston Street, Annandale, Alfred Deakin said of him that:

... though not rich or versatile, his personality was massive, durable and imposing, resting on elementary qualities of human nature elevated by a strong mind. He was cast in the mould of a great man and though he suffered from numerous pettinesses, spites and failings, he was himself a large-brained self-educated Titan whose natural field was parliament and whose resources of character and intellect enabled him in his later years to overshadow all his contemporaries.[31]

In his later years, Parkes did not, however, escape scandal. His second wife had been his mistress and had two children by him before the relationship was formalised and, on account of this indiscretion, the doors of Government House were closed to him.[32] He raised eyebrows again when he married his 23-year-old housekeeper shortly after his second wife died, against the strong wishes of his closest friends. He died shortly after his third wedding, just before his eighty-first birthday. Parkes had twelve children from his first marriage. Five of them died in infancy and six survived him. He had another five children from his second marriage, one of whom, Cobden Parkes, became the Government Architect responsible for the design of the Dixson and Mitchell wings of the State Library.

Like other cities throughout the western world, the increase in Sydney's population was dramatic. Between 1851 and 1901 the population rose from 54 000 to nearly 500 000. In the twenty years from 1881 to 1901, the population more than doubled from 225 000 to 497 000. The second half of the nineteenth century, particularly between 1870 and 1892, was the time the suburbs now called the inner-city suburbs were built.[33] In 1851, more than 80 per cent of Sydney's population lived in central Sydney. Fifty years later, only 23 per cent did.

From the 1880s, the middle classes started their exodus from the inner city. The developing public transport network made this possible. As people left, the areas closest to the city started a long period of decline that was not reversed until the mid-twentieth century. These suburbs included Newtown, Glebe, Redfern, Surry Hills, Enmore, Paddington and Woolloomooloo.

In 1901, the outer suburbs of Sydney were Strathfield, Concord, Lane Cove, Hunters Hill and Waverley. Sydneysiders were keen (sometimes inexpert) builders, and little attention was paid to landscaping their private domains:

There are few cottage gardens about Sydney. Land is too valuable and too much cut up into fifty feet sections, to admit of horticulture. What gardening there is, is in the hands of chinamen [sic], whose prosaic souls do not rise above the level of culinary roots and herbs. There are few flowerpots about the workmen's houses of Sydney. There are still fewer back gardens. The pot-herb patches, the mushroom beds, homely cabbage rows, or artisan dwellings in western Europe, are altogether wanting. The cottages are dependent entirely on purchased poultry and meat for the requirements of their *cuisine* ... it is not considered worth the trouble to keep pigs or poultry in the back yard.[34]

Perhaps the reaction against cultivating and improving one's garden was a consequence of the attendant risks and disappointments of gardening and small-scale horticulture. Rainfall was unreliable, soil quality poor and, in periods of long drought, the water supply at times precarious.

In the poorer parts of inner Sydney—Woolloomooloo, The Rocks and Surry Hills—groups, or 'pushes', of larrikins roamed around and harassed the general population in the latter years of the nineteenth century. This was not a phenomenon unique to Sydney; similar groups of young men roamed other cities across the world, menacing strangers and loitering in public places. Some observers such as Mark Twain thought Sydney larrikins were more sociable and less threatening than their counterparts elsewhere.[35] This was a rather rosy view of things—larrikins often picked fights with the Chinese and raided their vegetable gardens and shops. Many members of the wider community were also harassed. Sydney's larrikin streak was reflected in the crime rates of 1892. Twice as many people appeared before the magistrates' courts in New South Wales than did in Victoria which, at the time, had a higher population, and there were also twice as many serious charges dealt with in Sydney.[36]

The larrikin ethos was readily grafted onto Sydney's overall character. Louis Stone wrote a novel in 1911 where the central hero, Jonah, was a larrikin. The Cardigan Street push of Waterloo, an inner-city, working-class suburb to the south of Sydney, used to gather under the veranda of an unoccupied shop smoking cigarettes and spend their time:

> discussing the weightier matters of life—horses and women. They were still young—from eighteen to twenty-five—for the larrikin never grows old. The Cardigan Street Push, composed of twenty or thirty young men of the neighbourhood, was a social wart of a kind familiar to the streets of Sydney. Originally banded together to amuse themselves at other people's expense, the Push found new cares and duties thrust upon them, the chief of which was chastising anyone who intruded with their pleasures. Their feats ranged from kicking an enemy senseless, and leaving him for dead, to wrecking hotel windows if the landlord had contrived to offend them. Another of their duties was to check ungodly pride in the rival Pushes by battering them out of shape with fists and blue metal at regular intervals.[37]

The lack of interest on the part of the more affluent social classes in reducing the menacing aspect of larrikinism through philanthropy and the encouragement of benevolent institutions such as night schools was remarked upon.[38] Private philanthropy has, until recent years, not been a prominent or a widespread feature of Sydney's culture, though there are always exceptions, the most prominent of these being David Scott Mitchell and William Dixson. Each of these men devoted much of his life to collecting books, artworks and manuscripts later donated to the State Library. As 'Maori' Inglis put the lack of fellow feeling of the privileged towards the less fortunate:

'Am I my brother's keeper?' they ask. 'We are too busy gambling, and pot hunting and plundering the treasury and rigging the market, to lose time over mawkish sentimentality. Let the parsons, and the police, and the government look to it. They are paid to put down larrikinism. What have we to do with it?'[39]

Literature and the arts flourished in Sydney in the late nineteenth century. Larrikinism and life in the bush were drawn upon as an inspiration and source for many writers of the day. Another feature of the decades leading up to Federation in 1901 was the emergence of nationalism. Sometimes this nationalism had racist overtones. The Aborigines and the Chinese were heavily discriminated against. The Aborigines were often treated as primitive savages and figures of fun. The spectre of cheap labour from Chinese immigration threatened the rise of the union movement.

120

The *Bulletin*, founded in 1880 and published in Sydney, was one of the centres of this nationalistic political and literary activity. The motto on its masthead was: 'Australia for the White Man'. The *Bulletin*'s politics were radical and republican. Its leading lights were Francophile publisher J. F. Archibald and, later, A. G. Stephens, the literary critic. Both these men helped many poets and writers find their voices and their feet. Famous poets and writers such as 'Banjo' Paterson, Henry Lawson, Joseph Furphy and Victor Daley had their poems

LEFT: Poet and balladeer, and author of 'Waltzing Matilda', A. B. ('Banjo') Paterson.
BELOW: Henry Lawson (c. 1910), another famous Sydney poet of the late nineteenth and early twentieth centuries.

and short stories published in the *Bulletin*, and it was often referred to as 'the bushman's bible' because of its wide readership in the more remote areas of Australia. The *Bulletin* appealed to the common man. The illustrations were as well regarded as the literature. The most famous illustrators were political cartoonist Livingstone Hopkins ('Hop'), Phil May and Will Dyson. Like many Australian nationalists of his day, Archibald was less than enthusiastic about extolling the glory of the colony's convict past, and the *Bulletin* boycotted the centenary celebrations of 1888. Archibald and his *Bulletin* colleagues preferred to celebrate the anniversary of the Eureka Stockade. One of the *Bulletin*'s writers, Price Warung (his real name was William Ashley), published stories in the magazine that gave gruesome and brutal accounts of the early days of the colony and the nation.[40]

Henry Lawson and 'Banjo' Paterson mythologised Australian bush culture at a time when urbanisation and the erection of paddock fences had created a gap between reality and the romantic images depicted in their poetry. The literature of the late nineteenth century drew on the oral balladeering tradition of the convicts and the bushrangers and bushmen in Australia's past, rather than on the more academic and traditional works of mid–nineteenth-century poets Henry Kendall and Charles Harpur.

121

Lawson and Paterson were born within three years of each other, but came from different backgrounds. Paterson came from a prosperous family of graziers who lived near Yass. He enjoyed a happy childhood. He attended Sydney Grammar School and the University of Sydney then practised as a solicitor. Paterson's other non-literary interests were gentlemanly: he liked to hunt and play polo. He wrote verses that are as well known (often by heart) and loved today as they were when they were published. Some of these are 'The Man from Snowy River', 'Clancy of the Overflow', 'The Geebung Polo Club' and, most famous of all, 'Waltzing Matilda'. Lawson, on the other hand, grew up the child of an unhappy marriage in a poor mining town. From his late teens, he suffered a permanent major hearing loss and this made him even more introverted and isolated. His mother, Louisa, was a feminist who left her husband and the outback for Sydney, and, from 1889, published *Dawn*, one of the first Australian women's magazines. She also started a feminist and temperance discussion group called the Dawn and Dusk Club, which met in Quong Tart's tearooms in the city. Louisa Lawson became a committee member of the Womanhood Suffrage League of New South Wales in 1891.

Lawson served an apprenticeship as a coach painter and went to night school. He was more emotionally tortured and politically motivated than Paterson. Lawson published his first poem, 'A Song for the Republic', when he was twenty-three. Two years later, in 1889, he wrote 'The Faces in the Street'. His best work is probably his short stories. He found making a living as a writer difficult, and often relied on the goodwill of his publisher, George Robertson (co-founder of Angus & Robertson) and other friends and acquaintances for money to tide him over.

In 1892, Archibald sent Lawson off to the bush, where he saw the effects of the drought and rural recession. This visit was the source of inspiration for many of his short stories, some of which appeared in *While the Billy Boils* (1896). Lawson's trip to witness the suffering of those living in the bush did not lighten his already gloomy temperament. Unable to heed the warnings of his temperance-minded mother, he often lapsed into bouts of heavy drinking. He was increasingly prone to alcoholism and depression, and had an unhappy personal life. His literary efforts suffered from 1900 onwards, and he died in 1922.

Bohemianism was a popular cultural movement of the mid to late nineteenth century in Europe, and Sydney did not escape its influence. The bohemian life was made popular by Frenchman Henri Murger's play *La Vie de Bohème* (1849), which was later adapted into Puccini's opera *La Bohème*. Bohemians lived a carefree, artistic and very unconventional life by the strict standards of the Victorian era. In Sydney, bohemianism developed within the walls of clubs such as the Athenaeum Club in Castlereagh Street and the 'Growlers' Corner' at the Café Francais. Unlike the European capitals and Melbourne, it was also easy to be a bohemian in the outdoors, especially in the bushland around Sydney Harbour.

The 1880s and 1890s were a golden era for art in Sydney. In 1880, the Art Society was established. Headquartered at the Garden Palace in the Domain, it held art classes and art exhibitions. When the palace burnt down in 1892, more than 300 paintings were lost. In 1883, English-born artist and art teacher Julian Ashton arrived in Sydney, and became president of the Art Society and later trustee of the Art Gallery of New South Wales, and was also a leading figure in promoting the visual arts. He led a successful battle to convince the government that the Art Gallery should spend £500 per annum on Australian art, making it possible for the gallery to buy important artworks of the period. Throughout the 1880s, he took his students to the bushland and beaches around Sydney so they could learn to paint in the *plein air* style. Ashton's students included Charles Edward Conder, Benjamin Minns, Sydney Long and George Lambert.

In the mid-1890s, Tom Roberts and Arthur Streeton, two of Australia's most famous and well-loved artists, arrived in Sydney from Melbourne. Streeton and Roberts soon fell in love with the bushland around the harbour, which was so well suited to the *plein air* style, and visited the Curlew Camp at Little Sirius Cove over many years. The men came and went between the camp, the city and other parts of the bush, often moving elsewhere to paint and sell heroic works such as Streeton's *Fire's On, Lapstone Tunnel*, and Roberts's *The Golden Fleece* and *Bailed Up*. Roberts also became one of Sydney's leading portrait painters.

Roberts reacted to a conservative coup of the Art Society by establishing with the bohemians the breakaway Society of Artists (of which he was to be the president) on the steps of the General Post Office in Martin Place. A by-product of this secession was the sacking of Julian Ashton from the Art Society and the creation of the Julian Ashton Art School, which still exists and is based in Lower George Street at The Rocks.

In 1895, Sir Henry Parkes opened the first exhibition of the Society of Artists. The bush was a great inspiration to these artists, as it had been for Paterson and Lawson. In a sense, these artists depicted bushland around Sydney with the pastoral image they also gave the more remote interior—except many of the Sydney bushland paintings are more personal and intimate than the larger, heroic works upon which the artists' reputations were built.

There was an exodus of these and other leading artists from Australia at the end of the 1890s. Streeton, Roberts, Charles Conder and Benjamin Minns spent many years in England and Europe. Henry Fullwood returned to England and became the official Australian War Artist. Julian Ashton, unlike the others, stayed behind and ran his art school. A one-time companion of those who stayed at the Curlew Camp was art patron and businessman Howard Hinton, who lived at Cremorne. He collected the works of Streeton, Roberts and Ashton, and other Sydney artists such as George Lambert and Elioth Gruner. He endowed both the Art Gallery of New South Wales and later the University of New England with his extensive collection.

The most popular forms of theatre in Sydney in the late nineteenth century were melodrama and vaudeville. Examples of melodramas with Australian themes were *Robbery Under Arms* and *For the Term of His Natural Life*. The Tivoli Theatre specialised in vaudeville, an art form that became bawdier and more titillating as time went on, much to the disgust of the more religious and morally upstanding members of the community, who in some quarters were referred to as 'wowsers'.

123

The second half of the nineteenth century saw many important developments in the growth of amateur sports. Throughout the British Empire notions of athleticism meant that sporting activities were seen as more than just another opportunity for gambling and passing idle hours. Athleticism improved the mind, character and spirits—and prepared men for the idea of combat (and war). This notion of 'muscular Christianity' was sometimes connected with the temperance movement. Sport would get men out of the pubs and into the fresh air.

Inter-colonial cricket matches had been held with Victoria from 1856. Melbourne, flush with gold wealth, soon had better facilities for competitive cricket in the form of the Melbourne Cricket Ground (MCG). It also had the advantage of being built on a flat landscape, where cricket grounds were easier to lay out on the regular, grid-like street system. Melbourne's regular planning was something which Sydney, first settled in the eighteenth century, was both too old and too topographically uneven to be able to achieve.[41] Soon Victoria was winning the inter-colonial matches. They had better cricket grounds, greater loyalty in local district areas as there were more grounds to play on, and the sport was better administered.

Sydney had to make do with the Domain. Finding a permanent home for representative cricket games in Sydney took a long time. The site that later became the Sydney Cricket Ground was offered in the 1850s, but then it was too far from the city to be attractive. By 1876 the city had grown so much that the same offer was accepted.

There were no district cricket competitions in New South Wales until the season of 1892–93 when Sheffield Shield cricket matches between the Australian colonies were introduced. Leading cricket clubs of the middle of the nineteenth century were dominated by the well born and well connected. One of these was leading lawyer Septimus Alfred Stephen. Stephen was the son of a former chief justice, Sir Alfred Stephen. The gentlemanly nature of cricket in Sydney restricted its development as a district-based competitive sport—as was the case with rugby. Most of the early rugby clubs were run by gentlemen and the game was played by gentlemen. The cradle for the introduction of rugby to Sydney was the University of Sydney, which had one of the few rugby ovals. From the university, rugby trickled down into private boys schools such as The King's School, Sydney Grammar and Newington. The Sydney-based Southern Rugby Football Union was formed in 1874 to act as governing body for the game. Rugby had been played on unenclosed land at Moore Park since the early 1870s. The park was not enclosed until 1881.

The evolution of football mimicked what was happening in Britain. There was no formal split between what later became the two major football codes, rugby, developed by Rugby School in England, and soccer, which was first played at the prominent boys school Eton until 1863. Meanwhile, in Victoria, the game closely related to Gaelic football which would later become known as Australian Rules was played from the 1850s.

In the late 1870s, rugby in Sydney was almost taken over by Australian Rules. One city club, the Waratahs, based at the Freemasons' Hotel in York Street, threatened to secede, possibly disgruntled by the gentlemanly bias in the administration of the game. The club even held the closest thing to an inter-colonial Australian Rules match with Carlton—but they lost miserably. For a couple of seasons, even the Sydney University Rugby Club appeared to be wavering towards the Victorian code, but it fell back into line, as did the Waratahs. At the same time there was a movement for the adoption of soccer as the main football code in Sydney as the result of injuries sustained on the rugby field, but there was not a great deal of support for this. The halcyon era for rugby union in Sydney was the 1880s and 1890s. Unable to play against Melbourne with her own local football code, Sydney sought representative matches against rugby-loving New Zealand.

The stranglehold of gentlemen on the administration of rugby caused a split in the Metropolitan Rugby Union in 1908 between the amateurs (gentlemen) and the professionals who could be paid, albeit a token amount, and compensated for injuries sustained on the field. Rugby league soon became Sydney's professional code.

Horseracing and sculling were other popular sports. The Australian Jockey Club held its races at Randwick from 1860. Its biggest carnivals were (and still are) held in autumn (Easter) and spring. Other horseraces were held on other smaller racetracks around Sydney, such as at Canterbury and Rose Hill.

Saturday nights were busy in the city in the 1870s and 1880s. Shops were open till late through the week and on Saturday. There would be throngs of people in the city's streets until about ten in the evening. The crowds would turn out in:

> countless swarms … and throng the streets in thousands … there is a densely packed, slowly surging mass of people occupying the breadth of the street … the whole population is out of doors … It is rough, doubtless but it is hearty, jovial, good humoured roughness, and everything bespeaks rude plenty, a vigorous, well-contented, well-fed, well-housed, well-clad, well-paid, working population. When we can add well-

governed, and thoroughly well-educated, we shall see a magnificent race, and the future is not without signs of hopeful promise.[42]

However, the influence of Methodism, Sabbatarianism and general wowserism was increasing. We shall meet John Norton, the journalist and politician who invented or claimed to have invented the expression in the next chapter, but the meaning and import of 'wowserism' was clear. No less a literary figure than H. L. Mencken tried to import the expression into American English. He defined it as:

> a drab souled Philistine haunted by the mockery of others' happiness. Every Puritan is not necessarily a wowser; to be one he must devote himself to reforming the morals of his neighbours, and, in particular, to throwing obstacles in the way of their enjoyment of what they choose to regard as pleasures.[43]

The wowser element in New South Wales agitated for a referendum in 1882 to determine whether people could vote to have hotel licences withdrawn in their local municipality. The wowserist middle-class constituencies voted to close many hotels in their local areas. Opening hours were restricted to eleven in the evening, and had to close on Sundays as well. The rule against Sunday trading was not closely observed. In 1887 a commission of inquiry found that only 193 of the 822 Sydney hotels obeyed the law.[44]

The 1880s boom was fed by enormous inflows of capital. The New South Wales statistician, T. A. Coghlan (who certainly ought to have known such things) referred to it as a deluge. Most speculation involved land. This meant that financial institutions were heavily exposed to the property market. The greatest period of capital inflow was between 1886 and 1890. The boom spread to the rest of the economy. The amount of inbound and outbound trade was considerable. The tonnage of shipping in New South Wales almost doubled between 1871 and 1881, and then doubled again in the following ten years to 1891.[45] In 1892, Sydney was the largest port in Australia in terms of the value of the goods shipped.[46] Only London, Liverpool and Hull had goods of a greater value passing through their ports. In those days, Australia's major trading partner (by a huge margin) was Britain, which accounted for 75 per cent of its trade. The United States came second, but amounted to slightly more than 7 per cent of the total.

Following the Queen's Jubilee in 1887, Sydney and New South Wales began to focus on the centenary celebrations of 26 January 1888. Sydney celebrated the centenary with the opening of Centennial Park by the governor-general, Lord Carrington, which was attended by 50 000 people. The area set aside was at the time little more than sandhills and swamp. A foundation stone for the Trades Hall on the corner of Sussex and Goulburn streets was laid. The building, designed by John Smedley, was built as a meeting place and learning centre for working men.

Also, a statue of Queen Victoria was unveiled outside St James' Church before an enthralled procession which had marched up King Street. The opulent and optimistic spirit of the centenary celebrated the pride shared by all Australians in how far the colonies had travelled in a hundred years of white settlement—especially when the very humble beginnings as a penal colony (which was often euphemistically referred to) were taken into account. Now Australia was a prosperous and successful geographic entity, if not yet a nation.

The centenary celebration of 1888 took place at the apogee of the boom period, as the bicentenary did in 1988. These booms soon collapsed under the weight of serious economic downturn—although the stock market had already collapsed by 1988, there was still another year of boom-time property speculation to run.

A drought took hold from the mid-1880s and the level of rural unemployment increased. The rural population drifted into the cities in search of work and unemployment soon spread beyond the rural economy. The New South Wales government commissioned public works, using unemployed labour at the Kurnell industrial site and in building the tramline from Waverley to Randwick. Another widespread economic downturn started in the early 1890s with the cooling of the British economy. Again as in the 1840s, the price of wool and other commodities fell and capital inflow from Britain dried up.

Heavily indebted companies and lending institutions with low liquidity were the first to fail. Just as in the 1980s, the negligent and criminal activities of the directors of many of these businesses exacerbated the situation for shareholders, depositors and creditors. Many high-fliers became bankrupt. By late 1891, two banks had failed. The cooling economy coincided with industrial action encouraged by the growth of the labour movement as a political force.

In early 1892, there was a run on the Savings Bank of New South Wales. This run was fed by rumour and panic caused by the high failure rate of smaller lending institutions and two banks in Melbourne. The government stepped in to support the bank, but that was not the end of the crisis. During 1892, many New South Wales land banks and other financial institutions failed. Several directors of lending institutions were sent to Darlinghurst Gaol in that year.

The economic crisis deepened to its lowest point in the middle of 1893. In that year, fourteen of the twenty-five trading banks across Australia failed. The Commercial Banking Company (CBC) of Sydney, New South Wales's largest bank, suspended payments in mid-May. One-third of all deposits were compulsorily converted to equity (shares) in the bank. Other deposit funds were frozen.

The collapse of the banks (or freezing of their assets) had a devastating effect on depositors and their families. Many people faced economic calamity; there was no safety net in the form of social security. The unemployed had to beg and scrounge for food and sleep wherever they could. Homeless people (called 'sundowners') camped out every night in the parks of Sydney, particularly in the Domain. They wrapped themselves in newspapers and whatever else they could find. They fished for food and washed themselves in the horse troughs.

By the end of 1894, the immediate financial crisis was over. A drought that set in from 1895 until 1903, however, meant that the economy did not recover until several years into the twentieth century. The rate of immigration was severely affected by the depression of the 1890s. The levels of immigrants declined from 1891 and, in the early years of the twentieth century, there were more people leaving than entering Australia.[47]

English financial institutions were gaining the confidence to advance further loans to New South Wales by the end of 1895, but the hard climb out of the depression for the unemployed took much longer. At Christmas time in 1898, the government stepped in to try to improve matters by giving 2000 men work scraping and painting the iron railings on Hyde Park and Centennial Park. In the late 1890s, a scheme was introduced where the more fortunate ones wrapped scraps of food in clean paper which they left for the less well off. The depression was felt even more severely in 'Marvellous Melbourne'. There was even more debt-financed land speculation in that city. In the 1890s, Victoria lost population to New South Wales and Western Australia, so that, by 1900, New South Wales's population exceeded that of Victoria.

The labour movement gathered momentum during the harsh years of the 1890s. In the Great Strike of 1890, employers resisted demands for 'closed shops' or complete union coverage of the workforce. The strike started in the rural sector and spread to the maritime industry. It lasted for three months and wrought havoc throughout Australian commercial life. It was also, in the end, defeated. The strike tested where people's political sympathies lay: with the union workers or with capital and non-union ('scab') labour, of which there was a bountiful supply during the depression. The police, then under the administration of Henry Parkes, were often called in to assist in loading and unloading the goods from Sydney's wharves.

In the aftermath of the strike, the labour movement resolved to organise politically at the Trades Union Conference held in Sydney in 1891. The Labor Party was formed on a colony-by-colony basis. From Sydney, the Trades and Labor Council set up local branches of the Labour Electoral League. After the election of 1891, the Labor Party held thirty-five seats in the Legislative Assembly and held the balance of power. The discipline and 'pledge' these men signed as members of the party made it compulsory for them to abide by its electoral platforms and policies. This led to a political discipline that had previously been lacking in parliamentary politics.

Another outcome of the maritime strike was the gradual implementation of the conciliation and arbitration system (rather than collective or enterprise bargaining). These changes meant that the influence of the unions became much stronger than it was in other English-speaking countries, such as Britain or the United States, where there was no centralised wage-fixing.

One of the biggest political controversies of the second half of the late nineteenth century in Australia was the debate between protectionists and free traders. New South Wales politics was dominated by free traders and Victorian politics by protectionists. Protectionists thought (and still think) that jobs and high employment rates should not be threatened by cheap imports, and that tariffs should be imposed to prevent this from happening. Free traders thought (and think) that tariffs should be avoided as they cause a rise in the cost of living and inefficient 'featherbedding' of industries and businesses which should not be artificially propped up. In the nineteenth century, free trade generally suited the squatters, importers of goods and consumers who wanted access to cheaper goods. Protection favoured the economic interests of the manufacturers and those who worked in the manufacturing industries. This was the section of the economy that was least able to compete against a tide of British manufactured goods. Trade protection also made good economic sense to colonial governments. In the years before income tax was introduced during World War II, one of the main sources of funds for colonial governments was from levying customs duties. The differing opinions about trade policy in the Australian colonies delayed the path to federation.

The protectionist–free trade debate also inflamed inter-colonial rivalry between Victoria and New South Wales. The newer colony of Victoria was determined to reduce its reliance on imports (including imports from New South Wales), and used high tariff as a means of achieving this. The debate was stoked by the newspapers in each capital city. Melbourne's *Age* newspaper asserted, firstly, the general dominance of Melbourne over Sydney and secondly, the benefits of protectionism versus free trade. The *Sydney Morning Herald*, on the other hand, was pro free trade in its editorial views. Now both these newspapers are controlled by the same company, the Sydney-based John Fairfax & Sons Limited.

Despite this inter-colonial rivalry, the benefits of federation, or at least coordination, soon became apparent. An inter-colonial postal conference in 1867 resolved to form a federal council. At this conference, Henry Parkes gave a stirring speech in favour of federation. The next inter-colonial conference took place in 1870. Predictably, the colonies could not agree on a customs or uniform tariff policy. However, the colonies did agree on the need for cooperation with respect to postage and the enforcement of the criminal laws of each colony.

The issue of restricting high levels of Chinese immigration was one on which all the colonies agreed. It was a central political objective that had widespread popular support. The opposition to cheaper Chinese labour became a rallying call for the union movement. In 1878, employees of Sydney's Australasian Steam Navigation Co., headquartered at Circular Quay West, went on strike to protest against the company's use of Chinese 'coolie' labour on its ships. Rioting unionists tried to set fire to the workshops of Chinese cabinet-makers in Lower George Street, where the Regent Hotel now stands.

Although the number of Chinese living in Australia had dropped significantly from the end of the gold rush up until the 1880s, there was strong apprehension that unrestricted Asian immigration would lead to the swamping of the European population. As one commentator said at the time:

> The Chinese are sure to come, if allowed to come, in such vast numbers that Australia will be more Asiatic than European. As they come now, to live for a time but not to settle, their labour is no profit to the community … The very virtues of the Chinese may prove

more dangerous than their vices. We want English institutions, English social life, dominant and predominant in Australia …[48]

The Chinese, not unreasonably, thought they were being dealt with harshly:

In the name of heaven, we ask, where is your justice? Where your religion? Where your morality? Where all your sense of right and wrong? Where your enlightenment? Where your love of liberty? … Which are the 'pagans'—you or we?[49]

The political temperature intensified in the lead-up to the centenary. There was a large increase in the number of Chinese people seeking to immigrate to the Northern Territory. Reports of the discovery of ruby deposits in the MacDonnell Ranges raised the spectre of a large wave of Chinese immigration, in the manner of the gold rushes of the 1850s. The Queensland government was particularly anxious about the 'threat' from the north. The Chinese were showing signs of creating a naval force, and Queensland feared its newly discovered mineral wealth in the sparsely settled far north would make her perilously attractive to possible invaders.

At the same time as these fears of invasion were escalating, China saw that her national dignity required that some protection be afforded to her nationals living in foreign countries.[50] The Australian colonies were not alone in their mistreatment of the Chinese. The Dutch in the islands of the East Indies and the United States were acting in a cruel and discriminatory manner as well—although the United States government at least provided some monetary compensation for its wrongdoing.

Chinese emigration commissioners visited Australia in 1887, among many other nations and colonies on the Pacific Rim, to see how members of the Chinese community lived. Some Australians thought that this could be a foretaste of something more sinister, such as mass invasion. The Chinese Minister in London made a formal protest to the British government (which was then responsible for the colonies' relations with foreign nations). The 'mother country' then had the challenging task of explaining the wayward racial policy of her Australian colonies. This was an embarrassing situation for a British government keen to maintain good relations with China and Japan.

The colonies were not prepared to delegate the power to make an immigration treaty with China to the British government. On the other hand, Britain could not be seen to approve the creation of overtly discriminatory colonial laws. The challenge was to find a way of attracting high levels of non-Chinese immigration at the same time as excluding less desirable Chinese immigrants. Henry Parkes cabled the British Secretary of State about the urgent need for New South Wales to introduce restrictive immigration legislation.

While the British government prevaricated, a special inter-colonial conference into the Chinese question was held in June 1888. It was resolved that there should be uniform laws restricting immigration along the same lines of legislation in the United States.[51] Only one

Chinese person was permitted to enter for every 500 tons of inbound shipping, and they needed consent to move to another colony. After the conference, traffic in Chinese immigrants from British Crown colonies (particularly Hong Kong) also ceased. The new uniform legislation had the desired effect: the Chinese-born population declined from about 50 000 in 1888 to 32 000 in 1901.[52]

In 1891, however, the 'problem' had still not gone away. Four ships carrying Chinese passengers arrived in Sydney Harbour. A large protest meeting was held in Sydney, presided over by the mayor. As Henry Parkes explained (or justified), 'If the Chinamen had attempted to land in the usual way, there could be little doubt that violence, and possibly serious bloodshed, would have taken place.'[53] The noisy meeting was adjourned and reconvened at Parliament House. The crowd only dispersed when Parkes announced that the boats would not be allowed to land. Parkes wrote that:

> It is mainly because the influx of the Chinese, or of persons of any other inferior nationality, is a disturbing cause to social peace and contentment that it should not be tolerated. No advantage to employers, no convenience to a limited number of citizens, can compensate for loosening the consanguineous ties which bind the state together.[54]

A Chinese deputation led by the leader of Sydney's Chinese community, Quong Tart, implored Parkes not to cave into the public hysteria. Quong Tart was Cantonese-born, arriving in Australia at the age of nine. He prospered on the goldfields, visited China in 1881, and returned to Sydney later that year to open a chain of teashops and, later, restaurants in King Street and the new Queen Victoria Markets, which opened in 1898. He advocated the restriction of opium imports and spoke out for the interests of the often oppressed and victimised Chinese community. Quong Tart married a woman of European descent. He died at the age of fifty-three of complications following an attack upon him by an intruder at his Queen Victoria Markets restaurant.

In 1896, it was agreed at a colonial premiers' conference that uniform legislation should be enacted to restrict *all* coloured immigration, irrespective of whether people were British subjects. Japan, starting to flex its new muscles as an emerging world power, objected to being lumped together in the 'coloured' category, together with the Chinese and Indians. Another exclusionary device, therefore, that did not expressly refer to racial background had to be found.[55] The compromise method adopted after Federation in 1901 was the use of the dictation test that had been pioneered in Natal, South Africa. The dictation test could be given to intending immigrants in any European language. This test was sometimes even used to exclude politically undesirable Europeans as well.

Meanwhile, non-Asian immigration continued. Between 1860 and 1890, 310 000 people migrated to New South Wales, and the population grew from 320 000 to 1.1 million.[56] Of the overseas-born population in 1891, 93 per cent came from the British Isles, with more than half of these from England.[57]

ABOVE LEFT: Quong Tart, a leader of Sydney's Chinese community in the late nineteenth century.
RIGHT: Magazine cover of the 1890s whipping up anti-Chinese sentiment and popular fears of Asian invasion.

It was assumed at the time of the centenary celebrations that federation would eventually take place, but not in the short term, as there were too many hurdles to overcome, such as the ideal level of trade protection, what powers the federal government and the senate should have, and the issue of how to balance the competing interests of the larger and smaller colonies. Some people feared federation might necessarily coincide with complete severance from Britain. Henry Parkes continued to be the strongest advocate for federation. He gave two influential speeches in 1889. One was held on the Hawkesbury River to inaugurate the new railway bridge which finally linked Brisbane and Sydney by rail, and the other in his electorate, at the opening of the railway at Tenterfield.

Parkes, always the orator, appealed to his audiences by conjuring up the image of the 'crimson thread of kinship that runs through us all'; that crimson thread was the Britishness of all the colonies. It was an image that was invoked many more times, especially in the middle of the twentieth century by anglophile Liberal Prime Minister, Sir Robert Menzies.

The first federal convention was held in 1890. Parkes adroitly used the bogeyman of defence (and Asian invasion) by asking how a group of colonies could defend themselves jointly against external aggression. In the depression of the early 1890s the issue of federation was far less important than the financial crises gripping the colonies—at least for many politicians of the day. It was the people, rather than the politicians, who revived federation at the convention held at Corowa, a town on the border of New South Wales and Victoria in 1893. At that conference it was agreed that each colony would pass legislation for the election of representatives to attend a constitutional convention. There, a new constitution would be agreed to and put back to the electors of the Australian colonies. Things did not move as quickly as had been hoped. Another people's convention was held in Bathurst in 1896, shortly after Parkes died, and it became apparent just how difficult achieving federation was going to be.

After the Bathurst convention, elections were held in each colony to elect delegates to the constitutional conventions. Three of these conventions were held in Adelaide, Sydney and Melbourne between 1897 and early 1898. Finally, the new constitution was put to a referendum. Of the colonies, New South Wales was the most reluctant to federate. Further negotiations took place to make the constitution more appealing to the voters of New South Wales. The deal struck was that the new capital should be in New South Wales, but more than 100 miles (160 kilometres) from Sydney—as close as the other colonial capitals would allow. After many discussions, deliberations and journeys across the country-side, the area to be known as the Australian Capital Territory was chosen. This is where Canberra was eventually built. The new law was nicknamed the 'Surrender to Sydney Influences Act'.[58] The new draft of the constitution with this and other amendments was put back to the people, and the majority in favour of federation in New South Wales increased enough to enable federation to proceed.

Australia was federated on 1 January 1901 in Centennial Park, at a ceremony attended by about 50 000 people. Australians voted in the first national poll that same year. There was broad consensus that the federal parliament should promptly enshrine the White Australia policy in federal legislation and the European-language dictation test as a means of screening prospective immigrants. Protection from manufactured imports by means of a tariff wall was another early policy of the new national government.

The public works of the 1880s and 1890s were on an impressive scale. The Queen Victoria Building by George McRae (grand, but never, until recently, a commercial success) and Sydney Hospital, designed by Thomas Rowe, were built, as were many of the public buildings in Bridge Street, such as the Chief Secretary's Building and the Lands Department Building. Many unemployed labourers were put to work on another major late–nineteenth-century work, the Royal Prince Alfred Hospital at Camperdown.

When Walter Vernon succeeded James Barnet as colonial architect in 1890, the style of public architecture became more restrained. Vernon built the Central Police Court in Liverpool Street and the Art Gallery of New South Wales. He also made several additions to the roofline of some of Barnet's buildings. Examples of this are the Chief Secretary's Building and the General Post Office. From the middle of the 1890s onwards, there was a tendency to scale down all forms of architecture, brought about by a combination of economic circumstances and changing aesthetics.

The idea of federation provoked a more independent development of architectural styles from the 1890s right up to World War I. The English Arts and Crafts Movement influenced architects such as Vernon. Two examples of Vernon's version of the Arts and Crafts style were the Ritz Carlton Hotel (formerly the Health Department Building) in Macquarie Street, built between 1896 and 1898, and the later City Coroner's Court Building (1906) in Lower George Street. Another is the Darlinghurst Fire Station.

Another popular style of the period was the Romanesque Revival style which was pioneered in the early skyscrapers of the United States. Good examples of this are the Société Générale Building in George Street near Martin Place, designed by American architect Edward Raht. A more stripped-down variation of this style was used in the design of warehouses and factories to the west of George Street and close to Darling Harbour, then the centre of most of Sydney's industrial activity. These industrial buildings replaced the tenement housing that used to dominate that part of Sydney.

On the domestic front, the Federation-style bungalow emerged. The Federation style of architecture dominates many Sydney suburbs, particularly on the lower North Shore and Inner West around Haberfield and Ashfield. This style is an eclectic Australian mix of the Californian bungalow style and the more ornate Queen Anne and Arts and Crafts styles. Federation architecture uses dark brick, and has wide verandas. The dominant feature is the red-tiled roofline. The adoption of the California bungalow style was one of the earlier examples of Australia's cultural reorientation towards the United States. In early decades of the twentieth century, the taste for ornate European-derived architectural detail faded and the typical Sydney house was a bungalow, modelled along Californian lines. This was a harbinger of the nation's greater focus on the United States for new cultural developments in the visual and applied arts, literature and technology.

133

CHAPTER SIX

PROUD
PROVINCIAL CITY

For every pie shop wafts an ode
And every terrace window rhymes,
And there's a folk song in the slowed
Crescendo of a tram that climbs
At night, some wet, black shining road.

The modern rhythm of soaring flats,
The old refrain of quarried stone,
The merry note of cricket bats,
All mingle with the overtone
Of half a million grey felt hats.

COLIN WILLS, 'Song of Sydney'

ONCE AUSTRALIA was federated on 1 January 1901, the nationalist literary and artistic movement, promoted by the *Bulletin* and substantially based in Sydney, seemed to run out of steam. Sydneysiders, like other Australians, were torn between loyalty to a nation which did not yet have any defining moments or symbols, and loyalty to the British Empire which was strong and successful, and which, during the early months of 1901, was still ruled by the greatest imperial symbol of them all—the Queen Empress, Victoria.

Her passing later that year intensified, rather than weakened, the sense of loyalty to Empire. The concept of nationhood was still nebulous, and it was easier to cling to colonial or imperial loyalty than it was to grapple with the concept of Australia or being Australian. This is why

ABOVE: A parade held during Federation celebrations in Sydney in 1901.

Australians could have accurately been described as Britannic Australians.[1] At the time of Federation, Australia had no separate foreign policy, no army or navy, no flag (until later that year), the loyal toast was always given at official functions and the British national anthem was played.

A clear indication of Australia's loyalty to Britain was her engagement in the Boer War with the British army from 1899–1902. More than 16 000 Australians volunteered for service in a war which had no strategic significance beyond the borders of South Africa. Attachment to empire also implied attachment to the significance of cultural life of the metropolitan centre of empire—and that was London.

The British Empire was so popular in the early twentieth century that New South Wales Premier Carruthers successfully promoted a new national public holiday, Empire Day, from 1905, which was celebrated on Queen Victoria's birthday, 24 May, until 1955. This date had long been celebrated in the British Empire for this very reason—and a sceptic might argue that Empire Day was proclaimed because people had become used to the habit of taking a holiday on that date throughout Victoria's long reign. The focus of the celebrations was on children: sporting events, parades and flag-waving connected young Australians more closely to the mother country and the rest of the British Empire, indicated in atlases of the day in crimson pink. By the time Empire Day was abandoned in the post-colonial era, the year after Queen Elizabeth's 1954 tour of Australia (the first visit by a reigning British monarch), the concept of empire had withered away.

In the time leading up to Federation, Sydney's citizens were being titillated by more scandalous matters. Dr Denis O'Haran, a dashingly handsome Irish-born Roman Catholic priest, was the administrator of St Mary's Cathedral and secretary to Cardinal Patrick Moran. Arthur Coningham, a former Test cricketer and chemist who had become a bookmaker at Randwick racecourse, sued his wife, Alice, for divorce on the grounds of adultery with O'Haran in the priest's rooms at St Mary's Cathedral. He also sought a sum of £5000 as compensation. Mrs Coningham admitted in court that her third child was O'Haran's, and confessed of her wrongdoing with the priest—enthusiastically, extensively and in great detail under cross-examination from Coningham himself. Coningham's lawyer had resigned in the middle of the proceedings, possibly sensing the collaboration between husband and wife after Coningham had admitted in the court that he was still sleeping with his wife after the adultery proceedings had begun.[2]

As this marriage was 'mixed'—Coningham was a Protestant and his wife Catholic—the scandal provoked a strong sectarian response. More than 5000 people stood outside the court to await the jury's verdict in December 1900, but the jury was discharged as it could not agree that adultery was proven. The second trial was held in March at the same time as the campaigning for the first federal election was in progress. A Presbyterian minister stepped in to organise a fighting fund for Coningham. A counter-campaign was launched by O'Haran's supporters, led by notorious lawyer, politician and fixer, Paddy Crick. It was claimed that the case was baseless and nothing but a conspiracy between the Coninghams to extort money from the Catholic Church. There were double agents in each camp, one of them being another well-respected Catholic priest, code-named 'Zero', who was giving advice to the other side. He had the task of trying to explain his actions to the cardinal, who was most displeased. The priest was shipped to the United States for his treachery. Paddy Crick also wrongfully used his powers as postmaster-general to intercept and copy mail between Mr and Mrs Coningham. His doing this gained much insight into the total extent of the Coninghams' collaboration. Father O'Haran won a verdict in his favour and his reputation was almost completely restored. The Coninghams moved to New Zealand, where Alice Coningham later successfully sued her husband for divorce on the grounds of adultery.

Another event which coincided with Federation and had a significant effect on Sydney was the outbreak of bubonic plague in the wharf areas around The Rocks and Millers Point. In 1900, there was a worldwide epidemic of the disease. A wharf labourer who lived in Pottinger Street at Millers Point was the first to be struck down. Three hundred Sydneysiders caught the plague and one hundred of them died. This was the first epidemic of the plague where it was established beyond doubt that the disease was carried by fleas on rats. Sydney's chief officer of public health, J. A. Thompson, did much of the work that traced the origins of the plague;

however, in the early stages of 1900, there was considerable emphasis on less direct methods of containing the plague, such as disinfection and garbage disposal, rather than on rat eradication itself.[3] Areas where plague broke out were instantly barricaded and quarantined. Unemployed people from the labour bureau were inoculated and then sent in to clean up the houses, yards and alleys. Hundreds of tonnes of rubbish were punted out to sea. Rubbish was dredged out of the harbour, and the underbelly of the wharves cleaned out and sprayed at high pressure with boiling water.

The plague was met with a zealous response that also suited those who were well disposed to improving Sydney through slum clearance and modernisation. 'Uninhabitable' housing was destroyed in The Rocks, around Kent and Sussex streets, and in parts of Surry Hills. This demolition created opportunities for road widening, as well as the improvement of Sydney's port facilities. It also allowed construction of the approaches to the Sydney Harbour Bridge some years later. Much of the land around The Rocks and Millers Point was expropriated and placed in the hands of the Sydney Harbour Trust, precursor to the Maritime Services Board (now known as Sydney Waterways).

Other parts of Sydney to be improved and modernised were Oxford Street and Wentworth Avenue. These streets were widened at the cost of much working-class housing. There may have been racist forces at work here as well. This area was the centre of Sydney's Chinese community. Further north, around Circular Quay, access to the harbour and the northern end of the city was improved by widening and raising the level of George Street north of Grosvenor Street. Before 1908, the area was a low-lying one with poor housing which often flooded. It was at this time that the Federation–Edwardian-style buildings along the street, such as the Johnson's Overall Building, were erected. The facade of the Johnson's Overall Building was retained when Grosvenor Place was built in the 1980s, against the protests of the architect of Grosvenor Place, Harry Seidler.

Apart from the road widening and slum clearance in the inner-city area, the other major change in the city in this era was the introduction of cantilevered street awnings. The old demountable canvas awnings disappeared forever, and the street level of the city's architecture was permanently truncated from what stood above the ground level. This may have given welcome respite from the hot summer sun, but the overall visual effect of the awnings on Sydney's streetscape was not a happy one. Shop frontages underneath the awnings could be modified without any reference to the style of the building as a whole, and the original architectural detailing was stripped away. The City Council did not have the interest, discipline or resolve to maintain the integrity of the old Victorian buildings, and the architectural mishmash at street level below the new awnings probably made fewer people aware of the fine quality of the buildings that came under the wrecker's hammer in the 1960s and 1970s.

Australia was becoming increasingly urbanised from the late nineteenth century. In 1901, 13 per cent of Australia's population lived in Sydney. In 1931, this proportion had grown to 19 per cent.[4] This proportion has not increased as greatly throughout the rest of the twentieth century: in 1991, 21 per cent of Australians lived in Sydney. The three factors which created the high level of urbanisation were the poor economic outlook on the land, the growth of industrialisation and city-based factories (predominantly in Sydney and Melbourne), and the high immigration rates from 1904 to 1913, most of these Britons who settled in the cities.

The drought that began in the 1890s and continued until 1905 made life on the land even tougher than it already was. The sheep population was halved. The rabbit plague also devastated many farms that had already been severely affected by the drought.

A consequence of the growth of the large cities was that the balance of political power in Australia swung further away from the pastoralists and farmers to the urban industrial workers. These people worked in light industries such as food processing, textiles and footwear, the transport industry and other commercial areas. Many of these workers and their employers thought that economic protection would help their businesses and employment and wage prospects, and it was from the cities that the demand for tariff protection came. It was not until World War I that Australia developed significant heavy industries, such as iron and steel.

138

At Federation, all state governments handed over authority to the new Commonwealth government in several key areas: foreign policy (although in fact this was dictated by the British Foreign Office until 1942), interstate and international trade and commerce, taxation, banking, insurance, postal and telephone services, citizenship and immigration. In future, state politics would have fewer areas of responsibility and would be mainly concerned with schools, railways, health and unemployment relief.

Until 1901, the main source of New South Wales's revenue was customs duty—thus the grandeur and location of the Customs House at Circular Quay, built by James Barnet at the end of the nineteenth century. Although the right to collect customs duties passed to the Commonwealth government in 1901, three-quarters of the money raised was returned to the states for the first ten years after Federation. The other quarter of the customs raised went to fund the costs of running the new nation. There was no income tax until World War I.

Sydney's reputation was not entirely wholesome in the late nineteenth and early twentieth century. John Norton did more than most to give the city and its residents a certain reputation for tawdriness, corruptibility and corruption, by revealing (and often being part of) its less wholesome underbelly. Norton had an uncanny ability to tap into the larrikin sensibility of the city through the use of his colourful, often alliterative and outrageous turn of phrase.

An English-born journalist, Norton arrived in Sydney in 1884 at the age of twenty-six. His early political sympathies lay with the labour movement and the Labor Party, though he was later to fall out with them. In 1896, he bought *Truth* which, although always tabloid in content and outlook, Norton transformed into a sensationalist, salacious, rude and irreverent newspaper. His political enemies were often at the receiving end of Norton's editorial bile, as were members of the royal family. The people loved it. Norton was a hard drinker and womaniser who thrived on controversy, litigation and libel in particular.

One of his greatest enemies was Paddy Crick, the lawyer and parliamentarian, with whom he feuded whenever and wherever they could. Norton's—and Crick's—conduct was quite untempered by their membership of the Legislative Assembly in the early years of the twentieth century. Crick, to Norton's great satisfaction, withdrew from the Legislative Assembly and was struck off the roll of solicitors in the aftermath of a corruption scandal following a royal commission into the Lands Department. Norton, like artist Norman Lindsay and many others, was opposed to censorship and mean-spirited, often hypocritical puritans—though he was not above hypocrisy himself. He coined the term 'wowser' to describe anyone who didnot share his libertarian views of what was permissible conduct or suitable material for publication.

The first person Norton described as a 'wowser' was Alderman Waterhouse, the 'white, woolly, weary, watery, word-wasting wowser Alderman from Waverley'.[5] Norton was charged with sedition in 1896 for writing in *Truth* that Queen Victoria was a 'flabby fat and flatulent looking scion and successor of the most ignoble line of Royal Georges' and her son, Edward, Prince of Wales was a 'rascal of a turf-swindling, card-sharping, wife-debauching, boozing, rowdy of a son'.[6] The charge against Norton did not stick. The jury was 'hung'—that is, it was unable to reach the unanimous decision that was required. Norton revealed that the juryman who held out against the rest was an unnaturalised German. Norton was not a stranger to jury tampering.

From 1905, Norton lived in a large villa at Maroubra called St Helena, named after the final residence of his greatest hero, Napoleon Bonaparte. It is there that Norton's extensive art collection, much of which depicted his hero, was contained. Norton also had a philanthropic side: during World War I, he donated St Helena to the government for use as a convalescent hospital for wounded soldiers.

Australians were not the only people who were taken aback when the *parvenu* world power, Japan, won a war with the great Russian Empire in 1905. The victory of Japan, however, had immediate ramifications for Australia. There was now a military power to our immediate north and our defence forces had to be designed around the possibility of future aggression in the Asian region.

As a means of flexing its new industrial and military muscles, the United States, in a gesture of friendliness and goodwill, sent the Great White Fleet around the world and, in August 1908, it visited Sydney. The sixteen white-painted warships in the fleet sailed into Sydney Harbour to a rapturous welcome by Sydneysiders. The visit of the Great White Fleet was a harbinger of Australia's future dependence on the United States for defence.

By the following year, it was quite apparent that Australia needed a small fleet of ships which would be part of the British Eastern Fleet, and the government ordered three destroyers. Soon afterwards, in 1910, the first ships of the Royal Australian Navy sailed into

Sydney Harbour. Large and enthusiastic crowds came to welcome the new fleet at Farm Cove. In another defence move, Lord Kitchener, the famous British soldier who had relieved the besieged British army at Khartoum, was sent out to advise on Australia's military defence. All males between the ages of twelve and twenty-five were liable to undergo compulsory training. This was not a move which was universally approved, and it sowed the seeds of the anti-conscription movement which divided the nation during World War I.

After the depression and the long drought, the economy boomed. The gross domestic product doubled between 1904 and 1913. There was increased agricultural, mineral and industrial production.[7] State governments were keen to increase agricultural production, and assisted immigration schemes were introduced to provide a source of new Australian farmers to work the land. As with most of the other assistance schemes, this objective was rarely achieved. Not many British yeoman farmers, or other British immigrants, were tempted to settle in the wide, arid spaces of the Australian bush and till the ancient, often infertile soil. Most of the nearly 400 000 British people who immigrated in that period made their homes in the cities and large towns of the nation.

Australia automatically joined in the war effort in August 1914. As Opposition Leader (shortly to become prime minister) Andrew Fisher said just before the outbreak of the war, Australia would support the war 'to our last man and our last shilling'. Australia's contribution to the war was motivated by patriotism to the mother country and the Empire. Britain's possible demise was seen as being linked with Australia. A small expeditionary force left Sydney for (German) New Guinea in late August 1914 and hoisted the British flag. In November, the navy had its first and successful engagement when the HMAS *Sydney* sank the German ship *Emden* off the strategically significant Cocos Islands. This was a huge fillip for national morale.

By late 1914, volunteers of the Australian Imperial Force (AIF) were boarding ships for the Middle East. The first major engagement was against the Turks at Gallipoli, in the Dardanelles. It lasted from April until December 1915. Altogether 7600 Australians died and 19 000 were wounded in that campaign. This battle was an heroic defeat, and its commemoration developed into an event of national significance. Sadly, however, it was only the first of many major campaigns that cost thousands of Australian lives. The morale of the Australian army throughout the war was enhanced by the insistence of Brigadier-General William Bridges (who was killed at Gallipoli) that the AIF remain intact, and not be absorbed into the British army. The diggers wore a distinctive uniform, with an even more distinctive slouch hat with an upturned brim, upon which was pinned a badge depicting the rising sun.

At the outbreak of the war there was a rush of volunteer enlistments, and a sudden revulsion towards anything German, including German imports and merchandise for sale in the shops. Many of the soldiers were trained on the larger sporting grounds in the city. Men and boys of all ages and backgrounds wanted to join in; those who did not enlist were often ostracised by their friends and family, or presented with white feathers symbolising cowardice. By July 1915, 75 000 Australians had gone to war and, by October, there were as many again in training. There was a massive collection throughout Sydney to support the war effort. Trains and trams were decorated with wattle, a native tree which blooms with yellow flowers in the late winter and early spring. Wattle, then and now one of our most popular national symbols, was for sale everywhere.

A less glorious incident of World War I happened on the outskirts of Sydney at Casula near Liverpool in February 1916. There was a mutiny of about 15 000 troops. Soldiers grabbed liquor from nearby hotels. Some hijacked trains and rampaged through the streets, abusing pedestrians. There was looting of Sydney's pubs and shops. A *mêlée* at Central Station ensued between rioters and the authorities. One man was killed and six were wounded, and the shops near Central were looted. The causes of the mutiny were never really agreed upon. Some blamed alcohol and others the fact that none was available. Others blamed it on the youth and inexperience of the troops. The immediate cause seemed to be that an order was given to the troops to train for an extra hour and a half a day.

141

One lasting outcome of the Casula Riot was the introduction of early closing in Sydney's pubs. This made the wowsers happy. A referendum was put to the people on the basis that early closing would be a wartime measure only. Patriotism was used as a marketing tool by the temperance movement. One typical advertising slogan cried 'In the Great Tug of War help Britain—by Abstaining from Drink.'[8] In 1923, early closing became permanent, with little opposition from the hotel trade, which learnt to earn as much money in a shorter working day.

That grotesque Sydney institution, the 'six o'clock swill', became a regular feature of the city's life. Workers would leave their offices or factories, head for the nearest pub, and drink as much as they possibly could in the narrow window of opportunity available to them. Sydney's pubs were redesigned to allow for the huge late afternoon crowds and many old buildings were modified. Furniture was dispensed with, as was anything that took up valuable floor space, such as billiard and pool tables. The early-closing era, which lasted until 1955, was the heyday of the pub with tiled walls. The tiles made it easier to wash the places down after the customers departed, often in a very inebriated state. Pubs became utilitarian and basic drinking establishments, as they had been in the early days of the colony.[9]

Australian manufacturing thrived during World War I. British exports of manufactured goods were not as forthcoming as they had been before the war as much British manpower and shipping was diverted to assist with the war effort, and, as a consequence, Australian industry stepped in to fill the gap. Although Australia was not capable of manufacturing the arms the soldiers needed, the clothes and boots the diggers wore were Australian-made. Primary producers enjoyed guaranteed prices: the British government agreed to buy the entire Australian wool clip for the duration of the war, and all the beef and mutton exports. One side effect of the war was the use of female labour, particularly in clerical jobs. Women were paid less than half the wage their husbands and brothers could earn.[10]

Another side effect of the war was the development of the metals industry. Up until 1914, a handful of German companies had had long-term contracts for the purchase of Australian metal ores. These companies controlled the markets for these metals, and, in the case of zinc, the market for refining as well. With the coming of war, metals were an essential strategic ingredient in the arms-making industry. Contracts with German companies were cancelled and the Australian metals-processing industry developed.

A great deal of this new economic activity, as well as the cost of the war, was funded by increased borrowing from Britain and by new taxes such as death duties and income tax. The federal government issued an Australian war loan bond which was oversubscribed. Australia's public debt rose at the end of the war to £350 million, at a time when our population was just five million.

In October 1915, William Morris Hughes, one of Sydney's greatest (and most controversial) political figures, became prime minister. Hughes was raised in Wales, and emigrated to Australia in 1884 at the age of twenty-two.[11] He was only 5 feet 6 inches tall and was partially deaf. This, and his indomitable character demonstrated during the war, led to him being nicknamed 'the Little Digger'. In the late 1880s and early 1890s he lived in Balmain and ran a small shop there. Hughes joined the Labor Party in its earliest days in the 1890s. As well as being a parliamentary politician in New South Wales and, from 1901, in the federal parliament, he was a driving force in organising the wharf labourers' movement, and turned it into a national union—the Waterside Workers' Federation. He held the federal seat of West Sydney from 1901 until 1916.

After visiting Britain in 1916 as prime minister, he was convinced that conscription was the only way that the supply of manpower to the battlefields could be sustained. As 1916 progressed, the casualty list of the diggers had been growing. In the unsuccessful Battle of the Somme, which lasted for seven weeks, Australia lost 23 000 men. The rates of enlistment were falling off through 1916 and were considerably short of the target. The issue of conscription soon divided the young nation. The first referendum was put in October 1916, and won by the anti-conscriptionists. In New South Wales, 57 per cent of the people voted against conscription.

Conscription was one of the most divisive political issues Australia has ever faced. The trade unionists were opposed to conscription and therefore to their former ally, Billy Hughes. A huge anti-conscription rally was organised by the New South Wales branch of the Labor Party and held in the Domain, which between 60 000 and 100 000 people attended.

Hughes was expelled from the Labor Party for his efforts, and held in great contempt. He abandoned his past allegiances and his parliamentary seat of West Sydney, and formed a new party, the National Labor Party, with his former political opponents. In November 1916, the National Labor Party came to power. Hughes moved from Sydney to a new parliamentary seat in Bendigo. Undeterred by the divisive consequences of the first referendum, he called

142

another which was even more passionately fought by both sides. The referendum was lost by a greater majority. In New South Wales, 59 per cent of the voters were opposed to conscription. Remarkably enough, he did not lose office as there was no clear successor worthy of the job.

During the war, the prices of food and other essential items were rising, sometimes dramatically, at the same time that wages were frozen. The drop in living standards was quite at odds with the concept of conciliation and arbitration which was adopted in the years after Federation, and particularly with the principles of wage-fixing as laid down in 1908 in the landmark decision of the Harvester case. That case dramatically affected the course of industrial relations for eighty years. Mr Justice Higgins of the Commonwealth Court of Conciliation and Arbitration said that the minimum wage for an unskilled worker should be determined by looking at the normal needs of an average employee, living in a civilised community, with a wife and children to support.

Centralised wage-fixing was a policy which was bundled up with trade protection for the manufacturing industry. If businesses were protected from international competition, their proprietors were to perform their side of the bargain by paying a 'fair wage' assessed on the basis of economic need, rather than on the performance of the business itself. Both these policies combined to give Australians—both employers and employed—a limited view of their level of productivity and competitiveness in comparison to the other economies of the world.

143

In August 1917, workers in New South Wales went on general strike, in protest against their declining standards of living. They could see the profits being made in many of the newly created industries, and they wanted a share of the spoils. They demanded higher wages and better working conditions. The strike began in the railway workshops and soon spread to coal miners, the transport workers, the meat industry, seamen, and waterside workers. A camp of strike-breakers came down from the country and camped in the Showground and Taronga Zoo. The government fed and clothed the strike-breakers and called them patriots and loyalists. Many of the strikers and their families faced starvation, and the hand of charity was neither as warm nor as open as it had been in the depression of the 1890s. The strike was broken within three weeks.

When peace came in 1918, Australia had sent 330 000 troops to the war. Half the male population aged between eighteen and forty-five had enlisted. Sixty thousand men were killed, and 170 000 were wounded. Proportionately, this was the highest casualty rate of any of the British Empire's armies. It took slightly more than a year for all the troops to be shipped home. The newly returned diggers had to find employment and soon clashed with trade unionists over who should have preferred employee status. Some of them took up the offer of land from the government as part of the soldier settlement schemes.

The 'Digger', the nickname the Australian soldiers gave themselves, had, as an Englishman observed, particular characteristics:

> No more original figure than the Australian soldier has appeared in the war … Hard to manage in camp, he improved in morale as he neared the firing line. He was fearlessly

144

TOP: When victory in World War I was announced in 1918, thousands of Sydneysiders turned out for peace celebrations.
ABOVE: World War I victory celebrations in Martin Place in the city's centre. The circular hut in the foreground was used as a recruiting booth for volunteer servicemen. The Cenotaph, the city's best-known memorial to fallen soldiers, was built on the site of the hut.

himself. He behaved in the Strand as he would have done on a Saturday night in Wagga Wagga. Defiance of convention was his one pose ... but there was no body of men who so triumphantly satisfied the supreme test of discipline, the test of being ready in the field when they were required, and of moving under fire to whatever point they were asked to occupy. The German High Command marked the Australians as First Class Storm Troops. The courage of the Australian was not the courage of the savage or the devotee. It was never buoyed up by sentiment or illusion. Its most wonderful feature was a wide-eyed habit of facing things as they really were—of looking at the worst and defying it. This clearness of vision gave him that initiative, that skill under fire, which made up so large a part of his value in the field.

On the human side, few soldiers have had in such measure the supreme soldierly gift of comradeship. Whenever they were in a fight, breaking King's regulations, or raiding the Hun trenches, they stuck together. The Battalion was the digger's home, and he was never truly happy, or a really first-class soldier away from it. The thing, however that made the Digger the perpetual delight of all who love human nature is his constant play of humour. In this he expressed his soul, his criticism of life, with its wonderful range of insight and feeling, now grotesque, now gay, now grim and sardonic, feeding on the terrible contrasts of life around him.[12]

Without falling into sentimentality, it is not hard to see a strong connection between the currency lads of the 1820s, the diggers of the goldfields from whom the soldiers borrowed their name, and the Australian Diggers of World War I.

After the war ended, Hughes insisted that Australia be represented at the Peace Conference at Versailles in 1919. A person with fewer persuasive skills and less persistence probably would not have been able to achieve this. Australia, for the first time, was represented on an equal footing with other nations. Australia never hitherto enjoyed an independent role and was not yet an independent nation, at least in formal terms, as foreign policy was still determined at Whitehall. Hughes, having won the right to speak on the grounds that he spoke for 'sixty thousand dead', argued doggedly for the successful resolution of issues affecting Australia. His first objective was that the term 'war reparations' should be widely defined so that Australia and other combatant nations could be compensated for the costs of the war effort. Secondly, he sought and won an Australian mandate over formerly German New Guinea to create a defence buffer zone against Japanese aggression. Thirdly, Hughes fought against a Japanese demand that the covenant of the new League of Nations include a clause forbidding immigration policies which were racist in outlook. This was Hughes's most difficult and narrowly won victory.

In February 1923, Hughes resigned as prime minister and was replaced by Stanley Melbourne Bruce. Hughes moved back to Sydney from Victoria and represented the seat of North Sydney, which he retained until 1949. Later, in the inter-war period, he, like Winston Churchill in Britain, foresaw the need to rearm and prepare for another war much earlier than a lot of his political colleagues. Unlike Robert Menzies and Prime Minister Joseph Lyons, Hughes was not convinced of the sincerity of the undertakings Hitler had given British Prime Minister Neville Chamberlain at Munich in 1938. Hughes and the United Australia Party were in opposition during most of World War II, though Hughes did sit on the War Advisory Council. In 1949, Hughes, then aged in his late eighties, became the Liberal member for Bradfield on Sydney's North Shore, which he held until his death three years later.

From November 1918 to February 1919 many Sydneysiders suffered in the worldwide influenza outbreak. It was estimated that it killed more of the world's population than the war did. More than one-third of Sydney's population caught the flu badly and more than 6000 died in New South Wales alone, more than half the Australian total of 11 500. At the peak of the outbreak, church services were prohibited, and theatres and small hotels closed. Sporting events were cancelled. Many pedestrians wore face masks, and incoming ships were quarantined at North Head.

Australia's industrialisation continued after the war: in 1921, for the first time, workers in manufacturing exceeded those in primary production. New industrial suburbs reflecting the growth in manufacturing sprang up in Alexandria and Waterloo, in turn making the areas less attractive to live in because of the population that was generated, further diminishing the quality of life in Sydney's inner ring of suburbs.

After the war, Australian manufacturers had to face competition from imported goods again, although the United States, now a capital exporter, helped with the establishment of Australian industries which, with the high tariff wall, could compete with overseas manufactures. An example of this was the manufacture of motor vehicles at General Motors' Marrickville plant from 1926. In 1931, General Motors took advantage of the commercial opportunities afforded by the Depression and merged with Holden, an Adelaide-based Australian car manufacturer.

The early twentieth century was not a great period for Sydney's public works. One of the more significant efforts in the early 1900s was the opening of Central Station in 1906, on the site of the old Sydney cemetery.

Central Railway made access to the city a little easier for commuters, but not easy enough: commuters still had to get off the train and onto a tram to go any further north towards Circular Quay. From the time that Central Station opened, a new business and retail precinct grew around it. Lord Mayor Allen Taylor used the new location of Sydney's main railway terminus as an opportunity to widen the thoroughfares leading to the station.

From 1900 onwards, there was growing discussion of how Sydney should be planned and its

ABOVE: An aerial view of the Sydney Harbour Bridge during the latter stages of construction in 1931. Work on the Bradfield Highway on the southern approaches to the bridge can be clearly seen in the centre right of the picture.

147

growth regulated. The population of Sydney was growing quickly. Between 1901 and 1921, Sydney's population nearly doubled from 500 000 to 970 000 people.[13] This population growth promoted the outward sprawl of Sydney and the decline of the inner-city suburbs.

The desire for central coordination of Sydney's growth was a reaction to the city's unplanned, random development, an outcome of the *laissez-faire* planning politics of the late nineteenth century, combined with high population growth. The first decade of the twentieth century was the heyday of the movement to create a hybrid entity between municipal and New South Wales government, called the Greater Sydney Movement. Haussmann's work in improving Paris—and, particularly, widening her streets—was universally admired at the time, and some thought it should be emulated in Sydney. So, in 1908, the New South Wales government, prompted by an active City Council, set up a royal commission called the Improvement of Sydney Commission to inquire into improving the transport and planning of Sydney.

At the time, the most urgent consideration was given to the city's transport problems. These were the isolation of the North Shore, the lack of train lines to the east of the city, and the lack of connection between the railway at Central and Circular Quay. The Sydney

Commission recommended that a bridge be built across the harbour, while another royal commission, considering the question of connecting the North Shore alone, recommended a tunnel. Now, of course, the city has one of each. Sydney's political leaders have never been shy about creating royal commissions and governmental inquiries, many of which are capable of running at cross-purposes with each other, as these ones did. The Sydney Commission also recommended an underground city rail loop, an idea which was adopted later in the 1920s. Many of the other recommendations were never put into effect on the grounds of expense. Some of these unsuccessful proposals were extending Macquarie Street down past College Street to Central Railway, and an amphitheatre of multistorey buildings facing Central Railway across Belmore Park.

The Sydney Commission also thought that the city needed a planning regime to regulate building heights and densities. These laws took a while to come to pass, and when they did, their introduction was in phases, in 1912, 1919 and 1935, in the form of the *Local Government Act*. In the meantime, there was not enough legislative will to give municipal councils sufficient power to prevent heterogeneous sprawling development, even along the foreshores of the harbour, so the conditions for the dense and often disorganised development of suburban Sydney were created.

The turn of the century saw the great era of the electric tram begin in Sydney. The first line ran down George Street from Central Station to Circular Quay in late 1899. The tram network was completed in 1922, filling in the gaps left by the railway system, and speeding up the pace of the suburbanisation. Nearly all the lines terminated at Circular Quay—unlike the less convenient railway system. Suburbs which could be subdivided and suburbanised with easier commuting from 1900 to 1914 by tram were Haberfield, Kensington and Drummoyne. The ferry and tram systems were making high population on the North Shore possible: the municipalities of North Sydney, Mosman, Willoughby, Ku-ring-gai and Lane Cove were growing at a rate of 10 per cent per year.

There was some debate on the relative merits of the tram versus the railway system. The Sydney Commission of 1909 noted the increasing congestion of the city's streets with trams and recommended that a suburban and city railway system needed to be developed to ease this problem, and that suburban trunk tramlines should be replaced by trunk railway lines.[14] Trains went faster and were better suited to development beyond the then limits of Sydney's development. In the 1920s, the metropolitan train lines were electrified: first, the Illawarra and Canterbury lines were converted in 1926 and, by 1929, the Parramatta and North Shore lines were as well. By the 1930s, trams were considered to be feeder services for the train system, which provided the main arterial or trunk lines in and out of the city. These new fast routes out of town made the suburbs closer and more attractive, and the inner suburbs deteriorated more rapidly.

In the early twentieth century, the motor car reached Sydney. Trunk (long-distance) telephone calls to Melbourne, and then further afield, were introduced. In 1904, the opening of the Pyrmont power station provided electric light to the city's streets. This came later to

148

ABOVE: View of the city from Martin Place looking northwards to Circular Quay, c. 1925.

Sydney than it did to many other parts of Australia, as there were insufficient funds and a lack of will at the local government level to create a sufficient power supply. There was also disagreement between the City Council and the Australian Gas Light Company about who should be responsible for supplying electricity. The council won. It saw its capacity to monopolise the generation of power as a means of implementing its 'Greater Sydney' objective.[15]

The new motor vehicles threatened the safety of other vehicles and pedestrians, and left clouds of dust behind. The *Motor Traffic Act* was passed in 1909. This gave magistrates discretion on what driving speed was negligent. Some thought the speed limit should be 4 miles (7 kilometres) per hour; others thought it should be 10 miles (16 kilometres). The New South Wales Automobile Club (later Royal) was formed in 1903. The car, which was the catalyst for Sydney's great, uncontrolled sprawl, was now in the city's midst. It would not be until after 1947, however, that its presence would have the most drastic effect on the shape and size of Sydney.

Growing traffic congestion prompted the conversion of some of the city's thoroughfares, including King, Bligh and Castlereagh streets, to one-way streets by 1914. Cars were expensive because of the high duty (22 per cent) payable on them. Cars were not made locally until the 1920s. Their high price, however, did not appear to affect their popularity. By 1929,

Australia was ranked sixth of all nations in the total (not per capita) number of motor vehicles on the road.[16] The number of vehicle registrations in New South Wales rose from 29 000 registered in 1921 to nearly 330 000 in 1939, and then to nearly 750 000 in 1957.[17] The first traffic lights in Sydney were installed in 1933 at the corner of Kent and Market streets.[18] The advent of motor vehicles meant that sealed roads had to be built for the cars to travel on, and many streets were widened.

The motor bus began putting pressure on the tram systems from the late 1920s. The labour costs on the buses were cheaper than on trams because tram workers were unionised, whereas bus workers were not. There were accusations of obstruction made by bus drivers about trams. Gradually, the financial position of the tram system began to deteriorate. Taxes were imposed by the Lang government in 1931 on bus services, to try to restore the viability of the tram services. The tax on buses was very unpopular and this added to Lang's political difficulties. In 1930, 2000 bus workers marched from Eddy Avenue near Central Station to the Domain in protest against the tax on bus services. There they were met by another 20 000 people who also objected to the government's discrimination against the private bus operators.

150

After Lang's dismissal by the New South Wales governor, Sir Philip Game, the new conservative government decided that some form of coordination of Sydney's public transport was needed. In late 1932, a government-operated bus company was established so that both bus and train services were in the government's hands. The government, no longer competing with bus services, resolved that no more tramlines would be built.[19]

There were now two factors at work in shaping the future spread of Sydney: the ever-growing suburban railway system and the growing use of the roads by the motor car and public bus system. By 1961, the trams were no more. Now, fashionable attitudes to particular forms of public transport have turned full circle. In 1997, the Sydney Light Rail system was introduced between Ultimo, Pyrmont and Central Station, and there are proposals to extend it to other inner western suburbs.

Throughout the western world, the 1920s were the Jazz Age and the era of the 'Flapper'. Everyone (including women) wanted to have fun, to escape from the horrors of the Great War, which had claimed brothers, lovers and friends alike. It was the behaviour of women which changed the most in the 1920s. They threw away modesty by shortening their skirts, they drank, smoked, danced the Charleston, and, in Sydney, went to the beach and surfed with the boys.

That new breed of handsome, bronzed male lifesaver was coming to the fore as an image of Australian manhood, and there were plenty of examples of them to be seen at Bondi, Manly and the many other surfing beaches around Sydney. This was the first time that the image of the heroic Australian male could be at home as much on the beaches and in the city as he could be riding a horse in the outback, which had long been the customary domain of Australian folk heroes. Increasing political apathy (or maybe people were just having too much fun) meant that voter turnout at elections started to slide. In 1924, the federal government made voting compulsory and, in 1928, it became compulsory to vote in New South Wales.

House parties were popular in the 1920s, and these were much more lively than they had ever been before, helped greatly by the introduction of the radio and the wind-up gramophone. Away from home, dance halls sprang up. The high point of Sydney's social calendar in the 1920s was the annual Artists' Ball, held in the Town Hall. These fancy-dress balls were wilder and more debauched than anything ever seen before—or afterwards—until the Sleaze Ball and Gay and Lesbian Mardi Gras became annual events in the late 1970s and 1980s.

The first Artists' Ball was held in the Town Hall in 1922. Two thousand people attended.[20] The staid old Centennial Hall was decorated with brightly coloured friezes depicting figures doing the same thing as the guests: chasing each other, dancing and mingling around the room. The balls became wilder and wilder. The souvenir for the 1924 ball, based on a theme of childhood and innocence—'be a kid again' was the motto for the evening—did not give any indication of the bacchanalian orgy that party became. Funds raised were to be used to encourage art in New South Wales and go towards establishing a chair of Fine Arts at Sydney University. The police had to be called in to restore order. That was the last time that alcohol could be served at the Artists' Balls legally, although the ball of 1927 was supposed to be the most fun of all.

The less rigid and more fun-loving 1920s were a decade when the bohemian spirit was revived in Sydney from the dormant state it had been in since the departure of many of the Australian artists for Europe in the early years of the century. In the 1920s, bohemianism was centred on the weekly literary publications, the *Bulletin* and *Smith's Weekly*. Poet and journalist Kenneth Slessor was one of those who worked at *Smith's Weekly*, a newspaper established by John Joynton Smith, Clyde Packer (grandfather of present-day mogul, Kerry) and Claude McKay in 1919. Bohemianism was still a very blokey affair in the Sydney of the 1920s, and dominated by personalities such as Norman Lindsay and his adoring son Jack. There were women bohemians, but they were more likely to be objects of desire and adoration than they were equal partners. One exception was Dulcie Deamer, who played a leading role in a loosely affiliated bohemian dining society, which called itself the 'Noble Order of i Felici, Litterati, Cognoscenti e Lunatici'.[21]

Post-impressionism was gaining a foothold in the Sydney art scene, in the work of Margaret Preston (who was one of the first artists of European background to be influenced by Aboriginal art), Thea Proctor, Grace Cossington Smith, Roland Wakelin and Roy de Maistre, but the art establishment, in the form of the Art Gallery of New South Wales, did not embrace the new modernism with any enthusiasm. A brighter spot in the firmament was Sydney Ure Smith's publication, *Art in Australia*, which brought, through reproductions, many modern works to a wider audience of connoisseurs and collectors.

A significant step for Sydney's visual arts was the generous decision of J. F. Archibald to endow the annual Archibald Prize. The winner is selected by the trustees of the Art Gallery of

New South Wales, and their decisions today still attract a great deal of popular attention. They are often criticised for their conservatism, their radicalism, their perversity or their arbitrariness.

Bohemianism of the 1920s produced some interesting literature. The centre of Sydney's bohemian life was Kings Cross, Elizabeth Bay and Darlinghurst. The main cafés where bohemians of both sexes could meet on more equal terms than at pubs were Betsy Matthais's Café La Bohème (long demolished) at 5 Wilmot Street in the city, where the Coopers & Lybrand building is today, and later at Madame Pura's Latin Café, the Roma Café (both in Pitt Street in the city) and, most risqué of all, Theo's Club at Campbell Street in Chinatown.

Many of these cafés and clubs served liquor after six in the evening in breach of the licensing regulations. This made them vulnerable to police raids and closure. On the other hand, wine bars were downmarket establishments, for very serious and committed, if not desperate, drinkers. Not many people drank wine in those days, and what was on offer did little to lift the reputation of the wine industry. The wine bars in the city were not uncommonly used as fronts for brothels. One of the better, more bohemian wine bars of the period was Pellegrini's, at 85 Elizabeth Street in the city.

Norman Lindsay and Christopher Brennan were the leading stars in the bohemian firmament of Sydney in the early twentieth century. Brennan was a poet, philosopher and classicist. The son of Irish immigrants, he was a brilliant scholar educated by the Jesuits at St Ignatius College, Riverview, and at the University of Sydney where, despite an unruly reputation, he performed well and won the University Medal for logic and philosophy. Like Henry Lawson (a poet for whom he had little respect), he had a melancholic personality, drank heavily and had an unhappy personal life, despite his reputation as a *bon vivant* and stalwart of Sydney's café society. Although Brennan's poetry was less popular and more scholarly than that of Paterson and Lawson, since his death in 1925, he has achieved the status of being a Sydney literary legend—even if many people are unfamiliar with his work. Like poet Hugh McCrae and artist Norman Lindsay, Brennan had an international perspective and was not inspired by the Australian landscape or way of life. Brennan, rather, was inspired by the ideals of the French symbolist poets, such as André Mallarmé. One of his most famous poems is 'The Wanderer' (1901–02).

Norman Lindsay came to Sydney in 1901 to work as an artist and cartoonist on the *Bulletin*, and contributed to the magazine until 1958. He is famous as both an artist and as a writer. As an artist, he is best known for his florid and often lustily overblown treatment of women. Lindsay had a strongly internationalist perspective. He thought that the artists of the 1880s and 1890s had overworked and overused the Australian bush and other nationalistic symbols—although he did use the bush and Australian images in lighter (and arguably more durable) literary works such as *The Magic Pudding* (1918), which is still a very popular children's book. One of his most famous illustrative collaborations was with poet Hugh McCrae in the work *Satyrs and Sunlight* (1928), where both poet and illustrator drew on Greek and Roman mythology. The theme of Lindsay's work was far more often Dionysian and epicurean than it was heroic.

Lindsay deplored post-impressionist art, so his taste and style had dated by the middle of this century. He was a libertarian and therefore a strong opponent of any wowserist or puritanical tendencies that often prevailed in the Sydney of the early and middle twentieth century. Those who disapproved of him were often busily—and successfully—engaged in trying to suppress his more controversial and titillating works, such as his novel *Redheap* in 1930. An alliance between the moralising wowsers and those whose political views were conservative and pro-censorship meant that many controversial books were banned in the mid-twentieth century, including the works of Marx, Lenin and Stalin, and Aldous Huxley's *Brave New World*.

Jack Lindsay was Norman's son and acolyte, who followed in his father's footsteps, in the literary field at least (he was a classical scholar). He published a four-issue publication, *Vision*, which had an influence that belied its short life. It launched other Sydney poets such as Kenneth Slessor, Douglas Stewart and R. D. FitzGerald.

Of these poets, the one who was most inspired by and preoccupied with Sydney and her harbour was Kenneth Slessor, born in 1901. In the early 1920s, he was working as a journalist on the *Sun*. He later worked at *Smith's Weekly* from 1927 to 1939, as its editor, lead writer and frequent contributor.

In 1939, Slessor wrote his most famous poem, 'Five Bells', an elegy to his friend and former *Smith's Weekly* colleague, the black-and-white cartoonist Jack Lynch, who, while on his way to a party in Mosman in May 1927, fell from the rails of a ferry into the harbour. Laden down with a heavy overcoat and bottles of beer stuffed in its pockets, Lynch drowned. His body was never recovered. The poem was later used as the inspiration for John Olsen's *Ode to Five Bells*, the mural which sadly is now covered so it can be protected from the destructive force of Sydney's strong sunlight, at the northern end of the Concert Hall of the Opera House:

> Deep and dissolving verticals of light
> Ferry the falls of moonshine down. Five bells
> Coldly rung out in a machine's voice. Night and water
> Pour to one rip of darkness, the Harbour floats
> In air, the Cross hangs upside-down in water …
>
> I looked out of my window in the dark
> At waves with diamond quills and combs of light
> That arched their mackerel-backs and smacked the sand
> In the moon's drench, that straight enormous glaze,
> And ships far off sleep, and Harbour-buoys
> Tossing their fireballs wearily each to each,
> And tried to hear your voice, but all I heard
> Was a boat's whistle, and the scraping squeal
> Of seabirds' voices far away …

In a sudden career change, soon after writing 'Five Bells', Slessor became the official war correspondent in 1940. He wrote little poetry after 1944. After the war, he continued to work as a journalist in Sydney on the *Sun* and the *Daily Telegraph*.

Radio was of far more significance to many Sydneysiders than literary and artistic endeavour, and was introduced to Australia in Sydney in 1923. By Christmas, both Radio 2BL and 2FC were broadcasting. The first national election where radio was used by the political leaders to put their messages across was in 1931. Today, both these stations are operated by the Australian Broadcasting Corporation established in 1932. From 1937 to 1953, the radio serial 'Dad and Dave' was heard in Australian homes, and many more followed, such as 'The Argonauts' (1941–71) and 'Blue Hills' (1944–76). One of the more significant decisions taken by ABC management in the 1930s was to establish symphony orchestras in some Australian cities, including Sydney.

At about the same time as radio became established, the influence of the cinema, much of it imported from the United States, was felt in Australian life. Cinemas went up in the city and the suburbs, many in the Art Deco style of the day. Some cinemas and theatres were 'themed' fantasy retreats, such as the Capitol and State theatres in the city, which are still standing today. The State Theatre is in more original condition and one of the best examples of Art Deco architecture in Sydney. In the 1920s era of the silent movie, several famous

154

ABOVE: William Morris 'Billy' Hughes (1862–1952), prime minister of Australia from 1915 to 1923.
RIGHT: Wurlitzer Organ in the State Theatre, c. 1947.

movies were made in Australia, such as *Breaking the Drought*, *Robbery under Arms*, *On Our Selection*, *While the Billy Boils*, *For the Term of His Natural Life* and *The Kelly Gang*.

Many of the city's old theatres were now under threat from the moving pictures, especially when the 'talkies' took over in the summer of 1928–29. The city cinemas which first played talking movies were the Regent and the Lyceum, both of which no longer exist. One of the first and most successful early talking movies was Al Jolson's *The Jazz Singer*. The decade had been a prosperous time for 'live' theatre, but the decline set in quickly after the introduction of the 'talkies', and many old 'live' theatres closed down in the 1930s or became cinemas. By the late 1930s, musical tastes were changing as well: the Charleston gave way to swing music, and records and gramophones became cheaper and more plentiful.

In the 1920s, Sydney's main theatre districts were based around Pitt Street between King and Park streets, around the Theatre Royal in Castlereagh Street, and Central Railway. By 1935, only two of the ten live theatres operating in the city in 1929 remained. Examples of these casualties were Her Majesty's (which became the site of a new Woolworths building in 86 Pitt Street, near the corner of Market Street, later still the site of Centrepoint Tower) and the Palace and St James's theatres, both of which became cinemas. Movies soon spread through the suburbs as well, often in the exotic Art Deco style. By 1933, there were 112 suburban cinemas and twenty-two in the city.[22]

The Australian talking-film industry had a brief flowering in the 1930s with movies such as *Diggers*, which was produced in 1931 by Frank Thring, well-known actor and managing director of Hoyts Cinemas. Other movies of that era were Charles Chauvel's *In the Wake of the Bounty* and *Heritage*, and Ken Hall's *The Squatter's Daughter*, *Tall Timbers* and *Strike Me Lucky*. By the end of the 1930s, however, the economics of movie-making and changing fashions favoured the big-budget American blockbusters, made by new Hollywood moguls such as Cecil B. De Mille. These portrayed the glamorous and affluent American high life.

The domestic film industry languished until the early 1970s. Government did not see fit to nurture and protect Australia's own film industry in the same way that the manufacturing industry had been, despite the recommendations of a royal commission into the moving-picture industry. Australian culture and content were easier to detect on the radio and in the theatrical revues by comedians such as Roy Rene, who often portrayed larrikin and irreverent characters.

This Americanisation of Australian culture was not restricted to the cinema: the increased access to electrical power through the 1920s created the demand for appliances and gadgets, which would change the character of domestic life—the radio, refrigerator, electric fan, kettle and washing machine, for example. Sydney was rather backward compared to the rest of Australia in adopting electrical power. In 1922, only one in six New South Wales homes used it, compared with half of the households in smaller states, but electrification both domestic and public spread in the period up to the Great Depression. The consequences of the introduction of electrical appliances was commented upon humorously, yet nostalgically, by Kenneth Slessor in the 1920s, in his poem 'Good-bye Iceman!':[23]

155

Ladies always standing on the first-floor landing
Ladies in the el

       e

          vator,

Ladies looking, looking, while the sausages are cooking,
Looking at the ice in the refrig

               er

                 ator—

Once there was an Iceman, full of burning smirks,
Cupid's Casanova from the freezing works;
Now there's only porcelain, cupboards and duplicity
Pipes and wheels and switches, and stupid electricity,
And girls grow sick of the cold click, click
Of the

      New

         Re-

           frig-

              er-

                 ator.

New, protected companies were founded, dedicated to the manufacture and sale of these appliances. One was Hallstrom Industries, a refrigerator manufacture based at Willoughby where the Nine Network television studios are today. Travelling salesmen had a completely new line of business to chase after—consumers in need of electrical appliances—even if these customers did not yet know it. The growth of the advertising industry was also assured. At the end of 1924, there were 100 000 Hecla electric fires, tens of thousands of electric kettles, as well as stoves and hot-water services in use throughout Australia.[24]

Between 1919 and the mid-1930s, there was a building boom in Sydney, particularly in the eastern and beach-side southern suburbs, and the Inner West. This boom was the result of immigration and the increasing urbanisation of the Australian population. The patterns of rural labour were changing with increased mechanisation and the advent of the tractor in particular, so workers continued to drift into cities.[25] Between 1921 and 1931, the growth rate of Sydney's population was 3 per cent each year.[26] Averages, however, can be misleading: the population of the municipalities which were most affected by the boom in building bungalows and high-density flats, such as Woollahra, Vaucluse, Randwick and Waverley, grew by 43 per cent in ten years.[27] These municipalities covered the eastern and southeastern suburbs down to Maroubra.

The reason these municipalities grew faster than the others was the felicitous combination of being on an extensive tram network, close to beaches and parks, and with easy access to sewerage and water supply. This meant that flats were both in demand and easy to develop as part of the existing urban infrastructure. Most of the houses built in this period throughout Sydney were single-storey, Californian bungalows, often in liver brick. The building blocks were larger than they had been in the inner city, and it was possible to build the bungalows across, rather than down, the blocks. This meant that the houses were sunnier and better ventilated. Sydney, by 1938, had spread itself out so far to the west that Parramatta became a city within the metropolitan region. Today, it is close to the demographic centre of the Sydney metropolitan area.

The boom in flat building continued up to World War II. For the better off, this was the age of the Art Deco mansion apartments. Only a few of these were built. Examples are Macleay Regis in Macleay Street, Potts Point; The Astor in Macquarie Street; and others on the ridge of Edgecliff. Self-sufficient flats were a convenient solution to the shortage of domestic staff, who were both expensive and in short supply after World War I. The combination of wartime deaths and casualties, the growth in industrial jobs and the boom in the building industry meant that work was usually available in less servile circumstances. This taste for luxury apartment living did not survive the war and the onslaught of the motor vehicle, which made possible the mass exodus to the suburbs after 1945. Inner-city apartment living for the well-to-do only re-emerged in the late 1980s.

157

As well as mansion flats, less grand flats and bungalows were built on formerly unoccupied land at Bondi, Rose Bay, Randwick, Waverley, Manly and, after the bridge was opened in 1932, North Sydney and the harbour-side suburbs of the lower North Shore. The 1930s also saw many flats and bungalows being built in the inner-western municipalities of Ashfield, Petersham and Marrickville, usually along street blocks closer to railway lines. The transformation of some parts of Sydney was remarkable. In 1918 the suburb of Bondi mostly consisted of scrubby sand dunes. By 1939, it was a densely built area of flats and single-storey bungalows.

The building boom also meant a rise in the proportion of home ownership.[28] Although the goal of home ownership had been emerging from the late nineteenth century, it was in the inter-war period that the boom took off. Long-term loans with small deposits were more easily available through banks and building societies. Creating a new life in the clean and unpolluted air of the suburbs became a dream for many families. The Royal Commission into the Improvement of Sydney (1909) even recommended that people should be encouraged to live in separate suburban houses. The *Housing Act* of 1912 encouraged the construction of freestanding homes with gardens and, in 1918, federal legislation made cheap, government-funded housing loans available to ex-servicemen. This was not just a way of rewarding the veterans for the war effort—promoting home ownership was also a good way of reducing popular support for socialism and communism. It gave the impression, if not always a true one, of general prosperity—at least for the middle classes—even though unemployment rates were high for much of the inter-war period.

By the end of the 1920s, most householders owned, rather than rented, their homes.[29] During the Great Depression, Jack Lang's successor, Bertram Stevens, maintained a policy of promoting home ownership by ensuring access to cheap credit through the government-owned Rural (now State) Bank, and promoting the growth of cooperative building societies. A consequence of government policy in favour of home ownership was the rise of the slum-clearance movement, aimed at reducing the health risks of inner-city life, and promoting even more migration to the suburbs.

With all the suburban growth, the boundaries of Sydney spread outwards and more infrastructure was needed to service the newly developed area. Roads, electricity, sewerage, schools and hospitals followed, sometimes fitfully and long after the new home owners had moved in. During World War II, government policies in favour of home ownership and the building industry were suspended, so that productive activity could be more completely diverted to the war effort. There were restrictions on the amount of money which could be spent on home building and renovation. When added to the shortages of building materials and labour, this meant that, after 1945, there would be a huge, pent-up demand for housing.

158

The inter-war period was the heyday of the international cricket Tests between England and Australia, known as the Ashes. Five Test series were played in Australia, and five in England. In the 1932–33 series in Australia, the notion of fair play and sportsmanship, and even the nature of Australia's relationship with the mother country, were all sorely tested in the 'Bodyline' Tests, where English bowlers aimed directly at the Australian players, rather than at the wickets. Local heroes included Bill O'Reilly, Stan McCabe and Don Bradman.

The rugby league football code became more popular in Sydney when it was introduced in state schools. In 1932, 70 000 people attended a rugby league Test match at the Sydney Cricket Ground. Rugby union continued to be an amateur game, played in private boys schools, and the local clubs never attracted widespread popular support.

One spectator sport introduced in the 1920s was greyhound racing. Its audience was working class, and the staging of events in the evenings at Harold Park made it easy for people to attend after work. Gambling, one of Sydney's most popular pastimes since 1788, became more organised and controlled by the government in the postwar period. The government discovered that taxes on betting were a valuable source of state revenue. Government-run totalisators, which computed odds and dividends mechanically, were introduced on racecourses. While the government muscled in on what was a thriving field of private enterprise, illegal off-course SP (starting price) bookmaking continued to flourish in Sydney, greatly helped by the widespread use of the radio from the 1930s. Many SP operations were (unofficially) run from pubs. The illegality of this form of betting created a fertile ground for police corruption and organised crime.

Another old (and illegal) gambling institution was the game of two-up. One of the bastions of the game in Sydney was Thommo's two-up school, run by Joe Thomas. Because of the game's illegality, the school often moved from place to place, from empty house to empty factory, and only members of the club could get in. Two-up is a simple game to play and to bet on—there are two coins thrown in the air and participants bet on the outcome. It was popular with the diggers during World War I, and the game has evolved its own vernacular. The police often turned a blind eye to the school, but when King George died Thommo's two-up school was raided twice in one evening.[30] Usually, the proprietors were given due notice of police raids, so took the opportunity of tipping off important clientele. In memory of the Anzacs' fondness for the game, it is legal on just one day of the year—Anzac Day, 25 April.

In late 1927, Sydney experienced serious political scandal. The City Council was dismissed amid allegations of large-scale corruption and bribery, including taking 'backhanders' for granting council contracts for the construction of the Bunnerong power station at Botany, and providing sinecures for friends and relations. A royal commission was held to inquire into the tendering process, which uncovered a consistent and bipartisan disposition of the city's aldermen to receiving bribes. It was the Labor Party aldermen, however, whose reputations suffered the most.

One outcome of this scandal was the decision in 1935 by the conservative state government to remove the responsibility for generating the city's electricity from the council and to place it in the hands of the Sydney County Council (later the Electricity Commission, and later still Pacific Power).

After the war, emigration schemes sponsored by the British government were stepped up, but the inflow of migrants was well below that of the 1870s and 1880s. In the 1920s, 260 000 immigrants arrived from Britain, of whom nearly 80 per cent were assisted. Intending immigrants could qualify for assistance by being nominated by friends or prospective employers. The idea underlying Imperial immigration was to encourage agricultural production in the dominions on one hand—even though few immigrants went onto the land—and expanded foreign markets for Britain's manufactured goods, on the other.

In 1929, the metropolis comprised 181 square miles (464 square kilometres) from the Georges River to Bankstown, Granville, Parramatta, Ryde, Eastwood, the Ku-ring-gai municipality, Willoughby and Manly.[31] The population in 1931 was 1.25 million. But by 1929, even before the Wall Street Crash, unemployment was rising in Australia, and the prices of Australia's export commodities were falling. More goods and capital were being imported than were being exported, which made the crash worse when it came.

The downward pressure on prices turned into a rout in September and October of 1929. Again, in that old familiar way of the 1840s and 1890s, overseas capital dried up. Unemployment rose quickly from 8 per cent in the early 1920s to 18 per cent in 1930, 27 per cent in 1931 and 28 per cent in 1932.[32] There was no systematic unemployment benefit along the same lines as today's 'dole', but there was unemployment relief to those who could establish that they had realised all their assets, excluding their homes.

159

There was a large demonstration by unemployed people in Sydney in late February 1930, but it seemed that there was little that politicians could do to solve the economic crisis. The federal Labor government, led by James Scullin, tried to remedy the situation by seeking the advice of Sir Otto Niemeyer, an economist nominated by the Bank of England.

At the time there was considerable concern among Australia's British creditors about the country's creditworthiness, as Australia's debt had been rising steadily through the 1920s. The Niemeyer plan advocated a strongly deflationary policy of reducing wages, costs, tariffs and prices, and, most significantly, reducing government expenditure. This often meant sacking government employees. Niemeyer strongly criticised automatic cost-of-living adjustments to industrial awards and the centralised conciliation and arbitration scheme. This advice from the mother country was not warmly received in many quarters. One of the most vocal opponents of Niemeyer was Jack Lang.

In 1930, Jack Lang's Labor Party swept the Nationalist–Country Party opponents from power in New South Wales. As Lang put it, at an electoral rally held on 23 October 1930 at the Grand Opera House in Castlereagh Street, the choice was clear:

> You are asked to vote for a Labor Party which stands for the maintenance of our Australian idealism and our standard of living, or to vote for a Nationalist Party, which unashamedly advocates poverty, unemployment and degradation.[33]

The voters swung to Labor resoundingly: 55 per cent of the vote compared to 43 per cent at the previous election. These elections were the first ones in New South Wales where voting was compulsory. Lang had previously led a Labor government between 1925 and 1927, and in his first administration had introduced many significant reforms, including child endowment and the 44-hour week for workers. The 44-hour week had been suspended during the Nationalist government's term in office. Kenneth Slessor commented on Lang's return to power with a tongue-in-cheek poem in *Smith's Weekly*:[34]

Imagine that bankers were banished,
Imagine that prices are down;
Depression has utterly vanished,
We're all of us dining in town;
Endeavour to keep up your pecker
By copious draughts of champagne—
We'll go to the Ritz in a Checker
And fare back to foxtrots again …

    And fare back to foxtrots again—
    Hurrah, for the pop of champagne!
    A trifle informal,
    Ferociously normal,
    We'll fare back to foxtrots again!

Let 'Merry and Bright' be our motto
Forget the financiers' price;
If gloom be the ransom of Otto,
Good God, we ha' purchased him twice,
And why should we groan for 'em doubly,
Those faults of our palmier days?
Go, pour me a pint of the bubbly,
And bring out the prawn mayonnaise!

> And bring out the prawn mayonnaise,
> We're back to the happy old days;
> There's time to be solemn,
> In some other column,
> But bring out the prawn mayonnaise!

The Lang government soon got to work. It opened soup kitchens. The *Fair Rents Act* was amended to make it harder to evict tenants. Debtors were given some relief from their onerous financial obligations with the *Moratorium Act*. A state lottery was set up to provide essential funds for hospitals, and was instantly a popular and financial success, emulated to this day by governments of all persuasions as an important source of revenue. Other steps taken by Lang created increasing levels of consternation among employers. These included the introduction of compulsory insurance for workers, payable by the employer, and the return of the mandatory 44-hour week. Lang also established the Government Insurance Office, designed to prevent private insurance companies from overcharging for their services. To the middle classes and owners of capital, the financial sacrifices Lang extracted were much too high. At every turn, the tax burden upon them was growing and they protested loudly. One particularly unpopular move in middle-class circles was the introduction of the *Unemployment Relief Tax Act*, calculated at the rate of 9 pence in the pound of income earned.

Again during the Depression, 'sundowners' came into the parks and other open spaces to sleep every evening, congregating in the Domain after dark just as they had in the 1890s. They sheltered in caves when it rained, wrapping themselves in newspapers and anything else they could find. They also congregated in Happy Valley at La Perouse and in a hastily built shantytown at Lidcombe. The St Vincent de Paul Society, run by an order of the Catholic Church, did much to alleviate starvation and suffering by providing charitable assistance, as did other benevolent institutions.

One of the more remarkable outcomes of the Depression was the new suburb of Hammondville, near Liverpool, in the southwest of Sydney. It was started by Canon Hammond of St Barnabas's Church on Broadway at Ultimo. In this new and distant suburb, families who had been evicted from their homes were relocated with moneys raised from the public, away from the greater temptations (such as alcohol and vice) of the inner-city suburbs. Each family was given a small weatherboard house with half an acre of land, on which they were to grow vegetables and raise poultry so they could be self-sufficient. After the Depression, many of the families settled there permanently.

Another phenomenon, closer to the city centre, which Hammond was largely responsible for was the conversion of Arthur Stace. Stace, who was born to alcoholic parents, grew up in Balmain. By his early twenties, Stace was a petty criminal and, by his thirties, he was a serious alcoholic. In 1930, at the age of forty-five, he attended an address by Hammond at St Barnabas's Church and began the process of Christian conversion. The conversion worked so well that Stace spent the rest of his life writing the word 'Eternity' in chalk across the pavements and streets of Sydney, until his death at the age of eighty-three in 1967. There is a memorial to his efforts in the form of a permanent facsimile of the word 'Eternity', which is set in paving near the fountain in Sydney Square.

The police were less tolerant about the sundowners in the Domain than they were about shanty communities further away from the centre of the city. The *Labor Daily* was incensed when the sundowners were evicted from the Domain in the wintry month of August 1930, as soon as the worst weather had broken. About the only good news Sydney had all through 1930 was the brilliant performance of Donald Bradman in the Test matches held in England and the exploits of Phar Lap on the racetrack.

To try to alleviate the hardship, public works, especially on roads and in parks, were commissioned to occupy the thousands who were unable to find work. Roads such as the Wakehurst Parkway were levelled and improved, as were the roads around Ku-ring-gai Chase and Centennial Park, and at Randwick and Maroubra. The main roads out of Sydney were also concreted at this time: the Pacific Highway, the Princes Highway and Parramatta Road between Lidcombe and Homebush.

The political temperature rose in the Depression; in 1931, there were riots in inner Sydney to protest against the eviction of tenants. The windows of Grace Bros Broadway and Anthony Hordern's were smashed and many people were critically injured. There were other anti-eviction riots at Bankstown. Some people thought that Lang did not go far enough to alleviate the misery of the unemployed, particularly the Communist Party and the Unemployed Workers' Movement (UWM). The UWM deeply resented the efforts of the police force in evicting tenants from housing, and did everything in their power to prevent families being forced to leave their inner-city homes. Paddington evictions were strongly contested, and protest meetings were held in Paddington Town Hall, where long questionnaires which determined eligibility for the dole were burnt because of the absurdity of the questions. Stan Moran, an executive member of the UWM, created a network of court advocates who challenged evictions in the courts, and often had the terms of occupancies extended.[35]

As the level of unemployment rose, the procedure for receiving dole coupons (cash was never provided) became more complicated. Tickets were given out at Number 7 Wharf, Circular Quay, but there was a 2-mile (3.2-kilometre) walk to the offices of the Benevolent Society at Central Station for the food hand-outs.

Much of the labour available in and around the city was casual day labour. Sometimes the scrabble for the daily job tickets on the wharves was cruelly set up. Foremen sometimes threw job tickets into the air and the seething mass of job seekers behind the fence would have to scramble for them, often pushing and treading on those further in front.[36]

All the residential areas around the waterfront were very depressed. With the shortage of work, territoriality became more important. One area of the wharves, on Hickson Road on the eastern side of Darling Harbour, was known as 'the Hungry Mile', because of the number of unemployed seeking jobs there. That section was worked by labourers who lived around Sussex Street. Millers Point residents worked on the wharves around Walsh Bay. It was not until 1942 that a roster system for waterside labour was introduced, putting an end to the daily tussle and grab for job tickets.

In 1931, Jack Lang took on New South Wales creditors by defaulting on the state's loan obligations, owed mostly to British banks. This was an audacious move. In doing this, Lang was throwing down the gauntlet not only to the state's creditors, but also to all those people who had deeply embedded kinship and emotive ties with the 'mother country'. For many, defaulting on the debt to Britain was like spitting in a parent's face—a parent who was still heavily relied upon throughout Australia as a source of capital. The federal government had guaranteed to pay any losses due to default by a state on its loan obligations and so took legal action to recover the interest New South Wales owed as a result of the Lang government's act of default. There was a popular run on the state-owned Savings Bank, and it closed its doors. It merged with the federal government's Commonwealth Bank.

In February 1931, at the Imperial Services Club in Sydney, the right-wing New Guard—consisting largely of ex-soldiers and led by Lieutenant Colonel Eric Campbell, DSO—was formed. Its objective was to defend society against communists and anarchists in general, and Jack Lang's illegal and disloyal acts in particular. The movement soon became popular and had about 36 000 members within months. It took on the role played by fascists and Nazis in Europe by breaking up meetings of communists and socialists, and soon came into head-to-head confrontation with the government of the day. The heartland of the New Guard was in conservative middle-class areas of Sydney, such as Drummoyne and the North Shore.

Lang, in a gesture of heroic but doomed defiance, refused to cave in to the demands of foreign capital and did not abide by the judgment of the High Court handed down in 1932. The High Court had said that Lang did not have the power to suspend loan repayments. This meant he was acting unconstitutionally and it was on this ground that Governor Philip Game dismissed him in May 1932, just two months after the opening of the Sydney Harbour Bridge. Lang had snubbed Game at the opening celebrations when he boldly dispensed with the vice-regal protocol of the day and insisted that he, rather than Governor Game, officially open the Harbour Bridge. A member of the New Guard, Captain de Groot, stepped in to defend the status quo on the day of the official opening of the bridge by charging ahead of the official party on his horse to cut the ribbon, shouting as he went that he was doing it 'for King and Country'.

New South Wales went to the polls after the dismissal of Lang and the Labor Party was roundly defeated, losing more than half its seats. Lang continued to blame his downfall on the scourge of foreign bankers, and to declaim that his dismissal was a very sorry day for the people of New South Wales.

The Great Depression continued for much of the 1930s. The worst period was 1932–33. Gross domestic product declined by 25 per cent between 1928 and 1933.[37] In June 1933, 500 000 people of a total Australian population of 6 630 000 were unemployed. The only country where the percentage of unemployed was higher was Germany.[38] Slowly, world commodity prices rose and unemployment started to decline. The emergency wages cut of 10 per cent was cancelled and life started to return to normal, although the recovery was muted.

The flow of migration was interrupted by the Depression. The Australian government could no longer afford immigrant-assistance schemes and Britain had lost interest in Empire settlement schemes, as her population was both ageing and declining. In the future, the British Isles could no longer be relied upon as the sole source of Australia's migrants. Even in the period between the wars, there was a higher intake of non-British migrants, in particular Italians and Greeks.

For these immigrants, the process of chain migration was as important as it had been for some British and Irish immigrants in previous years, and in some cases it was dramatic. For example, two families from Kythera arrived in Sydney in the 1870s. By 1911, the number of Kytherans had grown to 400. Similarly, Greeks from Castellorizo migrated in large numbers, resulting in a strong local community. Many Castellorizians settled around Kensington and other southeastern suburbs.

The small but significant Jewish community in Sydney was augmented in the prewar years by those who could foresee trouble in Europe. At first, the Australian government was unable to see the gathering political storm clouds in Europe and was suspicious of the motives of Jews seeking refuge in Australia. Some of the Jewish refugees settled around Kings Cross, Bondi and other parts of the eastern suburbs. As time proceeded, however, the government's attitude to people seeking asylum from the rise of Nazism in Europe softened, and 5000 refugees arrived in Australia. One of these was Edouard Borovansky, who later became a major figure in the development of ballet in Australia. There were many others who helped create, through their skills and their expectation of access to higher forms of culture (particularly music), a supply of talent and a demand for higher culture. In 1940, another 2542 internees arrived on the *Dunera*. This small inflow of continental European immigrants was a foretaste of what was to come after 1945.

In 1938, Sydney and Australia celebrated the sesquicentenary of white settlement. Sydney's taller buildings and the Harbour Bridge were illuminated. Hyde Park was floodlit with low-intensity floodlights which, according to the *Sydney Morning Herald*, 'provided the gayest spectacle of all'. The floodlights were submerged in the pool of the Archibald

ABOVE: Bronzed lifesavers on a float in a parade along Macquarie Street, part of sesquicentenary celebrations in 1938.

Fountain, transforming the fountain's water streams to flame-coloured jets. Many saw the celebrations as the final nail in the coffin of the Great Depression. A million people watched a pageant through the city and a carnival was held at Sydney Showground. The only dark spot, noted by the *Sydney Morning Herald*, was the omission of any reference to Australia's contribution to World War I, although the ominously gathering war clouds might have been partially responsible for this. The Empire Games, convincingly won by Australia, were hosted by Sydney in 1938.

The year 1938, however, was not a good one as far as the safety of Sydney's waters was concerned. Three freak waves at Bondi washed 200 people out to sea, and five died. In the same month, a ferry capsized in Sydney Harbour and nineteen people drowned. As early as 1935, when Italy invaded Abyssinia, former wartime prime minister William Morris Hughes spoke out strongly about Australia's unpreparedness for war. There was popular apprehension about Japan's increasing militarism.

In 1939, Robert Menzies declared that Australia was at war as a result of Britain's declaration of war on Germany—unlike in Canada, where the nation had seven days to reflect on matters. Two days later, the Second AIF was formed. It was four months before the first contingent of 6000 men left Australian shores for the Middle East. On 3 January 1940, thousands of Sydneysiders saw them off from Woolloomooloo.

In this coming war, Australia was to be less reliant on imported machine tools and manufactured goods. The upgrading of Garden Island to provide maintenance services to allied fleets during the war was an engineering marvel on par with the construction of the Harbour Bridge. Any Allied naval ship could be docked and repaired there. Thousands of people, including many engineers from the Maritime Services Board, worked on the project. To an even greater degree than had been the case in World War I, World War II gave much impetus to Australian industry. The menace of German submarines made the sea lanes hazardous, and Britain was very closely focused on preventing invasion from Germany.

It was not until 1941, when petrol rationing was imposed, that the ordinary lives of Australians were seriously affected by the war—at the time, Australia was entirely dependent on imported oil. The bombing of Pearl Harbor in December 1941 brought the war right into our geographic region. From late 1941, the news of Japanese advances continued: Hong Kong, the Philippines and northern Malaya had all been invaded by Christmas 1941, and the British navy lost two ships off the Malayan coast, threatening Allied naval supremacy in the Far East. For the first time, Australia could no longer look to the British Isles for its security. That task would now fall onto the shoulders of the United States. As Prime Minister John Curtin said in his New Year's message in 1942, 'Australia looks to America, free of any pangs as to our links or kinship with the United Kingdom.' Air-raid precautions were put in place and shelters were built. Some people evacuated to the Blue Mountains.

Just as Australia looked to the United States, so did the United States look to Australia as a base for the South-West Pacific military operations. General Douglas MacArthur, who was based at Brisbane, became supreme commander of the region.[39] Many of the naval forces were also stationed in Sydney, because of the strategic importance of Sydney Harbour and the dock at Garden Island, which was used to service American ships. The Australian general Sir Thomas Blamey was appointed commander of Allied land forces under the American supreme commander. After the Allies won the Battle of the Coral Sea and the Americans defeated the Japanese at the Battle of Midway, the threat of hostile action against Australian cities diminished.

The presence of members of the US military forces in Sydney during the war meant that there was a strong growth in the nightlife and entertainment available in the city and around Kings Cross. Paradoxically, the city, during the war, became more glamorous and fun. Nightclubs and bars were popular, as were the leading restaurants of the era, Prince's and Romano's. This was despite the fact that many Sydney men were off at war, or, even worse, were being held as prisoners of war. The Eighth Division of the AIF had been captured in the fall of Singapore in 1942, held at Changi prison and later put to work on the infamous Burma railway.

However, the possibility of invasion could never be discounted. Public buildings were sandbagged and glass windows were netted so that damage from bombing could be reduced. The clock tower of the GPO—one of the tallest landmarks in Sydney—was dismantled. In May 1942, Japanese submarines entered Sydney Harbour. One of these was sunk and one was tangled in netting and blown up by its crew. The third escaped after blowing up the *Kuttabul*,

ABOVE: Sydneysiders once again turned out to celebrate Allied victory at the end of World War II.

LEFT: Crowds of people thronged the city's streets on VJ-Day (15 August 1945) to mark the Allied forces victory over Japan in World War II.

a ferry converted into a naval depot ship. Nineteen sailors died. Two months later, parts of Sydney Harbour and Bondi were shelled one night, and two Australian steamships were torpedoed by the Japanese off the New South Wales coast.

By the end of 1942, the tide of the war seemed to be turning in the Allies' favour. There were no more assaults on Sydney Harbour. Australian troops recaptured Kokoda in late 1942 and Buna in early 1943. By the end of 1943, Bougainville and New Britain had been recaptured by the Allies, and the island-hopping campaign by Allied soldiers moved onto the Indonesian archipelago.

At the end of the war, Australia's population was 7.4 million. Thirty-four thousand soldiers and other servicemen lost their lives in the war, and 180 000 were wounded. The end of the war with Japan was met with wild celebration and jubilation all around the city, especially around Martin Place.

The federal Labor government, led by Ben Chifley, won the election in 1945. Shortages and price regulation were to last for a few more years, though people were prepared to put up with these restrictions, as they could anticipate an end to the hardship. Rationing of meat and clothing did not end until 1948, and petrol and butter rationing were not finally lifted until 1950.

168

The threat of Japanese invasion during the war created the belief among many Australians, including the wartime prime minister, John Curtin, that we had to increase our population up to 20 or 30 million, or be forever vulnerable to external aggression. 'Populate or perish' was the common catch cry. Rapid population growth, combined with the increasing number of families with cars, meant Sydney spread out and diversified from the 1950s onwards, in a way that was unimaginable at the turn of the century.

GROWING UP AND SPREADING OUT

169

If Australians have learnt one lesson from the Pacific War now moving to a successful conclusion, it is surely that we cannot continue to hold our island continent for ourselves and our descendants unless we greatly increase our numbers … Our need to undertake (development and settlement) is urgent and imperative if we are to survive … Our first requirement is additional population. We need it for reasons of defence and for the fullest expansion of our economy … Australia wants, and will welcome, new healthy citizens who are determined to become good Australians by adoption.[1]

Minister for Immigration and Information Arthur Calwell, March 1945

THE POSTWAR YEARS from 1949 to 1965 were the Menzies era. There is some disagreement about the nature and extent of Prime Minister Sir Robert Menzies's political achievements. What is clear, however, is that the 1950s and 1960s were, politically and culturally, a case of 'steady as she goes'. The ship of state was being maintained at the same time as the economy was growing and the demographics of the population were changing, particularly in the big cities of Sydney and Melbourne. This change was fed by a huge surge in immigration from many different nations, including non–English-speaking ones. In 1955, Australia welcomed its one millionth postwar immigrant. The social changes which were bubbling under the surface in the immediate postwar period would not come to light until the middle of the 1960s.

None of the three key governmental policies of the first half of the century was abandoned. High tariff protection to encourage Australian industries, centralised wage-fixing and the White Australia policy were all steadfastly maintained. There was still a great deal of

ABOVE: Newly arrived immigrant children, c. 1948—the younger generation of 'New Australians'.

170

respect for, if not adulation of, Britain and her institutions, especially towards the new, young queen, Elizabeth, on her royal visit to Australia in 1954. Despite the attitudes of the fond, if not fawning, Prime Minister Menzies, increasingly people no longer saw themselves as Australian Britons in quite the same way as they had in 1901. The relationship between Britain and Australia would continue to evolve after Britain joined the European Community from the late 1960s and the level of trade between Australia and Britain declined.

In 1949, the populate-or-perish policy was enthusiastically adopted by the new Menzies Liberal–Country Party coalition government. The bipartisan political objective was to increase the population by 2 per cent every year, half through immigration and half through natural increase. There were many potential immigrants from the United Kingdom. In the aftermath of the war and the Blitz, continued shortages and rationing, the bleak climate and a bleak economy in Britain made Australia look sunny and attractive. The Australian government offered British migrants a £10 passage out, if they stayed for a minimum of two years. These new arrivals, many of whom were skilled, helped reduce the labour, materials and housing shortages Australia was experiencing in the postwar period. During the 1940s and 1950s, however, British immigrants were only one-third of the new arrivals.[2]

Postwar immigration from non–English-speaking countries energised and invigorated Sydney in a way that it had never been before. It became a much livelier and more interesting place to live in, or visit. Postwar immigration policy fitted in well with the concerns about the growth of communism in Asian countries, particularly around the time of the beginning of the Korean War in 1950. In the Cold War hysteria, one of Menzies's election promises in 1949 was to ban the Communist Party in Australia. Menzies was thwarted in this move, however, by the High Court, which ruled that the government did not have the power to do this unless it was at war, as it could only do so on the grounds of national security. In late 1951, a referendum was held to determine whether the government should be given the constitutional power to ban the Communist Party. By a narrow majority, the population decided that it should not.

The fear of communism marginalised postwar radical politics. The Australian Security Intelligence Organisation (ASIO) busied itself by seeking out signs of nascent communism through the 1950s and 1960s. One of the less likely radicals in Sydney was (Lady) Jessie Street, the wife of the eminent chief justice of New South Wales, Sir Kenneth Street. Jessie Street was a feminist pioneer who was Australia's only female delegate at the United Nations' founding conference in 1945. She played a continuing role at the United Nations as Australia's delegate on women's issues, founded the organisation which later became the Family Planning Association, and advocated Aboriginal rights. Her loose affiliation with the Australia–Russia Society captured ASIO's attention, and her political activities and public addresses were closely monitored. At the time she stood as a Labor candidate for the seat of Wentworth, in the conservative heartland of Sydney's eastern suburbs, her opponents tickled the strong popular anti-communist sentiment in the election with the slogan 'The way to Moscow is Jessie Street'. A small park in front of the Gateway Building in Macquarie Place is named after her and her papers are held by the City of Sydney Library.

171

The 1950s was not a good decade for the Labor Party. The first split came at the time of the move to ban the Communist Party—the left wing was opposed to banning it, and the right wing supported Menzies's move. In 1955, there was another more official split when the right-wing Catholic group in Victoria led by B. A. Santamaria seized control of many left-wing trade unions. The end result was the formation of the Democratic Labor Party. The split was most effective in Victoria and Queensland. It did not spread so noticeably in New South Wales, where the Labor Party held together. The major result of the split was to consign the federal Labor Party to opposition until 1972. However, because the state branch of the New South Wales Labor Party remained unified, Labor was able to hold on to power in New South Wales until 1965. To do this, it had to abandon any pretence of radicalism and move to the right. Its Catholic Celtic constituents and membership embraced conservatism and political pragmatism.

The overall growth in the workforce from immigration was very high in the prosperous postwar years to 1973. About 60 per cent of the new workers were born outside Australia.[3] Many women immigrants sought work in new industries such as textiles, footwear and food processing. In order to save and prosper, many immigrant families relied on two incomes. Like other female workers, migrant women worked either part-time or on a piecework basis, and so did not have any of the economic safety nets—the minimum wage, annual and sick leave—that male full-time workers had. The structural inequity between male and female workers was not formally removed until the 1970s.

From the 1950s, immigration policy favoured family reunions. The reason for this was that, with the fall in export prices in the early 1950s, unemployment rose (to 2.3 per cent!). In the short term, with the family reunion policy, there would be less pressure from immigrants in the jobs market. Family reunion schemes, such as the 'Bring out a Briton' campaign, were strongly encouraged. Started in 1957, the objective was to encourage young British families to immigrate to Australia. British migrants were given the same rights to social security benefits as Australians sooner than other immigrants were. Times have changed, and so has immigration policy. Since 1996, the family reunion policy has been cut back in favour of business and skilled immigration, which, in recent decades of high unemployment, is seen to be more clearly in the national interest.

From 1947 to 1954, more than 170 000 displaced persons arrived from countries behind the newly created Iron Curtain, such as the Baltic States, Poland, Yugoslavia and Czechoslovakia. These new arrivals were not as costly as the £10 migrants, as the United Nations paid for their trip out. They had to work where the government dictated for the first two years, often in heavy industry such as the BHP steelworks at Port Kembla, in the timber industry or later on the Snowy Mountains Hydro-Electric Scheme. Outnumbered by the Anglo-Celtic majority, and often with limited English skills, many of these new arrivals—colloquially called 'DPs' or 'reffos'—clung together in this strange new land, where they were often made to feel isolated and unwelcome. Many chose not to assimilate with the mainstream Anglo-Celtic culture once they had mastered the English language. Total assimilation was sometimes, implicitly or explicitly, expected of them.

Apart from the displaced persons, many non-British migrants were Italian and Greek. Unlike the British and the Greeks after 1952, the Italians were not given assistance. Despite this, between 1947 and 1951 more Italians immigrated to Australia than any other non-British group. Many Italians settled in areas where earlier Italian immigrants lived. There had been an Italian presence around Leichhardt from the late nineteenth century, and the process of chain migration continued. Further out west, around Liverpool, other groups of Italian-born migrants established market gardens, and relations, friends and friends of friends followed. Most of the Italian community is now dispersed throughout Sydney, although Leichhardt is still a commercial centre for the Italian-speaking community, and the municipalities of Leichhardt and Liverpool still have a relatively high concentration of Italian-born migrants.

One of the great Italian-immigrant success stories is that of Franco Belgiorno-Nettis and Carlo Salteri. They founded the engineering firm Transfield in 1956. Today Transfield is one of Australia's largest engineering and construction companies, building, among many other things, the Sydney Harbour Tunnel in the late 1980s. Nettis was born in Puglia in southern Italy. He was drafted into Rommel's Afrika Korps during World War II, captured by the Allies and spent time as a prisoner of war in India, where he learnt to speak English and studied engineering. Belgiorno-Nettis is also a keen patron of the arts. The Sydney Biennale art exhibition held at the Art Gallery of New South Wales is sponsored by Transfield.

The Italians brought about a big change in Sydney's dining habits. In 1954, spaghetti bolognese was an exotic foreign dish. Now it is just as ubiquitous in homes and restaurants (if not more so) than roast dinners. Beppi Polese was one of the Italian immigrants who can take much credit for bringing Italian cuisine to the attention of Sydneysiders. In the early postwar period, the French international style predominated at fashionable restaurants.

Polese was born in the Veneto region and trained at various restaurants in Rome, Milan and Florence. When he first arrived in Australia in 1952, he worked at Romano's restaurant and nightclub in the city. Polese opened Beppi's on the corner of Stanley and Yurong streets, East Sydney, in 1956. At that time, there were only two other Italian restaurants in Sydney. There was the Chianti and, down the road in Stanley Street, La Veneziana, a cheap, *mensa*-style Italian restaurant which served the Italian community—and other Sydneysiders who were willing to take the risk with cheap, but non-traditional food. Beppi's is the oldest Italian restaurant to remain in the hands of its original owners.

When the Poleses took over the lease of the premises, it was a small coffee lounge serving Yugoslav food. At the time, Polese had to borrow all his capital at high (12 per cent) interest rates during the high inflation of the mid-1950s. He could not afford to threaten the cash flow of the business by changing its operations dramatically, so business continued there, Yugoslav-style, for another year, while he gradually introduced Italian dishes onto the menu. In those days, it was risky to introduce more sophisticated seafood and exotic vegetables such as artichokes. Appropriate ingredients were also hard to find. Beppi drove to the Spit Bridge to buy mussels freshly collected from the rocks around Middle Harbour, and bought calamari and octopus directly from the Italian fishermen who kept their boats nearby at Woolloomooloo. Many vegetables could only be bought directly from Italian market gardeners on the outskirts of the city.

Sydney's gourmets and *bon vivants*—Rudy Komon, Nevile Baker and 'Snow' Swift, to name just a few—supported Beppi through their patronage, and by word of mouth. These men were all members of the Wine and Food Society, which promoted newly established restaurants like Beppi's, and Australian wines. Until then, wine had a somewhat tawdry reputation. Wine drinkers were widely thought to be alcoholics and indigent derelicts who frequented seedy inner-city wine bars. By 1964, there were so many Italian restaurants that Alitalia, which had recently started its Australian operations, held a competition between restaurants for the best Italian food. Beppi's popularity grew, especially among journalists and advertising executives. As restaurants such as Beppi's gained in popularity, by the late 1970s, Italian food had eclipsed French food as the dominant European cuisine. Beppi's still serves the best traditional regional Italian cuisine in Sydney.

The Polese family also runs a modern-style Italian restaurant, Mezzaluna, in Victoria Street, Potts Point. The building has been owned by the Polese family for twenty-five years and the restaurant is run by Norma and her son Mark.

173

Greek immigrants first arrived in Sydney during the gold rushes of the 1850s.[4] The religious centre of gravity for the Greek community since 1898 has been the Holy Trinity (*Ayia Trias*) Greek Orthodox Church on the corner of Bourke and Ridge streets, Surry Hills. In the first half of the twentieth century, Greek immigrants to Sydney came from the islands of Castellorizo, Kythera and Ithaca. Many of them worked initially as wharf labourers, builders' labourers or market gardeners, to earn enough money to start their own businesses, such as cafés, milk bars, oyster bars, restaurants, groceries and fish-and-chips shops, often in the city, inner city and eastern beach and bayside suburbs of Sydney.

These new small businesses run by Greeks became a source of employment for new Greek arrivals, which was just as well, as many narrow-minded Australian employers were unwilling to employ them. Greek clubs were formed: the Kytherans Brotherhood of Australia was formed at a café in Oxford Street, Darlinghurst, in 1922. The Castellorizian Club was formed in 1926 at a shop in Park Street owned by the Confos family. In the same decade, the first Greek-language newspapers were published in Sydney. By 1940, there were between 2000 and 3000 Greek people living in Sydney.

174

From 1952, Greek immigration was encouraged by the Australian government with assistance given to single men and heads of households. The Greek government had an official policy which prohibited the emigration of unmarried Greek women until 1961, when prolonged lobbying by the Australian government and Greek-Australian community leaders succeeded in ending it.[5] This made the male-to-female ratio of Greek immigrants very high and, for many, the only form of social contact was in the local Greek community clubs in the inner-city suburbs. After married men established themselves, their families followed unassisted.

Many postwar Greek immigrants who came from Crete, Cyprus and the Peloponnese settled in Surry Hills and Redfern, close to the religious heart of the community.[6] Initially, these Greeks had little in common with their compatriots who were part of the previously established chains of migration, and who by then were well established in their new home. Today, the Greek community is relatively more concentrated than the Italian community, predominantly in the municipalities of (in descending order) Canterbury, Marrickville, Rockdale, Randwick and Blacktown.

The inner-city suburbs were the first to be affected by postwar immigration from non–English-speaking countries. By 1961, 20 per cent of the Greek and Italian communities were employers or self-employed, and the businesses they ran added much life to decayed urban areas. Coffee shops, corner shops, milk bars and small restaurants sprang up, which, in turn, attracted a new type of resident to these areas, for whom the lure of the remote garden suburbs was less compelling than it had been for their parents and grandparents.

There are many Greek families who have made a significant contribution to Sydney. One example is the Kytheran-born Andronicus family, who in 1910 established a café and confectionery business in George Street near Circular Quay, on the site where the Regent Hotel is today. Andronicus Coffee was bought by Nestlé, the Swiss-based food multinational, in the boom of the 1980s. The Andronicus brand is still a market leader for coffee in Australia.

Another success story is Peter Manettas, a Castellorizian who arrived in Sydney as an orphan in 1927 to live with his uncle and has built up what is today one of Australia's largest wholesale seafood distributors. His first business was the Victory Café in George Street, which he opened in 1938. The business is now managed by Manettas's sons.

Another significant source of Sydney's postwar immigrants was Hungary. The number of Hungarian-born people in Sydney today is not great—only 11 000—but this belies their influence.[7] The Hungarian presence in suburbs such as Double Bay in the postwar years meant that the pattern and nature of retail activity there was altered significantly. Hungarians, used to café society, introduced it to Double Bay in the early 1960s at a time when there were only two milk bars, run by Greek families. In creating these new small businesses, they helped other migrant businesses, such as Andronicus Coffee, to prosper. They, like the Italians, Greeks and other non–English-speaking immigrants, gave other Australians a chance to enjoy a more cosmopolitan lifestyle.

The Hungarian influence soon extended far beyond the eastern suburbs. Many Hungarians became successful businessmen. Some well-known people from Hungarian backgrounds are Sir Peter Abeles, who founded the transport empire TNT; the late Larry Adler, the well-known share trader of the 1980s who founded FAI Insurance; and founders of Westfield Holdings, Frank Lowy (born in Czechoslovakia) and John Saunders. These last two started their business life in Australia as delicatessen owners at Blacktown; by the 1960s, they had become important players in developing and operating the new, large district shopping centres. In the process, these shopping centres transformed the retail industry and the pattern of development of many of Sydney's suburbs. Now Westfield is one of the largest owner-operators of shopping malls in the United States as well. In Sydney, Westfield 'Shoppingtowns' can be found throughout the Sydney metropolitan region.

Many other, smaller Hungarian-born property developers have left a distinct mark on Sydney's built environment. One highly visible example is the apartment developments on the western edge of Potts Point in Victoria Street (of which more later) which were conceived by Frank Theeman. The Hungarian contribution to Sydney, however, extends beyond commerce. Leading artist Judy Cassab, literary critic and author Andrew Riemer and former *Sydney Morning Herald* cartoonist George Molnar have made a significant though less obviously tangible contribution to Sydney's fabric. Hungarian-born Nick Greiner was premier of New South Wales between 1988 and 1992.

During the 1950s and 1960s, there was substantial immigration, assisted and unassisted, from the Netherlands and Germany. Altogether, a quarter of a million northern Europeans settled in Australia between 1947 and 1969. When Indonesia became independent in the late 1940s, many middle-class Dutch people resettled in Australia rather than returning 'home'. It was these northern European immigrants who found the task of assimilation easiest. Some of them started new restaurants in the city, which gave Sydneysiders their first taste of Asian cuisine. Not many Sydneysiders were adventurous enough to take their chances in Chinatown, near the Haymarket. In the early postwar period, Chinese restaurants were considered

175

unworthy of genteel patronage. Indonesian food was the only exotic cuisine that was available within the central business district itself.

One Dutch immigrant was Dik Dusseldorp, founder of Lend Lease, now, like Westfield, one of Australia's largest companies. Dusseldorp's career began in Australia when he was sent here as managing director of a Dutch engineering company. He decided to stay and founded an Australian-based engineering company, Civil and Civic, which was involved in the construction of the Snowy Mountains Hydro-Electric Scheme from the middle of the 1950s. Dusseldorp then founded Lend Lease as a property development company, which later bought Civil and Civic. Many of Lend Lease's founding shareholders were Europeans, including Queen Beatrix of the Netherlands. Lend Lease hit Sydney with a bang in 1957, when it built Caltex House, the first high-rise to be built after the abolition of the 45-metre height control limits.

Dusseldorp used his engineering skills to imbue in Lend Lease's city buildings a level of structural innovation sometimes missing in other late–twentieth-century architecture. These buildings include Australia Square (1967), which had been inspired by the Rockefeller Center in New York; the MLC Centre; and Darling Park, on the eastern side of Darling Harbour. In the late 1960s, MLC, a Sydney-based insurance company, became one of Lend Lease's major clients, and, as time wore on, Lend Lease bought a large interest in MLC. This was being closely observed by Ron Brierley's Industrial Equity Limited, an opportunistic share-trading company which made its money investing in undervalued, sleepy companies often run by members of the 'old school tie' brigade.

Dusseldorp's entrepreneurial skills also led him to create Australia's first property trusts in the late 1960s. The General Property Trust was one of the first property trust companies in the world. It enabled small investors to become indirect owners of large commercial city developments. In this way, and through MLC, Lend Lease became a big player in the financial services and funds management industry. It later took over Capita and Australian Eagle, and promoted other various property funds. Dusseldorp also initiated and organised the drafting of the Strata Titles law which revolutionised—and clarified—property ownership of residential flats. Lend Lease was a leader in residential subdivisions. One of the earlier subdivisions was on rocky, vacant land at Castlecrag. From the 1980s, Lend Lease started its successful offshore expansion. Dusseldorp retired as a director in 1988 and now lives in Tahiti.

Wowserism was not yet dead in Sydney in 1945, but it was starting to fade. Social dissent was still not encouraged and conformity was the order of the day. In 1946, liquor licensing laws were relaxed so that clubs such as the Returned Servicemen's League (RSL) clubs and sporting clubs were allowed to serve alcohol after six in the evening, and wine and beer could be served in restaurants. The state government held a referendum in the same year to test the electorate's willingness to abandon early closing. A big majority—two-thirds of voters—were against abandoning it. In the following eight years, the public's resolve weakened. Another referendum was held in 1954. Early closing was narrowly defeated—by only 10 000 votes. After that pubs could stay open until ten in the evening.

One unintended consequence of the end of early closing was the demise of the city pub. In the years of early closing, the pub closest to work was the only place office workers could get a drink in the narrow window of opportunity between the end of the working day and closing time. After its abolition, people could go back to their local pub or club. From 1956, clubs had another advantage: they were able to install that great vehicle for gambling in Sydney, the poker machine, or 'pokie'. Poker machines were not allowed in pubs until 1997. The city pubs lost business, they lost profits, and they lost value. This made it easier for city blocks to be consolidated by property developers. The greatest (and saddest) example of this was probably Adams's Hotel with its famous Marble Bar, where the present-day Hilton Hotel stands. It went, along with the Palace Theatre and the Royal Arcade, in the 1960s, so that that great mediocrity of Sydney architecture, the Hilton Hotel, could be built.

In 1995, the City Council stepped in to protect pubs, which were by then an endangered species. Many of them are fine examples of Art Deco, or older, architecture. They now pay lower rates to the City Council than the skyscrapers and other commercial buildings which tower over them, even though profitability has soared with the introduction of poker machines.

The mid-1950s saw not only the end of early closing in the pubs, but also the introduction of television. This created an even stronger vehicle for the Americanisation of our popular culture than even the cinema had been. It also contributed to greater suburban isolation, as it could be enjoyed in the seclusion of one's own lounge room. Through the 1950s and early 1960s, television became cheaper and more accessible. Then, in 1975, when colour television was introduced (much later than in many other English-speaking countries), the television-buying frenzy began all over again.

Sundays were dead quiet in Sydney in the 1950s and early 1960s, as they had been from the late nineteenth century when the population drifted out to the suburbs. The pubs were shut on Sundays and there was little public entertainment available—cinemas, theatres and sporting venues were not allowed to charge admission. The rules about Sunday entertainment and sport were not relaxed until 1966, and normal Sunday hotel trading was not legalised until 1979.

All this Sabbatarianism meant that Saturday was the big day for outings such as sport and the movies, nicknamed 'the flicks'. Children used to go to their local suburban cinema to watch the matinées, and their parents and older siblings would go on Saturday nights. About the only thing to do on Sunday was to go on a slow tram ride or head for the beach.

On a higher cultural plane, literature and art flourished from 1950 in a way it had not since 1900. Two of Australia's greatest writers, Patrick White and Tom Keneally, emerged from Sydney in the 1950s and 1960s, and the works of some of Australia's leading painters, John Olsen, Lloyd Rees and Brett Whiteley, became vital—and vibrant—elements of Sydney's cultural landscape.

By the early 1950s, Sydney's younger artists were growing tired of the profound con-servatism of the art establishment. The conservative mood had set in early in the twentieth century. In the 1880s and 1890s, the Art Gallery of New South Wales had been one of the first institutions to buy Tom Roberts's and Arthur Streeton's work. This sense of adventure had long since withered away. There had been a brief change of wind in 1944, when Sydney portrait painter William Dobell was awarded the Archibald Prize by the trustees of the Art Gallery of New South Wales for his portrait of Joshua Smith. For their efforts, the trustees were promptly taken to court by two disappointed competitors on the grounds that the work was a caricature and not a portrait. Dobell won the day, but the case was an epic struggle between the old and the new.

The reactionaries lost the legal battle, but they won the war. The trustees of the Art Gallery must have been terrified—trustees of public institutions are not usually famous for their bravery. They buckled under and awarded the Archibald Prize six times in the following twelve years to the same academic and conservative painter, William Dargie. In January 1953, their highly conservative decision to award the prize to Ivor Hele provoked a demonstration by about twenty young Sydney artists, led by Olsen.

The artists of Sydney from the late 1950s had a much greater appetite for innovation than the artists of the previous generation. Painters were quickly influenced by, and adopted, overseas trends. Olsen lived, like many other young and emerging artists, at Victoria Street, Potts Point, in the early 1960s. He used the energy of the city, Potts Point and the harbour as a major source of his inspiration. He also had plenty of his own energy to draw on and was able to communicate to others both as an art teacher and as an engaging and articulate *bon vivant* and mentor. With this personality and optimism, Olsen imbued his Sydney works with a larrikin-like, sometimes vulgar and irreverent quality. On more than one occasion, he looked to the poetry of Kenneth Slessor for inspiration.

A more dynamic market for art developed under the influence of a new breed of art dealers, such as Thelma Clune and Rudy Komon, a Czech immigrant. Up until then, the art market was more genteel and restrained, in a sleepy, Anglo-Saxon kind of way. The only commercial galleries were Macquarie Galleries, the David Jones Art Gallery and the Blaxland Gallery, located within the Farmer's (now Grace Bros) store in the city. Thelma Clune's gallery at Macleay Street, Kings Cross, became a haven for young artists such as Olsen in the 1950s. Later, in the 1970s, it was the home of the alternative art gallery run by Martin Sharp, called the Yellow House.

Rudy Komon opened a gallery on the premises of an old wine bar on the corner of Jersey Road and Paddington Street, and this added momentum to the early stages of Paddington and Woollahra's urban renewal. Komon was a mentor to many of Australia's best postwar artists, Olsen and Rees included, and a formidable presence in the Sydney art scene until his death in the early 1980s. Komon employed and trained many people such as Barry Stern and Frank Watters, who would, in turn, establish their own art galleries. His thickly accented English was mimicked by Patrick White in his novel *The Vivisector*: 'Zese faht you see are all early lyrical veuorks. Zere is gfeater Kraft—depth—later; but purity—ze lyrical purity of youss has its appeal, I sink you vill agree.'[8] White was a patrician Australian who was, like many others, getting accustomed to the new, more diverse postwar society.

The Australian-born and English-educated novelist and playwright Patrick White returned to Sydney in the early postwar period and lived from 1964 at a house in Martin Road, Centennial Park. His prolific writing career spanned nearly half a century. White was the first Australian writer to receive the Nobel Prize for Literature in 1973. His novels include *The Tree of Man* (1955), *Voss* (1957), *Riders in the Chariot* (1961) and *The Vivisector* (1970). In the early 1970s, White became involved in local conservation issues, such as the preservation of Centennial and Moore parks, and in weakening the already faltering wowser grasp on censorship when he gave evidence about the literary qualities of Philip Roth's *Portnoy's Complaint*, which was then, like many other books in those days, still banned.

Tom Keneally's first novel, *Bring Larks and Heroes* (1967) won the Miles Franklin Award for Literature. Other novels by Keneally include *The Chant of Jimmie Blacksmith* and *Schindler's Ark*, both adapted for film. In 1988, Keneally wrote *The Playmaker*, which was about the staging in Sydney's earliest colonial days of *The Recruiting Officer*, the first play ever performed in the new settlement. *The Playmaker* was performed as a double billing with *The Recruiting Officer* in the Bicentennial year.

179

One indomitable figure in Sydney from the late 1950s to the middle of the 1970s was Welsh-born Len Evans. Evans arrived in Sydney in 1955 with £10 in his pocket, and spent his first night in Sydney at the People's Palace Hotel in Pitt Street, a building which has since been transformed into city apartments. For many years, Evans eked out a living washing glasses at the Ship Inn at Circular Quay and as a freelance wine and food writer for the *Observer* and the *Bulletin*. Evans soon fell into the company of the leading lights of the Wine and Food Society. All the members of that society were enthusiasts, keen to share their knowledge with anyone who was interested.

Evans started work at the newly built Chevron Hotel in 1960, and soon worked his way up the managerial ladder there from bar manager to food and beverage assistant manager, then deputy general manager. Evans started the cellar on the ground floor of the hotel, which was for many years the best in Sydney. Wine makers and growers such as Max Schubert and Geoffrey Penfold-Hyland nurtured and encouraged him. The cellar at the Chevron was very successful. For the first time, wine was being properly merchandised. By 1965, wine was becoming more common on Sydney tables than beer, and Evans can claim a considerable amount of credit for this. In the process, he was promoting a wine industry whose reputation soon spread beyond Australia.

Between 1969 and 1989, Evans ran a restaurant and wine bar and cellar in an old, run-down nineteenth-century building at Bulletin Place. Simple, unadorned meals were served to complement the vast range of wines available there. When the area of the city near Macquarie Place was altered almost beyond recognition in the late 1980s, with the construction of the Renaissance Hotel and Gateway Building, Evans closed the doors of Bulletin Place and

BELOW: Immigrant children, mostly from England, in the school playground of the migrant hostel at Bradfield Park on Sydney's North Shore in 1961. The hostel was made up of a collection of huts from a wartime training camp.

concentrated his efforts on wine making at Rothbury Estate. Evans is now recognised as one of the world's most knowledgeable people on the subject of wine. He was awarded the Man of the Year prize in 1997 by British wine magazine *Decanter*. Evans has contributed far more than his knowledge of wine to Sydneysiders. He also brought with him a mischievous Celtic charm and outspoken *bonhomie*. For many years, he was a television personality and made regular appearances on 'Beauty and the Beast'.

The biggest problem facing both state and local governments in the postwar period has been how to manage growth. The state Department of Housing could foresee even before the end of the war that a housing shortage would occur. The population increased sharply because of postwar immigration and the baby boom. To ease the immediate shortage, the department took over buildings which had been used by the defence forces during the war as temporary accommodation for migrants and other homeless people.

In 1945, even before troops were demobilised, it was estimated that there was a shortage of 69 000 houses in Sydney.[9] In the early postwar period, people took matters into their own hands by building their own homes, often in fibro, as this was cheaper and easier to find than bricks. The Housing Commission had been established in 1941, with a policy which favoured the suburban location of public housing. Often the urgency brought on by the housing shortage was used as a convenient excuse to cut aesthetic corners and not provide the parks and other facilities which these new housing estates should have had.

Public housing was built in the suburbs of Westmead, Cabramatta, Liverpool, Granville, Fairfield, Bankstown, Canley Vale, Green Valley, Rydalmere and, particularly, Villawood, which was the commission's largest land holding. There was also some high-density public housing built in the inner city where land was cheap, as in Surry Hills, Redfern and Waterloo.

The postwar economic boom did not really gather momentum until the early 1950s. The Korean War, which lasted from 1950 to 1953, had a very positive effect on the economy by creating a strong demand for wool. In the years before synthetic quilting, it was the only thing that could keep the members of the United States and United Nations forces (including Australians) warm in the cold, north Asian winter. This war produced an economic boom with high inflation, which peaked in 1952 at 21 per cent and lasted until the mid-1950s.

A boom in building soon followed, fed by pent-up demand and by the cheap housing loans available to ex-servicemen. It was from the 1950s that the suburban sprawl started in earnest. While the population was rising, the number of people in households was decreasing. In 1947 there was an average of four people per household. In 1971, this figure had shrunk to 3.3, and to 2.9 in 1986.[10]

From the 1950s, factories moved further out to the new population growth areas on the fringes of the city. The remaining inner-city factories were often staffed by non–English-speaking migrants, who formed a key component in Sydney's industrial workforce. Industrial expansion was quick and substantial. Between 1950 and 1955, the amount of factories in New South Wales increased by 30 per cent.[11] In the second half of the 1950s, the inner-city suburbs lost nearly 400 factories, and this trend has persisted to the present day, especially as land values have risen from the 1970s onwards.

The period of high postwar growth coincided with agitation for a Sydney-wide development scheme, along similar lines to the Greater Sydney Movement of the early years of the century. The closest Sydney ever came to having a Council of Greater Sydney was the Cumberland County Council.

The County of Cumberland was a body of ten councillors elected by the forty constituent local councils. There was no particular status accorded to the City of Sydney when the council was established, and this proved to be a source of difficulty later on. The Cumberland County Council's task was to prepare a plan for Sydney within three years which would be an outline of the entire city's needs. The main issues to consider were: the size and location of arterial roads; the zoning and usage of land; water supply; the location and size of green belts and recreational areas; and the areas where new settlements and future population growth should be located. The council succeeded in completing its task well within its time limit, but it took another three years for the government to move with sufficient energy and vigour so that the scheme became law. Many municipal councils were hostile to the county council, as they saw it as an attack on their political autonomy.

Two of the key objectives of the scheme were to contain Sydney's sprawl with the use of the green belt and other open spaces, and, secondly, to decentralise Sydney's industry and commerce with the creation of district and county centres. The green belt, which no longer exists in any significant form, was a strip of open country surrounding the metropolitan area, terminating at the Royal National Park at its southern end and Ku-ring-gai Chase National Park to the north. The green belt was to be maintained to encourage the denser settlement of the metropolitan area and to discourage undesirable ribbon development along highways.

The protection of Sydney's rural areas was another objective of the scheme: at the time, market gardens, orchards, dairies and poultry farms within the County of Cumberland at Ryde, Penrith, Liverpool, Campbelltown, Sutherland, St Ives, Warriewood and Eastwood were major sources of Sydney's fruit, vegetables and poultry. The last three of these rural areas were under threat of subdivision at the time the report was written. Casula and Chipping Norton were right in the middle of the green belt. They had many vineyards until the land was subdivided.

Main roads and expressways, such as the Warringah Expressway, were also planned to ease traffic congestion within the city. The location of new, decentralised industrial zones were agreed upon. Some of these zones were identified at St Marys, Sutherland, Bankstown, Brookvale, St Leonards and Regents Park. Once the policies were set, the implementation was left in the hands of the local councils. As Denis Winston wrote:

> it is for the municipalities and shires to put the meat on the bones of the scheme by filling in the details … which fit the overall network, by zoning for local industries … and above all by supervising all new building developments, whether public or private, to see that they conform to the intentions of the scheme and make the County a better place instead of worse.[12]

This was a little like leaving a fox to mind the chicken coop. Soon the green belt was under serious threat. Rates could not be levied on unoccupied land. Some of this land was carved out for residential and industrial use before the scheme became law. Areas within the built-up area which the government had agreed to buy and convert into open land had become too expensive for the government to afford. The estimated £15 million cost simply was not available.[13] By 1967, a large portion of the green belt had been released for development.[14]

Nowadays, the former green belt along the Hume Highway from Casula to Campbelltown is an unending sprawl of low-density suburbs. Suburbs which have devoured the green belt are (to the west and the south) Bossley Park, Greystanes, Prairiewood, Bonnyrigg, Green Valley, Sadleir, Hoxton Park and Lurnea. Further to the north, the green belt has been gobbled up by Winston Hills, Kings Langley, parts of Baulkham Hills, Carlingford, Cherrybrook and West Pennant Hills.

Beyond the green belt, in 1951, was much rural land. This is no longer the case. One politician who can take much of the credit for the destruction of the green belt is Pat Hills, former City of Sydney alderman and later Labor minister for local government during the 1960s. The release of new, cheap (green-belt) housing land to the public was a vote winner which overcame lofty planning considerations. Cumberland County Council was disbanded in 1964 and replaced by the State Planning Authority.

The objectives of the Cumberland Scheme that were easier to achieve were those which created commercial opportunities. The creation of district shopping centres and the zoning of industrial land were made possible through the entrepreneurial contribution of the private sector. A major weakness of the Cumberland Scheme was the underestimation of future population growth. It was assumed that population growth in Sydney would peak in 1980 at a level of 2.3 million people, in line with the assumption that the Australian population would decline from a maximum of 8.5 million people in 1980. By as early as 1957 alone, however, Sydney's population was already nearly 2 million. The other practical weakness was the lack of political will and determination to stick to the plan.

183

In the 1950s, the city was still the heart of Sydney. Suburban shopping centres ran along main roads, with their Art Deco cinemas, milk bars, butchers' and grocery shops. The gargantuan district shopping centre did not arrive in Sydney until the late 1950s, although they were gleams in the government's eye well before this under the Cumberland Scheme. These district centres diminished the importance of the city itself. Nowadays it is possible (although most inadvisable) to live for years, if not a lifetime, without venturing into the central business district.

Some of these district centres can be found at Parramatta, Bondi Junction, Hurstville, Burwood, Chatswood, Ryde and Bankstown. The idea was to replicate in each district the services then only available in the centre of the city. These new centres were an essential ingredient in Sydney's postwar suburbanisation, and they have certainly had the desired effect of regionalising Sydney. They succeeded brilliantly in dispersing retail trade from the city: in the late 1940s, more than half Sydney's retail sales were in the city. By 1980 this figure had declined to just less than 10 per cent.[15] Two of the earlier models of the district shopping centre were Top Ryde (1957) and Warringah Mall at Brookvale (1959).

In 1947 the north, south and west of Sydney were not yet densely settled. The Barrenjoey Peninsula, Warringah, Bankstown, Sutherland and Fairfield were not fully developed, and much of the land in these areas was in a semi-rural or native state. This vacant land was soon gobbled up between 1947 and 1961. The municipalities with the fastest-growing populations in this era were (in descending order) Sutherland, Bankstown, Blacktown, Fairfield, Warringah, Ku-ring-gai and Hornsby–Ryde. Sutherland's population quadrupled, and the population of Hornsby–Ryde, at the bottom of the high-growth list, was still a high 90 per cent.[16] Bankstown was an area which benefited from the boom in industrial production with the location of many industries there. Its population grew from 60 000 in 1947 to 152 000 in 1961.

While Sydney was spreading outwards, its centre was emptying out. Population was moving from the inner city towards the outer suburbs. Prosperity, cheaper motor vehicles and available credit made life in the suburbs attainable for the working classes. Between 1947 and 1961, the percentage of Sydneysiders living in the inner city and eastern suburbs (as far south as the municipality of Randwick) shrank from 38 to 25 per cent.[17]

The abolition of rent controls in the late 1950s provoked a building boom for flats. Strata title legislation was passed in 1961, with the strong support of property developer and Lend Lease founder, Dik Dusseldorp.[18] In the 1960s, flats were increasingly part of the transitional stage for young couples on the road to home ownership.

The flats built from the 1960s often went up in the same municipalities as the ones that had been built in the inter-war period: beach and harbourside flats were popular, as were flats along major transport routes such as the East Hills, Illawarra and North Shore lines. As time wore on, more outlying suburbs such as Canterbury, Auburn and Ryde were more densely built up with low-rise suburban flats. The amount of flats as a percentage of total dwellings in the Sydney region has grown dramatically from 21 per cent in 1961 to 34 per cent in 1986, and this trend will continue.[19] Nearly a quarter of Sydney's population lives in medium- or high-density housing.[20]

The most concentrated and visible building boom in Sydney was in the city itself. In 1957 the restriction on building heights was lifted. The first buildings to go up after this were the first generation of office buildings: Caltex House in Kent Street, Unilever, ICI House and the Lend Lease headquarters on Circular Quay East. These were in the new, modernist style. They could be glassy, transparent and as tall as the market determined and the City Council would allow. The 'old' AMP Building on the site of Mort's Wool Store soon followed. It was completed in 1961, at about the same time as the Cahill Expressway.

The transformation of this northern part of the city from its early status as a port into the dress circle of the business and financial centre was now under way, but the new buildings along Circular Quay East did not last as long as the nineteenth-century wool stores they replaced. Now, in turn, they have been demolished or refitted as residential or hotel accommodation, provoking much heated controversy about their bulk and appearance.

By 1955, North Sydney (which had gone into something of a decline in terms of residential status with the construction of the Harbour Bridge) started to find a new role in life as a commercial centre. Insurance companies such as the AMP and MLC began the move, and a land boom for commercial property in North Sydney followed. In fact, the MLC Building (1955) in Miller Street, North Sydney, designed by Harry Seidler, was the first postwar office building which used a modular, lightweight, curtain wall system of construction.[21] Many of the new modern buildings were designed without much architectural inspiration. As Leo

ABOVE: View of Sydney's central business district from Australia Square looking towards the southwest in 1967. The Ultimo power station (now the Powerhouse Museum) can be seen in the background to the right.

185

Schofield put it, most of the skyscrapers of the 1960s 'look as if they came out of a curtain wall catalogue'.

On the other hand, it was in the early postwar period that architects began to take a fresher and less derivative approach to domestic architecture. The Californian bungalow had dominated residential architecture for decades since the 1920s. One of the agitators for a new style of domestic architecture was Walter Bunning. His book *Homes in the Sun* advocated that the designs of homes should take into account the peculiarities of the Australian environment. Sunlight should be encouraged in winter and discouraged in summer, and houses should be designed to benefit from cooling breezes.

In the early postwar era, materials were hard to get, so decoration was abandoned in favour of functionality. Sydney Ancher and Harry Seidler were two architects practising in Sydney who advocated a move from the designs of the past. Later, in the 1960s, companies which designed and built project homes concentrated on architectural elements that adapted the house to its environment. Pergolas, verandas, increased glazing and the use of native plants were examples of this.

Transport patterns started to change in the early postwar period. By 1961, there were no more trams running in Sydney. The decline set in quickly when petrol rationing was abolished.[22] The auditor general reported in an unpublished internal document that the replacement of trams with buses was justified on financial grounds.[23] Buses, it was argued, were faster and more efficient, and less disruptive to traffic. They were not beholden to the paths of tramlines, so needed less special infrastructure. Today, many older Sydneysiders who still remember the trams are nostalgic about them, but, at the time, their demise was seen as a fine example of progress.

The city railway network was expanded in the 1950s when Circular Quay Station opened in 1956—the first new city railway station since Wynyard opened in 1932. Investment in transport infrastructure was, however, sporadic at best. No further railway lines were built in the inner-city area after 1956 for another twenty-one years when the Eastern Suburbs Railway to Bondi Junction was completed in 1977. On the other hand, suburban train travel became quieter and more user-friendly, with wide-scale electrification of the train lines as far as Lithgow, Campbelltown and Gosford. Sydney's private ferry companies, already knocked about by the opening of the Harbour Bridge, suffered again with the rising dominance of the motor car. Many commuters could now afford to drive to work. By the early 1970s, all the old ferry companies had passed into the state government's hands. The ferries themselves had become old and unreliable, and the fleet was not upgraded until the early 1980s.

In the fourteen years between 1947 and 1961, Sydney's population grew by more than a third, from 1.5 to 2.2 million.[24] In the next twenty years to 1981, Sydney's population increased by 50 per cent to 3.3 million. The age of convenience (and consumption) had truly arrived, indicated by the rise in the per capita consumption of electricity throughout the state from 776 kilowatt hours in 1947 to 2670 per capita in 1961. New South Wales's electricity grid, largely fuelled by coal from the Hunter Valley, was expanded to satisfy rising demand. A new dam, the Warragamba Dam, was built to increase the water supply. In the 1990s, it is becoming apparent that Sydney's water supply needs to be expanded yet again.

The high-water mark of Sydney's suburbanisation was in 1967 when the State Planning Authority (SPA) published its *Sydney Region—Growth and Change: Prelude to a Plan*. The Sydney area by then covered 370 square miles (960 square kilometres), compared with 240 square miles (620 square kilometres) in 1947.[25] The SPA blandly stated that the space needed for urban uses in the Sydney region would more than double in the next thirty years, and that infrastructure would just have to keep up with this requirement.[26] Now that the gaps to the north and south had been filled in, the only direction Sydney could grow was towards the west. The alternative of increasing the density of Sydney's then existing footprint was briefly discussed, and dismissed, without much examination of the issues, with the following words: 'Only a modest proportion of the population will wish to live in home units ... it is not wise to assume, at this stage, that much additional population capacity will result.'[27]

It was clear that money was no object in the late 1960s. The relative cost of extending new infrastructure services such as water, sewerage and electricity (as opposed to increasing the population density) was stated in the report. The comparisons were stark, but the economies of higher-density developments had no effect on the outcome. Cost was not considered a weighty enough factor to affect Sydney's planning.[28] The SPA advised that any new plan for Sydney would have to be more adaptable to the unexpected changes, such as population growth and the encroachment on the green belt that had blighted the County of Cumberland Scheme. The question the SPA never answered was: how flexible and adaptable can a plan be before it ceases to be one?

The SPA had the power to overturn council decisions, and compel councils to develop planning schemes. In 1967 the role of the City of Sydney Council was drastically eroded when the SPA was given the power to control developments of more than 45 metres in height. The SPA was delighted to use its wide powers to encourage development in the city, and this was the beginning of the biggest boom in building Sydney has ever witnessed, changing the city almost beyond recognition. Small laneways were sold off so bigger buildings could go up, and streets which had once been bathed in sunlight became sunless and windy canyons. Both the scale and the ambience of the city were transformed forever.

187

The Labor Party held control of the state parliament until 1965 when Robin Askin became Liberal premier, partly by stoking the political controversy over the construction of the Opera House. The Askin era was a low point in Sydney's political and planning history. Venality and greed were unrestrained and this had major consequences for the nature of some of the high-rise developments of the era. There are still many unfortunate legacies remaining within the city itself. The City Council euphemistically refers to these buildings as 'opportunity sites'. One of the few bright spots in the area of urban planning was the creation of many national parks, most notably the Sydney Harbour National Park.

The newly elected Liberal government led by Robin Askin shared Pat Hills's vision for the future of the central business district; it was a high-rise dream and it was not a pretty one. Askin sacked the (Labor) City Council in 1967, and the commissioners in charge of the City of Sydney adopted the government's point of view. Development application after development application was approved by the commissioners, and some of the city's greatest architectural atrocities were the result. Applications for millions of square metres of office space were approved.[29] Soon, buildings built between 1970 and 1976 accounted for 30 per cent of all office space available.[30] In the boom, which really lasted from 1968 to 1976, 210 buildings went up in the CBD and eighty-four of these went up after 1971.[31]

The 1950s were the time when the virtues of materialism and progress were rarely questioned. Life in the suburbs was the ideal of most members of the middle and working classes. Menzies astutely championed the voting inhabitants of this new world. They were his 'forgotten people', the frugal, austere, even self-denying middle class of the late 1940s and

1950s whose recreational existence was based around hearth and home, and saving for their children's welfare and education.

One of the first indicators of prosperity was the rising proportion of home ownership. The goal—sometimes expressed as a right—of home ownership is bundled up with the egalitarian aspiration of a 'fair go', and it still exists today as much as it did in the Menzies era. Home ownership was an automatic ticket to a higher social plane, even if it meant that, because of the high cost of housing, disposable income shrank. Governments encouraged home ownership with regulated low–interest-rate loans: the family home is the only asset which is immune from capital gains tax since it was introduced in 1985. The percentage of Australians who owned their own homes was growing steadily in the postwar boom period, from 52 per cent in 1947 to 71 per cent in 1966.[32] Another expression of this right to a fair go is the guarantee of a minimum wage for full-time employees. The wisdom of having a minimum wage is now controversial. From the middle of the 1970s onwards, it has been strongly criticised for adding to the level of unemployment.

The 1950s was the beginning of the era of consumerism. Suburban life could be made easier with the convenience of the Victa lawn mower, the Hills Hoist, the automatic washing machine, steam iron, new bigger and better refrigerators, toasters, electric kettles, and the supermarkets which made selecting the new myriad of household products so easy. Kleenex tissues, prepared Heinz baby food, clothes detergent and other 'essential' household cleaning products, and a maze of new Kellogg's breakfast cereals were all within arm's reach.

Consumerism was not only fun and convenient, but it also became more easily affordable, in theory anyway, with easy access to consumer credit such as hire purchase. Many of the banks set up their own finance company offshoots which could operate in this new growth area with little prudential supervision. The most important postwar consumer item, however, was the motor car. In 1948, the new affordable Holden, 'Australia's Own Car', was launched on the public. In fact, it was manufactured in Australia by an American motor giant, General Motors-Holden's, but the fact remained that owning this car, or something like it, became not only a suburban dream, but a necessity as well. The public transport network did not keep up with the postwar suburban sprawl. In the mid-1950s, 40 per cent of the people living in the County of Cumberland did not have access to public transport.[33] A new family pastime was now possible—the Sunday drive to the country or the beach. Meanwhile, motor vehicle registrations rose from nearly half a million in 1950 to 1.3 million in 1965. This was an average of one motor vehicle per family.[34] The increased pressure on the roads of the city was commensurately dramatic.

Members of the new generation of 'baby-boomer' Sydneysiders were more hedonistic than their parents. They quickly took to the new craze for surfboard riding (or the boys did anyway—the girls mostly just watched) and rock 'n roll. In 1955, radio station 2UE launched a 'Top 40' pop music format which was directed at the new teenage market. One early pop tour promoter, Lee Gordon, brought modern heroes such as Bill Haley and the Comets, and the Platters out to Sydney, where they performed at the stadium at Rushcutters Bay to excited young audiences. Sydney produced its own rock 'n roll legends as well: Johnny O'Keefe, Col Joye and the Joyboys, Little Patti, the Delltones, and Billy Thorpe and the Aztecs. Rock 'n roll came to television in the form of Johnny O'Keefe's 'Six O'Clock Rock' and Brian Henderson's 'Bandstand'. Teenagers were looking to make themselves different from their parents and their older brothers and sisters, as no other teenagers had been able to do before.

Early forms of teen culture such as 'bodgies' and 'widgies' appeared. They observed strict and rather extreme dress codes which caused much consternation among their elders. Some observers thought they heralded a dangerous wave of rebelliousness and disobedience. Bodgies and widgies used to hang around public places, go to milk bars and the movies in groups, and had as much fun as they could—and certainly more than their parents seemed to be having. As they grew older, these children of self-sacrificing parents brought about dramatic changes in popular attitudes and values.

The great sporting heroes of the mid-1950s were the tennis players—Lew Hoad and Ken Rosewall. In the following decade, John Newcombe and Tony Roche were the rising stars. Australia won the Davis Cup eight times in the 1950s. Its reputation as a nation of great tennis players has never reached such heights since. Other famous athletes, especially during the 1956 Melbourne Olympics, were swimmers Dawn Fraser, Lorraine Crapp, and Murray Rose, and runner Betty Cuthbert.

189

LEFT: Johnny O'Keefe, known as the 'Wild One', was one of Sydney's home-grown rock legends, with popular hits such as 'Shout' and 'Move Baby Move'.

It was not until the 1950s that governments became interested or involved in funding theatre, opera or ballet. In 1954 the Elizabethan Theatre Trust was established under the aegis of eminent economist and federal public servant H. C. 'Nugget' Coombs, *Sydney Morning Herald* editor and journalist J. D. Pringle and ABC supremo, Sir Charles Moses. The trust was the government-funded organisation from which the Australian Opera (now, since its merger with the Victorian State Opera, called Opera Australia) and the Australian Ballet were spawned. At the time of its creation, there was not, and never had been, a government-funded national theatre. Its Sydney venue was the old, Victorian-style Elizabethan Theatre at Newtown. The idea of a national theatre never worked. Today, the leading publicly funded theatre in Sydney is the Sydney Theatre Company (STC). It was founded by the Wran government and is based at the Wharf Theatre, Walsh Bay. Piers Four and Five were specially remodelled for the STC and the Sydney Dance Company by architect Vivian Fraser.

In the 1950s and early 1960s, the locus of much cultural activity was Sydney University, then simply known as 'the University' for want of any rivals. The university in those days was, in the words of Leo Schofield:

> full of people who wanted to be glamorous personalities who made much of being 'identities'. There was an entire group of people who were interested in politics, journalism and the theatre. The university was a wonderful, languid and relaxed, leafy retreat. There was little pressure to pass exams—although the swots always did.'[35]

The objective of these proto-celebrities, who included Schofield, present critics and writers Clive James and Robert Hughes, actors John Bell and John Gaden, and film director Bruce Beresford, was to enliven the dull, grey and bourgeois atmosphere of Sydney. In those days, most of the commercial theatre on offer was run-of-the-mill. The main commercial theatre, the Theatre Royal, staged biennial Gilbert and Sullivan seasons, and imported the more successful mainstream West End plays from London. There was the Independent Theatre, which was run by Doris Fitton, but there was also a demand for the amateur theatrical productions of the Sydney University Dramatic Society (SUDS). New members of this and similar societies were signed up on Orientation Day. In those days, Commemoration ('Commem') Day in April was a big event, not only at the university, but in the city as well. Students would dress up and parade around the streets in a light-hearted and spirited fashion. The Commem Day parade tradition had died by the mid-1960s.

Many of our brightest university students left Sydney for overseas, sometimes for a few years, and sometimes, as in the case of Clive James and Robert Hughes, permanently. As Schofield put it: 'It was almost as if we had a chip in our heads that said we had to go leave the country.'[36] Luckily for Sydney, Schofield was back after five years away in the mid-1960s. In the 1950s and early 1960s, career advancement was much easier if you had the great *cachet* of overseas experience, no matter what that experience was—waiting tables, pulling beer or minor clerical work. This deference to foreign life and foreign culture *per se* is often referred to as Australia's 'cultural cringe'. It was derived from Australia's early colonial status, when London and England were the source of all the finer things in life. The cringe proved hard to erase.

One small but vocal group of people who did not agree or accept the political and social conformity of the 1950s and early 1960s was the 'Sydney Push', whose guiding light was libertarian-minded professor of philosophy at the University of Sydney, John Anderson. The push was the postwar version of bohemian life in Sydney. It was easy for members of the push to ignore the *mores* of the day: for the most part, they operated in a self-contained, libertarian social milieu. The push boldly appropriated the collective term used by the many groups of inner-city larrikins in the late nineteenth and early twentieth centuries. It swam against the strong tide of mainstream, often wowserish values. Members of the push were sceptics and anarchists, philosophers and punters. Their interest and preoccupation with intellectual discussion also set them apart. Push women were pre-women's movement sexual libertarians who lived their lives the way unrestrained bohemians often do. They congregated in pubs around the city, most notably the Royal George Hotel in Sussex Street and the Tudor Hotel in Phillip Street, thereby perpetuating, in their choice of venue, the essential 'blokey-ness' of Sydney culture, sexual promiscuity notwithstanding. Ambitious career plans were not highly regarded. One of the core members, Roelof Smilde, worked as a wharf labourer. Other members of the push included Darcy Waters, poet Harry Hooton, film producer Margaret Fink, writer Frank Moorhouse, journalist Lillian Roxon and academics Germaine Greer and Liz Fell. In a sense, they were the harbingers for the more widely dispersed mood of social dissent and scepticism about traditional values which emerged in the middle of the 1960s.[37]

191

CHAPTER EIGHT

THE PAST THIRTY YEARS

Sydney has much to be proud of. Our city has an attractive natural and built environment. It is generally regarded as one of the world's most livable cities. We have a skilled labour force, high quality 'hard' infrastructure and an improving reputation as a place to do business. We are also experiencing a pre-Olympic growth period.

Our multi-cultural population is contributing to our reputation as an Asian hub. The latest *Fortune* magazine survey of the most improved cities for business in Asia over the past five to ten years ranked Sydney second.

Price Waterhouse Coopers Report for the Committee of Sydney 1998

MENZIES RETIRED from office before the political dissent and confrontations of the 1960s and 1970s became apparent. The new generation of baby-boomers challenged the traditional values and assumptions of their parents, and what they saw as dull suburban lives. Through television, the younger generation could observe and then rapidly adopt overseas cultural influences such as the Beatles, Rolling Stones and the hippie movement more quickly than was ever possible in the radio era of the 1930s and 1940s.

The political dissent and defiance of the younger generation were expressed in Sydney in the late 1960s and early 1970s during the Vietnam War, and later in the battle by residents' action groups, environmentalists and the Builders' Labourers Federation to preserve precious parts of Sydney. Sydneysiders have a lot to thank these resident activists for today. Without their agitation and intervention, parts of the inner city such as The Rocks and Millers Point (now one of Sydney's biggest tourist attractions) and Woolloomooloo would have been lost forever.

From the 1970s onwards, the social and demographic effects of large-scale non–English-speaking immigration, and the abandonment of the White Australia policy had a large, colourful and positive impact on life in Sydney. The old parochial, Anglo-Celtic intolerance towards difference sometimes re-emerges, but is much weaker than it once was. Sydney is now a culturally richer, livelier and more interesting place to live than ever before.

Many Australians did not agree with the federal Liberal government led by Menzies and Harold Holt that Australia should be involved in the Vietnam War, and in particular that young men should be conscripted into the army by means of the *National Service Act*. Conscription has never been a simple issue in Australian politics. Australia's involvement in the Vietnam War was the outcome of the strong anti-communist fervour of the 1950s and 1960s, and Australia's reliance on the United States for international defence, evidenced in the ANZUS defence treaty of 1951.

In 1962, Menzies sent army instructors to Vietnam at the request of the US government. National service was actually introduced in 1964 as a response to political unrest between Indonesia and Malaysia, in the unpredictable years when Sukarno was president of Indonesia. In 1965, an infantry battalion was committed to Vietnam. The *National Service Act* made it compulsory for all men of more than eighteen years of age to register for a ballot that

193

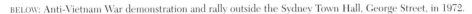

BELOW: Anti-Vietnam War demonstration and rally outside the Sydney Town Hall, George Street, in 1972.

determined whether they would be called up or not. Those who refused to comply with the outcome of the ballot were labelled conscientious objectors.

Australia's involvement in the Vietnam War was unpopular. Many Australians were affronted by Prime Minister Holt's fawning catch cry that Australia should go 'All the way with LBJ'.[1] There were many demonstrations between 1966 and 1972, some of which were peaceful and some of which were less so. In 1966, Premier Robin Askin inflamed anti-war dissent when he urged police to 'ride over the bastards' at an anti-war rally held during President Johnson's visit to Australia. The anti-war movement intensified between 1967 and 1971.

The biggest year for the anti-war movement was 1970. The creation of the Vietnam Moratorium campaign in March brought a greater level of political organisation. Moratorium Day took place on 8 May 1970. It was one of Sydney's biggest and most peaceful protests, with about 20 000 participants. There were 1700 police on duty, and only seven arrests were made. High school and university students marched in the streets, and lunch-time rallies were held around the city which office workers could attend, such as at Macquarie Place and Hyde Park, where a large trade union meeting took place. There was only one ugly incident in Hunter Street where a protester was dragged away by two police and allegedly hit.

September 1970 was another big month for anti-war demonstrations. On 18 September approximately 8000 moratorium demonstrators battled with police and there were 200 arrests. Leading moratorium figure and draft resister, Mike Jones was arrested after being beaten repeatedly by police in the doorway of the Regent Street police station. The march became even uglier when police, using loudspeakers, directed marchers away from the Town Hall and towards Hyde Park. The police then formed a line that prevented access to the Town Hall, and a crush and *mêlée* followed.

By June 1971, the temperature had cooled as the Australian military presence in Vietnam was winding down. Marches were more peaceful. At one rally in Hyde Park, the peace activist and well-known US paediatrician Benjamin Spock spoke to an audience of between 5000 and 6000. Spock had written an authoritative book on child care and development which the parents of younger baby-boomers had used as the bible for raising their now rebellious children.

The mood of political dissension was not limited to the Vietnam issue. In 1971, there were violent demonstrations against the South African policy of apartheid when the Springboks rugby team toured Australia. A member of the Builders' Labourers Federation (BLF) tried to sabotage one of the Test matches at the Sydney Sportsground in Moore Park by cutting the goal posts down.

Another major issue to emerge in the late 1960s and early 1970s was the women's movement. There had been faint stirrings of the emerging battle for equal rights in 1966 when married women were finally allowed to become permanent employees in the public service. Then, in 1969, the Arbitration Commission decided that women should be entitled to equal pay for equal work. The pragmatic response to many employers was to downgrade the pay

194

scales of all jobs in which women were heavily concentrated.[2] In 1972, the injustice of this was reversed when a new equal pay was won before the commission. All federal awards imposed the same wage rate for similar jobs. The Women's Electoral Lobby was formed in 1972 to persuade governments to adopt policies which redressed the gender-based imbalance within society, in particular, the issue of equal pay. The principles of the women's movement were adopted with great gusto by the federal Labor government between 1972 and 1975. In 1974, the minimum wage for women was made equal to the minimum male wage. The government also promoted many women to high-profile positions. However, more entrenched forms of sexual discrimination are still apparent in Australian society. These are as hard to legislate against as they are elsewhere in the world.

In 1970, one-time member of the Sydney Push, Germaine Greer, published her ground-breaking *Female Eunuch*, and life for many families was never quite the same. Its relatively libertarian, even anarchic ideas, appealed to many women in Sydney and throughout Australia. In the same year, the abortion issue reached a climax in Sydney. Under political pressure from anti-abortionists, the police raided a well-known and well-run abortion clinic in Bondi, which they had long turned a blind eye to. Three doctors and the owners were charged. The judge who heard the case, Aaron Levine, decided that there had been no breach of the law: abortion was justified if continuing a pregnancy would cause physical or mental harm to the mother, as certified by two medical practitioners. This law still applies in New South Wales. The Right to Life movement has never gathered enough political momentum in liberal New South Wales to bring about any changes to it.

Women were drawn more closely to the focus of power in the 1980s with the considerable assistance of the Hawke and Keating governments from 1983 to 1996. The Office of the Status of Women (OSW) played a big role in institutionalising the women's movement. Affirmative action programs were adopted in the public service and encouraged elsewhere.

195

For Sydneysiders, perhaps the most significant popular cause of the early 1970s—in an era where there were so many forms of dissent—was the reaction against the plans some property developers had for Sydney. Many developers and politicians thought that the decrepit and decayed inner-city suburbs should be replaced or sacrificed to road widening and development wherever they thought appropriate. Entire suburbs and precincts such as Woolloomooloo, Victoria Street in Potts Point, Paddington, Millers Point and The Rocks were faced with modification and extinction. But by the end of the 1960s, opposition was growing to these radical plans. Not everyone agreed that the old Georgian and Victorian architecture was worthless.

The artist Sali Herman was partly responsible for showing Sydneysiders the beauty of the past. Herman was born in Switzerland and came to Australia in 1936, wisely foreseeing the tide of Nazism and anti-Semitism in Europe. At first he worked as an art dealer, then took up painting, which he had studied in Europe. His main subject matter was the Victorian architecture and streetscape around Kings Cross, Potts Point, The Rocks, Woolloomooloo and Paddington. His painting of the McElhone Stairs that run from Potts Point's Victoria Street down to Woolloomooloo won the Wynne Prize for landscape painting in 1944. This was an unlikely subject, at the time, for a landscape painting.

Herman lived in Kings Cross and won the Wynne Prize three more times, using as his subjects Sydney's older buildings and streets.

Another ingredient that awakened Sydney's consciousness of its architectural past was the growing popularity of Victoriana in the hippie era of the late 1960s. The revolt against the wishes of the developers and the state government of the day was partly also a cultural reaction by baby-boomers against the creeping dominance of grey suburbs and the transformation of the city's skyline during the long and untrammelled building boom of the 1960s and early 1970s.

The first outbreak of activity by a residents' action group was in Paddington to protest against the widening of Jersey Road. As result of this proposal and others which would have seen terrace housing demolished to make way for blocks of flats, the Paddington Society was formed. Mahla Pearlman (now Chief Judge of the Land and Environment Court) and Leo Schofield were two of the early prime movers. By 1970, many more residents' action groups had been formed. One on the North Shore was opposing the occupation by Readymix Concrete of harbour foreshore land belonging to AGL. There was much (ultimately unsuccessful) agitation in Balmain against a proposed chemical plant and the construction of a container terminal at White Bay.

Then, in the middle of 1971, the BLF led by Jack Mundey imposed a 'green ban' on the destruction of Kellys Bush at Hunters Hill for a large residential development. This was the first time a union had intervened in an issue which did not directly affect the position of its members. In fact, imposing green bans was not in the short-term economic interests of the BLF as no work would be available for building workers on sites which were affected. So the improbable alliance of middle-class residents and left-wing unionists was created. Soon the green bans spread. By the end of 1974, much of Potts Point and Woolloomooloo was affected, as was The Rocks. Another groundswell of local activism was the Save the Parks campaign which preserved Centennial Park from becoming a large car park.

In October 1973, just as the building boom was starting to teeter on the brink of the economic abyss, green-ban and residents' action–group protests reached a head at The Rocks and Victoria Street, Potts Point. There, resident activism was combined with left-wing political agitation. Politically inspired squatters moved in to protect the housing after the harassed and frustrated tenants had given up and moved on to less contentious accommodation. The police took the side of the developers in the conflict, and demonstrations and rioting ensued.

The battle was over in late 1973, when the state branch of the BLF fell under the control of more conservative political forces led by Norm Gallagher. Although the green bans remained in force, the potency of the resistance to development weakened, at the same time

196

as many of the developers such as Sid Londish and Frank Theeman were feeling the financial distress brought on by the collapse of the economy. The halcyon days of populist and politically radical agitation against demolition of the inner city were at an end.

Sydney's property boom between 1968 and 1974 was the biggest in its history, even by the standard of previous booms such as that of the 1870s, the 1880s and the 1920s.[3] The government's policy helped the boom along, of course, but there were many other factors at work. One of them was the mining boom of the era, the biggest since the 1850s. This had a positive effect on Australia's terms of trade, and therefore on the level of optimism about Australia's economic prospects.

The economic boom fed into the property market. New and bigger financial institutions, stockbrokers and merchant banks needed bigger and better offices, and more lawyers and accountants, which also led to an increase in the demand for office space. Many financial institutions lent large sums of money to property developers. Much of the high level of capital inflow went into the property market and the booming share market. Sydney was at the epicentre of this economic boom, and its property market heated up.

British property developers such as Abbey Capital, the Grosvenor Estate and MEPC saw great opportunity in Sydney's CBD. The return on investment was higher and rents, they thought, could only move up. In the short term, they were right. Even staid old industrial companies such as CSR went into property development. Financial institutions and insurance companies formed joint ventures and other partnerships with property developers. AMP joined forces with developer Stocks and Holdings to build the Imperial Arcade (1966). The big banks formed subsidiary finance companies which were not constrained by banking regulations in the same manner as the banks. This way, they could more easily share the profits to be made in the property business and be more readily exposed to the consequences of any downturn or credit squeeze.

From late 1971, the federal Liberal government, in a flawed bid to buy votes at the federal election in 1972, lowered taxes and raised pensions. This led to a huge increase in the money supply. Inflationary pressure built up. Then, in December 1972, E. G. (Gough) Whitlam led the Labor Party into office for the first time since 1949. The new Labor government went further still and introduced worthy, but costly, social reforms, such as equal pay and greater expenditure on public housing. Money supply kept rising; the boom, fed by money supply and high liquidity, continued. The property market kept on the boil until the oil shock of 1973, when the price of oil quadrupled. Inflation took off and interest rates soon followed.

Whitlam then took another bold move and reduced tariff protection across the board by 25 per cent in a single step—which was brave, if not suicidal. Until then, Australia had been one of the world leaders in the high level of protection given to its manufacturing industries.

Many industries could not cope with this strong dose of international competition from cheaper foreign imports and had to close their doors forever. The de-industrialisation of the Australian economy began, creating high levels of suffering and hardship. Many industrial

ABOVE: Union leader Jack Mundey campaigning for 'Green Bans' at a protest meeting at the Newcastle Hotel in 1972. Mundey imposed the work bans in many parts of the city, thereby preserving areas and buildings such as this hotel in The Rocks from wholesale demolition.

198

sites across Sydney were closed, and for many the nature of work changed forever. For the more unfortunate ones, long-term unemployment would become a way of life. Some of the people most affected were the core Labor working-class voters. The Labor Party held office for only three years.

From the middle of 1973, the Sydney property market became jittery. Money fled the country and interest rates kept rising. Property was no longer changing hands as quickly as it had been. Some property companies had liquidity crises on their hands, and many of them, highly geared and reliant on easy loan finance to repay their short-term borrowings, lost the battle for survival. In August 1974, one of the biggest developers of the day, Mainline, crashed, despite AMP and MLC's attempts to shore up its share price. The company had been responsible for developing Goldfields House, Centrepoint and the Exchange Centre in Bridge Street.

A few weeks later, Cambridge Credit collapsed as well. Later casualties of the shake-up in the property market were Hungarian-born knight, Sir Paul Strasser's Parkes Developments (1977) and the finance company Australian Securities Limited (1979). Some bank-owned finance companies such as CAGA, owned by the Commercial Banking Company, only survived because their parent companies propped them up.

By 1978, however, rents were rising again, the supply of property was falling and property was once again on the move. This time there were opportunities in the new district centres such as Chatswood, St Leonards and North Sydney. This was also when the early signs of

ABOVE: Aerial view of the wharves at Walsh Bay. These wharves were built in the early twentieth century after the outbreak of bubonic plague in 1900. The new wharves were better suited to the larger cargo ships that dominated maritime trade until the advent of containerised shipping in the 1970s, which transformed Sydney's wharf facilities once again. (*Marcus Clinton*)

RIGHT: The Harbour Bridge and Circular Quay West today. (*Marcus Clinton*)

ABOVE: Lyons Terrace at Liverpool Street at the southern end of Hyde Park in 1844. View from Lyons Terrace, Hyde Park, Sydney, New South Wales, *1844, George Edwards Peacock (Rex Nan Kivell Collection, National Library of Australia)*

LEFT: Aerial view from the North Shore looking south over the northern approaches to the Harbour Bridge and the city beyond. Botany Bay, further to the south, can be seen in the background. *(Marcus Clinton)*

ABOVE: The Macquarie Gates, part of the original Macquarie Wall, built in 1810, which, rather like the 'pale' in Ireland, was built to protect respectable residents within and keep unruly (in this case convict) elements without. Only a small section of the wall remains standing today. *(Marcus Clinton)*

ABOVE: View of the Harbour of Port Jackson, and the country between Sydney and the Blue Mountains, New South Wales, *c. 1823, Major James Taylor (Image Library, State Library of NSW)*
BELOW: Millers Point and the Flagstaff, *c. 1840, Joseph Fowles (Image Library, State Library of NSW)*

luxury high-rise residential construction in the city could be seen, in the form of the Connaught in Liverpool Street and The Quay apartments.

Many suburbs that had been the heartland of early postwar growth and industrialisation were hard hit from the 1970s. Motor vehicle plants in inner-city Waterloo and Pagewood closed, as did many smaller factories and workshops.[4] The manufacturing industry accounted for only 17 per cent of the workforce in 1986, down from 31 per cent in 1971. In the same period there was a parallel growth in the tertiary services sector: finance, the professions and the communications industry. Manufacturing moved out of the western and southern fringes of the CBD, and the city's share of the retailing dollar shrank, causing many shops, such as Anthony Hordern's in the southern part of the city, to close.

By the middle of the 1970s, there was a popular reaction against the reformist tendencies of the federal Labor government. The government was moving too fast and many people found it hard to keep up. Laws that improved the legal status of women and disadvantaged members of the community were being imposed too quickly for some people's comfort. The economy was in a bad state as well, with high inflation and unemployment. Whitlam was sacked in dramatic circumstances by the Governor General, Sir John Kerr, who exercised his reserve powers on the ground that Whitlam's government could not ensure the passage of Supply Bills through the senate. The dismissal of the Whitlam government by the unelected Queen's representative, Sir John Kerr, divided the nation, and led to demonstrations and marches. It was reminiscent of Sir Philip Game's sacking of Jack Lang in the 1930s, and embroiled the office and role of the governor general in even greater controversy.

The manner of Whitlam's dismissal did not have any effect on the electoral outcome. The subsequent federal election was a landslide win for Malcolm Fraser's Liberal–National Party coalition. Fraser held onto power for eight years and opinion is divided as to whether his promise to 'turn on the lights' was kept.

Almost miraculously, six months after Labor's 1975 electoral defeat, the voters of New South Wales elected a Labor leader, Neville Wran. Wran's Labor Party held office in New South Wales until 1988. His term in office, which lasted from 1976 to 1986, was a great era for Sydney, the likes of which had not been seen for quite a while, possibly since the centenary in 1888.[5] Neville Wran is one of the major political figures in twentieth-century Sydney. Balmain-born, Wran, a Queen's counsel, succeeded as a Labor politician because of his sharp political skills and his pragmatism. He was also aware of the importance of enhancing the culture and general quality of life in Sydney and New South Wales.

For the first time, issues of preserving the past, as well as planning for the future, were addressed seriously by the state government. Wran was ably assisted by the state government's long-term *über* bureaucrat, Gerry Gleeson (head of the Premier's Department), a young Laurie Brereton (the enthusiastic Minister for Public Works) and Paul Landa (Planning Minister), among others. The government adopted the fight to preserve historically significant

199

ABOVE: A cruise ship berthed at Circular Quay's Overseas Passenger Terminal. Much of Circular Quay was remodelled for the Bicentenary in 1988. A walkway now runs along the foreshore from the Opera House, around Circular Quay, to the wharves at Walsh Bay on the western side of the southern pylon of the Harbour Bridge.

architecture; the *Heritage Act* was passed, making it possible to prohibit the demolition of historic buildings. The Heritage Council was created, as was the Historic Houses Trust, a body charged with the task of maintaining buildings of high heritage value. Heritage issues were no longer cast onto the political fringe and dependent on union support. A consequence is that there is less direct citizen-based involvement in planning and heritage issues than there was in the heady days of the BLF's green bans. Another achievement during the term of the Wran government was the reform of the Legislative Council into a democratically elected upper house. Up until then, members of the Legislative Council were still appointed, not elected.

There was every good reason to improve the city. The Bicentenary of 1988 was approaching, and, perhaps even more significantly, there was federal government funding to pay for public works to commemorate the 200 years of European settlement in Australia. Sydney would, as the cradle of European settlement, take centre stage on Australia Day when the eyes of the world would be focused on the nation.

Improvements to Sydney for the Bicentenary included the extensions to Parliament House and the State Library in Macquarie Street, the renovation of Hyde Park Barracks and the Mint, additions to the Art Gallery of New South Wales, and the remodelling of Circular Quay and the Opera House forecourt. Most controversial of all was the decision to transform the disused industrial land at Darling Harbour into a major work of urban renewal. Public access to the harbour was improved with new walking tracks, and Bicentennial Park at Homebush, the first major new park since the Centenary in 1888, was dedicated. This park was the first stage of the long-term regeneration of the Homebush Bay area.

There was, as there nearly always is, a political reaction against the grand vision and the scale of public works—which are never cheap. Wran retired from office in 1986, leaving the city a far better place than he had found it ten years before. Sydney became, under Wran's administration, a city that could proudly assert that it had shaken off its dull, grey, provincial mantle. As a result of these Bicentennial-induced improvements, the tourist industry has become, since the 1980s, an increasingly important source of revenue and employment. The optimism of the 1980s about Sydney's great qualities and its rosy economic future as an important regional centre in the then booming Asia-Pacific region coincided with the financial excesses of the late 1980s that swept the developed world.

The best indication of Sydney's transformation is its new-found popularity as a tourist destination, particularly for Asian tourists. In 1995, more than 2.1 million foreign tourists visited Sydney, and there were another 6.1 million visits by non–Sydney resident Australians. In 1996, 1997 and 1998, Sydney was voted Tourist Destination of the Year by the magazine *International Traveller*. This could never have happened without the physical improvements to the city that took place during the Wran years, and the contribution of Sydney's non–English-speaking residents in enhancing Sydney's culture. From 1988, the phenomenon of urban revival and renewal has continued, if not with the same gusto, then steadily enough but without the same highly engaged involvement on the part of state government—with the possible exception of government projects associated with the Olympics.

The works associated with the Olympics will be heavily concentrated at the primary Olympic site at Homebush. After the Olympics, a new 400-hectare Millennium Park will be created around Homebush Bay, near Bicentennial Park. Many of the developments at Homebush have been undertaken and financed by private enterprise. The biggest example of this is the Olympic Stadium. Another focus of building activity in preparation for the Olympics is at Darling Harbour. The City Council is also spending more than $20 million improving the public spaces and thoroughfares in the city, including George Street between Town Hall and Railway Square, Pitt, Castlereagh and Market streets, Chifley and Wynyard squares, and Central Station, as well as the restoration and renovation of the Customs House at Circular Quay.

One of the most highly charged issues of the late 1990s has been the nature and scale of redevelopment of the harbour foreshore, at Circular Quay East in particular. Some of the passions that had last been witnessed almost a generation ago during the era of the green bans have re-emerged. The appearance of the building cruelly dubbed 'the Toaster' on the foreshore of Sydney Cove damaged the faith many Sydneysiders had in the planning process. How could such a thing have come to pass? How did it slip through the net of the local and state governments and the public?

ABOVE: Circular Quay East in the mid-1980s, before the advent of the controversial second generation of twentieth-century buildings, showing the line of private developments erected along Macquarie Street in the 1950s and 1960s.

Approval was granted by the Central Sydney Planning Committee (CSPC) in September 1994 by an overwhelming (eight to one) majority. There was consensus between the state government and the Council of the City of Sydney that the proposal was the best that could be achieved. The process of winning planning consent had dragged on for five years through a change of government in 1988 when the Labor Party lost to the Nick Greiner–led Liberal coalition. The developer's original idea was to build two 50-storey office towers. Over time, the height of the development was scaled down. The new development was stumpier (about half the height) but chunkier than the previous buildings on the site had been. At the time that planning permission was given, the proposal was described by planners at the City of Sydney as 'an architecturally restrained and elegant addition to Circular Quay'. The council was paid about $5.5 million for the part of the roadway it sold to the developers.[6]

The council was not alone in its enthusiasm for the project, as finally approved. The Royal Australian Institute of Architects supported it.[7] Even the *Sydney Morning Herald* editorialised in favour of the development:

> The latest proposals for the redevelopment of East Circular Quay meet virtually all the aesthetic and practical requirements demanded by such [an] historic and visually valuable site. This is a remarkable achievement.[8]

One dissenting voice was the chairman of the National Trust's conservation committee, Peter Johnson, who argued that the quality of the architecture was not good enough.[9]

Those who were part of the decision-making process argued that they had little alternative. The land was not publicly owned, and the cost of resuming it would have been prohibitive.

The government did not offer to step in to swap the land or resume it, so the only room to manoeuvre was to pursue diminished heights for the series of buildings. The controversy over what has been built at Circular Quay East has, for the time being at least, energised opinions and attitudes against the destruction of the foreshore and the ambience of this harbour city, and created an atmosphere of vigilant concern about new developments. For many, it is harsh consolation to be told that the development could have been much worse.

Defenders of Circular Quay East are not easy to find, although, in all fairness, the CSPC and the City Council did the best job it could, in the circumstances, to constrain the magnitude of the building. Everyone's attention was focused on height, not footprint or bulk. The federal government even stepped in to ensure that the height of the building was kept to a minimum as part of an agreement with the City of Sydney. In return for the council agreeing to share the permanent air-space rights above the new buildings on Circular Quay East with the federal government, they granted a long-term lease over the Customs House. It has turned out that even Jørn Utzon, architect of the Sydney Opera House, anticipated that buildings of about thirteen storeys would line Circular Quay East. The final act in the Circular Quay East saga was the decision by the John Howard government not to set aside part of the Federation Fund to resume the land. Perhaps, in the longer term, the issue will be whether the buildings of Circular Quay East are significantly better, or worse, than what stood before.

203

In 1997 and 1998, Sydney's collective angst about planning was transferred to vocal concerns about the way in which the finger wharves at Walsh Bay will be restored and redeveloped, and the extent of the building works to the Conservatorium of Music in the Botanic Gardens. Opinion is divided over how much architectural and developmental interference there should be at Walsh Bay. Sadly, too much interference is, in some circumstances, a less desirable outcome than total demolition. Concern about Walsh Bay has also been elevated by redevelopment of the finger wharf in Woolloomooloo Bay.

At Walsh Bay, an intelligent compromise between the economic aspirations of the developers and preserving the heritage of some of the old wharves there is required. One outcome of the rise in public concern about the redevelopment along the harbour and the Parramatta River is the move by the Minister for Urban Affairs and Planning, Craig Knowles, to create an advisory panel of eminent architects to consider strategic design issues for the foreshores. In August 1998, Knowles took the further step of taking control of many significant sites around the harbour and Parramatta River. Any overall 'master-plans' for those sites will have to be approved by the state government before being adopted by local councils. For many of the most significant sites—for example, the defence sites on North, Middle and Georges heads and around Sydney Cove—the state government will have to approve not only master-plans, but any specific redevelopment proposals as well. The sometimes bewildering maze of different governmental authorities, local and state, has become easier to negotiate with the amalgamation of the Sydney Cove Authority, the Darling Harbour Authority and the CityWest Development Corporation into one entity, the Sydney Harbour Foreshores Authority. This authority also controls the use and development of significant harbour sites.

The growth in Sydney's population in the period from 1961 to 1981 was taking place even further out than in the period up to 1961. In its 1967 strategic plan, the Sydney Planning Authority nominated future population-growth areas on the ever-expanding periphery. These included Gosford–Wyong, Campbelltown, Fairfield and the northwestern fringe of Sydney around Castle Hill and Rouse Hill. As such, the plan became a valuable guide for property developers. More and more semi-rural land was gobbled up. The population in the inner- and middle-ring suburbs was stable, or in decline.

There has been, since the late 1980s, a more concerned attitude towards Sydney's physical growth than the attitude which prevailed in the 1960s. No one believes—least of all state governments—that Sydney can afford, on either economic or environmental grounds, to spread indefinitely. In 1988, the Department of Urban Affairs and Planning published the successor to the high-growth, high-sprawl 1967 vision of the growth of Sydney published by the Sydney Planning Authority. In the new plan, the objective of higher-density development was spelt out for the first time since 1948. Density would be built up by decreasing the average size of lots of new subdivisions, and increasing the permissible density of houses in built-up areas. Certain areas were earmarked for intensive development: especially the northwestern sector around Rouse Hill and Baulkham Hills. A new industrial park there was planned to provide valuable employment opportunities. With the 1988 strategic plan, access to public transport (in the form of the railway line to Windsor) was an important factor in selecting this area for future growth. Other areas for future expansion are the Central Coast area around Wyong and Tuggerah, and the Camden–Campbelltown region.

Another priority is to slow the westward sprawl of the city by encouraging medium-density housing in the inner and middle suburbs. The Department of Urban Affairs and Planning has estimated that 10 000 houses must be built in these suburbs if the sprawl is to be contained. Land at Concord, Bankstown, Randwick, South Sydney, Auburn, Ashfield, Ryde, Turramurra, Paddington, Manly, Pyrmont, Ultimo and Botany, much of which was formerly industrial, has been identified as suitable.

Planning the containment of the sprawl is one thing. Making it happen, however, is another. Development of Parramatta as a second central business district is another important objective of the state government. It became even more important with the development of another urban strategy called 'Cities for the 21st Century' in 1993. Parramatta lies close to the demographic centre of Sydney. Public works there like the Riverside Stadium are calculated to provide the same services as are available closer to the city. Commercial activity in western subregional centres such as Liverpool, Mt Druitt and Blacktown is also being encouraged. Meanwhile, however, the cost of housing in Sydney is higher than it is anywhere else in Australia, and rising at a much greater rate than inflation.[10]

204

The issue of how to limit the physical growth of Sydney will never be resolved to everyone's satisfaction. The city is one of the least densely built-up cities of a comparable (or larger) size. The Sydney statistical area covers more than 12 000 square kilometres. State governments try to do their best to create a framework that will contain the city, but they are pilloried by the combined forces of their political opponents in state parliament, on the one hand, and local government and local interest groups on the other.

Local interest groups and councils are the ones who most stridently disagree with anything that involves change, or any deviation from their regional version of the suburban norm. As negative as this is for the objective of containing Sydney within reasonable limits, their point of view is not impossible to comprehend. For them, medium-density housing is synonymous with lower cost housing, and the consequent decline in socio-economic status of the neighbourhood. Any move away from the standard quarter-acre block is a deviation from the social ideal that has persisted in Sydney since the early decades of the twentieth century. It is firmly embedded in popular culture and is very hard to dislodge.

The Liberal government that held office from 1988 to 1995 tried to contain the urban sprawl by permitting the subdivision of suburban blocks. This would encourage dual occupancy, and denser settlement and housing. The plan was not warmly received by local interest groups. Local councils, as a rule, do not appreciate the urban policies of state governments being foisted upon them. The government's policy was criticised as nothing more than an opportunity for some to make windfall gains by selling their property either before or after it had been subdivided and redeveloped. Then, in 1993, the government held a competition to promote environmentally responsible medium-density housing.

The local residents of the outer suburb of St Clair were very unhappy with the proposal for their area. Luckily for them, they lived in a marginal electorate. The local member of parliament persuaded the planning minister not to proceed, but still lost her seat in the next state election. As the example of St Clair shows, the greatest reaction against medium-density housing comes from the parts of Sydney where it is most greatly needed—on the margins of subdivision areas. Another example is Wyong on the Central Coast, where the cost of building infrastructure such as roads, sewerage, electricity, schools and hospitals is high—even before the environmental cost of consuming ever-expanding chunks of Sydney's bushland is taken into account.

In 1996, the Labor government tried a gentler approach. In order to dispel the perception of medium-density housing as being cheap and undesirable, models for denser development were designed so that there is a maximum amount of sunlight and individuality for each dwelling and a minimum of interference with the existing suburban streetscape. Each local government authority had the task of demonstrating how it was promoting medium-density housing—otherwise the state government would step in and show them the way and rezone areas for denser development. Most of the councils in the Sydney area have demonstrated to the satisfaction of the Department of Urban Affairs and Planning that they have plans to encourage medium-density housing.

Further in towards the old centre of the city, the results of this shift in policy towards denser inner-city development are evident. One development is at Raleigh Park, Kensington (the site of a former cigarette factory), and along the former industrial land at South Dowling Street and Rushcutters Bay. Other examples are at Pyrmont and the southern and western sectors of the CBD. Developments such as The Peak on top of Paddy's Markets, the residential development of hundreds of apartments on the western corridor of the city, and Harry Seidler's Horizon apartments at Darlinghurst (built on land formerly occupied by the ABC) are typical examples of this. Lend Lease has a large plan for medium-density development of the old CSR industrial site on the tip of the Pyrmont peninsula called Jackson's Landing.

It is the present boom which has facilitated the construction of the inner-city apartments, and they have had a major impact on the appearance and ambience of central Sydney in the past ten years. The economic recession of the late 1980s and 1990s meant that there was an oversupply of commercial floor space in the city, so many developers decided to convert their property to residential use. While the rental value might not be so high, at least tenants were easier to find in uncertain economic times. Residential developments can also be sold off the plan. There has been a shift in council policy in favour of residential development with the Living City plan.[11]

The Department of Urban Affairs and Planning expects the population of the CBD to rise from about 7300 in 1995 to almost 40 000 in 2021, which would make the population growth rate in the city higher than that of any other local government area in the Sydney Statistical Region.[12]

One of the most active companies in the inner-city residential building boom is Meriton Apartments. Meriton, founded and owned by Russian-born Harry Triguboff, has been a big player in the apartment-building business since 1962. The company has left an indelible mark upon Sydney. Parts of Sydney which have been, or are in the process of becoming, 'Meritonised' include the city fringe and particularly Pyrmont, where the otherwise low skyline makes the additions of these new buildings easy to identify. There are many old industrial sites in Meriton's inventory beyond the city fringe. Some of them are the old Clark Rubber site at Caringbah, Ashton Square at Rockdale, near Hornsby railway station and at Ashfield on former industrial land once owned by AWA (which was one of the many companies whose fortunes declined with economic deregulation). It was at this site that the (compulsory) standard-issue Australian telephone was manufactured for many years. Meriton's construction costs are usually 20 to 25 per cent of the price achieved per unit sold.[13]

The 1980s was a decade of great change for Sydney and Australia. Like the rest of the developed world, Sydney experienced the excesses that marked the economic boom of the period, but the hangover was worse than it was in most other countries. The after effects were magnified as a result of significant shifts in Australia's economic policy and the preference of many Australian business leaders of the day for highly leveraged speculation. During thirteen years of the federal Labor government from 1983, Australia's political landscape changed almost as much as Sydney's skyline had since 1960.

For the first time since Federation, the Australian economy was internationalised and deregulated. Tariff protection was reduced, gradually this time, and the dollar was floated. With lower protection and a floating exchange rate, Australia had to learn to compete internationally in the world's markets after years of economic isolation. The impact of centralised wage-fixing by the Industrial Court was reduced by the use of voluntary 'accords' with the trade union movement. As a result, real wages declined for the first time since the Great Depression.

The economic reforms were not without unintended consequences: there was a collapse in the dollar between 1985 and 1986 and a blowout in Australia's trade deficit, which increased its foreign debt. The paradox the government had to cope with was the way that strong economic growth and demand for goods led to deteriorating trade and foreign debt statistics. It soon became clear to everyone that Australia was living beyond its means and that its standard of living was in decline, certainly in relation to other nations. Because of the economic isolationism in the past, Australia had missed out on the postwar surge in international trade. Its market share of total world exports fell by 35 per cent between 1960 and 1987, while those of its trading partners and regional neighbours were exploding.[14] The nation could no longer be content with being an exporter of wool, cattle and minerals alone. This made Australia just as vulnerable to variations of international commodity prices as it had been from the 1830s.

Panic set in in 1986 when Treasurer Paul Keating said on John Laws's Sydney radio talkback program that Australia risked becoming a 'banana republic'. The only way the government could reduce its own debt was by budgetary cutbacks and general belt tightening. State governments were not immune to this, and the main item on the agenda for the premiers of New South Wales and other Australian states from the mid-1980s has been how to manage the economy responsibly. In the long term, foreign debt (both public and private) would only be reduced by increased national saving and the selling-off of assets, such as the Commonwealth Bank and Telstra. By means of a compulsory superannuation (pension) scheme, saving was encouraged. This also led to a huge boom in the size of the financial services industry.

In the aftermath of banking deregulation, the older, established banks and the new foreign entrants went into a lending frenzy. To get or keep market share, corners were cut, standards of credit assessment were relaxed, and the quality of risk management became poor. A great deal of the new foreign debt capital found its way into the hands of the new generation of Australian entrepreneurs, who worked the newly deregulated system to their own advantage.

In 1987, the government was faced with another crisis, strangely enough, in the shape of a worldwide boom. Just as the McMahon government had failed to prevent the economy from overheating in 1971 and 1972, so too did the Hawke government. Commodity prices rose, the dollar rose and fevered stock-market speculation followed. Sydney was a hotbed of this, and no one was immune—not individuals, fund managers nor large companies.

Then, in October 1987, the Australian stock markets crashed, harder and for longer than many other countries. It took almost a decade for the stock-market index to recover to pre-crash levels. Many experts believed a recession would quickly follow the crash, just as the Depression had followed Black Tuesday in 1929, but they were wrong. It took two years to hit, due partly to a reluctance on the part of governments to tighten monetary policy. However, when the recession set in in Australia, it did so sharply and severely for three years. The Sydney property market went into another of its dramatic declines—the worst in living memory.

Few of the key self-made entrepreneurs who played the takeover game so aggressively in the 1980s were born or based in Sydney. The most notorious one of all, Alan Bond, was an English-born resident of Perth. Robert Holmes à Court, the man who took on the establishment when he made an audacious takeover bid for Australia's largest company, BHP, lived in Western Australia as well. The two largest moguls Sydney produced in the 1980s were Kerry Packer, Australia's richest man, whose father and grandfather had built up the Consolidated Press empire before him, and Hungarian-born Larry Adler, a successful share-market speculator and founder of the insurance company FAI.

208

Many of the targets of takeovers in the 1980s were well-established, family-owned Sydney businesses that soon fell into the hands of the 'new boys'. David Jones was raided by Latvian-born John Spalvins's Adelaide Steamship Company; Grace Bros was bought by Myer, a large Melbourne-based retailer (Myer was in turn later taken over by Solomon Lew); Waltons was taken over by Bond Corporation; the brewers Tooths were bought by Adsteam again; and Tooheys also became Bond's. Well-established brand names in the textile business changed hands at least once. Speedo, the once Australian-owned maker of swimsuits, is now owned by a US company. King Gee, a name which for many years was synonymous with clothes for the working man, is also now in foreign hands.

Not even that bastion of the Sydney establishment, the *Sydney Morning Herald*, was immune from takeover fever. This time the raider came from within the Fairfax family itself. Warwick Fairfax Junior borrowed nearly $2 billion from the ANZ bank just before the stock-market crash and went ahead with the purchase. In 1990, 150 years after the family empire was founded, Warwick Fairfax lost control of the business when he defaulted on his debt obligations. The Sydney-based company Arnott's, for many years synonymous with the word 'biscuit' in Australia, was bought by an American food giant, Campbell's.

Many, if not most, of the newly founded entrepreneurial empires collapsed when interest rates rose. They left, as their legacies to the banks, a mountain of bad debts and illiquid assets. The aftermath of the recession and the deregulation of the early 1980s is still being felt today in the form of higher unemployment, but we do enjoy a sound, transparent and better governed financial system than before the recession of the early 1990s. This has made the economy better able to withstand the slowdown in Asian economies. The balance of trade is still negative, as it always has been, and our dependency on foreign debt is still alarmingly high.

Combined with the after effects of the recession has been the economic rationalisation of the banking and finance industries, brought about by the revolution in information technology. The shedding of workers and middle management ('downsizing') is exposing people from all classes of society to the effects of economic change. Job security may soon largely be a thing of the past, and the level of service for customers seems to be deteriorating rather than improving, though the profits of the largest banks continue to climb.

One of the more interesting postwar events which has had a dramatic effect on Sydney's culture and ambience has been the dismantling of the White Australia policy. By 1959, Australia was in a self-congratulatory mood. The population had reached 10 million, a growth of 3 million from 1939. The aim was to grow by a further 10 million by 1988.[15] It was not clear where the huge numbers of immigrants would come from if this target was to be reached. Economies in Western and northern Europe had recovered from the war, and West Germany was even welcoming guest workers from Turkey because of a labour shortage. The European appetite for emigration was disappearing. As Foreign Minister Downer would say later:

> We have reached the stage where good migrants with the skills we want are not just growing like cherries on the tree; nor are they available just when we feel that we can absorb them comfortably ... we shall have to 'sell' the idea of migrating to Australia much harder ... Recent moves among European countries for economic integration under the European Economic Community, previously called the European Common Market, are intensifying the problem.[16]

209

Downer was right, in part at least. Immigration from northern Europe dried up from 1960, but British and southern European migration grew and peaked in 1969, when 185 000 migrants arrived in Australia. The slow melting of the White Australia policy from the mid-1950s through to the 1970s was a result of many factors, some of them pragmatic and self-interested rather than altruistic. The moral conundrum of maintaining a racist immigration policy had been, from the late 1950s, a topic of much debate. The White Australia policy became embarrassing as we traded more with our Asian neighbours. From the perspective of the high economic growth levels and low levels of unemployment in the 1960s, it became apparent that a wider net would need to be cast to maintain a high rate of immigration. Immigrants would need to come from further afield (or closer to home).

In 1956, Asian refugees who came to Australia in World War II and other Asians who had been in Australia for a long period were given permanent residency. In 1958, shortly after Australia signed a trade agreement with Japan, the *Immigration Restriction Act* was repealed. There would be no more 'dictation test' and 'distinguished and qualified' people could settle here, bringing with them the skills the nation needed. In 1965, the Labor Party dropped the White Australia policy and the Liberal Party followed suit the next year while Harold Holt was prime minister. From 1966, a wider range of people with different skills were allowed to immigrate, although the extent to which skills learnt overseas were recognised was heavily

ABOVE: Members of the Asian community at Cabramatta, 1990. (Reproduced with the permission of Mark Tedeschi/Image Library, State Library of NSW)

210

weighted in favour of English speakers. Between 1963 and 1973, 60 per cent of the qualifications from English-speaking countries were recognised compared with only 40 per cent of those from non–English-speaking countries.[17]

From the 1970s, with higher inflation and unemployment, political support for high levels of immigration weakened. The Cold War era was behind us and external aggression and invasion had become a very remote prospect, so the 'populate or perish' slogan had less potency. The Labor government reduced the immigration numbers, but moved away from the assimilationist policy which had been strongly expressed by the former Liberal immigration minister, Billy Snedden:

We must have a single culture—if immigration implied multicultural activities within Australian society, then it was not the type Australia wanted. I am quite determined we should have a monoculture, with everyone living in the same way, understanding each other and sharing the same aspirations. We don't want pluralism.[18]

From 1973, new policies were introduced to help immigrants settle into their new home. Government assistance was given to disadvantaged immigrants, so that they would get their right to a 'fair go'. All remaining discriminatory aspects of government policy were removed, and 'multiculturalism' became a key platform of social policy. The central idea behind this frequently misunderstood concept is that it is possible to be part of Australian society without abandoning the language and culture of the land of one's background: diversity should not only be tolerated, but also appreciated. Some conservative politicians, including Prime Minister John Howard, are so wary of the expression that they prefer not to use it, as for them, in its more extreme manifestations, it has connotations of the fragmentation of Australian society into smaller minority interests.

Throughout the 1970s, multiculturalism was not only a worthy social policy, it was good politics, too. Not all voters were the monocultural Australians Snedden had in mind. Multi-language or 'ethnic' radio was introduced in the mid-1970s and, in 1980, SBS Television started broadcasting. The New South Wales Ethnic Affairs Commission was created by the Wran government in 1977. It was charged with the task of looking after the interests of non–English-speaking people in New South Wales.

From 1981, immigration assistance was restricted to refugees only. The first major wave of late–twentieth-century refugees were the Indochinese from Vietnam, Cambodia and Laos. The Indochinese 'boat people' caused far more political controversy than any other group of refugees in the 1970s and 1980s. At the end of 1975, 1000 Indochinese had come to Australia, mostly in refugee boats which were often dangerously overcrowded and barely seaworthy. One of these boats can be seen berthed outside the National Maritime Museum at Darling Harbour.

In 1982, the numbers of Indochinese immigrants continued to grow when the Australian and Vietnamese governments agreed that further migration to Australia on the grounds of family reunion should be encouraged. This created a huge change to the cultural complexion of many Sydney suburbs, and the policy has come in for much criticism in more recent years, on the grounds that there is insufficient regard for the skills, age and employability of prospective immigrants.

From the middle of the 1980s, there has also been a strong increase in the Chinese-born population in Sydney. The pattern of Chinese immigration in the wake of the demonstrations in Tiananmen Square is a good example of chain migration through family reunions. The federal government granted residency to all the 15 000 Chinese students living in Australia in 1989. It is estimated that between 75 000 and 80 000 other Chinese people will immigrate as a result of the promotion of immigration.

In 1991, there were 42 000 Chinese-born people in Sydney. In the next five years, this figure grew to more than 62 000. China is now Sydney's third-biggest source of immigrants after the United Kingdom with nearly 200 000 immigrants and New Zealand with 67 000.

There have been some unfortunate developments in the wake of high levels of Indochinese and Chinese immigration. The drug trade and organised crime based in certain sections of the Vietnamese community in Cabramatta have usurped the dominant position the drug and crime czars of Kings Cross previously enjoyed. The owner of a Vietnamese community club faces charges for the brutal murder of his longtime political rival, local state politician John Newman, outside the latter's home in 1994. This was the first political assassination in Australia. People with Vietnamese backgrounds form a disproportionate level of the prison population, just as Aborigines and Lebanese people do. Unemployment rates in these immigrant groups is much higher than the national average. There have been allegations of social welfare fraud. Asian and Middle Eastern gangs operate in the city and in some suburbs of Sydney's west and southwest. Criminologists are sounding alarm bells about the arrival in Sydney of Chinese criminal gangs and the increasing rate of home invasions and extortion of small businesses, as well as the rise of organised crime in Asian communities. On a happier note, the academic performance of some high school students from Asian backgrounds is brilliant, and these high achievers go on to excel at university and at their chosen professions.

Asian immigration has not been the only significant source of non–English-speaking immigration in recent decades. There are almost 170 000 people living in Sydney who were either born in the Middle East (mostly Lebanon) or have at least one parent who was born there. Many of Sydney's Middle Eastern population live in the municipalities of Canterbury and Bankstown.

212

The rate of increase in proportion of Sydneysiders who were born in Asian countries has been accelerating. In the five years to 1991, there was an 88 per cent increase in Sydney's Asian-born population (from among the top thirty-six sources of immigrants), from 131 000 to 245 000. In 1996, the rate of change had slowed considerably to 28 per cent. The total number of people living in Sydney who were either born in an Asian country or born in Australia with at least one Asian parent is approximately 370 000, or 10 per cent of the population.

In 1996, 31 per cent of Sydney's population was born outside Australia. Two-thirds of these immigrants were born in a non–English-speaking country. Like other big cities the world over, Sydney has been a huge gateway for inbound migrants. It receives almost double its share of immigrants compared to the rest of the Australian population. Nearly 6 per cent of Sydney's population are immigrants who arrived in the past five years.

In the past decade, there has been a steady rise in the number of South African immigrants. Some of these immigrants share some of the same characteristics that Hungarian immigrants did in the period from 1947 to 1960. Their education, business acumen and creative skills have meant that many of them have settled easily into life in Sydney, and made a mark which belies their relatively small numbers. In 1996, there were almost 19 000 South Africans living in Sydney, many of them in the middle-class suburbs on the upper North Shore and in the eastern suburbs.

The settlement patterns of English-speaking and non–English-speaking immigrants in Sydney are distinct. English-speakers tend to cluster around the harbour, the coast and the northern and eastern suburbs, as well as in the outer west and southwest, Penrith, Camden and Campbelltown. Non–English-speaking immigrants are concentrated in a crescent that runs southeast from Fairfield, Bankstown, Auburn, Canterbury and Ashfield to the northern side of the Georges River, covering the local government areas of Marrickville, Canterbury and Rockdale. Fairfield has the highest population of people who do not speak English at home (50.4 per cent).[19]

Despite the high concentration of non–English-speaking migrants in certain areas of Sydney, there is, for the most part, a diverse mix of national backgrounds within each area. Fairfield–Cabramatta is one exception to this, with its high concentration of Indochinese immigrants. Canterbury has a high proportion of people of Middle Eastern origin. These areas might be the first in Sydney—and Australia—to have the characteristics of a ghetto or, less dramatically put, a racial enclave. For the most part, however, Sydney is unlike other melting-pot cities such as Los Angeles and London, which also have many non–English-speakers. Both these cities draw most of their immigrants from a smaller range of countries and language groups, such as Spanish in Los Angeles and Hindi in London.

One of the leaders of the Chinese community in Sydney is Deputy Lord Mayor Henry Tsang. Born in China, his family were Nationalists who fled to Hong Kong after 1949. Tsang's father was concerned about Hong Kong's fall to communism after the handover of the Crown colony back to China in 1997, so he strongly encouraged his son to leave Hong Kong and find another country in which to live. Tsang did his final years of high school at Vaucluse High, then studied architecture at the University of New South Wales. This way, he would be able to 'rescue' his family from communism if the need arose. This desire to be able to flee from the strong grasp of communism has driven many other Hong Kong Chinese to immigrate to Australia since the abolition of the White Australia policy in the mid-1960s.

In recent years, these immigrants have also brought with them substantial capital, as well as skills and high levels of motivation. Although Tsang left Australia to live in the United States for several years, he did return. As he says:

> [In the early 1970s] I compared the United States with Australia. While both are new nations, Australia is a fairer society. Australia has a lot of potential. Everybody can fit into this society. You don't *have* to be successful. There is not such a strong competitive edge to life in Australia.

Tsang's parents now live with him and his family on Sydney's North Shore. For many years, Tsang had an architectural practice. His firm designed the Dixon Street shopping mall and another mall at Cabramatta, as well as hotels and serviced apartments.

Many of Tsang's largest architectural works have been done in an honorary capacity. He planned the improvements to Dixon Street in the late 1970s and early 1980s, designed the Chinese Garden at Darling Harbour, another Chinese garden at the New Children's Hospital, Westmead, and several Chinese temples. Since the late 1970s, Tsang has been an interpreter and spokesperson for the Chinese community, holding the position of vice-chairman of the Ethnic Communities Council of New South Wales. He has also spoken out at rallies against the political oppression of the human rights movement in China. Spotted by the Labor Party, he was encouraged to stand for election as an alderman on the Council of the City of Sydney.

Tsang has been witness to a big change in sentiment felt by the Chinese community towards Sydney and Australia. Back in the late nineteenth and early twentieth centuries, many Chinese people worked on the edges of society as market gardeners, for example working plots on the fringe of the city. Some of the vegetable plots can still be seen near the Botany Cemetery and around the periphery of Kingsford Smith Airport. For these people, Sydney and Australia were never considered to be 'home'—it was just a place to work to earn money to send back to their families in China. Their remains were often returned home to China for burial. Since the abandonment of the White Australia policy in the mid to late 1960s, the Chinese have felt it was possible to put down permanent roots here. The renovations to Dixon Street in the 1970s with the collaboration of the Chinese community were an indication of this. Since then, Chinese businesses have been more involved in Sydney's commercial life. Property developer Ipoh Gardens (owned by Chinese Malays) has renovated the Queen Victoria Building and the Capitol Theatre, and the Grace Bros Building in Market Street; and around Chinatown there are many other developments financed by the Chinese, including the Peak Tower.

214

Despite some popular misconceptions, the 'Asian' communities are not homogeneous in a cultural, economic or political sense. There was a long-term political division between Chinese nationalists and communists. The influx of Chinese Vietnamese people from the mid-1970s created another subgroup within the Chinese community. Some of these divisions are diminishing with the liberalisation of trade and close political links between China and the rest of the world. Around Sydney's Chinatown, the Chinese Vietnamese are active in the supermarkets and jewellery trade, while the restaurants there are mostly owned by the Hong Kong Chinese.

Many of the more recently arrived immigrants from northern Asia (especially Hong Kong and Taiwan) have also settled in middle-class neighbourhoods on the North Shore of Sydney, such as North Sydney, Willoughby, Castlecrag, Middle Cove, St Ives and Chatswood, and on the southern fringe of the central business district near the Haymarket and Chinatown, Sydney University and the University of Technology. Many of Sydney's Indian and Sri Lankan population live in the northwest, around Ryde and Macquarie University.

It is the greater presence of Asian immigrants on the North Shore and around the harbour-side and inner city that is giving the centre of Sydney a heightened flavour as a city perched on and part of the Pacific Rim. The Chinese community, both mainland Chinese, Hong Kong and Taiwanese, and the overseas Chinese from Singapore and Malaysia, are playing an important role in providing Sydney's services, and are big players in the prestige-property market. In some of Sydney's prime high-rise apartments, such as Quay West and The Peak, 50 per cent of the units are owned by people living overseas, mostly in Asia. Many people buy property in Sydney as a second home and use it for vacations and as accommodation for children who study here. The consequences of the economic recession in Asia are having their inevitable impact on the property market in Sydney and the general buoyancy of the

ABOVE: Enjoying the amenities of the Royal Botanic Gardens in the late nineteenth century. *Engraving by Gibbs, Shallard & Co. for the Illustrated Sydney News, 1884 (Image Library, State Library of NSW)*

BELOW: Picnic at Mrs Macquarie's Chair, *c. 1855, artist unknown (Image Library, State Library of NSW)*

ABOVE: Cockle Bay in the early days of the colony—it is hard to equate this open stretch of land with the bay of today, with its hemmed-in strip of water, stark white, late-twentieth century architecture and Darling Harbour container wharves. Cockle Bay, *c. 1819, J. Taylor (Image Library, State Library of NSW)*

BELOW: Old Government House at Sydney Cove. The Museum of Sydney is now sited on what little remains of this, the colony's original Government House. Government House, *1791, William Bradley (Image Library, State Library of NSW)*

ABOVE: The current Government House, a Gothic Revival edifice complete with turrets built from 1837 to 1845, stands within the Royal Botanic Gardens and is in complete contrast to the simplicity of the first Government House. *Government House, Sydney, c. 1845, Joseph Fowles (Image Library, State Library of NSW)*

BELOW: Cricket matches were very much part of the early life of Hyde Park, which was named by Governor Lachlan Macquarie in 1810 and intended for the 'recreation and amusement' of Sydneysiders. St James' Church can be seen behind the park, with Elizabeth Street on the left and Macquarie Street on the right. *The old days of merry cricket club matches, c. 1843, Thomas H. Lewis (Image Library, State Library of NSW)*

ABOVE: Hyde Park Barracks, designed by convict architect Francis Greenway and built in 1819, began their life as housing for 600 convicts. Today, it is a museum displaying the history of the site and its early occupants. *(Marcus Clinton)*

ABOVE: The city skyline as night closes in. *(Marcus Clinton)*

Australian economy, but it is not as great as many feared.

Another leader of the Chinese-speaking community in Sydney is Cathy Chung, the former President of the Sydney-based Australian Chinese Community Association (ACCA). The ACCA's task is to help Chinese immigrants settle in, and deal with the alienation and loneliness which recent immigrants often feel. Chung is a Hong Kong–born solicitor and company director who came to live on the North Shore of Sydney at the age of sixteen to attend school and later university. Her family owns the large and very successful Marigold restaurants, which were established in response to an unsatisfied demand for Chinese banqueting. As a result of the increased commercial activity in the Chinatown area near the Haymarket, this area of the city is booming and teeming with life long after office workers have gone home, and on weekends.

While, in some quarters, there is opposition to the high rate of Asian immigration, Australia's—and Sydney's—population is now a mixture of different ingredients, and the egg cannot be unscrambled. The issue of Asian immigration is sometimes confusingly co-mingled with the issue of the level of overall immigration (from any source), and what level of population increase is sustainable and in the public interest. These are important issues which need to be addressed without strident accusations of racial intolerance. In a national newspoll taken in September 1996, published in the *Australian* newspaper, 71 per cent of the 1200 people questioned said they thought present immigration levels were too high, most of them saying they were much too high. Those most highly opposed to high levels of immigration were older people, and people on lower-than-average incomes.

The Howard Liberal government, elected in 1996, has responded to the public mood. It has shifted immigration policy away from family reunions in favour of attracting business and skilled migrants, so that the overall cost of immigration can be reduced. There is a two-year waiting period before immigrants are eligible for social security. The overall level of immigration has been reduced as well.

Residents of social melting pots such as Sydney may prove to be more able to adapt to the demographic change in their midst than those who live in more provincial and regional areas, where diversity is more of an abstract notion than a reality. Sadly, it is proving harder to erase the long-held Anglo-Celtic views about the cultural ideal of a white Australia than many believed it would be in some quarters.

It will be interesting to see the cultural consequences of the waves of immigration which have occurred since the mid-1970s, as the second generation of these diverse immigrant groups continue to work their way into the city's cultural and social fabric. Henry Tsang gives a good example of the changes Sydney (and Australia) is undergoing. When talking to someone who was concerned about the rate of demographic change within society and disgruntled that Chinese parents did not speak English to their children at home, Tsang gave a recent example of the New South Wales high school debating team who won the World Debating Championships in 1996. Tsang was at a function held to welcome them and congratulate them for their efforts.

The captain, Gerald Wong, was born in Australia of Taiwanese parents, and speaks Chinese at home. The vice-captain was female and born in New Zealand and had a mixed Maori, Chinese and Anglo-Saxon background. The third speaker was male, born in Scotland and spoke English with a strong Scottish accent. The fourth speaker was a South African–born female and spoke with a South African accent. Tsang asked the woman: 'Would you pick on him because he spoke Chinese at home? He is a world champion communicator in English, and he was the only one in the team actually born in Australia. We might have to learn to change our perceptions of what being Australian means.'

One example of trying to change Australians' perceptions is the increasing support in the 1990s for replacing the British monarch with an Australian head of state. 'A resident for president' has been the slogan of the Australian Republican Movement (ARM), the major force behind this campaign. The ARM was officially launched in Sydney in July 1991. Most of the founding ARM members were Sydneysiders—Tom Keneally, Neville Wran, Malcolm Turnbull, journalists and broadcasters Geraldine Doogue and Mark Day, architect Harry Seidler, designer Jenny Kee, controversial member of the Legislative Council Franca Arena and playwright David Williamson. The motivating idea behind the move for a republic is that there should be no office under the Australian Constitution (especially at its apex) that is not available to all Australians on the basis of merit alone—without any limitations imposed because of a person's sex or religious beliefs. The importance of reinforcing the core values of democracy, promotion based on merit, openness and tolerance seems more imperative in the closing years of the twentieth century than it has ever been. Ensuring that Australia's head of state is Australian is a tangible way of acknowledging the social, demographic and cultural journey Australia has taken since the post-colonial period began in 1947.

A constitutional convention was held in 1998. It overwhelmingly endorsed the move to a republic. In 1999, the Australian people will have the chance to vote for or against a republic at a referendum. If this vote is successful, the ceremonies associated with the Olympic Games and the centenary of Federation in January 2001 will have an even more celebratory flavour.

The old chestnut about the philistinism of Australian culture has now been put to rest. Australia is the largest market, per capita, for English-language books and, after the United States, is the second-largest importer of British books published.[20] The performing arts is now a major industry, often promoted and financed with the significant assistance of state and federal governments. Nearly 250 000 tickets were bought for the Australian Opera in 1995 for performances in Sydney, almost 40 000 for the Sydney Dance Company's performances, and more than 1 million tickets were sold for concerts and performances at the Opera House. The Sydney Theatre Company is just one of many which produce stage plays.

This strong growth in the audience for opera and classical music started after 1945 with the growing number of European—and especially Jewish—immigrants. Musica Viva, which performs chamber music, was founded in 1945 by the musician and inventor, Richard Goldner. The government-run Australian Broadcasting Corporation (ABC) has been the cradle of much creative endeavour deemed too risky for commercial media companies. Until the mid-1990s, it sponsored the Sydney Symphony Orchestra. It also assists in bringing cultural events, such as Opera Australia's annual Opera in the Park, which is staged in the Domain every January during the Festival of Sydney. This festival is a highlight on the Sydney cultural calendar. It has been revamped and improved under the guiding hand of chairman Leo Schofield.

ABOVE: Looking down Phillip Street from Bridge Street to Circular Quay in the late nineteenth century. On the left is the Blacket-designed Mort's Wool Warehouse, which was demolished to make way for the AMP Building.

CHAPTER NINE

COVE, QUAY, ROCKS, BRIDGE

SYDNEY COVE is the cradle of European settlement in Australia. It was named after the home secretary, Lord Sydney, an otherwise undistinguished politician who was an early supporter of the idea of establishing a penal colony in New South Wales. The cove had a happy confluence of a ready supply of fresh water (in the form of what later became known as the Tank Stream), safe anchorage for the ships of the First Fleet and good defence prospects. The V-shaped cove used to extend further south, as far as the corner of Bridge and Pitt streets. It was surrounded by alternately bushy, swampy and rocky land. The original 'zoning' of the land at the head of the cove by Governor Phillip still resonates to the present day. Rockier land on the western side of the Tank Stream was allocated to the convicts, sailors and marines, and Phillip and his administrative staff occupied the grassier and lusher eastern side of the city beyond tidal mud flats at the head of the cove. Hence the location of the public buildings on upper Bridge Street and Macquarie Street, and the location of the Governor's Domain, and the original focus of the commercial centre of the city along George Street.

Circular Quay plays many roles: it is the northernmost edge of the central business district, and therefore the home of some of Sydney's showier skyscrapers. It is the bustling terminus for the city's harbour ferries and many of its bus routes. It is, together with The Rocks, Sydney's greatest tourist attraction. It is also the closest thing Sydneysiders and many Australians have to a sacred site, reminding Australians of the beginning of European occupation of Australia and the roots of nationhood. Governments of all levels interfere with Sydney's beloved cove and quay at their political peril.

At Circular Quay, the observer can watch Sydney's own particular *zeitgeist* at its most exuberant and energetic. On weekdays, it is easy to tell the locals from the tourists. Hasty, pressed commuters look purposefully ahead (and nowhere else) on their journey to work or home again. Tourists and sightseers from Australia and all over the world take in Sydney's most popular tourist attraction more slowly. Any first-time visit to Sydney should start at Circular Quay.

On weekends, the tourists and the watchers far outnumber the workers, and the pace slows down. Buskers and street vendors abound (or at least they used to until their activities were banned in early 1998), as do crowds of people enjoying a day out in the city. From the mid-1980s, there have been great improvements to Circular Quay. Before then, the quay was not so accessible for pedestrians and there were limited—very limited—entertainment facilities, other than a few seedy, run-down pubs. Now there are walkways, inviting green lawns and sunny cafés that have cannily been built under the gruesome, massive Cahill Expressway that slices through the quay, separating it visually from the city that lies to the south. Proposals to tear down the expressway may yet, with a lot of goodwill and even more money from government, come to pass, but no one is holding their breath in expectation. The presence of the Cahill Expressway is one of Sydney's best illustrations of why road authorities should not be given a free rein by government when determining the city's most efficient traffic flows.

When the Sydney Harbour Bridge opened in 1932, Circular Quay was temporarily eclipsed. It was no longer the central link between the northern and southern sides of the harbour. Ferry traffic declined dramatically and business in Lower George Street slumped. The area became a sad shadow of its former busy self. It had been one of the liveliest parts of the city since 1788. It was not until the containerisation of Sydney's port facilities and the building boom of the 1960s and 1970s that Circular Quay and The Rocks entirely sloughed off their early maritime origins. Until then, the area had the salty character that could be found in port cities around the world—the smell of rum and pipe tobacco mixed with the briny flavour of the sea, the sound of hauling and shouting, and the spectacle of loading and unloading the greasy wool clip and other more exotic cargoes.

In the 1950s, the main businesses around the quay were relics of Sydney Cove's days as a port. Dalgety, Elders, Burns Philp and other old wool-trading and maritime firms still have their offices there today, although the clippers and trading ships have long since moved on.

Although the quay has changed beyond recognition in the past fifty years, especially since the removal of the 46-metre building height restriction in 1957, precious remnants of the past remain, and it is well worth exploring the quay on foot to look at the contrast between old and new, and to gain a better understanding of the way Sydney grew and developed. A good place to start a visit to Circular Quay is the Sydney Cove Bicentennial Map (1988) in First Fleet Park, to the south of the Museum of Contemporary Art near Alfred Street, on the spot where the old Tank Stream ran into Sydney Cove at high tide. Designed by Beverly Atkinson in sixty-three

ABOVE: The James Barnet–designed Customs House at Circular Quay in the late nineteenth century.

different varieties of coloured terrazzo tiles, the work is based on maps, charts and pictures of Sydney Cove executed between 1788 and 1808. It is a pity that there is not more landscaping in the area which gives more of an idea of the cove's original topography.

One of the most imposing earlier buildings on Circular Quay is the Customs House. Like nearly all of Sydney's other government buildings of the second half of the nineteenth century, it was designed by Colonial Architect James Barnet. Of all Sydney's public buildings from that century, the Customs House most strongly evokes the idea of empire and New South Wales's colonial status during that time. Until World War I, customs duties and tariffs were the principal source of government revenue. The building was located and designed to reflect the importance of customs levies to the colonial economy. In those days, most of New South Wales's trade was with Britain and the other parts of the British Empire. Thus the medallions on the upper levels of the building remind observers of Australia's most important cultural and economic connections, and the significance of our imperial bonds—South Africa, New Zealand, India and Singapore, to name just a few. Barnet's Customs House was completed in 1887, on the site of an earlier, smaller building designed by one of his predecessors, Mortimer Lewis, in 1850. The decorative clock, installed after the completion of the building, was illuminated to be visible from all parts of the quay at night. The Customs House and the handsome square in front of it have now been restored by the City of Sydney. One of the occupants of the building is the Australian Museum's Djamu Gallery on the second floor (*Djamu* is Eora for 'I am here'). Important items from the museum's anthropological collection from Australia, the Pacific and elsewhere will be on public view, some of them for the first time. On the third floor is the Centre for Contemporary Craft's Object Gallery.

The City of Sydney has also installed an exhibition space on the fourth floor, displaying a model of the city's buildings and any proposed redevelopments, as well as other items of interest relating to the City of Sydney's built environment. There is retail and dining space on the ground floor, and a restaurant on the top floor.

On the corner of Alfred and George streets stands Herald Square. The fountain spouts water from the Tank Stream. The work was created to mark the sesquicentenary of the *Sydney Morning Herald*. Sculptures depict the animals that would have inhabited the banks of the stream: lizards, goannas, pelicans and frogs.

Architectural remnants of what Circular Quay used to be like can be seen in Young and Loftus streets. Hinchcliffe's Wool Store lies immediately behind the Customs House, overshadowed to the east by the looming AMP Centre. The Hinchcliffe's Wool Store buildings were erected in the second half of the nineteenth century. Until the 1950s, most of the buildings around the quay were of a similar scale to those that fringe Campbells Cove. The building now contains a Marist Chapel and a foreign language school. One block to the west, the Gallipoli Club in Loftus Street was also a wool store until 1946, when it became a club for Gallipoli veterans. These veterans have passed into history and the club remains a memorial to these early–twentieth-century Australian heroes and, like so many others in Sydney, is now the home of many poker machines.

The commercial centre of Sydney grew ribbon-like, southward and away from the cove along George Street, hemmed in by the two sandstone ridges lying to the east and west. George Street is still the city's main street. In the early years of the colony, people both lived and worked around Sydney Cove, The Rocks, Millers Point and the eastern side of Darling Harbour. The better-off members of society were the first to leave for the clearer air of the suburbs from the late 1840s and 1850s. Others followed them over the next 130 years. In the past two decades of the twentieth century, this outward dispersal has been reversed. Some of the earlier examples of the new generation of high-rise residential apartments can be seen at Circular Quay, such as The Quay apartments on the eastern side and the Quay West apartments near the ANA Hotel.

One of the important early jobs in the penal camp was to link the eastern and western parts of the town by building a bridge over the swampy tidal area at the mouth of the Tank Stream. It was constructed near the corner of Pitt and Bridge streets, and called Bon Accord Bridge.

The bridge was an important feature of Sydney Cove until the stream was consigned to its fate as an underground waterway from the mid-nineteenth century. The City of Sydney is considering whether it should uncover parts of the Tank Stream in recognition of its historic significance.

To the west of the bridge, on the corner of Bridge and George streets, stood the infamous Lumber Yard. This was a euphemistic label for what was, in reality, a workhouse for convict labour. The pillory which was often used as the place to flog convicts for any wrongdoing lay within the yard. The other principal centre of convict labour was the government dockyard. Well-preserved archaeological remains of this dockyard have recently been discovered beneath the Museum of Contemporary Art.

The town itself, especially the Lumber Yard, was a busy hive of forced activity in the years up until the 1820s, when Sydney's principal role was as a penal colony:

> The principal place of convict labour in Sydney, is the lumber yard … [T]he trades carried on in this place, are those of blacksmiths, locksmiths, nailers, iron and brass founders, bellows makers, coopers, sawyers, painters, lead casters, harness and collar makers, tailors and shoemakers, carpenters, joiners and cabinet makers. All the different sheds in which the workmen are employed, front towards the yard that they enclose, and in the centre is deposited the wood that is brought from Pennant Hills and Newcastle … [T]he dockyard likewise furnishes employment to a considerable number of workmen, either in construction of the quays, or in the building and naval equipment of boats and vessels. The gaol gang are generally employed at this place, in unloading the cargoes of the colonial vessels, and in delivering them on the quays of the dock yard, and they are made to work in chains … The office of the principal superintendant [sic] of convicts is in the lumber yard, and two convict clerks are constantly employed there, in keeping the books and making entries, copying returns of labour, writing orders for the signature of the superintendant [sic], numerical and nominal lists of the gangs of workmen and labourers, and in receiving the applications of individuals for convicts.[1]

223

Convicts were a regular sight around Sydney Cove until the more structured assignment system, recommended by Thomas Bigge, was implemented from the 1820s. In 1788, however, the convict 'system' was embryonic. Convicts built whatever shelters they could and wore whatever clothes they brought with them, made or otherwise obtained. There were no uniforms issued to them. As the administration of the convicts became more institutionalised during the Macquarie era, most of the convicts in the town were consigned to Hyde Park Barracks in Macquarie Street or Carters' Barracks at the bottom of Brickfield Hill to the south. These convicts wore uniforms with either 'HPB' or 'CB' painted on them to make them identifiable from the rest of society and to indicate in which barracks they should be after curfew.

On the opposite side of Bridge and George streets stood the Orphan School. The house was originally built by Lieutenant William Kent, commander of the *Supply* and a nephew of

ABOVE: Looking eastward down Grosvenor Street from Church Hill. St Patrick's Church is at left and the government buildings of Bridge Street can be seen in the background.

224

Governor Hunter. When Kent returned to England in 1800 he sold the house to Governor King, who used the building to house some of the large number of children roaming the streets of Sydney. It was used as an orphanage until 1828, when James Underwood, a successful emancipist businessman, bought the house and the surrounding blocks. For many years, it was one of the more imposing buildings in the colony.

The site now occupied by the Regent Hotel in George Street was once the location of Sydney's early gaol. It stood in the shadow of the guard house on the corner of George and Grosvenor streets. The stone gaol was built on the site of its timber predecessor, which burnt down in 1799. Just behind the stone gaol was the aptly named Hangman's Hill or Gallows Hill. Even Commissioner Bigge, not known for his humanitarian zeal, was so appalled by the conditions in the notorious gaol that he recommended its demolition and that a new one be built at Darlinghurst.

In the early days of the colony, the security at the gaol was so inadequate—or the penal system was so primitive—that many of the convicts had to be kept in heavy leg-irons and sometimes wore spiked iron collars as well. The first gaoler was an ex-convict called Henry Kable, after whom the exclusive Kable's Restaurant in the Regent Hotel was named. Kable went into the boat-building business with James Underwood just behind Underwood's house, on the western bank of the Tank Stream. In the second half of the nineteenth century, many workshops and businesses operated by members of Sydney's Chinese community were located on the site of the former gaol.

Before Hyde Park Barracks were built, marines and soldiers kept a watchful eye on the convicts living in the town and the gaol from the parade ground near the corner of George and Grosvenor streets. More permanent barracks in Wynyard Square were completed between 1809 and 1817. These barracks were designed by Lieutenant Colonel William Foveaux. When they were built, they were said by Governor Macquarie to be 'perhaps the best and most Compleat [sic] of any in His Majesty's Foreign Dominions'.[2] The lieutenant-governor lived next door, to the north of the barracks. The location of his house on the southern corner of Grosvenor and George streets explains the irregular intersection of Bridge, George and Grosvenor streets today. The National Australia Bank building stands where the lieutenant governor's home once did. The site has always been a piece of prime Sydney commercial real estate. After the lieutenant-governor had moved elsewhere, his residence became a hotel, then Samuel Lyon's auction rooms and later still the premises of the P&O shipping line.[3]

225

One of the larger and more important public buildings constructed in the early nineteenth century that added an air of permanence to the city was the Commissariat Stores—designed, like the barracks, by Foveaux, with the objective of keeping the food and other supplies in and convicts and thieves out. All incoming goods were stored there in an effort to prevent smuggling. The Commissariat Stores stood on the western side of the cove, just behind the King's (later Queen's) Wharf. The building was demolished in the middle of the twentieth century—a great loss to Sydney's early heritage—to make way for the Maritime Services Board building, now the Museum of Contemporary Art. If it were still standing today, its demolition would be as inconceivable as a proposal to tear down Hyde Park Barracks in Macquarie Street.

In 1800, Sydney Cove looked exactly like what it was: a penal camp. In the next ten years, as money was made by members of the Rum Corps and prosperous emancipist traders, new buildings appeared around the cove. Macquarie Place was home to three of Sydney's earliest and most successful emancipists—Simeon Lord, James Underwood and Mary Reiby.

Macquarie Place, located close to Circular Quay today, is much smaller than it used to be. It lies on the eastern bank of the old Tank Stream. Until Circular Quay was built, Macquarie Place extended to the muddy head of the cove. For the first forty years of the nineteenth century, Macquarie Place was one of the focal points of Sydney's commercial and civic life. This is why Greenway's obelisk, from which all distances in the colony were measured, was erected there.

Unlike the exclusives, Lord, Underwood and Reiby had no qualms about being in 'trade' and living 'above the shop'. By 1808, Lord had made enough money to be able to build the most imposing house in the colony. It stands prominently in the sketches of the early nineteenth century and was not demolished until 1904.

To the north of Lord's house and warehouse, on the corner of Macquarie and Reiby places, lived Mary Reiby. Mary Reiby was the first successful emancipist businesswoman. Sentenced as a young girl, in 1790, to seven years' transportation for stealing a horse, her first job was to work as a nursemaid in Acting Governor Francis Grose's household. She married whaling captain Thomas Reiby, an employee of the East India Company, who retired from his post and was soon running a prosperous trading operation in Sydney. When he died at the age of forty-two, he left Mary with seven children, a successful business, a warehouse in George Street, near Argyle Street, and the cottage in Macquarie Place.

Reiby significantly increased the family's empire. She owned and developed property in George and Castlereagh streets, and had other significant property holdings at Newtown, Hunters Hill and Windsor. In 1817, Reiby leased her cottage in Macquarie Place to the newly founded Bank of New South Wales, now renamed Westpac. Later she sold the buildings to the government for use as customs houses.

Macquarie Place was one of Sydney's smartest addresses until the 1840s. After its early residents had moved on, the area became closely connected with Sydney's maritime trade. Lord's house, for example, became a boarding house for sailors. It was years before Macquarie Place began to resemble what it is like today. The Francis Greenway–designed obelisk used to stand in the centre. Much of the space was whittled away over the intervening years, a result of the growth of the city and the contraction of the Governor's Domain. Loftus Street was extended in the 1840s to the newly built Circular Quay, and most of the proud Moreton Bay fig trees planted in the 1860s under the supervision of the director of the Botanic Gardens, Charles Moore, were pulled out between 1905 and 1910 so that surrounding streets could be widened.

Sydney's only two First Fleet relics, the anchor and cannon from the *Sirius*, were placed there in the early twentieth century. The other commemorative work in Macquarie Place is the statue of Sir Thomas Sutcliffe Mort, businessman, pastoralist and founder of the AMP Society. On the southern side of the place stand two plane trees planted by Queen Elizabeth in 1954 to mark the beginning of Remembrance Drive. This drive runs along the Hume Highway and commemorates those who died in war.

Macquarie Place is hemmed in and badly overshadowed by late–twentieth-century buildings. The Renaissance Hotel and the triangular-shaped Gateway Building now dominate the northern end of Macquarie Place. The Gateway also dominates the skyline of Circular Quay. Massive as it is, the reflectiveness of the glass and its siting on the western side of Macquarie Place reduce (to a certain extent) the impact of its scale on the place below; the Renaissance Hotel, however, casts a long and dreary shadow over the once sunny, green space.

Sydney Cove had to wait until 1837 before it began to take its present form. Sydney's population growth and the wool boom of the 1830s meant that more wharves were badly needed. Before Circular Quay was built, it was often impossible for ships' passengers to

ABOVE: Circular Quay looking west to George Street, c. 1920, when trams were still running in Sydney.

BELOW: Aerial view of Circular Quay and the city centre in 1931. The Commissariat Stores, demolished to make way for the Maritime Services Board Building (now the Museum of Contemporary Art), can be seen at centre right.

227

embark or disembark. The only landing jetties were primitive and makeshift, so smaller vessels had to ferry goods, convicts, immigrants and livestock on and off the ships. This process was tedious and inefficient.

In the late 1830s, the arrival of ships was still a big event. Upon casting anchor in the 'stream' they were boarded first by harbour and customs officials and then by doctors, who checked on the health of the incoming passengers. If there were no companion ladders on the ships, passengers were winched over the side and deposited into the sterns of watermen's boats. They were then rowed ashore, and alighted at the Queen's Wharf below the commissariat stores. This was obviously inconvenient for women wearing restrictive clothing.

Before Semi-Circular Quay was built, ships were secured by mooring ropes surrounding the cove. The process of loading and unloading the cargo from the ships was slow: it could take as long as three months. Bales of wool brought from the remote interior by bullock dray were stored in warehouses or dumped close to the shore of the cove and pressed just before they were loaded. As Sir James Fairfax reflected in 1900 on Sydney in the late 1830s:

> It was quite an event when the ship's loading was complete, hatches closed and covered with tarpaulin, and everything ready to unship the ponderous gangway or stage. The full rigged ship moved from Sydney Cove to the 'stream' … and oftentimes days elapsed before the sea pilot came on board, waiting for a favourable wind. With the anchor weighed and a light westerly wind, and sail gradually unfurled, it was a fine sight to see the good ship passing down Port Jackson, past Bradleys Head, then past South Reef [Sow and Pigs Reef] and through the Heads, finally dropping the pilot and setting her face towards Good Old England.[4]

Circular Quay was built in two stages, the first from Circular Quay East to the Tank Stream. Circular Quay East was part of the governor's exclusive Domain until he moved to his new residence in 1838. At that time, the Governor's Domain contracted to the eastern side of Macquarie Street. When the first stage of Semi-Circular Quay was built, 10 acres (4 hectares) of tidal mud flats around the head of Sydney Cove were reclaimed under the direction of Major George Barney, the colonial engineer responsible for public works. This land reclamation was very ambitious by the standards of the day. The depression of the 1840s slowed progress, and the abolition of transportation dried up the most easily accessible labour pool. Barney was also responsible for the engineering and construction of Victoria Barracks, Fort Denison and the fortification of Bradleys Head.

Thousands of convicts were employed cutting stone and carting rubble and other infill from Pinchgut (Fort Denison), the Argyle Cut and the Tarpeian Way, which was hewn out of rock to make way for the flat apron of land around Circular Quay East and Bennelong Point. All this material was needed to build the sea wall as far as the Tank Stream. This was the last and most significant convict work undertaken in the colony.

In the 1850s, after Sydney had recovered from the economic recession of the 1840s and absorbed the effects of the gold boom, the decision was taken to extend the quay again over the Tank Stream around to Campbell's Wharf. When that work was completed, the area became known as Circular Quay. The rocky shoreline on the western side of Circular Quay West was covered up forever. In the 1890s Circular Quay was remodelled and more land was reclaimed. In the process, the government dockyard was subsumed beneath the surface of the land. Timber wharves were replaced by stone and other more permanent materials.

The only reminder of the natural waterline in the cove is Cadman's Cottage, the front wall of which was built on the water's edge. This gives a good idea of the extent of land reclamation on the western side of Circular Quay. The shape of the footpath to the right of Cadman's Cottage has been designed to show the location of the wharf that used to stand outside the coxswain's home. This is such a subtle and unheralded detail that few people are aware of it.

The period between the gold rush of the 1850s and the turn of the century was the quay's heyday as a bustling port. Generally, from the middle of the nineteenth century, the eastern side of the quay was used by wool fleets, and the western side by ships carrying other cargoes, while the head of the quay was used by ferries. From the 1860s onwards, as the volume of trade and ferry traffic increased, port facilities became more concentrated at Darling Harbour, and further to the west at Pyrmont and White Bay. Despite this, wool loading and unloading were still important activities around the quay and many wharves were built there to accommodate the new clippers and, later, steamships.

Steamships began to carry the lion's share of cargo by the 1880s. By 1900, only 20 per cent of the total tonnage in Sydney's ports were sailing vessels. Twenty years later, these vessels were an oddity. With the modernisation of other wharf facilities in Woolloomooloo, Walsh Bay and Darling Harbour in the 1920s, Circular Quay was from then on mainly used by overseas passengers and ferry commuters.

The Rocks is Sydney's oldest residential area. It is no longer easy to discern the craggy sandstone rocks which gave the area its name by looking west from Sydney Cove, as the area is heavily built-up with office towers, hotels and apartment buildings. The rocky topography is more clearly visible from the western side, at Millers Point. Some of Sydney's finest early colonial town houses of the 1830s were built at Millers Point. They still loom proudly over the sandstone cliffs above Walsh Bay which were cut, as Circular Quay East had been before, to make way for new port facilities.

The Rocks is an area that has been shrinking over time, at least in the minds of Sydney's planners. Before the construction of the Sydney Harbour Bridge, The Rocks began at Grosvenor (formerly Charlotte) Street. The name of the street was changed to help erase the unpleasant memories of the colony's convict past in the late nineteenth century. The construction of the Cahill Expressway and twentieth-century skyscrapers meant that the area known as The Rocks now begins on the northern side of the expressway. Despite these twentieth-century assaults upon its original integrity, The Rocks has retained some of its early colonial character, although the pressure of being Australia's greatest tourist showcase has been intense. The area is a premium retail and tourist precinct. Some of the more unusual shops have disappeared, and duty-free stores and designer boutiques proliferate along Lower George Street. One of the saddest losses was the old shell shop on the northern end of Lower George Street. This shop could keep a fascinated amateur collector busy for hours. It survived until the early 1980s and displayed a staggering variety of diverse and beautiful shells and pieces of coral, and other maritime curios from around the world. In some ways, its disappearance seemed to be a symbolic severance of The Rocks from its maritime past.

The Rocks has always been a lively place. It was where the convicts, marines and early immigrants lived, and where the first hospital was built (where the James Barnet–designed police station now stands in George Street). In the nineteenth century, as well as being the centre of Sydney's maritime activity, The Rocks was the location of Sydney's first 'Chinatown'.

Nearly all the remaining old houses in The Rocks have been restored. Millers Point begins on the western side of the Argyle Cut. There, the streets are wider and quieter, and the atmosphere is more tranquil and less obviously dominated by the bustle of retail activity.

For most of the nineteenth century, the area of The Rocks around the northern end of George Street was like any other dockland area: noisy and sometimes unwholesome. Unlicensed taverns and inns sprang up where they could. The area had an exotic flavour. Seamen from all around the world came ashore from ships engaged in the whaling and sealing trades in the Pacific and Great Southern oceans. Europeans, Americans, Maoris, Chinese and South Sea islanders worked, rested and played in the Millers Point–Rocks area. Gradually, as the wool industry grew, bigger warehouses were built to store this valuable cargo.

From the 1830s, Lower George Street was the address of many businesses of various shapes and sizes. They ranged from ships' chandlers to newspaper publishers, including Sydney's earliest newspapers—the *Sydney Gazette*, the *Monitor* (both now defunct) and the *Sydney Morning Herald*—butchers, bakers, the Post Office, 'crimping houses' where sailors could cash their bills of exchange at a discount, and all the other services which were available in any small seaport town.

Typically, criminal activity was part of life's tapestry. In the 1840s, one of Sydney's most gruesome murders was committed in Lower George Street. A shipping agent, Mr Warne, was cruelly hacked to death with an axe by his French valet, Mr Videll, while Warne was working at his desk. Having committed the crime, Videll then had to work out how to dispose of the body. His attempts to burn the body failed—he nearly set fire to the chimney in Warne's rooms, thereby attracting some attention. He was able to deflect this by hiding the body, dragging it from room to room to escape detection. His next gambit was to try to dispose of the corpse by cutting up the body, putting it in a box and throwing it in the harbour.

Videll dragged the box across the road to the nearby Queen's Wharf and hired a waterman

ABOVE: Aerial view of Bennelong Point and the Sydney Opera House, with Circular Quay and the city centre in the background. *(Marcus Clinton)*

BELOW: Aerial view of Farm Cove and the Royal Botanic Gardens. The popular harbour vantage point of Mrs Macquarie's Chair is in the foreground to the left. *(Marcus Clinton)*

ABOVE: Looking westward from the sweeping curve of Bondi Beach over the eastern suburbs towards the city. (*Alan Lever, Australian Tourist Commission*)

BELOW: Children with pose with Chinese 'dragons' in Sydney's Chinatown. (*Australian Tourist Commission*)

ABOVE: Central Railway Station and clock tower. (*Marcus Clinton*)

ABOVE: Aerial view of the city with Darling Harbour container terminal in the foreground. *(Marcus Clinton)*

BELOW: Looking eastward over the Pyrmont Peninsula over Darling Harbour to Millers Point, the Harbour Bridge and the North Shore. *(Marcus Clinton)*

to take him across the harbour, telling the waterman that it contained bad pork. The waterman's suspicions were aroused by the sight of blood oozing from the box. The police were called, and Videll was arrested and later hanged at Darlinghurst Gaol. Some ghoulish residents of Sydney mounted the stairs to view the blood-soaked, messy murder scene.[5]

An archaeological dig on the 2800–square-metre site of demolished terraces between Gloucester and Cumberland streets opposite the King George V Recreation Centre has revealed much about life in The Rocks in the nineteenth century.[6] Some of the houses on the site date from the 1840s. The houses were demolished soon after the land was reclaimed by the Sydney Harbour Trust after the outbreak of bubonic plague in The Rocks in 1900.

The site contains some of the only remaining intact remnants of early Sydney. It shows the degree to which Sydney was an eighteenth-century, pre–Industrial Revolution town. It was built organically, more like a medieval town in Europe than a nineteenth-century city of the New World, many of which, including Melbourne, were laid out in a grid pattern. At The Rocks, houses were densely packed together, in all their motley variety. Imposing homes stood close to small cottages, and rich and poor lived within a stone's throw of each other rather than being isolated within their respective socio-economic groups.[7] The hilly topography accentuated the organic and unplanned appearance of the early town. Gentleman ship and wharf owners, such as whaler and trader Robert Towns, and members of the professions and their families lived a short distance away from seamen, artisans and general labourers.

Because of the abundance of local sandstone, most housing for the working classes was built in stone, while more gracious villas and town houses were built in brick. Victorian prosperity, industry and rectitude and the nineteenth-century expansion of Sydney beyond the old town eliminated the diverse social mix in The Rocks and Millers Point. The area became a working-class suburb with a reputation, deserved or otherwise, for criminality, drunkenness and depravity.

Sometimes the unplanned nature of The Rocks had undesirable consequences. Suez Canal, so-called by the locals from the late nineteenth century, presumably because of the torrents that poured through it every time it rained, is only one of many narrow alleys that acted as a thoroughfare in the early nineteenth century. The lane was a haven for drunks and larrikin pushes in the late nineteenth and early twentieth centuries. Now it is part of a maze of alleys which, together with Surgeons Court and Nurses Walk, cater almost exclusively to tourists.

231

Today, older buildings from Sydney's maritime and industrial past sit alongside towering skyscrapers, but a leisurely stroll through Circular Quay West and The Rocks provides an interesting glimpse of Sydney over time.

West of the ferry terminus is First Fleet Park and the Museum of Contemporary Art. The building was designed for the Maritime Services Board as an assertive gesture of bureaucratic authority. It is a very late manifestation of Art Deco architecture, completed after World War II and one of the last buildings in Sydney where sandstone was used structurally rather than decoratively. It is more massive and stripped of detail than other, pre-war Art Deco buildings in Sydney.

The Museum of Contemporary Art was founded with money bequeathed to the Power Institute of Sydney University by doctor and artist John Power. His works are contained within the building, as are many contemporary artworks by local and international artists. Unlike Sydney's other major cultural institutions, the MCA does not (yet) rely to any significant degree on government money, but rather on the goodwill of its patrons. It has ambitious expansion plans, with one object being the construction of a cinémathèque. Any extensions to the building will need to take into account the recent discovery of remains of the old government dockyard, built in 1797. These are some of the earliest remnants of old Sydney, and of priceless heritage value.

Further to the north between the MCA and the Overseas Passenger Terminal is Cadman's Cottage, built between 1815 and 1816. This is the oldest remaining building in Sydney, and gives some idea of the scale of the architecture around Sydney Cove in the early colonial period. The cottage was originally built just above the high-water mark. It is a miracle that this Colonial Georgian building has survived. Some believe that Francis Greenway, who lived close to the cottage in George Street, had a hand in its design, although this claim has never been verified.

John Cadman came to Sydney in 1798. He had been sentenced to transportation for life for the theft of a horse. He was pardoned by Macquarie in 1821, when he was officially appointed government coxswain. By 1827, he had been promoted again to the position of superintendent of government craft. He held this position for nineteen years until he died, at the age of ninety, in 1848. Cadman had lived in his cottage until 1845 with his wife and two daughters. The boat crew lived in small adjoining huts.

In the early years of the colony, before roads or railways were built, transport of goods by water up the Parramatta River was the most important form of transport to the west, before Parramatta Road became passable and safe from bushrangers. This meant that the person in charge of the government transport fleet held a very important position. The government coxswain not only had to transport goods, but performed the roles of the water police and customs department as well.

After Cadman's death, the cottage was used as headquarters for the water police. When the land was reclaimed to build the western side of Circular Quay, the police moved on to the James Barnet-designed building which is now the Justice and Police Museum in Phillip Street. Even more land in front of Cadman's Cottage was reclaimed to build the Overseas Passenger Terminal in 1964. Cadman's cottage was vacant and derelict by the 1960s, until its historical significance was finally recognised in the early 1970s. That same decade, it was restored by the Sydney Cove Authority. The National Parks and Wildlife Service has offices and an information centre for Sydney Harbour National Park in the building.

Today, the largest monument to Circular Quay's twentieth-century role as an ocean liner terminus is the oversized Overseas Passenger Terminal. It stands on the site of many smaller

232

wharves. Apart from the handful of days each year when there is a large passenger ship in port or when a large social function is held, the terminal is empty. Ocean travel is an indulgence few people have the time or the money for these days. In an attempt to reduce its dinosaur-like status, the steel and glass building was reduced in scale in the 1980s, so that Cadman's Cottage is once again exposed to the harbour. The Passenger Terminal has taken on new roles, as a function centre and as a location for two fine restaurants, Quay and Doyle's. The balconies in the terminal offer fine night-time views of the harbour and the Opera House on the other side of the cove.

Immediately to the west of the Overseas Passenger Terminal is the Australasian Steam Navigation Co. Building. It was built in 1883 and designed by William Wardell, who also designed St Mary's Cathedral in College Street. It was restored in the early 1990s. Its roofline and northern tower are northern European in style and appearance. This is an unusual architectural style in Sydney, where nineteenth-century architects usually limited themselves to the Gothic or Classical Revival styles of architecture. The construction of this building and James Barnet's Customs House at the head of the quay changed the scale of the place in the late nineteenth century—but to a much smaller degree than the changes that came about from the 1960s onwards.

233

The little cove between the Overseas Passenger Terminal and Dawes Point is called Campbells Cove. Today, it is ringed by nineteenth-century warehouses and the exclusive Park Hyatt Hotel. Robert Campbell, a merchant and trader who arrived in Sydney from Calcutta with his brother in 1798, built the first private wharf in Sydney in 1802.

Campbell acquired leases covering 3 acres (1.2 hectares) of land on the western side of Sydney Cove. He became an extremely successful merchant. Campbell was one of the founders of the Australian sealing and whaling industries. His success as a trader chiselled away at the monopolistic and predatory pricing of the Rum Corps, and he was an ally of the emancipists and free settlers, lending them money on reasonable terms, and generally looking after their interests. Campbell retired to his property, Duntroon, which is now the site of Australia's Defence Force Academy, located just outside Canberra.

An early-nineteenth-century name for Campbells Cove was 'the Go-down', a nineteenth-century expression for a warehouse. Robert Campbell's home stood on the site of the Australasian Steam Navigation Co. Building at the southern end of the cove. Peacocks, turkeys and other poultry used to roam around the grounds of the house. In the nineteenth century, the Campbells later moved to a Wardell-designed home in Bligh Street, which was later converted into the Union Club. Another branch of the family built a home in Lower Fort Street, Millers Point.

Within three years, Campbell had constructed, in addition to the wharf, a number of storehouses behind it which have long since been demolished. The warehouses around Campbells Cove date from 1838 to 1861. The storehouses have been owned by the government since 1887. The third storeys were added in the 1890s. Restoration of the buildings took place between 1975 and 1978, as part of the work of the Sydney Cove

234

ABOVE: Looking north over Pitt Street while the Harbour Bridge was under construction, c. 1930. At the time, Pitt Street extended as far as Campbells Cove. The old Commissariat Stores, one of the earliest and most significant buildings of the early colonial period, can be seen just behind the trams to the left. This building was demolished in 1940 to make way for what is now the Museum of Contemporary Art.

Authority. These storehouses are now occupied by several restaurants, including the Waterfront, Wolfie's and the Imperial Peking Harbourside. Outside the Imperial Peking Harbourside is an old hydraulic whip (hoist), which was used to load and unload goods in and out of the warehouses.

At the northern end of George Street, opposite the luxury Park Hyatt Hotel, is the former Earth Exchange (Geological and Mining Museum). The museum was originally designed to operate as a power station for The Rocks area—but it was never used as such. While it was being built, bigger power stations at Balmain and Pyrmont were already under construction, so it was never commissioned. In 1908, the Government Architect proceeded to draw plans to convert it into a museum. Until 1995, the building housed the mineral and fossil collection gathered from the Geological Survey of New South Wales, now called the Department of Mineral Resources. The future of the old mining museum is uncertain. Eventually, it may be converted to mixed retail, commercial and residential use, and may be used as an Aboriginal cultural centre.

In Argyle Street, just below the Argyle Cut, is the Argyle Centre, now renamed and repositioned as a fashion and design emporium, The Argyle. On the top floor is bel mondo, one of Sydney's smartest modern Italian restaurants. The complex of buildings of which The Argyle forms a part used to be a collection of bond stores, built between 1826 and 1887. Four of these are built around an old cobblestone courtyard just off Argyle Street. The eastern store is the earliest—it was also the first customs house in the colony, operating as such from 1830 to 1850, until Mortimer Lewis's Customs House in Circular Quay was completed. Some of the occupants of the bond stores in the nineteenth century were Mary Reiby, customs collector Captain John Piper and brewers and businessmen Robert and Edwin Tooth.

It was the renovation of the Argyle Tavern (which had earlier been the haunt of larrikins), the Argyle Arts Centre and the nearby Spaghetti Factory from the late 1960s that heralded the arrival of tourism in the area. The earliest tourists to visit were curious, and/or hungry Sydneysiders. When the Argyle Arts Centre was renovated by the McMahon family, artisans and craftspeople, often inspired by the cottage industries of the hippie era, opened small businesses there. It never completely lost the *Zeitgeist* of the early 1970s, though this spirit of twenty years ago had faded considerably by the time it was closed for renovations in 1993.

Just west of The Argyle up Argyle Street are the famous Argyle Steps, the Argyle Cut and the underbelly of the Harbour Bridge. On the other side, the ambience changes. Many of the streets of Millers Point exude a sedate, early colonial atmosphere not found anywhere else in Sydney. Argyle Place is surrounded by town houses, many of them dating from the 1840s. Some of these houses have views up to Observatory Hill.

On the corner of Argyle and Lower Fort streets is the Garrison Church, the first military church in the colony. It served the soldiers garrisoned at Dawes Point. The Garrison Church was designed by architect Henry Ginn in 1840 and extended in 1878 by Edmund Blacket. It houses what is said to be the best stained-glass window in the southern hemisphere, a gift of Doctor James Mitchell, whose son David founded the Mitchell Library. The Mitchell family lived in an old Francis Greenway-designed mansion called Cumberland Place near Cumberland Street in the 1830s. This building is gone. The Garrison Church served the British army until it departed in 1870, and the New South Wales Army Regiment subsequently adopted it. Within the grounds of the church is a museum of local history.

Lower Fort Street had been popular from as early as the 1820s: Bligh House (1833) and Clyde Bank are fine examples of Colonial Georgian architecture. Bligh House, built by Robert Campbell Junior, at 43 Lower Fort Street, is the only remaining Georgian freestanding town house (as opposed to a terrace house) in the city area.[8] Richmond Villa, at 120 Kent Street, used to be located in the Domain behind Parliament House. Built in 1849, it was designed by Mortimer Lewis as his own home. It shows an interesting architectural transition between the early Colonial Georgian style and the Victorian architecture of the late nineteenth century. Richmond Villa was relocated when Parliament House was extended in the 1980s.

After walking to the northern end of Lower Fort Street and back along George Street, opposite the corner of George Street and Hickson Road, one can visit an old 1840s building which now contains a 'museum branch' of Westpac Bank. The architect of the building was John Bibb, who also built the Bethel Union Chapel (now called the Rawson Institute). The Westpac building was designed in the manner of a late-nineteenth-century banking chamber, although the building has never before been used as a bank. A little to the north of George Street is the Merchant's House, a Greek Revival-style town house built in the 1850s, which has been recently renovated and is now administered by the Sydney Harbour Foreshores Trust, and is open to the public during Heritage Week.

Further south along George Street, on the eastern side, is the old Coroner's Court. It was built in 1907 and designed by architect Walter Vernon in the Federation style. This style of architecture, which borrowed freely from the British Arts and Crafts movement of the late nineteenth century, is identified by its asymmetrical appearance. Today, it is the home of an antique shop.

Just along the street is the Sailors' Home, now The Rocks Visitors' Centre, built in 1864 to provide comfortable lodging for visiting seamen. On the ground floor was a reading room and sitting room, and down in the basement were the kitchen and dining rooms. It was closed as a sailors' home in 1979, nine years after it had been resumed by the Sydney Cove Redevelopment Authority. By then there were no sailors left in the area because of the exodus of cargo handling. The Rocks Visitors' Centre is a multistorey mine of information about Sydney's early days. Downstairs is Sailors Thai, an excellent Thai restaurant.

Two doors up from the Sailors' Home stands the Rawson Institute for Seamen, separated from the Sailors' Home by the old Coroner's Court. The Rawson Institute was built by philanthropic Sydneysiders who were concerned about the moral wellbeing of sailors in the port. It was operated on non-denominational, evangelical lines. The building was completed in various stages, the first chapel being completed in 1859. In 1895, the Bethel Union merged with the adjacent Sydney Seamen's Mission, which provided reading and club rooms. The building was extended in 1909, and again in 1947. These extensions now dwarf the original chapel, sections of which can be seen from the building's eastern side near the Overseas Passenger Terminal. In more recent times, it was briefly home to the Story of Sydney Exhibition. The institute has been relocated to the old public school in Sussex Street near the corner of Liverpool Street.

The site of Sydney's first makeshift canvas hospital is marked on the wall of the old police station at 127–131 George Street. The station was designed in 1882 by James Barnet in the heyday of The Rocks pushes, and the building's stern severity is a serious reminder of the power and authority of the law. It was intended to discourage the criminality and lawlessness of the members of the various pushes. The station is built in the style of a Palladian water gate. The lion's head keystone has a police baton in its mouth.

The doctors of the first hospital in the colony who had to battle to save lives with scarce supplies and wholly insufficient human resources are remembered today in Surgeons Court, located just off George Street. Just behind Surgeons Court is Nurses Walk. The early nurses were selected from the convict population, and maintained at government expense, with no wages. It was not until the late 1860s that nurses with any kind of professional training practised in Australia. In that decade, Lucy Osburn, a nurse trained by Florence Nightingale, arrived with a handful of her colleagues.

There are some very fine buildings at the northern end of Lower George Street, between Alfred Street and Argyle Street. One of Sydney's finest restaurants, The Rockpool, stands almost anonymously alongside a maze of tourist and duty-free boutiques.

Millers Point was originally called Cockle Bay Point. This was where the first windmills were built in the late 1790s. Jack Leighton was the first miller; he owned three flour mills on the ridge of Millers Point. Leighton met an untimely death in 1826 when he fell, drunk, from a ladder which was leaning against one of them.

In the early days of the colony, Millers Point was a rocky outcrop with access limited to a narrow footpath running along the top of the precipitous ridges. One of the first activities there was stone quarrying. The recasting of the rocky terrain of Millers Point and Walsh Bay went on, in fits and starts, throughout the nineteenth and early twentieth centuries, gradually moulding the place into the more regular shape it is today.

Observatory Hill was formerly known as Windmill Hill, then Flagstaff Hill. Fort Phillip, built by Governor King as a reaction to the Irish insurrection at Vinegar Hill, used to stand there. The fort had a very short life and was dismantled during the Macquarie era.

The old stone Sydney Observatory, built in 1858, stands on the site of the old fort. It was used until 1982, when clear views of the sky were no longer possible due to smog and the

237

reflection of Sydney's bright city lights. Today, the only reminders of the days when the skyline was dominated by windmills is the name given to Windmill Street. On the corner of Windmill and Lower Fort streets is the Hero of Waterloo, the Lord Nelson's rival to the claim of Sydney's oldest pub. The Lord Nelson was built in the 1830s, and licensed in 1842. The Hero of Waterloo was built in the 1840s with sandstone hewn from the Argyle Cut. Further down, in George Street, another old hotel, the Orient (1844), stands on the corner of George and Argyle streets.

The construction of Argyle Place from 1810 enhanced the ambience of Millers Point. In the 1830s the well-to-do built town houses in Cumberland Street, Lower Fort Street and Princes Street. Princes Street was demolished in the 1920s to make way for the Harbour Bridge. Poorer quality housing was built further down the hill, often in an unplanned and almost haphazard way. Important colonists such as Bishop William Broughton, Sydney's first bishop and founder of The King's School at Parramatta, lived in Cumberland House in the 1830s, as did the Mitchell family, one member of which was David Scott Mitchell, who endowed the Mitchell Library.

238

The Argyle Cut, hewn out by both convict and free men between 1843 and 1859, was built to link the western and eastern sides of the rocky promontory. As well as the need for infill to build Semi-Circular Quay, east–west access across The Rocks and Millers Point had long been considered a worthwhile objective as it would make Millers Point more accessible to the centre of the town. In fact, making Millers Point more accessible to George Street and the commercial centre probably accelerated the rate of the area's socio-economic decline and the drift of more affluent people out of the area, until the mid-twentieth century.

As with Semi-Circular Quay and Fort Denison, the end of transportation and the shortage of government funds meant that building the Argyle Cut took much longer than it should have. The overhead bridges along Gloucester, Cumberland and Princes streets were not all finished until 1868. By that time, Millers Point's days as a genteel address had passed.

By the late nineteenth century, The Rocks and Millers Point were in a run-down state. The social diversity had faded, and the area was predominantly working class. Some of Sydney's most notorious larrikin pushes roamed the streets there, often fighting each other on the Argyle Cut, which forms the boundary between The Rocks and Millers Point.

One of those who spent time living at The Rocks was the legendary boxer of the late nineteenth and early twentieth century, Les Darcy. He won some of his earliest fights in the backstreets competing against members of rival pushes and, in beating them, earning the sobriquet 'the Captain of the Push'. Another famous boxer who perfected his skill in the back alleys of The Rocks was Albert Griffiths ('Young Griffo'), a newspaper boy who, as a slightly built ten-year-old, learned how to defend himself from local bullies, beat them, and later became a local hero.

It was for people such as Les Darcy and Albert Griffiths that the anonymous ballad 'The Bastard from the Bush' was penned:

As the shades of night were falling
   over town and bush
From a slum in Bludgers' Alley slunk
   the Captain of the Push.
He scowled to the north and he scowled
   to the south
Then crooked his little finger in a
   corner of his mouth
And with a long, low whistle woke
   the echoes of The Rocks
And a dozen ghouls came, sloping,
   'round the corners of the blocks.

They say naught to raise their anger
   yet the oath that each one swore
Was less fit for publication than the
   one that went before.
For they spoke the gutter language with
   the easy flow that comes
To men whose children know the brothels
   and the slums …

239

Many of the local families, including Albert Griffiths's, were involved in maritime trade. The men worked as seamen or wharf labourers. Life as a wharf labourer was more uncertain in those days. Men queued up every morning for casual work, and many were disappointed. The system was sometimes arbitrary and capricious. Union men and 'trouble makers' were avoided and denied work by employers wherever possible.

The Great Maritime Strike of 1890 was a tough time for these men and their families who had worked in the shipping industry since the earliest years of the colony. The strike was broken by free or 'scab' labourers who loaded wool onto the waiting ships. The bitter memory of these years lived on in the small maritime communities, such as Millers Point.

Economic conditions for the wharfies did not improve in the early twentieth century. The advent of larger cargo ships meant that work was less regular, and the Depression was a miserable time for them. The wharfies exacted a heavy price from the stevedores during the labour shortages of World War II. The Waterside Workers' Federation (WWF) wasted no time in negotiating the maximum pay and working conditions it possibly could. Its members felt bitter and angry about the way their fathers and grandfathers had been treated in earlier years, forced to scrounge for job tickets along the 'Hungry Mile' of Sussex Street and Hickson Road. A roster system for labour was introduced in 1943. There are still outbreaks of hostilities between the maritime workers and the stevedores, most notably in 1998 between

Patricks Stevedores and the Maritime Union of Australia, the successor to the WWF. As a result of the acrimonious dispute between Patricks and its workforce, there has been much improvement to work practices and the level of productivity. Featherbedding and overstaffing have been reduced, and the rate of pay for workers is now more closely linked with increases in the rate at which goods are processed through Sydney's wharves.

In 1900, The Rocks and Millers Point were stricken by an outbreak of bubonic plague that other parts of Sydney also experienced. This sad event made the area even more demonised for its squalor and unfitness as a place to live. In fact death rates from typhoid fever were higher than they were for the plague[9] but the plague was more easily localised, and the cause of it more easily identified as the unsanitary conditions on the wharves and in some of the tenement housing of the area. Victims of the plague were quickly shipped off to the quarantine station at North Head.

After the plague, 53 hectares of land was resumed and placed in the hands of the Sydney Harbour Trust, later called the Maritime Services Board and recently renamed Sydney Waterways. Although the land was resumed on the grounds of public health, the timing of the resumption was propitious. It dovetailed neatly with the need to upgrade Sydney's motley, old-fashioned wharf facilities. Just as significantly, it made the construction of the southern approaches to the Harbour Bridge more easily achievable in the 1920s. A harbour crossing by road had long been in the minds of Sydney's planners, and the possibility that the outbreak of the plague served as a pretext for land resumption is not entirely fanciful.

With the construction of the bridge, the division between Millers Point and The Rocks became more marked, as it had been in the days before the Argyle Cut was built. The approach to the bridge sliced through the top of the once rocky promontory. Old streets such as Princes Street were completely demolished. Major sections of Cumberland and Gloucester streets were other casualties.

Throughout the late nineteenth and early twentieth centuries, The Rocks and Millers Point became tightknit communities. Many of the residents worked for the Sydney Harbour Trust and the trust also owned the roofs over their heads. Some of the state government's first attempts at public housing can be found at numbers 46 to 56 Gloucester Street opposite the Australia Hotel, and in High and Fort streets. The new workers' housing only partially arrested the decline in the amount of housing available in the area due to the construction of the bridge and other land reclamation.

The trust also built new hotels to replace those demolished to make way for new, wider and longer wharves. Some of these are the Palisade, the Dunbarton Castle and the Harbour View. Tucked away in Cumberland Street on the corner of Gloucester Street is the Edwardian–Federation hotel, the Australia Hotel (1913). The Australia Hotel is built with a split-level bar which follows the contours of the sandstone rocks underneath, and is frequented by city business people during the week and exclusively by out-of-towners on the weekends.

In 1936, the Sydney Harbour Trust became more closely connected with government when it was absorbed into a new governmental body, the Maritime Services Board (MSB). The

ABOVE: Schoolboys during the 1930s Depression on an excursion to Moore Park from Fort Street school to learn about the making of Akubra hats. Note the number who did not wear school shoes, which in those days were a status symbol.

'Maritime', as it was called by locals, had the task of maintaining, or at least saving from ruin, the housing at The Rocks and Millers Point which had escaped demolition. The MSB did not take a very active role in looking after its non-wharf properties in the area, and it was a responsibility it tried to pass on to other authorities without success. As a consequence many people drifted out to enjoy life in the suburbs. The enrolments of students at Fort Street Primary School tell the story of the ageing population and the exodus to the suburbs. In 1955, there were 270 children enrolled; in 1963, there were 153; and, in 1975, there were only forty-eight students.[10] St Brigid's Catholic School, founded in 1835, still stands on the corner of Kent Street and Argyle Place; it closed recently due to a lack of enrolments.

In the late 1950s and early 1960s, the area was adversely affected once again, this time by the construction of the Cahill Expressway, and The Rocks was even more isolated. By 1970, less than half the buildings standing in 1890 had survived. In 1968, the Sydney Cove Redevelopment Authority was created to deal with the area. The Askin government had the large-scale demolition and development of The Rocks specifically in mind. In 1971, the authority proposed to raze The Rocks and build two 50-storey office blocks and eight blocks of 30 storeys each. Proponents of the demolition of The Rocks included Harry Seidler and many others.

Fortunately, the Builders' Labourers' Federation (BLF) combined with residents to oppose these plans, and 'green bans' were imposed by the union. The union would not allow any of its members to work on redevelopment sites there. These bans led to acrimonious exchanges between the government and the unions: the leader of the BLF, Jack Mundey, was called a traitor to his country by the then minister for local government, Charles Cutler. Many developers would have agreed with this assessment. Undeterred by the combined forces of local opposition, the BLF *and* the National Trust, the Askin government forged ahead with its plans.

Bulldozers moved into Playfair Street in October 1973. Protesters barricaded streets and occupied half-demolished buildings. Despite the ostensibly inflexible stance of Premier Robin Askin's Liberal coalition government, The Rocks was saved from demolition. One or two buildings, such as the box-like Sirius apartment complex which rises above the height of the bridge, slipped through the net. About the only good thing which can be said about the Sirius block is that the assumption underlying it is admirably egalitarian: Housing Commission accommodation is just as entitled to breathtaking views of the harbour as accommodation and office space for the more prosperous. One of the leaders of the residents' action groups was Nita McCrae, who lived at 35 George Street. Her earliest Australian ancestor had lived in The Rocks from 1806.

By the mid-1970s, the urge to conserve this historical precinct had prevailed over the desire to rebuild it entirely. The trade-off was that high-rise development south of the Cahill Expressway would fund the restoration of residential and tourist precincts. The Sydney Cove Authority was sitting on some of the best undeveloped pieces of city real estate, such as the sites upon which Grosvenor Place and the Regent and ANA hotels were built. These buildings were leased and the income is used to look after the rest of the property owned by the Sydney Cove Authority, recently merged with the Darling Harbour Authority and CityWest Development Corporation into the Sydney Harbour Foreshores Authority. In 1996, the Sydney Cove Authority earned annual rentals of more than $20 million.

The growth of the tourist industry throughout the 1980s has increased the strength of the winds of change brought about by changes in the maritime industry. The transfer of the housing once owned by the Maritime Services Board to the Housing Commission has been another important factor in changing the atmosphere of the area. Although this was only a transfer between government departments, they had widely marked differences in culture and approach. The MSB had a policy of allowing tenancies to be passed down generation to generation, reinforcing connection between the traditional residents and their work. The Housing Commission, on the other hand, often gives priority to people who need housing on an emergency or temporary basis. As a result, there are more short-term tenants in the area than there used to be.

As traditional grocers and other small businesses gave way to duty-free opal shops that could afford higher rents, the amount of facilities available to local residents shrank. Until the

1980s, buildings north of the Regent Hotel mostly served the local, maritime and ship-providoring markets. Now, chemists, newsagents and other small businesses are given subsidised rents to encourage them to stay.

What is intriguing about the more residential areas of Millers Point and The Rocks is that there are still some people who can trace a family connection with the area going back to the early days of the colony, though this connection is becoming increasingly rare. With the advent of containerisation and roll-on/roll-off cargo in the shipping industry from the late 1960s, the maritime trade has shrunk, and many of the wharves have become obsolete. Some of them have been converted to other uses. Throughout the 1970s, traditional jobs were lost and people who had stoically survived the land reclamation and building of the Harbour Bridge earlier in the twentieth century finally moved on.

One example of a family that has long been connected with the area is Dave Jackson's. Dave works as a building services manager for two buildings in the city. His mother, Val, can trace a connection to The Rocks as far back as the 1830s. Her earliest ancestor was a convict who had worked on a chain gang and lived at Pyrmont before he moved to The Rocks. Since then, her family has always lived there, close to their work. Her grandfather was a wharf labourer born in 1894. Her great-grandfather, born in 1851, was a sailor.

243

Last century, Val's family owned a pub in Princes Street called the Bee Hive. Val, unimpressed by the changes to The Rocks, moved to Dee Why in 1986. Many of her friends had moved out as well, often to the Central Coast. Only three of Dave's old schoolmates still live in the area. According to the Reverend Brian Seers of the Garrison Church, one old man who could trace his family's uninterrupted residence in The Rocks back to the First Fleet, and whose family had lived there continuously since those far-off days, had recently moved on.

Reverend Seers came to the Holy Trinity (Garrison) Church in late 1983, and in that relatively short time has seen significant social change. The parish is comparatively tiny; 650 yards (595 metres) long and 500 yards (460 metres) wide, running from the Cahill Expressway to Dawes Point, and from the Overseas Passenger Terminal to the Maritime Services Board tower on Walsh Bay. Despite the size of the parish, there were three distinct communities when Seers arrived: Church Hill, which was a strong and self-contained community of about 200 people, Millers Point and Dawes Point.

In 1983, the area was much more tribal than it is now. Often these tribal animosities could be traced back through generations, to the fights and the pushes the protagonists' parents and grandparents had been part of. There were sometimes fights on the Argyle Steps. Seers was amazed when he discovered that these tight little communities really existed at the end of the twentieth century. From about 1987, the area became just one community, according to Seers. More and more members of the old, permanent community who relied on the maritime industry as a source of work—old, middle-aged and young—are moving out. Even Dave Jackson moved to Beacon Hill near Sydney's northern beaches in 1995.

The focus of the Sydney Cove Authority has been to promote visits to The Rocks, by both overseas and local tourists and sightseers, and to encourage businesses that would bring income in the area. Examples are the advertising industry, and architects and designers. More of the Sydney Cove Authority's budget was allocated to marketing, also aimed at bringing in more visitors. It is estimated that almost 5 million people visit The Rocks each year, 60 per cent of whom are Australians.

There is much more colour and movement at The Rocks than there was ten years ago. On Sundays, at the northern extremity of George Street, just outside the Mining Museum, The Rocks Markets are held. These markets are the brainchild of the Sydney Cove Authority and its consultant, Frank Elgar. Having created the renovated historical backdrop at The Rocks, the next step was to continue to expand the vibrancy of the area with new, well-planned markets. They were located well to the north, so that people would be drawn right through The Rocks and spill back into the area's other laneways and squares, such as Playfair Street, The Rocks Centre and Rocks Square.

Special events and festivals have also been conceived to attract more visitors to The Rocks, such as the Bald Archy Exhibition in the Australasian Steam Navigation Co. Building in April and May of each year. This is a send-up of the Archibald Prize and exhibition, held concurrently at the Art Gallery of New South Wales. Other regular events are The Rocks Spring Fair, The Rocks Arts Festival and, last but not least, Frocks on The Rocks, which coincides with the Gay and Lesbian Mardi Gras Festival and features drag shows.

The Rocks is in a period of transition. New, affluent residents, attracted to inner-city life, are moving into refurbished buildings such as Highgate and Observatory Tower in Kent Street, two of the more glamorous and exclusive city residential developments of the 1990s. Ensuring quality control of these new residential developments is an important task. Some developers have a nasty habit of changing architects halfway through construction and sometimes drastically varying the original plans for the building once they have been given development consent, so that the finished product has less resemblance to the original idea than it should.

Closer to the water's edge and along Hickson Road and Walsh Bay, residential development will add thousands of metres of luxury waterfront living to this once solidly working-class area. The area will never be the same—and the city will lose even more connection with its maritime past. Another sort of vibrancy will develop, however, replacing the one that has been lost with the decline in the residential population and changes to the shipping industry.

The Walsh Bay area between Millers and Dawes points covers 8 hectares. There are nine wharves, built between 1910 and 1922, each 200 metres long, built on the site of smaller, private wharves demolished after the outbreak of the plague. They are named after the chief engineer, H. D. Walsh, who designed the wharves with rat-proof walls.

The construction of the wharves at Walsh Bay was made possible by the land resumptions effected by the Sydney Harbour Trust after 1900. Whole streets of housing on the upper part of Millers Point were demolished and the sandstone upon which they lay hewn away for the construction of Hickson Wharf, named in honour of the first chairman of the trust. Hickson Road is one of the widest in Sydney. It was designed not only as a roadway, but also as the path for a train between the railway goods yard at Darling Harbour and Walsh Bay and Millers Point, which was never built (but should have been). At the same time as the wharves were being built, the harbour was being dredged to accommodate the newer, bigger ships.

The wharves of Walsh Bay, like the Woolloomooloo finger wharf, are built on turpentine piles. They were primarily used for wool loading. The first wharf, known as Pier One, has been converted to a hotel. Most of the wharves are subject to a permanent conservation order. Wharves 4 and 5 at Walsh Bay accommodate the Sydney Theatre Company, the Sydney Dance Company and the Australian Theatre for Young People. The restoration and remodelling by architect Vivian Fraser was a more sympathetic adaptive reuse of the old wharf buildings. The restaurant right at the end of Pier 4, appropriately called the Wharf, is well worth visiting for its close-up view of the harbour and the bridge.

These and the other, unused wharves are subject to much attention from developers. How many and, if not all, which particular wharves will be preserved was a topic of much discussion between planners and developers during the middle and late 1990s. Many of the wharves are now infested with white ants, and also suffer from damp. A developer, Walsh Bay Properties, has retained a French architect, Phillippe Robert, to come up with a plan for recycling the old wharves without destroying their integrity.

In 1997, a development was proposed which would keep only some of the wharves intact. Wharves 6 and 7 are to be demolished, and the land-based ends of the other wharves will be remodelled so that there is a pedestrian walkway. There has been some disagreement between the National Trust about what constitutes acceptable development on these heritage buildings, and the developers, for whom the project must be economically viable. The National Trust is opposed to the scale of proposed demolition.[11] Further around towards Darling Harbour, wharves 9 and 10 will be converted to retail and residential use.

245

The southern pylons of the Sydney Harbour Bridge rest on the shore of Dawes Point, which was named after Lieutenant William Dawes, an astronomer with the First Fleet. It was here that the first observatory was built, in 1788, so that Dawes could observe the Great Southern Comet that year. Actually, that first observatory was probably in a tent, but a slightly more permanent construction was built soon after arrival. Dawes was also responsible for the supervision of the construction of a temporary fort, mounted with eight guns from the *Sirius*. This became known as Dawes Battery, and it was later built into a permanent defensive position complete with soldiers' quarters and a commanding officer's residence. Five cannons remain in Dawes Point Park below the southern approach to the Bridge, and the outline of the old battery can be seen from the Harbour Bridge overhead. Dawes Point Park provides magnificent views of the harbour. In 1995, archaeologists excavated part of Dawes Point to explore the old fortifications, which were extended by Greenway in 1819 and by George Barney in the 1850s. One of the more intriguing discoveries, apart from champagne and brandy bottles, was a Roman coin dated 150 BC.

The Sydney Harbour Bridge and the Opera House are Sydney's most visible, and possibly most recognisable, icons. Entering Sydney from the bridge along the Warringah Freeway and Cahill Expressway is one of the shortest, and most magnificent journeys which can be taken by car anywhere in the world, by day or by night.

In 1998, it became possible to take another dramatic journey across the bridge on foot. BridgeClimb is based in Cumberland Street under the southern approaches to the bridge. It organises walking tours to the top of the bridge in groups of up to ten. Walkers are put into bridge-grey jumpsuits and shown how to use cables for their trek to the top of the bridge. Observing Sydney from the summit of the bridge is a remarkable experience for both Sydneysider and tourist. It also provides one of the best views of Sydney Harbour, the lower reaches of the Parramatta River, the city skyline and the harbourside suburbs. Climbing the bridge is not nearly as frightening as it sounds and is the best way of coming to terms with the bridge's structural grandeur.

The Harbour Bridge is the largest steel arch bridge in the world, and its completion had wide implications for the development of Sydney. It could be said that Sydney was fated to have the bridge—not just any bridge, but particularly a single-arch bridge: in the first year of Sydney's settlement, Erasmus Darwin, Charles Darwin's grandfather, having seen a picture of the young colony, wrote about how it would be in the future:

> There the proud arch, Colossus like, bestride
> Yon glittering streams and bound the chafing tide …

Before the advent of ferries, passage across the harbour was provided by watermen who rowed or sailed their small boats wherever they were bidden. Billy Blue was one of the harbour's first ferrymen. He was probably a native of the West Indies, and he arrived in Sydney in January 1801 as a convict. The next year he was appointed water bailiff, which entitled him to a residence on Sydney Cove. He lived in an octagonal watch tower on Bennelong Point.

Architect Francis Greenway's dream of a bridge across the harbour was premature. The bridge had to wait for the settlement of the North Shore in the late nineteenth century. By 1890, Circular Quay was so crowded with heavy ferry traffic competing for space with cargo and passenger ships that a royal commission was established to report on whether a bridge or a tunnel should be built across the harbour. The royal commission reported that each year

ABOVE: Giraffes at Taronga Zoo. Aside from the drawcard of its animal and reptile exhibits, the zoo has unparalleled views of the harbour and the city beyond. *(Australian Tourist Commission)*

ABOVE: An aerial view of Potts Point and Woolloomooloo looking towards The Domain and the city centre. The finger wharf at Woolloomooloo Bay was the disembarkation point for many of Sydney's postwar immigrants. *(Marcus Clinton)*
BELOW: Darling Harbour at night, looking eastward towards the city. The area today is a far cry from its early industrial roots, although traces of this can still be seen at Pyrmont and Ultimo. *(Hamilton Lund, Australian Tourist Commission)*

ABOVE: An aerial view of Sydney Harbour looking east towards the heads. The harbour is integral to Sydney's image of itself and also to that of outsiders. *(Marcus Clinton)*

BELOW: Sydney's smaller harbourside beaches, such as this one in the eastern suburbs, can provide an almost peaceful haven on summer's days, often in stark contrast to packed surf beaches such as Bondi. *(Marcus Clinton)*

ABOVE: Looking back to the town of Sydney from New South Head Road, Vaucluse. Panorama from New South Head Road, *1848, Janssen (Image Library, State Library of NSW)*

BELOW: Pinchgut—later to become Fort Denison—in the early years of the colony. Pinchgut in the Early Days, with gibbet, *1802, George Barrington, in* The History of New South Wales *(Image Library, State Library of NSW)*

ABOVE: Traffic crossing the Sydney Harbour Bridge in 1947, with the North Shore railway line on the left.

247

5 million people crossed the harbour, as did 378 500 vehicles and 43 800 horsemen. It rejected the notion of a tunnel on the basis that 'so little is known as to what the waters of the harbour hide from view', and concluded that a bridge was needed to carry pedestrians, road traffic, railways and trams, all at a height sufficient to enable sailing vessels to pass beneath.

In 1900, competitive designs and tenders were called for by the New South Wales government, all of which were rejected for various reasons. It was not until 1911 that another proposal for a bridge was outlined, and advice was sought from Dr J. J. C. Bradfield at the Public Works Department. In 1912, Bradfield was appointed chief engineer in charge of the design of an electric railway system for Sydney, including the design of a bridge. His plans were completed by 1916, but action was postponed for the duration of World War I. In 1922, tenders were invited for the construction of the bridge.

The political decision to build the bridge was dogged by the old rivalry between city and country interests in railway building and public works. The city interests, less concerned with

ABOVE: The Sydney Harbour Bridge under construction in the 1930s, with Circular Quay in the foreground. The arch is almost completed, ready for the deck along which the road and railway line runs to be hung beneath.

extending transport infrastructure in New South Wales's hinterland than in creating growth opportunities for the city, prevailed. A band of Nationalist Party members who lived on the North Shore were gaining ascendancy in the party and they were no doubt looking forward to the increase in accessibility and property values that a link to the north side would bring. The Labor Party also supported the building of the bridge, because it would open up new residential areas and have the symbolic effect of uniting two sides of the city.

Six companies from around the world submitted a total of twenty tenders. Bradfield was initially in favour of the cantilever style, but changed his mind when the tenders were received. The successful tender was one of seven submitted by British company Dorman Long & Co. Ltd: a two-hinged arch with abutment towers faced in granite, at an estimated cost of £4 217 722. Dorman Long already had two well-established steel-fabricating shops in Australia (one in Sydney and one in Melbourne)—a certain advantage for them, as the invitations to tender wisely included requirements about Australian-made content of both materials and labour. One of the engineers, Ralph Freeman, had designed the 150-metre span of the arched bridge across the Zambezi River near Victoria Falls, and this was another point in Dorman Long's favour.

There was some grumbling about appointing a British firm, but Bradfield was quick to emphasise that the bridge would be fabricated at Milsons Point by Australian workers. The piers and abutments would be constructed of Nepean River sand and New South Wales cement, and the whole bridge would be erected by Australian hands. Construction finally began in April 1924, with all aspects of the work being subject to Bradfield's approval, although Freeman was largely responsible for the technical and creative control of the project.

At the same time as the bridge was being built, the underground railway which would then go over the bridge and up the North Shore was under construction. The length of the road crossing from Grosvenor Street to the Pacific Highway on the north side is called the Bradfield Highway; at 2.4 kilometres, it is the shortest and most-used highway in Australia.

The total weight of the steel in the bridge is 52 800 tonnes, of which 39 000 are in the arch. The rivets alone weigh 3200 tonnes. Most of the steel came from England, including all the silicon steel used for the arch. The remainder was Australian-made. The pylons are faced in granite from Moruya on the south coast. Many people quibble that they were never necessary in a structural sense, and so should not be there. Although they are purely decorative and as such unnecessary, they do squarely place the bridge in its historical period, when monumental ziggurat-style Art Deco architecture was in favour. Other nearby works associated with the bridge which also give the area a period flavour are Luna Park and the North Sydney Pool (which both stand on the site of the former bridge workshops) and the North Sydney railway station.

The main arch of the bridge, which is 134 metres high, was the tallest construction in Sydney from 1932 until 1967, when the Australia Square Tower was built. The high clearance from the water was necessary to give easy access to ships loading and unloading at the wharves of Walsh Bay, Darling Harbour and Pyrmont. On hot days, the top of the arch rises an extra 18 centimetres as the bridge heats up and expands. The arch sets its weight on two steel bearings at each end, which are set in 12-metre–deep concrete foundations, embedded in sandstone.

Construction of the bridge was not a universally popular undertaking—a fact which is often forgotten now that the bridge has become a symbol of the city. Hundreds of residents on either side of the harbour were dislocated as their land was resumed to build the approaches to the bridge, with only a minimum amount of notice given, so that for many it was very hard to find new homes. Some of Sydney's most historic streets were lost forever. From the moment the bridge was opened, the noise of trains, cars and buses would change the character of The Rocks forever. On the north side, much land was resumed for the Warringah Freeway, and the busy, village-like character of North Sydney came to an end.

Sixteen workers died in the construction of the bridge. One of the most horrific accidents was the death of James Campbell, who fell from the northwestern pylon in January 1932. According to the *Sydney Morning Herald*, 'Horrified watchers in the streets below saw him shot out from the pylon, turning over and over as he clutched wildly for something to stay his flight.' The watchers may well have been horrified, but in those days such a sight must have been a chilling reminder to Campbell's colleagues that the safety precautions left much to be desired, and that this was very dangerous work. Martyrdom in the cause of public progress would have been little consolation to the victims and their families. There was never a significant outcry about the industrial safety on the bridge, as there would be today. There were many disputes over wages during the bridge's construction. The terms of the contract stated that the government had to pay for increases, so Dorman Long was less troubled by wage claims than it was by the costs associated with improving the level of safety for those who were working on the bridge. Many of the workers found it hard to get other jobs in the era of the Great Depression once their employment had finished.

The Harbour Bridge opened on Saturday, 19 March 1932, and it was an occasion celebrated for weeks. Having cost £6 million, with an extra £3.75 million for associated roadworks, the bridge was celebrated as an engineering phenomenon and, moreover, as a symbol of the unity of the people of Sydney and of hope for the future. After its opening, however, it seemed to be plagued by death. It was unfortunate that this engineering marvel provided ample opportunities for people to commit suicide. In the seven months after it opened, many people had leapt to their death. Access to the top of the bridge was made more difficult, which was a pity for those who were not suicidal as the walk over the bridge and from the pylons offers some of the most dramatic views of the city and the harbour.

Apart from being a functional necessity in modern Sydney life, the bridge has become a central ingredient of the city's celebrations. Each year, on New Year's Eve and Australia Day, the Harbour Bridge is the centre of attention as Sydneysiders gather on the foreshores to watch the spectacular fireworks displays.

More visually prosaic than the bridge, the harbour tunnel is nevertheless one of Sydney's great engineering works. By the early 1950s, it had already become apparent that the bridge was not going to be able to handle the increased traffic volumes in the future. Another harbour crossing was seen as essential.

Between 1957 and 1984, various proposals were considered. Nothing was accepted until 1986 when a firm of engineers, Wargon Chapman partners, submitted a proposal to the minister for public works, Laurie Brereton. A tunnel, which would minimise the amount of land resumption and have the least impact on the population and the environment, was proposed. Another elegant component of the plan was that four of the existing twelve approach lanes to the bridge could also be used. The tunnel became New South Wales's largest privately funded civil engineering project.

Wargon Chapman consulted Transfield and Kumagai Gumi, two companies that had previously been involved in a joint venture building the Perisher Valley ski tunnel. They formed the Sydney Harbour Tunnel Joint Venture, and appointed Wargon Chapman to oversee the designs. The Sydney Harbour Tunnel Joint Venture will run the tunnel until 2022, after which time it will be owned by the state of New South Wales.

The tunnel is an immersed tube, which links the northern and eastern suburbs of Sydney. Like any of the major public works undertakings in Sydney, the Harbour Tunnel was not a universally popular concept. There was general public outrage over the fact that the toll on the bridge would rise to $2 in order to help pay for the tunnel; local North Sydney politicians condemned the enormous cost of building something which, it was felt, would ultimately benefit only a very few. The effects of building the tunnel on the environment of the harbour, both under and above the water, were not inconsiderable. Many residents complained about the noise of air extractor fans at Kirribilli and the deterioration of the air quality.

Unlike Darling Harbour, which was plagued by industrial disputes, construction of the tunnel in the years 1988 to 1993 lost virtually no time to strikes, and was completed on time and within budget—and no lives were lost. It cost $750 million and has the capacity to accommodate about 1700 vehicles per lane, per hour.

ABOVE: Bridge Street in the late afternoon, looking east to Macquarie Street (1947).

CHAPTER TEN

THE LOCUS OF GOVERNMENT: THE EASTERN EDGE OF THE CITY

JUST AS THE ROCKS and the area of the city around Sydney Cove are the cradle of Sydney's civilian and maritime life, and the city that lies behind the cove is the hub of finance and commerce, upper Bridge Street and the eastern edge of the city have, since 1788, been the seat of government.[1] This area is also the location of the city's greatest public spaces—the Domain, the Royal Botanic Gardens and Hyde Park—and its oldest and greatest cultural institutions—the State Library, the Australian Museum, the Art Gallery of New South Wales and, since 1973, the Opera House.

Bridge Street provided a link between the colonial administration and the rest of Sydney's population. It was up Bridge Street, on a hot summer's afternoon on 26 January 1808—the twentieth anniversary of white settlement in New South Wales—that members of the New South Wales Corps, led by Major Johnston, marched from their barracks in George Street, with their bayonets fixed, to arrest Governor Bligh.

The Museum of Sydney stands on the site of the old Government House. Above it soars Governor Phillip Tower. This and its smaller sibling, Governor Macquarie Tower, are two of the finest examples of contemporary high-rise architecture in Sydney. The democratically elected premier of New South Wales wields power over the state's people from the upper

254

ABOVE: The first government house, built in 1788–89, stood on the corner of Bridge and Phillip streets. In those early days, Government House was the locus of absolute power in the colony. The Museum of Sydney has been built on this site at the base of the Governor Phillip Tower. The sculpture *The Edge of the Trees*, by Janet Laurence and Fiona Foley, stands in front of the museum. This installation evokes the earliest contact between the Aborigines and the Europeans.

levels of Governor Macquarie Tower, almost directly above where governors once wielded absolute power in old Government House.

The Museum of Sydney, small but very well formed, commemorates the site of the original Government House and displays the early archaeological history of Sydney and the early contact between the colonial government and the indigenous community. In front of the museum stands an outstanding piece of sculpture, *The Edge of the Trees*, created by Janet Laurence in collaboration with Fiona Foley, an indigenous Australian contemporary artist. The work is a tribute to both indigenous and European cultures. The twenty-nine piers are made of native turpentine (recycled from a demolished foundry in Pyrmont), Sydney sandstone and steel. Some of the pillars are engraved with the botanical names of plants which would have grown on the site before white settlement, and others are engraved with the names of the clans and tribes of the Eora people who occupied the Sydney area in 1788. The names of members of the First Fleet are also engraved. The windows depicted in the pillars are 'windows of memory' and the sound of recorded Aboriginal voices can be heard. This is one of the most haunting and thoughtfully conceived and executed works of public sculpture in the city. The background of nineteenth-century terrace buildings reinforces the historic symbolism of the site, and the sculpture that stands there.

Bridge Street was extended from Phillip Street up to Macquarie Street in 1845. To this day, the area around Bridge Street and Macquarie Place is still occupied by government departments, such as the Chief Secretary's Building (1875), the Lands Department (1888), and the Education Department Building (1914). The first two of these were designed by Colonial Architect James Barnet. More notable than the overall exterior of the Lands Department Building are the sculptures on the facade commemorating the early explorers of this continent. The explorers depicted include Blaxland, Lawson and Wentworth, Mitchell, Oxley and Leichhardt. The building still houses all the original surveys of New South Wales.

In 1995, urban design guidelines for the Bridge Street and Macquarie Place precinct were published by the City Council. A height limit similar to the present height of the older buildings of Bridge Street has been imposed, so that the architectural integrity of this historically and architecturally significant area can be preserved. Although not *entirely* a case of closing the stable door after *all* the horses have bolted, it is a pity that these guidelines were not in force in the early 1960s.

255

Sadly for us today, the old Exchange Building built between 1853 and 1857 that stood between Gresham and Pitt streets did not survive the architectural vandalism of the 1960s. Together with the other buildings on the southern side of Bridge Street, the old Exchange Building formed part of a wall of nineteenth-century architecture, and its loss to Sydney is great. This was where Sydney's first stock exchange developed. For many years, it was also the centre for the wool auctions and other trade in the city. A soulless piece of mid–twentieth-century architecture replaced it. If only the demolishers had not got to it so quickly, a new building would probably have arisen from the grand old facade, as happened with the Treasury Building, now the nucleus of the Inter.Continental Hotel.

The Treasury Building was used as government offices, most notably by treasury officials and as the office of the premier until 1967, when they were relocated to the old State Office Block, or 'black stump' as it used to be known, until it was demolished in 1997 to make way for new buildings designed by Italian architect Renzo Piano on the corner of Bent and Macquarie streets. The buildings will be an architectural fantasy of a magnitude rarely seen in Sydney. The estimated cost will be about $500 million.

Further down the western side of Macquarie Street is the Ritz Carlton Hotel. It used to be the headquarters of the Board of Health. Of all the bars in Sydney's hotels, this is one of the city's smartest and more comfortable. The original architect of the building was Walter Liberty Vernon who also designed the Coroner's Court and the Mining Museum in George Street at The Rocks. One of the more notorious services offered by the Board of Health was the 'blue-light clinic' which specialised in the treatment of sexually transmitted diseases until 1987 when the extensions to the hotel began.

No other impressive street could have been so appropriately dedicated to the achievements of Lachlan Macquarie than Macquarie Street. Together with architect Francis Greenway,

Macquarie is responsible for some of the street's more notable architectural achievements: the Hyde Park Barracks, St James' Church and, further north, the Governor's Stables, now used as the Conservatorium of Music. Without Greenway's architectural assistance, Macquarie commissioned the building of the Rum Hospital. Two of the wings are still standing, the northern wing now containing Parliament House and the southern wing the former Sydney Mint and the administrative offices of the Historic Houses Trust.

Macquarie Street has a most stately air. Not only is it the seat of government, but it also has an elevation and aspect unsurpassed by the city's other streets lower down the valley of the Tank Stream, which are mostly dedicated to commerce and retail activity. The relocation of Government House from Bridge Street to the Domain in 1845, and the contraction of the Domain to the eastern side of Macquarie Street made it a fashionable place to live from the late 1840s. The street, perched on the eastern flank of the town, was far away from the bulk of the population living to the west.

The middle of the nineteenth century, particularly the 1850s to 1870s, was Macquarie Street's heyday as a smart city address. By the 1870s, the middle classes had started to drift towards the suburbs and the houses of Macquarie Street were gradually converted to commercial or professional use, boarding houses, or gentlemen's clubs. Between 1879 and 1894 the new Sydney Hospital designed by Thomas Rowe was built on the site of the mid-section of the old Rum Hospital. This attracted medical practitioners to the area, and the street is still a well-known address for doctors, especially specialists, though the relative importance of Sydney Hospital has diminished. Many of the later makeshift additions to Sydney Hospital have been demolished and the building restored to its former elegant state. It is easy to see and walk through the hospital grounds to the Domain.

Macquarie Street profited greatly from the resurgence of publicly funded building activity and restoration work done in preparation for the bicentenary of European settlement in 1988. Due to the aesthetic concerns of the Wran government, and of the Government Architect of the day, Andrew Andersons, these late–twentieth-century developments really can be described as improvements, unlike much of the public architecture of the 1960s and 1970s. There is much greater sensitivity for the streetscape and the street's history than there is on the western side of the street, developed commercially from the 1960s. Most of the fine town houses on that side were demolished, and very little of outstanding quality remains.

A significant portion of the extensions to the State Library and Parliament House were underground, so the heights of the buildings were limited. At the same time as these extensions were under way, the old colonial buildings of Macquarie Street were restored to their former glory. Parliament House and the Mint were painted in colours which were fashionable during the centennial celebrations, rather than in the lighter colours of the earlier Georgian era.

The earlier section of the State Library, the Dixson and Mitchell rooms, are around the corner in Shakespeare Place. The main reading room of the State Library was designed by Henry Parkes's son, Cobden, and built between 1939 and 1941. This is late for Classical Revival architecture, making the buildings appear older than they are. Like Sydney's other significant

ABOVE: Macquarie Street near Sydney Hospital in the late 1880s, before the demolition of Burdekin House and widening of the street. Burdekin House can be seen on the right-hand side, immediately behind the woman in the foreground.

cultural institutions, the Australian Museum and the Art Gallery of New South Wales, the building has a Greek portico.

Inside the older section of the State Library is the remarkable Tasmanian blackwood–panelled Shakespeare Room, decorated in the manner of a Tudor English library in Shakespeare's era. It contains an impressive period chandelier given by one of the library's principal benefactors, Sir William Dixson. In the entrance hall of the library is a marble inlay of an early map of southeastern Australia. The work was executed by the Melocco Brothers, the pre-eminent mosaicists of early–twentieth-century Sydney.

The older section of the State Library now contains the Mitchell and Dixson collections. David Scott Mitchell was a socially withdrawn, wealthy gentleman whose life was almost entirely dedicated to book collecting. His passion for book collecting was first directed towards Elizabethan literature and manuscripts. Later he specialised in collecting works relating to Australian history, at a time when few other people showed interest in the subject. Another one of his interests, never mentioned publicly until recent years, was literary and photographic erotica. Mitchell spent most of his adult life living in a relatively modest terrace house in Darlinghurst Road, which groaned under the weight of his vast collection of books, maps and paintings. All the booksellers of the day used to compete for Mitchell's business, as he was the only serious collector in the field.

The principal librarian of the Public Library of New South Wales (precursor to the State Library) soon realised that the library could not outbid Mitchell. Instead of competing with him, the librarian, H. C. L. Anderson, courted him vigorously. As Mitchell's health declined, he undertook to leave the library his entire collection and an endowment to pay for future book acquisitions, on the condition that the government design a building to contain it so that it would be available to the people of New South Wales. It took eight years before the foundation stone of the library was laid in Shakespeare Place, and Mitchell at one stage was so frustrated that he threatened to leave the collection to the University of Sydney instead.[2] The building was completed in 1910, after Mitchell's death. The Mitchell Library is the priceless key repository of books, maps and letters which have a bearing on Australia's early history.

The State Library has also benefited incalculably from the generosity of Sir William Dixson. His family fortune was made in the tobacco industry. Like Mitchell, Dixson was a bachelor. He started collecting in the 1890s. His interest was Australian history, with a strong bias in favour of pictures and other works of art, which complemented and added depth to Mitchell's collection. Although they were both keen collectors, Mitchell and Dixson never met. The Mitchell wing of the library was extended to contain Dixson's art collection and books. The Dixson wing was opened in 1929. Dixson also provided £4000 to pay for three bronze entry doors to the library, which are dedicated to the memory of David Scott Mitchell. The doors depict Aborigines and important figures in early Australian history. He also gave the stained-glass windows in the Mitchell Library Reading Room, which are dedicated to Geoffrey Chaucer.

Next to Hyde Park Barracks is the southern wing of the old Rum Hospital, the former Sydney Mint. The novel means of financing the construction of the Rum Hospital, Sydney's oldest public building, have already been described. From 1855, the southern wing was used as the colony's first mint. Recently discovered gold was brought in from the goldfields and processed into coinage, bullion or ingots. The mint closed in 1927. In the late 1970s and early 1980s, the building was restored to the condition it was in 1870. There were more renovations in 1995 designed to emphasise the building's original function as a mint. After a brief period as the Sydney Mint Museum, it is now administered by the Historic Houses Trust.

When the Rum Hospital was first built, the level of sanitation left a lot to be desired. Sick convicts were locked up overnight in the hospital rooms with almost no sanitary facilities. Meals were cooked in the hospital wards. Gradually, the level of health care improved as the nineteenth century progressed and the convict system wound down.

The northern wing of the Rum Hospital was later converted into the Legislative Council, which first gathered there in 1829 (although it had been formed in 1824). The northern wing of Parliament House was designed as the parliamentary chamber for the Legislative Assembly in the 1840s by Mortimer Lewis. The Legislative Assembly still sits in this chamber. On account of the vituperative nature of many parliamentary debates in the late nineteenth and twentieth centuries, the chamber of the Legislative Assembly earned the nickname 'the Bear Pit'. The southern end of the building is used as the Legislative Council. That section of the building was made of prefabricated cast iron. It was originally intended for use as a church in a Victorian town.

Two rare examples of the residential architecture of the mid-nineteenth century which have survived are History House at 173 Macquarie Street and the Royal College of Physicians at 145–147 Macquarie Street. The latter was built in 1848 by John Fairfax, joint founder of the *Sydney Morning Herald* with Charles Kemp. Fairfax and his family lived in Macquarie Street until 1858, when he moved to Ginahgulla in Bellevue Hill, now part of Scots College. The building was one of a terrace of five buildings, originally Georgian in appearance, and only two storeys tall. In the late nineteenth century, the third storey was added, then, in 1910, storeys four and five were added on for the Warrigal Club, one of the many gentlemen's clubs which flourished in those days. In 1937, the building was purchased by the Royal College of Physicians. It has recently undergone restoration work.

History House is another former gentlemen's town house. It was built in the mid-1850s as a house, later converted into a gentlemen's club and then used as medical consulting rooms. In 1968, the Royal Australian Historical Society bought History House with funds from the sale of its former headquarters, an old wool store in Young Street, which was sold to the AMP and demolished to make way for the new AMP Centre.

The architecture of the early twentieth century is represented by two impressive mansion flats: Wyoming (1909), on the corner of Hunter and Macquarie streets, and the Astor, built in 1923 by the same property developer, John O'Brien. The Astor is still one of the smartest places to live in the city. It was an architecturally adventurous building in its day, and its design was heavily influenced by the Chicago School of architecture. The facade does not hide the underlying structure, enabling the size of the windows to be increased. Another example of relatively adventurous inter-war architecture is the British Medical Association (BMA) Building (1929). It pays muted homage to the stepped ziggurat style of Art Deco architecture. The ziggurat style is an uneconomic use of space, particularly when there is a height limit of 46 metres, as there was when this building was erected. The building is faced with coloured faïence glazing and uses Australian flora and fauna as its theme. It was built as doctors' consulting rooms. The BMA Building is now called the Australian Medical Association Building.

Further south, the Reserve Bank Building on the corner of Martin Place is one example of the style of public architecture circa 1963, and it is interesting to compare the quality of this architecture with the improvements to the public buildings in the 1980s. It looks like the sort of building any good (or bad) authoritarian would feel at home in. Further south there is another inferior example of public architecture of the mid-twentieth century. The pebblecrete-faced Supreme Court and Federal Court Building stands opposite Hyde Park Barracks and overlooks St James' Church. Its height dramatically increases the wind tunnel effect at the top of Macquarie Street and around Queen's Square.

View from St. James' Spire looking east
Sydney N.S.Wales June 1894

ABOVE: View of Queen's Square and the Domain from St James' spire in 1894. Hyde Park Barracks can be seen at right.

Burdekin House (1841–1933) used to stand on the site presently occupied by St Stephen's Church just to the north of Martin Place. Burdekin House was one of Sydney's greatest architectural wonders—and casualties. The house was built by Thomas Burdekin, a merchant and ironmonger who arrived in Sydney in 1831 and soon prospered. Burdekin had several property investments in the city, including large portions of Darlinghurst which he bought from the Riley estate. He started one of Sydney's first mutual insurance businesses, the Mutual Fire Insurance Association.

The architect of Burdekin House is unknown. It was probably designed in England. The construction of this, and other impressive buildings like it, demonstrated to some that:

> [T]he hovels which have long been eye sores in many of our best streets are rapidly disappearing and substantial and comfortable houses are being erected on the ground formerly occupied by them … those who have been absent from Sydney for one or two years only are surprised at the change which has taken place. One of the finest buildings is the house … which has been built by Mr Burdekin and which would not disgrace any square in London … All that is wanting is a general lighting with gas, and we hope that it will not be long before this takes place.[3]

The house was Georgian and symmetrical, divided by a central hallway. Although the house had an English flavour from the outside, the interior was decorated in the more ornate French

Louis XIV style. Burdekin himself was not universally popular. He was considered by some to be what we would now call a loan shark. Those who were unfortunate enough to be in his debt probably took great delight when an impecunious stranger, thought to be long deceased, arrived from England and was able to demonstrate that he had good title to the land as he was its original (colonial) owner. The stranger proceeded to take possession of the property. Humiliated and furious, Burdekin entered into an arrangement whereby he paid the stranger an annual rent of £600 for the stranger's life. Burdekin's health collapsed as a result of these troubles, and he described himself as a 'victim of mortification'.[4] The colonists who were financially indebted to him probably said he deserved such a fate.

Two of Burdekin's younger sons, Marshall and Sydney, became members of parliament and went on to join the Legislative Assembly. Sydney became the member for East Sydney from 1884 until 1892, and was a supporter of the Free Trade Faction and of Sir Henry Parkes.

Burdekin House was looked after by trustees from 1913 until the 1920s, when the Royal Australian Historical Society and the Institute of Architects urged the government to purchase the house. Sadly, this opportunity was not taken up. In 1922, the entire contents of the house were auctioned off and, in the early 1920s, the house changed hands.

The earliest manifestation of the urge to conserve old Sydney buildings emerged when Burdekin House's fate was under consideration. Leading Sydney historian and state librarian, Charles Henry Bertie, expressed this concern at a meeting of the Royal Australian Historical Society that:

> Burdekin House is suffering from century disease ... as our old buildings approach their centenary mark, almost inevitably circumstances arise which suggest their removal. As a consequence we have only about four buildings which are actually more than a century old.[5]

By 1935, Burdekin House had been demolished and St Stephen's Church dedicated. As we look at the architecturally uninspired St Stephen's Church we should wistfully try to imagine what once stood there.

Hyde Park Barracks is one of Francis Greenway's finest buildings. The barracks were built in fourteen months and Greenway was deservedly given a full pardon upon its completion in June 1819. This was Greenway's second building in Sydney—his first was Macquarie Lighthouse at South Head, for which he was conditionally pardoned.

It was during the construction of his early works that Greenway was faced with the daunting task of training many of his fellow convicts to become skilled stonemasons and bricklayers. The labour pool of skilled workers was very small in the early years of the colony.

The barracks were used to house up to 1000 male convicts. They were also a clearing house for newly arrived convicts and a place of punishment for those who were guilty of misconduct, or a shelter for those who were incapable of earning an independent income. Before the barracks were built, all convicts were expected to accommodate themselves wherever they could, and pay for their accommodation from the fruit of their own labour, which they could perform after three in the afternoon. One effect of the construction of the barracks was to institutionalise the convict system to a greater degree than it had been when convicts were responsible for finding their own shelter. This new wave of institutionalisation came just in time for the growing influx of convicts through the 1820s and 1830s.

The convicts slept in hammocks, each one just more than half a metre in width, and just 2 metres in length. Seventy men slept in the larger rooms, which were 20 metres by 6 metres, and thirty-five in the smaller rooms, which were 9 metres by 6 metres.

Sydney became a safer place in which to live after the barracks were built. Macquarie noted that in the three months after the barracks were opened, 'there were not a tenth … of the former Night Robberies and Burglaries'.[6] Commissioner Bigge in his inquiry into the colony thought that form had unfortunately triumphed over function—that is, it did not have to look so fine. It was only a convict barracks in a remote penal colony. No one would agree with Bigge today.

In January 1848, as the transportation system was winding down, the barracks were used as temporary accommodation for newly arrived assisted female immigrants, and provided offices for the colony's immigration agent. Convicts were relocated to the more isolated Cockatoo Island. The site was also used for many other purposes, including as a vaccination depot and as administrative offices. A jumble of ill-conceived architectural clutter inevitably resulted, as it often has, due to bureaucratic indifference and neglect.

From the late nineteenth century until the 1970s, the barracks were also used as courts, notably the Arbitration Court. The myriad of outhouses built in the old convict muster yard obscured Greenway's architecture. They were demolished from the late 1970s, while the barracks themselves were restored. The old cell block on the northern side of the muster yard is now occupied by the Barracks Café. During the restoration, the site proved to be an archaeological treasure-trove. Objects both tiny and large were found between the floorboards and under the ground. An old convict shirt was found in a rat's nest on the second floor. The Hyde Park Barracks have been restored to give an idea of what convict life in the 1820s was like. It is owned by the Historic Houses Trust. There is a permanent exhibition of the early history of the barracks and the convicts who lived there. The Greenway Gallery houses many fine temporary exhibitions.

Opposite the Hyde Park Barracks is St James' Church. The barracks and the church are perfect foils for each other. These buildings are Greenway's greatest contribution to the city and the colony. Each one is a fine example of early Colonial architecture, and the fact they are close together is an added bonus. Their fine proportions are accentuated by the lack of embellishment.

St James' Church was originally intended as a courthouse, but following the recommendations of Thomas Bigge, the uses of this building and the present-day courthouse behind it were switched in the interests of prudence and economy. The courthouse (which was still at the planning stage) became a church and the proposed school behind it became a courthouse. Architect John Verge added the eastern vestry and porches to the church in the 1830s. The courthouse was built after the church, and Greenway's hand is less discernible.

The Georgian School was built opposite the courthouse on the western side of Elizabeth Street. It remained a school until it was demolished in 1926 to make way for the new commercial developments around the St James's area which followed the completion of the new underground railway line.

Hyde Park was proclaimed by Governor Macquarie soon after he arrived in Sydney in 1810. In that year, the newly arrived 73rd Regiment was encamped at the southern end of what is now the park. Macquarie was determined to lift the civic tone of the place and to prevent the inclusion of the brick pits into Hyde Park from the south, and the military officers and administrators of the colony were happy to assist in this task if it meant that a racecourse could be built on it. Up until then, it had been known as 'the Common' or 'the Exercising Ground'. By October 1810, enough land had been cleared to be able to hold the first horse-race in the colony. The advent of horseracing brought a flurry of illegal gambling dens along Elizabeth Street. Cricket was also played there.

Hyde Park was not fenced until the 1840s. In 1834, Park Street was extended through it. Busby's Bore, the main source of the city's water supply on the corner of Park and Elizabeth streets, was completed in 1837. The bore pumped water underground from Lachlan Swamp, near Centennial Park.

Before Hyde Park was landscaped in the 1850s and 1860s, a lane called Lovers Lane ran across the park, starting at St James' Church and ending on the western side of Lyons Terrace in Liverpool Street. It was a well-known promenade and meeting place for lovers, who sat on the benches interspersed along the laneway. As one visitor to Sydney described it:

> In the evenings, on Sundays especially, this place is crowded with all classes, and sometimes with people of all nations. The temperature of the air is generally agreeable on summer nights. There is always a gentle breeze blowing from some quarter, but chiefly from the direction of the Heads. Its situation is high, and commands a very extensive view of the magnificent harbour, which is often illuminated with numbers of moving lights from the vessels resting upon its placid waters, and the beautiful villas along its shores. Far in the distance, the revolving light upon South Head flashes its bright gleams towards the land, and again turns quickly out to sea, to tell the approaching mariner that he is nearing a haven of rest and safety.[7]

From 1854, Hyde Park was administered by the Hyde Park Trust, and the park's use became more respectable and decorative rather than sporting, at least by day. At night the park was unlit, and destitute vagrants slept there—and they still do. From the 1850s onwards the cricket players and soapbox orators moved onto the Domain, the park was landscaped and Lovers Lane was no more.

One of the first acts performed by the City Council as the new manager from 1904 was to install lighting in the park. It took many years before the trees which now dominate the park grew to maturity. Most of the park was dug up to accommodate the underground city-loop railway in the 1920s. The central avenue of Moreton Bay figs was planted between 1927 and 1934.

Underneath St James's Station is an underground tunnel which had been, and remains, flooded by water seeping through the porous sandstone. The progress on the tunnel, designed to provide another railway route through the city, was halted during the Depression. Some enthusiasts even today enjoy the unusual pastime of swimming in the lake.

The best way of seeing the layout of the park is from the observation deck of Centrepoint Tower. The greatest threat to the park is overshadowing by the city's skyscrapers. It has been estimated that in winter, half the park is in shade. The current design of the park seeks to balance shade in the central and radial axes with sunny and grassy areas on the fringes.

All the major structures in Hyde Park commemorate those who were lost in World War I. At the southern end is the War Memorial and the Pool of Reflection. The memorial was built in the Art Deco style between 1932 and 1934. Around the Hyde Park memorial and the Pool of Reflection were planted seedlings of pines from the Lone Pine and Pine Ridge battlefields at Gallipoli.

The Anzac Memorial was built out of Bathurst granite as a shrine of remembrance by members of the Returned Services League (RSL) of Australia. The stars on the ceiling represent the soldiers. The sculpture below is of three women holding a slight, dead soldier. On the floor of the memorial are engraved the words 'Let Silent Contemplation be Your Offering'.

At the northern end of the park is one of Sydney's finest statues, the Archibald Fountain (1933). This was generously donated to the people of Sydney by the editor and publisher J. F. Archibald, the longtime editor of the *Bulletin* during its golden decades of the late nineteenth and early twentieth centuries. The fountain, which was designed by François Sicard, commemorates the casualties of World War I, and Franco-Australian cooperation during the war.

Throughout the 1990s, the park has undergone extensive renovations and replantings, starting from the southern end. Liverpool Street at the southern end of Hyde Park is the meeting point between the 'pink', or gay, entertainment zone of Oxford Street and the southern end of the city. A mediocre slew of tall office buildings menaces the southern edge of the park. On the eastern edge at the corner of Wentworth Avenue are the Connaught apartments, one of the first luxury city apartment buildings to be built in the early 1980s. It stands on the site of the old Paris Theatre—one of the many demolished Art Deco–style cinemas that had disappeared by 1980.

Further down Liverpool Street, on the corner of Elizabeth Street, is the old Mark Foy's Building, now known as the Downing Centre, where many courts are located. The management of Mark Foy's tried to revive the store in the 1970s by calling it a 'piazza store', but no amount of marketing and renaming could compensate for a bad location: as the heart of the retail area moved northward with the opening of Town Hall and Wynyard stations, Mark Foy's was left behind. There are still mosaics on the exterior of the building to remind us of its former role. The building had the first escalator for customers in Sydney, as well as boasting a fine coloured tile roof.

At the southern end of Hyde Park there stood, until 1905, an impressive row of six terraces built as investment properties by a prosperous emancipist merchant and auctioneer, John Lyons. The grand terrace, intended to be occupied by gentlefolk (as opposed to the middle and working classes), sadly did not survive the widening of Liverpool Street and the construction of Wentworth Avenue. The loss of these buildings is great. People who lived in Lyons Terrace include Sir Alfred Stephen, chief justice for nearly thirty years from 1844, and other judges and barristers including Richard Windeyer and Roger Terry. Miss Moore's School for Ladies was another one-time occupant.

Lyons Terrace was designed by John Verge and his assistant, John Bibb, in the Post-Regency style. It was completed in 1840. Many of the architectural features seen for the first time in Sydney on this building were to be repeated in the city for the rest of the nineteenth century: the use of cast-iron decoration, particularly on the first-floor verandas; supporting cast-iron (as opposed to wooden) columns; French windows on the first floor, and the extension of party walls above the roofline.[8]

The earliest use after 1788 of the land on College Street, on the eastern side of the park, was as a garden worked by convicts quartered in the nearby Hyde Park Barracks. In the late twentieth century, at the park's southern end between Stanley and Oxford streets, there is another grim parade of mediocre, late–twentieth-century architecture, including a hotel and police headquarters.

Between Stanley and William streets are two imposing examples of early– and mid–nineteenth-century architecture still serving their original purposes. One of them is Sydney Grammar School, established in 1854, but the building was occupied by an earlier school before that time. The oldest section, still called 'The Big School' by pupils and teachers, was designed by Edward Hallen and built by Robert Cooper between 1831 and 1834. This building contained one of the few halls where concerts and meetings could be held in the early years of the colony. The two later classical wings on either side of it were designed by Edmund Blacket and built in 1857. Blacket was better known for his Gothic Revival architecture, especially on the newly built grounds of the University of Sydney.

Sydney Grammar was intended as, and still is, a non-denominational school. Its original objective was to prepare its students for the recently established University of Sydney. Apart from the fact that there are now several more universities in Sydney, its objectives remain unchanged. Sydney Grammar is a selective boys school and one of Sydney's Greater Public (GPS) Schools.

Next door to Sydney Grammar is the Australian Museum, one of the country's earliest scientific and cultural institutions. It was established in 1827. The museum is devoted to natural history and the natural sciences, such as biology, anthropology and geology. For first-time visitors to Australia, as well as for locals, it is an excellent way of getting to know Australia's natural environment and indigenous culture.

The first section of the museum was designed by Mortimer Lewis in 1846, but it was not opened to the public until 1857. Lewis's building was in the Greek Revival style favoured by him in other public works such as the Darlinghurst Courthouse. It faced north towards William Street (which was then much narrower than it now is) and the harbour beyond. The main remaining section of this building is the Long Gallery, which now contains the Skeleton Gallery.

Soon after the museum was opened, it became clear there was not enough exhibition space. From the turn of the nineteenth century there was a steadily growing fascination with the wonders of science and nature, and the strangeness of Australian nature in particular. At the time, Sydney did not have a public library or art gallery. The government gave the newly appointed Colonial Architect, James Barnet, his first major task. Seizing the opportunity to make his reputation, he designed the museum in the monumental proportions that were becoming increasingly fashionable in Britain and its colonies. The grandeur of the building would also reflect the growing public interest in science and the increasing stature of the city.

Barnet's extensions indicated that the scale of public buildings was changing markedly from the scale of early colonial architecture, easily seen further to the north at Hyde Park Barracks and St James' Church. The extended building was opened to the public in 1868. At the time, the only other large building under construction was Blacket's Gothic Revival–style St Andrew's Cathedral, which could then be easily seen from across Hyde Park.

It is amazing that, so early in the Colonial Architect's career, Barnet's reputation survived the political furore whipped up during the construction of the museum. Relations between the Museum Trust (which included Barnet as a member) and the museum curator, Gerard Krefft, were frosty. Krefft was vocal in indicating what the defects of the new building were. He hated its size and height, and thought it impractical and overdecorated.[9] The trustees accused Krefft of insubordination. A select committee (upon which two of the trustees sat) inquired into the condition of the Museum. The committee agreed with Krefft that the design of the museum had many faults. Yet these defects did not stop the visitors: there were 240 000 visitors in 1872.[10]

The museum was extended in the early twentieth century, and again in the 1960s and 1980s. The extensions of the early 1960s, which can be seen along William Street, appear to be an overreaction to Barnet's work—here, function was followed to the detriment of form. The building's stern exterior belies the enormous range of exhibits, temporary and permanent, that lie within. In the darker and less accessible areas of the Australian Museum, there is a staggeringly wide range of scientific research undertaken. On the other side of William Street stands a new aquatic and leisure centre at Cook and Phillip Park, mostly built underground, on the site of a former bowling club.

The foundation stone of the first St Mary's Church was laid by Governor Macquarie in 1821, shortly before he ended his term in office. Much smaller than the present St Mary's Cathedral, it stood on the eastern side of Hyde Park, across from the Church of England's St James'

Church. Like the present cathedral, it was in the Gothic Revival style. Due to a shortage of subscription funds, the early church, like its successor, took a long time to build. The first mass was held in 1833, but the roof was not finished until 1839. The church was not consecrated as a cathedral until 1843 when Bishop Polding became the first Catholic archbishop in Australia. In 1865, uninsured, the cathedral burnt to the ground.

William Wardell was appointed as the architect for the new cathedral. He had already designed St John's College at Sydney University. Wardell had previously been Colonial Architect in Victoria from 1858 and was a favourite architect of the Catholic community. The foundation stone was laid in 1868, the same year as the foundation stone of the Town Hall. Although dedicated and used since 1882, it was not officially opened until 1900, nor consecrated until 1905. The cathedral is built from Pyrmont sandstone on an unusual north–south axis, because the fall of the land could not accommodate the proportions of the new cathedral on the more traditional east–west orientation. Work on the cathedral's spires did not commence until 1998.

The best way to view the cathedral is from Victoria Street or Brougham Street in Potts Point, preferably on a sunny winter's day when the lower sun creates deep shadows on the stone mouldings. The cathedral is one of the city's few architectural landmarks which can be seen from a distance. Although most were designed to be seen from afar, they have now been hemmed in by growth and progress.

The stained-glass windows were executed by John Hardman & Co. of Birmingham, the same firm which made the stained glass in St Andrew's Cathedral. There are two altars in the central axis, the main one and the tabernacle altar. There are three smaller chapels within the cathedral: two are on the sides, opposite the sanctuary. The chapel on the left (western) side is the Chapel of the Sacred Heart, and on the eastern side is the Chapel of the Irish Saints. The third chapel, at the northern end of the cathedral, is the Blessed Sacrament Chapel. In the crypt, six archbishops of Sydney are buried.

The inlaid terrazzo floor in the crypt is based on the Celtic Book of Kells, with a huge Celtic cross along the central axis. Peter Melocco designed and laid the marble and terrazzo floor. He also created the floors in the baptistry, opposite the bookshop and information office, and in the Chapel of the Irish Saints.

Across Art Gallery Road from St Mary's is one of Sydney's last attempts at Tudor Gothic Revival architecture, designed by Walter Liberty Vernon to complement the cathedral. The Registrar-General's Department Building was built in 1911. The relative austerity of the Gothic detailing compared to what had gone before in the previous century is easily seen. The sandstone used is decorative only: beneath lies a concrete and steel substructure.

The Art Gallery of New South Wales is very well situated at the northeastern corner of the outer Domain, on the crest of the southern precipice created by the construction of the Cahill Expressway in 1962. The gallery enjoys sweeping views down to Woolloomooloo Bay.

The New South Wales Arts Society agitated for a permanent home after its collection was burnt in the Garden Palace fire of 1882, and the Art Gallery of New South Wales was the result of this campaign. The Colonial Architect, James Barnet, whose grand high Victorian star was fading, was overlooked by the trustees of the society in favour of Horbury Hunt. Because of insufficient funds, he only built a small portion of the gallery. The depression of the late 1880s and 1890s intervened. The gallery was added to between 1896 and 1906 by Walter Liberty Vernon, who designed the facade, the portico and the southern wing. Like many other public buildings, the facade is made of Pyrmont sandstone. There are many empty panels on the exterior western elevation which have beneath them the names of the intended subject in each panel. Like the incomplete spires of St Mary's Cathedral, these empty panels are a reminder of the strong boom–bust cycles in Sydney's history—and the related unpredictability of government funding.

There have been many additions to the gallery since. In 1972, the new southeastern wing was added, and in the 1980s Andrew Andersons designed the significant extensions to the northern and lower levels. This greatly increased the exhibition space and other public areas. The New South Wales Art Gallery is the best example of the harmonious blending of old and new architecture in any public building in Sydney. The scale of the interior is inviting, rather than daunting. In the impressive, yet intimate spaces of the gallery, the artworks are displayed to maximum effect. The combination of its fine proportions and the quality of its collections renders it one of the city's most successful public spaces. It is still the epicentre for the enjoyment of the visual arts in Sydney, despite recent competition from the Museum of Contemporary Art at Circular Quay.

As well as the outstanding examples of early and contemporary Australian art, the Yiribana Gallery is dedicated to indigenous art. There is also an impressive collection of Old Masters and Italian paintings from the Florentine and Sienese schools. The additions to the gallery itself and its collections have been greatly augmented during the directorship of Edmund Capon. Capon has been in charge of the gallery since 1979. The improvements over the past twenty years are a great testament to his ability and determination. One of the finest and best-displayed collections of Asian art in Australia is contained within the gallery.

> I know no more pleasant lounge than the public gardens, sheltered as they are by the heights of Darlinghurst Hill from the chill south winds of winter, and in summer shaded from the sun's rays by trees … nothing can be more delicious during the hot days of summer, than to seek the deep shade in the sylvan recesses of the gardens … Plants from the Cape and China, Peru and Japan, Madagascar, South America and the Canary Isles, Van Diemen's Land, Hindostan, and New Zealand, are thriving within a stone's throw of each other. The oak and the bamboo, the hawthorn and sugar cane, the Scotch fir, plantain and mango—the last, however not looking happy—almost mingle branches.[11]

Lieutenant Colonel George Mundy's comments describe the gardens of today as well as they did 150 years ago. Nowhere else in Sydney is it easier to appreciate the city's location on the boundary of subtropical and temperate climates, where almost anything will grow within the sheltered, gently northward-sloping gardens, situated on one of the most beautiful harbours in the world.

The outer Domain and Royal (since 1958) Botanic Gardens are the sizeable (64-hectare) green lungs which divide the eastern side of the city from Woolloomooloo Bay. The gardens themselves cover 30 hectares. As well as their aesthetic and recreational attributes, they are an important scientific research and educational centre for the study of botany.

The Royal Botanic Gardens were the site of the earliest, unsuccessful agricultural experiment in Australia by Europeans, commemorated today in the First Farm exhibition near the Visitors' Centre. Only some of the exotic plants from Rio de Janeiro and the Cape (of South Africa) planted in the valley of Farm Cove thrived. By the end of the first summer of European settlement, it was apparent that a new spot for agriculture would have to be found, so agricultural efforts were relocated to Rose Hill (Parramatta). Some of the land upon which the gardens now lie was leased to colonial administrators; one small plot was leased to Joseph Gerrald, one of the Scottish Martyrs, who is buried near the creek.

Although Governor Phillip, who granted the leases over this area, never intended that the land should be built upon, his successors, governors Hunter and King, were not so resolved, and cottages appeared. One of the acts of imperiousness Governor Bligh was accused of was prohibiting the grazing of livestock in the gardens and the Domain, by ordering that a ditch be built to set the boundary of the Governor's Domain. Bligh also ordered the dismantling of houses built on the Domain land, close to Government House.[12] In those days, however, governmental edicts were often ignored. Nor did the policy prevent Commissary General John Palmer of Woolloomooloo House from building flour mills and a bakehouse on the crest of the hill along which Macquarie Street runs, where the Governor's Stables (now the Conservatorium of Music) were built. Other mills, such as Boston's Mills, were also constructed.

The original intention of sealing off the Domain was to provide security and privacy. Governors wanted to be quarantined from the *hoi polloi* of the town—and in those days that meant anyone who was not part of the governor's household. Macquarie carried on the task begun by Bligh to make the governor's access to the Domain more exclusive by removing Palmer's and Boston's small industrial concerns when the leases expired. He also built a sandstone wall around the Domain and improved the area with road building, particularly Mrs Macquaries Road which ran from Government House to Mrs Macquarie's Chair. Some of the Macquarie Wall still stands in the gardens today, east of the Gardens Restaurant. This wall made it possible for Mrs Macquarie to drive or walk to her 'chair' in privacy, without being overlooked by the public.

Elizabeth Macquarie had excellent taste. The panoramic view of Sydney Cove and the harbour from this spot is one of Sydney's greatest vistas, and even more popular—and more accessible—today as a spot used by Japanese newlyweds as a backdrop for their wedding photos. Now the presence of large tourist buses around Mrs Macquarie's Chair is a lively political issue. Mrs Macquarie would not be impressed if she could see them now.

Macquarie's defensive, even fanatically exclusivist attitude to the Domain added to the governor's political woes, just as it had to Bligh's. On one occasion, he took the unusual step of summarily lashing three men, none of whom were convicts, for encroaching on the land.[13] To do this, Macquarie had improperly constituted himself as a magistrate, despite his personal interest in the matter, as occupant of his domain. To explain himself, after the matter had been raised by his political enemy, Judge Jeffery Hart Bent, the governor wrote to Undersecretary Goulburn of the Colonial Office in the following terms:

> Notwithstanding the Prohibition (of trespass) the Wall had been repeatedly broken down or Scaled by idle and vicious Persons passing into the Domain, although a Road had been constructed … (this) did not suit the Persons going thither for vicious and disorderly purposes, namely secreting stolen Goods, which have been found there frequently, and for which many parts of (the Domain) are well Calculated, being wild, rocky Shrubbery, which had remained undisturbed by the Hand of Civilized Man. This Shrubbery was also much frequented by lewd, disorderly Men and Women for most indecent and improper purposes …

Keeping the people out of the gardens and the Domain was a vexing issue until the Middle and Lower Botanic Gardens were opened to the public in 1831, at about the same time as the site for the new Government House was selected by the Surveyor General, Thomas Mitchell. The land resumed for Government House was considerable, effectively the northwestern portion of the gardens. By 1871, the only part of the Botanic Gardens which was not open to the public was the Upper Garden. Since 1996, even Government House and its grounds are open to the public on weekends, and are under the administration of the Historic Houses Trust.

Englishwoman Louisa Meredith, who lived near Homebush for some years, was amazed how unpopular the Domain was in the late 1830s. In those days, people preferred to take walks in the newly developed urban centre, along George Street. The new buildings and emerging urban streetscape of the town were far more remarkable, it seemed, than the native bushland which surrounded the town. The Botanic Gardens were yet another expanse of native countryside. The attempt to tame and fashion the natural bushland into a botanic garden would preoccupy its supervisors for decades to come.

> [The Domain is] a most picturesque rocky promontory, thickly wooded and laid out in fine, smooth drives and walks, all commanding most exquisite views … we generally found ourselves the only visitors. It was unfashionable in fact, not the proper thing at all, either to walk or drive in the Domain. It was a notorious fact, that maid-servants and their sweethearts resorted thither on Sundays, and of course that shocking circumstance

ruined its character as a place for their mistresses to visit; the public streets being so much more select …[14]

But in the next ten years, as the novelty of having a smart, newly built-up township wore off, access to open space was more greatly treasured, and the Domain became a popular gathering spot for Sydneysiders, particularly on Sundays, and also on Monday afternoons between two and four o'clock when:

[T]he Domain is resorted to by fashionables and unfashionables of Sydney, eager to listen to the harmonious strains of the band of the 99th Regiment. There you may see elegant ladies, in their splendid carriages, on the doors of which some favoured gentlemen are wont to lean, and chat with the admired ones within. There too are settlers from the interior whose immense beards and moustaches, monkey jackets, and cabbage tree hats, give them a Robinson Crusoe–like appearance.… There are not a few gentlemen on horseback or on foot, while crowds of the humbler classes are resting on the greensward, listening with pleasure to the lively polkas, and enjoying the charms of the beautiful scenery …[15]

271

Recently arrived immigrants could, at a stretch, imagine the pleasures of home by visiting the exotic European plants in the gardens. Annual horticultural exhibitions were held in the gardens where colonial produce could be inspected and keenly sought prizes were awarded. The only place where swimming was allowed in Sydney was at the Fig Tree Baths, on the eastern perimeter of the Domain, which had shark-proof netting to protect bathers.[16]

While the Domain and the gardens were becoming one of Sydney's most popular recreational spots, the scientific and horticultural role of the Botanic Gardens had been growing. Specimens of new, exotic trees were given to governors, and planted in their Domain. Early in the nineteenth century, King George III's patronage of the natural sciences, and Joseph Banks's role in the establishment of the settlement, were important factors in the early stages of the development of botany in the colony.

Allan Cunningham, the king's botanist, visited the colony to collect specimens for the Royal Botanical Gardens at Kew in the second decade of the nineteenth century.[17] His journeys around New South Wales, and especially the Illawarra region south of Sydney led to the discovery in 1809 of the Illawarra flame tree. One of these trees is still in the gardens, and is numbered (eleven), as are all other heritage trees. This tree is on the western side of the Palm Grove. Also near the Palm Grove are specimens of trees which would have grown around Farm Cove before 1788, such as the prickly paperbark, pieces of which were used by Aborigines for inhalation.

Commissioner Thomas Bigge advocated a greater scientific role for the gardens. He spoke highly of Macquarie's botanist, Charles Fraser, who was also working on collecting samples of Australian flora. Fraser was the first man to be formally appointed as Colonial Botanic

Gardener. As time wore on, the gardens' botanic function included acclimatising and distributing exotic plants—which sometimes irritated nurserymen in the same line of business.

A later candidate for the position of Colonial Botanical Gardener was Ludwig Leichhardt, the Prussian explorer who later disappeared while exploring the interior of Queensland. Leichhardt declined the offer because he thought gardens were more a place for amusement and recreation than a scientific institution. The nature of the appointment of one of the longest-serving directors of the gardens created a political storm and a tension in the relationship between the colonial administration and the British Colonial Office. Both Governor FitzRoy and British Colonial Secretary Earl Grey wanted to appoint a Colonial Botanic Gardener. Earl Grey won (after all he was the boss), and Charles Moore was appointed to the position in 1848, which he held until his death in 1896.

Moore's responsibilities extended to the Botanic Gardens, the Domain and Hyde Park. His performance soon soothed bruised colonial sensibilities such as those of the Macleays and the Macarthurs. Even the Anglophile 'exclusives' were alarmed at the high-handed manner of Moore's appointment and his lack of familiarity with Australian botany. Colonial Secretary and natural scientist Alexander Macleay, his two children Elizabeth and William, and Elizabeth Macarthur and her son James had been active early supporters of the gardens, in their capacities as keen amateur botanists and horticulturists.

William Macleay collected many botanical specimens and introduced the camellia to Australia. His sister used her considerable artistic skills to illustrate botanical specimens, as well as playing the more usual role for ladies of those days of assistant to her father and brother. She was an early convert to the beauty, botanical richness and subtlety of the Australian bush, unlike many botanists of the nineteenth century, such as Charles Moore, who were cultivated in the European tradition.[18]

Moore's experience was limited to botanic gardens at Dublin, Kew and Regent's Park. At the time of Moore's arrival, the gardens were in a run-down state. In the transitional period between Macquarie's era and 1840, the assignment system had reduced the amount of convict labour for government work, and the winding-down of the convict system had also taken its toll. The gold rush further reduced the labour pool, and made whatever labour was available more expensive.

Moore set to work repairing the carriageways, footpaths and overgrown garden beds. He reclaimed some of Farm Cove by rebuilding a sea wall partially with stone from the site of old Government House. He also planted the Palm Grove, one of the finest in the world, containing many native and exotic palms and cycads, the most primitive plant on earth. Moore usually resisted governmental moves to allow encroachments on the Domain—the City Council wanted to build a gravel pit near the present site of the State Library, for example, which he rejected. While Moore was away on a botanical expedition, however, the government permitted the church authorities of St Mary's Cathedral to build a stone quarry at the Domain. Much later, in the early twentieth century, a proposal to extend Sydney's wharf facilities around to Farm Cove was rapidly suppressed.

A battle for the rights to use the Domain developed in the 1860s between cricketing enthusiasts, who wanted an enclosed ground upon it, and those who wanted it kept as open recreational space. New South Wales's dominance in the inter-colonial cricket matches had faded in favour of Victoria, a colony which was by then flexing her political, economic and sporting muscle. There was even a parliamentary inquiry into what usage of the Domain should be permitted. It was recommended that the newly built cricket fence be removed because it was unsightly.

In the 1860s, cattle and horses grazed in the Domain—they served a useful purpose in the era before lawn mowers were available. The native trees and plants, which were dying off, were replaced with exotic specimens, such as Moreton Bay figs, still the dominant tree there today, and other trees such as Asian camphor laurel and English elms, oaks and plane trees. Fig Tree Avenue, now marooned by the Cahill Expressway, divided the Domain from the Upper Botanic Garden. A keen amateur botanist, Helena Scott, a cousin of David Scott Mitchell who lived in the Hunter Valley to the north of Sydney, wrote in 1862 of how the gardens and the Domain had been in earlier days:

> How beautiful the native flowers are at this season! Our railway line is positively resplendent with yellow dogwood, blue campanula and scarlet bottlebrush. Somehow the scent of native flowers is always associated in my mind with the days when we were tiny little children and Mamma used to take us in the early morning for long rambles in the fragrant bush then around the Botanic Gardens. It is wonderful how these early recollections associated with the sight and scent of peculiar flowers cling to us …[19]

273

The Garden Palace, the main venue for the Sydney International Exhibition of 1879–80 stood at the western end of the inner Domain. It was the high-water mark of the optimistic architecture of the boom period in Sydney in the 1870s and 1880s. If it had lasted to the present day, it would look like an oversized example of unrestrained Victorian grandiosity. But at the time it was seen as a harbinger of New South Wales's centenary in 1888, and of Australia's growth into a mature and proud member of the British Empire, although nationhood was still twenty-one years away.

Countries which exhibited at the Garden Palace included the United Kingdom, the United States and many European nations. Each Australasian colony was also represented. More than 1 million people were admitted to the exhibition at a time when the population of Australia was only 2.2 million. The construction of the Garden Palace and the timing of the exhibition were one of the most visible illustrations of nineteenth-century Sydney–Melbourne rivalry. Each city's newspapers observed closely the progress of the other's exhibition building, in an inter-colonial version of outdoing the colonial neighbours.

The building, designed by the Colonial Architect, James Barnet, was vast—244 metres by 152 metres. It covered the area between the Conservatorium of Music and the State Library. At the centre of the building was a 30-metre–wide giant dome of 47 metres, under which stood, naturally, a large statue of Queen Victoria. The Garden Palace completely dominated the western horizon from Farm Cove. Construction started on the the building in January 1879, and the entire project was subjected to a very tight deadline for completion in September of that year. Recently introduced electric lights made it possible for labourers to work around the clock.

The objective of the exhibition was to encourage international trade and show the public the latest engineering, technological and scientific developments. Naturally, most of these developments and innovations would have to be imported as New South Wales was at the time, above all, a producer of wool and other primary products. The exhibition was therefore arguably more of a marketing opportunity for the industrial exporters such as the United States and the United Kingdom than it was for exporters of primary commodities, such as the Australian colonies. After the exhibition closed, the big question was what should be done with the building. Predictably, it filled with government offices and was used as document storage space.

On the morning of 22 September 1882, the Garden Palace caught fire. The *Sydney Morning Herald* reported that '[T]he scene was the most imposing as it was the most pitiful ever seen in the colonies.'[20]

274

Cinders ignited the roof of a house far away in Potts Point and sheets of iron fell in the grounds of Elizabeth Bay House. The entire collection of botanical specimens belonging to the New South Wales branch of the Linnean Society was burnt, as was the the nucleus of the Technological and Mining Museum, and several hundred paintings to be shown by the New South Wales Arts Society, the progenitor of the Art Gallery of New South Wales. Thirty thousand ornamental plants around the Garden Palace were also destroyed.

The present-day memorials to the Garden Palace are the gates to the Botanic Gardens at the Macquarie Street entrance, designed by James Barnet in 1888, and a plaque in the Pioneers' Memorial Garden section of the Botanic Gardens. One less tragic consequence of the fire was that the area of land became open space once again.

Late Victorian morality took its toll on the gardens and the Domain. Charles Moore even prosecuted a husband for displaying 'uxorious affection' within the gardens. Acceptable behaviour in the area became more restricted. No games were to be played, and no one was allowed to lie on the grass near the walks, or on the benches.[21] On the more positive side, Moore was instrumental in introducing large numbers of jacarandas, pepper trees and the hibiscus around the streets and parks of Sydney,[22] and his horticultural expertise was used in the laying out of Centennial Park, Moore Park, Government House, Admiralty House, Garden Island and many railway station gardens. Moore died at his home in Queen Street, Woollahra, close to Centennial Park, in 1905. Joseph Maiden, a keen scientist and student of Australian botany, particularly eucalypts, succeeded him.

By then, the Domain had become a popular recreational spot—it was estimated that on a fine Sunday afternoon, 15 000 people would assemble there, strolling, reclining or listening to regimental bands and to the discourse of the many orators, some of whom were rather eccentric, who held court there.

For many years, the Domain was the place where people would air their strong (and sometimes crackpot) political and social opinions. Speakers stood on ladders or makeshift podiums opposite the steps of the Art Gallery of New South Wales. There they would address (or berate) their audience on matters they felt passionate about—the threat of fascism, the dangers of communism, the yellow (Asian) peril, the Vietnam War, the dire consequences of a liberal society, or whatever else took their fancy. As one observer noted in 1895:

> [O]n Sunday afternoon the Domain is crowded with a variety of men whose object is to talk their particular hobby to death. I have seen men who indulge freely in intoxicating drink during the week face an audience in the Domain on Sunday afternoon and deliver stirring lectures on the evils of intemperance. The same feeling causes the clergyman to read all the debatable novels he can secure, in order to be able to properly dissect their contents …[23]

The audience would gravitate towards the most interesting or controversial speakers. In the past twenty years, the speakers and their audience have melted away. Perhaps the old speakers went on to the great soapbox in the sky, or maybe their audience lost interest at a time when political extremism lost its potency and support.

Street vendors used to ply their trade at the St Mary's entrance to the Domain. During tough economic times, 'sundowners' gathered there to sleep. In 1900, 25 000 people gathered in the Domain to farewell the troops who were off to the Boer War, and in 1908, 3000 members of the American Great White Fleet landed at Farm Cove, at the Fleet Steps, which had been purpose-built to receive them. The Fleet Steps later became a landing spot for royal and state visits, and were the spot from which the Federation procession to Centennial Park began.

During World War I, soldiers gathered at the Anzac Buffet in the Domain near St Mary's Gate to meet their families or have a cup of tea on the long journey between the battlefields and home. For some diggers, shell-shocked and wounded, the sight of the Domain and its large canopy of Moreton Bay figs was the first glimpse of home for many hard, long years. Some of the soldiers returning home brought with them seeds of plants taken from the French and Belgian battlefields. The school children of Villers-Bretonneux sent poppy seeds to the Botanic Gardens to commemorate the efforts of the Anzacs in European battlefields. These were keenly sought by people who wished to plant these European cornfield poppies as a form of remembrance.[24]

Relief workers were used to improve the gardens and the Domain in the Depression years. The ponds in the lower garden were cleaned, and stone from the excavated Harbour Bridge site was used to strengthen the pond walls. Several hundred people slept in makeshift shelters around the Domain, and fences, seats and trees were used to build fires for warmth. In 1938, the Domain was a focal point for the Sesquicentenary celebrations. During the construction of the dock and naval facilities at Garden Island, a replica of the Choragic Monument of Lysicrates, which stood from 1870 in the garden of Sir James Martin, former governor and

Supreme Court judge in whose honour Martin Place was named, was relocated in the Lower Botanic Garden from Potts Point.

The 1950s and early 1960s were not a good era for the Domain nor for the Botanic Gardens. The postwar dominance of the motor car created the need for expressways such as the Cahill Expressway, and this meant the end of Fig Tree Avenue, as well as the appropriation of Domain land, and many fine trees which stood upon it, to build a car park. In 1958, as a delayed response to the royal visit to Australia in 1954 which began at Farm Cove, the title 'Royal' was added to the Botanic Gardens, ironically at a time the British Empire was passing into history. At the beginning of the royal visit in 1954, the conundrum about who should welcome Queen Elizabeth to our shores—the prime minister or the premier of New South Wales—was neatly resolved when a pontoon was constructed at Farm Cove upon which prime minister Robert Menzies warmly welcomed her ashore, then handed her over, so to speak, to the premier once they had reached *terra firma* of New South Wales.

In the late 1970s, the Wran government removed responsibility for the gardens from the Department of Agriculture and gave it to the Premier's Department, so that the administration of the Domain, the gardens and other reserves, such as Centennial Park, could be improved. This was the beginning of a period of positive change and improvement of the gardens and the Domain. A new herbarium, named after Robert Brown, a leading nineteenth-century botanist who visited Australia and travelled with Flinders on the *Investigator* in 1802, was built, as was the Pyramid Glasshouse, housing tropical plants.

Today, the Domain is the venue for open-air musical performances such as Opera in the Park, Symphony Under the Stars, Jazz in the Domain and Carols by Candlelight, part of the Festival of Sydney.

The Sydney Opera House is Sydney's most internationally recognised symbol. Built to emulate the shape and sweep of sails on the harbour, without any regard for traditional architectural forms, it is not surprising that it has been called one of the seven architectural wonders of the twentieth century. The Opera House sits on Bennelong Point, first called Cattle Point; this is where the first cattle in the colony were landed and quickly escaped from, to be rediscovered years later at The Cowpastures, now known as Camden, about 70 kilometres away to the city's southwest.

By 1790, Arthur Phillip decided to build accommodation for his friend Bennelong, but Bennelong's hut soon fell into disrepair and was dismantled in 1795. Governor Macquarie built a stone fort which bore his name on Bennelong Point and filled in the tidal channel which used to run between the point and the nearby land. Fort Macquarie stood until 1902 when it was replaced by a tram shed. In 1959, the tram shed was demolished to make way for the Opera House.

The cultural awakening of Sydney after 1945, which coincided with the beginning of postwar immigration from Europe, created a greater demand for higher forms of entertainment. Up

ABOVE: The former tram depot at the northern end of Macquarie Street in the mid-twentieth century. Phillip Street and the Mort's Wool Warehouse (since demolished) can be seen at left, while Macquarie Street is to the right.

until then, Sydneysiders mostly had to look to visiting artists for their artistic experiences. Onto this fairly fragmented and nascent postwar artistic stage walked English composer Eugene Goossens, who would become the driving force in the moves to commission a permanent opera house and concert theatre for Sydney on the site at Bennelong Point. Goossens came to Sydney in 1947 to take up his appointment as chief conductor of the Sydney Symphony Orchestra and director of the State Conservatorium (at a salary which was widely rumoured to have been greater than that of the prime minister). In 1949, it was Goossens who gave Joan Sutherland her first big role. He led a group of Australian citizens in lobbying for a theatre suitable for first-class productions. By 1952, he had enlisted the support and encouragement of J. J. Cahill, the premier of New South Wales, who had initially been noncommittal, but established a committee to advise the government on its options.

Originally, the favoured site was above Wynyard Station, but Goossens was vehement in his opposition to this plan, arguing instead for the site at Bennelong Point. This had been set aside for the Maritime Services Board to build a new international shipping terminal. Fortunately Goossens won, so the Opera House could be built on Bennelong Point rather than the Overseas Passenger Terminal. Goossens, who had initially been lionised by many

Sydneysiders, suddenly fell from grace when officious customs officers found pornographic publications and other dubious material in his luggage upon his return to Sydney from an overseas trip.

The Goossens affair was, like the dismissal of the Opera House's architect Jørn Utzon in the 1960s, one of the events which convulsed Sydney's cultural life, and divided people into starkly opposing points of view, creating a great deal of disappointment and bitterness in the process. In the case of Goossens, the wowsers appeared to gang up against people with more liberal views who valued high culture and the right to privacy. In the case of Utzon, opinions divided broadly between the fiscal pragmatists and philistines in government and the architectural and cultural purists, though it must be said that there were differing views within Sydney's architectural community about the merits of the 'Opera House Affair'. The faltering of the careers of these two great artistic talents, Goossens and Utzon, during the long and arduous process of conceiving, designing and building one of the world's greatest works has given the Opera House added historical weight and drama beyond its extraordinary physical uniqueness and the wide range of cultural experience available within its shells.

In 1955, the government announced a competition for the design of an Opera House. The prize was a heady £5000. Altogether, 230 designs were submitted from thirty-two countries. The original brief was to design a building containing two halls: a major hall for concerts, opera and ballet, seating between 3000 and 3500 people; and a smaller hall for more intimate performances, seating about 1200. The winner was Jørn Utzon, a Danish architect who had worked for leading modern architect Alvar Aalto in Helsinki in Finland. The plans Utzon submitted were diagrammatical rather than precise, with little engineering detail, but the vision was exciting enough to overcome these shortcomings.

The sculptural quality of the building was probably strongly influenced by Utzon's family background. His father was a highly regarded yacht designer, and another member of his family was a sculptor and professor of fine arts. The central sculptural idea was for there to be a solid, granite-clad base upon which three linked shell- or sail-shaped vaults would soar. The constant interplay of sun, sky, sea and cloud upon the building's shells would give it an almost living and kinetic quality. The geometry of the building's shells is in fact derived from a segmented orange. Designing and building the shells was one of the greatest engineering challenges of the project. Initially, Utzon had drawn the shells in freer sculptural form. The final engineering solution was, rather than casting the shells on site, to build pre-cast concrete ribs, all of which were based on the same spherical shape, creating a crisper and more rhythmic effect than Utzon had initially conceived. The issue of timing was creating its own stresses. The conundrum of how to design and build the shells was proceeding as the podium was starting to rise from Bennelong Point. Then, later as the ribs of the shells were becoming visible, the issues of how to design the interiors within were being worked out with furious effort and intensity.

The construction of the Opera House was plagued with political controversy and cost blowouts. A British engineering firm, Ove Arup and Partners, was commissioned to work with Utzon in developing his ideas to the engineering stage. The first cost estimate was $7 million; this went drastically skyward to a final $102 million.

To finance construction, a public appeal was conducted. This raised $990 000, but the real revenue raiser was the Sydney Opera House Lottery. This lottery financed almost the entire project, but was shrouded in controversy when, in 1960, eight-year-old Scots College student Graeme Thorne was kidnapped and murdered after his parents won $100 000 in the lottery. Since that time, only very foolhardy lottery winners have ever revealed their identities.

Despite the success of the lottery, the cost of building the Opera House was still a lively political issue and a contributing cause of the Labor Party's loss in the state elections of 1965, which paved the way for the Askin years.

The change of government in 1965 spelt the end of Utzon's connection with the Opera House. He resigned in 1966 after arguing with Davis Hughes, the new Liberal minister for public works. By then, Utzon had also lost the support of engineers Ove Arup, who had different views on how the exterior glass walls and interior ceilings should be built. Davis Hughes froze Utzon out by refusing to pay his architectural fees, leaving him with no alternative but to resign. Utzon left Sydney a bitter man and he has never returned to see his greatest work—which turned out to be substantially different in detail to what he had in mind. Peter Hall, then aged thirty-four and a designer in the government architect's office, Lionel Todd and David Littlemore succeeded Utzon. Hall was principally responsible for the design of the interior.

Hughes defended his position by saying that Utzon had developed no workable ideas for the interior of the Opera House. This view has some superficial appeal—the interior of the Opera House is far less impressive than its exterior, but it is hard to believe that the work would not have been better executed if the original creator had been involved, despite the valiant efforts of the architects who succeeded Utzon, and the exasperation felt by the government at the uncertainty of the construction and design process and the costs involved. In 1995, Utzon's daughter Lin tendered a scale model prepared by her father which indicates that the plans were more advanced than some of his opponents had asserted. At the time the Opera House was opened, Utzon gave his architectural records to the Mitchell Library.

The City of Sydney went some way towards trying to heal the rift with Utzon when the lord mayor, Frank Sartor, presented Utzon with the keys of the city in July 1998. The only way the circle can ever be closed, however, is for Utzon to return to the city he once considered to be his home, and see his greatest work.

In 1967, the Australian Broadcasting Commission, then responsible for the Sydney Symphony Orchestra, insisted that, if the move from Sydney Town Hall, with a capacity of 2400, was to be justified, there would have to be much more seating available for concerts than for opera, and the acoustics would have to be good for concerts. Acoustic and sightline requirements for symphonic concerts and opera productions are not the same. The main, multi-purpose auditorium was converted into what is now the Concert Hall, with a platform only and no pit for an orchestra. Stage machinery for opera and ballet which had already been installed was dismantled. The second-largest hall, originally intended as a drama theatre, became the Opera Theatre, but the stage is too small for many large opera productions.

A month before the official opening of the Sydney Opera House on 20 October 1973 by Queen Elizabeth, the premiere performance at the Opera House was Prokofiev's opera *War and Peace*, staged in the Opera Theatre. Later, at the official opening, there was a huge display of fireworks and much fanfare. Thousands of small and large boats came to watch the launch and the fireworks. The concert program featured Beethoven's Ninth Symphony. The members of the Askin government present glowed with pride, and foreign dignitaries, including Imelda Marcos, were present as well, yet there was little reference made to the contributions of Eugene Goossens, or Jørn Utzon. Since 1973, the Opera House has also been one of the most popular vantage points for Sydney's fireworks displays.

When the Opera House was officially opened, it was not complete. The forecourt was a hastily built expanse of black bitumen and there were no car-parking facilities. Final completion of the approaches to the building had to wait for the advent of the Wran Labor government in 1976. Then Government Architect Andrew Andersons designed the two-level walkway in time for the Bicentennial celebrations in 1988. The bitumen was torn up and the area was paved in granite cobblestones. The circular car park at the end of Macquarie Street was completed after the Bicentenary.

Joan Sutherland had her debut Opera House performance in 1974. She and her husband, Richard Bonynge, played regularly in the Opera House as honorary members of the Australian Opera. In 1978, she performed the Sydney premiere of Bellini's *Norma*, a role which had made her world-famous. She also performed in a concert with Luciano Pavarotti, in 1983, when both performers were still at the height of their powers.

Despite the conflicts and internal design deficiencies, the Opera House is one of Sydney's greatest assets. The giant building houses nearly 1000 rooms, including the Concert Hall (seating 2690), the Opera Theatre (1547 seats), the Drama Theatre (554 seats) and the Playhouse (398 seats).

The Opera House is where the Australian Opera, the Sydney Symphony Orchestra and the Sydney Theatre Company perform. It is administered by the Opera House Trust, under the state government's Ministry of the Arts.

The building, which weighs 157 800 tons, is supported on 580 concrete piers sunk up to 25 metres below sea level, and the roofs are supported on thirty-two concrete columns. The walls, stairs and floors are faced with pink granite quarried at Tarana in New South Wales, and the interiors are decorated with brush box and white birch plywood. The tiles of the Opera House roof have a shiny but waved, glazed finish, so that they are self-cleaning in heavy rain. Their wavy finish also reduces the glare being reflected from Sydney's bright sunlight. They have been laid in a ribbed pattern, designed to emulate the fronds of a palm tree.[25]

The Sydney Opera House is, however, a high-maintenance building: the roof tiles, for instance, have already undergone renovation and replacement. The question of how to preserve artist John Olsen's *Salute to Five Bells* is not yet resolved. Olsen has proposed that the painting be replaced by a work to be executed in ceramic tiles, which are impervious to the sunlight.

The Opera House is one of Sydney's most popular tourist attractions. On any day of the week, particularly during the summer months, the whole area is bustling with tourists who come not only to view the great architectural feat that is the Opera House, but also to admire its position on the world's most beautiful harbour. During performances of the opera, tourists also come to listen and watch from the television screens in the foyer. The complex has four restaurants and a number of souvenir shops, and, on Sundays, markets are held on the forecourt. The issue of whether to pursue World Heritage listing for the Opera House is controversial. Keating's Labor government was strongly in favour of this, as the state government still is, but the federal Liberal government led by John Howard does not share this fervour, as it would not make any difference to its status as a tourist attraction.

CHAPTER ELEVEN

THE CITY

FIFTY YEARS AGO, Sydney was still a Victorian city. As a leading architectural historian, Morton Herman, described it in 1956: 'Here and there in the commercial centre appears a towering building of steel and glass somewhat like a gold tooth in a discoloured Victorian mouth.'[1]

This was a slight exaggeration: there were many examples of twentieth-century architecture to be seen, particularly in Elizabeth Street near Hyde Park, but these new buildings did nothing to change the essential scale of the city. This was because building heights were restricted to 46 metres until 1957. Sydney was still the compact, organically grown, walking city it had always been. Straight, wide streets had not been an indulgence Sydney could afford. Its topography (situated between two ridges) and eighteenth-century penal origins dictated this outcome. Although the grandeur of younger nineteenth-century cities such as Melbourne and Haussmann's Paris have their attractions, the narrow streets of Sydney give it a certain character as Kenneth Slessor wrote before the transformation of old Sydney began:

> [B]road avenues, … boulevards and esplanades … have their beauties of space and perspective, but they are mathematically impersonal, as remote and supernaturally perfect as peacocks … they separate and isolate human beings whose impacts and contacts make a city's character. Sydney's citizens are brought up against each other violently and impetuously as they go about their business, dart across the traffic, collide and mingle with each other …[2]

Some of this mingling is a thing of the past. Almost all Sydney's old laneways and the nineteenth-century architecture that gave Sydney much of her former character have gone. The ghosts of the city lanes lie beneath the city's tall buildings, such as the AMP Centre, the

MLC Centre, Goldfields House and Australia Square. Not one city block, not one of Sydney's streets is unaffected by the changes to the city since 1960.[3] By the late 1970s, the vibrancy and atmosphere had been sucked out of the once energetic city, particularly after business hours when cold winds howled down the empty canyon-like streetscape. City planners and the City of Sydney are well aware of the cost of architectural 'progress' and they have been hard at work trying to bring back some of the energy and verve of earlier years.

On a more positive note, fifty years ago, the glorious architecture of the city's early colonial era (1788–1820) was tatty, unloved and obscured by later, less noble additions. Hyde Park Barracks and the old Rum Hospital are two of the best examples of this. Now they are two of the city's great architectural jewels. Sydney is now one of the regional financial centres of the Pacific Rim. This would never have been possible without the changes to the city's scale and skyline.

Until the abolition of height restrictions in 1957, it was impossible to build skyscrapers. The restrictions on building heights had been imposed since the early decades of the twentieth century, and provoked by the construction of Culwulla Chambers in Castlereagh Street, near the corner of King Street. However, even without the height limits, it is by no means certain that many towering skyscrapers would have been built. Sydney did not undergo the economic boom of the early twentieth century in the same way that cities such as New York and Chicago did. There were no Fords or Chryslers wealthy or eager enough to leave their mark for posterity. So, for fifty years, Culwulla Chambers was the tallest building in Sydney. The AWA Tower in Wynyard Square only slipped through the net because it was a communications tower, not a building. Completed in 1940 and 110 metres tall, the AWA Tower was not beaten for height by the AMP Building until 1961, and then only by a small margin.

Substantial examples of the architecture of the boom years of the 1960s and 1970s are Australia Square (1967), the AMP Building (1961), the AMP Centre (1976) and the MLC Centre (1977). There are countless others, too numerous to mention.

By the middle of the 1980s, after the lull of the 1970s property crash, the city was ready for another building boom. The approaching Bicentenary created a strong desire in the heart of the government to leave an indelible mark on the landscape (or cityscape) in time for the celebrations, just as there had been the century before. There was also a boom in the tourist industry. Many of Sydney's great hotels—the Park Hyatt, the Inter.Continental, the Ritz Carlton and the ANA Hotel—were built in the 1980s.

Most of the city's landmark buildings were holes in the ground or gleams in the developers' eyes in 1985. Sydney's skyline is dominated by buildings which went up from this date. Examples include the Quay West apartments, Grosvenor Place, the Gateway Building, Northbourne House at 1 O'Connell Street, Governor Phillip Tower, Governor Macquarie Tower, Chifley Tower and many buildings in the city's western corridor, such as the MMI Building and twin-towered Darling Park.

In the closing years of the twentieth century, the retail sector of the city and the southern edge of the CBD are undergoing great change. The most obvious example of this is the giant

ABOVE: The city looking southward from the clock tower of the General Post Office in the late nineteenth century.

BELOW: George Street in the late nineteenth century looking south, near the corner of King Street. Note the wool bales destined for Circular Quay.

hole in the ground that is the former Walton's site, a victim of the Bond empire's *folie de grandeur*. It is being built on after a lapse of more than a decade—not before time.

Meanwhile, some of the early postwar-boom skyscrapers are being torn down to be replaced by a second generation of tall buildings. Many of the newer skyscrapers have extensive retail space at and near ground level. This means that office workers have no need to venture outside their building until it is time to go home. In the 1970s the ambition of promoting pedestrian traffic through retail space was more extreme. In the MLC Centre and the American Express Tower, pedestrians were lured, yellow brick road–like, into the web of retail activity that lay within. Paradoxically, this never really worked as a means of drumming up passing trade. Pedestrians, this writer for one, would avoid that side of the street, as a form of mute protest against the building's obvious intentions. The internal design of these two buildings has now been updated along less authoritarian lines.[4]

For many years until the middle of the nineteenth century, the walled army barracks in George Street, on the site of today's Wynyard, acted as a long 'buffer zone' between the commercial activity in the centre of the town, in George and Pitt streets, and the emerging financial centre. The barracks stretched from Margaret to Barrack Street between George and Clarence streets. Relations between the soldiers and the populace were often strained: the soldiers sometimes picked fights with local civilians, using their big belt buckles as assault weapons after having too many drinks in the many local hotels. To prevent this, they were not allowed to wear their belts out at night.[5] Some of the finest houses in the town in 1848 were on the eastern side of George Street opposite the barracks, and later some of Sydney's finest commercial buildings were built here. One of the few remaining buildings from the 1840s is Skinner's Hotel on the corner of Hunter Street, built in 1845, now occupied by a bank.

From the middle of the nineteenth century, the financial centre was dominated architecturally and commercially by the Royal Exchange Building (1857–1964). Insurance businesses, such as the AMP, and banks had large offices in this precinct near Bridge Street and Spring Street, and along Pitt and George streets, close to the Royal Exchange. But financial precincts, important though they may be, seldom bustle.

Wynyard was a precinct destined for indiscriminate demolition (and desecration). Not only did the area stand on top of a railway line, but it was also close to the burgeoning financial district. The fine old buildings of western George Street were demolished to make way for their banal and graceless successors. Poet Kenneth Slessor wrote in 1962, just as the buildings were disappearing, of his memories of the area in the 1920s:

> On the spot where thousands of suburban travellers go down into the earth to catch the 5.15 for Roseville [at Wynyard], there stood the fabled Café Français—pub, chop house and billiards-saloon combined … There were no less than three delightful old-fashioned

hotels with their bars concentrated in less than a hundred yards of 'The Lane'. It became, naturally enough, a popular Saturday walk for writers, cartoonists and eccentrics—not that they had to walk farther than across the lane.

In Pfahlerts and the Café Français there were dim religious grillrooms of a kind no longer seen in Sydney, filled with the smoke and splutter of mutton chops and T-bone steaks, sizzling over red-hot charcoal which now and then burst into flame as the fat fell down. The tables were large and solid, the chairs leather padded, the napkins snow white and forced into intricate frills, and in the centre of each table there was a circular mahogany cruet-stand which spun when you revolved it, presenting a merry-go-round of Worcester sauce, anchovy sauce, mushroom sauce and other pungencies.[6]

One of the few places in the city where it is possible today to try to imagine the scale of mid-1950s Sydney is at York Street at the southern end of Wynyard Square, looking southward towards Town Hall. A proud cluster of nineteenth-century buildings can still be seen, as can the Art Deco Grace Building (1930) on the southwestern corner of King Street. The Grace Building itself has an interesting history. It was to be the alternative flagship building for Grace Bros after it became apparent that the store at Broadway was not well located for passing trade—it was much too far south of the retail precinct. The site in York Street was not much better. During World War II, the building was expropriated by the government, and for many years it was run-down and disused. A Malaysian property group has refurbished the building that is now occupied by a 300-room hotel, The Forum.

The City Council led by Lord Mayor Frank Sartor since 1991 has been busy making big changes to the parameters of the development of central Sydney. The objective of the new policy is to reverse the negative effects of much of the city's modern developments of the 1960s and 1970s. Sartor is the first politically unaligned lord mayor the city has had for many years. He straddles the middle ground between the two major political parties.

The overall objectives of the Living City Program are to draw people back into the city, especially after office hours, by enhancing the public spaces within the city and promoting a diversity of uses—commercial, residential and tourist-related. Some large development projects have only been permitted on the condition that they will build auditoriums and public function rooms. The Westin Hotel on the site of the General Post Office will have a huge dining and function room, and the AMP has to build a recital hall within its Ash Street development.

The council has also tried to change the appearance of new city buildings. Alienating windy tunnels, euphemistically called 'forecourts', that act as a no-man's-land between public and private space have been discouraged. At ground level, buildings are built closer to the street, and there are step-backs at the upper levels so that there will be more sunlight on the city's streets. This encourages trees to grow and will make the city's footpaths less gloomy and overshadowed.

One example of the Living City Program in action is at Chifley Square. The council has flattened the alienating original design in the forecourt of Chifley Tower, executed in the early 1990s, and planted rows of indigenous cabbage tree palms and built a restaurant, which add energy to what was once badly laid-out public space. A sculpture of Ben Chifley, the former train driver and wartime prime minister, graces the forecourt. A more ambitious task is the refurbishment of Martin Place. Footpaths throughout the city have been widened, sometimes to the consternation of motorists.

Some of the city's greater eyesores have been tactically referred to in the program as 'opportunity sites'. These sites may be redeveloped with favourable floor-space ratios, if as a result the amenity of the surrounding public domain will be improved. Other innovations in the new planning strategy include the retention of whatever is left of the city's old laneways and the construction of some new ones. Overhead skyways, the scourge of the 1960s and early 1970s, will no longer be permitted, and demolished wherever possible.

The implementation of the City of Sydney's strategic plan depends on a high level of goodwill between the council and state government, and agreement by the majority of members of the Central Sydney Strategic Planning Committee. Members of the CSSPC are appointed by the state and local government. It has the task of giving planning consent for buildings and developments with a value of more than $50 million. The pinnacle of the administrative ladder for development approvals is the Department of Urban Affairs and Planning. It has the right of veto over any large development. The planning regime for Sydney can appear mystifying to the uninitiated, although it is gradually becoming less so.

287

The council's Living City strategy had its detractors. One has been Harry Seidler, a highly regarded, multi–award-winning architect, and Sydney's illustrious scion of the international school of architecture. He has criticised the council's vision, accusing it of attempting 'to re-create nineteenth-century street architecture'.[7] The disagreement between Seidler and the City Council is really a result of two opposing approaches to how the city should look and the functions it should serve. Should future developments be constrained, as the council believes, by looking at the pre-existing environment including the streetscape and building heights, so that a reasonable amount of physical cohesion results? Or should cityscapes be seen as blank canvases or greenfield sites for modern architecture to work its miracles upon, with little regard to history and context? It would appear that the tide of opinion is now mostly on the council's side. Darling Park on the city's western corridor is a good example of trying to bring warmth and human convenience to city buildings. Built by Lend Lease and designed by architect Eric Kuhne, it is occupied by John Fairfax and Sons Limited, IBM and Price Waterhouse Coopers.

Recent planning controls have pegged the maximum height of the city buildings at 228 metres. This is the height of the MLC Tower and Governor Phillip and Governor Macquarie towers. The pinnacle of Centrepoint Tower, at 305 metres, would not be given building approval today. Its observation tower, at 252 metres, will, as long as the policy holds, be the highest viewing spot within the city.

George Street has been the main thoroughfare in Sydney since 1788. Three of Sydney's most imposing pieces of architecture—the Queen Victoria Building, the Town Hall and St Andrew's Cathedral—lie on the last stretch of this great artery.

The Queen Victoria Building (QVB) stands on the site of the old markets built by Governor Macquarie, just uphill from the Market Street wharf at Cockle Bay, now Darling Harbour. It was the 1890s replacement for the original markets that were once a bustling centre of commercial life in the colony. The old markets, though unimposing, were crowded, noisy and congested with traffic. The QVB, an ambitious work of architecture, never really worked in the nineteenth and early twentieth centuries as a market, perhaps because it was too vast and grand. It soon fell into disrepair and was used as storerooms and artists' studios, and as the City Lending Library. The street level was occupied by a murky blend of low-rent, shabby shops.

The Queen Victoria Building is in the 'American Romanesque' style with more than a few Byzantine flourishes, designed by the City Architect, George McCrae.[8] It is of the same vintage as another important work of the American Romanesque style, the Société Générale Building in George Street, near the corner of Martin Place, which was designed by American Edward Raht. The Chinese Malaysian property group Ipoh Gardens redeveloped the QVB in 1986 as an exclusive retail precinct. It now possesses some of Sydney's smarter shops, and the main Sydney ABC Shop. The restoration work entailed the manufacture of cast-iron work, mosaic and stained-glass work of a very high quality. The addition of the clock surprised some Sydneysiders, as it was difficult to reconcile with the aesthetic whole. On the second floor is the grand old ballroom. The retail area is linked by underground walkways to Town Hall railway station on the other side of Druitt Street, and the Grace Building, home of Grace Bros department store on the corner of Market and George streets.

In the nineteenth century, the City of Sydney selected its permanent home in the southern part of the city near the markets and the small businesses that were its political constituency. The site of the Town Hall was also a healthy distance away from its sometime political rival, the colonial, later state, government, in Macquarie Street.

There had been intense negotiations and disagreements with the government in Macquarie Street over the site of the Town Hall. The city aldermen wanted it to be a healthy distance from the government at Macquarie Street, close to their constituency, and adjacent to the city markets the council then owned. The colonial government had other ideas. It would have preferred the Town Hall to be in its own territory, further east, near Parliament House, on the site where Governor Phillip Tower now stands.

The main part of the Town Hall that stands on the site of the old burial ground was completed in 1874 in the Second Empire style, a form of architecture popular in Paris in the middle of the nineteenth century. The idea of this form of architecture, in France at least, was to outdo in grandeur and splendour the works commissioned during the rule of the first emperor, Napoleon. The adoption of this ornate French architectural style in faraway, Anglophone Sydney was possibly a conscious decision by the council to make the building entirely unlike the relatively more restrained Classical and Italianate styles of James Barnet. At the time, Barnet was busy designing other great landmarks, such as the GPO, the Chief Secretary's Building on the corner of Macquarie and Bridge streets, the Lands Department Building in Bridge Street, and the Customs House at Circular Quay.

There were many architects and aldermen involved in building the Town Hall, and maybe its almost frantically overworked ornateness is partly due to this. Despite its elaborate external appearance, the building is well loved by Sydneysiders, and the steps of the Town Hall are still an important meeting place for people in the city.

The saga of the building of the Town Hall is long and tortuous, in the same way building the Opera House was to be a century later. Before the construction began, the remains of the dead were moved south to the Devonshire Street cemetery, the present site of Central Railway. The first architect employed was J. H. Wilson, who said the cost would be £35 000. Wilson passed away, and the task was handed on to two different firms of architects, as well as to the first and second city architects, Albert Bond and David McBeath. Then in 1879 another architect, Thomas Sapsford, was appointed.

289

After construction began, the cost (predictably) increased. Meanwhile, an inquiry by the aldermen of the day revealed that the workmanship was substandard and that there was a pressing need to underpin the foundations. The problems were rectified, and the scale of the building was enlarged to contain Sydney's largest auditorium. When Sapsford died in 1886, the official task of completing the building fell on the new City Architect, George McCrae, who also designed the Queen Victoria Building and the Capitol Theatre.

The total cost of the Town Hall blew out to a final £500 000.[9] This was even after some of the more ornate fripperies had been cut back on the grounds of cost.[10] It is hard to imagine a more detailed and excessive building, and we can be thankful that the more restrained version was realised.

One of the many architects involved in the design of the Town Hall, Albert Bond, designed the vestibule with its exquisite white and gold plasterwork. The clock tower, which rises 58 metres, used to be a landmark on the Sydney skyline. The Centennial Hall section of the Town Hall was added in 1889, a year too late for the centenary celebrations themselves. Before the Opera House was opened in 1973, the Town Hall was one of Sydney's most important venues for musical concerts. The capacity of the Centennial Hall is nearly 5000 people, and the orchestra platform can hold 600. The organ in the Centennial Hall is enormous. It has six keyboards and nearly 8800 pipes.

Public access to and use of the Town Hall has always been strongly encouraged by the city aldermen, for meetings, balls, banquets and sometimes political rallies, although at various times controversy has raged as to who should or should not be permitted to use the Town Hall. For example, the decision by the council not to permit the Australia–Russia Society to meet there in 1948 at the height of the Cold War was unpopular in left-wing circles.

Next door to the Town Hall is St Andrew's Cathedral. It was built earlier than the Town Hall and, like the GPO, is sited in such a way that it is very difficult to enjoy the exterior as a great work of architecture. The site for the cathedral was originally chosen by Macquarie and Greenway on the assumption that they would be able to build a grand city square to cover the area now bounded by Liverpool, Kent, Druitt and Pitt streets.

The foundation stone for the cathedral was laid shortly before Commissioner Bigge's arrival in the colony, but Bigge swiftly put a stop to the extravagant plans. Such a scheme could never be justified in a tiny town with a population of only about 7000. Despite a delay, work on the cathedral recommenced in 1837 at the instigation of the first bishop of Australia, William Broughton. The first architect, James Hume, worked under the bishop's strong guiding hand, who also rather fancied himself as an architect. This collaboration continued until 1842, when funds ran out during the depression. In that same year, Edmund Blacket arrived in Australia, armed with a letter of introduction from the Archbishop of Canterbury. In 1846, he was appointed architect for the cathedral, having already designed or completed several smaller churches. The cathedral, designed in the Victorian Gothic style, was not finally completed until 1868.

290

The western side of the cathedral was intended to be the most imposing facade. Now it is obscured by Sydney Square and the cathedral school. The cathedral is best viewed from the north. The earlier (mostly pre-Blacket) southern transept faces Bathurst Street. This style of Gothic Revival architecture is more restrained than the later romantic Gothic Revival style of the western facade, which becomes more highly embellished with Gothic decoration as the towers, topped with ornately detailed pinnacles rising 39 metres, ascend towards heaven.

The piers and arches inside the cathedral were built of Sydney sandstone, to replicate the manner in which Gothic-style churches were built in medieval times. This was one of Blacket's innovations. In Sydney's earlier churches, piers and arches were built in timber. The proportions of the cathedral have an enlarging effect.

From inside, it looks much larger than its 48 metres, and taller than its height of nearly 21 metres. The stained-glass windows were beautifully executed by Birmingham-based John Hardman, who worked with, and was greatly influenced by, the famous Gothic Revival architect, A. W. Pugin. The alabaster reredos behind the altar are extremely fine, adding a warm glow to the sanctuary area. Behind the baptismal font flies the Union Jack that was secretly kept in Changi prison during World War II, and flown there after the war ended.

One of Sydney's great eccentric figures, Bea Miles, used to stand on the corner of George and Park streets in the middle decades of the twentieth century. Dressed in a greatcoat and sandshoes, with a placard slung around her neck, she used to recite Shakespeare—for a price—to fascinated (or horrified) onlookers on their way to and from Town Hall station, in her well-modulated middle-class voice. The eccentricity did not stop there: she was one of the

291

ABOVE LEFT: The Société Génerale Building (former Equitable Building) on the corner of George and Ash streets, which was intended to stand opposite the GPO in Martin Place. In the 1890s, the land covered with tin sheds was sold off, so Martin Place became much narrower than originally intended.

ABOVE RIGHT: View of George Street south from the Queen Victoria Building, the Town Hall and St Andrew's Cathedral down Brickfield Hill.

greatest clients the Sydney taxi industry has ever had. Miles once travelled to Perth by taxi to gather some wildflowers for the National Herbarium in the Royal Botanic Gardens. Her family owned the leading menswear store, Peapes, in George Street near Wynyard. Her father, William Miles, a notable figure himself, was not amused by her foibles. As well as being a prosperous businessman, he had many diverse political interests. He was a nationalist, a leading anti-conscriptionist during World War I and opposed to British imperialism. He was also a sometime sponsor of literary endeavour, notably Xavier Herbert's *Capricornia* and P. R. ('Inky') Stephensen's work, *The Foundation of Culture in Australia*.

In the 1920s, William Miles had Bea committed to Gladesville Psychiatric Hospital. One of the journalists working on *Smith's Weekly* fell in love with her. The magazine campaigned successfully for her release from hospital.

Bea Miles spent most of her life running from the constraints of middle-class life. She lived her adult life on the streets of the city and around Rushcutters Bay. Miles died in 1973, and was buried at Rookwood Cemetery to the tunes of 'Tie Me Kangaroo Down Sport', 'Waltzing Matilda' and 'Advance Australia Fair'.

In the early days of the colony, there was no postal system. Everyone had to keep their eye on incoming ships to see if they had any mail, and wait to see the flag raised at Flagstaff (now Observatory) Hill to see if any ships were coming around the heads and down the harbour. The first post office in Sydney was set up during the period of the Rum Rebellion by Lieutenant Governor William Paterson. The first postmaster was the emancipist Isaac Nichols, a man who had risen to the office of assistant naval officer, which then included the job of assisting with the collection of customs duties. Nichols ran the postal service from his George Street store, close to the old marketplace at Sydney Cove, at about the spot where the Cahill Expressway crosses George Street. This was conveniently close to inbound shipping. By 1838, there were daily postal deliveries in Sydney.

In 1830, the Post Office had moved down George Street, to opposite Barrack Street. It was a graceful, Neoclassical building with six Doric columns. Curiously enough, some of these Doric columns were later sprinkled across the city when the building was demolished, in one of the earliest examples of building recycling. One of these columns still stands on the tip of Bradleys Head.

292

The Post Office moved to temporary premises in Wynyard Square between York and Carrington streets, where it remained until Barnet's monumental GPO was ready for occupation in 1874. The GPO was Barnet's greatest architectural legacy to Sydney, and the planning and construction spanned much of his career as Colonial Architect from the time he took office in 1862. Barnet's active lobbying for extending the GPO site to Pitt Street indirectly helped make Martin Place possible.

The building stands on a long and narrow site. The clock tower, finally completed in 1887, was a city landmark and for this reason was dismantled during World War II. The stone carvings on the George Street and Martin Place facades were well received by the people of Sydney; they fitted neatly into the mould of Classical Revivalism and featured subjects suitable for public buildings in the prevailing tastes of the day. The carvings on the Pitt Street facade had a different reception. Classical themes were abandoned and ordinary men and women of the day were depicted toiling away as mortals do.

The controversy about the appropriateness of the carvings gathered pace. The matter was even debated in the Legislative Council, and a board of inquiry was established, presided over by leading men of taste and perceived judgment in the arts.[11] The board criticised Barnet's works, but Barnet boldly ignored them. In 1890, the Legislative Assembly finally agreed with Barnet, and his determination finally paid off. Thank goodness they were allowed to remain; it is one of the few quirky things Barnet has left to us. It is a relief for us to know that he was capable of occasionally breaking out in an era when breaking out (especially by government architects) was very unusual.

Modern communications have reduced the pivotal importance of the post offices in daily life, and the skyscrapers of mid-city Sydney have reduced the significance of the once proud building, both physically and otherwise. For many years it has looked sad and unloved. Unsympathetic but utilitarian additions detracted from its grandeur. The gawky additions have been torn down, and a five-star hotel and office building have been built within its walls. As long as the original building is not completely overpowered by the additions, the new hotel should lift the sombre mood of the southern end of Martin Place a little and bring back some nightlife and energy.

After Governor Macquarie and Francis Greenway's great vision of a civic square centred on the site of St Andrew's Cathedral had been quashed by Thomas Bigge, such a concept lay dormant for many decades. By the time the idea resurfaced in the late nineteenth century, it was almost too late. The city had grown so much that it was no longer possible to fashion a large and great open space of a similar magnitude to Greenway's grand plan. The area identified as a future city square was lower Martin Place, between George and Pitt streets. Its primary task was to enhance the GPO. Martin Place also provided another badly needed east–west axis for the city's streets. It was not closed to traffic until the early 1970s.

Just before the depression of the 1890s set in, the colonial government bought land on the northern side of Martin Place and earmarked it for use as open space. The square was intended to extend as far north as Ash Street, one block further than it does. In the early 1890s, the land, so recently resumed, was sold off because of a shortage of money. The possibility of a grand, wide square vanished forever. The GIO Building was built on the site instead. This obscured the impressive southern facade of the Société Générale Building forever. Photographs of the Société Générale Building show the shed next to the laneway which was to have been torn down to widen the space. The only direction Martin Place could grow after that was lengthways, and it proceeded to stretch in an easterly direction all the way up to Macquarie Street. That is why the more recent buildings are on the eastern end of the place.

In 1890, a fire in Moore Street, the pedestrian walkway that ran from Pitt Street to Castlereagh Street, burnt out buildings as far east as the recently completed Hotel Australia. While the fire left a wake of destruction, it did create the possibility of an extension to Martin Place. Lord Mayor Burdekin used his casting vote at a council election to vote in favour of the extension from Pitt to Castlereagh streets.

The next stage had to wait until the beginning of the twentieth century. When the extension of Martin Place was advocated, the Royal Australian Institute of Architects opposed the move, arguing that it would just become a long street rather than a grand public square. They were probably right, but their views were unheeded. It took until 1932 for the council to resolve to extend Martin Place all the way to Macquarie Street, on the basis that it would increase the prestige (and hence rateable value) of the precinct that was then considerably east of the heart of the city.

The finest inter-war building in Martin Place is the Commonwealth Savings Bank Building. Built in the massive but well-proportioned Beaux Arts style, it proudly stands diagonally opposite the MLC Centre. Another example is the Commonwealth Trading Bank that stands on the corner of Pitt Street, opposite the GPO. For many years, this building was the model

293

ABOVE: Anzac Ceremony at the Cenotaph
in Martin Place in 1930.

LEFT: Detail of the Beaux Arts style
Commonwealth Savings Bank (1928),
48–50 Martin Place, one of the city's more
monumental and imposing buildings.

for money boxes given by the bank to children and other keen savers. Both these Commonwealth Savings and Trading Bank buildings were designed at the end of a long and continuous era of imposing public buildings, in the days before the International style of architecture came to Sydney. In those far-off days, consideration of maximising net lettable area was less pressing than the desire to create inspiring and imposing monuments.

The section of Martin Place between Elizabeth and Phillip streets was not developed until the 1930s during the heyday of Art Deco architecture. The old Rural Bank Building (now demolished and the site of its successor, the Colonial State Bank Building) and the APA Building were two of the first to be built. The last section of Martin Place to be built is also the least attractive. This part is flanked by the Reserve Bank Building to the south and the Westpac Building to the north. The Westpac Building has recently undergone positive architectural enhancement.

However, despite its design defects, Martin Place has been an important gathering place at critical times in Australian history. The Cenotaph (1927), containing an empty tomb guarded by images of a soldier and a sailor, stands outside the GPO on the site of the old booth where troops were recruited during World War I. The Cenotaph is one of Sydney's two great shrines to our fallen heroes. The other is the Anzac Memorial at the southern end of Hyde Park. Martin Place was the venue for many patriotic wartime rallies from 1914. Since Anzac Day was inaugurated in 1916, the Cenotaph has been the focal point of the Anzac Day Dawn Service. In the early autumn morning mist, the image of veterans standing to commemorate the fallen is a moving one.

Before the development of public spaces around Circular Quay, Martin Place was one of the most popular gathering spots in the city. It was where people celebrated New Year, the end of World Wars I and II, and other important moments. Martin Place before the building boom was clearly drawn by Slessor in 1952:

> If the Bridge is the sign manual of Sydney from six miles at sea, Martin Place is the centre, the circus, the fulcrum, the Trafalgar Square … But it resembles the heart of the city less than the mentality of the city's officials. Its jumble of architecture … its cement lamp posts, its public lavatory … might be a symbol of the honest, practical point of view which has never yet succeeded in designing the heart of a living city on a blueprint. In the corner of the canyon there are flower sellers, diligently numbered and ticketed by the City Council. They stand like elderly hobgoblins, in stalls with lolly-painted awnings, offering flannel flowers, which seem the blossoming of blankets, Christmas bush, daffodils, violets and nut-coloured boronia, that scent which, far more sharply than gum leaves, disturbs the hearts of Australians in far countries. And through this valley of sandstone successive columns of Australian fighting men have marched, going to the wars and returning from the wars. Here managing directors and office-girls danced hand-in-hand and tore up snowstorms of paper on what they thought was Victory Day. And here every procession pauses to look silently at the bronze figures, the stone covered

with dying flowers, the Cenotaph which is our fumbling expression of something that can never be expressed.[12]

There has until recently been a constant series of visual interruptions leading all the way from George Street to Sydney Hospital in Macquarie Street, and little of the sense of gravity and stateliness one would expect in a great civic square. The newspaper and green ticket huts diminish the scale. The challenge is to design an attractive and imposing public square on sloping land. The red plastic moulded benches which were a sad marriage of the ugly and the uncomfortable have gone. The pebblecrete paving is being replaced with granite.

With the recent renovations to the MLC Centre near Castlereagh Street, parts of Martin Place are finally starting to look more animated, certainly at night-time. There are signs of greater human activity after hours, and not only in the form of daring, if not dangerous skateboarders who use the contours of the amphitheatre as a launching pad for death-defying tricks. The Dendy Cinema, bars, cafés and restaurants attract a large clientele.

Some of the old glamour of the past is returning as well. Banc Restaurant, owned and managed by Stan Sarris, provides the smart ambience and fine food that disappeared entirely from this quarter of the city in the aftermath of the architectural devastation of the 1960s. Sarris also brought smart espresso cafés and the Mediterranean-inspired fast food that has so improved the lunch-time fare for city workers when he opened Paradiso Café further north in Macquarie Place in 1991. This sort of café has proliferated through the 1990s, to the extent that the old-fashioned sandwich bars—with their restrained offerings of smallgoods looking well past their prime, grey-looking tuna and salad selections of fanatically thinly sliced iceberg lettuce, tasteless tomato, tinned asparagus and beetroot—are almost an endangered species.

In recent times, Martin Place has started to sprout a new, very fashionable image: it is at the tail end of the ribbon of designer boutiques that begins at Giorgio Armani on the corner of Elizabeth and Market streets, coils around Castlereagh Street, turns again at Martin Place, and terminates at Emporio Armani opposite the GPO. This new breed of shops caters to tourists and locals alike, selling clothes in tune with the northern hemisphere, quite out of kilter with the prevailing climate on the streets outside—hence the plethora of overcoats on display in summer, and shorts and sandals in winter.

Like Castlereagh Street, Bligh Street was, until the 1960s, one of the prettiest quarters of old Sydney. The New South Wales Club (1884) designed by William Wardell is all that remains. On the other side of the road was the Union Club, also designed by Wardell, and formerly the home of the Campbell family. This lovely old building was demolished to make way for the Wentworth Hotel in the middle of the 1960s. The nineteenth-century Savoy Theatre was another landmark. It had plush, red velvet curtains upon which were appliquéd representations of the Eiffel Tower in Paris. Like so many others, the theatre was converted into a cinema and specialised in exotic French subtitled movies from the 1950s until it was demolished.

In the past fifteen years, Castlereagh Street has become the closest thing Sydney has to the exclusive shopping of Bond Street or Madison Avenue. Exclusive boutiques, including Chanel, Salvatore Ferragamo, Hermès and Gucci, are sprinkled along the street.

Castlereagh Street begins at Hunter Street in Johnson Square, named after Richard Johnson, the first clergyman in the colony. It was the site of the first church service in 1788, over which Johnson presided. The memorial there refers to the psalm read out to the colonists and marines:

> What shall I return to the Lord
> For all his bounty to me?
> I will lift up the cup of salvation
> And call on the name of the Lord
> I will pay my vows to the Lord
> In the presence of all his people …
>
> Psalm 116, verses 12–14

297

The early colonists were not God-fearing; it took until the 1830s when there were high levels of free immigration for religion to catch on with the majority. Not many of the convicts at that first religious service would have agreed that God had been so bountiful to them.

Until the middle of the nineteenth century, Castlereagh Street was solidly residential. One famous former resident was Henry Browne Hayes, baronet, heiress abductor, convict and original owner of Vaucluse House. Hayes lived in a cottage on the site now occupied by the Prudential Building on the corner of Martin Place.

Over the years, nineteenth-century cottages gave way to larger buildings, and the ubiquitous corner pub. From 1855, the block on the corner of King Street where the MLC is today has always had a theatre upon it. The descendant of these theatres is the Theatre Royal, which is underground and subsumed within the MLC. Its predecessor was far more worthy of the title. The first three theatres on the site were burnt down. The last one was rebuilt in 1921. It was one of the many victims of the redevelopment of the block when the MLC Centre was built.

Other casualties of the MLC Centre were nineteenth-century Rowe Street and the Hotel Australia. For many decades, until the early 1960s, the Hotel Australia was the smartest in Sydney. Sarah Bernhardt was one of the earlier visitors there who arrived in 1891 with an astounding menagerie of animals in cages and tons of luggage and boxes. The *Sydney Morning Herald* reported:

> [T]he animals were soon quite at home in their richly carpeted snuggery. The big St Bernard was hugged, the pug dog rewarded with a dish of milk and a kiss, the little comical bear was encouraged to be friendly, and the cage of possums, parrots and other unconsidered trifles ranged about her rooms and balcony.

An adoring crowd swarmed around the Hotel Australia and Castlereagh Street as she drove down the road towards the grand, domed Her Majesty's Theatre (on the site occupied by Centrepoint Tower) to perform in *La Dame aux Camellias*. Later, when Dame Nellie Melba performed in Sydney, a whole suite was configured and furnished to her taste, and afterwards christened the 'Melba Suite'.

Until the late 1960s the Long Bar and the Art Deco–style Wintergarden—decorated in black onyx with silver stars on the ceiling—at the Hotel Australia were the two best public rooms in Sydney. Journalists, actresses and radio stars would lunch or dine at the Wintergarden—some people had tables each day of the week. Graziers' wives held huge, elegant balls there during the Easter season. The hotel was a good place for looking at people—and trying to pick some of them up, if one was so inclined—especially in the busy lobby, nicknamed the 'Snake Pit'.

On the other side of the street was the Prince Edward Theatre. Nearby there were many more: the St James's, the Mayfair and the Embassy. Two of Sydney's famous nightclubs, Prince's (underground at the Hotel Australia) and Romano's (underground again), next to the Prince Edward, were nearby. These nightclubs opened up near the Hotel Australia because that was where all the night-time activity was. Grand descending staircases led down to the tables, and beyond these were the band and the dance floor. Pretty girls were usually given the best tables, so they could more easily be seen.

Over the street, the old Victoria Arcade stood on the site of the Carlton Arcade now being rebuilt. It had a curious collection of speciality shops and one of Sydney's famous Italian restaurants, Florentino. Florentino was not only good, it was affordable, and was frequented by the eclectic mix of people living and working in that part of town: lawyers, art students, office workers, actors and journalists. Usher's Hotel on the corner of Castlereagh and King streets was a favourite of Sir Robert Menzies during World War II. There are few architectural remnants from those days. One is the Trust Building, now a branch of Westpac bank, built in the early twentieth century in an early–twentieth-century version of the Italianate style.

Rowe Street ran along the southern boundary of the hotel, between Pitt and Castlereagh streets. Called Brougham Place until 1875, it was named after Thomas Rowe, an architect of note who married one of Captain John Piper's daughters and designed the synagogue in Elizabeth Street, Sydney Hospital and many buildings in Pitt Street. Rowe Street was described by writer Isidore Brodsky in 1962 as 'old world and Continental'.[13] The Strand Arcade is all that is left to remind us of this vanished era in Sydney's retail history.

All that remains of Rowe Street is a dismembered, dead-end access to the shopping area of the MLC. Before it disappeared, the laneway was nicknamed 'Little Bond Street', after its English counterpart. There was a collection of small shops with hand-painted, old-fashioned street awnings depicting the area's history. Afternoon tea parties attended by artists and writers were held at Roycroft, an old book and art shop. The owner of Roycroft, Frances Zabell, hoarded copies of Norman Lindsay's *Redheap* there after it was banned in the 1930s. There were other coffee shops, small restaurants, speciality shops (such as Kenneth Slessor's sister Maud shop, The Jade Tree, selling Chinese curiosities, antiques and Japanese woodblock prints), and a shop where exotic fabrics were elegantly displayed in the shop front. Some of Sydney's leading artists, Donald Friend, Loudon Sainthill and Thea Proctor acted as window dressers. During World War II, when clothing was scarce and austere, fashion-conscious women bought exotic, handblocked upholstery fabrics to make sun dresses.[14]

There were also small bachelor studios in Australia Chambers above the shops where artists Lionel Lindsay and Italian-born Dattilo Rubbo, and literary figure A. G. Stephens, of the *Bulletin*, lived until 1933. Rubbo once challenged Lindsay to a duel after the Italian artist had been gravely offended by one of Lindsay's cartoons which disparaged the achievements of great Italians such as Michelangelo, Leonardo Da Vinci, Dante and Garibaldi. Rubbo approached Stephens to arrange the duel, but the crusty old editor, after recovering from his mirth, averted any bloodshed by introducing the pair. They later became good friends.

In the late nineteenth century, lovers used to drift to this dark, narrow street, much to Rubbo's consternation. He was the Rowe Street vigilante of his day. He sometimes tripped over couples while returning to his studio. To deter them, he dressed a wooden artist's model in a policeman's uniform—but this only worked for a while, until larrikins poured beer on the dummy. On another occasion, he chased a streetwoman waving a sword. Many years later, in the 1950s, art critic, *bon vivant* and later editor of *Art in Australia*, Mervyn Horton, ran one of the first coffee shops in Sydney to sell espresso coffee there. Rowe Street was one of the last outposts of old bohemian Sydney.

Although the MLC Centre (1977) was built at great cost to the social fabric and played a key role in changing the tone of the city, the building was an assertive and fine expression of architectural purism designed by Harry Seidler. The 1-acre (0.4-hectare) site was aggregated during the 1960s, and Rowe Street was bought from the council. Imposing as it is, the huge set-back from Martin Place created an open, cold and uninviting space which has only been made more user-friendly since the improvements of the early 1990s. Now there are outdoor cafés, restaurants, a myriad variety of convenience-food outlets, and the Dendy Cinema.

The Commercial Travellers' Club sits uncomfortably right on the corner of Castlereagh Street and Martin Place on the MLC site, like a scaled down Centrepoint Tower. It is a bizarre building that looks a little like a compressed toadstool. It is hard to understand why the commercial travellers chose not to occupy part of the MLC proper, rather than insisting on being accommodated in their very own architectural protuberance.

Whatever the consequences of building the MLC were, the effect of the building boom on the eastern side of Castlereagh Street is far worse. None of the buildings is of any architectural significance—the Prudential Building and the Carlton Arcade, to name just two, were so ugly as they were built that they have already been redeveloped in the last years of the twentieth century. Despite fresh efforts, this part of Sydney may never entirely recover its lost soul.

On the intersection of Market Street and Castlereagh Street stand the two city stores of David Jones. David Jones was originally established in George Street near the corner of

Barrack Street in 1838. Retail activity in the city drifted east in the 1920s to coincide with the construction of the city-loop railway system from Central Station to Circular Quay, but it was not until the late 1970s that the store that stood on the site of the original flagship was closed down. By that time, it sat incongruously beside sober financial institutions and office blocks. David Jones is one of the city's leading department stores. The competition between it and rival Grace Bros further down Market Street is often intense.

The food hall in David Jones's Market Street store is a Sydney institution. Below ground level, an enticing maze for the hungry and keen gourmets awaits. In spring, the elegantly designed ground floor of the Elizabeth Street store, dedicated for the most part to women's fashions, is ablaze with a springtime festival of flowers.

Like so many other great Sydney-based businesses and institutions, David Jones succumbed to takeover fever in the early 1980s when it fell into the hands of John Spalvins's Adelaide Steamship Company. With the demise of Adsteam in the recession of 1989–92, David Jones went through a turbulent period in its ownership. It is now, once again, listed on the stock exchange, and is emerging from a state of upheaval.

Grace Brothers has been much improved and modernised, and will continue to compete for retail supremacy with David Jones. On the other side of the street, Gowings is one of the few retail businesses in Sydney to remain in family hands. The first Gowings store was opened in George Street in 1868. For nearly a century, Gowings has promoted the popularity of Australian-made clothes, such as King Gee overalls and Speedo swimwear. The store we see today was opened in 1929. The Sydney expression 'Gone to Gowings', meaning that someone has gone absent without leave, or just taken off, was first coined by Darcy Dugan, famous Sydney criminal and gaol escapee, who wrote the words just before fleeing his prison cell at Long Bay.

Like the other north–south city streets, Pitt Street moves through the financial district and into the retail core of the city. In the early days of the colony, much of Pitt Street south of Hunter Street belonged to the prosperous emancipist Samuel Terry. He lived near the corner of Angel Place, and had a tavern nearby. In those days, Pitt Street ran along the eastern side of the Tank Stream, north of present-day Martin Place. The stream was not covered up until the 1850s. Now there are proposals to uncover parts of the old Tank Stream so that people can catch a glimpse of Sydney's earliest source of fresh water.

The commercial activity in Pitt Street was concentrated near Market Street where the Pitt Street Mall is. That is where Sydney's first theatre, the Royal Victoria Theatre, was built. This theatre soon eclipsed the earlier Royal Theatre, which was actually built within the confines of the old Royal Hotel in George Street. The Victoria was also the venue for public meetings and balls. Perhaps the most famous performer ever to grace the stage of the theatre was Lola Montez, who performed her famous Spider Dance there in 1855. There were many other famous old theatres in Pitt Street in bygone days: the Lyceum and Palace theatres, the

ABOVE LEFT: Interior of Her Majesty's Theatre in 1903, before it was replaced by Woolworths flagship store.
ABOVE RIGHT: One of Colonial Architect James Barnet's greatest works, the General Post Office in Martin Place.

Criterion and, grandest of all, Her Majesty's. Her Majesty's stood in Pitt Street between 1887 and 1933, when it was replaced by Sydney's flagship Woolworths store. Later still, in the late 1960s, Woolworths gave way to Centrepoint (AMP) Tower.

Running between Pitt, Castlereagh and George streets were a number of gracious nineteenth-century arcades that gave the city so much of its old character. The only one of these still standing is the Strand Arcade. Those which have fallen under the wrecker's hammer are the Royal (now replaced by one of Sydney's plainest buildings, the Sydney Hilton hotel), the Piccadilly, the Sydney, the Imperial and Her Majesty's arcades. The Royal Arcade was not the only casualty the Hilton Hotel claimed. Other landmarks that stood on the site were Tattersalls Hotel, with its famous Marble Bar (now trimmed down and relocated in the Hilton Hotel), and the Palace Theatre (1896). The loss of these fine old buildings was a great one for Sydney. The early School of Arts (originally founded in 1833) still stands next to the Hilton Hotel. This is the oldest building in Pitt Street. For many years during the nineteenth century, the School of Arts offered Sydneysiders the only access to adult education and self-improvement. It organised public lectures, discussions and instruction classes, provided access to books through its lending library and helped people develop their debating skills. As time went on, with the establishment of the Sydney Technical College, the school became more dedicated to general, rather than trade-based, education. It was one of many similar institutions spread across Sydney in the nineteenth century.

With the exception of the Strand Arcade, the facade of the Skygarden retail centre and the Soul Pattinson chemist shop, there is little nineteenth-century architecture remaining in Pitt Street. The Strand Arcade is a fragmentary treasure of what Sydney once was. It was designed by J. B. Spencer in the Classical Revival style. One of the financiers of the Strand Arcade was Sir Hugh Dixson, father of William, who left his large collection of books and art to the State Library. The arcade is loaded with old-world charm, enhanced by the openness to natural light that pours through the glass roof and bathes the whole arcade in a manner quite unlike the city's other shopping arcades. The cast-iron balcony that runs along the upper levels increases the sensation of space. The Strand Arcade is home to some of Sydney's more successful clothes designers and jewellers.

Although built as one arcade and completed in 1892, by some accident of fate it fell into two separate hands in the 1920s, and remained in separate hands until the Prudential Assurance Company bought both ends of the arcade in the early 1970s. The accident was probably a lucky one, as it may have saved the arcade from demolition.[15] The Strand Arcade almost burned to the ground in 1976. The decision of whether to demolish the building or restore it was finely balanced.[16] Again, blessed by luck, this meant that there was much reconstruction work to be done, and this time it was done sympathetically with awareness of the building's heritage value. After the reconstruction and renovation, the building was brought closer to its original condition. By the time of the fire, not much money had been spent on the building for many years. Rent controls imposed in the middle of the twentieth century meant that tenants had protected low rents, and eviction was a practical impossibility.

The Strand has always been occupied by artisans, couturiers, milliners, glove- and shoe-makers. Fifty years ago the best millinery boutique was owned by the French mother of journalist and publicist Georgie Swift. Georgie herself was also one of Sydney's *doyennes* of fashion and style from the 1950s. The family millinery business thrived in an era when everybody wore hats, and all hats on sale there cost less than £1. In the Depression years of the 1920s and 1930s, hats were the only affordable means of adding to women's wardrobes. The basement of the Strand Arcade, now occupied by a duty-free store, was the home of Sydney's first ballroom–nightclub, Ambassadors. Azzalin Orlando Romano, who later opened Romano's nightclub in Castlereagh Street, was the chef there. Before its reincarnation as a nightclub, Ambassadors had been a large, grand restaurant with ballroom, palm court and separate dining saloons, until the Great Depression in 1930. From the early 1970s, a new generation of artisans occupied the Strand. Jenny Kee and Linda Jackson opened the colourful Flamingo Park. Le Café, owned by Patrick and Chrissie Juillet, thrived and brought passing traffic back to the arcade. Lloyd Lomas opened one of Sydney's most fashionable hairdressing salons, and more clothing designers such as Robert Burton moved in. The place became an oasis of creativity in a sea of commercial redevelopment.

The Pitt Street Mall (along with Martin Place and Dixon Street) is one of the city's few attempts at street closure. Whether the idea has worked to improve the ambience of these streets is arguable. Just around the corner from the mall in Market Street is the State Theatre

(1929), now the only theatre of its period left in the retail precinct. The State Theatre was built in the same year that talking movies were starting to threaten the dominance of live theatre. It is a fabulous, but solitary, remnant of an era when going to the cinema or the theatre was a major outing. In those days, entertainment in the city's theatres was not limited to what you saw on stage or screen, but part of a themed, total experience, which enveloped you as you crossed the threshold. In the case of the State Theatre, the theme was a Spanish Gothic Palazzo fantasy.

Elizabeth Street was, until the development of the city-loop railway line, too far east to be part of the retail, entertainment and commercial heart of the city. It was more commonly used for residential purposes, or as professional rooms for lawyers and doctors. One of the earlier significant architectural works in the street is the Great Synagogue (1873), designed by Thomas Rowe. It stands just north of the Park Street corner. It was built in the Free Gothic style, appropriately so-called because it drew on Byzantine, Romanesque and Gothic details.

Although the first Jewish people arrived on the First Fleet, it was not until 1844 that Sydney's first synagogue was built at York Street, close to the markets. Most of the Jewish community immigrated from England, and religious and dietary laws were not closely observed.[17] Few Russian and Eastern European Jews, fleeing pogroms and anti-Semitism, migrated to Australia in the nineteenth century. One important early Jewish immigrant was Isaac Nathan, a musician who composed the first opera written in Australia, *Don John of Austria*. Others pursued legal and political careers. One of these was Sir Julian Salomons, a barrister and politician who was appointed briefly as chief justice of the Supreme Court, but in fact was never sworn in on the grounds of ill health. In those days, there was also adverse comment on the grounds of his religion.[18] Since the 1930s, there has been Jewish immigration from other European countries, and there are now many other synagogues throughout Sydney. Many are in the eastern suburbs, including the Orthodox Central Synagogue in Fletcher Street, Woollahra, and the liberal Temple Emanuel in Ocean Street, Woollahra.

Half a century after the synagogue was built, the new city railway loop prompted the next building wave in Elizabeth Street. Classically proportioned early–twentieth-century buildings include David Jones, the St James' Trust Building (formerly the Manchester Unity Building) and the former Tattersall's Club were built. The elegant Art Deco T & G Building, on the corner of Elizabeth and Park streets, was floodlit at night, adding an air of dazzle and gravitas at the same time. Many of these buildings have now been demolished. Perhaps saddest of all is the loss of the old T & G Building and its replacement by the inelegant Pacific Power Building in the 1970s. The Tattersall's building was another casualty. It stood on the site of the Sheraton on the Park, one of Sydney's smart newer hotels.

Further north, the GIO Building is an impressive example of inter-war Gothic Art Deco style. It was built in 1929 as the headquarters of the *Sun* newspaper and the imposing sculpture of the sun on top of the building bears witness to this.

303

Of all the streets in the city of Sydney, King Street provides one of the city's greatest cavernous vistas and best snapshots of the magnitude of change Sydney has experienced in the past century. There are only a few remaining examples of nineteenth-century architecture, such as the now tiny-looking building on the corner of Pitt Street abutting the MLC Centre that towers above it. In the nineteenth and early twentieth centuries, King Street east of George Street had been famous for its pubs, its fish cafés and oyster bars. Now it is flanked by skyscrapers. Most of the earlier architecture in King Street is concentrated at the lower, western end. There are still some late–nineteenth-century and early–twentieth-century industrial buildings built at a time that industry and warehousing were major activities within the city itself. In the 1970s, the City Council in one of its less enlightened periods consented to a pedestrian bridge over King Street, from the MLC Centre to the other side of the street. This obscured the vista as far east as Queens Square and Macquarie Street. It can only be hoped that the walkway will not be there in another hundred years.

The former American Express Tower, an almost unique expression of architectural modernism when it was built in the 1970s, stands on the northern corner of King and George streets. It was an adventurous and innovative work of architecture of its day, but has been drastically remodelled by Lend Lease, to the lament of some purists. Its new tenant is the National Roads and Motorists Association (NRMA), a large, cooperatively owned financial organisation based in Sydney that has grown from its humble origins as provider of emergency road service and lobby group for motorists. Another new, late–twentieth-century building is being built by BT Property Trust on the opposite side of the street at 400 George Street, next to the famous Darrell Lea chocolate shop. In the nineteenth century, this corner was the transition point between the commercial, financial and retail centres of the city, and was known as the 'Golden Corner', as its real estate value was so high.

CHAPTER TWELVE

DARLING HARBOUR AND THE CITY'S SOUTH

305

RUNNING DOWN THE SLOPE of Brickfield Hill is the city's entertainment district. Most of Sydney's cinemas and theatres have been concentrated there since the old theatres and cinemas sprinkled throughout the city were closed and demolished to make way for large shops and office buildings. This part of the city is the epicentre for after-hours and holiday entertainment. All the leading cinema houses are there: Hoyts, Village and Greater Union, and also some independent cinemas. Restaurants and amusement arcades have sprung up to complement what is offered to movie-goers, and on Friday and Saturday nights the place is packed with people looking for fun—and sometimes trouble as well. It is now, sadly, one of the city's hot spots for crime. A short distance from the cinemas are the many restaurants of Chinatown. One of the city's few remaining laneways, Albion Lane, runs alongside the Greater Union Cinema to Kent Street.

In the early days of the colony, the road up Brickfield Hill was steep and dusty, and became treacherously muddy in wet weather. The southerly wind in the town of Sydney was known as a 'Brickfielder' because dust would blow from the roads and clay pits over the city to the north. It was not until later in the nineteenth century that this unpleasant phenomenon ceased as the roads were sealed. Brickfield Hill was the site of the city's earliest clay pits and kilns. Clay was dug out of pits on the eastern side of George Street.

Many convicts built huts in the area around Brickfield Hill, close to their work, and drinking, whoring and cockfighting were not uncommon. On the southwestern corner of Goulburn and

George streets one of the early colony's grislier murders took place, and for a long time the ground was thought to be haunted.[1]

The Reverend Mr Clode was a missionary on his way home from Tahiti. He met a soldier called Jones who lived at Brickfield Hill with his wife and two other soldiers. Clode lent the man some money, but Jones was disinclined (or unable) to repay it. Clode's badly mutilated body was found in a nearby sawpit. Ghoulish evidence pointed to Jones's guilt, but he refused to confess. He was found guilty of murder anyway, along with his wife and one of his lodgers, and all three were sentenced to a spectacular hanging on gallows erected on the site of his house, which had been burnt down on Governor Hunter's orders. The bodies of the two hanged men were left suspended until they rotted, and Mrs Jones's body was given to the hospital.

The slope of Brickfield Hill was flattened under the administration of governors Bourke and Gipps in the late 1830s. The top of the hill was pared down and the debris used to raise the incline lower down the hill. This work, like the construction of Circular Quay, the Argyle Cut and the levelling of the road from Cockle Bay up to Bathurst Street, was done with convict labour. It was estimated that 1 million cubic feet of debris (much of it sandstone) was moved during the levelling of Brickfield Hill. After this was done, a busy, bazaar-like retail trade flourished in the later nineteenth century. Almost anything could be bought there. With the construction of Central Railway Station in the early twentieth century, more substantial retailers such as Anthony Hordern moved in.

Retail patterns changed from the 1930s with the opening of new railway stations at Town Hall, Wynyard and St James, and the heart of Sydney's retail precinct shrank to the north. The fortunes of Anthony Hordern's went into decline, along with those of other department stores in the city's south, such as Mark Foy's, Marcus Clark and Beard Watson.

Today, the ambitious World Square is gradually being built on the Anthony Hordern's site building by building. The project was a casualty of the recession and industrial unrest in the building industry in the 1980s. Work ceased completely for several years, and the rate of progress is still not as good as was hoped.

South again of Brickfield Hill lies the Haymarket, so called because a cattle and corn market operated there from the middle of the 1830s, as it was too hard to negotiate a bullock cart full of produce up Brickfield Hill to the city market. Now this area is part of Chinatown.

Sydney's earliest members of the Chinese community lived around The Rocks, and particularly around George Street North. Chinese indentured labourers came to Sydney in the 1840s to do the work formerly done by convicts, and many more free immigrants came during the gold rushes. In the 1890s, the Chinese, possibly because of harassment from larrikins of the notorious Rocks Push, moved south to the area around Wexford Street in Surry Hills. Wexford Street was demolished in the early years of the twentieth century so that Wentworth Avenue could be built as the eastern approach to Central Railway. The Chinese then started

ABOVE: Hay Street in the Haymarket in the 1950s, when Paddy's Markets was still Sydney's major produce markets and much of that produce was supplied by Sydney's Chinese market gardeners. Although the produce section of the markets has moved to Flemington, Paddy's still runs in the Haymarket and is a much-loved Sydney institution. There have been markets on or near this site almost continuously since 1869.

307

to settle around Campbell Street in the Haymarket, and later around Dixon and Sussex streets. By 1900, there were 3500 members of Sydney's Chinese community, nearly all of whom were from the Pearl River delta in Guangzhou province.[2]

In the late nineteenth century and early twentieth centuries, many Chinese people in Sydney were market gardeners who sold their produce at the city markets at Belmore Park and later at Paddy's Market. The shops and restaurants around Dixon Street served the Chinese residents and those who worked at the nearby markets.

In the 1970s, when the city markets moved out to Flemington, the Chinese restaurants and shops lost their clientele and the businesses went into decline. Many of the buildings became vacant and dilapidated. Local property and business owners searched for a solution. Architect Henry Tsang, now deputy lord mayor, was one of the community leaders who revived the area. Tsang was a member of the first wave of professional Chinese people practising in professions in Sydney.

He agreed to act as voluntary architect to try to find a solution for Chinatown. In the early 1970s, the City Council and the local community provided money for landscaping Dixon

Street. Archways and pavilions were built, the road was closed to traffic and repaved, and trees were planted. As the White Australia policy was beginning to fade into history, a time capsule was put under the archway to Dixon Street in 1980, to symbolise the change of sentiment about the Chinese–Australian relationship.

The capsule contains Chinese sand and pebbles—the closest thing to Chinese soil permitted by the quarantine officials in the Australian customs department. The mixing of this soil with Australian soil signified the fact that Chinese people no longer needed to return to China. Australia could become the home it had never been to the Chinese during the years of the White Australia policy. With the sand and gravel is buried a lucky golden tortoise, signifying long life and prosperity, and old Chinese coins, to bring luck and engender a new sense of belonging in Australia. Historically, the Chinese had been reluctant to bring capital into the country. The Chinatown area was one of the prime targets for this new investment.

The improvements to Dixon Street and Chinatown were a turning point in the attitude of the Chinese community towards Sydney—and Australia.[3] They also attracted new businesses and a new generation of Sydneysiders keen to come to the area to eat and shop. The nearby cinemas in George Street ensured a steady supply of patronage. The next great improvement to the area was the creation of the Chinese Garden. It had a long period of gestation. The premier, Neville Wran, came to Dixon Street during political campaigning for his re-election in the early 1980s, promising a garden to complement the improvements to Dixon Street. The Chinese Garden is probably bigger than anyone had seriously contemplated.

In the early 1980s, New South Wales and Guangdong became sister provinces, and the governor of Guangdong offered to assist the Chinese community build the garden near Dixon Street. Premier Wran took a trade delegation to Guangdong, and part of the memorandum of understanding was that each government would jointly fund a Chinese garden in Sydney which was to be a symbol of the new, closer relationship. The timing of this agreement was excellent. Darling Harbour was being rebuilt, and a cluster of industrial buildings on the southeastern side of Darling Harbour close to Chinatown was identified as the future site for the garden. It was to be designed by Henry Tsang. Both Chinatown and the Chinese Garden at Darling Harbour are two of Sydney's most popular tourist destinations, particularly on weekends.

The southern end of the city and the Pyrmont peninsula are expected to be the engine room of population growth in the city in the coming decades. The southern and western sections of the city will have the highest population growth rate of the whole Sydney region:[4] the population in the central business district is forecast to grow from 7300 in 1995 to 40 000 in the year 2021. Evidence of this is the apartment-building boom south of Park Street. The level of construction is quite phenomenal.

One of the largest examples of this new building activity is The Peak, a large tower of apartments on top of Paddy's Markets. There are many others to come. This type of development activity, much of it by Chinese property developers, is a reminder to the city of its role as an important commercial and residential base for the Chinese diaspora. There is no better way of witnessing this than to visit the Haymarket–Chinatown area on weekends. The many shops and restaurants teem with life and an energy that was missing a decade ago.

Like the similar area in San Francisco, Chinatown in Sydney is a self-sufficient community. Import and export firms, professional services, eating houses, social clubs, food stores, herbal medicine shops and other retail outlets can all be seen. The old and new facades of Sydney's Chinatown visible today are a testament to the hard work and the self-reliance of Sydney's Chinese community.

Central Railway Station, on the southern fringe of the city, was built in 1906. It is an imposing example of Federation-style public architecture. Around the corner in Broadway opposite the University of Technology is the old, long-disused post office, built in a quirkier and freer Federation style. It is being converted to hotel accommodation. Central Railway Station's location so far south of the port facilities of Sydney was at least some improvement on the location of the previous railway terminus at Redfern.

309

The infamous Carters' Barracks, later called the Belmore Barracks, used to stand on the eastern side of Pitt Street between Belmore Park and Railway Square. They were pulled down to make way for the building of Central Station and its approaches. These barracks were one of the most gruesome buildings left to us from the early, penal-colony days. They were built in 1822 to accommodate up to 200 convicts whose job it was to cart bricks and timber up Brickfield Hill to the city. The barracks replaced the series of huts the carters used to live in, near the brick pit at Brickfield Hill. The treadmill at Carters' Barracks was worked by convicts, as a form of punishment, to thresh grain. This was harsh punishment indeed, involving endless forced climbing. A committee constituted in 1825 to look into the treadmill noted:

> [I]f coercive labour and restraint are calculated to reform, or deter from crime, no system of discipline can be better calculated for this purpose, than that of labour on the tread-wheel, which admits of being regulated, and enforced, with more strictness and exactitude than any other ...[5]

Railway Square, the area to the west of Central Railway Station and Belmore Park, has been greatly affected by the building booms of the past few decades. The McKell Building is the headquarters of the Department of Public Works. It is named after one-time Labor Party premier, later governor general, William McKell. Around the corner in Pitt Street is the Sydney Central Building, which provides office space for many federal government departments. The late–twentieth-century streetscape in this area now almost completely overpowers the Gothic Christ Church St Laurence, built in the early nineteenth century with later additions by Edmund Blacket.

To the north of Central Railway is Belmore Park, the site of the Belmore Markets. They were the city's produce markets in the late nineteenth century, after the old George Street markets were demolished to make way for the Queen Victoria Building. In 1893, the original markets were replaced with the new, George McCrae–designed Belmore Markets in the Neoclassical style. The quality of the architecture could not overcome the problem of the Belmore Markets not being close to any railway terminus—Central Station was not yet built—and the growers were agitating strongly to relocate the markets towards the railway goods line at Darling Harbour. They finally got their way in 1909, and the markets were relocated to where Paddy's Markets now stand, under The Peak apartments on the block bounded by Ultimo, Quay and Hay streets. The first Paddy's Markets grew up around the Belmore Markets in the 1860s and 1870s, near the Capitol Theatre. Paddy's Markets became a popular place for entertainment, as well as being a general market. They still are, even though Sydney's produce markets have been relocated to Flemington in Sydney's west.

In the 1920s and 1930s, the old McCrae-designed Belmore Markets building was converted into what is now the recently reopened Capitol Theatre. When the markets moved to the other side of George Street, the building was used as a hippodrome and circus, then in 1926 it reopened as an atmospheric picture palace, with decoration and furnishings to match. The Great Depression spelt the end of its glory days, and it reopened along more austere lines again in 1933. For many years, it was a cinema featuring B-grade movies. Then, under the aegis of theatre impresario Harry M. Miller, it was transformed in the 1970s to accommodate the production of *Jesus Christ Superstar*. After that closed, the Capitol fell into disuse for many years. It has recently been remodelled by Ipoh Gardens into a lyric theatre, with a capacity of 2000 people, and is a popular venue for musicals.

The western side of the city has been undergoing much change in recent years, in tandem with the development of Darling Harbour. Until the early twentieth century, many tenement houses could be seen in Kent, Sussex, Clarence and York streets, but these gradually gave way to warehouses. Since the mid-1980s, several tall office buildings, such as the MMI Building and the Darling Park building, have gone up along the western corridor of the city.

On the corner of Bathurst and Sussex streets is an older building, now converted into office accommodation and called Vintage House. It was built in 1893 and used to be the City of Sydney Roller Flour Mills. The location close to the Darling Harbour railway yards meant that wheat could easily be transported to the mill. From the 1920s until the 1970s, the building was used as a warehouse for Seppelt's wines.

At 531 Kent Street stands one of Sydney's oldest buildings, the Judge's House. The house was built between 1821 and 1822 for William Harper, a surveyor, and is the second-oldest domestic building after Cadman's Cottage. At the time it was built, it had water views down to Darling Harbour and was surrounded by open land. The house got its name when it was occupied by the Supreme Court judge James Dowling, who later became chief justice.

ABOVE: Darling Harbour and Pyrmont docks, c. 1948, when the area was still very much an industrial and maritime hub.

Dowling later built Brougham Lodge at Woolloomooloo. Gradually, the area around the house was developed for industrial use, and the status of the area, and that of the tenants of the house, declined. In 1868, the house became a shelter for the destitute and then part of the Dixon Street Soup Kitchen. The Sydney City Mission occupied the house from 1945 to 1970. The Grosvenor Trust bought the building and the refuge buildings which surrounded it, and proposed to demolish them and build an office tower. Thankfully, this did not proceed, although the refuge buildings were demolished by the Grosvenor Trust in 1978 and a Japanese restaurant was built there instead. The restored Judge's House was opened in the same year. It is now used as commercial premises.

The narrow body of water between Millers Point and Peacock Point at Balmain is the main entrance into Sydney's old industrial and maritime heartlands. Although the many bays that lie within still provide port facilities, nearly all the industry is gone. Until the late 1970s, the names of Walsh Bay, Darling Harbour, Blackwattle Bay, Rozelle Bay and White Bay were synonymous with Sydney's industrial and working-class history.

In the early 'hunger years' of the colony, the colonists fed on the cockles of Darling Harbour, just as the Aborigines had done. Thus its first European name was Cockle Bay. For many years, the eastern side of Cockle Bay was uninhabited. The steep terrain made the area hard to build upon, and carting building materials down the sandstone bluffs was difficult. The first buildings were built when Macquarie established the George Street markets and levelled land to build Market Street down to the bay. Boats and barges used the Market Street wharf to load and unload their produce on the way to and from market.

In 1813, the industrial revolution came to Cockle Bay—and Sydney—when John Dickson imported the components of a steam engine. The engine threshed grain for nearly ninety years at the head of Cockle Bay from 1815, and was not decommissioned until 1903.[6] Before the steam engine was put into use, power for grain grinding in the colony was provided by windmills. Dickson was granted 15 acres (6 hectares) covering the area between George, Hay, Sussex and Goulburn streets, down to Darling Harbour. The steam engine was housed on Harbour Street, just to the north of the present-day site of the Sydney Entertainment Centre.

A second steam engine was built by Thomas Barker near the corner of Sussex and Bathurst streets, alongside Cockle Bay, in the 1820s. Over the years, manufacturing activity increased. During the wool boom of the 1830s, more industries moved into the area, including Dickson's brewery, later bought by the Toohey family. In that same decade, Governor Darling also took a leaf out of Lachlan Macquarie's book and renamed Cockle Bay after himself.

Many new forms of industry and technology were built near Darling Harbour. Thomas Sutcliffe Mort, a pioneer of refrigeration, built Sydney's first freezing works there. These freezing works and the refrigeration technology developed by Mort were a breakthrough for the Australian economy, which resulted in the beef export industry.

By the end of the nineteenth century, Darling Harbour was a crowded centre of maritime and industrial activity. Private wharves were built along Sussex Street, and the coastal shipping trade was based on the eastern side of the bay. This was the only means of transport and communication available in the era before the railway network became well established. One of the more important commodities transported by the coastal trade was coal, the essential form of energy for the great steamships of the nineteenth and early twentieth centuries. Darling Harbour was the main depot for loading and unloading the coal shipped down from the Hunter or up from the Illawarra.

The once pre-eminent Australasian Steam Navigation Co. was one of the biggest companies in Darling Harbour. Its wharf stood in Sussex Street at the bottom of Margaret Street. Its slipway was at the bottom of Erskine Street. As the company grew and prospered, it built new grand headquarters at Circular Quay West, but many of its main shipping and

ABOVE: Sussex Street at Grafton Wharf in the late nineteenth century, when ferry and shipping wharves flanked the western side of the street.

cargo-handling activities were still based at Darling Harbour.

The growth of Sydney's role as a port during the decades of high growth from 1850 to 1888 promoted the development of working-class housing near the wharves and warehouses, especially around Sussex Street and in Millers Point and Pyrmont. In this period, both population and trade were growing dramatically. Large wool stores, such as the Goldsbrough Mort Building, went up to provide warehouse space. The swamp at Blackwattle Bay was reclaimed to form Wentworth Park, and Blackwattle Bay became a centre for the timber and coal trade.[7] The presence of industry intensified in 1879, when the Colonial Sugar Refinery's factory was built on the tip of the Pyrmont peninsula. Because the area was such a stronghold of labour, many of Sydney's early trade unions were located close by. For many years, the Trades Hall and Labor Party headquarters were also located on the western side of the city, close to the industrial workers of the city, Darling Harbour and Pyrmont.

In the solidly working-class areas of Pyrmont, Ultimo and Darling Harbour, there was little infrastructure and few public amenities. Hygiene was poor. Raw sewage was pumped into the harbour at the bottom of Liverpool Street. Residential pockets were thrown together with factories, wharves and warehouses. This was a paradoxical outcome for Pyrmont, which had

314

ABOVE: Traffic crossing the second Pyrmont Bridge shortly after its opening in 1902. The construction of a crossing over Cockle Bay (the first bridge was built in 1858) did much to transform the Pyrmont peninsula into a busy industrial area. Note the steamships berthed at the wharves.

been originally so named because it reminded one visitor to it of a restful spa retreat in Germany, Bad Pyrmont. Earlier in the colony's life, Pyrmont had been the domain of exclusive families. A 55-acre (22-hectare) estate there was owned by the Macarthur family from 1799. The John Harris estate called Ultimo Farm, upon which he built a gracious early colonial home, ran from the southern boundary of the Macarthurs' land.

The first Pyrmont Bridge was built in 1858. This created easy access to the Pyrmont peninsula, and the level of industrial activity grew. A branch railway line connected Darling Harbour to the new railway system. This bridge was replaced in 1902 with the bridge we know today—the world's oldest electrically driven swing bridge, designed and built by the New South Wales Public Works Department. At the time it was commissioned, the bridge was internationally renowned as an engineering marvel.

In the 1880s, and later in the 1920s, the swampy land at the head of Darling Harbour was reclaimed and used to expand the goods railway yards. These were the major rail–sea goods interchange in New South Wales for nearly a century. Much of the infill used for land reclamation in the 1920s was sandstone dug up in the course of building the city's underground railways.[8] Before this land reclamation, the harbour extended as far south as Pier Street, which runs between the Chinese Garden and the Entertainment Centre. The head of Darling Harbour was swampy and mostly unusable as far south as the intersection of Hay and George streets.

From the early years of the twentieth century, the rebuilding of most of Sydney's port facilities changed the face of the inner harbour completely. Between 1901 and 1922, the newly created port authority, the Sydney Harbour Trust, built the many finger wharves that stretch from Walsh Bay to Glebe Island. With the twentieth-century revolution in cargo handling brought about with roll-on/roll-off containerisation, some of these have been recycled, and others torn down.

Hickson Road was built to connect Circular Quay, Walsh Bay, Darling Harbour and Pyrmont. This had a remarkable effect on the throughput of Sydney's wharves: the tonnage of goods going through the Darling Harbour goods yard rose from nearly 2 million tonnes in 1900 to 3.3 million tonnes in 1909.[9] Coal for the power stations at Pyrmont and Ultimo was unloaded at White Bay. From the 1930s, the number of ships using the inner harbour declined—ships were getting bigger, so there were fewer of them, and trains and trucks soon replaced most of the coastal shipping trade.[10]

From the late 1960s, container terminals were built at Mort Bay, Balmain, Glebe Island and White Bay. As trade increased, there were insufficient facilities, so in 1979 Port Botany was commissioned. Warehousing of containers has now spread as far afield as Chullora and Villawood. In the inner city, the industrial corridor that grew to complement Sydney's maritime activities extended from Darling Harbour to Botany through Alexandria, Waterloo, Zetland, Beaconsfield and Mascot. Many of the old harbour wharves in the area became obsolete.

By the 1970s, Darling Harbour, Pyrmont and the southwestern section of the city area were little more than sad, run-down relics of Sydney's industrial past, although the railway goods yards were still operating. The changes to Darling Harbour, Pyrmont and the western side of the city from the 1960s are starkly illustrated by a contemporary account given by P. R. Stephensen in 1966:

> All the streets in that western slope of the western ridge of the City of Sydney are dominated by the busy life of the wharves. In that zone are most of the warehouses of the importers of merchandise, the bond and free stores, the wool stores, the offices of stevedores and of shipping and customs agents, the depots of carriers and of ship providores, the engineering workshops connected with wharves and shipping, and the pubs where seamen and waterside workers quench their thirsts; but there are in this district very few dwellings, or retail shops, or large blocks of offices tenanted by members of the learned professions … it is here that the wealth of a seaport emporium-city accumulates and the profits of trade originate, to be spent more showily elsewhere.[11]

Darling Harbour is one of the city's prime tourist attractions, as well as being a popular recreational spot for Sydneysiders on weekends. Covering 54 hectares, the area contains a sometimes baffling combination of attractions. The more significant ones are the Powerhouse Museum; the Exhibition and Convention Centre; the Harbourside Shopping Centre; the National Maritime Museum; the Sydney Aquarium, the Chinese Garden of Friendship; the IMAX Cinema; the SegaWorld entertainment centre and Cockle Bay.

In 1971, the first assessment of the potential for redevelopment of Darling Harbour was published by the Sydney City Council. It proposed that a Bicentennial Park of open space, markets and residential development be built. Studies of the area continued throughout that decade. However, it was not until the project was taken up at a state government level during Neville Wran's administration, with Laurie Brereton serving as minister for public works, that final plans for what was to be one of Australia's largest and most controversial redevelopment projects were prepared.

The unsatisfied need that drove the overall development of Darling Harbour was the fact that Sydney did not have a convention centre, an essential ingredient in earning tourist dollars, which were being spent in other cities which offered convention facilities. A study undertaken by the Department of Environment and Planning in 1983 concluded that the potential of the largely obsolete area would best be harnessed by building a large complex that was compatible with public access to the harbour foreshores of Sydney. In 1984, Premier Wran announced that Darling Harbour would be redeveloped as Sydney's major undertaking for the Bicentenary. Wran's government immediately took the whole project out of the hands of the Sydney City Council, sparking yet another revival of the debate about the appropriate roles of state and local governments in planning, and fuelling political controversy. The council had expected that the project would be theirs. Darling Harbour, however, was an undertaking of such magnitude that only the state government had the capacity and resources to proceed with the vision.

The Darling Harbour Authority was created to put the plans into action. The struggle to complete the project in the three years from mid-1985 to 1988 was monumental. Plagued by industrial disputes and unfriendly weather, the project was not, as so many had predicted, entirely completed by January 1988, when Queen Elizabeth came to Sydney to open Darling Harbour. In the meantime, the costs had nearly doubled to more than $700 million.

The most controversial ingredients in the planning of Darling Harbour were the monorail and the casino. Many architects and planners, including some from government departments, thought that the most appropriate link from the city to the new complex should be a light rail system, which they claimed would be cheap and easy to build. The impact of the monorail upon the streetscape of the city was ignored by the government. This was unfortunate. The monorail's ugliness and the awkward course it takes through the southern end of the city has meant that it has never been popular, nor has it been a commercial success. It would have been better to build a light rail system to link Darling Harbour with the northern half of the city and Circular Quay.

ABOVE: Aerial view taken in 1992 of the redevelopment of Darling Harbour. The Sydney Entertainment Centre can be seen centre left. Note that the swingspan of the Pyrmont Bridge (at right) is open to allow a barge to pass underneath it.

Some of the animosity towards the monorail rubbed off onto Darling Harbour. As the only tangible part of the overall development during construction, the extramural manifestation of the monorail did not create much public confidence in, or warmth towards, the overall project. Unhappy with the scale of the project, and the speed with which Darling Harbour was being foisted upon them by a determined government, Sydneysiders did what they sometimes do very well—they whinged, dug their toes in and harshly criticised the entire project as a further example of governmental arrogance. The shouting has died away, except for the ongoing aesthetic objections to the monorail. It now seems, as with Circular Quay East, that its owners would be prepared to pull it down—on satisfactory financial terms. Despite the early glitches, the facilities of Darling Harbour have become a well-respected part of Sydney's late–twentieth-century public infrastructure. Cockle Bay has helped to make the facilities more accessible from the city and the east. Darling Harbour will be a venue for some events at the 2000 Olympics, including weightlifting and basketball. Not many Sydneysiders would agree today that the development of Darling Harbour was nothing but a waste of time and money. In the late 1990s, more visitors come to Sydney because of conventions held at the Exhibition and Convention Centre than any other city in the world. On weekends, it is plain to see

Sydneysiders voting with their feet (and their wallets), as they come to Darling Harbour to have fun or simply stroll around.

In 1988, the question of building a large hotel-casino complex was shelved by the incoming Liberal government led by Premier Nick Greiner. No casino licence had been issued during the term of the Labor government because no one could be found who was able to pass the necessary probity checks. In 1991, the temptation to raise revenue and tourist numbers by granting a casino licence had become too great for the Greiner government to pass up, and tenders were called again.

The result of this process is the massive Sydney Harbour Casino, the dominant feature on the northwestern side of Darling Harbour, which looms over the water like a fortress. It is hard to believe that the architect responsible, Philip Cox, was the same person who designed the handsome National Maritime Museum nearby. As well as the obvious gambling facilities (1500 poker machines and 160 gaming tables) there are thirteen restaurants, twelve bars, a lyric theatre with the capacity to seat 2000 people, a 350-room hotel and a shopping centre. The appetite for gambling at the temporary casino, which operated for three years before the present casino was built, turned out to be less than expected. After all, there are already 72 000 poker machines elsewhere in Sydney, as well as other avenues for gambling. The casino is not, however, just for gambling. The tropical underwater theme is strong at the casino. The brightly coloured carpet of tropical fish and the huge tanks displaying fish from the coral reef add to the theme-park ambience. The casino has been affected, along with others, by the demise of the Asian financial and property markets, and consequent reduction in the number of 'high-roller' gamblers coming to visit and 'spend up big'.

Darling Harbour bustles on weekends, albeit at a suitably relaxed pace, and there are many ways to be entertained. Tumbalong Park, which fronts the Exhibition Centre, is a regular venue for street performers and bands. Organised festivals, exhibitions, sports, games and community events are regular features of the area on weekends. For those more inclined to recline, there is the shade provided by Fred, the 15-metre tall, 42-tonne Port Jackson fig. Fred was planted in the park in 1987, following a three-day barge journey down the Parramatta River from Homebush Bay in Sydney's west, where the tree had spent the past seventy years.

The Exhibition Centre houses the largest column-free exhibition space in Australia, with an open area equivalent to about five football fields. Trade shows and other exhibitions are held here. Other attractions include the National Maritime Museum, which has regular marine exhibits, as well as periodic special attractions, such as the $17 million replica of the *Endeavour* which was launched in 1993. Many boats and ships of historic significance are moored alongside the museum.

At the southwestern end of Darling Harbour is the Powerhouse Museum of Applied Arts and Sciences in Harris Street. The main strengths of the Powerhouse are its collection of decorative arts and its sociological and technological exhibits. It was designed by Lionel Glendenning and opened in 1985, and features many interactive exhibits for children and curious adults. Together with the Art Gallery of New South Wales, the Australian Museum and the smaller Museum of Sydney and the State Library of New South Wales, it is one of Sydney's leading cultural institutions. Glendenning also designed the wide-screen IMAX cinema on the eastern side of Darling Harbour.

The density of development in Darling Harbour and Pyrmont has intensified since 1988 and will continue to do so. Cockle Bay provides an almost bewildering choice of restaurants and entertainment. Sadly, the network of roads and overpasses in Darling Harbour seems contrived to make access, whether pedestrian or vehicular, a maze-like challenge for the unwary who are visiting the area for the first time. The buildings seem to be turning their backs on the city. The colourful Sega Entertainment Centre and a mixed commercial/residential development north of the Sydney Aquarium will add much weight and volume to the original brave and bold concept of renewing the redundant industrial and maritime land in old Cockle Bay. Darling Harbour is as removed from its historical roots as it is possible to be.

One of the few remnants of Darling Harbour's industrial and maritime past is the Pumphouse Tavern, now a boutique brewery. It was only saved at the urging of the National Trust and, later, the intervention of the Heritage Council, which placed a stop-work order on its demolition. The pumphouse was where hydraulic power was first generated in Sydney. Hydraulic power was the only source of power available in the days before electricity. It was used to drive the city's lifts, wool presses and the hydraulic cranes used for loading cargo around Darling Harbour, Pyrmont and Woolloomooloo, as well as the huge, old metal bank doors in the city. Even though electrical power had become dominant by the middle of the twentieth century, the pumphouse was still in use until 1975. Water was pumped to the power station where it was pressurised and sent through special cast-iron pipes laid under the city. The original steam plant was not replaced by an electrical plant until the early 1950s. The supply of hydraulic power in Sydney was phased out in stages between 1974 and 1975.

Darling Harbour is still a work in progress, particularly its northern and eastern arms, although the pace of change will have slowed by 2000. To the west of Darling Harbour, in Pyrmont and Ultimo, development is transforming the precinct in a manner unlike any other part of Sydney, with the possible exception of Homebush Bay. Nearly all the old bridges and crossings, except for the Pyrmont Bridge, now used as a footway, have gone.

The new Anzac Bridge (formerly the Glebe Island Bridge), like the Sydney Harbour Bridge, is one of Sydney's great engineering landmarks, especially for people who live and work around the inner harbour. The bridge is the first concrete cable-stayed bridge in Australia. (A cable-stayed bridge is one which has at least one tower supporting a system of straight cables holding up the main span.) Two 121-metre towers hold up 128 steel cables, with the middle span extending 345 metres.

The Pyrmont peninsula, upon which both Pyrmont and Ultimo are situated, has been undergoing drastic changes since the late 1980s. Expressways and overpasses transect the area, dividing formerly cohesive residential neighbourhoods into stranded islands. The Better

Cities Program, launched in 1991 by the federal government, set aside $117 million of the $816 million fund to help with the regeneration of Pyrmont and Ultimo. Some of this has been applied to building the new light rail system between Wattle Street, Ultimo, Pyrmont and Central Railway Station. Extensions to this railway, which was built by a private consortium, are proposed. There are plans to extend it further into Leichhardt in the Inner West and also from Central Station to Circular Quay via Pitt and Castlereagh streets, thus making it more useful for Sydneysiders and tourists; however, no firm government commitment to do this has been made. The western extension will follow the old goods line through Glebe and Annandale.

In 1992, planning responsibilities for the area were placed in the state government's hands and the CityWest Strategy was developed. The objective of the strategy was to create a compact and high-density mix of commercial and residential space, with no marked division between commercial and residential building. Most of the designated residential-only sections run down Jones and Harris streets, along the ridge of the Pyrmont peninsula. This policy for the CityWest area fits as a component of the government's overall objective of encouraging medium- to high-density housing.

This strategy, combined with the essential ingredient of market forces, has triggered a boom in medium- and high-density housing, the like of which has not been seen since the building boom in Potts Point–Kings Cross in the 1920s. It is expected that the residential population of the CityWest precinct will rise from 3000 in 1993 to 20 000 by the end of the twentieth century. Combined with the construction of more expressways, flyovers and the Anzac Bridge, Pyrmont–Ultimo has been completely transformed from its previous working-class, inner-city industrial origins. Much of the old Victorian architecture has gone, as have many examples of early twentieth-century industrial architecture, including Walter Burley Griffin's incinerator, which was demolished in 1994.

The process of transformation is astounding, if not alarming. The Goldsbrough Mort Building, once a wool store, has been converted into 500 apartments, some of which are tiny. Meriton is one of the busiest developers in the area. Its distinctive high-density architectural style is very apparent on the Pyrmont skyline. There is some concern that too much high-density, relatively low-cost housing will lead to an aesthetically inferior outcome for the area. Despite the development, the Pyrmont peninsula has retained much of its former charm.

At the same time as new buildings are being added to the skyline, a new type of industry has been attracted to Pyrmont–Ultimo: the media. The ABC, Channel 10 and Foxtel are all located there, and John Fairfax & Sons is not far away, in Darling Park on the eastern side of Darling Harbour.

The Fish Markets still occupy the same site they have for decades, on the southeastern side of Blackwattle Bay. On weekends, they become an inner-city food-shopping mecca. The Sydney Fish Markets are an interesting slice of Sydney life, with their own peculiar bustle and ambience. From the late 1980s, the markets were redeveloped and retail space grew substantially. Today, they are probably the best shopping precinct for food within 3 kilometres of the city, not only for the amazing variety of fish on display, but for other food as well. The mix of people on weekends is almost as interesting as the fish.

The process of change on the Pyrmont peninsula will continue. One of the biggest ingredients of change in the short term will be the redevelopment of the old CSR Sugar Refinery site at the northern end of Pyrmont by Lend Lease. This is a 12-hectare site, bought by the developer in 1996, due for completion in 2004. The mixed commercial-residential development will cost about $900 million. It will, after the project is completed, be possible to walk from Darling Harbour to the Anzac Bridge. Altogether, 1500 apartments will be built and, along the Harris Street axis, 50 000 square metres of commercial floor space will be created. Buildings of heritage value, such as the Rum Store and twenty terrace houses, will be restored and readapted where necessary.

It will be intriguing to see what sort of place the Pyrmont peninsula will be in another ten years, when it will be one of the city's most notable examples of mixed-use medium- and high-density inner-city living.

321

CHAPTER THIRTEEN

THE HARBOUR

THE HARBOUR'S COURSE runs southward from North and South heads to Bradleys Head, then westward through the soft sandstone bed of the drowned valley of the Parramatta River. Along its shores are the well-covered, bushy, grey-green headlands with their honey-coloured cliffs and golden, sandy bays. The land tumbles down from the harbourside ridges to create dozens of naturally shaped, amphitheatre-like bays—some large and expansive, others close and intimate. This curved, sandstone scenery, combined with the harbourside suburbs that cling to the water's edge with their brightly coloured red-tiled roofs, the city's skyline and the icons of the Opera House and the Harbour Bridge all mix, with a dash of alchemy, to make Sydney unique.

Many of Sydney's most talented artists such as Arthur Streeton, Lloyd Rees, John Olsen and Brett Whiteley have captured the mellifluous course and topography of the harbour in their paintings and drawings. This has been referred to as the 'Sydney line'. The ephemeral interplay of light, colour, wind and weather creates constantly changing scenery. The atmosphere can transform dramatically in the course of a few minutes with a summer storm or freshening of the wind from sapphire blue to stormy black and back again, as Kenneth Slessor described it:

> The character and the life of Sydney are changed continually and imperceptibly by the fingers of the Harbour, groping across the piers and jetties, clutching deeply into the hills … The water is like silk, like pewter, like blood, like a leopard's skin, and occasionally merely like water. Its pigments run into themselves, from amber and aquamarine through cobalt to the deep and tranquil molasses of a summer midnight. Sometimes it dances with flakes of fire, sometimes it is blank and anonymous with fog, sometimes it shouts as joyously as a mirror.[1]

ABOVE: An early engraving of Vaucluse Bay and Vaucluse House when it was owned by Henry Brown Hayes.

Much of the land around the harbour is still in a relatively untouched state. The 400-hectare patchwork mosaic of the Sydney Harbour National Park constitutes only some of the bushland along the shores. The harbour foreshores have been protected on the grounds that they were of military significance. For almost a century, the main headlands of the harbour were the first and only line of defence against external aggression. Most of Sydney's old defence fortifications at Middle, Georges, North and South heads are still occupied by Australia's defence forces. Ensuring an orderly transfer of these lands from the defence forces to the public has been a lively issue of political debate in the closing years of the twentieth century. In the election campaign of 1998, the prime minister, John Howard, undertook to set aside $96 million from the Federation Fund to buy most of the land around Sydney Harbour owned by the Commonwealth. If the promise is fulfilled, most of the government-owned land would become accessible to the public and be administered by the Sydney Harbour Federation Trust. Although Howard's promise has been criticised as a political sleight of hand, as the money would flow from one branch of government—the Federation Fund—to another—the Department of Defence—with a net cost to the government of almost zero, the promise is a far better alternative than allowing undeveloped foreshores to be sold off and redeveloped. The critical issue is ensuring that no key public foreshore land is sold off to help pay for any improvements.

There is not much evidence today of the presence of the indigenous occupation of the harbour. More than 200 years of European settlement have erased almost all the marks of Aboriginal occupation, although there are some rock paintings and shell middens which can be found most easily in the bushy reserves around the harbour. Many of the shell middens near the city itself were dug up and burnt for lime as they were the only source of badly needed mortar for Sydney's early colonial buildings. Nearly all the sandstone shelters the Aborigines used have given way to European development.[2] The few remaining Aboriginal sites are managed in consultation with the Metropolitan Land Council.

The harbour is one of the city's great recreational resources: spending time on or near it is one of the most enjoyable experiences in Sydney. The variety of boats is vast, ranging from the huge ocean-going maxi yachts that display their prowess and practise their finer manoeuvres in calmer waters down to tiny dinghies sailed by small children. There are not as many enormous, flashy boats on the harbour as can be found, say, in the south of France or on the east coast of the United States. This is part of the harbour's charm. The contact between Sydneysiders and the water seems a lot closer than is ever possible on huge yachts and 'gin palaces'.

Perhaps the most typically Sydney-style sailing boats are the light, agile skiffs (open boats without side decks or foredecks) that run twice as fast as keeled boats of similar size. The most famous of these are the 18-footers. Not only are these boats fast and exciting, but they are also (traditionally) inexpensive and so within reach of anyone who cares to sail. Bigger yachts seem to lack the derring-do of wet sailing in a skiff in a strong breeze. There are few other harbours in the world better suited to dinghy skiff-sailing than Sydney Harbour. The water never gets too cold, so wet sailing is always possible—although wetsuits are advisable in winter.

The first skiffs were built in Sydney for speed, and they have been built for speed ever since. In the early nineteenth century, watermen raced out in their skiffs as fast as they could to greet incoming ships. With luck, the providores they worked for would win the lucrative contract to provision the inbound ship for the next stage of their voyage, thereby earning the watermen an extra reward. Skiffs were also used to transport passengers around the harbour. If there was no wind, the watermen pulled out the oars and rowed passengers and cargo from place to place.

Earlier this century, fine, varnished-timber 18-footers, with their huge, billowing sails, graced the harbour. Today, lightweight, high-technology, expensive carbon-fibre engineering feats skim across the water with far less sail and fewer hands on board. Nowadays, the standard crew on a racing skiff is three. In years gone by, sails were so overwhelmingly big that boats would often sink when the wind dropped and the sails collapsed into the water, and the rules of racing were rough and ready. There was no limit on the size of the sails. Rigging became so big that crews of fourteen men were not uncommon. If the wind dropped and the boat needed to offload some weight, men would jump off the boats and tread water near the markers until the rest of the crew came back and picked them up. This is no longer allowed.

The dominance of the 18-footer is being challenged in the late 1990s by the newer, 16-foot (4.9-metre) '49ers'. The main advantage of the 49ers is that they can race with a two-person crew, one less than an 18-footer. This class has been accepted to run in the Olympics in 2000. This is the first time that a skiff has been selected as a class for an Olympic event.

The 18-footer racing season lasts from spring to the end of autumn, and is run from the Double Bay Sailing Club, which races on Sundays. Since the late nineteenth century, racing skiffs have used brightly coloured sails so that they would be easily recognisable by the large crowds of spectators who thronged around the harbour to watch the races.

One person who can claim credit for the emergence of the 18-footer races as a key feature of Sydney Harbour on weekends is Jimmy Giltinan. Giltinan had earlier agitated for the introduction of a professional rugby code in Sydney, which became rugby league. In 1935, Giltinan founded a breakaway 18-foot sailing club at Double Bay because the Sydney Flying Squadron would not accept new, faster, narrower 18-foot skiffs. Watching the skiffs sail on Sundays soon became a popular pastime for Sydneysiders, in an era when there was little else to do on the Sabbath.

On racing days, hundreds of spectators queue along the foreshore to watch, enthralled by crews leaning out on aluminium wings on trapezes, like circus acrobats. Some watch from the land, especially at Bradleys Head. Others prefer to follow the races closer up on ferries where, it is rumoured, bets are taken on the outcome—with a sublime indifference to the legality of the wagers taken.

325

Competitive sailing was one of Sydney's earliest regular sporting events. The anniversary regatta was held on the harbour on 26 January from 1827 on what is now called Australia Day. At these early regattas, rowing, sculling and sailing races were held.

Yacht racing has traditionally been the domain of 'gentlemen' sailors. The oldest yacht club in Sydney is the Royal Sydney Yacht Squadron (RSYS) at Kirribilli, established in 1862. The founders of the RSYS included the original proprietor of Sydney Ferries, James Milson Junior, and Mosman resident, businessman and property speculator Richard Harnett. The Sydney Amateur Sailing Club, based in Mosman Bay, is another old Sydney sailing club. It was founded in 1872 and appeals to those with more modest-sized traditional wooden yachts. This club used to be based at Bennelong Point, in the shadow of old Fort Macquarie, near where the Man o' War Steps jetty is today. As Sydney grew, so did the number, and wider geographic range, of her sailing clubs—from Pittwater to the Parramatta River, and down to Port Hacking in the city's south.

The other great sailing event on Sydney Harbour is the start of the annual Sydney–Hobart Yacht Race on Boxing Day from the Cruising Yacht Club at Rushcutters Bay. The Sydney–Hobart race, along with the Fastnet and the Cape Town to Rio races, is one of the great ocean sailing races. Its course is 960 kilometres down the southeastern coast of the continent across Bass Strait to Hobart. The race has been held every year since 1945, sometimes in heavy and dangerous conditions. Sometimes the racing fleet has to sail straight down the coast into the teeth of a strong southerly 'buster', bringing with it gale-force

ABOVE: Sailing an 18-foot skiff on Sydney Harbour, the ideal environment for these fast, agile boats which seem to skim across the water at lightning speed in a strong breeze.

headwinds. Farewelling the boats as they leave the harbour is a popular Sydney activity—either on boat or from any house or parkland which enjoys a view of the yachts as they take off from Bradleys Head and sail out through the heads.

That other famous institution, the Sydney ferry, has been part of the harbour for a century and a half. It was an essential ingredient in the development of the North Shore in the second half of the nineteenth century. The trip by ferry to Manly, Taronga Park Zoo and other spots around the harbour is one of the great treats for visitors to Sydney, and for Sydneysiders, too, who often take one of the cheapest and most beautiful trips in the world for granted. Looking astern and seeing Sydney Cove disappear from view, and then observing the boat life on the harbour, its sandy curves and headlands, and eventually arriving at one's destination is an essential Sydney experience. From every perspective, the harbour has something different to offer—so the trip back to the quay is just as good as the outward journey.

Until the Sydney Harbour Bridge was completed in 1932, the journey by road across the harbour was long and arduous. Even after the Gladesville and Fig Tree bridges were built across the Parramatta and Lane Cove rivers in the mid-1880s, road travellers had to travel 12 miles (19 kilometres) to get to parts of the North Shore and cross five bridges: the Pyrmont Bridge, the Glebe Island Bridge, the Iron Cove Bridge, the Gladesville Bridge and the Fig Tree Bridge. Ferries were the only practicable alternative.

The first passenger boat was launched in Sydney in 1789. The Rose Hill packet was built by Robertson Reed, a ship's carpenter in the First Fleet. It was propelled by a single sail. Often, when there was not enough wind, oars and elbow grease were needed to move the 'Lump', as she was colloquially called. Sometimes it took a whole week to do the round trip to Parramatta—there was no road there until some years later.[3]

The earliest forms of today's ferries were the small and uncomfortable passage boats operated by watermen (and women). Many of the watermen were emancipists. They were not allowed to transport convicts, and to enforce this rule, watermen had to pay a good-behaviour bond. The boats also required a government licence. One of the most famous old watermen of Sydney was Billy Blue, a Jamaican by birth, who came to Sydney as a convict. He ran passage boats between Dawes and Milsons points.

Billy Blue's sons and his son-in-law, George Lavender, one-time bosun on a prison hulk moored at what is now called Lavender Bay, ran Blue's boating business after Blue retired. Lavender ran Sydney's first large ferry, the paddle-steamer *Princess*, in the 1840s between Sydney Cove and the North Shore. This first attempt at a proper ferry service soon failed, as the charms of the North Shore were not as obvious then as they are today. By the end of the 1850s, however, seven or eight steamships were involved in ferry services around the harbour.[4]

The water taxis that sprint around the harbour today like brightly coloured beetles are the descendants of the early watermen's boats. These water taxis are the fastest form of transport across the harbour, and to the islands dotted upon it. They are most commonly used to take commuters into and out of the city, to harbour-side restaurants, social events held around the harbour and performances at the Opera House. The taxis are sometimes used for more unusual purposes: as a romantic way of proposing marriage or even to sprinkle the ashes of the deceased on the blue waters of the harbour. These water-taxi skippers, like the old watermen, are well acquainted with the harbour and its foibles. A ride in a water taxi is a worthwhile (if sometimes bumpy) experience.

In 1860, James Milson, one of the first European landowners on the North Shore, established a ferry service between Milsons and Dawes points. By the mid-1880s, ferry operators were supplementing their regular weekly work by transporting picnickers on the weekends to places such as Cremorne, Cabarita, Clontarf and Manly.

Milson's son took over the family business, which was later named the North Shore Ferry Company, and later still, in 1900, Sydney Ferries Limited. This company dominated ferry traffic in the harbour, and to and from the lower North Shore in particular. In 1886, the business benefited from new cable tram networks which covered North Sydney and Mosman. Then, in 1893, the North Shore train line was completed. All this transport created a boom in settlement on the other side of the harbour, and inevitably in the passenger trade of Sydney

327

Ferries. Between 1871 and 1903, the population on the North Shore as far as Roseville grew from 3600 to almost 42 000. The Milsons Point service contributed significantly to the development of North Sydney, Kirribilli, Cremorne and Mosman, and the route to Blues Point serviced other parts of the lower North Shore: Crows Nest, St Leonards, Artarmon and Chatswood.

The only other major ferry company servicing the outer harbour was the Port Jackson and Manly Steamship Company, which operated the famous Manly ferries. The largest of the Manly ferries were the *Dee Why* (1928), the *Curl Curl* (1928) and the *South Steyne* (1938), which could carry 1600, 1600 and 1800 passengers, respectively.[5] Today, the *Dee Why* sits at the bottom of the sea near Long Reef as an artificial reef (it was sunk deliberately for this purpose). The *South Steyne* is moored outside the National Maritime Museum in Darling Harbour and is available for hire as a party venue.

One of Sydney Harbour's worst disasters occurred on a ferry trip from Circular Quay to Watsons Bay in November 1927. The ferry steamer SS *Greycliffe*, with about 125 passengers aboard, many of them boisterous school children on their way home from an athletics carnival at Moore Park, was overtaken by the ocean liner SS *Tahiti* just off Bradleys Head. Suddenly, there was a collision and the ferry was cut in half. Forty-two people drowned.[6] In the court claim by the owners of the *Greycliffe*, Sydney Ferries Limited, against the owners of the *Tahiti*, the judge found that both had contributed to the disaster.

Sydney Ferries' high point was in 1928, just before the Great Depression and the opening of the Harbour Bridge. In the 1920s, there were large ferries with a capacity of 2000 people each which acted as a permanent 'bridge' between Circular Quay and Milsons Point. During the Depression years, ferry services up the Parramatta River and to Balmain and Watsons Bay declined. Then the bridge had its obvious effect. Passenger traffic on the company's ferries declined from 47 million trips in 1927 to 15 million in 1933 and to fewer than 9 million in 1950. The fleet declined from fifty-one ferries in 1927 to only fifteen in 1951.[7]

Everything was working against the viability of the ferries after the Harbour Bridge was opened. Other events—the opening of the Spit Bridge, the post–World War II boom in the use of the motor car, and the dismantling of the tram services which acted as feeder for the ferry system—all took their toll. Sydney Ferries fell into the government's hands in 1951, as it was no longer commercially viable. By the 1970s, even the service to Manly was looking extinction in the face. The Manly ferry fleet was taken over by the government in 1974.

In the 1980s, ferries became popular again, as traffic congestion in peak hours built up to unpleasant levels and the price of petrol rose. Sydneysiders again began to recognise that the ferries were an important part of the city's culture. From 1980, the Great Sydney Ferry Race was run on the harbour on Australia Day, as one of the attractions of the Sydney Festival. The safety of the old wooden ferries became a lively political issue when the *Karrabee* sank after running in the Great Sydney Ferry Race on Australia Day in 1984. In 1985, the last of the 'old' Manly ferries, the *North Head*, was sold and is now in operation in Hobart.

Meanwhile, the collapse of the bridge over the Derwent River in Tasmania in 1975 led to the design of a new type of fast ferry, to prevent isolation on either side of the River Derwent. These ferries were the prototype of the catamaran ferries, known as Jetcats, in Sydney which ply the harbour today. They have run up the Parramatta River since 1987. The first Jetcat on the Manly run, *Blue Fin*, went into service in 1990.

Sydney's ferry fleet consists of twenty-seven vessels, which carry between 14 million and 15 million people a year. The passenger numbers are rising by nearly 10 per cent per annum.[8] There are four Manly ferries, all of which have been built since 1968, and four 'Lady'-class ferries, which are smaller than the Manly ferries and up until this year have been a key feature of the annual Sydney Ferry Race. Three Jetcats, which reach speeds of up to 30 knots, operate in the harbour, while smaller and slower (24-knot) Rivercats navigate the shallower waters of the Parramatta River. There are nine first-fleet catamarans which serve the harbour and travel more slowly than the Jetcats and Rivercats, at about 11 knots. There are still other privately owned ferry companies which operate on the harbour, Pittwater, the Georges River and the Hawkesbury River.

The question of how to defend the harbour and Sydney from hostile attack was an issue which emerged sporadically in the nineteenth century. Sydney's remoteness and insubstantial strategic value made defence a low priority for much of the nineteenth century, though there were flurries of alarm from time to time. These prompted the construction of fortifications along the foreshores and, most visibly today, the works on Fort Denison. The first attempt at creating a defensive perimeter for Sydney was the construction of batteries at Dawes Point, Bennelong Point and Garden Island in the years up to 1800. One of the oldest defence structures still remaining is a carved sandstone parapet at Georges Head. After the riots at Vinegar Hill in 1804, Governor King commissioned the construction of Fort Phillip, on Observatory Hill, to repel attack by both sea and land. It was never completed.

During Macquarie's term as governor, Fort Macquarie was built on Bennelong Point to deter both invasion and any unauthorised departures from the harbour (by escaping convicts, for example). It was designed in a rather romantic castellated style to complement the Governor's Stables up the road, and was never considered to be anything more than a decorative embellishment to the harbour's foreshore. The battery on Dawes Point was far more useful, and was built to defend the inner harbour on its own, without the assistance of Fort Macquarie.

It was not until 1835 that the Colonial Office sent out a troop of Royal Engineers, led by Captain George Barney, to examine the defences of Sydney. Barney's preferred strategy was to protect the inner, rather than the outer, harbour from attack. At that stage, the main perceived threat was from privateers rather than from any world power, real or putative. In 1836, Barney, with the help of 200 convicts, built defence lookouts at Bradleys Head and Pinchgut (Fort Denison).

The work at Fort Denison was hard. The 25-metre–high, scrub-covered rocky outcrop was chipped away, blasted and excavated. The lonely island had been the spot that recalcitrant convicts were often sent on short rations (hence the name 'Pinchgut'), the first only two weeks after the arrival of the First Fleet.[9] The island was used as a penitentiary for misbehaving convicts until, in November 1796, Francis Morgan was found guilty of a particularly unsavoury murder and, as an example to the rest of the colony, Governor Hunter ordered that Morgan be hanged in chains and his body left on the gibbet to rot. There he stayed for four years, sparking little reaction from the convicts and the other settlers, but terrifying the Aboriginal population who had used the island they called *Mat-ye-wan-ye* for recreation purposes. Believing that the island was now cursed, they never returned. This was not the only occasion when the Europeans' criminal justice system baffled the Aborigines.

When Barney was excavating the tiny island in 1836, some of the stone from Fort Denison was used in the reclamation of Circular Quay, which was then under construction. Barney's view was that defence fortifications should be concentrated at Fort Denison—any enemy ships could be shot at as they sailed up the harbour. In 1837, Governor Gipps ordered Colonial Engineer George Barney to keep levelling the island and build a fort. Working on Pinchgut was some of the toughest work to which convicts could be put. They had to live on the island while they were working on it and the conditions were terrible—even worse than working the treadmill at Carters' Barracks near present-day Railway Square.

In 1839, Sydney's lack of defences was underlined when four (friendly) American warships slipped into the harbour undetected. No one had heard a sound, let alone attempted to ask the ships what their business was. As the American officer in charge, Commander Wilkes, pointed out, they could very easily have reduced the city to ashes before anyone had the slightest idea they were there. This finally galvanised the many arms of government to consider defence issues more seriously, although the depression of the 1840s soon overwhelmed anyone's determination to bolster the harbour's defences.

At the time that work was stopped due to lack of finances, Pinchgut had been levelled, but no fortifications—apart from a 1.2-metre–high perimeter wall—had been built.[10] When Barney was succeeded by Lieutenant James Gordon in 1843, the tactical approach to defending the town swung in the opposite direction. Gordon and Barney were rivals in the Royal Engineers. Gordon thought it would be better to protect the outer harbour from the elevated positions of the headlands, rather than rely on defences at sea level. There was never enough money available for Gordon to be allowed to have his way, and few permanent guns were placed on North, South, Middle or Georges heads.

The Defence Committee of Port Jackson was set up in 1853, the same year as New Caledonia was annexed by France, bringing the issue of the harbour's defence to the fore once again. It was feared that the island could be a launching platform for raids on shipping and, even worse, for invasion. In the meantime, Gordon had been replaced by his old rival, George Barney, and the plan for Sydney's defences swung back to the original plans to fortify Pinchgut. Fort Denison was finally completed in 1857, when fears of Russian aggression was foremost in the eyes of the colonial administration. It was named after the governor of the day, who, like Barney, was an officer in the Royal Engineers.

While it is probably the finest example of stone craftsmanship in Sydney, the fort was always criticised as being useless as a defence stronghold. By the time it was finished, Martello towers were out of fashion. They were a hangover from the Napoleonic Wars, when British ships had been repulsed by guns placed in a similar tower in Martello, Corsica. Heavier guns and artillery had made them less useful than they had been in the late eighteenth and early nineteenth century. Fort Denison's strength has, luckily for Sydney, never been tested. The only other Martello towers in the southern hemisphere are at Cape Town in South Africa.

The building adjacent to the tower itself contains barracks, a mess hall and storage cells. It was built from 8000 tonnes of stone quarried from Thrupp's quarry at Kurraba Point, immediately to the north of the island. The walls are almost 4 metres thick at the base and 3 metres at the top. During the Japanese submarine invasion of Sydney Harbour in World War II, a shell from an American cruiser ricocheted off the top of the tower; the special construction of the tower protected it from serious damage, but a thin crack can still be seen.

331

Guided tours of the fort show well-preserved items of weaponry from the last century, as well as providing a great view of the beautiful harbour. The island has a navigational beacon and a tidal gauge from which tides in New South Wales are measured. For many years, from 1906 to 1942, a time gun used for standardising chronometers was fired at Fort Denison at one o'clock in the afternoon. From 1901, Fort Denison was under the control of the Sydney Harbour Trust and its successor, the Maritime Services Board. In 1994, it was handed over to the National Parks and Wildlife Service and is part of Sydney Harbour National Park.

At the same time that Pinchgut was being transformed into what we can now see, Barney was completing the execution of the rest of his defence strategy. New batteries were built at Kirribilli on the site of Admiralty House, at Mrs Macquaries Point on the eastern side of Farm Cove, and also at Dawes Point, Bradleys Head and Fort Macquarie. Barney lived at Kirribilli House while building Fort Denison. Barney's rival, James Gordon, had the last say when sitting on another committee inquiring into the defences of the harbour in 1867. He recommended that these inner defences be dismantled, but Fort Denison survived. The fort was a barracks for some of the Royal Artillery until 1870, when the Imperial Forces went back to Britain, and volunteers were trained there until the 1890s.

From the 1870s, when New South Wales was largely in charge of its own defences, there was a period where many of the harbour headlands, such as Shark Point and Bradleys Georges, Middle and South heads, were upgraded. The fortifications on Middle Head are possibly the most rewarding to visit as they are still reasonably intact. Guns were dragged along a road to the points on the northern side of the harbour, which became known as Military Road. Locals were paid 10 shillings for each tree stump they removed.

Cobblestone roads and defensive ditches were built, as well as three brick beehive casemates at Georges Head and gun emplacements and a rifle wall at Bradleys Head. In the later years of the nineteenth century, more powerful guns were placed on strategic headlands. In 1871, Dobroyd Point (near Middle Head) was resumed for defence purposes. In World War II, concrete command posts, range-finding stations, observation posts and gun emplacements were built on many of the headlands of the harbour. Australia's coastal artillery was taken out of commission during the 1960s when technological advances rendered them obsolete, although during Australia's involvement in the Vietnam War, officers were trained to withstand torture in the corrugated-iron cages at Middle Head.

The remnants and ruins of the defences of Sydney Harbour are the most diverse collection of defence sites in Australia.[11] One of the largest remnants of Sydney Harbour's years as a base for defence facilities is the military school at Chowder Bay, named after the soup American sailors used to make from oysters when they anchored there in the nineteenth century. There is also HMAS *Penguin* and the Centre for Pacific Development and Training at Middle Head, and the North Head Army Barracks and School for Training with the National Artillery Museum. On South Head is the military reserve and HMAS *Watson*. The best place to view the historical layering of the defences of Sydney Harbour is at Middle Head.

The first commercial threat (apart from the inevitable threat caused by the growth of Sydney's population from the 1850s onwards) to the harbour's foreshores was coal mining. Coal lies deep (about 800 metres) under the harbour and the rest of Sydney. In the late nineteenth century, a British mining company was granted a lease over Bradleys Head and started to clear the land to build a mine head. Thousands of trees were cut down.[12] Artist Arthur Streeton and others lobbied against the mine, and the atrocity was averted. Streeton painted *Cremorne Pastoral* in 1895, which was bought by the then-fledgling Art Gallery of New South Wales.

The painting still hangs there and remains a reminder of what would have been lost forever if the colliery and the government of George Reid had had their way. As the judge who heard the case between the government (which had by then seen the light) and the colliery seeking to have a wharf built nearby said:

> no consideration in the nature of rent could be any compensation or consolation for the disfigurement of a harbour [which Australians] had been taught to cherish as one of nature's choicest masterpieces.[13]

The colliery decided that, to avoid further fuss, the mining operations should be relocated to the more industrial Balmain peninsula. Working-class residents there did not object to this in the years of high unemployment in the 1890s. The ratepayers of Balmain voted by a comfortable two to one margin in favour of handing the park over to the colliery. But the mine never made any money. It closed in 1931 and the Birchgrove Public School stands on the site.

From the late 1890s onwards, the spread of population around both sides of the harbour and the threat to public access to the foreshores was causing concern to some far-sighted people. Some of those who lived along the harbour showed little brotherly inclination towards those who were stranded on boats in trouble on the harbour. A tragic example of this was when a sailing boat, *Iolanthe*, was ordered off private land in Vaucluse in a strong gale in the early 1900s. The boat later capsized and seven people were drowned. Concern over public access to the foreshores mingled with civic pride in the early years of the twentieth century and more people turned their minds to public-spirited endeavour.

One of those who took up the cause of public access to the harbour was amateur yachtsman William Albert Notting. In 1905, Notting set up the Harbour Foreshore Vigilance Committee, whose object was to agitate for public resumption of land on the original Wentworth estate at Vaucluse, including Shark Bay and Bottle and Glass Point. As Notting put the case rather forcefully in 1907:

> It is useless … to talk about Sydney possessing the most beautiful harbour in the world, unless steps be taken to prevent it becoming a private lake. At present it is little better than a pond in a privately-owned paddock … if mistakes have been made in the past [as far back as 1795], the time has now arrived when these lands must be resumed. Otherwise the rapid expansion of the city will cause them to be sub-divided, and thus make future resumptions … practically impossible for future generations.[14]

The Royal Commission into the Improvement of Sydney was the ideal forum for publicly airing Notting's views, as he was getting nowhere with the government of the day, and his agitation had achieved little in three years to 1908. Many of the royal commissioners agreed with Notting that the foreshores of Sydney needed some form of protection. Some of them lived in leafy and prosperous harbour-side suburbs of Sydney themselves, and could see the benefits of a more publicly accessible harbour.

The royal commission's report did not directly endorse Notting's wishes for land resumption. They came up with an even more expensive and grandly ambitious proposal to resume all the harbour foreshore land in the eastern suburbs for a public driveway. This required much more land resumption than was practicable, even in those days, and was not followed up; but it did create a paradigm in favour of public access.

The next step was taken by the first Labor government which came to power in New South Wales in 1910. The new Minister for Lands, Niels Nielsen, a Danish-born, Cootamundra-raised Australian, had been active in the formation of the Australian Workers' Union and the labour movement generally. In 1911, at Ashton Park (an area which included Bradleys Head and later Taronga Park Zoo), Nielsen announced a program of foreshore land resumption and set aside £150 000.

Nielsen Park, the Hermitage Reserve, Ashton Park and other land between the Spit Bridge and Manly were reclaimed. Fittingly enough, Mr Notting was one of the original trustees of the new Nielsen Park. The park is now a fragment of the Sydney Harbour National Park, and is administered by the National Parks and Wildlife Service, headquartered at Greycliffe House, Nielsen Park.

The Sydney Harbour National Park was created in 1975. It was one of the more innovative and public-spirited acts of an otherwise mediocre period in Sydney's development and governance. Nielsen Park still has a wonderfully beguiling turn-of-the-century atmosphere. Thankfully, the original improvements to it, such as the dressing shed and the kiosk, have been relatively untouched by renovation and progress. The park is one of the most popular picnic spots in the eastern suburbs. Unlike many other harbour beaches, it has parkland behind which provides shade from the hot summer sun, and it is also netted—which is unusual for the beaches of Sydney Harbour. In winter, during a strong southerly swell when the surf at Bondi becomes dangerously wild, surfers can be seen catching waves at the eastern end of Nielsen Park outside the net.

Further towards the heads, at the outermost limit of the southern side of the harbour, Lady Bay (often misnamed Lady Jayne Beach) is one of Sydney Harbour's nudist beaches. On the northern side, Obelisk Beach is another. Last century, Lady Bay was known as Lady Beach because it was a secluded beach where 'ladies' could swim and cool off.

It would be a great complement to the walking track on the northern side of the harbour from the Spit Bridge to Manly if a similar track was built on the southern side of the harbour to commemorate the centenary of Australia's federation in 2001. Such a track would run from the Gap past the outside perimeter of HMAS *Watson* to the Hornby Lighthouse, just inside the heads. Currently, the walk from Camp Cove runs past Lady Bay to the Hornby Lighthouse, but stops at HMAS *Watson*.

Further around to the south lie Camp Cove and Watsons Bay. Camp Cove is very popular with that vanishing breed of dedicated 'sunbakers', who look for long hours of northwesterly afternoon sun, with protection from the strong northeasterly onshore summer breezes. Camp Cove is so named because it is where Captain Phillip and his men first slept when they entered Sydney Harbour. In the early days of the colony, Camp Cove and Watsons Bay were used as landing points for newly arrived ships, where their status and the cargo they were importing could be checked before they went further up the harbour.

Lying treacherously off Camp Cove is the Sow and Pigs Reef, a shallow shoal of rocks dividing the harbour into two shipping lanes, west and east, up as far as Bradleys Head. Obelisks were built off Laings Point on the southern end of Camp Cove and off Obelisk Beach to help ships navigate up the harbour and avoid the Sow and Pigs Reef. There are other reefs off South Head, Bottle and Glass Point, to the north of Bradleys Head and another off Shark Island, which can trap the unwary or unprepared.

Since 1788, Watsons Bay, named after the first harbour master and superintendent of the Macquarie Lighthouse, Robert Watson, has had strategic value as the first vantage point for seeing ships coming into the harbour. Accordingly, a pilot station was built there, near the present Watsons Bay baths. By 1792, the area was one of the most prolific fisheries in the harbour and, until the late 1960s, it provided one of Sydney's dining institutions, Doyle's Restaurant, with much of the catch later served there. Access to Watsons Bay was difficult in the early years of the colony, before Governor Macquarie built (Old) South Head Road in 1811. The village-like atmosphere of Watsons Bay somehow manages to survive, in a muted form, despite the motor car and the other changes of the twentieth century. It is still a popular weekend destination. Watsons Bay is 11 kilometres from the city centre, at the end of Old and New South Head roads. The relative remoteness of Watsons Bay adds to its character, a factor which is only accentuated by the vista down the harbour to the city's twentieth-century skyscrapers. This distant view is framed by the bushy headlands of the harbour.

Watsons Bay was one of the earliest destinations for weekend ferry services, with services running from 1854. In 1881, a local resident, Sir John Robertson, MLC, set up his own daily ferry service. Robertson's service eventually became the Watsons Bay and South Shore Ferry Company, which was later subsumed by Sydney Ferries Limited.

John Robertson lived at Clovelly House at Watsons Bay until 1891, in what is now called Robertson Park. Dunbar House, also in Robertson Park, used to be the Vaucluse Council Chambers before the municipality was merged with Woollahra Council. The fine, old, sandstone St Peter's Church (1864) stands a little up the hill on Old South Head Road. It was designed by Edmund Blacket. In 1880, a replica of Francis Greenway's Macquarie Lighthouse (1816) was built. Building of the later version was supervised by government architect, James Barnet.

The cooling sea breezes, fresh air and isolation made Watsons Bay a haven in hot weather. People took the ferry, and later the tram, to spend the day there. Excursions out of town were often the only way of spending an otherwise dull Sunday, when there was no publicly available sport or entertainment. As a result of the tram's popularity, the ferry service to Watsons Bay was discontinued in 1933.

One of the most notorious events ever to occur near Watsons Bay was the shipwreck of the *Dunbar* in 1857. During a wild southerly gale in heavy winter weather, the *Dunbar*, an emigrant ship carrying 122 people, crashed into rocks below the Gap. The captain of the ship had mistaken it for the entrance to Sydney Harbour. The ship broke into thousands of pieces and all on board were lost, except for an Irish sailor named James Johnson. The wreck was discovered the next morning. Bales of goods, bedding, children's toys and even a sofa and piano could be seen drifting and rolling in the sea.

The identity of the ship was not discovered until the postal bag was found floating in the water. Hundreds of onlookers flocked to Watsons Bay to see the ghoulish spectacle of bodies being washed on and off the rocks below. Many pieces of wreckage landed at Middle Harbour and twelve bodies came ashore there. Sharks were seen devouring the carcass of a cow. Johnson survived the disaster by hanging on to a plank while he was washed out to sea.

It is perhaps not surprising, given the tragic history of this part of the coast and its bleak, windswept cliffs, that the Gap is one of Sydney's most popular suicide spots. The Hornby

335

ABOVE: The village of Watsons Bay in the late nineteenth century.

336

Lighthouse on the tip of South Head, not far from the Gap, was built after the *Dunbar* disaster to ensure that nothing like it ever happened again. The stone cottages around the lighthouse were once the home of the lighthouse and assistant lighthouse-keepers. They are now subject to a permanent conservation order.

In 1880, the first marine station in Sydney Harbour dedicated to biology was established at Watsons Bay by Russian baron and natural scientist Nikolai Nikolaievich Mikluho-Maclay. Mikluho-Maclay's fieldwork took him far from his native home to New Guinea, the Pacific islands and the Philippines. He arrived in Sydney in 1878 with a large collection of anthropological and zoological specimens, and became an active member of the Linnean Society. His observation station at 31 Pacific Street was a laboratory for the study of marine biology in Sydney Harbour. Mikluho-Maclay married the daughter of John Robertson. Unfortunately, much of the scientific collection was lost during the Garden Palace fire in the Royal Botanic Gardens in 1882.

From 1900, much of the waterfront land between Watsons Bay and Parsley Bay was subdivided. The advent of the motor car and the postwar building boom meant that much of the change came about from the 1950s onwards, when the village lost much of its old nineteenth-century character.

Since the 1960s, it has become impossible for Sydneysiders to think about Watsons Bay without thinking of Doyle's Restaurant on the beach. It is one of Sydney's enduring dining institutions. The Doyle family has been connected with the area since the 1830s, when matriarch Alice Doyle's English forebears settled there and started a fishing business.

For more than a century, nearly everyone at Watsons Bay was either in the fishing business or worked as harbour pilots, taking large ships safely past the treacherous Sow and Pigs Reef near Watsons Bay—which was also an excellent fishing spot. Alice Doyle and her children all grew up there. Many small fishermen's cottages can still be seen around Watsons Bay, some of them much renovated, almost beyond recognition.

Peter Doyle, one of Alice's sons, is one of Sydney's (and Australia's) great fishermen and raconteurs. Peter Doyle vividly remembers the late 1930s and 1940s when he was a boy growing up on the beach, and loves to talk about the characters who lived in the small fishing village and kept their cotton and linen fishing nets in a communal shed on the beach.[15] One of the fishermen was 'Black' Peter, a tall African American who had jumped ship when the Great White Fleet visited Sydney in 1908.

The local fishermen used to catch the fish that Peter Doyle's grandmother cooked and sold at the family fish-and-chip shop, located within the oldest part of today's Doyle's Restaurant. This original part of the restaurant was built on the site of an old, tumbledown wooden shed which was demolished and replaced in preparation for the arrival of the Great White Fleet in 1908.

Doyle's parents started the restaurant after World War II on a shoestring budget. In those days, finding capital to start a business was tough—despite empty promises by the government that veterans would be able to get easy access to low-interest business loans. His parents went to auctions of second-hand furniture to buy the tables and chairs, and bought a lot of the plates and cutlery used in the restaurants from pig farmers. In those days, food scraps from hotels, restaurants, cafés and ships were collected by pig farmers and used as pig feed. The pig farmers had a handy sideline in selling knives, forks, spoons and plates that had accidentally been thrown into the rubbish when the food scraps were discarded. Doyle still has some of the old motley collection of plates that had their origins emblazoned on them for everyone to see: 'Sargent's Pies', the 'Orient Line', 'Hotel Australia', etc.

For some years, the Doyles leased out the restaurant at Watsons Bay and concentrated their activities at the Pier Restaurant, Rose Bay, until 1967. From the 1970s onwards, Doyle's Restaurant at Watsons Bay has continued to expand, in step with the growing popularity of restaurants in the postwar era. It now seats 400 people. As well as the original restaurant, the family also owns the restaurant on the wharf at Watsons Bay, the Watsons Bay Hotel and another restaurant at the northern end of the Overseas Passenger Terminal at Circular Quay West. The Doyles pioneered the legalisation of outdoor dining in Sydney, which at the time was severely frowned upon by bureaucratic local councils, state government and wowsers within the community. Doyle's restaurants are still serving the same fresh, unpretentiously cooked seafood that they have done for more than half a century.

Peter Doyle bought his first fishing boat at the age of twelve and, until a recent illness, has been fishing all his life. His favourite pastime as a boy was to go out on weekends with the net fishermen, one of whom was his uncle. Beachcombing occupied many of Watsons Bay's residents—to such a degree that there was a fair amount of territoriality involved, with each person having their own patch of sand.

People would hunt for coins and other lost treasures, and pick up onions and other vegetables which would bob along the water and wash up on the beach after ships dumped them into the harbour. (Quarantine regulations prohibited the importation of any plant matter.) Many of the onions were collected and planted in local gardens. Pieces of coke fuel would also drift onto the beach from the old steamships, to be used as fuel to protect the fishermen and their families against the cold westerly winds in winter, which whipped the sea into heads of angry, white foam.

When the Japanese midget submarines entered the harbour during World War II to torpedo the USS *Chicago*, which was moored off Bradleys Head, Doyle and his family watched the searchlights and tracer bullets light up the night sky like a fireworks display. Transfixed and terrified, Doyle's only regret was that his local school, Vaucluse Public, had not been hit by the Japanese. The next morning, hundreds of dead and stunned fish were washed up on the beach at Watsons Bay, and Doyle did his best to throw them back into deeper water.

During World War II, Watsons Bay was heavily populated with the Australian and the American defence forces. This added a touch of modernity to what up till then had been a reasonably isolated and insular community. The American presence was a harbinger of the postwar modernisation to come to the sleepy fishing village, and Sydney as well.

Fishing in the harbour has always been seasonal. Before the demand for fish rose in the 1950s and 1960s, however, the harbour was, in the words of Peter Doyle, 'absolutely alive with fish'. There were bream, mullet, whitehead, crayfish and prawns. Fish and crustaceans could most easily be caught in nets on the mud flats at Rose Bay. The best fighting fish in the harbour were kingfish and bluefin tuna. Tuna were also netted at Rose Bay. In those days, flocks of black swans fed on the sea grass in the shallow water there. The tuna numbers dropped dramatically in the late 1950s and early 1960s when commercial fishing methods became devastatingly effective. There were whales in the harbour as well, and even sea lions. When there were not enough fish caught to serve at the restaurant, Doyle or one of his brothers would catch the tram to Woolloomooloo and buy fish from the larger, Italian-owned fishing boats which were based in Woolloomooloo Bay.

Porpoises, then common in harbour waters, were killed by Doyle's uncle, among others, off Green Point and other parts of the outer harbour—sometimes as berley for sharks, sometimes for other reasons. Their snouts were cut off, and their teeth were sold to Burns Philp, which used them as trading articles with the New Guinea Highlanders. Doyle was turned off catching porpoises forever after hearing the haunting cries of a young calf who had lost its mother to the fishermen.

Experienced fishermen knew that seasonal changes were a vital factor in determining

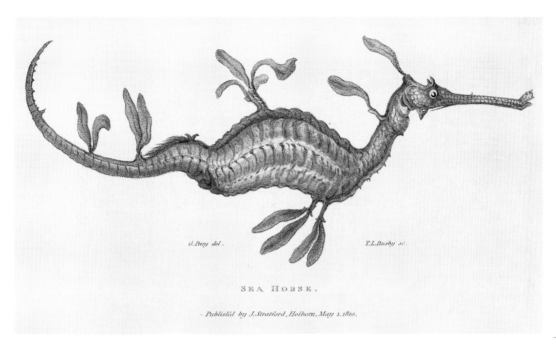

G.Perry del.   T.L.Busby sc.

SEA HORSE.

Publish'd by J.Stratford, Holborn, May 1.1810.

ABOVE: 'Hippocampus'—an engraving of a sea horse by T. L. Busby, after a drawing by G. Perry. Sea horses abound in the waters of Sydney Harbour.

which fish could be found in the harbour. For example, when the wattle bloomed in late winter, the flathead arrived in the harbour. When the westerlies of late winter and early springtime arrived, mullet travelled down the Parramatta River on their way to breed in the sea. In October, one of the local fishermen from Watsons Bay used to go across the harbour to Georges Head, and from a vantage point near the water's edge, look to see whether the bream were running. Like most fish, apart from the more audacious kingfish, bream shelter near the rocky ledges of the harbour. The shadows of the bream (otherwise invisible) would show up on the sand below the shallow water near Georges Head and Clifton Gardens.

The clarity of the water in the harbour improves greatly beyond Bradleys Head and it is in this outer part of the harbour that schools of kingfish and sea horses can most easily be seen today. Sea horses thrive in the area around Nielsen Park, where kelp, their main source of food, floats past on the tides and currents in the outer harbour. Sea horses are possibly one of the most ancient (40 million years old) and passive sea species living in the harbour today. They can be seen, often just floating, curled up, as they were born, or clinging onto nets such as that at Nielsen Park. They may not be seen there for much longer, however, as they are coming under increasing threat from fishing. Sea horses are an important ingredient in traditional Chinese and other Asian medicine, and are believed to prevent asthma, baldness and depression, as well as promote virility.

Environmental initiatives applying to boats, such as the ban on copper-based anti-fouling paint have already had a beneficial effect on marine life in the harbour. The construction of ocean outfalls further out to sea in the late 1980s has also meant cleaner water and a better marine environment. The Department of Fisheries has introduced guidelines that set aside exclusive zones within the harbour to protect seagrass habitats. The biggest seagrass beds are in the northern harbour, near Manly Cove and Fairlight, and, to a lesser degree, at Rose Bay. In the summer months of early 1998, scientists from the Australian Museum found nearly 500 species of marine life in the harbour's depths between Lady Bay and South Head. These included many tropical species carried southward in warm tropical currents. The range was enormous: the largest was a 20-kilogram mulloway or jewfish.

Improved water quality has led to the establishment of new, small colonies of fairy penguins in the northern harbour; in 1997, a sea lion visited the beach and rocks around Nielsen Park. Bird life abounds around the harbour: at least forty-four species of birds breed there. In quieter and leafier parts of the harbour foreshores, superb blue wrens, willie wagtails, king parrots, rosellas, rainbow lorikeets, sulphur-crested cockatoos, silver gulls, kookaburras and pelicans make their homes.

340 Rose Bay is the largest bay in the harbour. The land between Rose Bay and Bondi is a large sand spit. The width of the bay, its northerly aspect and the protection it enjoys from harsh weather from the south and west have meant that it is now one of the main spots on the southern shore of the harbour for sea-based pastimes such as sailing, rowing and sailboarding. Two of Sydney's best restaurants, Catalina and The Pier, lie on the shores of Rose Bay.

On the north side of the harbour are many pretty bays, beaches and headlands, including McMahons Point, Neutral Bay, Cremorne Point, Balmoral Beach, Clontarf, Forty Baskets Beach, North Harbour Reserve, Manly Cove and Little Manly Cove. Some of the coves and bays on the lower North Shore, such as Mosman Bay (Sirius Cove) and Neutral Bay, were used as bases for whaling and ship-repair stations in the early years of the colony. By the 1860s, these industries were in decline and sharp-eyed businessmen saw opportunities to turn these areas into recreational spots for which admission was charged.

In 1788, Bradleys Head was the home of the Bororegal clan, named after the headland they called 'Burrogi'. Much of the inner harbour would have looked as Bradleys Head does today, including Sydney Cove, Darling Harbour, Neutral Bay and Cremorne. Just around the corner to the east, at Taylors Bay, the forest is more moist and thicker. On other more exposed cliffs and headlands around the harbour, scrubby heathland is the dominant form of vegetation. Examples of this can be seen on North and South heads, and on the upper reaches of Middle Head. Quite remarkably, a completely new species of plant, *Allocasuarina portuensis*, was found in the Hermitage Foreshore Reserve by a national parks ranger and keen botanist, Peter Brookhouse, in the early 1990s.

At Bradleys Head, the mast of the cruiser HMAS *Sydney*, which sank the German ship *Emden* in 1914, can be seen, as can one of the Doric columns which used to stand at the old Post Office in George Street before the current General Post Office in Martin Place was built. For many years, this column was used as the the finishing point for the nautical-mile course from Fort Denison, to check the speed and efficiency of ships' nautical equipment.

One of the more remarkable domestic settlements in Sydney is at Crater Cove, just off Dobroyd Head. There is a cluster of huts built from as early as the 1920s, shortly after a walking track to Reef Beach was built. Two huts were built before the 1930s Depression years by Bob Cadwell and Fred Williams (not the well-known artist), and later more were added. The community built its own rock swimming pool. In the 1970s, the huts were lived in by hippies who did a reasonable job of maintaining the huts, but they were moved on in the 1980s by the National Parks and Wildlife Service. Some of the descendants of the original hut builders, sensitive to the cultural heritage value of the old settlement, volunteered to maintain the huts in original condition and formed the Crater Cove Huts Association. It is possible to be shown around the huts and the association now works with the National Parks and Wildlife Service to make the huts available for interested observers.

North Head was used as a quarantine station between 1832 and 1972. In the 1830s, it was feared that a cholera outbreak in Europe would spread to Sydney, and later smallpox became an even greater concern. The captain of each and every inbound ship would have to provide a bill of health for passengers and crew entering Australia. If they could not, the ships and every person upon them would be quarantined there upon arrival to protect the town from epidemics such as smallpox, typhoid, influenza and plague.

In a manner evocative of days gone by, the standard of accommodation at the station was arranged in accordance with the class of accommodation that had been paid for on the inbound journey, as the cost had to be borne by the owners of the ships which had carried the passengers to Australia. Asian travellers were put in fourth-class accommodation, and they were not treated well. The Commonwealth government became responsible for the running of the quarantine station in 1909, and handed it back to the state government as part of the Sydney Harbour National Park in 1984. The station is the largest and oldest intact quarantine facility in Australia, and as such is of significant historical interest. Many of the inmates fought off boredom by carving names and inscriptions into sandstone at the station, and there are nearly 600 people buried there.

Now, as part of the Sydney Harbour National Park, the quarantine station is managed by the National Parks and Wildlife Service. The North Head Scenic Drive is a popular route for joggers and walkers, as well as motorists. The National Parks and Wildlife Service is planning to extend the walk from Scenic Drive down to Shelly Beach.

The waters west of the Harbour Bridge are known as the inner harbour. It has long been home to Sydney's port facilities. At Yurulbin Port (formerly Long Nose Point) at Birchgrove, the harbour meets the tidal Parramatta River. The slopes and bays become gentler as the hilly sandstone country flattens out. The Parramatta River drains a very small area to the east of

Blacktown, to the north of Parramatta and to the south of Castle Hill. Most of the land to the west of Sydney drains into the larger Hawkesbury River, which skirts around the Cumberland Plain and empties into Broken Bay to Sydney's north.

Sharks have always been present in the waters of the harbour, and in the waters of Sydney's ocean beaches, but there have been few attacks, and no fatalities, since 1964. In fact, according to shark expert Sir Victor Coppleson:

> [M]ore people are killed by snakes, bulls and spiders than by sharks, three times as many are struck by lightning, and many more are killed by horses. Still more are killed by firearms or drowning.[16]

Despite this, the ghoulish and morbid fear of Sydneysiders and visitors alike about what lurks in Sydney's waters has not disappeared. Most shark attacks take place in late summer and early autumn when the water temperature is high, and there are more swimmers in the water. Shark attacks within the harbour and other enclosed waters have been more frequent between December and February.[17] One grisly shark attack took place when an 18-footer capsized in a southerly gale off Shark Island in 1850. Five of the crew were drowned. The owner prevailed on a brave person to dive below and find the boat and missing crew. As the bodies were dragged out of the murky depths, sharks dismembered the corpses.[18]

The first shark attacks recorded in the twentieth century were two fatal attacks at Sirius Cove, one in 1913 and another in 1916. That same year, a married couple were attacked while swimming at Seven Shillings Beach, Double Bay. The wife was the first to be attacked, 10 metres from the shore, and, as her husband was dragging her in, the shark also attacked him fatally.

The ocean beaches have, at various times, been the scene of fatal and near-fatal attacks. In 1922, a lifesaver at Coogee was taken by a shark with such force that his body was lifted out of the water, and the crowd at the beach watched as his arm was torn off. He did not survive the attack, despite the efforts of his lifesaving mates, including Olympic athlete Frank Beaurepaire, to save him. Beaurepaire established one of Australia's leading industrial companies with the bravery award he received. Beaurepaires for Tyres is still an Australian market leader.

Two months later, another swimmer was taken at Coogee. Then, two years later, a woman's legs were torn off by a shark at nearby Bronte Beach; shortly after that, another young man was attacked at Coogee. The focus of shark attacks then moved to Bondi, where two swimmers were killed and one was injured in the space of a year between April 1928 and February 1929. Just three days later, another swimmer was killed off Maroubra, 4 kilometres south of Bondi.

The northern beaches were next. Five attacks took place north of Manly in the two-year period from January 1934 to February 1936, most likely as a result of the work of a single, angry rogue shark. Meshing was introduced to many of Sydney's beaches from 1936 onwards.

There were still further attacks, however, along the Georges River and around Botany Bay. In the harbour itself, there were two shark attacks, at Bantry Bay and Middle Harbour. In 1942, a woman was bitten in half in a particularly vicious attack, and, less than a year later, a fifteen-year-old girl was also taken and died instantly. There was a thirteen-year reprieve before there was another pair of shark attacks, also in Middle Harbour—one off Edwards Beach, Mosman, in 1955, and another one month later off Sugarloaf Bay in Middle Harbour. In 1960, a thirteen-year-old boy was fatally attacked near the Roseville Bridge, again in Middle Harbour.

In the January holiday period in 1963, as many as sixty-six sharks were spotted off the coast of Sydney, one just 40 metres away from bathers at Maroubra Beach. In Middle Harbour (again), off Sugarloaf Bay, actress Marcia Hathaway was bitten by a shark when she was just waist deep in water. While Hathaway's life was ebbing away, the ambulance that had come to take her to hospital became stuck on the steep driveway leading to the water. Hathaway died before a second ambulance was able to get her to the Mater Misericordiae Hospital at North Sydney.

For whatever reason—possibly increasing levels of water pollution and the reduction in the amount of fish in the harbour—there were no more shark attacks in the harbour or along the beaches of Sydney until 1996, when a swimmer was attacked at night by a bronze whaler shark while swimming across the Parramatta River. Then, in February 1997, a shark attacked the rowing shell of a woman who was sculling in Iron Cove Bay near the Leichhardt Rowing Club.

343

When the First Fleet arrived in 1788, Sydney Harbour had thirteen islands, ranging from small rock platforms to large forested landforms where the Aborigines lived. Of these, five have, through land reclamation, been joined to the mainland: Garden Island, Bennelong Point, Berry Island (which has been joined to Wollstonecraft), Glebe Island and tiny Darling Island, now reclaimed and part of Pyrmont. Others have been quarried to the point where they bear almost no relation to their original appearance. The best examples of this are Fort Denison and Cockatoo and Goat islands. Of all the harbour islands, or former islands, the ones which most closely resemble their natural state are Clark and Berry islands.

Shark Island, located about 500 metres from Rose Bay, was officially given its name in 1879, when it, Clark and Rodd islands were dedicated as the first public recreation reserves on Sydney Harbour, but it had been unofficially so named since the early nineteenth century, due to its vague resemblance to the shape of a shark. In fact, in the early years of the nineteenth century, the island looked as though it would prove to be as treacherous as its name suggested. In 1826, Shark Island claimed its first victim when the *Newcastle* ran aground on its rocks and had to limp back to Cockle Bay (Darling Harbour). A month later, the vessel sank, killing all on board, due probably to the damage that had been caused during the accident.

Shark Island was briefly used as a quarantine station in the late nineteenth century. Between 1900 and 1920, old dilapidated buildings were removed and a program of improvement was started, with the construction of walkways and a pavilion. In World War II, the island was occupied by the Royal Australian Navy as a storage depot, but, since 1975, it has been under the control of the Sydney Harbour National Park, and it can be used for parties and visited by prior arrangement with the National Parks and Wildlife Service.

Clark Island lies 350 metres to the north of Darling Point. In November 1789, Lieutenant Ralph Clark rowed to the island from the fledgling colony at Sydney Cove, and determined that he would use the island in order to develop his horticultural talents and grow some food. Since there was a serious shortage of food in the colony at the time, however, Clark's agricultural efforts were not left undisturbed for long. His garden was raided and his efforts came to nil.

Clark soon abandoned the island and, for the next century, the only life on it was a steady stream of picnickers. During World War II, the island was transferred to the navy for defence purposes. Like Shark Island, it is now part of Sydney Harbour National Park. Its vegetation is in a more natural state than that on Shark Island and smaller groups of people (up to fifteen) may use it, with permission from the National Parks and Wildlife Service.

344

Located on the Parramatta River, off the Balmain peninsula, lies Goat Island. It was known to the Aboriginal inhabitants of Sydney as *Mel-mel*. According to Bennelong, it belonged to his tribe, and there was, before 1788, much 'feasting and enjoyment' on the island. Unfortunately, any archaeological evidence has been destroyed as the island is mostly cleared and levelled. Feasting and enjoyment on the island did not survive European settlement. In 1826, a prisoner hulk, the *Phoenix*, was towed to Goat Island: 'To this island it is considered that the filth [excrement not prisoners] from the hulk might be conveyed.'[19]

By 1831, a site on the island's eastern side had been established as a quarry to be worked by convicts, with the high-quality sandstone produced being used in the construction of many of the city's buildings. After the quarry was closed, Goat Island was chosen as a central and secure magazine for gunpowder and other explosives.

The arms magazine was built over six years using convict labour, its construction being supervised by George Barney. Work on Goat Island was given as a form of punishment for disobedient convicts, who were put to work there on chain gangs.

One convict, Charles Anderson, is commemorated in 'Anderson's Couch', which can be seen today on the southern side of the island. Anderson was a convict who had been sentenced to transportation at the age of eighteen, after being in a bar-room brawl. He neither repented nor changed his ways. He was finally sentenced to be chained to a rock on Goat Island for two years. Anderson's Couch is the result of these two years of solitary confinement. Anderson was fed by a long pole, and the only protection from the harsh climate was a wooden box that was fixed over him at night. Free settlers who passed by the island persuaded Governor Bourke to give Anderson a reprieve. By then, his back was burnt and infested with maggots.

Meanwhile, Goat Island was serving an additional purpose: the water police moved there as it was easy to see the flow of activity around the harbour. Mortimer Lewis designed the police-station building. A ditch was built across the island so that its functions as a magazine and a station for the water police could be separated. The military won the later competition for sole occupation of the island, and the water police moved to Kirribilli.

Most components of the original magazine complex can still be seen on the island. Like Victoria Barracks, Fort Denison and Circular Quay, Goat Island is a testament to colonial engineer George Barney's engineering skills, as well as the forced labour of the convict gangs. In 1861, an observer commented that Goat Island stored enough gunpowder 'quite sufficient to send half of Sydney to the other world'.

From 1901, Goat Island was the centre of operations for the Sydney Harbour Trust, and during the plague epidemic it was used as a bacteriology station. A residence for the harbour master was built and navigation markers were installed. The island was also used as a base for firefighting on the harbour. Just after World War II, a conscious attempt was made to boost the morale of the twenty-six firefighters who lived on the island with their families. The erection of a recreation hall was aimed at fostering community spirit and providing entertainment for these people who were deprived of the usual benefits of city living, and it became a raging success, with visitors from the mainland regularly rowing to the island for the Saturday-night dances. The hall, which was a wooden building with Doric porches, was demolished in the late 1960s. The popular television series 'Water Rats' is filmed on the island. In 1994, Goat Island was transferred to the New South Wales National Parks and Wildlife Service, and can be visited, like most of the other islands on the harbour, by prior arrangement.

Further to the west, up the Parramatta River, is Sydney's biggest island, located near the junction of the Parramatta and Lane Cove rivers and Iron Cove. It was to Cockatoo Island that the convict workers were sent after the first main works on Goat Island were completed. The conditions there were no less harsh, and the island was infamous. Cockatoo Island is the most built-up of Sydney's harbour islands and the most polluted. For many years, it was used as the government dockyards. Its future use is uncertain. As a result of chemical contamination of the island, developing it is a challenge which has not yet been met. Access to the island is not easy. Part of the Federation Fund for government-owned harbourside land has been earmarked to pay for remediation.

The island was called *Biloela* by the Aborigines which means cockatoo. The birds liked the red gum forest that stood upon it. Looking at the denuded island today, it is hard to imagine that this area was once heavily forested and buzzing with squawking native birds. First use of the island by the colonists occurred in 1833, when Governor Bourke ordered the construction of a cell complex. The gaol in George Street was hopelessly overcrowded, and the funds were not yet available for the proposed new Darlinghurst Gaol. All traces of the prison, however, were demolished later in the nineteenth century during excavation works for a dry dock. Many of the convicts from Goat Island were transferred to Cockatoo Island to build the prison. Governor Gipps, at the suggestion of George Barney, commissioned the construction of grain silos on the island. This was the first government attempt to store grain. The silos were huge, each holding between 84 and 140 tonnes. They were remarkable public works. To make them airtight, they were chiselled into the solid rock, in the shape of enormous bottles, and access to them was sealed off with concrete after the grain had settled. Although built with unskilled labour, the silos served their purpose well. The idea of the government storing grain did not, however, coincide with the *laissez-faire* policy of the day in Britain. Food storage by the government in the colonies was an intolerable interference with the free market, so the silos were abandoned, before later being used as water-storage tanks.

When convict transportation from New South Wales to Norfolk Island was abandoned, Sydney soon had numbers of convicts awaiting further distribution and Cockatoo Island was the place they were sent. The island remained a prison until 1871, when it was finally closed down because of the constant litany of complaints. It developed a reputation as a penal hellhole and a den of infamy.

After two official inquiries, the Cockatoo Island prison had finally become too embarrassing for the government, and its inmates were transferred to Darlinghurst Gaol. The island was renamed Biloela, in an unsuccessful attempt to erase the island's penal connotations.

The convicts on Cockatoo Island built the Fitzroy Graving Dock in the 1850s. It was extended afterwards so that it would be able to service large ships. In 1913, the Commonwealth government acquired the island for use as a defence installation. Little was done on the island until after the end of World War II, when the island served for many years as a shipbuilding and submarine-refitting site. Cockatoo Island's future use is uncertain.

To the west and south of Cockatoo Island lie Spectacle and Snapper islands. Both of these islands have been occupied by the navy. Spectacle Island (originally called Dawes Island after Lieutenant William Dawes, but renamed because of its shape) was used as a powder magazine and armaments depot in the nineteenth century. Convicts from Cockatoo Island built the three earliest sandstone buildings there. Building work progressed in the haphazard fashion that was typical of the manner in which the military and other government bodies worked in those days. By 1910, there were forty buildings on the island, some of them obscuring the finer earlier architectural works. Spectacle Island was enlarged using infill from the Balmain coal mine. The chief function of the island is for the storage of naval artefacts and memorabilia, only some of which have found their way to the National Maritime Museum at Darling Harbour. Tiny Snapper Island, only 200 metres off Drummoyne, was used for many years as a naval cadet base. From 1932, the island was levelled and cadets were used to build the sea wall around the island.

Further south, in Iron Cove, is Rodd Island, just beyond the Iron Cove Bridge. Like Clark and Shark islands, Rodd Island is in a reasonably natural state and has a house on it which was converted to a dance hall early in the twentieth century. Between 1888 and 1894, Rodd Island was used as a research base for experiments into rabbit eradication by the Pasteur Institute, and as a quarantine station for imported animal stock, to supplement quarantine stations on Shark Island and at Bradleys Head.

CHAPTER FOURTEEN

THE INNER CITY

THE FIRST DIRECTION the town spread was eastward. In Sydney's first boom period, the 1830s, Woolloomooloo, Potts Point, Elizabeth Bay and Darlinghurst were settled. At first these suburbs, and others that were built up shortly afterwards, such as Surry Hills, Redfern, Newtown and Camperdown, were lived in by genteel members of the upper classes who lived on the land grants made by the early governors. As the high rate of population growth increased throughout the remainder of the nineteenth century, these were the first areas to feel the impact of the Victorian housing boom. Large land-holdings were sold off for denser development.

From the middle of the nineteenth century onwards, row after row of terrace houses lined the dusty streets of the inner suburbs. Water supply, sewerage and sealed roads often took a long time to catch up with this urban growth. From the early twentieth century, these suburbs began their long period of decline, brought on by the outward sprawl of Sydney's population, attracted to the open spaces along the growing tram and railway networks. Some of the inner suburbs, however, particularly Potts Point and Elizabeth Bay, were witness to the building boom of the 1920s and 1930s, when dozens of tall (for those days) blocks of flats grew up on the city's skyline. This new high-density, low-cost living, which became possible during the inter-war and early postwar period, created the environment where the earliest manifestations of a more cosmopolitan lifestyle could be experienced and enjoyed.

Since the 1970s, Sydney's inner-city suburbs have undergone a period of urban renewal sometimes referred to as 'gentrification'. The first stage in this process was the advent of non–English-speaking migrants, often from southern Europe, who brought their culture and their skills at running small, family-owned businesses to the inner suburbs. They opened fruit and vegetable shops, delicatessens, cafés, milk bars and cheap restaurants. In doing so, they exposed Sydneysiders to a different way of life. Dull brown, run-down and sometimes derelict terraces were given a fresh coat of brightly coloured paint. Then, from the mid-1960s, the Australian-born home buyers moved in, and started renovating old homes (many of which had been used as boarding houses) into fashionable residences. The older occupants passed away or moved out to the suburbs, so land values started their long ascent. As the amount of available entertainment and nightlife dried up in the city itself during the building boom of the 1960s and 1970s, a lot of the after-hours action moved out to the inner suburbs. Today, it is the inner-city suburbs which offer the biggest, liveliest and most diverse range of entertainment activities, as well as Sydney's quirkier shopping precincts.

The inner-city suburbs have witnessed, and have played a big part in, the social changes in Sydney over the past thirty years. Since the larrikin pushes and the razor gangs of the late nineteenth and early twentieth centuries, these suburbs have been at the centre of Sydney's seamier activities: illegal gambling, extortion, and the drug and sex industries. Until the mid-1990s, this side of life in the inner city had been accompanied by a staggeringly well-institutionalised regime of police corruption. Despite many attempts from the time of the Moffitt Royal Commission in the early 1970s onwards, it was not until the Police Royal Commission presided over by Justice James Wood in the early and mid-1990s that there was any significant change in improving this dark underbelly of corruption that lay close to the surface of inner-city life. It remains to be seen whether the improvement will be permanent.

In the early 1970s, Woolloomooloo and Potts Point were two important battlefields for the fight to save Sydney's urban heritage. The battle between developers and conservationists culminated in the green bans imposed by the Builder's Labourers Federation (BLF), led at the time by Jack Mundey. Sometimes, those who were strongly on the side of development enlisted the aid of the underworld crime figures who already ran their operations and prospered in the inner city around Kings Cross, and this made the achievements of the BLF and others even more heroic. One local agitator was Juanita Nielsen, publisher of a local Kings Cross newspaper, who disappeared without trace. This political activity by urban conservationists, combined with the downturn in the property market, eventually ensured that whole suburbs were not razed in the name of 'progress'. The efforts of these people should never be forgotten—although more than a few ugly buildings slipped through the net.

The residential flat building boom of the 1920s and 1930s also indirectly contributed to the emergence, fifty years later, of a strong gay culture that characterises many of the inner suburbs today, centred on Oxford Street. It is easier to lead a nonconformist life anonymously, with little or no attention from the neighbours in residential flats than it is in suburbia, where one's actions and habits can be observed by hawk-like neighbours. Sydney's beauty and socially libertarian outlook (compared to some other Australian cities) are other factors that have led to the emergence of a strong gay culture in the city's inner suburbs.

Woolloomooloo was Sydney's first suburb to be subdivided in the nineteenth century. With the construction of the Eastern Distributor and high-rise residential accommodation, its character is changing once again. The 'Loo has the added physical disadvantage of being scarred by the eastern suburbs railway viaduct, completed in the 1970s, which bisects the valley. The lasting legacy of the resident activism during the green bans in the early 1970s is the public housing on the eastern side of Woolloomooloo. Built by the Housing Commission (the organ of state government responsible for providing low-cost housing to those on welfare or low incomes), it is one of the more heroic attempts at urban renewal funded by government.

Darlinghurst Road and William Street at Kings Cross are at the epicentre of the sex industry in Sydney, and a walk down either of these roads is not for the faint-hearted on a Friday or Saturday night. But behind the main arteries lie many interesting and sometimes gracious streets, such as plane tree–lined Victoria and Kellett streets, Challis Avenue and Roslyn Street.

To the south of Kings Cross is Darlinghurst. In the past fifteen years, this has become a fashionable and lively area, especially along Victoria Street between William and Burton streets, and down in the valley in Stanley and Crown streets. Dividing Darlinghurst and Surry Hills is Oxford Street. To the south of Oxford Street is Surry Hills, a suburb that is what it always has been—an unplanned mixture of residential, commercial and industrial uses. Surry Hills has risen to the challenge posed by being on the route of some of the city's major north–south roads and is now a much more interesting place than it was twenty years ago. Surry Hills used to be the centre of Sydney's garment industry or 'rag trade'. With the decline of this industry from the 1970s, many of the old factories and warehouses have closed down or moved further afield and the buildings have been converted into residential apartments.

To the south and west of these inner-city suburbs lie Redfern, Camperdown and Newtown. These areas experienced gentrification later than the eastern inner-city fringe, but the revival of these areas is well under way.

349

Woolloomooloo is separated from the city by the Domain and is neatly contained by the harbour, the Potts Point escarpment and William Street. Until the 1850s, Woolloomooloo covered a much greater area—as far south, in fact, as Oxford Street. For nearly a century, until the 1960s, Woolloomooloo Bay was a bustling centre of Sydney's maritime industry and location of the city's fish markets.

The name 'Woolloomooloo' is derived from the Aboriginal name for the place, *Walla Mulla*. This name was adopted by its first European landowner, Commissary General John Palmer, instead of the blander Garden Cove, which it was first called by the colonists. Palmer built a house near the head of the cove, on 100 acres (40 hectares) of land he was granted by Major Francis Grose. Here he built the best house in Sydney of the day, where he lived for twenty years. The house stood near the corner of Woolloomooloo (now Cathedral) and Riley streets until the 1850s.

In the first decade of the nineteenth century, Palmer kept his fleet of commercial schooners in Woolloomooloo Bay. His flour mill stood on the hill within the Governor's Domain, until it was torn down by government order. Palmer's fortunes declined during Macquarie's term in office, and in 1822 he sold his heavily mortgaged estate to Edward Riley, a merchant and a director of the Bank of New South Wales. In 1825, Riley committed suicide, and in 1842 the land was subdivided. Two of its main streets, Palmer and Riley streets, are named after these two early European landowners. The Burdekin family, creditors of one of Riley's heirs, received part of the Riley estate in settlement of a debt. In the late 1820s, further land grants were made in large 8- to 10-acre (3.2- to 4-hectare) lots to men of high status. Two of the grantees were Supreme Court judges, Sir James Dowling and John Stephen.

In Woolloomooloo and Potts Point, there was an early and, for Sydney, atypical attempt to ensure quality control over land development imposed by Governor Darling in the 1830s. Houses were to be built for no less than £1000 and set back a certain distance from the street. If a house had not been built within three years, the grant lapsed. This was all part of Darling's scheme to create a private and exclusive suburb dotted with substantial homes. He also had plans to relocate Government House to Elizabeth Bay. As a result of these land-grant conditions, about ten large villas were built in the area during the 1830s, including Sir Thomas Mitchell's Craigend, Judge Stephen's Orwell, Attorney-General Alexander Baxter's Springfield, and Judge Dowling's Brougham Lodge. Most of these were complete or nearing completion by 1835, four years after Governor Darling had left the colony, in accordance with the grant conditions.

Bourke Street is the dividing line between the older and the newer Woolloomooloo. The Riley estate lay on the western side and went all the way south to Oxford Street. It was the first to be subdivided in 1841. The earliest remaining Woolloomooloo buildings are here. The area east of Bourke Street was subdivided from the estate of Judge Dowling's Brougham Lodge. The lodge stood on the site of the Kings Cross Hotel and many of the nearby streets bear this judicial legacy—Dowling, Brougham and Judge streets and Judge Lane. Some of the streets near the ridge had to be hewn out of the sandstone cliff formerly known as Windmill Ridge, upon which Victoria Street sits.

The trend towards subdivision intensified in the middle of the nineteenth century, stimulated by the gold rush and the growth of the shipping industry. In the 1850s, the tidal mud flats north of Harmer Street were reclaimed. This made disembarkation from ships much easier. Woolloomooloo's days as a port were about to begin in earnest. Woolloomooloo's new life as a port had predictable consequences. The pace of daily life quickened and the density of the housing increased. Pubs sprang up on many street corners to satisfy the thirst of those working on or near the wharves. The area acquired the same salty flavour that The Rocks had displayed since the colony's earliest days. An observer of Sydney in 1879 thought that:

> The entrance to Wooloomaloo [sic] Bay [is] magnificent. McQuade Point and Garden Island are perfect gems of living verdure; the Botanical Gardens, enriched with the plants and flowers of every clime, look green, cool, and secluded; … Wooloomaloo seeming a huge city by itself … and far ahead, the piled-up masses of the buildings, all

ABOVE: During the 1930s Depression, this unemployed man was forced to live on a rock ledge overlooking Woolloomooloo Bay, having lost his job at St Luke's Hospital in 1932. His one ambition was to return to his mother, who lived in London.

of solid sandstone loom out in the morning mist, vague, shadowy and undefined against the sky-line …[1]

By the 1880s, cheap tenement buildings were being erected to provide housing for dockside workers and sailors; warehouses and timber mills were built close to the water and the fish markets near Cowper Wharf added to the working-class atmosphere in the postwar era. Italian families used to live around Woolloomooloo, using the bay for their fishing operations. They moved on in the late 1960s.

Until the sewerage system was rerouted to Bondi, one of the inner city's largest sewers ran down the valley to Woolloomooloo Bay, making the area unswimmable. It was not until 1908 that the water quality improved sufficiently for new baths to be built, near where the Fig Tree Baths, the city's first swimming enclosure, had originally been situated. The Boy Charlton Swimming Pool is built near the site.

By the 1890s, the area was becoming notorious for its larrikins and groups of pushes, as were other inner-city areas such as The Rocks and Millers Point. The name 'Woolloomooloo' had by 1905 become so synonymous with violence and the influence of pushes that Woolloomooloo Street was renamed Cathedral Street in an attempt to redeem its reputation. A private hospital in the street claimed that its address was so disreputable that people were deterred from visiting the sick.[2]

The imposition of 6 p.m. closing time in the pubs during World War I created a whole new industry at the 'Loo, the sly grog shop. There were plenty of brothels as well. Two of the 'Loo and Darlinghurst's most famous working girls were Tilly Devine and 'Diamond Kate' Carney, who wore a diamond in each tooth. The Depression of the early 1930s was possibly the lowest ebb for the 'Loo and other nearby inner-city suburbs. The economic and social misery provoked younger generations of the old pushes to become more violent, and razor gangs developed. Local shop-owners had to pay protection money for their safety, and people who were not local were not safe to walk the streets at night. In an effort to encourage better behaviour, Australia's first police–citizens' boys club opened in Woolloomooloo in 1937. The clubs were established in this period to encourage the young and the out of work to become engaged in healthy physical activity, such as boxing and the martial arts, rather than loitering in the streets of the inner suburbs.

352

The notoriety of the 'Loo persisted until the middle of the century. Growing up in Woolloomooloo was synonymous, in the opinion of some, with growing up in the closest thing Sydney had to a bona fide slum. To be referred to in the expression of the day as someone who 'must have been educated at Plunkett Street [Public School]' certainly did not suggest that the person had reached a high level of education or social achievement.

Cowper's Wharf at Woolloomooloo, named after New South Wales's first premier, Charles Cowper, was the main departure point for many soldiers on their way to the Boer and both world wars. The wharf was completed in 1913 by the Sydney Harbour Trust as part of the modernisation of Sydney's port facilities. During World War II, Cowpers Wharf Road was known as the 'Burma Road' to many soldiers, as leaving Sydney from the Woolloomooloo wharf ultimately meant the start of a journey to work as a prisoner of war on the Burma railway for some.

Woolloomooloo wharf was, for many postwar immigrants, the place where they first stood on Australian soil. Some of them walked through the streets of Woolloomooloo and Darlinghurst searching for a room to live in in one of the many boarding houses in the area. The worn and peeling grey paint and the rhythm of the detailing of the timber walls were familiar and distinctive Sydney landmarks until the mid-1990s.

All these nostalgic aspects of Woolloomooloo wharf provoked a huge public outcry when the demolition of the old finger wharf was proposed by the state government in the late 1980s. As a consequence, the wharf—or certain small and arguably insignificant elements of it, such as the old turpentine wooden piers—have been preserved and the rest of it has been demolished and rebuilt as apartments and a hotel. Most of the old timber has been taken away, recycled and advertised for sale in Western Australia (of all places). The finger wharf was the largest covered wharf in the world—350 metres long and 70 metres wide. Sometimes it seems

ABOVE: Scrambling aboard the tram at the junction of William Street and Bayswater Road, Kings Cross, c. 1908.

almost impossible for Sydney's old buildings to be recycled for new purposes in a way that is both sensitive to the building's historical context and progressive and forward-looking.

From the 1950s, Woolloomooloo started to develop a more bohemian *mien*, like other inner-city suburbs around the world. Artists, designers and dancers lived, drank and worked there, alongside others who practised many of the older professions. From the 1920s, organised crime and gang warfare thrived. A notorious policeman in the Vice Squad, Inspector 'Bumper' Farrell, was renowned for his aggression.

A former first-grade rugby league prop for Newtown, Farrell was accused of biting the ear off one of his opponents on the football field. He denied the charge, but the victim did spend a long time in hospital recovering from his injury. Farrell was for many years deputy head of the Vice Squad at Darlinghurst Police Station. According to one of his police colleagues, Farrell was a legend, particularly in street fights, immune to fear and pain. Once he and a colleague found well-renowned gunman 'Tosser' Corbett and three of his cronies standing over and threatening some prostitutes in a back lane in Darlinghurst. Farrell told his colleague not to join in the fight, as he was wearing his best suit following a court appearance. Farrell took on the four gangsters and arrested them.[3]

By the 1960s, a wharfie remarked upon how respectable the 'Loo was becoming.[4] The next major threat Woolloomooloo faced was not from crime, but from progress. Kings Cross and Woolloomooloo were starting to feel the effects of the postwar building boom. In 1964, it was designated for planning purposes as a comprehensive development area. One of the first buildings to go was an old mansion in Cathedral Street that was replaced by an ugly car park. Car parks were popular with planning authorities in those days. A large tranche of the eastern Domain was destroyed to make way for the Domain car park in the early 1960s. Then, in 1969, the Askin government decided to proceed with the comprehensive redevelopment of Woolloomooloo. Land developers became active in the area, aggregating sites for future construction. One of the most active was local Woolloomooloo boy Sid Londish.

The state government was in favour of high-rise development in the area; it also wanted to improve road access to Potts Point by building an overhead viaduct from Plunkett Street to Victoria Street, along similar lines to the Cahill Expressway. In 1971, the Civic Reform Council disagreed with the state government and stepped in to limit the scope of the redevelopment, and argued that the suburb should remain predominantly residential.

354

The confrontation between the developers and the residents heated up in 1972. While Londish was pushing for planning approval, the Woolloomooloo Residents' Action Group was formed. The federal government decided against going ahead with the high-rise Commonwealth Government Centre. The Commonwealth's role became even more important when the Labor Party came to power in December 1972. Saving Woolloomooloo was one of the new government's election promises. Tom Uren, the minister for urban and regional development, took this promise seriously. The government's work was greatly assisted by the decision of the Woolloomooloo Residents' Action Group to enlist the help of the Builders' Labourers Federation (BLF) led by Jack Mundey. A union ban was imposed on all demolition and construction work in the area. The only building to slip through the net was an office tower opposite the Domain Parking Station. It has since been converted to residential apartments. The rest of Woolloomooloo would have been redeveloped on a similar scale if the Liberal state government led by Bob Askin and developers like Sid Londish had had their way.

By mid-1973, the property boom was teetering on the brink of collapse and Sid Londish wanted to be bought out. By 1974, all three tiers of government agreed that the valley of Woolloomooloo should have medium-density housing only, to be provided by a combination of renovating old buildings and building new ones. The Housing Commission needed some convincing—it was used to high-density solutions to public housing in the inner city—but eventually it was persuaded. Woolloomooloo proved to be a Bermuda Triangle for several property developers, including Londish. Many well-known property development companies in Sydney in the late 1960s and early 1970s which became insolvent owned significant amounts of land in Woolloomooloo.[5]

In the meantime, the stock of housing and the occupancy rates in Woolloomooloo had been declining. People were moving out of the area in large numbers. In 1976, only 430 houses were occupied, down from 1100 in 1966.[6]

A more consultative method of planning was adopted. Architect Colin James was appointed by the federal government as the advocate for the residents before the Woolloomooloo Steering Committee, which Uren also set up. James was also the BLF's adviser on green bans.

In 1975, the Housing Commission started resuming properties. Today, Woolloomooloo is one of our better architectural attempts at public housing. The low-density, traffic-free areas with the amenities of the city over the ridge beyond is a great testament to the efforts of the determined residents and their supporters, especially Tom Uren and the BLF; however, Woolloomooloo is far from being a social utopia. It is not quarantined from the drugs, violence and criminality of Kings Cross and probably never will be.

With the pressure brought on by the city's high growth rate and the growing acceptability of inner-city living for the affluent, there is a growing cluster of late–twentieth-century luxury high-rise developments in the Woolloomooloo and William Street precinct. These include Crown Gardens and the Harry Seidler–designed Horizon Apartments, which stand behind William Street on the site of the old ABC studios at Forbes Street. There are more on the drawing board, for example, one on the site of the Sydney Eye Hospital.

355

There are still many old pubs in Woolloomooloo, established at a time when the area bustled with wharf labourers and other people in the shipping industry. The men in blue singlets have disappeared and the pubs cater to a younger inner-city crowd. There is one institution, however, which has survived the changes in Woolloomooloo in its original form: Harry's Café de Wheels, on the eastern end of Cowpers Wharf Road. Nowadays, it is one of Sydney's culinary landmarks, open all night on Fridays, Saturdays and Sundays, and it is very popular with late-night revellers and workers, particularly taxi drivers. Harry's was started by Yorkshireman Henry Edwards in 1945, and the classic dish served there, a pie floater, is true to these northern English origins.

Until the 1940s, Garden Island was still an island and Potts Point was a point. The two were separated by 600 metres of water. Garden Island was named within three weeks of the First Fleet's landing in 1788, as it was one of the first places where land was cultivated in the colony. Since the mid-nineteenth century, Garden Island has been a naval base. Its future is less certain now that the headquarters of the navy are to be located in Jervis Bay on the south coast. When the navy vacates Garden Island, it is proposed that the land and the heritage buildings on it will become an accessible part of the Sydney Harbour National Park.

Sailors on the the *Sirius* were sent to Garden Island to cultivate vegetables for their fellow marines in 1788, but like the other early attempts at cultivation, this was not con-spicuously successful in curbing the shortage of food in the colony. Other ships of the Royal Navy later occupied the island, including, in 1795, another ship of the First Fleet, the *Supply*. From the nineteenth century, preoccupations with defence matters led to the erection of two guns on the north of the island, but these guns were not well maintained. In 1857, the

ABOVE: An inner-city corner grocery store, East Sydney, in the mid-twentieth century.

New South Wales government handed the island over to the Royal Navy for use as a naval base. It was during the second half of the nineteenth century that the utilitarian but attractive buildings on the island were constructed. These included those that are now visible from the eastern side of the island—the administration building, the naval stores and the barracks building. The newly formed Royal Australian Navy took possession of Garden Island in July 1911. During World War I, the island was used to refit and arm ships. The question of who owned Garden Island—the federal or the state government—led to a battle in the High Court in 1923. The state government won the claim, but the victory was a hollow one: the federal government used its emergency powers after the outbreak of World War II to reclaim the disputed land.

In 1938, spurred on by signs of Japanese militarism, Garden Island was chosen as the site of a dry dock for repairing the largest ships in the world. Altogether, 14 hectares of land were reclaimed in one of the greatest engineering works ever undertaken in Sydney. The pressure to complete the dry dock increased greatly after the fall of Singapore in 1942, and completing the work became a wartime emergency. The Captain Cook Dry Dock was the result. It was built to British specifications and paid for by the Australian government. Wylde Street (named in honour of the original grantee of 11 acres (4.5 hectares) on Potts Point, James Wylde, during Macquarie's term as governor) was built to connect Cowpers Wharf Road with Potts Point up the hill. Until then, the only direct access from Potts Point to Woolloomooloo below were the stairs that run down the escarpment—the Butler, McElhone and Hordern stairs.

The construction of Garden Island had the indirect effect of making Potts Point and Kings Cross a lot more accessible by road from Woolloomooloo than before. Visiting sailors were no longer relatively contained within Woolloomooloo Bay. This had a significant effect on the flavour of Kings Cross. Some activities traditionally associated with port areas around the world, nefarious and otherwise, crept up the hill. The US soldiers and sailors were the most common visitors, and the sort of businesses which cater to lonely soldiers and sailors developed at that time: bars, nightclubs and, of course, the sex industry.

Kings Cross sits on the sandstone ridge between Woolloomooloo and Elizabeth and Rushcutters bays. Geographically, it is best defined as the area to the northeast of William Street, covering the area between Darlinghurst and Bayswater roads to the El Alamein Fountain. More important than the geography, Kings Cross is a state of mind. The huge range of entertainment caters to different tastes.

From the 1960s, the main streets of Kings Cross, particularly Darlinghurst Road, became seedy and unsafe places. The attempt to rid the area of crime has proceeded with varying degrees of success in the wake of the Police Royal Commission.

Between 1994 and 1997, crime in Kings Cross and the role of the police force in protecting and even promoting crime were two of the most closely explored subjects of the Police Royal Commission presided over by Justice James Wood. The revelations of an endemically rotten culture within the police force stunned even the most scandal-weary Sydneysiders. The level of corruption in the New South Wales Police Service had a macabre resonance with the colony's early years during the rule of the Rum Corps.

There has been a long history of police corruption, ever since convicts were elevated to positions as night watchmen and constables.[7] The first police commander was appointed in 1833 and stood down following allegations of impropriety in 1840. For many years, there was a complex power-sharing and power-rotating arrangement between Catholics and Masons. Also, there has long been a rivalry between plain-clothes detectives and the uniformed members of the force.

In the 1920s, razor gangs of the inner city fought for the control of criminal activities. The *Vagrancy Act*, passed in 1929, made consorting with known criminals a crime in itself. This applied to police just as it did to the general public, and over time, these razor gangs faded from the city's streets. In the 1930s, however, the opportunities for corrupt members of the police force blossomed with the introduction of widespread illegal starting price (SP) betting, made possible by easy access to race broadcasts on the radio. In the middle of the twentieth century, increasing specialisation within the police force, especially within the Criminal

357

Investigation Bureau (CIB), meant that 'elite' enclaves within the force flourished. These enclaves were apparently immune from investigation or internal surveillance. Police did not only have investigative powers, but they also prosecuted those accused of crime in the courts. This consolidated their power within the justice system itself. Any police misconduct uncovered during an investigation was unlikely to be reported by fellow police acting in the role of prosecutors.

During the 1940s and 1950s, the Vice Squad became notorious for promoting vice. Gambling dens openly flaunted the law by operating, to the knowledge of many, if not most Sydneysiders, through the 1960s and early 1970s, when the Gaming Squad assumed direct responsibility for 'preventing' gambling. From the 1960s, the Drug Squad became infamous for its involvement in the drug trade. In the 1970s, the Armed Hold-up Squad became notorious for their role in 'green-lighting' armed hold-ups. It was all very neat, in its perverse but orderly way. The Vice, Consorting and No. 21 Special squads were all based in the Darlinghurst–Kings Cross area. Together with Darlinghurst and Kings Cross police stations, these organs of the police force in the inner city created a safe haven for much of the organised crime in Sydney.

In 1974, a royal commission presided over by Justice Athol Moffitt found that police officers during their inquiries and reports had masked the nature of links between a major poker-machine manufacturer and organised crime. The Criminal Intelligence Unit (CIU), formed at the recommendation of the commission, was created, but little else was achieved. The CIU's attempt to uncover police corruption was brought to an abrupt end when the tapes of telephone taps were seized from it. Later, in 1981, it was enlarged, separated from the CIB and renamed the Bureau of Crime Intelligence.

One of the great scandals in the history of crime and police tolerance of it in Kings Cross was the disappearance of Juanita Nielsen in 1975. Her disappearance and presumed death demonstrated clearly that there was serious police corruption and a very unhealthy relationship between crime and law enforcement at Kings Cross. Nielsen came from a prominent family which owned the department store Mark Foy's.[8] She operated a local newspaper from her home in 202 Victoria Street. In July 1975, she went to an appointment at the Carousel Club to discuss selling advertising space in her publication. She was never seen again. The Carousel operated as a transvestite nightclub where Les Girls had once performed. At the time of Nielsen's disappearance, the Carousel was run by Abe Saffron, a leading identity in Sydney's criminal underworld, and James McCartney Anderson. Nielsen, among many others, opposed developer Frank Theeman's plan to raze the Victorian terraces of Victoria Street and build high-density housing on land then occupied by terrace houses at numbers 55 to 115 Victoria Street.

Theeman had collaborated with Detective Sergeant Frederick Krahe, who organised thugs to induce tenants of these properties to leave them. Krahe was well known to Saffron and Anderson. There were also financial dealings between Anderson and Theeman which were, in the words of a parliamentary joint committee:

... capable of supporting the conclusion that at about the time Nielsen disappeared, Theeman paid money to Anderson for a purpose that may have been other than its stated purpose. This invites the question whether the true purpose was to pay Anderson for dealing with Nielsen's opposition to Theeman's Victoria Street plans.

At the inquest into her disappearance, the jury found evidence that the police inquiries were hampered by an atmosphere of police corruption. There was only a cursory attempt to link Anderson with the disappearance, and Anderson acted in a high-handed manner towards police investigators. His alibi was never checked out and the police inquiry moved very slowly. Subsequently, Anderson and Saffron fell out, and Anderson tried to extort money from Saffron in return for giving favourable evidence in his trial on tax charges. Two of Anderson's business associates served prison terms for trying to abduct Nielsen on a previous occasion, but there was not enough evidence to connect anyone directly with her disappearance. Her killers have never been punished.

In order to break down the dominance of the CIB culture within the police service (renamed as such in 1987, after a merger between the police force and the police department), the CIB itself was disbanded in 1987 and absorbed within four geographical police regions. Instead of eradicating the corrupt culture within the CIB, this merely spread it further afield.

In the late 1970s and 1980s, a 'barbecue set' of senior police officers, mostly from the CIB, appeared to dominate the police service, immune from any internal investigations. Over time, the more senior members of the CIB had acted as mentors and role models to younger police, so the cycle of corruption was perpetuated, unchecked by internal investigation. One member of the elite CIB group was Detective Sergeant Roger Rogerson, who shot drug dealer Warren Lanfranchi in Chippendale in 1981, apparently while trying to arrest him. Although a jury declined to say that Rogerson shot Lanfranchi in self-defence, the matter never went any further. A series of of gangland murders in Sydney in 1984 and 1985 claimed the lives of many drug dealers and organised crime figures. Rogerson was eventually dismissed from the police force in 1986, and convicted on a charge of conspiring to pervert the course of justice.

As is often the case, some of the criminals who were part of the culture of organised crime have fallen out with each other. Leading crime figure Neddy Smith has testified in his own murder trial that he made hundreds of thousands of dollars selling heroin and running illegal betting operations while his activities were protected by Rogerson and others. Perhaps most disturbing of all, the Joint Task Force (JTF) between federal and state police, set up to deal with serious drug trafficking, had within its own ranks police officers who were heavily involved in the drug trade. The JTF was wound up in 1988.

In May 1994, the Wood Royal Commission was established to examine the nature and extent of police corruption following allegations made by an independent state parliamentarian, John Hatton. The range of the commission was extended later that year when allegations of corrupt dealings between police and paedophile networks were made under parliamentary privilege. The commission undertook extensive undercover work in pursuit of corrupt police officers. Many Sydneysiders will never forget the sight on television of wads of money being handed over from one corrupt police officer to another, filmed on a 'crotch cam' secretly installed on the dashboard of a police vehicle. One of the policemen filmed was Trevor Haken, who testified before the commission of police involvement in the drug trade and sex industry in Kings Cross.

The latter stages of the commission focused on the issue of whether there was police protection of paedophile rackets. One parliamentarian, Franca Arena, did not think the commission was trying hard enough to bring paedophiles to justice. She took matters into her own hands by revealing the names of suspected paedophiles under parliamentary privilege in 1996. One of those named by Arena, a retired Supreme Court judge, committed suicide shortly afterwards. The next year, Arena's allegations became even more febrile. She alleged that the premier, the leader of the opposition and Justice Wood were involved in the cover-up. Arena did not stand by her allegations at an inquiry established to find if there was any substance to them.

Justice Wood found that there was a consistent course of police misconduct endemic within the culture of the police service. Police took bribes, lied on oath, fabricated evidence, misappropriated and resold seized drugs, 'fitted up' people with drugs and later arrested them, fixed cases, took drugs and drank on the job. They also shared hundred of thousands of dollars of money earned in the drug trade. A police vocabulary of euphemisms and slang was brought to light during the royal commission, which will be remembered for many years to come. The 'laugh' was corrupt moneys received to be shared among police colleagues. The 'joke' was the way the money was handed around between policemen. A 'gorilla' was a bribe of $1000. A 'scrumdown' was a meeting between policemen to get their (false) evidence straight. Accused criminals were able to bribe the police to 'gut' prosecution briefs of important documents and information.

The main recommendations of Justice Wood were that criminal prosecutions be taken out of police hands and become the responsibility of the director of public prosecutions; that the government consider the legalisation of licensed 'shooting galleries' for drug addicts; and that public awareness of the drug problem and available drug rehabilitation therapies be raised through advertisements. On the critical issue of police-force structure, Wood recommended a general flattening out of the hierarchy. Promotions should not be based only on seniority, but on merit as well. Wood also recommended that the police should work in multidisciplinary teams and be employed contractually for a certain term.

The Police Integrity Commission, similar in structure to the royal commission itself, has been established to detect, investigate and deal with allegations of corruption and police misconduct. Other persons and bodies with a supervisory role to play are the ombudsman, the Independent Commission Against Corruption and the New South Wales Crimes Commission, with a specific role of combating drug trafficking. One response to the findings of the royal commission was the recruitment of an outsider as police commissioner, Englishman Peter Ryan, who would be able to evaluate and run the police service with fresh, unprejudiced eyes.

As an outsider, he has had to endure an unconscionable level of criticism. The fact that he, as an Englishman, is in charge of the New South Wales police service has teased out all the anxieties that usually lie well beneath the surface of Australia's once colonial relationship with Britain. Ryan has championed discussion of controlled legalisation of heroin, but not enough have followed this brave move.

The Cross seems to have been cleaned up to a certain extent. The owners of local strip joints, some of whom have been dubbed the 'Kings of Sleaze', can no longer flout the law with impunity, and some of them have paid heavy fines. The law has also caught up with many of the key figures in the drug trade. There are reports that the drug trade has simply moved elsewhere, to Cabramatta (where the heroin is often purer), Campbelltown and Bondi, and started to drift back to Kings Cross. Wood's recommendation to promote an elevation in the standards and ethics of police conduct by setting professional standards internally seems altruistic in the light of what is now known about police corruption in the past. The highly structured, adversarial, long chain of command system has not, however, worked either.

Kings Cross is not, however, just a seedy dive. There are glimpses of its old cosmopolitan and bohemian years. There are quiet enclaves and handsome tree-lined streets with fine Victorian and Art Deco architecture and good restaurants. Some of these are Victoria and Kellett streets, the northern end of Macleay Street and along Challis Avenue.

Potts Point was named after an early landowner in the area, James Potts, who bought half of Wylde's 11 acres (4.5 hectares) of land. Potts was the first employee of the Bank of New South Wales. He lived at the bank in Macquarie Place and never occupied the land he had acquired. He became insolvent, like so many others, in the 1840s. Only a decade earlier, the land had been in its original state and occupied by Aborigines. The authoritarian Governor Darling moved the Aborigines on at the time of the land grants in 1831. Many of the houses built from this time have since been demolished, such as Goderich House (designed by John Verge), which stood on the site of today's Hampton Court Hotel in Bayswater Road. Commissary General James Laidley built Rosebank, near tiny Rosebank Street. Politician Sir Stuart Alexander Donaldson built Kellett House near Bayswater Road. Surveyor Sir Thomas Mitchell lived on the other side of Kings Cross Road at Craigend, on land granted to him in 1828. He lived there for several years before moving further east and building Carthona at Darling Point.

Craigend was a grand villa with a Doric colonnade and a tessellated pavement modelled on the Roman ruins at Herculaneum. It stood on 10 acres (4 hectares), with gardens, vineyards and an orchard, close to present-day Craigend Street, above the Kings Cross Tunnel.[9] Mitchell was a perfectionist home builder. When he was unable to find any stonemasons with sufficient talent to carve the columns of the house, he did it himself.

One of the earliest and most celebrated early inhabitants of the Kings Cross area was Alexander Macleay, the Colonial Secretary after whom Macleay Street was named. He arrived in the colony in 1826. Macleay was a keen scientist and fellow of the Linnean and Royal societies. He was particularly interested in entomology and ornithology, and had before his arrival in Sydney been developing a very impressive collection of entomological and other specimens. This collection was later added to by his son William, and formed the nucleus for the Macleay Museum at Sydney University. Macleay also took on many other official roles, and it was Macleay who promoted the creation of the Australian Museum in College Street, as well as the Public Library and the Botanic Gardens.

Macleay's popularity declined with Governor Darling's, and both were criticised for their high-handedness. They were members of the class of exclusives, whose instincts towards convicts and emancipists were never populist or democratic. Macleay objected to moves to permit emancipists to sit on juries and assisted Darling in his unsuccessful attempt to impose press censorship. Macleay was adroit at looking after his own interests. He was given (or gave himself) many good and extensive land grants all around the state, and thus greatly profited from his position. His exclusivist tendencies drew him into head-to-head combat with Darling's successor, Governor Richard Bourke, and he was forced to resign as Colonial Secretary in 1837 in very acrimonious circumstances. That same year, he moved into the newly completed Elizabeth Bay House, designed by John Verge. The house stood on a grant of 54 acres (22 hectares), which was generous even by the standards of the day. The extensive landscaped gardens ran down to the harbour. Macleay was appointed as speaker to the first (partially) elected Legislative Council in 1843, much to the annoyance of his arch political enemy, W. C. Wentworth.

Macleay found it hard to survive without his £2000 annual stipend as Colonial Secretary and, by 1839, he was almost insolvent. Elizabeth Bay House had cost £10 000. The family's finances were reorganised by his son William Macleay along more frugal lines. Expenditure on the exterior of the building was halted and large amounts of the estate were sold off, as was his large library.

Through marriage, the house passed into the hands of the Macarthur Onslow family, and it was occupied by them until 1903. After that it became a boarding house and even briefly, in the 1920s, a nightclub. Well-known lodgers in the house included artists William Dobell and Donald Friend. The house is now administered by the Historic Houses Trust and is open to the public. It is the finest piece of Regency architecture left in Sydney; the oval-shaped stair-case is one of the city's great architectural jewels. The land around Elizabeth Bay House has been densely built up, particularly during the flat-building booms of the 1930s and 1960s.

Other Regency-style houses built by John Verge are sprinkled around Potts Point. Two of these are Rockwall and Tusculum. When they were built, their grounds spilled down to the eastern shore of Woolloomooloo Bay. Tusculum was built by Verge on a 9-acre (3.6-hectare) block for Alexander Spark, a merchant, woolbroker and shipowner. This was only one of his houses—Spark's favourite was Tempe on the Cooks River, after which the suburb was named. Spark was another victim of the recession of the 1840s.

Tusculum was later lived in by Bishop Broughton, and later still was used as a hospital. During World War II, it was a base for the Red Cross. It is now the offices of the Royal Australian Institute of Architects and is rented out for exhibitions and fairs. Next door, Judge

Stephen's Orwell stood on 11 acres (4.5 hectares) of land. The house itself stood where the Metro (formerly Minerva Theatre) once stood. The Metro is occupied by Kennedy Miller films. Rockwall in Rockwall Crescent has recently been restored. It was originally built for surveyor John Busby, the man in charge of connecting the water supply from Lachlan Swamp in Centennial Park to the town of Sydney. The old house is now occupied by the Landmark Hotel and used as meeting rooms.

By the 1860s, the subdivision of the earlier estates around Kings Cross and Potts Point was well under way. Ithaca Road and Billyard Avenue were built after the subdivision of the grounds of Elizabeth Bay House, and large homes were also built on Elizabeth Bay Road. Tresco, once the official residence of the admiral of the Royal Australian Navy, at the northern end of Elizabeth Bay Road, was built and lived in by architect Thomas Rowe from 1868. Italian stonemasons who had worked for the Joubert brothers in Hunters Hill were employed on the job. This house has recently been sold by the Department of Defence. Other large houses at the end of Elizabeth Bay Road were Toft Monks and Kincoppal, which was built by John Hughes. Toft Monks, built in the 1890s, was demolished to make way for apartments, but Kincoppal still stands with much diminished grounds as part of a substantial luxury apartment development of the late 1970s.

363

One grand old house of the nineteenth century was Marramanah, which stood on the southeastern corner of the Macleay Elizabeth estate. Now the El Alamein Fountain occupies this site, sporadically sending out sharp sprays of water which can be drenching in windy weather. Robin Eakin wrote a witty account of life in Marramanah in the 1940s in *Aunts up the Cross*.

The late nineteenth century was the era of the terrace house, and some of the grandest in Sydney were built in Potts Point and around Elizabeth Bay. One of the more impressive rows of terraces is still standing in Roslyn Street. For many years, they looked almost derelict and unloved, and were used as boarding houses like so many other big houses in the area. In the nineteenth century, the large terraces in Victoria and Macleay streets were popular addresses for the Jewish community, as the Grand Synagogue in Elizabeth Street was within walking distance.

The next big growth period transformed the area completely. In 1920, some parts of Elizabeth Bay were still sparsely built-up. The area around Billyard Avenue remained covered with bushland. Ten years later, the water's edge had been developed, most notably by the Del Rio Apartments and Sydney's greatest Hollywood Spanish fantasy, Boomerang. Large, red-brick blocks of flats provided mansion-flat and other cheaper accommodation. There were more mansion flats built in Potts Point and Elizabeth Bay than in any other part of Sydney. Some examples of these are Macleay Regis in Macleay Street, Beverly Hall in Elizabeth Bay Road and Kingsclere on the corner of Macleay Street and Greenknowe Avenue. After-hours activity soon followed this denser development. In 1929, the first restaurant in the area opened its doors. The American-owned California at the top of William Street introduced the triple-decker sandwich to Sydney. The Arabian Café and others followed throughout the 1930s.

The ambience of Potts Point and Kings Cross evolved from the 1920s onwards. Non–English-speaking Europeans, many fleeing the political situation in Europe in the 1930s, were attracted to the low rents, and undeterred by the anonymity and scale of high-density living. They opened delicatessens and fruit shops. The area had a freer and more tolerant air than the rest of Sydney of the 1920s, 1930s and 1940s, when there were few people whose native tongue was not English. The foreigners made the place appear very exotic to Sydneysiders living elsewhere. The Cross became even busier during the war, when US and British forces visited the city.

By the 1940s, many artists living and working in Sydney were attracted to Kings Cross and Potts Point and the nightlife in the bars, coffee shops and restaurants. Artists Donald Friend, William Dobell, John Olsen, Sali Herman and publisher Sydney Ure Smith all lived at the Cross in the mid-twentieth century. Ure Smith had been a leading influence in the dissemination of Australian art to a wider audience with the publication in the 1920s and early 1930s of *Art in Australia*, which featured high-quality photographic reproductions of art of the day. He lived there with his mistress in the 1940s, at a time when doing such things was not a common event. As well as being a publisher, Ure Smith owned an advertising agency, based in the city, where artists Lloyd Rees, Adrian Feint and Roland Wakelin worked at various times.

Another writer and art critic who lived in Potts Point at Victoria Street was Mervyn Horton, a leading writer and later editor of *Art and Australia*, which was published by Ure Smith's son, Sam, from the 1950s.[10] Still another, rather notorious resident of the Cross was Rosaleen Norton, a self-professed witch and artist who operated a coffee shop which she decorated with her own mystically inspired and highly coloured, garish artworks. For Sydneysiders used to the more homogeneous bungalow-covered suburbs, the Kings Cross area had an allure and glamour that was hard to find anywhere else.

In the 1950s and early 1960s, the seamier side of the Cross remained behind closed doors, while outside in the street, the building boom which was to make the area one of the most densely populated in Australia gathered pace. Many of the gracious old homes used as boarding houses were ripe for demolition in the following decades. Casualties were Springfield House, Goderich House and, on the site where the Landmark (formerly the Chevron) was built, a row of ornate terraces called the 'Himalayas'.[11] The building boom of the 1960s created an even bigger transient population than that of the 1930s. The old cafés gradually gave way to milk bars and most of the old theatres and cinemas closed. Retailing was getting bigger, too—Woolworths was built on the site of an old theatre.

From the middle of the 1960s, the Cross was once again the Sydney base for US servicemen on rest and recreation, or 'R&R', leave. Judging from the tone of the new businesses, such as striptease nightclubs, recreation was a higher priority than rest was. This time there was a new enemy the Cross had to face: illegal drugs. The Wayside Chapel, set up by Ted Noffs in 1964, has been offering drug counselling since 1967—obviously a response to a real need which has steadily and sadly worsened.

ATTEMPTED ESCAPE OF PRISONERS FROM DARLINGHURST GAOL.—[SEE PAGE 3.]

ABOVE: An illustration of an attempted prison breakout at Darlinghurst Gaol from *The Illustrated Sydney News* (1884).

William Street is a huge thoroughfare to the eastern suburbs, which follows the track the Aborigines used in the early years of the colony to access the town from the east.[12] These days it is noisy, congested and less than charming. Working girls and transvestites stoically ply their trade on even the coldest, windy winter nights.

William Street was, until the late nineteenth century, a narrow track to the eastern harbour-side suburbs. It was first graded in the 1830s to provide access to the city from the new villas being built at Potts Point and Elizabeth Bay. Its proximity to the increasingly working-class suburbs of Woolloomooloo and Darlinghurst meant that terrace houses lined the street from the 1850s. Boarding houses and pawn shops abounded. The most imposing of the blocks was Burdekin Square, built by the Burdekin family. Burdekin Square ran between Palmer and Crown streets on the southern side of William Street.

By the end of the 1870s, the social and ethnic mix had changed. Small businesses were based there, catering to the carriage trade in Potts Point and further east. William Street was a popular business address for the Jewish pawnbrokers[13] and Italians and Chinese people who ran fruit shops.[14] Launderers, tailors and dressmakers also worked there. The biggest

change to the street occurred in the early twentieth century when the street was widened following the recommendations of the 1909 Royal Commission into the Improvement of Sydney. Every building on the southern side was resumed in 1916 and razed, and the street widened from 40 to 100 feet (12 to 30 metres). The close-knit community that had lived or worked on William Street for decades dispersed. Some of the residents relocated to nearby accommodation in Woolloomooloo and Darlinghurst. New pubs sprang up behind where the old ones had been.

From the 1920s until the present day, William Street has been a centre for the trade in motor cars, particularly, these days, prestige cars. In the 1920s, automotive repair shops and garages sprang up to service this quite new activity in the backstreets of Darlinghurst and Woolloomooloo. The value of the property has risen so that these old garages are now uneconomical. Fashionable restaurants occupy many of these old workshops.

The development boom of the second half of this century affected William Street more quickly and comprehensively than Darlinghurst and Woolloomooloo. William Street was marked out as a high-rise boulevard in the 1960s. Developers such as Westfield were much wiser in selecting William Street than Sid Londish was in identifying Woolloomooloo as a redevelopment zone. From about the time the Kings Cross Tunnel was completed in the early 1970s, the traffic on William Street increased even more. Deprived of passing trade, small businesses were driven away. At the top of William Street, the new high-rise Elan apartment

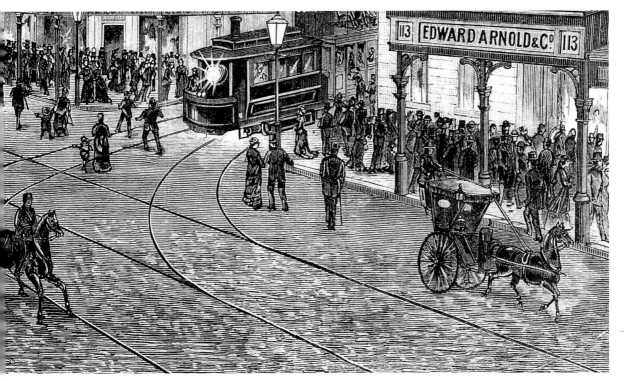

113 EDWARD ARNOLD & Cº 113

ABOVE: An engraving of Saturday night on Oxford Street in the late nineteenth century.

building developed by Sid Londish towers over the Kings Cross Tunnel. It is a much less notable work of architecture than Harry Seidler's Horizon, and it is sad that the top of William Street will long be dominated by this and the nearby Millennium Hotel with the famous Coca-Cola® sign.

Darlinghurst is a mecca for gourmets and coffee drinkers, but it was not always so. Victoria Street has been beautified and landscaped in recent years and the area has lost a lot of its grimier ill-kempt characteristics. New cafés, restaurants and small hotels have sprung up to cater for the new inner-city clientele and the area has a fashionable, design-conscious air, unaffected by self-consciousness or frippery.

Darlinghurst was well wooded in 1788. 'Hurst' is an old English word for 'wooded hill'. The first water mill in the colony was built at Darlinghurst by Thomas West, on the site now occupied by the old Darlinghurst Gaol. He named his property Barcom Glen.

By 1820, the George Street Gaol had become increasingly overcrowded. Even the miserly commissioner, Thomas Bigge, could see how badly a new gaol was needed. Darlinghurst was chosen as the site for it. Its prominent position on the escarpment between Woolloomooloo Bay and South Head Road (Oxford Street) would be a constant reminder of the consequences of law-breaking. Francis Greenway, who pegged the site, was also attracted to the ready supply of sandstone for building in Forbes Street, now the site of the Horizon. The outer wall was built by convicts between 1822 and 1824 under Greenway's supervision. Along Darlinghurst Road is 'the Wall' where male prostitutes, often frighteningly young, ply their trade.

Many of the stones on the wall at Darlinghurst have numbers engraved upon them. Each convict was assigned a number so that his productivity could be observed scrupulously.[15] Greenway's services were dispensed with after the exterior was built. The task of designing the interior of the gaol was left to the Colonial Architect Mortimer Lewis, who also designed the Darlinghurst courthouse. Lewis used the Philadelphia penitentiary, then a modern work, as his architectural model.

The core of the design was the central roundhouse (which was the chapel and is now the library). The cell blocks radiated out from this. Administrative buildings were placed on the periphery. The most significant of these buildings was the governor's residence, close by the Forbes Street entrance to the complex. The first two cell blocks were finished in 1840. One was for male, and the other for female prisoners. The old women's block is now the Cell Block Theatre. The ominous gallows stood near the corner of Darlinghurst Road and Burton Street. The gaol was closed in 1912 when the new Long Bay Gaol was completed. It was opened again during World War I when German enemy aliens were detained there. After the war, the gaol was converted into East Sydney Technical College, and it has been used by various public educational institutions since then.

When the gaol was finished, the prisoners from George Street marched along to their new compound watched by a crowd of jeering citizens. In the nineteenth century, hangings were well-attended events. In October 1841, Robert Hudson and George Stroud, two convicted murderers, were the first men publicly hanged, in front of about 600 people. Three years later, thousands of people turned out to watch the hanging of John Knatchbull, a distant relation of Lord Mountbatten, who had brutally murdered his landlady in her boarding house at Margaret Street.

By the 1860s, Darlinghurst, despite the presence of the gaol, was the address of many of the city's successful doctors, lawyers and businessmen. They, like today's residents, wanted to be close to the city, but in those days, they also appreciated the tranquillity. When the exodus to the outer suburbs increased in the late nineteenth century, many of the old houses fell into disrepair. In Darley Street, there is an interesting grouping of old nineteenth-century mansions in various architectural styles. Around the corner in Liverpool Street is a large row of late–nineteenth-century terraces. One of the earliest houses to remain in the area is Barham (1833), contained within the grounds of the Sydney Church of England Girls Grammar School in Forbes Street. It was designed by John Verge and built by Alexander Macleay's successor as Colonial Secretary, Edward Deas Thomson, after whom nearby Thomson Street is named. At the time it was built, it had wide views to the town of Sydney that lay to the west and Woolloomooloo Bay to the north.

The eastern valley of Darlinghurst that runs down to Rushcutters Bay was called the Valley of Lacrozia in the early nineteenth century. Most of the land east of the ridge was subdivided

ABOVE: Oxford Street on the corner of Liverpool Street. c. 1908.

369

and built up during the building boom of the 1880s. Until then, it was still part of the old Barcom Glen estate. As late as 1882:

> [It] had the appearance of a dark and dense forest, immense mahogany trees, blackbutt, and other of the eucalyptus species growing in great profusion, while in the glen leading up to the house a large number of cabbage trees used to grow ... [the swamp which is now part of Weigall and Rushcutters Bay Park] was a Slough of Despond, and could not be crossed. It swarmed with aquatic birds of every description.[16]

One cluster of interesting street life is along Victoria Street. The other is down in the valley around Crown and Stanley streets. The development of the Italian atmosphere in Darlinghurst has been evolving since Italian migrants first lived in the plentiful boarding houses and other cheap rental accommodation close to Woolloomooloo wharf, where many of them disembarked for the first time in their new country and later based their fishing activities.

The Stanley Street cafés and restaurants mostly concentrate on Italian food and snacks, whereas in Victoria Street there is a more diverse mixture of cafés and restaurants. Cuisines of many different nationalities are available, from Italian to Chinese, to Thai and even Turkish. Both these areas have developed since the mid-1970s from a nucleus of one or two small coffee shops and cheap restaurants. The earliest coffee shop in Victoria Street was the Bar Coluzzi, run by Roman-born Luigi Coluzzi, a boxer who beat the Australian middleweight champion in 1955. At his after-fight party, he met his wife Eleanor, a Romanian-born Greek, fell in love and stayed in Australia.

Coluzzi retired from boxing at Eleanor's suggestion and opened a coffee shop in William Street. He had experience working in a café in Rome as a small boy. The William Street café ran successfully until 1970, when the traffic patterns changed with the opening of the Kings Cross Tunnel. Coluzzi and his family moved the business around to 322 Victoria Street at a time when there was only one other coffee shop, which was run by a Hungarian. This is still one of East Sydney's great institutions for coffee drinkers, particularly in the early mornings. There is an enormous photo gallery of Coluzzi's patrons, both famous and infamous. The Bar Coluzzi is where Sydneysiders of every description can be seen, usually at the same time. Bar Coluzzi is now run by the next generation of Coluzzis, and Luigi Coluzzi now only works there on weekends. Since the café opened in Victoria Street, many other coffee shops and restaurants have followed.

370

In the 1920s and 1930s, Palmer Street was the headquarters of vice queen Tilly Devine and the infamous Darlinghurst Push, a razor gang which roamed the streets of inner Sydney in that period. Devine lived at number 391, now, ironically, renamed Bonne Femme restaurant, run and operated by leading chef Genevieve Copeland. Nearby, on the corner of Liverpool Street, stood the old Tradesmen's Arms Hotel, one of the more infamous bloodhouses of the era, patronised by many unsavoury characters and the site of many bloody fist fights. It has been renamed East Village. As the name implies, it has been relaunched as a smart bar serving the style-conscious residents of Darlinghurst. Like so many other inner-city pubs, these days it specialises in boutique wines and beers.

The development of the Italian quarter based around Stanley Street tells an interesting tale. In the late 1940s, some of the properties in the area were bought by Italians, often by people who already ran small businesses there. The number of Italian businesses boomed throughout the 1950s, and this prosperity has persisted—at the same time as many of the businesses have become much more upmarket in the past twenty years.[17] One of the older trattoria-style restaurants was La Veneziana, which served cheap meals to Italian immigrants. The terrazzo floor still exists on the site of the old restaurant, presently occupied by Restaurant Liago.

Oxford Street is the boundary between Darlinghurst and Surry Hills. Formerly known as South Head Road, it runs east–west, and was one of the city's first roads. In the nineteenth century, it was an important route for the Sunday drive, on horse, carriage, horse-drawn omnibus and, later, by tram. Spectacular views down through bushland to the harbour could be seen all the way to Watsons Bay.

In the early decades of this century, the street was widened between College and Bourke streets, and the City Council resumed much of the land. This is when Taylor Square was built, and named in honour of Lord Mayor Sir Allen Taylor, as well as the Federation Edwardian buildings, many of which the council still owns. These buildings give the Darlinghurst section of Oxford Street its distinctive architectural flavour.

Oxford Street is the centre of Sydney's gay nightlife, and part of the main procession route for the annual Gay and Lesbian Mardi Gras held each February. A huge parade of floats proceed along Liverpool Street, Oxford Street and Flinders Street to the former RAS Showground, where a huge party is held. The Mardi Gras was started in 1978 and its original objective was to protest against the then illegal status of homosexual acts between consenting male adults. The Mardi Gras of today is one of the biggest celebrations of gay culture in the world, and Sydney's most spectacular annual event. Only gays and lesbians are allowed to participate in the parade and tickets to the party at the former RAS Showground at the end of the parade are keenly sought.

By the 1960s, the social and legal repression of homosexuals was starting to ease. Part of the gentrification of the inner-city suburbs was effected by homosexuals, for whom the suburban ideal was anathema.[18] In the early 1970s, bars and nightclubs clearly directed at the homosexual market opened their doors. Beforehand, gay people used to congregate in the then social heart of the city around the old Hotel Australia, the old Carlton and Usher's Hotel. Some cafés in the city itself were also popular. When the demolishers and developers moved into the city, many of these old haunts disappeared. The main focus for gay (and straight) entertainment moved out to Kings Cross and Potts Point. The Bottoms Up bar at the Rex Hotel in Macleay Street was a popular gay bar. One of the earliest gay Sydney institutions in Kings Cross was Les Girls on the corner of Darlinghurst Road and Roslyn Street.

In the late 1960s, rising rents in Kings Cross made starting gay bars there riskier than in the lower-rent areas of Oxford Street and Darlinghurst generally. The drug trade, the straight sex industry and the prying eyes of gawking onlookers in Kings Cross made the area more dangerous for gay men, whose status was still illegal. 'Poofter-bashing' hoodlums were not unusual and terrorised gay men in public parks and dark alleys. Sydney's gay men had to contend with these violent outbursts of homophobia in a city where male, larrikin culture and pugnacity had been a dominant feature of the social geography since 1788.

The first gay bars on Oxford Street were run-down wine bars, which were soon smartened up and renovated. One of these was Enzo's near the Paddington Post Office. The first gay steam bath opened in Oxford Street, Bondi Junction, in 1968, near a gay wine bar called Ivy's. Capriccio's was one of the first gay nightclub–restaurants to open in Oxford Street, Darlinghurst. The popularity of the area grew from there. Well-known Oxford Street gay haunts which opened from the early 1970s included Patch's, the Midnight Shift, Palms and the Tropicana.

Another famous old gay nightclub was Jools in Crown Street, owned by local identity Dawn O'Donnell. This is where the Hard Rock Café is today. The proliferation of gay bars led, in turn, to the arrival of new shops and restaurants directed towards attracting the pink (gay) dollar. Politicians now court the gay vote in this part of the inner city as well.

Gay men in Sydney had to fight for the legalisation of homosexuality as they did in many other parts of the world. Homosexual sex between consenting adults (more than eighteen years of age) was legalised in 1984. The gay political movement was successful at pushing gay issues and gay consciousness into the mainstream—there was even a gay hero in the popular television soap opera 'Number 96', about the lives of people who lived in an inner-city block of flats, which was very radical at the time.

Oxford Street is now such a busy gay precinct that it is almost possible to miss the imposing Darlinghurst courthouse, on the corner of Bourke Street, built by Mortimer Lewis in the Greek Doric style. It was opened in 1842, conveniently close to Darlinghurst Gaol. It is one of Mortimer's most successful works. He designed the pedimented porch. The two wings on either side are later additions.

To the east of the Paddington Town Hall, Oxford Street passes through more residential Paddington. The Paddington Town Hall and the post office opposite are two prime inner-city examples of the grandiose late Victorian 'wedding cake' architectural style. From the Town Hall eastward, the nightlife becomes quieter, although by day the retail trade is very brisk. During the daytime on Saturdays, Oxford Street and the nearby blocks of side streets from Whitlam Square to Centennial Park are at their most interesting. The street life is just as distracting as the shops, if not more so.

Surry Hills lies to the south of Oxford Street. Surry Hills has always had a wide mixture of uses—residential, commercial and industrial—that reflects the unplanned nature of its development in the nineteenth century, although the presence of industrial activity has diminished over the past two decades. Major Foveaux was the first European landowner. He was granted the land now covered by Surry Hills in 1793. Foveaux never lived there, but the land was partially cleared with convict labour and cattle grazed there. When Foveaux left the colony, he sold the land to Commissary General John Palmer, who consolidated this land with the nearby Woolloomooloo estate. When Palmer's economic fortunes declined, he sold his Surry Hills estate in 1814.

Later, elaborate plans were drawn up and great things expected for this suburb, but ultimately business and financial interests proved stronger than planning interests. The suburb was divided into twenty-seven lots by Surveyor General James Meehan, but the streets marked on the survey were never officially proclaimed. Unplanned building works encroached on the streets with the result that many of them were never built.

As well as providing a residential centre close to the city (but still regarded as being out in the bush), Surry Hills provided materials needed for the building trade in the early years of the colony. Even before Foveaux received his land grant, the land had been used as a source of timber, sand, soil, sandstone and clay. This exploitation continued after the area fell into private hands.

In the 1830s, the area had the ambience of a small village. Some of the landowners worked market gardens providing fresh produce to the growing town. One of the suburb's grandest houses is the Colonial Georgian Cleveland House, in Buckingham Street, built by Daniel Cooper in the early 1820s. It is the oldest house standing in Surry Hills. It stood opposite the precursor to the Royal Sydney Showground, the Exhibition Centre in Prince Alfred Park. The house was later used as a rectory for Christ Church St Laurence and later as a girls school. It is now leased commercially.

Another Surry Hills landmark during the early part of the nineteenth century was the Albion Brewery, built on the corner of Albion and Elizabeth streets near Central Railway. This was built by the Terry family, led by patriarch Samuel Terry, leading emancipist, philanthropist and Australian nationalist, also known as the 'Botany Bay Rothschild'. Terry bought three of the original subdivisions of Palmer's estate. In 1826, he dammed a freshwater stream on his property and began building his brewery, which later became the biggest in Sydney. The brewery was later owned by Tooheys. The site was demolished in the 1980s to make way for office towers.

By the end of the 1850s, building activity in Surry Hills, as elsewhere in Sydney, was proceeding at a rapid pace. Working-class dwellings sprang up. Soon there was a mixture of workers' cottages and old colonial gentlemen's residences. Some of the larger residences were around Crown, Bourke and Albion streets. Two of these survive at the top of Albion Street. One was converted into the Italian restaurant Taylor's and the other, Durham Hall (1835) at number 207, is the office of the Royal College of Pathologists. Durham Hall was built on land once owned by Isaac Nichols, Sydney's first postmaster. Durham Hall was built in 1835 by George Hill, a publican who was one of the first aldermen elected to the City Council in 1842. He later became mayor of Sydney.

Mid–nineteenth-century workers' cottages were concentrated on the western side of Surry Hills. In 1850, a large amount of land known as the Cleveland Paddocks, between Devonshire and Cleveland streets, was resumed in preparation for the construction of the Redfern rail terminus. The other section of the old paddocks was set aside for Prince Alfred Park. In 1870, an exhibition building was constructed in the park to contain the first Inter-Colonial Exhibition. After this, it was used by the Royal Agricultural Society.

Work in light industry, especially the clothing industry, was available to the residents of Surry Hills, and clothing factories still operate there today. Between 1871 and 1891, the population of Surry Hills doubled to almost 30 000. With the exception of the construction of the Surry Hills Public School in Bourke Street in the early 1880s, this astounding growth was not accompanied by adequate provision of services and general facilities, and the standard of living continued to decline. At the end of the nineteenth century, charitable institutions began to move in, the signs of which can still be seen today—such as the Salvation Army Building in Foster Street. The public school in Crown Street is another notable architectural landmark and a reminder of the years when the area had a high population of young children.

373

The construction of Central Railway on the site of the Devonshire Street cemetery meant that many roads had to be widened and retail patterns changed. The area around Wexford and Campbell streets, widely known as 'South Sydney Hell', was reclaimed, demolished and rebuilt. Wentworth Avenue runs approximately where Wexford Street used to be. After World War I, huge areas of land were resumed by the government, by then under increasing pressure to clean up the terrible mess that Surry Hills had become. Hundreds of houses were demolished, facilitating even further industrialisation of the area.

Following World War II, the low property values and inexpensive accommodation attracted many of the immigrants escaping from Europe. The chronic housing shortage in Sydney following the war had prompted the City Council to put a stop to industrialisation of the inner-city areas, and large parts of Surry Hills were declared residential zones. Numerous council housing schemes were completed, and while many of the traditional residents of Surry Hills moved out, newly arrived immigrants often replaced them.

Like other parts of the inner city, these new residents were followed by members of the middle classes eager to establish themselves on the home-owning ladder. They were attracted to the delicatessens, cafés and restaurants the immigrants had established. Retail activity is very varied in Surry Hills. It is concentrated in the north–south streets of Elizabeth, Crown, Bourke and South Dowling streets. Some of the large warehouses in South Dowling Street are furniture and antique showrooms; Crown Street has many smaller shops catering to the building and design industries, and several good restaurants, including MG Garage, operating within a former car showroom. Near Oxford Street, there are many clothing shops. The liveliness and range of activities within Surry Hills today reflect its mixed uses in the nineteenth century—industrial, commercial and residential. Much of the manufacturing industry has moved on to cheaper premises (or gone completely), but retail commerce is still going strong. As a residential area, Surry Hills goes from strength to strength.

CHAPTER FIFTEEN

THE EASTERN SUBURBS

SYDNEY'S EASTERN SUBURBS begin at the fringe of the inner-city suburbs, at Paddington and Rushcutters Bay, around the southeastern foreshores of the harbour to Vaucluse and South Head, then down to Bondi, Tamarama and Bronte.[1]

The eastern suburbs include some of the most densely built-up residential areas of Sydney, and this has been a feature of the area since the flat-building boom of the 1920s and 1930s, the beginning of the region's period of greatest population growth. This density has given rise to some of Sydney's more cosmopolitan suburbs. The eastern suburbs have a reputation for affluence which can sometimes be crassly and brashly displayed—just as it can be anywhere else in the world. As with most other stereotyping, this may be true some of the time, but most residents of the eastern suburbs live their lives feeling (smugly) secure that they are living in the best part of the best city in the world.

The eastern suburbs provide a beguilingly wide range of recreational facilities—the harbour, ocean beaches and access to many fine open spaces and some of the city's great cultural and sporting facilities. Added to the area's close proximity to the city and the interesting, sometimes eye-popping variety of many of the various social subcultures Sydney has to offer, eastern suburbanites (this writer included) are probably quite reasonable in asserting their claim.

The geographic diversity is almost as great as the motley nature of the suburbs' inhabitants. The suburbs range from Paddington, one of the biggest and most intact Victorian suburbs anywhere in the world, to leafier and more genteel Woollahra and Edgecliff, down to the shores of the retail mecca of Double Bay, the exclusive residential harbour-side suburbs of Darling Point, Point Piper, Rose Bay and Vaucluse, past elevated Dover Heights which runs along the top of the sandstone cliffs of the coastline to the more densely built-up precincts around Bondi.

Paddington is shaped like an amphitheatre. It extends from the sandstone ridge of Oxford Street down to the shores of Rushcutters Bay. Its charming position and aspect drew prosperous businessmen such as Robert Cooper to the area in the early decades of the nineteenth century. Many built gracious homes along Glenmore Road. Paddington from the mid-nineteenth century was one of the earliest centres of the building boom in terrace housing, and Sydney's first commuter suburb. It was never the site of industry, as so many other suburbs which developed in the nineteenth century were. Paddington was also the first Victorian suburb to be 'gentrified' from the early 1960s.

In the immediate postwar years, rent controls in the form of the *Landlord and Tenant Act* kept the cost of housing low until the mid-1960s. This engendered an environment where artists, architects and small businesses such as art galleries could set up homes, studios, restaurants and galleries at a fraction of the cost of other more established areas.

Old wine bars and speakeasies were converted into restaurants and galleries. Examples of buildings which changed hands (and uses) in the early days of Paddington's revival were the Hungry Horse Restaurant, on the corner of Windsor and Elizabeth streets; the Rudy Komon Gallery, on the corner of Paddington Street and Jersey Road; and the old bakery at 2 Paddington Street. The contemporary uses of these buildings give some idea of the interesting manner in which Paddington has developed in the past forty years.

The Komon Gallery has passed into the hands of another art dealer, Christopher Day, who specialises in art of a more conservative kind. The Hungry Horse, once a haunt of impecunious artists, writers and other bohemians, is now one of Sydney's best Italian restaurants, run by Italian-born Lucio Galletto. Lucio's restaurant now caters to many of the same, rather more prosperous and well-upholstered clientele that the Hungry Horse once did. Galletto has continued the worthy tradition of encouraging his artist patrons by hanging their works on the walls of the restaurant.

The Old Paddington Bakery was used as a brothel during World War II. Later, it was one of the first buildings to be restored in Paddington, and the site of an art school run by John Olsen. Now it is the offices of a leading public relations consultancy.

Oxford Street, once known as South Head Road, was the first road built from the town eastward to South Head. In the early years of the colony, the strategic significance of South Head Road was considerable, as it was the only means of travelling on foot or by horse from the entrance to Sydney Harbour. In 1811, the same year the bush track was to be levelled into a roadway, Governor Macquarie also proclaimed and set the boundary of the Sydney Common. It covered the land where the Victoria Barracks, the Sydney Football Stadium, Sydney Cricket Ground, Moore Park and Centennial Park lie.

Nowadays, Paddington and Woollahra are home to some of Sydney's better fashion boutiques, antique shops and commercial art galleries—although some residents of the lower North Shore may disagree with this proposition. There are also many good pubs and restaurants with a much higher proportion of local patrons than is found closer to the city at The Rocks and Woolloomooloo. Most of all, however, Paddington and Woollahra are two of the best parts of Sydney simply to walk around and enjoy. The best time to do this is on a balmy summer's night while a cool northeasterly wind is still blowing from the harbour, or on a mild, sunny day in autumn, winter or spring.

Oxford Street, Paddington, is one of Sydney's most fashionable retail precincts. In the past decade, mainstream retailers such as Country Road, Esprit and General Pants Co. have moved into premises formerly occupied by smaller businesses. Higher rents have forced many of the smaller (and more unusual) boutiques further afield to other parts of the inner city, such as Surry Hills, Darlinghurst, and King Street, Newtown.

Oxford Street's fortunes have moved in step with Paddington's, and, like Paddington, it went into decline from the depression of the 1890s until the early 1960s. When New South Head Road became the main route to the eastern suburbs, its status as a main road declined as well. In 1970, Oxford Street was a hotchpotch of small retailers, with the many butchers, greengrocers and grocery stores interspersed with traditional cafés and fashion outlets catering to the cheaper and more eccentric ends of the market. Second-hand vintage clothing shops abounded, as they still do in King Street, Newtown.

Oxford Street started to climb out of the doldrums when the Paddington markets, held each Saturday in the grounds of the Uniting Church, opened in the early 1970s. The markets became very popular and this popularity rubbed off onto the whole of Oxford Street. Some of the more successful traders at the markets took the step of renting premises along the street in regular business hours. Gradually the butchers and traditional hot-food bars, old shoe and dress shops and Chinese restaurants closed down, and fashion became a dominant theme of the street. The only butcher left in Oxford Street shares the premises with a greengrocer and bakery outlet. Boutique beers and fine wines predominate where draught beer, port and sherry were once the area's staple alcoholic beverages.

One example of the old Oxford Street was George Warnecke's shop. Warnecke was an old stalwart of Paddington (and sometime Labor alderman). He operated, if that is the right word, a junk shop in Oxford Street until the early 1980s. It was an intriguing institution, made of galvanised iron with flimsy windowpanes and bars. Within the shop, or warehouse, a mind-boggling collection of bric-a-brac and memorabilia languished, or looked like it was languishing. And there it continued to languish, because the shop was hardly ever open for trade. It was hard to work out what was required to induce Mr Warnecke to open his doors. The shop and the building it inhabited have long gone and the site upon which they sat has been redeveloped.

In the process of the commercialisation of Oxford Street, some of its eccentric and bohemian flavour has been lost. Although it is churlish to complain about such progress, as it becomes more mainstream it is also losing some of its distinctiveness. In the past decade, the streetscape has been much improved, as a result of effective lobbying by the local chamber of commerce. The chamber president and other members, such as Warren Fahey, who owned Folkways Records there, and Frank Elgar can take much of the credit for the attractive appearance of the street.

The first house built in Paddington is still its largest. Juniper Hall (1824) was built by the emancipist and distiller Robert Cooper. Cooper was a man of property in London, and owned two public houses. He was convicted in 1812 for receiving stolen goods that included ostrich feathers and silk worth the considerable sum of £3000, and transported to New South Wales. Cooper's uncompelling defence was that he thought the goods were smuggled, rather than stolen. The judge hearing the case was unimpressed with the merits of his argument, and Cooper's death sentence was commuted to transportation for fourteen years. He arrived in Sydney in 1813. By 1815, Cooper had opened a shop in George Street. His commercial activities continued to flourish—he started an auctioneering business and was part-owner of a trading ship.

His largest business was the gin distillery he operated with James Underwood, another early Sydney emancipist magnate. The distillery was one of the only industrial activities ever conducted in Paddington. It was built close to the freshwater supply at the bottom of Cascade Street. The gin, hauled by cattle drays, was carted up the long track leading to South Head Road, and then into the town. The track is now Glenmore Road. This road is one of the few in Paddington to follow the natural gradient of the land. The course of most other roads and streets in the suburb was determined by the form of the original land grants and later subdivisions.

Cooper was also one of early Sydney's most prolific breeders, fathering in total twenty-eight children, with the considerable assistance of his three wives. He named Juniper Hall in honour of the berry used in distilling gin, the source of most of his wealth. Like so many other wealthy people, Cooper ran into financial difficulties in the depression of the 1840s. He mortgaged the house and, by 1852, it was used as an orphanage, then later as a college for young ladies. In the 1870s, Juniper Hall was occupied by property developer John Begg, who built Ormond Street between Glenmore Road and Juniper Hall so that he could have easy access to his developments.

In 1885, Juniper Hall was occupied by the government as a children's court, and, in 1925, it was converted into flats and used as such until it was restored by the National Trust in the 1980s as part of its program for the Bicentenary. For some years, it was open to the public, but it is once again in private hands and is leased to an advertising agency.

Juniper Hall is one of the few examples of Georgian architecture left in Paddington. Like many early houses built in the new colony, it was built to face south as if it were in the northern hemisphere, and thus was not designed so that the larger and more important rooms would catch the northerly sunlight. It took some time for architects and builders to re-orientate their works to suit antipodean conditions. With the cacophony generated by all his children, Cooper designed the house so that by closing two interior doors, the building could be divided into two residences. Juniper Hall, like nearly all Georgian architecture, would have been painted white. On sunny days in the early nineteenth century, the house would have been easily visible from the harbour as it glittered and sparkled atop the crest of the hill—Botany Bay was visible from the southern balcony.

Most of the other mansions and villas built in Paddington before the big subdivisions were along or near Glenmore Road. From that position, they could enjoy the northerly aspect and views, and cooling sea breezes rising from the harbour. There were at least fourteen mansions of ten rooms or more in Paddington in the nineteenth century.[2] Another early one was Engehurst, designed by Sydney's leading architect of the 1830s, John Verge. It is now demolished, but a fragment of it remains incorporated into the block of flats at 56 Ormond Street. Engehurst was built by Frederick Augustus Heely, a one-time superintendent of convicts. It stood on 7 acres (2.8 hectares) of land. The foundation stone was laid in 1834.

The Foy retailing family lived in the house on the corner of Liverpool Street and Glenmore Road. Another early mansion has long been the nucleus of the Scottish Hospital on the corner of Brown and Cooper streets. It was built by John Kinchella (a previous tenant of Juniper Hall) in the 1840s. A significant portion of the original grounds still exist to the north. These grounds give an interesting glimpse of what much of the lower areas of Paddington would have looked like before 1788. There are fine examples of New South Wales rainforest species such as Moreton Bay figs, cabbage trees and bangalow palms. The last of the Paddington mansions to be built was Olive Villa (1869), built by the Begg family. It is in Heeley Street, and is occupied by a kindergarten.

379

The early development of Paddington was closely linked with the construction of Victoria Barracks, selected for its then remoteness from the town. Governor Bourke set aside 30 acres (12 hectares) of the Sydney Common to provide space for the barracks, which are the largest concentration of early–nineteenth-century architecture in Australia. A small cluster of cottages on the other side of South Head Road appeared. At first, they were occupied by the stonemasons and other tradesmen engaged in the construction of the barracks, then later by the soldiers' families and by small businesses which soon followed the army out to its new headquarters. Some of these early houses can still be seen in Liverpool, Gipps, Prospect, Shadforth and Spring streets, near the junction of Glenmore Road and Oxford Street.

Victoria Barracks were built between 1841 and 1848. The project took much longer to complete than expected. The area was a semi-barren combination of sandhills, rocky outcrops and swamps, as was most of the Sydney Common. The problem of building a large stone barracks on shifting sandhills was not fully appreciated when the site was selected. The barracks were designed by George Barney, a royal engineer who had been appointed as Sydney's Colonial Engineer in 1836. Barney went on to to become commissioner of Crown lands in 1849 and chief surveyor of Sydney in 1855.

Some of the skilled stonemasons who built the barracks were Quebecois political prisoners, transported from Canada as punishment for their aborted insurrection in 1836. One of the architectural innovations Barney adopted was to use the cast-iron columns as downpipes from the roof. This economy of use reinforces the stark simplicity of the main barracks building. The run-off water was stored in a large, underground tank.

The main building in the barracks is 740 feet (225 metres) long and two storeys high. It housed up to 700 soldiers. The officers' mess stands on the eastern end of the site. Australian soldiers have occupied the barracks since 1871, the year the British garrison left the colony. Within the barracks is a museum of army memorabilia. Just outside Victoria Barracks is an outlet for Busby's Bore. For many years, this was the only source of fresh water in Paddington. The water travelled underground from Lachlan Swamp along Moore Park, then up to the barracks. Victoria Barracks is now the administrative headquarters of the Australian Army's Eastern Command in New South Wales.

Other early (1840s) examples of workers' houses in the Paddington area can be seen on the corner of Underwood and Union streets. In those days, workers' houses were often built in sandstone, and the houses for the middle classes built of brick and stucco.

James Underwood's estate was subdivided after he became insolvent in 1860. The estate extended from Jersey Road in the east to Cascade Street in the west, and from Oxford Street down to the shores of Rushcutters Bay. Paddington's main streets lie on the old estate— Underwood, Paddington, Windsor, Hargrave and Sutherland streets. This is the best laid-out and prettiest part of Paddington.

380

By 1863, three years after Paddington had been incorporated as a municipality, there were 535 houses in the area.[3] Most of these were simple cottages or small terraces with two rooms upstairs and two rooms downstairs. From the 1870s onwards, Paddington started to become the densely built, nineteenth-century suburb it happily still is. The remarkable rate of growth is best illustrated in the statistics: in 1873, there were 864 houses; in 1883, there were 2350; and, in 1893, 3800.

In the late nineteenth century, Paddington would have been a noisy, sometimes chaotic and muddy construction zone. Speculation was a popular economic pastime. Newly subdivided blocks of land changed hands at ever-increasing prices. Speculator owner–builders built one terrace, moved in, then built one next door, sold it or rented it out, and built another. This accounts for the more eclectic range of styles and architectural detail in the area. There are not many rows of terraces of more than ten houses in Paddington. There was no dominant developer who built entire streets or blocks in the same uniform architectural style, as was sometimes the case in London—a good example of this being the Grosvenor family who owned, built and still own much of the City of Westminster. Large-scale development was an indulgence far beyond the means of the small-scale owner–builders in the Paddington of the 1870s and 1880s. Yet, in the 1880s, four out of five tenants had landlords living in Paddington.[4] It was not until the 1890s, when the small 'spec' builders were squeezed out of the area when they were forced to liquidate their land-holdings in the harsh economic circumstances of the era. From then until the mid-twentieth century, absentee landlords became the norm in Paddington. As the more affluent tenants departed to more sylvan suburbs, land ownership became more concentrated in the hands of absentee landlords. They maximised their returns on the property by using the obvious device of restricting the amount of money they spent on repairs, and so the period of decay set in.

One of the larger-scale developers in Paddington was the Begg family, who built and lived in Olive Villa (1869). By 1876, the family owned 10 acres (4 hectares) in the Paddington area. They bought the distillery business from James Underwood and converted it into a tannery. The Begg family, however, did not aim to hold onto the property in the long term, but subdivided land and sold the vacant smaller blocks to speculators. The family ran into financial difficulties in the 1890s and was forced to sell its land-holdings.

Two of the later subdivisions of Paddington were the Duxford estate, owned by John Gurner and subdivided in 1885, and James Broughton's estate, which lay between Broughton, Union and Duxford streets. The latter was not subdivided until 1898. The scale of the houses built in Paddington from 1875 reflects the tastes of the more affluent lower middle classes and their preference for the Victorian Italianate style. Older terraces built before the late 1880s usually had arched windows and doorways.

One of Paddington's key advantages was that it was possible to commute to town by public transport. This was first in the form of the horse-drawn omnibus of the 1870s; the trip to town at that time took thirty minutes. The following decade, the development of the tram network shortened this ride even further, but it also laid the groundwork for the suburb's later social and economic deterioration. More affluent people could live even further east, in beachside suburbs such as Waverley, Coogee and Randwick. By 1922, Paddington was on three tram routes: one along Oxford Street going to Bondi, Waverley and Coogee; one along Glenmore Road which terminated at North Bondi, and the third along New South Head Road to Watsons Bay.

Indicators of Paddington's boom-time civic pride and high Victorian optimism are the Paddington Town Hall (built in 1890), the Post Office (1885) and Paddington Courthouse and Police Station (1888), designed by Colonial Architect James Barnet. Paddington Town Hall is still one of the most prominent landmarks on the horizon in the area. Its foundation stone was laid by Sir Henry Parkes. The 32-metre tower was built later and still dominates the horizon from the harbour.

By the 1940s, Paddington had become an overpopulated slum. The County of Cumberland Plan of 1948 declared that the whole area was substandard and needed total demolition. Thankfully, many southern Europeans chose Paddington as a place to set up home after their arrival in Sydney. Property was affordable, they were used to living in densely built environments and the trip to the city was short. Like other parts of the inner city, many bought or set up corner shops and other small businesses, and this gave the place a livelier, more interesting ambience. Paddington became attractive to other home buyers. Rudy Komon started the first large commercial gallery in Sydney in the early 1960s. Restaurants such as the Hungry Horse opened their doors, and artists and other people were drawn into the area. Bookshops and art schools soon followed.

Paddington is home to many of Sydney's best commercial art galleries. The Australian Galleries in Royston Street, the Ros Oxley Gallery in nearby Soudan Lane, the Sherman Goodhope Gallery in Goodhope Street and the Olsen Carr Gallery, just behind Lucio's restaurant, are all fine examples.

381

The best time to walk around Paddington is on Saturday when the area is busiest and the street life most interesting. More energetic walkers can take a stroll through time, starting near the Victoria Barracks, walking down Glenmore Road to Five Ways (a busy intersection and a village within Paddington itself) and along Gurner Street, up Cascade Street into Paddington Street and Jersey Road, and the other pretty streets that were once part of the Underwood estate.

Those with less energy, or time to spend, could explore either the small streets around Victoria Barracks and the top of Glenmore Road to see what the oldest part of Paddington looks like today, or the Woollahra end of Paddington between Jersey Road and Cascade Street. On the eastern side of Jersey Road near Oxford Street is a row of fine nineteenth-century mansions. There are many old pubs in this part of Paddington that are fashionable today: the Four in Hand in Sutherland Street, the Windsor Castle opposite Lucio's restaurant, the Grand National in Underwood Street, and the Bellevue in Hargrave Street.

382

The suburbs that lie to the east of Paddington—Darling Point, Woollahra and Bellevue Hill— were first settled from the 1830s, mostly by the well-to-do, many of whom built mansions with harbour views. Originally, the land was densely wooded, so land clearing was an early priority, as it was in many other parts of Sydney. New South Head Road was built in 1831 as far as Darling Point, then later extended to Double and Rose bays. Before New South Head Road was built, access to the eastern suburbs was by South Head Road, then Point Piper (now Jersey) Road.

The 'outer' eastern suburbs, unlike Paddington, were not affected by the building and population booms of the late nineteenth century, but they were not so immune to the building boom of the 1920s and early 1930s. Red-bricked bungalows and blocks of flats were often the result. The old estates were subdivided from 1900 onwards. These estates are too numerous to mention, but include the Mona estate between Mona and Darling Point roads, and many old estates along and near Edgecliff Road, including Merioola, Wallaroy, Quambi, Karoola and Hawthorndene.

Further east again, the remains of Daniel Cooper's land-holding, grandly titled the Belgravia estate, and other larger land-holdings at Point Piper were sold off in the same period. The land near the Belgravia estate, which is now Woollahra Park and Golf Course, was largely occupied by Chinese market gardens until the subdivision. The power of the Woollahra Council to resume this land was greatly assisted with the passage of the *Local Government Act* in 1919, which gave councils power to resume land in aid of beautification schemes.[5]

The eastern suburbs have seen many changes brought about by the postwar building boom, mostly in the form of houses built on land subdivided from larger estates, and higher-rise apartments that can be seen above the skyline along Darling Point and Edgecliff. The state government's policy of encouraging denser development in built-up areas is now affecting,

ABOVE: Aerial view Point Piper c. 1930, just before the demolition of Woollahra House.

and will continue to affect, the eastern suburbs. Although the population of the area is relatively static, redevelopments are driven by an ageing population in the area, and the diminishing average number of people in each household. The eastern suburbs may, in the coming years, witness and experience huge growth in the amount of medium- to high-density housing that will change its character, just as the building booms of the 1920s, 1960s and 1970s did.

The story of the development of the eastern suburbs would have been a much duller affair if Captain John Piper, after whom Point Piper was named, had never lived there. Piper arrived in Sydney as an ensign in the New South Wales Corps in 1792. By 1800, he had been promoted to the rank of captain. After serving on Norfolk Island, he returned to Sydney in 1811 and one year later resigned his commission. Piper became the naval officer for the colony, a position which included collecting customs. He received a generous 5 per cent commission on all customs duties levied by him. Soon Piper and his wife Mary Ann, a convict's daughter, prospered. Piper bought the 475-acre (200-hectare) estate from Henry Browne Hayes, where Vaucluse House now is, and, in 1816, he was granted 190 acres (77 hectares) on Point Piper by Governor Macquarie.

By 1822, Piper had built what was for a long time the grandest house in the colony. Piper's home, Henrietta Villa, was often used for lavish entertaining. It was perfectly situated on the harbour. Piper could see all shipping entering and leaving, and he would set off by boat to greet (and impose customs duty on) incoming ships. At its zenith, Piper's estate covered 1100 acres (460 hectares) in the Point Piper, Bellevue Hill and Rose Bay areas. These areas cover much of Sydney's prime eastern suburbs real estate. Piper had other large land-holdings in the Sydney area as well.

In a move which may have been partially motivated by Piper's extravagant lifestyle, Governor Darling inquired into the conduct of the customs office and the Bank of New South Wales, of which Piper was chairman. Piper resigned as chairman of the bank and was suspended as naval officer, not because of any dishonesty, but because of mis-management—£12 000 in customs duty seemed to be missing. Piper could not survive on the scale he was used to without the income he earned collecting customs, so in a dramatic gesture he tried to drown himself in the harbour, within view of his home to the accompaniment of his own musician. The suicide bid failed when his boatman rescued him. Most of Piper's estate passed on to Daniel Cooper in 1826 and Piper retired to Bathurst. Piper sold the land at Vaucluse to W. C. Wentworth.

The Piper estate was Daniel Cooper's first major land acquisition, and the story of the subdivision and eventual demise of what became known as the Cooper estate is a good example of the pattern of development of the eastern suburbs. Cooper was an emancipist convict who, like Piper, served as a director of the Bank of New South Wales. Cooper left Sydney in 1831 and Henrietta Villa was leased. The estate passed on Daniel Cooper's death to his nephew, another successful businessman, also called Daniel, in 1853. He lived in the John Verge–designed, recently restored Rose Bay Lodge, on the corner of Salisbury and New South Head roads. Cooper entered politics and became the first speaker of the Legislative Assembly in 1856. He decided that he needed a grander abode, to be built in the architectural taste of the day on the site of Henrietta Villa. But only the foundation stone was laid (with much fanfare) by Governor Denison in 1856. Cooper's health was not good and it would appear he did not have the stomach for the major building project, which would have resulted in the most vast and imposing residence Sydney had ever seen. Cooper left Sydney in 1861 for England. In 1863, he became an English peer and boasted the title, the Baronet of Woollahra. A smaller (but still very large) Woollahra House was built on the site of Henrietta Villa. The Rose Bay police station on the corner of New South Head and Wunulla roads was the gatehouse for Woollahra House. It was designed by E. Hilly, a leading architect of the day, and built in 1871. It is one of the finest works of architecture in the eastern suburbs.

From the 1850s, the Coopers began to subdivide the land at Point Piper. The three Tooth Brothers, Edwin, Robert and Frederick, leased a 50-acre (20-hectare) block and built Buckhurst (1856), close to Seven Shillings Beach, and later Cranbrook (1859). This is now occupied by a private boys school of the same name. In 1882, Cooper's son William built an even grander Woollahra House. It was a large, somewhat overblown example of the late

Victorian Italianate style. When William returned to England in 1888, the house was leased to Lady Martin, Sir James's widow, after whom nearby Lady Martins Beach is named.

In 1899, Woollahra House was auctioned off and even more of the estate was subdivided. By 1905, when Thomas Longworth bought the house and remaining land, only 5 acres (2 hectares) of surrounding land were left. After Longworth's death at Woollahra House in 1927, the rest of the land was sold off and the house was demolished to make way for a multitude of red-brick flats. The building that contained the old stables and servants' quarters was converted into flats called Wyuna Court.

Wunulla Road follows the old carriageway from New South Head Road to Woollahra House. In 1890, there were only twenty homes in Point Piper. With road building and sub-division, the ambience of the area began to change. More roads were built through the suburb: Wolseley Road (1890), Wentworth Road (1894) and Wyuna Road (1900). The crest of Point Piper is dominated by two large buildings which look as if they would be more comfortable in the Scottish Isles. One of them is a monastery and the other is being converted into luxury apartments.

Sadly, the only places in the eastern suburbs that commemorate the Cooper family, who dominated land ownership in the area for most of the nineteenth century, are Cooper Park and Cooper Street, Double Bay. Cooper Park was set aside and given to the Woollahra Council in 1917 by the Cooper estate. The park is situated in a steep gully that runs from the corner of Bellevue and Victoria roads down to Manning Road then into Double Bay.

385

Darling Point was one of the first of the outer eastern suburbs to be settled by the colonists. It was renamed from the Aboriginal Yarranabbee in honour of Governor Darling's wife. Lindesay (1835) was one of the first houses to be built. The first owner was the colonial treasurer, Campbell Riddell, and the house was designed by Edward Hallen. It was the first house built in the Gothic Revival style in Sydney. Lindesay originally stood on a 16-acre (6.5-hectare) grant. Surveyor General Thomas Mitchell bought and lived in Lindesay while he was building Carthona (1841) down the road. Mitchell fashioned the keystones on the arches and doors of Carthona himself. The last private resident of Lindesay was Walter Pye, who donated it to the National Trust in 1963. Carthona is still a private home owned by the Oxley family.

Another somewhat later but very prominent resident of the outer eastern suburbs was Thomas Sutcliffe Mort, one of Sydney's greatest industrialists. Born in Lancashire in 1816, he arrived in Sydney in 1838. Mort set up as a wool and livestock auctioneer and selling agent soon after his arrival in Sydney. He was one of the founders of the AMP, an early member of the Sydney Exchange, and a financier of Henry Parkes's *Empire* newspaper. In the mid-1850s he built Mort's Dock at Balmain and was responsible for developing a refrigeration system so that Australian beef and dairy products could be exported.

Mort lived in Greenoaks cottage at 38 Cross Street, Double Bay, while he built Greenoaks (now Bishopscourt) on the hill above it in 1846. The original building was designed by

John Hilly and extended in the late 1850s by another leading architect of the day, Edmund Blacket. One of the reasons the extensions were necessary was that Mort bought many artworks, furniture and items of historical interest, such as armour and coats of mail, which needed to be housed in a bigger space. Mort donated the land on which St Mark's Church and its rectory were built between 1848 and 1862. The spire was not added until 1875. Today, Bishopscourt is the home of the Anglican Archbishop of Sydney.

One of the grandest homes in Darling Point is The Swifts, built by the Tooth family on the site of a smaller cottage. Over the other side of the road is a dense cluster of high-rise apartments built in the 1960s which prompted the creation of the residential political lobby group, the Woollahra Action Committee in 1969. By 1971, this group had gained control of Woollahra Council. The council imposed planning controls that limited the amount of high-rise development in the eastern suburbs.

The Swifts dominated the western side of Darling Point and is one of Sydney's best examples of late–nineteenth-century Gothic Revival architecture. The building was designed by G. Morrell and vied with Government House for architectural prominence, being built in a similar style and on an equivalent scale. In its heyday, the house was a rich man's fantasy; apart from the usual rooms, there was a Moorish Room, a huge billiard room and a ballroom with minstrel gallery. Robert Tooth and his family moved to England. All his sons were killed in World War I, but the baronetcy granted to Tooth passed to the son of one of his daughters, who became Sir Hugh Lucas-Tooth. The Resch family, another brewing dynasty, bought The Swifts from the Tooth family. Edward Resch left the house to the Catholic Church. The church sold the property to a developer who became insolvent. The mortgagee, St George Bank, sold the property. The new owners have restored it to its former glory as a private residence.

Ascham, a private school for girls, covers several once privately held houses: Glenrock, built in the early 1870s; the Dower House, built for the widow of an early landowner; and Fiona (1864), designed by John Hilly and built by Edward Knox, the founder of the Colonial Sugar Refining Company (CSR). The Knox family lived at Fiona until 1946.

Double Bay was marked as a site for a village in 1834 as New South Head Road was being built from Rushcutters Bay to the east. The land upon which Double Bay Park lies was proclaimed and set aside at the same time for public use, but twenty-odd years later there was still only one building in Bay Street. Market gardening was the dominant activity in the area. One of the leading botanist–horticulturists of the day, William Guilfoyle, established a nursery near the corner of South Street and Ocean Street. There was a tract of alluvial soil along a stream of water that ran down the gully from Edgecliff to Double Bay. Guilfoyle later became the curator of the Botanic Gardens in Melbourne and played an active role in their design. He admired tropical exotic plants, and is credited with introducing the jacaranda tree to Australia. Guilfoyle's 2 acres (0.8 hectares) of land were sold and eventually became the site of the Double Bay Public School. He was not the only keen horticulturist in the area. Sir John Hay had a large garden along present-day Manning Road. Many of the exotic trees he planted can still be seen in the grounds of Overthorpe, a block of apartments in New South Head Road.

Daniel Cooper Junior applied to build a wharf at Double Bay in 1853, at about the same time as the foundation stone for the earlier Woollahra House was being laid. But apart from this and other large homes in the Double Bay area, there was little development there until the boom period commencing in the 1870s.

Glenyarrah, now known as Gladswood House, was built in 1856. Redleaf, the building which contains the Woollahra Council Chambers, was built in 1863. It was later purchased by the Busby family. Mrs Busby 'bought' the land around Seven Shillings Beach (named after the price of the bargain) from the Aborigines who lived there shortly after the family moved to their new home. After being moved on from Seven Shillings Beach, the Aborigines set up camp in what is now the garden of Rona.[6] Gurrah, the man who was paid the 7 shillings, later buried his treasure with the body of his wife, Nancy, on the corner of Bay and Cross streets, Double Bay. The last of the Aborigines who lived in the Double Bay area died in the 1870s. Seven Shillings Beach has recently undergone a period of controversy. There was some disagreement about whether public access to it should be permitted. Those in favour of access prevailed. Two of the most imposing houses in the eastern suburbs were built along Seven Shillings Beach: Fairwater and Elaine stand next to each other and are owned by different branches of the Fairfax family.

387

In 1871, Double Bay was described by the *Illustrated Sydney News* as a fashionable suburb with many trees such as palms, staghorn ferns and banana trees providing a tropical ambience. The Royal Oak Hotel was built in the 1870s. Terrace housing built before the end of the century can be seen opposite the park in William Street and in Bay and Cross streets. Access to the city was vastly improved when the new cable tram began to run along Ocean Avenue and William Street on the route to Watsons Bay.

From the turn of the twentieth century, the land around Double Bay was subdivided and became more densely settled. The flat-building boom of the 1920s and 1930s left a big mark on the area. Ocean Avenue and most of William Street were built up in the 1920s. As the density of settlement increased, so did the demand for shops and other services. Double Bay finally developed into the busy little village that had been anticipated nearly a century before.

In the early 1960s, Double Bay was still a small village, but the advent of the boom in supermarkets and shopping centres affected Double Bay and changed its sleepy, village-like flavour forever. The suburb also developed a cosmopolitan air. Double Bay, like many other parts of the eastern suburbs, was a popular address for postwar immigrants from Central and Eastern Europe, many of whom were Jewish. This further strengthened demand for shops, hairdressers and, particularly, cafés, such as the 21 in Knox Street.

Double Bay entered a period of hiatus at about the same time as Bondi Junction became a district centre from the 1970s. Double Bay has found a new role for itself as an important

ABOVE: The village of Double Bay in the 1870s, looking towards the Bay Street intersection.

388

quarter for after-hours commercial activity—cinemas, restaurants, cafés, pubs and book-shops, including the excellent Lesley Mackay bookshop, which is open at all hours and encourages browsing and reading.

With the recent improvements to the streetscape by the council and the addition of many more up-to-date, sleekly designed shops, cafés and restaurants, and the Ritz Carlton Hotel, Double Bay is recovering some of its old style in a more contemporary format.

Bellevue Hill has been one of Sydney's most exclusive suburbs since the 1850s. For many years, it has been home to generations of the Fairfax, Knox and Tooth families. The Fairfaxes were, until 1990, the proprietors of the *Sydney Morning Herald*. Large houses built or at one time owned by the Fairfax family in and near Ginahgulla Road include: Ginahgulla, built by the original John Fairfax in 1858 and now part of Scots College; Trahlee and Caerleon (1885); Barford, designed by Hardy Wilson and built by the Fairfax family in the 1930s; and Rona (1883), built and occupied by the Knox family, founders of CSR, and their descendants, until the 1980s. In recent years, Rona has been restored and the traditional gardens and grounds subdivided through the twentieth century have been consolidated by its new owners. Another branch of the Knox family built Leura, next door to Rona.

From the beginning of the twentieth century, rising land values and council rates promoted subdivision of Bellevue Hill, especially during the 1920s and 1960s. Many flats and smaller houses were built well back near the southern end of Victoria Road, down Bellevue Road and also along the grander old estates around Fairfax and Ginahgulla roads. One of the finer blocks of flats is Silchester (1930), designed by English architect Leslie Wilkinson. Wilkinson and Hardy Wilson were two of the first architects in Sydney to adopt architectural concepts from the Italian and French Mediterranean, such as courtyards, loggias and terraces. Both these architects skilfully fused these elements, which are so well suited to Sydney's warm climate, with the symmetrical forms and other conventions of Georgian architecture.

Some of the finest early examples of Mediterranean–Georgian architecture can be seen in the eastern suburbs, along Ginahgulla Road in Bellevue Hill, along Edgecliff Road and on the harbour's foreshores. It is a pity that this style was not more frequently adopted on the harbour, as it is better suited to the climate and topography than traditional bungalow-style architecture.

Rose Bay was also originally part of the Cooper estate. Early mansions in Rose Bay included Tivoli, now known as Kambala, which was built on a 60-acre (24-hectare) grant developed by Captain William Dumaresq, who married a daughter of Colonial Secretary Alexander Macleay. It was renamed Kambala when it was converted into an Anglican girls school in 1912.

In the earlier years of the twentieth century, much of the swampy and sandy land near Rose Bay used for market gardens was improved with drainage, and Lyne Park was reclaimed. Two golf courses were set aside, the Royal Sydney Golf Course and the Woollahra Municipal Golf Links. By 1923, there was no more market gardening in Rose Bay, and the bungalow- and flat-building boom gathered pace. Because of the relative high density of the building, three shopping villages developed there. One along New South Head Road, one along Old South Head Road near Dover Road, and the other at Plumer Road near the Woollahra Golf Course.

The first European settler at Vaucluse was Henry Browne Hayes, a nobleman transported to Sydney for abducting a Quaker heiress. Hayes lived in Sydney from 1802 until his return to Ireland in 1812. He bought 105 acres (42 hectares) at Vaucluse and proceeded to build a house, garden and orchard. Hayes successfully, it would seem, deterred the many snakes in the area by building a large trench around Vaucluse House and filling it with Irish soil. Captain Piper, who bought the land when Hayes returned to Ireland, said that snakes were never found within the trench, although there were plenty outside it.[7] William Charles Wentworth bought

Vaucluse House in 1827 from John Piper. He augmented his estate with land grants from the government. His land-holding stretched around the harbour foreshore from the present site of Kincoppal School to Parsley Bay. Portions of his estate were subdivided after the 1850s, when Wentworth went to live in England. When Wentworth died in 1872, his wife, then his daughter, received life interests in the remaining portions. Wentworth built the Gothic Revival Greycliffe House for one of his daughters.

By the late nineteenth century, there were no Wentworths living in Vaucluse House. A great deal of the old Wentworth land was resumed by the government for use as a public park, proclaimed in 1911. Vaucluse House was opened to the public in 1920. It grew in stages, as a series of additions, and still lies on generous grounds. The original cottage built by Henry Hayes is no longer discernible. Wentworth had grand plans for the extension of the north-facing facade, but these were never realised.

The Historic Houses Trust has restored the house and the grounds to the state they were in when the Wentworths lived there. The Tea Rooms, which were built in the 1920s, are very pleasantly situated and designed. Vaucluse House is at its best in spring and early summer when the azaleas, wisterias and jacarandas are in flower.

390

Greycliffe House is now the headquarters for the Sydney Harbour National Park and the National Parks and Wildlife Service, which looks after the park. On the same parkland stands Strickland House, once called Carrara. At the time of writing, its future use is uncertain. For many years, it was used as accommodation for the aged, but is now vacant. Strickland House was built in the 1850s by John Hosking, the first mayor of Sydney, who was married to Samuel Terry's daughter. Other houses built on land which was subdivided from the Wentworth estate along Vaucluse Road are The Hermitage, built in about the 1840s, and Claremont, upon which Kincoppal Rose Bay now stands on 17 acres (7 hectares) of prime harbourside land. The earlier portion of the building and the chapel were designed by leading architect of the day, Horbury Hunt.

Although The Hermitage's foreshore, running underneath the land at Kincoppal Rose Bay as far as Strickland House, had belonged to the local council since 1912, a lack of vigour in protecting it for public enjoyment was responsible for the limited public access to it during the twentieth century. Local political agitation was eventually successful and the land has now reverted to public use, despite considerable opposition from local residents who had become used to their privacy. The state government of the day, led by Neville Wran, ensured that public access was restored. The Hermitage Walk is one of the best harbour foreshore walks close to the city. It provides spectacular views of the city and the harbour.

Woollahra was always leafier and quieter than its more densely settled neighbour, Paddington, and house building started later than it did at Darling Point before the goldrush era. The land was a little less desirable, being further from the town and the harbour. One of the earliest mansions there is Rosemont (1858) in Ocean Street, for many years the home of the David

Jones retailing dynasty. Much of the land has been subdivided and built up into town houses. The grand red gravel drive is gone, and there is little land left to surround it. Next door to Rosemont is All Saints' Church, another Edmund Blacket building. The foundation stone was laid in 1876. Woollahra's Ocean Street is a busy arterial road, and many of the larger homes in the area are occupied by consulates. One of the more bizarre is the Russian Consulate in Fullerton Street, a brutal modern building that seems designed to intimidate any prospective intruder. The area to the west of Ocean Street is more densely built up with nineteenth-century terrace housing and town houses than the land which lies to the east.

With the introduction of the eastern suburbs railway to Edgecliff and Bondi Junction, the opportunity was taken up by developers in the 1970s and 1980s to build adjoining shopping centres on the corner of New South Head Road and Ocean Street. Useful as these shops are, this unfortunately also entailed the demolition of a large row of nineteenth-century terraces on New South Head Road. At the same time, the area known as the Glebe estate behind these two centres was sold by its owner, the Anglican Church. Many of the nineteenth-century houses in the old Glebe estate are perched on top of what used to be known as the Rushcutter Valley, the area now covered by Trumper Park, White City and Rushcutters Bay Park.

The shopping strip of Queen Street between Ocean Street and Oxford Street is the *ne plus ultra* of the antique and fine arts trade, and also accommodates many of Sydney's leading interior designers. It still has a village-like ambience, which has been enhanced in recent years with new coffee shops, restaurants and a bookshop. Queen Street is one of the smartest retail addresses in Sydney. One of the oldest antique dealers in the area is Bill Bradshaw, of Bradshaw antiques. His antiques business was the nucleus for the growth in the antique trade there in the past forty years.

Woollahra has the very good luck to be one of the suburbs that lie close to Centennial Park. Centennial Park, the Old Sydney Showground, Moore Park and the Sydney Cricket Ground and Football Stadium used to be part of the original Sydney Common, created by Lachlan Macquarie in 1811. It was originally set aside as a place to graze livestock after grazing animals had to be moved on from the recently created Hyde Park. As time went on, this alternately rocky, swampy, sandy and hilly countryside was appropriated for more organised public recreational uses.

Centennial Park is one of the largest and best-loved parks in Sydney. Its circumference is 8 kilometres. The five sets of entrance gates, designed by Louis Robertson, who worked in the Colonial Architect's office, are fittingly monumental for this park which, as the name suggests, commemorates the centenary of European settlement. In its early years, Centennial Park was a focal point for important national celebrations and events such as Federation in January 1901, the visit of the Great White Fleet in 1908, and various military parades in the early decades of the twentieth century.

The park is one of Sydney's most heavily used public recreational areas. It bustles and hums with life in a way that the Domain and the Royal Botanic Gardens do not. Unlike those areas, it can be actively as well as passively enjoyed. The variety of humankind that can be observed in Centennial Park somehow typifies what Sydney is all about. All sorts of people from all walks of life unselfconsciously enjoy the park in whatever manner they like.

The total area of Centennial Park is 220 hectares and it sits in the middle of the densely populated eastern suburbs, between Paddington, Bondi Junction, Randwick and Kensington. As is to be expected for such a large area, there are all sorts of terrain and pockets within the park, with something for everyone to enjoy.

Glimpses of the city to the west and the suburbs to the east can be seen from afar, but they do not overshadow or loom over the park. The reason Centennial Park was still open ground nearly a hundred years after Sydney was settled was partly topographical and partly historical. In 1811, Lachlan Macquarie set aside the area of which Centennial Park is a part as the Sydney Common, which precluded any development of the park. Much of the area is marshy, and Lachlan Swamp, located in the park, was the source of Sydney's freshwater supply from 1837 to 1859, after the Tank Stream became inadequate and too polluted. The colonial engineer at the time the water supply was routed from the swamp to the city was John Busby. With the considerable help of convict labour—he was not very keen on going underground— he built a tunnel from Lachlan Swamp, along Moore Park and Oxford Street, to Hyde Park.

Although the park was dedicated by Governor Lord Carrington in 1888, it was not in fact completed until much later. It was Carrington's idea to establish the park, an idea he conceived in 1885. Henry Parkes took the proposal up as a good way of celebrating the centenary of European settlement when he became premier again in 1887. On 26 January 1888, it would have taken spectators a lot of imagination to see what the park would become. At the time, it was still just sandhills and swampy land, with rocky outcrops. Much roadwork took place during the Depression of the 1930s, as part of the unemployment relief program operated by the government to alleviate hardship.

One of the interesting contrasts within the park is provided by the sight of both native trees and exotic species. The latter were planted at the time of the park's creation, under the supervision of Charles Moore, then curator of the Royal Botanic Gardens and an advocate of subtropical species in Sydney parklands. There are rocky outcrops on the northern side of Centennial Park, with many stands of casuarinas creating shady groves to hide in or stomp through. This area is a perfect place for children's games.

The park's best vantage point is in the northwestern corner at the hockey fields and children's park on top of the Centennial Park Reservoir, near the Oxford Street frontage. This position is on top of the sandstone ridge that runs from the eastern edge of the city, along Oxford Street to South Head. The ridge is the watershed for the harbour to the north and Botany Bay to the south.

Between the sandstone ridge and Grand Drive are the Federation Pavilion and the Centennial Hall (1988), built by noted architect Alexander Tzannes. The hall stands on the site where the Commonwealth of Australia was officially federated on 1 January 1901. That was where Australia's first governor general, Lord Hopetoun, and the first prime minister, Edmund Barton, were sworn in. Inside the hall is the Commonwealth Stone that commemorates the Federation of Australia in 1901.

Grand Drive, the circular road in the centre of Centennial Park, is just less than 4 kilometres in circumference and was one of the first roads built there after the park was dedicated. In those days, the *passeggiata* would have been taken in a more stately way, as befitted the times. These days, some cars whizz round at considerable speed, despite speed limits and speed bumps. Next to the roadway is a dirt track used for horse-riding and between that and the road is a walking and jogging track. On the outside perimeter of the road is a white line that marks the boundary of the bicycle track. Speeding packs of athletic cyclists race around this track in the early mornings and the evenings.

The shady trees between the walking area and the road were planted in 1889, and are mostly Port Jackson figs, holm oaks and Norfolk Island pines.

Straight ahead from the Bicentennial Pavilion, inside Grand Drive, there are stands of pine trees, planted by school children in the 1950s. At the centre of the park is the remaining fragment of Lachlan Swamp. In the swamp, native trees such as paperbarks and casuarinas abound. Much of the Lachlan Swamp has been fenced off so that more native plants can regenerate. Nearby on Dickens Drive, the park's layout becomes more formal again. An avenue of exotic palms lines the roadway. In the middle of the park is the formally laid-out rose garden, at its best in spring and autumn.

In the centre of the park are many lovely ponds in different shapes and sizes. Local ducks and swans waddle about, greedily grabbing pieces of stale bread from the pudgy hands of small children, who become quite alarmed at the sight of the approaching birds. One of the most popular ponds for duck feeding is just next to the Lachlan Swamp, called the Duck Pond. Next to it is the very pretty and much smaller Lily Pond, with its pretty wooden bridge. Near the Duck Pond is the Shelter Pavilion, typical of Federation architecture. Built in 1898, it is often screened out by an ice-cream van, which, in spite of its ugliness, serves a very useful purpose on hot days.

On the other side of the park, near the Robertson Road gate is the Ranger's House, another piece of Federation architecture. Fringing the park in this area are residential streets which provide many good examples of fine Federation architecture of the period. Some 104 acres (42 hectares) were subdivided and sold on the fringes of Centennial Park to help fund the construction and landscaping of the park. The finest Federation architecture can be seen at Martin, Lang and Darley roads.

The Centennial Park Café, opened in 1988 as part of the improvements to the park for the Bicentennial celebrations, is a good place for a well-deserved rest after walking around the park. The café stands on the inside of Grand Drive, opposite the spot between Parkes Drive and Hamilton Drive, on the site where the park was dedicated before 40 000 people on 26 January 1888. At the top of Parkes Drive is the Park Superintendent's House. It was built

393

earlier than the Park Ranger's House on the other side of the park, and is therefore more Victorian than Federation in appearance.

In Centennial Park, Sydneysiders of all ages and shapes can be seen at play or hard at work getting fit. The park can be explored on foot, or more quickly by bicycle, which can be rented in nearby Clovelly Road.

The park, like any other, has a daily rhythm and an ebb and flow of activities. On weekdays, in the very early morning, you can see cyclists, walkers and joggers racing to do their exercise before the working day begins. From about 8.30 a.m., the walking path starts to fill with parents who have just despatched the children to school or who are taking smaller children for a ride around the park in their prams. In the middle of the day, small children come out to play on the swings and the play equipment and feed the ducks, or come to learn how to ride their bikes on the bike training track on the southern side of Grand Drive. In the afternoon from about 4 p.m., the park fills again with serious exercisers—especially on summer evenings, as the gates do not close until sunset.

On Saturdays, the playing fields in the park can fill with school children playing Saturday morning cricket and rugby. Others come to ride horses or bicycles, or to walk or jog. Sunday is the park's busiest day. Family groups come for picnics and barbecues, especially near the children's bicycle track. The smell of sausages on the grills wafting over Grand Drive can be extremely distracting for hungry exercisers or hungry dogs being walked around the park.

On four Sundays a year (the first Sunday in December, March, June and September), the park is closed to cars. Anyone who is lucky enough to visit on one of those days can gain some idea of what the park must have been like before the advent of the motor vehicle. Some wonder wistfully why the park cannot be car-free every Sunday, or at least more frequently than four days a year.

To the west of Centennial Park is the site of the old Showground, recently leased to Fox Film Studios. Between 1882 and 1997, this was the site of the famous Royal Easter Show, which has been relocated to Homebush. When it was not in use as the venue for the show, the Showground was used as stabling for horses, including the police horses and the imperial troops during the Federation celebrations in Sydney in 1901. More significantly, it was used by the defence forces as an army camp when Australia was involved in armed conflict during the Boer War, World War I and World War II. During World War I, hundreds of thousands of soldiers poured through the Showground on their way to or from the battlefields. In Easter 1916 alone, more than 50 000 soldiers passed through the camp. Often the men were brought in from more outlying camps, such as the one at Casula to the west of Sydney, the night before they sailed off to war, and the ground was thrown open so that their relatives could visit them.[8] Then, in the influenza epidemic which followed the war in 1919, the Showground was used as an emergency hospital, holding 500 patients at one time. The Easter Show that year was cancelled because of the epidemic. The Show of 1920, which was the first since 1914, broke all attendance records when nearly 500 000 people went through the turnstiles.

Just before World War II, in 1938, the sesquicentenary of European settlement of Australia, the state government built the Commemorative Pavilion and the Manufacturers' Hall, as a prelude to mounting the biggest and most impressive Easter Show to date. Just more than 1 million people attended the show in 1938.

During World War II, more than 700 000 soldiers stayed at the Showground. The Easter Show was suspended again between 1942 and 1946. The Showground was a busy self-contained army town, with its own hospitals and messing centres, post offices, banks and other services. The soldiers trained there, and ceremonial parades were held in the main arena. To celebrate the end of the war years, more than 1.2 million people visited the Show of 1947 with such enthusiasm that, on one day, the ticket office was pushed over by a crowd of impatient people waiting in a queue.

The decision to relocate the show to Homebush was resented by many people who came to love the ambience of the Showground. Sydneysiders will long remember the grand old buildings such as the Royal Hall of Industries (1913), where sample bags used to be sold to eager children, the Royal Agricultural Hall (1913) that contained the ornately displayed agricultural exhibits from regional New South Wales, the Members' Grandstand and the Hordern Pavilion. The Hordern Pavilion is still used for concerts. There has been criticism of the government's decision to enter into a long-term lease of the Showground to Fox Studios, as it has been argued that this will diminish public access to land which was granted, as far back as 1811, to the people of Sydney and New South Wales. The Fox Studios proposal is far preferable to the previous proposal to build high-rise housing on the site. It will bring valuable new employment opportunities to the people of Sydney, and the film industry in particular. New, large cinema complexes and entertainment facilities are also provided.

Next to the Showground is the Sydney Cricket Ground and, on the corner of Moore Park Road and Driver Avenue, the Sydney Football Stadium, built in 1988. The area on which both these important Sydney sporting facilities are situated today was used from the 1850s as playing fields for the soldiers in nearby Victoria Barracks. The soldiers, colloquially called 'barrackers', supported their teams so loudly that, in Sydney and later Australia, the word 'barracking' evolved to mean 'cheering' and other forms of noisy support. As the population of Sydney spread and became closer to the area in the late nineteenth century, the use of the land was handed over to the public. The Sydney Cricket Ground was officially named in 1894. Shortly after, a sportsground was built next door for other sports.

The Sydney Cricket Ground was known as the Garrison Ground, and later the Military and Civil Cricket Ground. In 1877, the administration of the ground passed from the government to a trust, which became the owner of the land. In the early years, there were only two wooden grandstands, and the vacant, elevated land on the Randwick and Paddington sides were called the 'Hill' and the 'Paddo Hill', respectively. Now, these once open spaces have been built up with seating and little open space remains. Watching cricket, drinking beer and barracking for one's team from the Hill have become a famous Sydney institution. The first game of football played there was Australian Rules, between New South Wales and Victoria in 1881. The first rugby game was played there in 1882. The Sydney Cricket Ground was the main venue for the Empire Games in 1938. Because the Cricket Ground is circular in shape, it is large enough to play Australian Rules on—unlike the smaller, rectangular Sydney Football Stadium next door. There is growing popularity for Australian Rules in Sydney. The Sydney Cricket Ground is the home ground of the Sydney Swans.

Both grounds are administered by the Sydney Cricket and Sportsground Trust. The Football Stadium was designed by architect Philip Cox, who also designed the Aquatic Centre at Homebush, the Darling Harbour Exhibition and Convention Centre, the National Maritime Museum and the Star City Casino. The bulk of the building was kept low, so that it would not completely dominate the streetscape of Moore Park Road. The result is that the football field is 3 metres below ground level. The stadium was funded by selling gold memberships at $7500 entitling members to use of the sporting facilities, as well as attending sporting events. International soccer matches, rugby union and rugby league internationals, the State of Origin rugby league matches, and rugby 'Super 12' and 'World Sevens' matches, as well as club games for local teams, are held at the football stadium. Big blockbuster touring operas such as *Aida* and *Turandot* have been staged there, as well as concerts by popular performers such as the Rolling Stones, Madonna and U2. The capacity of the ground at football matches is slightly more than 40 000. The new stadium at the Olympic site at Homebush will hold almost double that amount.

The Sydney Football Stadium will compete for sporting fixtures with the Homebush Stadium after the 2000 Olympics. The Sydney Cricket and Sports Ground Trust was one of the unsuccessful tenderers to build the new stadium there.

Moore Park, which stands outside the Showground, Football Stadium and Cricket Ground, was named after Charles Moore, Coogee resident and local politician, who uncovered documents in 1866 that proved Macquarie had set aside the 1000 acres (405 hectares) of the Sydney Common for public use. The paperwork had been lost and, for many years previously, it had been wrongly assumed the area was Crown land. Moore advocated the construction of dams to improve the capacity of Sydney's then main water source, the Lachlan Swamp, which flowed (if that is the correct word) from Centennial Park to Botany Bay. Moore's other contributions as mayor of Sydney were to extend Macquarie Street to Circular Quay and build the Tarpeian Way into the rock just above Bennelong Point.

It took some time for the surf to become part of Sydney's and Australia's culture. From the 1830s, it was illegal (on the grounds of indecency) to swim on beaches within view of the public. In the 1860s, bathing boxes started to appear at Manly, Sydney's first beach resort, easily accessible by ferry from Circular Quay. Although daytime bathing was still forbidden, the bathing boxes permitted beach-goers to get wet without causing an affray. By the end of the nineteenth century, local councils had legal control over the issue of access to beaches. It was the proprietor of the local Manly newspaper who challenged the illegality of swimming in daylight hours in 1902. By 1904, surfing was permitted at most of Sydney's beaches and was made legal beyond any doubt by 1906.

The attitude of the local councils gradually softened. Despite protests from Archbishop Kelly, who thought that '[P]romiscuous surf-bathing [was] offensive in general to propriety, and a particular feature of that offensiveness is that attraction it has for idle onlookers.'[9] Kelly's particular concern was the commingling of the sexes and that this would lead to a reduction in proper moral standards. The mayor of Randwick, Alderman Cooper, took a different view:

> It is my belief that women who surf mix with the men more from a sense of safety than a desire to besport their figures in full view of admirers. And I also believe that the crowd who collect at the water's edge watching the parties diving under and riding on the crest of the breakers are animated by motives quite wholesome … the beauty of the human form has at all times appealed to the world's greatest painters and sculptors, and surely we, living in an enlightened age, can be permitted to add our quota of admiration without shocking our modesty.[10]

397

By today's standards, modesty was well protected: regulations required neck-to-knee swimming costumes. In the first decade of the twentieth century, local surf lifesaving clubs were formed as a voluntary service for surfers who got into trouble in the unpredictable surf and rips on Sydney's beaches. One of the first was the Bondi Surf Lifesaving Club (1906). The first person to be rescued, when he was a boy, was Charles Kingsford Smith. He later became Australia's greatest pioneer aviator. The lifesaving movement flourished quickly. By 1912, there were seventeen lifesaving clubs in Sydney. By the 1920s, surfing carnivals were a regular fixture of Sydney's summer beach culture. Lifesavers would demonstrate their skills and prowess in the water and on the sand. They still patrol the beach in their brightly coloured caps and swim out to rescue swimmers using a line and reel during competitions, but more modern equipment, such as small, inflatable rubber dinghies with outboard motors, has joined their lifesaving arsenal. Beach inspectors, employed by local councils, have the task of controlling bad behaviour and excessive immodesty on the beaches. In decades gone by, these inspectors, with their zinc-coated noses and white hats, imposed their values and taste on surfers and sunbakers with missionary zeal.

Sydney's most famous beach is Bondi. The alluring golden crescent of sand is one of the city's great lures and icons, however much people loudly proclaim the ugliness of the local architecture. In the years before British settlement, Bondi was a popular Aboriginal hunting and fishing ground, and families sheltered in nearby rock caves. Beneath the old Bondi sand hills that are now covered with roads, car parks and blocks of flats lie rocks that reveal that Bondi was once an important centre for Aboriginal tool and weapon making.

The 200-acre (81-hectare) Bondi estate was bought by newspaper publisher Edward Smith Hall in the 1850s for his daughter. Hall owned the *Monitor* and was an important political agitator in his day. He used the *Monitor* to protest against the way those charged with the Myall Creek Massacre were exonerated; this pressure led to a retrial of the perpetrators. At the second trial, seven men were convicted and sentenced to death. Hall's daughter Georgina married Francis O'Brien, who took over the running of Hall's newspaper in 1860. In 1881, 25 acres (10 hectares) of land along Bondi beach were resumed by the government so that the public would have permanent access to it. The dance hall built there soon after often became rowdy on weekends and public holidays. Members of various inner-city pushes would travel by tram on holidays and weekends, and, in 1884, there was a riot that took some time for the police to subdue. A popular but illegal two-up gambling school was a regular fixture on the sandhills of North Bondi. A quarry at Bondi was also for many years the source of some of Sydney's finest sandstone.

As surf bathing became more and more fashionable in the early decades of the twentieth century, land values around Bondi rose, and the process of subdivision began as it already had in so many other parts of Sydney. Bondi and Waverley in general were entirely transformed by the flat- and bungalow-building boom of the 1920s and 1930s. It was in this period that many hotels and shops were built—the Bondi Hotel, the Astra Hotel and the shops along Campbell Parade.

The Bondi Pavilion, Sydney's grandest bathing pavilion, was built in the 1920s. In an era when people no longer need to change at the beach into button-down shirts or dresses, flannel trousers and sensible leather shoes before travelling home on public transport, the pavilion seems to long for the days when it had a more important job to do. Despite its grace and beauty, it looks a little like a white elephant. The steps of the pavilion are one of the most popular meeting places at the beach. The aesthetic and political purpose of the pavilion was to launch Bondi as a world-class, premier beach resort and, although the building was a little grand for what was really needed, it certainly succeeded. The less imposing and less ambitious architecture of the North Bondi Surf Club is closer to the norm for such buildings on Sydney's beaches.

In February 1938, there was a major disaster at Bondi when freak waves crashed on the beach without warning. Five people drowned and nearly 200 people had to be rescued by the Bondi lifesavers. It was this incident, and countless other smaller ones, which led to the growing heroic status of the lifesaver. Today, the bronzed lifesaver and the surfing beach culture are two of Sydney's greatest and most enduring symbols.

In the postwar period, Bondi was the first home for many refugees and immigrants from war-torn Europe. It became one of the earliest suburbs in Sydney to experience this new diversity, and therefore one of the city's earliest demographic 'melting pots'.

The children of postwar refugees and immigrants sat in the classrooms of Bondi Public School next to the children of the mostly working-class Anglo-Celtic residents of Bondi. One school student at Bondi Public in the early 1950s, Richard Butler, was so affected by his witnessing, through his acquaintance of these 'new Australians', the effects of World War II and the Holocaust that he has made a lifelong professional commitment to military

ABOVE: Looking to the northern end of Bondi Beach in 1932.

disarmament and international diplomacy. Many of the children of these early postwar immigrants went on to great academic success, often at Sydney Boys or Sydney Girls high schools, and later at university. Bondi still has a strong Jewish community, a legacy of postwar immigration.

As the postwar immigrants established themselves and started businesses, other groups moved in. By the early 1970s, many New Zealanders had moved into the area, and Bondi was colloquially known as 'West Auckland'. In the 1980s and 1990s, many members of Sydney's 21 000-strong South African community came to live at or near Bondi.

Throughout the 1990s, Bondi has enjoyed a considerable real-estate boom. For young, unmarried people, it has become one of the more fashionable suburbs in which to live. Until the late 1980s, many streets in the area looked shabby and down-at-heel. The transformation of Bondi is one of the more remarkable aspects of change in the eastern suburbs in the last two decades of the twentieth century. Businesses such as coffee shops and restaurants arrived to more urbane tastes, and Bondi is now one of the 'cooler' places to spend sunny summer days. Young backpacker tourists also come to spend time there. But Bondi has not entirely lost its old, rakish charm, despite the addition of new layers of gloss and urbanity.

Even the reputation of Bondi's famous surf was eclipsed by dangerous levels of sewage pollution, until the ocean outfalls were extended in the late 1980s. These new outfalls had a direct and immediate effect on improving the quality of the water at Bondi and other beaches in the eastern and southeastern suburbs, and this made Bondi a more desirable address. At last, Bondi possesses the status to match its natural beauty. Bondi even boasts an hotel built in a loose and eclectic form of Spanish Mission Revival style. It is called, rather bizarrely, the Swiss Grand. Some elements of the old Bondi are disappearing. Two examples are the Diggers Club and the Bondi Icebergs, both subject to redevelopment pressure. Ravesi's Hotel and Restaurant now operates from a building that was once occupied by a greengrocer.

Bondi is the place where the eastern suburbs culture of physical fitness meets the surf culture. The walk (or run) from Bondi around the footpath to Tamarama, Bronte and Clovelly is busy, but still quite beautiful on weekday mornings and afternoons. On a hot day at any time of the year—weekend or weekday—Bondi is the best place in Sydney to witness the very broad cross-section of beach lovers. Surfers, young families and body-conscious teenagers are dotted along the beach in a fascinating array of human physical diversity. At the rock pool at the northern end, young children swim their first tentative laps and, later, catch their first waves in the flatter surf nearby. More serious surfers congregate either in the middle or at the southern end, depending on the conditions. Those who are very fit and unaffected by a fear of sharks swim right across Bondi from point to point beyond the breaking surf. The sight of thousands of people sunbaking on workdays is a vivid illustration of the high value placed on leisurely pursuits in Sydney.

On a weekday, it is often puzzling to look at the crowd lying on the beach and wonder how so many people can manage to spend their days at the beach without being burdened by the need to work regular hours—despite constant health warnings about skin cancer. One result of the extensive campaign to discourage overexposure to the strong Sydney sun is the absence of the wafting odours of coconut oil sizzling on warm human flesh. In days gone by, people could pay to have their bodies covered in this highly scented suntan oil.

Right at the southern end is the old Bondi Icebergs' club and swimming pool. The icebergs here are not large bodies of frozen water, but brave souls who swim during the winter months, as some of them have done since the club was formed in 1929.

Bondi is one of Sydney's major tourist attractions and, in recognition of this, there are substantial works in progress to beautify Campbell Parade and the Bondi foreshore. The coastal walk from Bondi to Bronte is one of the most popular in the eastern suburbs. It provides a remarkable view of Sydney's coastal scenery, both natural and suburban.

Around the corner from Bondi to the south is the much smaller Tamarama, sometimes nicknamed 'Glamarama'. Like Bondi and Bronte to the south, Tamarama has been going through a resurgence in its popularity as a place to live. There is far less commercial activity here than there is at Bondi. The beach at Tamarama is only 100 metres wide and its surf is usually more challenging than Bondi's. In the late nineteenth century, an aquarium and walking tracks were built at the expense of the dense natural vegetation. As well as fish, there was a shooting gallery, a dance hall and an ice-skating rink. The aquarium only lasted for four years, and was replaced in 1906 by Wonderland City, which was modelled on Coney Island. By 1911, it had also closed, just as the surf culture was becoming dominant in the area.

Bronte Beach is blessed with a generous amount of open parkland that provides a much more sylvan setting than exists at most of Sydney's other beaches. For this reason, it has long been a favourite spot for picnickers with small children. From the early 1990s, Bronte, too, has started to evolve into a newly fashionable, smaller and more intimate version of Bondi, with cafés and other businesses springing up to cater for a new clientele.

Elevated above the beach is one of the earliest houses still standing in the eastern suburbs, Bronte House (1845). The early–nineteenth-century Colonial Architect, Mortimer Lewis, owned 42 acres (17 hectares) of land at Bronte. He planned a house and built the foundations for it, but was forced, during the depression of the 1840s, to sell the land to Robert Lowe, who completed it. Lowe was a barrister, politician and keen advocate of the abolition of the convict transportation system. He later returned to London, where he entered parliament and became chancellor of the exchequer, and later became Viscount of Sherbrooke. Bronte House was one of the earliest Gothic Revival homes to be built in Sydney. The house now belongs to Waverley Council, and it is leased as a private residence. In recent years, the garden has undergone a great deal of improvement and restoration. Like Bondi and Coogee, Bronte was the terminus for a tram route that ran from the city. The tram made the suburbs accessible for residents and Sunday day-trippers.

Just to the south of Bronte, on the rocky shoreline, stands Waverley Cemetery, established in 1877. This is where poets Henry Lawson and Henry Kendall are buried, as well as George Johnston, leader of the Rum Rebellion. The contrast between the sandstone cliffs, the old marble and stone headstones and the sparkling blue ocean is dramatically spectacular—even if the selection of this prime oceanfront site as a cemetery seems somewhat peculiar.

ABOVE: Aerial view of the coastline from Manly along the northern beaches to the Barrenjoey Peninsula and Palm Beach.

CHAPTER SIXTEEN

THE NORTHERN SUBURBS

THE NORTHERN SIDE of Sydney Harbour was relatively isolated from the city for almost a century before the introduction of regular ferry services in the 1870s. Parts of Sydney's north were not developed until the North Shore railway line was built between Milsons Point and Hornsby in the late 1890s. The relatively late development of the northern suburbs has meant that much of the native bushland was left in a natural state for longer than elsewhere in Sydney. Even today, it is the bushland and open space on the North Shore that give the area much of its particular character and appeal.

The North Shore has a generous abundance of parks: the northern reaches of the Sydney Harbour National Park fringe the harbour's edge and the Lane Cove National Park runs along a large portion of the valley of the Lane Cove River. The other two major parks in Sydney's north are Garigal National Park and, biggest of all, Ku-ring-gai Chase National Park. It is the attractions of these open spaces and the ready access, by train, car and ferry to the city that have helped to make this leafy part of Sydney a pleasant and prosperous middle-class enclave. These attributes come at the price of a certain lack of bustle and cosmopolitan flavour found in other parts of Sydney; for many, however, the quieter ambience adds to the area's charm.

In recent years, the North Shore has seen an increase in the diversity within its resident population. There has been a rise in the number of Asian-born residents, who are often professionals and self-employed business people drawn to the solidly residential flavour of the area. Hong Kong Chinese, Chinese, Taiwanese and Japanese have made suburbs such as St Ives, Northbridge, Castle Cove, Castlecrag and Chatswood their home, as have many immigrants from South Africa.

The north of Sydney covers a wide geographical area from Sydney's northern foreshores up the North Shore line to Hornsby, and eastward across to Palm Beach. Within this area, there is a wide social and topographical range. The northern suburbs can be broadly divided into three subregions. The lower North Shore wraps around the harbour and covers suburbs such as North Sydney (which is for the most part an extension of the CBD), Wollstonecraft, Waverton, Willoughby, Crows Nest, Kirribilli, Neutral Bay, Cremorne, Mosman and Seaforth. Like the upper North Shore and parts of the eastern suburbs, the lower North Shore is considered one of the most socio-economically exclusive parts of Sydney.

The upper North Shore line begins at Roseville, just north of the area's main district centre, Chatswood, and the suburbs follow the spine of the North Shore railway line as far north as Hornsby. In general, the suburbs become leafier to the north. Examples of upper North Shore suburbs are Killara, Pymble, Turramurra, St Ives and Wahroonga.

The third region is the northern beaches. These run along many kilometres of coastline from North Head and Manly to Palm Beach. The social ambience of the northern beaches is quite distinct from the other parts of the north. Here there is a heavy overlay of Sydney's surfing culture upon the suburban sprawl, and parts of the northern beaches have a beach-resort flavour which makes them appear more remote from the city than they really are.

From Sydney Cove, the foreshores of the North Shore did not appear to be likely prospects for agricultural or pastoral activities, and indeed they were not. Consequently, there was no rush to settle there in the early years when agriculture and food production were the top priority for the fledgling colony. The best soil and land lie on the ridge of the North Shore line which runs up from Crows Nest to Hornsby, between the sandstone soils on either side of it in the Lane Cove River and Middle Harbour valleys. Rainfall on the North Shore line is higher than many other parts of Sydney. This was the perfect environment for the tall, blue gum forests to grow until timber cutters settled and cleared the area in the nineteenth century. Blue gums (*Eucalyptus saligna*) and blackbutt (*Eucalyptus pilularis*) grew up to 40 metres high, as did *Angophora costata*, grey ironbark (*Eucalyptus paniculata*), turpentine (*Syncapia glomulifera*) and forest oak (*Allocasuarina torulosa*).[1]

In the twentieth century, these advantageous conditions—the deep soil, cooler climate and higher rainfall—which made it possible for the blue gum forests to thrive, have also created an environment for fine domestic gardens to become established. The upper North Shore boasts many of Sydney's best gardens, and many of them are open to the public at certain times of the year.

The Aborigines of the lower North Shore were called the Kameraigal and the area where they lived was known as the Cammerra. The suburb Cammeray is derived from this place name. The Kameraigal were the largest and most powerful of the tribes of Sydney Harbour. A robust and muscular tribe, their power was derived from their physical attributes. The members of the Kameraigal were so superior that they had enough authority to be able to extract a tooth from the male members of other tribes who lived along the harbour and the 'sea coast'.[2] They were also consulted by other tribes when important decisions had to be made.

The first members of the First Fleet to visit the North Shore were Governor Phillip and nine companions. They set off in the middle of April 1788 on a four-day trek through the bush after rowing to Manly Cove. They walked a considerable distance to where Frenchs Forest, St Ives, Turramurra and Thornleigh are now situated. From the western edge of the North Shore, they could see beyond the Cumberland Plain to the Blue Mountains, which Phillip called the Carmarthen Hills. Although Phillip suspected there would be a river running beneath those hills, it would not be until the following year that the Hawkesbury–Nepean River was discovered.

With the exception of a brief sailing expedition up the Lane Cove River in 1790, the North Shore was not comprehensively explored and surveyed until George Caley, noted botanist, disciple and associate of Joseph Banks, arrived in Australia on a whaling ship in 1800. Caley was the first trained botanist since Banks to visit the Sydney area. In February 1805, after having explored the Camden area and attempting to cross the Blue Mountains and establishing a botanical garden for the governor at Parramatta, Caley set off to explore the North Shore on what would have then been a very long, rugged and arduous journey.

405

From the West Pennant Hills area, Caley travelled across country through present-day Thornleigh and Fox Valley to the head of the Lane Cove River. He then went eastward to the site of present-day Wahroonga and Turramurra, Ku-ring-gai Creek, St Ives and the head of Middle Harbour. He completed his journey via Belrose and Terrey Hills, and then cross-country to the sea at Narrabeen. He travelled back to where he had set out from, taking a more southerly path, through present-day Gordon and Turramurra. Caley noticed that the area had rich soil which would be suitable for agriculture, unlike much of the other bushland in and around Sydney.

The North Shore of Sydney was exploited long before it was settled. This exploitation took the form of whaling and sealing bases, as well as timber felling and stone quarrying. Whaling and sealing were the colony's first export industries. At first the whalers were based at Sydney Cove and Cockle Bay. The Campbell family, in particular, as merchants and traders based at Campbells Cove, were heavily involved in these industries. From 1814, the East India Company's monopoly on whaling and other trading, which had extended from the southern tip of Africa to the southern tip of South America, was cut back to the China tea trade only. This meant that merchant whalers could ply the southern waters on their own account and inter-colonial trade could proceed without the East India Company as an essential intermediary, although the import tariffs into Britain were still steep.[3] One of Thomas Bigge's recommendations was to promote whaling and sealing by eliminating the high tariff walls which discriminated against the export of seal skins and whale oil to Great Britain. This recommendation was adopted, and so the industries became more secure and profitable.

As Sydney Cove emerged from its early colonial state, and a reasonably civilised township started to develop around it, the idea of running smelly and messy whaling bases close to the town of Sydney became less acceptable.

In 1828, an application for a land grant on Darling Point to build a whaling base was rejected on the grounds that the area would be better suited for gracious residential development.[4] It was clear that the eastern suburbs were not going to be allocated for industrial use of any kind. The lower North Shore had to be the main locus of these profitable but unsavoury maritime activities. In 1828, there were nine applications for land grants which would be used as whaling bases in Sydney. Surveyor General Thomas Mitchell thought the North Shore was a suitable location. Areas chosen were the western side of Neutral Bay and Greater Sirius Cove. Six sites were selected at Neutral Bay and three at Great Sirius Cove in 1831.[5] The applicants for land in Darling Point were instead granted $2\frac{1}{2}$ acres (1 hectare) at Neutral Bay. The most committed of the grantees of harbourside land for whaling was Archibald Mosman. By 1851, however, it had completely collapsed in the Sydney area and had moved further down the coastline.[6]

Relics of Sydney's whaling days still exist, including whale jawbones at the waterside entrance to the Royal Sydney Yacht Squadron at Kirribilli and at the entrance to what today is the Mosman Boys' Scout Hall (the first in Australia) and what used to be Archibald

BELOW: Hunting for wallabies in the Turramurra area in the 1870s.

Mosman's whaling station. Whaling Road in North Sydney runs down towards Neutral Bay. By 1826, there were four vessels using Sydney as a base which were devoted to whaling and six vessels used exclusively for sealing.[7]

It seems hard to believe that the densely built-up lower North Shore (which broadly covers the municipalities of North Sydney, Willoughby and Mosman) was settled and suburbanised decades later than inner-city suburbs on the south side of the harbour. Military Road is now as busy as any other arterial road, both in density of traffic and in the level of commercial activity. Until the Sydney Harbour and Spit bridges were built, however, and people started to commute by car to the city from the northern beaches, the lower North Shore was secluded and remote. Like the upper North Shore, this air of separateness from the city and the southern side of the harbour still exists in some senses, and is most commonly manifested in pride and pleasure in living in a relatively quiet and leafy environment around the harbour, and yet being within easy reach of the city.

One of the earliest settlers north of the harbour, James Milson, was given a grant of 80 acres (32 hectares) of land for a farm in 1806. Milson owned a farm (among other land-holdings in the Sydney area) which extended for 50 acres (20 hectares) from Milsons Point to Kirribilli, including the area now occupied by St Aloysius College, and Kirribilli and Admiralty houses. Later in 1817, he was granted more land, covering Blues Point, as well as 5 acres (2 hectares) of land around Neutral Bay.

Milson used his land to grow fruit and vegetables, which he transported by boat over to Millers Point, for sale in the town. The boating became a profitable sideline for him when he started to ship passengers and goods. He, and later his son, James Junior, pioneered ferry services over the harbour between Milsons and Millers points. By the end of the nineteenth century, their North Shore Ferry Company dominated the harbour ferry business. Both James Senior and Junior were keen yachtsmen. James Junior was the first vice-commodore (and later commodore) of the Royal Sydney Yacht Squadron.

Milson Senior developed an abattoir and a quarry at Careening Cove to the west of Neutral Bay that provided ballast for ships. The system of land titles in the colony's early years was, unfortunately, often disorganised. When a bushfire destroyed his home and land in 1826, the title deeds to his land were also destroyed and Milson was forced to purchase the land he thought he already owned. Milson built a home called Carabella on the northeastern tip of Wudyong Point. He died there in 1872 at the age of seventy-nine. The site is now the home of the Sydney Yacht Squadron. There are other buildings in the area built by the Milson family, including Elamang, built by James Milson Junior, which is the administrative building of Loreto Convent, Kirribilli.

It was not until Macquarie's term as governor that significant land grants were made for land on the North Shore. The grant to Alfred Thrupp in 1814 was one of the earliest. Alexander Berry and Edward Wollstonecraft were granted 500 acres (200 hectares)—called the Crows

Nest Estate—in 1819, part of which now forms the suburbs of Waverton and Wollstonecraft. The houses these men lived in have since been demolished. They were involved in the shipping and whaling industries, and they based their operations at Berrys Bay, between McMahons Point and Balls Head. Both men were successful businessmen in the colony in the 1820s. When Wollstonecraft died, he left the land to his former business partner.

For many years, much of the land at Wollstonecraft was set aside for the North Shore Gasworks, which were built in 1917. With the use of natural gas, it no longer served any useful purpose. Predictably, there has been much residential land development there. Nowadays, Waverton and Wollstonecraft are residential areas with a combination of high-rise buildings, medium-density town houses and Federation architecture. At the end of Waverton is Balls Head Reserve, where Aboriginal shell middens and paintings can be seen on the eastern and western edges. The Aborigines chose this spot well. It affords spectacular views down the harbour to the east, and up the Parramatta River to the west. The reserve covers 24 acres (10 hectares), most of which was set aside in 1926 by the government of Jack Lang, the rest being set aside later in the 1930s following a campaign by Anne Forsyth Wyatt, first president of the National Trust. During the Depression years of the 1930s, unemployed people were used to landscape the area along similar lines to the landscaping at Cooper Park, Bellevue Hill, with paths, exotic trees and concrete 'caves'. The reserve is now being restored and regenerated along more natural lines.

Neutral Bay is so named as it was proclaimed by Governor Phillip after the outbreak of war between England and France as a place where foreign ships could be moored while waiting for their friendly or enemy status to be checked. On the eastern shore of Neutral Bay was Alfred Thrupp's 700 acres (280 hectares), which extended to Kurraba Point and across to Willoughby Bay. Alfred Thrupp was Captain John Piper's assistant and arrived in Sydney in 1814. He married one of Piper's daughters, but never lived on his North Shore land grant. In 1830, the land between Neutral Bay and Careening Cove to the west was subdivided into 4-acre (1.5-hectare) blocks and sold to people and companies involved in the whaling industry. Timber in the area was cut down and used in the shipbuilding industry.

At one time, Kurraba Point was also known as Ballast Point because of the sandstone quarry there. Stone from the quarry was also used in the construction of Fort Denison. The reserve on the western side of Kurraba Point was once the site of the Port Jackson Steamship Company's (later North Shore Ferry Company) repair workshops. These were moved to Balmain late in the nineteenth century. The tramline between Neutral Bay and Military Road ran down Wycombe Road to the Hayes Street ferry wharf on the eastern side of the bay. On the opposite side of the bay is HMAS *Platypus*, a submarine naval base which was the site of a gasworks from 1882, until they were relocated to Wollstonecraft.

Ben Boyd was a one-time landowner around Neutral Bay, and one of the North Shore's most colourful entrepreneurs. He came to Australia in 1842 with the aim of setting up branches of the Royal Bank. He became a substantial landowner and businessman, establishing a large whaling station and wool-scouring business at Twofold Bay on the

ABOVE: Sydney as viewed from North Sydney in the late nineteenth century.

New South Wales south coast. He built a home for himself on the waterfront at Neutral Bay which has since been demolished. Boyd ran into financial difficulties and sailed off for the California goldfields. Unsuccessful there, he returned to the Pacific, where he was seized and eaten by cannibals on the Solomon Islands.

Cremorne was not settled until 1853 when James Milson bought the land from the original grantee, James Robertson. Robertson helped Governor Brisbane in the manufacture and establishment of scientific instruments for astronomical purposes at Government House, Parramatta; for his efforts, he received the land grant on the North Shore. Robertson's son John went on to become premier of New South Wales on four separate occasions, and played a substantial role in nineteenth-century Sydney politics. Milson built a large home on the land at Cremorne, some of which he later leased for use as a pleasure garden. The Cremorne Gardens appear to have started grandly as a place for nocturnal balls and other revelry, but to have later fallen from favour when the revelry became too raucous and licentious for the public to tolerate. By 1862, the pleasure garden at Cremorne was no more. The advent of a regular ferry service operated by the Milson family made the place a more attractive weekend and public-holiday recreation spot for families. In 1891, when large-scale subdivision

ABOVE: A view of Lavender Bay, c. 1900, showing the separate swimming baths for 'ladies' and 'gentlemen'.

threatened Cremorne, the foreshores were reserved by the government for public use. This was a very early example of foreshore land resumption.

One of the people who was drawn to the remoteness of the lower North Shore, before the Harbour Bridge was opened, was May Gibbs, author of the famous Australian children's storybook *Snugglepot and Cuddlepie*. Gibbs called her home at Wallaringa Avenue, Neutral Bay, 'Nutcote'. It was here that Gibbs wrote many of her well-known and well-loved books. In the late 1980s, the house was threatened with demolition. Money was raised through a public appeal, and today it is administered by the National Trust. It is a fine monument to Gibbs's contribution to Australian literature, and offers a good insight into the way people lived in Sydney in the earlier decades of the twentieth century. The house and gardens are open to the public on weekends.

Mr J. G. N. Gibbes was the lessee of the land on which Admiralty and Kirribilli houses stand today. Gibbes was the Collector of Customs, and he built a substantial home he called Wotanga, which was well positioned to see the incoming and outgoing shipping in the harbour. In 1885, the New South Wales government bought the land for the British admiral to live in and it was renamed Admiralty House. The last admiral vacated the house in 1913 and it was lent to the federal government. It is the Sydney residence of the governor general.

The much smaller Kirribilli House was built in 1855 by businessman Adolph Feez, on 1 acre (0.4 hectares) of land, subdivided from the land on which Admiralty House stands. Kirribilli House was bought by the federal government in 1920 when it was threatened with subdivision. Originally, it was intended to be accommodation for visiting dignitaries, but it is now used as the Sydney residence of the prime minister.

Kirribilli is covered with a dense cluster of high-rise flats on the edge of the harbour which directly face Sydney Cove and the Opera House. Until the 1920s, much of the land was undeveloped; there was even a large wool store abutting Admiralty House, with a covered pier located where the Beulah Street wharf is today. Fire destroyed the wool store in 1921, and also threatened Admiralty House. Before the flat-building boom of the 1920s and 1930s, residents in many of the fine Victorian homes in Kirribilli Avenue would have had grand, uninterrupted views of the harbour and the city beyond.

The open land near the northern pylon of the Harbour Bridge is one of the best vantage points for New Year's Eve and other celebratory fireworks displays, as well as offering, all year round, one of the closest, and most spectacular views of Sydney Cove and the city skyline. There are still many beautiful and charming tree-lined streets in Kirribilli, and a walk around the area is highly recommended.

Much of the development at McMahons Point and Lavender Bay that lie to the west of the bridge had to wait until the middle of the nineteenth century. Lavender Bay's heyday as a busy harbourside suburb ended in 1886, when the cable car started its run from Milsons Point to Ridge Street, North Sydney. Until then, Lavender Bay was the main ferry wharf in the North Sydney area. Blues Point Road was the main access road down to the ferry at Lavender Bay. The road, named after early Sydney Harbour waterman Billy Blue, was flanked by shops, pubs and houses. With the construction of the cable tram and then the railway, business on Blues Point Road dropped off dramatically, and now it and the surrounding streets of McMahons Point have an isolated and village-like ambience, which somehow makes the suburb feel more removed from the late twentieth century. Other parts of the lower North Shore would have felt remote and detached in a similar way, before the train, the Harbour Bridge, the Warringah Expressway and other twentieth-century development changed them forever.

Large residences were built at Lavender Bay, some of which have survived, despite the construction of the railway line. One house standing above Lavender Bay, with a thatched turret, was lived in by artist Brett Whiteley, who painted the harbour from his studio window there. Within the Graythwaite Nursing Home at Edward Street, North Sydney, stands Euroka Villa, one of the earliest and largest residences built in the area in the 1850s. Euroka Villa was sold to leading politician Thomas Dibbs, and the name was changed to Graythwaite. In 1916, Dibbs gave the house to the Commonwealth for use as a hospital. During World War I, it was used by the Red Cross as a convalescent home for injured servicemen.

Another notable resident of Lavender Bay was Dick Cavill, whose family operated swimming baths there which were not demolished until 1975. Cavill was born in 1884 and perfected the Australian crawl, or overarm swimming stroke.

North Sydney itself was originally laid out in 1836, at which time it, and much of the lower North Shore, as far north as Chatswood, was collectively known as St Leonards. The first streets to be built were Miller, Walker, Lavender and Berry streets. The township grew and,

411

by 1880, the town hall and the courthouse, both designed by James Barnet, were built. In 1894, the Blacket-designed St Thomas's Church, the largest parish church in Australia, was dedicated. North Sydney was incorporated in 1890. The North Sydney municipality included Mosman until 1893.

The Dibbs family were prominent residents of North Sydney; Thomas was a banker and benefactor to charity, and his brother George was a politician and premier of New South Wales. They grew up at a house called Bujwa at Lavender Bay, which stood on the site of ferryman George Lavender's old stone house. Unlike many other banks, Dibbs's bank emerged substantially unscathed from the downturn in the economy of the 1890s, and Dibbs was praised for his efforts. He probably gave his brother, George, who was then premier, advice about how to avert a banking collapse in the same period. Thomas Dibbs bought a large house in the North Sydney area which had been built by German-born Otto Holtermann. It still stands today within the Sydney Church of England Grammar School (Shore), a private boys school. There is a street named after Holtermann in Crows Nest.

Holtermann arrived in Australia in 1858 and eventually prospered on the New South Wales goldfields. He was a member of the consortium that mined the famous and massive 290-kilogram 'Holtermann nugget' found in 1872. With some of the profits from gold-mining, he built a house in the 1870s on what is now called Holtermanns Hill. It became part of Shore in 1888. While Holtermann was working the goldfields around Hill End, he met two leading pioneers of photography, Beaufroy Merlin and his apprentice Charles Bayliss. Bayliss took two huge (1-metre by 1.5-metre) negatives of Sydney from the tower above Holtermann's house. These were used to advertise Sydney and her prospects as a place to settle in at international exhibitions such as the Philadelphia Exhibition of 1876 and the Paris Exhibition. Not only was the subject matter of the photographs produced from the negatives of interest, but so, too, was the technical feat of producing such large photographic works. The negatives were the largest ever made.

They were rediscovered intact in 1951 at Chatswood, in the home of Holtermann's son's widow. Holtermann entered the New South Wales parliament in 1882 as the member for St Leonards (North Sydney). He was a keen advocate for his local area and a supporter of immigration. He lobbied for the construction of North Sydney post office and courthouse, and the railway extension south of St Leonards. Like his photographer friend Charles Bayliss, Holtermann died in his forties.

What would amaze Holtermann and members of the Dibbs family is what North Sydney has become: in large measure a northern extension of the city's CBD. This high-rise development is mostly on the upper ridges of North Sydney, and further up to Crows Nest and St Leonards. The lower North Shore is home to many advertising firms, both large and boutique, graphic designers, publishers, publicists, and computer, high-technology and communications businesses, such as Optus. At another point in the cultural spectrum, one of the older institutions in North Sydney is the Independent Theatre at 269 Miller Street. The building dates from 1900 and was originally used as a tram shed until 1909. After that, it became a vaudeville theatre, then, in 1939, it became the Independent Theatre, run by Doris Fitton. The Independent Theatre was for many years one of the few venues for locally produced plays. Fitton retired from theatrical production in 1977 and the theatre closed down, with the building being used for a time as a drama school. It was restored in 1993.

Because of North Sydney's mixed residential and commercial uses, the density of development can change drastically, almost block by block. Miller and Walker streets, for example, have both high-rise architecture and late–nineteenth-century and early–twentieth-century architecture. There is very little transitional architecture of the early and mid-twentieth century linking the earlier architecture (such as the Playfair Terraces in Ridge Street, North Sydney) with the high-rise development that started in 1957 and still continues. North Sydney took a long time to recover and find a new character following the demolition associated with the construction of the northern approaches to the Harbour Bridge. Much of the heart of Victorian residential North Sydney was torn out, as were many old streets and quarters on the other side of the harbour. North Sydney had a new lease of life when insurance companies such as the AMP and Lend Lease decided to establish corporate offices there from the late 1950s. The suburb had to face another challenge in the 1960s when the construction of the Warringah Expressway bisected the area, and caused another wave of demolition.

There are, however, some outstanding examples of mid–twentieth-century Art Deco architecture to be found at Milsons Point and Lavender Bay, at the North Sydney Pool and Luna Park, both of which stand under the shadow of Sydney's most ambitious work of Art Deco architecture, the Harbour Bridge. Luna Park, which has always rejoiced with the motto 'Just for Fun', was built after the opening of the Harbour Bridge on the site of the Dorman Long engineering workshops, where the components of the Harbour Bridge were assembled. It was shipped up from Glenelg, South Australia, in 1935, and took only three months to reassemble. Luna Park's signature is the large clown's face at the entry gates. Seven versions of this face have been built. One of the former models can be found at the Powerhouse Museum. The latest facade emulates the version of the 1950s. This and the many other Art Deco–derived features of Luna Park, such as Coney Island, have long been highly treasured icons for Sydneysiders, as has the large ferris wheel, the wild mouse and many other rides and attractions.

In the 1970s, Luna Park was renovated with the considerable contribution of well-known artist, Martin Sharp. By the late 1970s, television and other late–twentieth-century forms of entertainment and changing public taste were making the financial survival of Luna Park precarious. Matters got worse when, in 1979, tragedy struck Luna Park—the ghost train caught fire because of an electrical fault. Six children and one man died in the fire. An inquiry by the National Crime Authority in 1989 found that the police investigation after the fire was inadequate. The site is one of the most valuable pieces of real estate in Sydney and redevelopment has long been a possibility, becoming ever more probable as time goes on.

After the fire, Luna Park closed for several years, but reopened in the mid-1980s. It was renovated and once again reopened, with a new, enhanced Big Dipper, in late 1994. Local residents, led by Harry and Penelope Seidler, protested loudly at the level of noise the Big Dipper generated, mostly from shrieking revellers, and the Land and Environment Court decided to restrict the use of the ride. This restriction, and lower-than-expected visitor numbers, put the new operators of Luna Park in the same financially delicate position of previous owners. Luna Park has now closed down and its future once again is unclear. Luna Park may disappear forever and the site become another medium-rise, residential harbourside development.

Next door to Luna Park is the North Sydney Pool on the former Dorman Long workshop site. The covering, in the form of a large bubble, comes off in the summer months, giving a spectacular perspective of the underbelly of the bridge. The pool was the venue for the swimming events of the Empire Games in 1938.

The other great sporting facility at North Sydney is St Leonards Park, within which is the North Sydney Oval, home of the North Sydney 'Bears' rugby league team until 1998, when the decision was made to move the team's base to the Central Coast. In 1983, the old 'Bob' Stand (so-called because of the price of admission—1 shilling) at the Sydney Cricket Ground, built in 1895, was removed and taken to the North Sydney Oval. St Leonards Park still has the flavour of an English village common, which is missing in many of Sydney's other parks dedicated to team sports.

In Mount Street, North Sydney, is Mary MacKillop Place, named in honour of the first Australian to be beatified. Blessed Mary MacKillop was beatified by the pope in a ceremony at Randwick Racecourse in January 1995. The building, which used to be a convent, is dedicated to Mary MacKillop's life and works. It is a popular place of pilgrimage for her many admirers, drawn to her on account of her ability to act independently and to triumph over adversity. Within the complex is the cottage in which she spent her last years. The miraculous acts which led to her beatification and possible future canonisation are depicted in the Miracle Room: it is claimed that she intervened to save the life of a woman who was dying of leukaemia. Her tomb is also within the complex, as is a commemorative chapel. Mary MacKillop founded the Order of the Sisters of St Joseph of the Sacred Heart, known as the Josephite Sisters, based in MacKillop Place. The order is dedicated to educating the poor and helping the infirm.

Mosman covers a very large area, and is bounded on all sides except to the west by the harbour. It includes nearly 20 kilometres of the harbour's foreshores. Mosman is really a cluster of bays with a spine in the middle, along which run Military and Spit roads, where the typical Sydney commercial ribbon development can be seen from Neutral Bay to Spit Junction. The bays and headlands of Mosman cover much of the northern side of Sydney Harbour and lower Middle Harbour. There are Great and Little Sirius coves, Athol Bay, Bradleys Head, Chowder Bay (named after the soup American whalers made when they were moored there in the nineteenth century), Georges Head, Obelisk Bay, Middle Head, Hunters

Bay (where Balmoral Beach is), Chinamans Beach (named after gardener Cho Hi Tick and where there was a joss house and a small village until the 1880s), Shell Cove, The Spit and Beauty Point. The earlier-built parts of Mosman are those southern areas which were initially served by ferry services on the harbour. The residential development on the northern side of Mosman came later.

Mosman's residents are loyal, sometimes fiercely so, about their suburb and what it has to offer. This entirely justifiable pride and parochialism—and feeling of self-containment close to the city, but within a verdant harbour-side environment—contributes to a great deal of Mosman's character. Mosman residents have defended themselves relatively well from undesirable incursions into their way of life. For example, in the 1960s, the council, at the urging of Alderman Barry O'Keefe, decided that the high-rise buildings, which were built predominantly along the spine of Spit Road, should not be allowed to spread any further, and regulations were imposed to prevent this. In 1967, Sydney's first tree preservation order was imposed by the council. Mosman Council was also one of the first local government areas to experiment with street closures. Perhaps most significantly for Sydney, the Bradley sisters, Joan and Eileen, residents of Clifton Gardens and lovers of the bushland and bird life around them, developed a system of weeding and regenerating the bush. This practice was adopted by the National Trust and other councils. The Bradley sisters are commemorated by a bushland reserve which bears their name at Middle Head near Rawson Park, where more than 13 000 native trees and shrubs of 100 species were planted.

The first European settler in Mosman was a pardoned convict, Thomas O'Neil. O'Neil farmed 40 acres (16 hectares) of land at Balmoral from 1811. His property and much of the lower North Shore were burnt out in a bushfire in 1826, which devastated the land from the Lane Cove River to Georges Head. By 1838, O'Neil had sold his land. The suburb is named after Scottish-born Archibald Mosman, who in 1831 set up a whaling operation in a deep and sheltered bay called Greater Sirius Cove now also known as Mosman Bay.

Mosman started off with a relatively modest land-holding of 4 acres (1.6 hectares) and built a large stone wharf and two stone storehouses and dwellings for whalers and ships' officers in the cove, as well as his own residence which he called The Nest. Mosman's home stood in Badham Avenue until 1921. The whaling business prospered and Mosman eventually accumulated 108 acres (44 hectares) of land. The whaling operations only lasted until 1838 when Mosman bought pastoral land in New England near Glen Innes. Mosman Bay was used for careening and repairing ships, including naval ships, as it had been used in the very early years of settlement when the storeship *Sirius* was repaired there, under the command of Lieutenant Governor John Hunter.

In 1859, Richard Harnett bought Mosman's land and lived at The Nest. He tried unsuccessfully to promote Mosman Bay as a weekend picnic spot. Harnett then developed a transport service, at first a horse-drawn omnibus from Mosman Bay to Military Road and later, from 1884, a ferry service to Circular Quay. Harnett subdivided much of his land and the speculators moved in.

ABOVE: The tranquillity of Mosman Bay in 1880, a time when the suburb of Mosman was just beginning to develop.

The population rose. A public school opened in 1880 and in 1893 the municipality of Mosman was incorporated—Harnett's son was the first mayor. There was a boom in residential development between 1890 and 1914 when Federation architecture was fashionable, and much of it can still be seen, especially in the parts of Mosman close to the tram and ferry services such as Clifton Gardens, Sirius Cove and along Rangers Road, at the end of which a Gothic-Federation folly built by Oswald Bloxsome once stood.

The northern side of Mosman was not subdivided until later; it was much further away from the harbour ferries and there was no commuter service to Balmoral. Killarney, a large estate of 11 acres (4.5 hectares), was sold off in sixty-one blocks in 1901. Beauty Point was not subdivided until 1921.

Taronga Park Zoo was established in 1912 and opened in 1916 on the eastern side of Little Sirius Cove (which lies to the east of Mosman Bay), on land within Ashton Park. It must be one of the most spectacularly located zoos in the world, covering 30 hectares of land, perched on a ridge of Mosman, and running, in the shape of an amphitheatre, down to the water's edge of Athol Bay. Breathtaking views of the harbour and the city compete with the animals for attention. The zoo is surrounded by natural vegetation, and has many native plants within its boundaries—angophoras, eucalypts and acacias. This may be the best spot in Sydney to see the city from across the harbour, looking through a hazy grey-green veil of eucalyptus leaves.

Before Taronga Park Zoo was opened, the zoo animals lived at Moore Park at the Billygoat Swamp, where the Sydney High playgrounds are today. The exodus of the animals must have been a sight to behold. Jessie the elephant and the other animals were punted across the harbour to their new home.

During the industrial unrest of 1917, the zoo was used to accommodate strike-breakers who had come down from the country. Nestling down to sleep in the open air surrounded by strange and sometimes noisy beasts must have been an interesting experience. One of the people who for many years had a great influence on the management and appearance of the zoo was philanthropic industrialist, E. J. L. Hallstrom. As well as donating a great deal of money to the zoo for buildings and other improvements, he commissioned safaris to Africa and New Guinea. Many species of exotic animals were added to the zoo, sometimes in unmanageably large numbers.[8] Hallstrom's views about what were appropriate living conditions for the animals were unusual, certainly by today's standards. Many cages and dens were built of concrete, which may have been easy to keep clean, but did not in any way replicate the natural environment the animals were used to. There was some suggestion of nature with handpainted bark and grain effects on some of the concrete cabins and rocks, but these subtle evocations were probably lost on the animals. During his term as executive chairman and later as honorary director, the Gorilla Villa was built, and King Kong placed within it. More gorillas were added through the 1960s.

417

Hallstrom cast a long and (financially) generous shadow over the zoo until 1967. His son, John, was also a trustee of the zoo for thirty-seven years until 1985. After Hallstrom's retirement, there was greater emphasis on developing the importance of zoological science within the zoo, and on exhibiting Australian animals. The Koala House, Rainforest Aviary, Waterfowl Ponds and Nocturnal House were built, the last so that visitors could see marsupials in night-time conditions,when they are most active. More attention was paid to creating a natural environment for the animals. Concrete floors were abandoned. New buildings such as the Chimpanzee Park and Gorilla and Orang-utan Rainforests have been designed with greater sensitivity towards the animals' wellbeing. In 1979, the popular Seal Theatre was opened and in 1987, the elephants were given more space in which to roam.

Since the 1980s, revenue from admission has been supplemented by sponsorship income. The government only provides money for capital works, not recurrent expenses. The zoo is open every day of the year. The best way to get to the zoo from the city is by ferry, and then taking the chair lift to the top where the main entrance is, then meander back down the hill to the water's edge. One of the best attractions at the zoo is the seal show, which takes place twice a day, at 1 p.m. and again at 2.30 p.m. Small children can enjoy contact with the animals at the Discovery Farm every day at 2 p.m. Until the lions' dens were relocated in recent years, their roars could sometimes be heard across the harbour on still evenings and in the early morning.

Near Bradleys Head, within Athol Park, stands one of the old dance pavilions, an architectural vestige of the days in the nineteenth century when the lower North Shore was a destination for fun and revelry on weekends, and the site of many pleasure grounds. One of the best harbour-side walks runs from the Zoo ferry wharf at Athol Bay, around the harbour's edge to Bradleys Head, then around Taylors Bay to Chowder Head and Clifton Gardens.

While the residential and suburban housing boom was starting to gain momentum in the 1880s and 1890s, Mosman also became a haven for bohemian life. The first artists' camp was built at Balmoral Beach. Later, in the 1890s, Curlew Camp was set up at Little Sirius Cove.

The artists' camp at Balmoral was set up on 50 acres (20 hectares) of land by American Livingstone ('Hop') Hopkins. Hopkins was a leading illustrator for the *Bulletin* in its heyday of the 1880s and 1890s. The conditions were jovial and rather more comfortable than most camps: there was a permanent four-room tent, built on the site of the Bathers' Pavilion, which had regular beds, and a special dining tent with cook—Old Ben, a retired sea captain—supplied. A regular visitor to the camp was Julian Ashton, who preferred to sleep out in the open air.[9] Robert Louis Stevenson visited the camp when he was in Sydney. Livingstone Hopkins loved the camp so much that he moved his household from North Sydney to Mosman. The spirit of the artists' camps is well summed up in the following lines by fellow bohemian Sydney artist, Benjamin Minns:

418

> To the ti-tree camp all painters we invite
> Including those who work in black and white
> Tired workers with the brush or pen
> Retreating from the busy haunts of men
> Enter our gates and stretch upon the grass
> Enjoy the soothing pipe and the cooling glass.
> Camped on this lonely seagirt shore
> Art is the mistress we adore.[10]

Other weekend camps set up alongside Hopkins's. Other people who lived at or spent time at these camps include Tom Roberts, Charles Conder, William Lister, Sydney Long and Sienese-born Girolamo Nerli.

In 1890, a new camp set up at Little Sirius Cove on the southern side of Mosman, near Taronga Zoo. Rather than looking out to the heads of Sydney Harbour, this camp looked across to the eastern suburbs, Circular Quay and the city beyond. Arthur Streeton spent time at the camp, as did Tom Roberts. Streeton arrived in Sydney in 1890, encouraged by the Art Gallery of New South Wales's decision to buy his painting *Still Glides the Stream and Shall Forever Glide*. One of the residents of the Curlew Camp, Reuben Brasch, used to row over from Parsley Bay. Brasch owned a haberdashery in Oxford Street, and he supplied Streeton and Roberts with the rectangular wooden 'dress boards' that fabric was folded around, which they used for their works. Artist Henry Fullwood moved to the camp as a refugee from the bank crash of 1893.

The inspiration of the harbour for the members of the artists' camps was well illustrated by Arthur Streeton, then aged twenty-four, when he wrote of a day in early summer:

> The Harbour is a wonder of spirit and life and movement today. Hundreds and hundreds of yachts are coursing over the purple sea (it is wine). The brilliant white sails cutting finely against the summer sky. Ferryboats puff and paddle along crowded with pleasure loving folk—the youth of Sydney in bright flannels hang out to windward, their bronze limbs all aglitter with the spray of salt waves—in every little nook and bay are numbers of boats full of gay costumes and laughter—some parties are singing in chorus others cooee and listen to the echo across the bright bay. The air is warm and soft like unto a drooping crimson poppy … Around the tent the Begonia and Clematis and Sarsparilla, the rough winds broken for us by an exquisite fusion of tender gum leaf.[11]

Bohemian artists' camps did not sit well alongside Mosman's burgeoning reputation as a pleasant residential harbour-side sanctuary from the city, and the council did not encourage campers to stay. The death knell for the artists' camps was the introduction of daylight swimming at Sydney's beaches in 1903. This made the beaches of Mosman less secluded than they had been in the 1890s. All the huts and camps, as well as Mosman's bohemian era, have vanished.

Mosman Council still takes great pride in having achieved and maintained a high level of surveillance over the quality of development and redevelopment at Mosman. The resolve of the council will be tested as the demand for medium- and even high-density housing in this pleasant suburb increases. Some people at Mosman are very willing to enjoy the convenience of easy access to the city, as long as this convenience does not mean that outsiders will come and enjoy the tranquillity and beauty of the place.

Some Mosman residents are apprehensive about what effect larger-scale dining and bar facilities will have on the relatively peaceful area and the tranquillity of the main harbour beach for the lower North Shore. There was protracted dispute between locals and developers when proposals to develop the old Bathers' Pavilion at Balmoral Beach were put before the council. After many years, the plans are finally going ahead. What is clear is that some, though not all, residents of Mosman do not want their treasured and relatively isolated bays and coves to be overused and over-visited in the same way as other Sydney natural landmarks have, such as Watsons Bay and Bondi Beach. This reluctance to host outsiders has been long-standing: in 1910, residents objected strongly to the visits of larrikin gangs to Balmoral on the weekends.[12] The council stepped in to protect Balmoral from the larrikin influence.

In the 1920s, Balmoral's emerging status as a pleasant harbourside suburb and beach had to compete with a group of people who were members of the theosophist Order of the Star of the East, led by a retired doctor, Mary Rocke, and her leader, Charles Leadbeater, who were busy preparing for the second coming of the Messiah. A Doric amphitheatre was built at the northern end of Edwards Bay at Balmoral in 1924 and performances were held there. It had a capacity of 3000 people. The idea of building the amphitheatre was that it should be:

[A] symbol in stone of what our daily lives should be … simple, pure, clean, dignified. Australia must not copy, she must lead … Australia must be a window through which the Empire looks upon the future of what awaits it.[13]

Theosophy was an attempt to create a new religion that drew strongly on Indian spirituality and belief in the concept of *karma* and reincarnation. Sydney was one of the stronger centres for theosophy between 1923 and 1926, which also was practised in many other parts of the British Empire. The members of the Order of the Star of the East believed that Krishnamurti would be revealed as the Messiah at the theatre/temple. This did not happen. The urban myth has since evolved that the members of the order expected the messiah to walk through Sydney Heads. Many theosophists in Sydney were based in a large house in Clifton Gardens called Bakewell's Folly, which they renamed The Manor. Theosophists established the still-active radio station 2GB in the 1920s, and were culturally active in fields of theatre, music and art, as well as being exponents of progressive education. They also published a magazine called *Advance Australia*. The use and popularity of the amphitheatre at Balmoral declined along with theosophy from 1926. It was sold in 1931 and demolished in 1951. A block of flats was built there in the 1950s by one of the first postwar property development companies.

Despite the demise of the artists' camps, and the disappearance of the theosophists from the area, Mosman has since the 1880s been a popular place for artists, writers and poets to live. Ethel Turner, author of *Seven Little Australians*, lived there, as did poet Christopher Brennan, his friend, poet and academic John Le Gay Brereton, writers George Johnston, Charmian Clift, Ruth Park and Gavin Souter, and well-known painters Lloyd Rees and Margaret Preston. Like other Mosman residents, these people were greatly attracted by the area's physical beauty and village-like charm, where the harbour and the bushland are never far away.

Military Road at Mosman is one of Sydney's better retail precincts, certainly for fashion and products for the home. Design and style seem to be an important ingredient in Military Road's retail success, if the nature of many of the shops is any indication, and Mosman residents talk proudly, even chauvinistically, of what there is to offer. Despite being almost bisected by Military Road, and on a main access road to Sydney's northern beaches, many parts of Mosman still have the flavour of being remotely situated at the end of the line.

The biggest blot on Mosman's recent history was the 'Granny Killer', John Glover, a travelling meat-pie salesman and Mosman resident who chose elderly women who lived alone as his victims. Between March 1989 and March 1990, he committed six murders, four of which occurred in Mosman. The murders were quite incomprehensible and staggeringly gruesome. His victims included Gwendolen Mitchelhill (82); Lady Ashton (84), widow of Mosman artist Sir William Ashton; Dora Cox (86), who survived the attack, but had no memory of it; Madge Prahud (85); Olive Cleveland (81); and Muriel Falconer (93). His final victim was a friend of his, the much younger Joan Sinclair (60), who lived at Beauty Point.

The police task force had attached an electronic surveillance device to Glover's car and waited outside Sinclair's house for seven hours. Finally the police entered the house and found his victim, who had been hammered and strangled to death. Glover had taken a large amount of sleeping pills and whisky, but survived. He was tried for murder. He was unable to convince the court of his insanity and was sentenced to life imprisonment.

It was not until 1924 that Spit Bridge was built. Before this time, Middle Harbour could only be crossed by ferry so there was little suburban settlement on the northern side of Middle Harbour. One early suburb on the northern side of the Spit Bridge was Seaforth. It was designed and subdivided by property developer Henry Halloran in 1907 in such a way that the contours of the area which sloped down to Middle Harbour were used as the basis of the layout of the streets.[14]

An interesting aspect of Sydney's industrial history can be seen at Bantry Bay, Middle Harbour, within the Garigal National Park. The first use for Bantry Bay was as a shipping base for timber felled up on the ridge in the area now known as Frenchs Forest (named after the first European landowner). In 1915, Bantry Bay was selected as the place for the government's explosives magazine. Nitroglycerine was very unstable at that time and needed to be stored in remote places. It was used by the government throughout Sydney and New South Wales for building railways and roads. Not only was Bantry Bay remote, but the high hills were also thought to be able to contain damage in the event of any explosion. The deep-water bay was also attractive as a place to build wharves. Employees would be taken by boat from The Spit each morning to do their day's work further up Middle Harbour. When explosives became safer and easier to store, remoteness was not such a critical requirement and the government stored them at the Australian Defence Industries site at St Marys. By then, explosives were manufactured in Australia by Imperial Chemical Industries (ICI) in Melbourne. Now the fine, old buildings of Bantry Bay are deserted. Entry to them is prohibited, but, by boat, it is possible to see one of the largest intact early–twentieth-century industrial sites in Sydney.

An unusual suburb of the lower North Shore is Castlecrag, initially designed by Walter Burley Griffin and his wife, Marion Mahony Griffin. The Griffins had worked with leading North American architect Frank Lloyd Wright in Chicago before arriving in Australia. They came to Australia having won the competition to build the new national capital in Canberra. As a foretaste of what Jørn Utzon was to experience many years later during the building of the Sydney Opera House, their scheme for the city was never fully implemented, and Castlecrag is the main architectural legacy the Griffins realised during their years in Australia. The Griffins promoted the land company that bought and subdivided the land, although the promoters made no windfall profits before they left for India.

The Griffins wanted Castlecrag's development to be in harmony with the natural topo-graphy, rather than being tamed into the same sort of homogeneous red-tiled and liver- or red-

421

ABOVE: The Spit in Middle Harbour before the Spit Bridge was built in 1924.

422

brick bungalow suburbs that were proliferating in Sydney during the 1920s. The use of local sandstone as a building material was a rare early–twentieth-century attempt to match the housing with its setting. The 'demonstration house' for the development project at Edinburgh Road has been restored by the Historic Houses Trust. It is subject to a permanent conservation order. Some of the other original houses at Castlecrag have been renovated in such a way that their original scale and many original features have been lost.

Willoughby Council used its legal powers under the *Local Government Act* of 1919 to proclaim Castlecrag, then harbourside bushland, as a residential district. Castlecrag and nearby Northbridge were suburbs built in anticipation of the completion of the Sydney Harbour Bridge. More houses were built in Northbridge in 1922 than in any other part of Sydney,[15] and the overall aesthetic result is vastly different to what the Griffins had in mind. In the early 1960s, Lend Lease Corporation continued the work of subdividing the suburb which Griffin had started.

The initial grantees of land on the upper North Shore exploited their land by clearing the vast stands of timber. Timber was felled and dragged by oxen along very rough dirt tracks, including Fiddens Wharf Road, westward to the Lane Cove River. From the river, the logs

ABOVE: Elizabeth Bay in the nineteenth century. Elizabeth Bay House can be seen in the background. *Elizabeth Bay House, c. 1840, Conrad Martens (Image Library, State Library of NSW)*

BELOW: View of the heads at the entrance to Port Jackson, *c. 1820, Joseph Lycett (Rex Nan Kivell Collection, National Library of Australia)*

ABOVE: Bondi beach has achieved almost iconic status worldwide as the beach that typifies Sydney. Although partisan locals may take exception to this description in favour of their particular beachside mecca, its arc of almost blinding white sand and green–blue waters still draws the crowds—ranging from families and sun worshippers through to overseas visitors and dedicated surfers and board riders. (*Marcus Clinton*)

BELOW: Balmoral Beach on Sydney's North Shore has a netted swimming pool popular with people who prefer to swim in the calm harbour waters and its original Bathers' Pavilion, these days a popular up-market restaurant. (*Marcus Clinton*)

ABOVE: Ducks on a pond in Centennial Park, which was dedicated to the people of New South Wales in the colony's centenary year of 1888. Covering 220 hectares, the park contains the source of what was once Sydney's water supply. It was also the site of the swearing in of the first federal ministry by the governor-general, when the Commonwealth of Australia was formed in 1901. (*Australian Tourist Commission*)

BELOW: View of harbour islands looking west towards the Harbour Bridge from the eastern suburbs. Shark Island is in the foreground of the picture, with Fort Denison visible in the centre. (*Hamilton Lund, Australian Tourist Commission*)

ABOVE: An older style Paddington store that no longer exists on this fashionable strip of Oxford Street. *(Australian Tourist Commission)*

LEFT: A row of Victorian terrace houses featuring characteristic iron lace balconies in Paddington. *(Australian Tourist Commission)*

were taken by barge down to Cockle Bay (Darling Harbour).

One of the first grantees of land on the North Shore was William Henry, an officer and close ally of William Bligh, who refused to side with Macarthur and the others in the Rum Rebellion of 1808. Henry was exiled to the Coal River (Newcastle) for this act of loyalty to his superior officer. He was later rehabilitated by Macquarie and given a small land grant on the North Shore, which he cleared for orchards. Although Henry had asked for 1000 acres (400 hectares) around Blue Gum Creek (where the eastern extremity of the Lane Cove National Park is in present-day Chatswood West), this request was declined. Instead, he was granted 1000 acres (400 hectares) of land around Burns Bay, on the Lane Cove River, where the private Catholic boys school St Ignatius Riverview now is. Burns Bay was used as a depot for transporting timber. Henry's descendants established orchards on the North Shore, and the family owned a large produce wholesaling business at the Sydney markets. Henry, like other early grantees of land, was an absentee landlord. He did not build a large home here, but probably stayed in a crudely built hut while visiting his land-holdings north of the harbour. Otherwise he lived in the town of Sydney itself.

Daniel Mathew was another early landowner. He was granted 400 acres (160 hectares) of land at Roseville, which at the time was known as Lane Cove. Mathew was what would have then been described as a gentleman. He was well connected in England, and possibly a remittance man. Remittance men had usually somehow disgraced the family by scandalising it in some way—by being profligate, by gambling, by acting immorally or even by making an inappropriate marriage. Remittance men were typically sent out to the colonies with enough money to become established, but were expected to make their own way.

Mathew lived and worked as an architect and developer in Sydney while his land was cleared with convict and hired labour. He could foresee the profitability of the timber industry on the North Shore, and decided to take a trip to England to invest in a plant that could make the timber cutting profitable. He sold his partly cleared farm to Richard Archbold, bought a sawmill in England, shipped it back and started to clear 800 acres (320 hectares) further north at present-day Pymble and St Ives. Mona Vale Road passes through what was once his land.

One of the biggest landowners on the North Shore was Thomas Hyndes. He came to Sydney as a convict, and was later appointed as an overseer of town and gaol gangs. He received grants of land covering much of the upper North Shore between Bobbin Head Road and Hornsby, thus covering present-day Turramurra, Warrawee and Wahroonga. Hyndes built himself a private wharf on the Lane Cove River, which was used by him and other timber cutters in the area. Hyndes was a major timber merchant, and the family home was situated close to the centre of the timber trade at Darling Harbour. Hyndes owned a wharf at the end of Druitt Street, which was the destination of much of the timber from his land on the upper North Shore. He also had a farm on the Cooks River.

Joseph Fidden was the primary shipper of timber down river from his eponymously named wharf at the western end of Fiddens Wharf Road at West Killara. Fidden also operated two sawpits near the wharf. The area around Fiddens Wharf became a social centre for timbermen and sawyers. As timber felling gave way to orcharding, Fidden's transport business continued to prosper as produce was transported down to the markets near Darling Harbour.

One of the first settlers in the area (as opposed to absentee landowners and timber getters) was Robert Pymble. He was granted 600 acres (240 hectares) of land in 1823 in the area of the North Shore which has been named after him. With convict labour, he built a timber cottage close to Pymble railway station. Pymble worked at clearing the land, transporting the timber to Sydney by oxen to Fidden's or Hyndes's wharves on the Lane Cove River, then had it shipped down the river and across to Darling Harbour. Pymble planted orchards in the land as he cleared. Some of the convicts employed by Pymble and Hyndes eventually settled in the area.

The population of the North Shore was small and isolated until the advent of the railway in the last years of the nineteenth century. In the early timber-gathering years, social life was much rougher and less refined than it is today. One of the earliest legal public bars in the area—as opposed to the illegal stills which were the focus of social gatherings—was an earlier version of today's Greengate Hotel on the Pacific Highway at Killara. Timbermen and other labourers could refresh themselves there. It was conveniently close to the junction of Fiddens Wharf Road and the Lane Cove Road (now the Pacific Highway). One of the first owners of the hotel was Tom Waterhouse. The Waterhouse family, members of which were later involved in the horseracing industry as well as having other hotel and business interests, held the hotel until 1903. The first post office on the North Shore, called the Lane Cove Post Office, was established in 1860. In 1879, it changed its name to Gordon Post Office. It stood on the current site of the Ravenswood School for Girls.

From the middle of the nineteenth century, Gordon increasingly became the main village on the North Shore. Gordon Public School, one of the rare older architectural landmarks on the Pacific Highway, was established as the Lane Cove School in 1876. By 1885, as development progressed, the area once known as Lane Cove began to be restricted to the area we now know it to be, on the lower and western part of the North Shore along the Lane Cove River. The second school on the upper North Shore was St Ives School (1889), and the third Lindfield (1903). The number of new schools increased with the completion of the North Shore railway line in 1890, and today some of Sydney's better-known private schools are to be found on the North Shore line, which adds to the area's attraction for families with young children.

Starting from the north, these schools are Abbotsleigh (1898), Barker (1896), Knox Grammar School (1923), Presbyterian Ladies College Pymble (1916), Ravenswood (1901), Shore (or the Sydney Church of England Grammar School) (1889), Wenona (1913), St Ignatius Riverview (1880), St Joseph's College, Hunters Hill, and Loreto Kirribilli and Normanhurst. Two of Sydney's best state high schools are also on the North Shore: North Sydney Boys High (1910) and North Sydney Girls High (1914). In 1963, Sydney's third university was established in northern Sydney. Macquarie University was created at the instigation of many North Shore residents and teachers. Critical to being able to attend this university was often the ability to own and drive a motor car. The only other alternative was a great deal of patience in coping with the ill-developed cross-city public transport network.

Until the introduction of the railway, transport in the area was rough and ready. Roads were unsealed and potholed, and the trip into town was usually an overnight journey by horse or on foot to the Lane Cove River, or later to the ferry wharves on the lower North Shore. In 1875, a petition was signed by North Shore residents campaigning for a railway in the area then called Lane Cove, which ran from Chatswood to Pearces Corner at Wahroonga. Finally, the agitation developed political momentum and, from 1882, it was supported by Henry Parkes. Everybody could agree on the northern terminus for the railway (Pearces Corner), but there was much less consensus about where its southern extremity should be. Possible candidates were Balls Head, Blues Point, Milsons Point and Cremorne. With all these choices, a final decision was deferred. The first stage of the railway was opened in 1890. It ran from Hornsby to St Leonards. Passengers had to make their way south from there by omnibus for the $2^1/_2$-mile (4-kilometre) journey to the ferries at Milsons Point. In 1891, the first sod was turned on the southern extension, from Milsons Point to St Leonards, and work was completed by 1893. The North Shore line was electrified in 1927 and extended over the Harbour Bridge in 1932.

In the late nineteenth century, houses and shops appeared along Lane Cove Road (later called the Gordon Road before it became the Pacific Highway after the completion of the Harbour Bridge). The Ku-ring-gai Shire Council was established in 1906. Just twenty-one years later, there had been so much residential development that it became a municipal council. The population in the Ku-ring-gai area grew from 4500 people in 1901 to 24 000 in 1925. In 1924, the Roseville Bridge across Middle Harbour was opened and, further down Middle Harbour, the Spit Bridge was completed. This made the subdivision of much of the land on the northern side of Middle Harbour possible. From the 1920s, these main roads were sealed. The suburban expansion through the twentieth century was greatly assisted by the construction of alternative northern routes such as the Archbold, Boundary and Arterial roads. Gradually, the orchards of the upper North Shore were subdivided into building blocks of 40 to 100 acres (16 to 40 hectares), then downwards to 10 acres (4 hectares) and then again, often to the standard housing-block size of 10 000 square feet (930 square metres).

One of the finest homes of the upper North Shore is Eryldene (1913), designed by Hardy Wilson, one of Sydney's most eminent early–twentieth-century architects, who often worked in the Georgian style. The owner of the house was Professor Waterhouse, an expert on camellias. In deference to the Asian origin of camellias, there is a Chinese teahouse within the gardens with the curious addition of Grecian pillars, as a gesture to both eastern and western architectural influences. The garden was designed as a visual extension to the house at a time when Federation-style architecture was dominant and most houses built at the time did not connect spatially or visually with the landscape within which they stood. Both the house and the fine, extensive (1-hectare) gardens are open to the public for one weekend during the camellia season as part of the Open Garden Scheme. Other gardens on the upper North Shore which can be seen are: the Phillips Garden in Chatswood, which features deciduous trees; Willow's End, Killara, which is open in the autumn; Craig Dhu and the Cummins Garden, in Pymble.

In the late twentieth century, there has been pressure on the housing densities on the North Shore. Its proximity to the city and the secondary business districts of North Sydney and Chatswood has promoted the growth in medium-density housing, especially south of Roseville and along the Pacific Highway. Further north again, there is even high-rise development at Hornsby near the railway station.

St Ives was one of the last suburbs to be developed on the upper North Shore. It was not as conveniently located close to the railway line as were other suburbs, as it lies considerably to the east. In the nineteenth century, orchards covered the fertile soil which lay west of Cowan Creek, and south of the sandstone country which lay beyond. It was a rural area until after 1918. The subdivision and residential development of St Ives had to wait until the 1960s and 1970s, when the motor car became the dominant form of transport. In recent years, there has been a growth in the number of Asian-born and Jewish residents. Members of the Jewish community, especially many South Africans, are attracted to the area because of the Jewish day school there.

St Ives ends abruptly at the edge of the bushland of Garigal National Park. The park runs from Middle Harbour up to the ridge of the upper North Shore. Other suburbs which adjoin this park are East Killara and East Lindfield. Within the park are several walking tracks leading down to the water.

One of the early settlers of the St Ives area was William Vernon, an accomplished gardener who had worked in Kent for the Earl of Cornwallis, then later in Sydney for T. S. Mort at Greenoaks, Darling Point, and for the Tooth family at Cranbrook, Bellevue Hill. Vernon was granted 48 acres (19 hectares) at St Ives in 1863, just north of the Pymble Golf Course.

Just to the west of St Ives, along present-day Pentecost Avenue at Turramurra, between Bobbin Head Road and Merrivale Street once stood Irish Town, probably so called because some of the residents there in the nineteenth century were timber cutters of Irish extraction. They and their descendants later owned orchards or were employed as orchardists.

From the advent of the railway in the 1890s, much of the land at Turramurra north of Eastern Road was subdivided and the orchards were converted into sites for large mansions. Streets which have many large homes built in this period are Ku-ring-gai Avenue and Burns Road. The huge rise in land values from 1947 onwards meant that many of the larger blocks were subdivided into smaller ones.

The remoteness from the centre of Sydney fostered a much deeper sense of civic pride than many other suburbs closer to the town enjoyed; this remoteness, though less extreme in the later years of the nineteenth century, still fosters an aura of the upper North Shore as a self-sufficient and strong community. An example of this was the move by local residents to subscribe to a club which bought and cleared the land that later became the Warrawee Bowling Club, where croquet, bowling, tennis and cricket were played. Entertainment was organised on a community or village basis as well. Trains would be chartered for the evening to take people into the theatre in the city. Residents travelled to Sydney to go to the theatre and enjoyed supper, organised by the Milsons Point stationmaster, on the train on the way home.[16] The train would stop wherever people wanted to get off, sometimes in the middle of what was then open countryside.

Before the creation of the Ku-ring-gai Shire Council in 1906, bodies such as the Wahroonga Progress Association were involved in the development and civic amenities of the area. Residents were rated on a voluntary basis. Street trees were planted, footpaths were built and roads were laid out and sealed. Roads such as Coonanbarra Road, Billyard Avenue and Burns Avenue were first sealed with funds voluntarily raised.

One of the early community leaders of the upper North Shore was Eccleston du Faur, an Englishman of French ancestry. He came to Australia in the gold rush and later settled in Sydney as a surveyor for the Lands Department. He drew up a map of New South Wales over many years which set out a systematic survey of lands available for selection. This map was one of the many governmental documents destroyed in the Garden Palace fire. Du Faur was also interested in the meteorological effect of Antarctica on the Australian climate. He supported and helped raise funds for Mawson's Antarctic expedition of 1910. In 1889, he built a large residence called Pibrac, which stands at Pibrac Avenue, Warrawee. Du Faur strongly advocated the creation of Ku-ring-gai Chase National Park in 1894 and was the managing trustee of it. The area was called a 'chase' rather than a 'park' as this connoted a large and unenclosed area of land, rather than a closed park. In 1895, du Faur built another house on the North Shore at the gates of the park, which later became the Lady Davidson Convalescent Hospital.

Du Faur was closely associated with the creation of the NSW Arts Academy in 1871, which grew into the National Art Gallery (now the Art Gallery of New South Wales) under his trusteeship and presidency, which lasted from 1892 to 1915. Du Faur's contribution to Sydney and New South Wales is not well commemorated. The only place named after him is the Du Faur Rocks at Mt Wilson in the Blue Mountains, which he settled and developed. Du Faur's daughter Emmeline grew up as a keen rock scrambler in the Ku-ring-gai Chase National Park and later became a keen mountaineer, and was the first woman to climb Mt Cook and many other mountains in New Zealand.

427

Architect John Sulman was another notable resident of the North Shore. Born in England, he originally settled at Parramatta, but moved to a house on the present-day site of Warrawee Public School on the Pacific Highway. He later built Ingelholme in Boomerang Street, Turramurra, now used by the Presbyterian Ladies College. He designed many large homes at Wahroonga and Turramurra, and many old English-style buildings in Coonanbarra Road, once the main road to Wahroonga station.

Sulman favoured the construction of a tunnel under the harbour, unlike fellow North Shore resident John Bradfield. Sulman served for many years on the National Capital Advisory Committee, and was the first president of the Town Planning Association of New South Wales. He also lectured in architecture at the University of Sydney. Like du Faur, he was heavily involved in the National Art Gallery of New South Wales. His family endowed the Sulman Prize in his honour, which is awarded each year for subject or genre painting at the Art Gallery of New South Wales. A Sulman Medal for Architecture was also endowed, and each year a prize is awarded to the architect of an outstanding piece of architecture in New South Wales.

The founder of the New South Wales branch of the National Trust, the organisation dedicated to the classification and preservation of buildings which have heritage value, was Anne Forsyth Wyatt. She lived on the North Shore, founded the Ku-ring-gai Tree Lovers Civic League in 1927 and helped in the creation of part of the reserve at Balls Head in 1931. The physical beauty of the North Shore attracted many artists from the late nineteenth century. Artists who lived on the North Shore were: Benjamin Minns, who lived at East Gordon; his neighbour, Sydney Long; Lionel Lindsay, who lived at Wahroonga; Robert Johnson, who lived at Lindfield; and Grace Cossington Smith, who moved from Neutral Bay to Turramurra in 1913 at the age of twenty-one. All were considerably inspired by the topography and the diverse native flora.

428

Much of the social activity of the upper North Shore still takes place within people's homes, rather than at cafés and restaurants, although this is slowly changing. This is part of the reason for its well-deserved reputation as a quiet, respectable suburban enclave, where gardening, as well as golf and tennis, are common forms of recreation. In the 1960s and early 1970s, the main difference between the upper North Shore and other parts of Sydney could be summed up in two words: swimming pools. In those days, before they were as common throughout Sydney as they are today (in some suburbs, they seem to be ubiquitous), the upper North Shore stood out for the number of sparkling, aqua-blue pools which could be seen by people flying into Sydney Airport. For many families, this reinforced the feeling of a happy, secure and self-contained suburban existence.

Although most social activity on the upper North Shore does take place indoors, there are many other ways of spending time. The abundance of public parkland is ideal for picnics and bushwalks in places such as the Lane Cove National Park and at Bobbin Head.

The northern beaches area of Sydney, more correctly known as the Manly–Warringah area, covers the thin northern strip of coastal land between Manly and Palm Beach. The southern section, from Manly to Mona Vale, is reasonably flat, with hills or plateau to the west. Often the pattern and the nature of the ribbon development along Pittwater Road seems contrived to make the area as unattractive and featureless as it can possibly be, in much the same way as any other suburban ribbon development anywhere in the world. The dull flatness of some of the landscape south of Mona Vale, and the unexceptional developments upon it, is only relieved by the beaches and occasional lagoons on one side and the natural landscape of Frenchs Forest, now part of Garigal National Park, on the other.

Most of the northern beaches lie on Sydney (Hawkesbury) sandstone, except for parts of the Barrenjoey Peninsula, which lie on earlier, darker and redder Narrabeen sandstone. This sandstone weathers to more fertile soil than does the more typical Sydney sandstone. Spotted gum (*Eucalyptus maculata*) thrives in the valleys and along the shoreline of Pittwater, as do other trees such as the bangalay eucalypts. For thousands of years, koalas lived in and ate the leaves of these trees. A bushfire on the headland in 1967 decimated the colony there. The only koala colony remaining in the area is in the Angophora Reserve at Avalon.[17] The native vegetation gives the area around Palm Beach and Pittwater north of Newport its lush and densely wooded character. The southernmost extent of this more fertile soil from Narrabeen sandstone is at Dee Why.

On the flatter, low-lying areas behind Narrabeen, Dee Why and Curl Curl beaches are lagoons or lakes, which do not appear anywhere else along Sydney's usually rocky and hilly coastline. The largest and northernmost of these is Narrabeen Lake and Lagoon. These lagoons were for many years a haven for anglers and prawning.

In the nineteenth century, there was little to attract many settlers to the northern beaches; most of the soils were light, sandy and often poorly drained, so the opportunities to work the land were limited. Wherever the soil was richer, such as at Mona Vale and Oxford Falls, market gardens were worked, often by Chinese immigrants. It was not until swimming in the surf became legal in the first decade of the twentieth century, and the establishment of a tramline from Manly to Narrabeen, that it was possible for the northern beaches to be developed as a holiday resort. There was a considerable amount of subdivision for weekend cottages, many built of fibro cement in the 1920s, leading up to and after the construction of the Spit Bridge, but this process of subdivision did not proceed far past Mona Vale.

Although there were bus services to the northern beaches in the inter-war period, real suburbanisation of the area, especially to the north, had to wait until after 1945 when the motor vehicle was the dominant form of transport. The completion in 1946 of the Wakehurst Parkway from Seaforth through Allambie Heights and Frenchs Forest to North Narrabeen made the northern beaches more accessible and amenable to denser, suburban settlement.

The most beautiful area of the northern beaches is the narrow Barrenjoey Peninsula, which starts at Mona Vale, and continues up to Barrenjoey Headland. Here, there are good surfing beaches on the eastern side and tranquil Pittwater on the other side of the coastal ridge, which is suitable for sailors and sailboarders. The undulating countryside creates many different vistas of the ocean, Pittwater, Lion Island and the Central Coast. This part of Sydney is warmer, lusher and more subtropical than other parts of the city. The bird life at Palm Beach is livelier, noisier and richer as well. Kookaburras, crimson rosellas, bulbuls, superb blue wrens, white-cheeked honeyeaters, peaceful doves, eagles, sulphur-crested cockatoos and galahs can be seen at various times of the year.

The pace of life is different, too—slower, less disciplined and only, it often seems, tenuously connected to the life of the city to the south, although many residents of the northern beaches commute to work. Surfing is the main activity for many young people—it is even a recognised school sport in many schools. Most of the surfing beaches also have rock swimming pools, usually situated at the southern end of the beaches, where people less drawn to the surf can swim more sedately, with no fear of sharks.

The two most famous of the northern beaches are Manly and Palm beaches, the southernmost and northernmost beaches, respectively. For eleven months of the year, the residential areas of Palm Beach and nearby Whale Beach are quiet residential havens which nestle into the cliffs, and look out to the sea and Pittwater below, 40 kilometres from the city's centre. At Christmas, the atmosphere changes. The peninsula is transformed into a playground for well-off Sydneysiders who appear to leave the city en masse, often on Boxing Day, for three to four weeks of vacation. Many of the locals wisely move off to more tranquil terrain.

High up on the hill behind Palm Beach is the Bible Garden, filled with plants selected because they were referred to in the Bible. The garden was bequeathed to a trust for use by the public. It is still open to the public and provides the most breathtaking views of the peninsula, Lion Island and Broken Bay. Another spectacular view of the area can be seen from the top of Barrenjoey. It can only be reached on foot.

430

Before the 1920s, the only residents of note since the Aborigines had been the lighthouse-keepers and customs officers, whose job it was to prevent smuggling of goods into Broken Bay and into Sydney via the Hawkesbury River. Chinese people also lived there seasonally, earning a living by drying and selling fish, and market gardening. From the 1920s, when the more affluent Sydneysiders were able to drive there in their own motor cars, Palm Beach became a summertime playground.

One of the families who have been permanent, rather than just seasonal, residents at Palm Beach is the Gonsalves family, who built their boatshed opposite Barrenjoey House. The Gonsalves family are of Portuguese descent. They have been active in the area as fishermen and boat-repairers for a century. Members of the Gonsalves family built the rock pool at Palm Beach and planted the Norfolk Island pines along the beach, under the direction of Samuel Hordern in the 1930s.[18] Portuguese Bay on the other side of Pittwater is named after the family.

Of all the Norfolk pines planted along Sydney's coastal beaches, those at Palm Beach have thrived the most. Closer to the city, airborne pollution has killed off many once fine specimens. It is the Norfolk Island pines which give Palm Beach itself much of its character.

One of the first houses built at Palm Beach was Sunrise Cottage, which still stands on Sunrise Hill. The most beautiful house at Palm Beach is Kahlua, built by the Hordern family in the 1920s, at the southern end of the beach. Palm Beach was once called Cabbage Tree Bay, because of the many cabbage tree palms which grew there.

The Palm Beach Golf Club was founded in 1924 to serve the holiday-makers. This issue of bringing modern forms of communication, such as the telephone, was often controversial in the area. Summer visitors, such as former prime minister William Morris Hughes, complained loudly (and, in his case, effectively) for better services.[19] For many years, the thousands of holiday-makers could only use one phone, which stood on the veranda of the post office, making confidential communication impossible.

Holidaying on the peninsula was so popular that there was a caravan park next to the golf course at Palm Beach until the early 1960s. To the north of the golf course and the caravan park stretches a narrow neck of sand, called a tombolo, which connects Barrenjoey Headland with the peninsula. In the 1970s, it seemed to be eroding to the point that the headland would soon be cut off. The erosion of the tombolo was arrested with a concerted effort to plant and propagate grasses, and restrict pedestrian access to marked paths only.

The headland itself lies on the largest volcanic dyke visible in the Sydney area. It can be seen on the northern face of the headland at sea level. There are two smaller dykes on the southern end of Palm Beach at the rock swimming pool. Above the dyke, the headland is made of Narrabeen sandstone. On the very top is a cap of Sydney sandstone. The different layers of rock create different soil types and environments for a wide variety of plants and trees to grow at the varying altitudes of Barrenjoey.

One of the oldest architectural features at Barrenjoey is the lighthouse, reached by a rocky, unsealed access road.[20] With the increase in coastal shipping and shipping up the Hawkesbury River from the mid-nineteenth century, a proper lighthouse was built at Barrenjoey by Colonial Architect James Barnet in 1881, which replaced two earlier, wooden ones. The new lighthouse, lighthouse-keeper's and the assistant lighthouse-keeper's accommodation were built of Sydney sandstone, quarried close by on the top of the headland. Fifty lighthouse-keepers and assistant lighthouse-keepers, and their families, lived on Barrenjoey in the fifty years the lighthouse was manned. Today, lighthouses are automated. A caretaker, Jervis Sparks, and his family still live on Barrenjoey. The other house there is leased. The first lighthouse-keeper, George Mulhall, met an untimely death when he was struck by lightning near the lighthouse in 1885. Tall structures such as lighthouses attract lightning, and there are about six lightning strikes on the top of the headland each year.[21]

431

The first access road up Barrenjoey was built by convicts and the coxswain whose task it was to set up a customs house at Broken Bay to deter smugglers who were not disposed to pay import duties on rum if they could avoid it. Any incoming boats had to report to the watch-house at Broken Bay before proceeding along the Hawkesbury River. In rough weather, the boatmen would light a fire both for warmth, and as a warning to nearby shipping. In the preparations leading up to the planned royal tour to Australia in 1937, a road built of massive sandstone blocks quarried on the headland was created especially for King George VI. Scrambling up the rocks like other mortals was not appropriate for a king. He would be driven over the new road to the summit for a view of Broken Bay, Pittwater, Lion Island and the coastline.

The royal tour did not go ahead as the king developed arteriosclerosis, and the road was only partly built. After heavy rain, the road is very hazardous and only sturdy four-wheel-drive vehicles can negotiate it. Today, the road is gazetted by Warringah Shire Council as a heritage item. A walk up the road for the moderately fit often seems easier than the bumpy trip by motor vehicle. At a casual pace, it only takes about half an hour to reach the top. The walk starts on the western side of the headland, at the end of Barrenjoey Beach. From the summit, near the lighthouse some of the best views in the entire Sydney area can be seen.

One of Sydney's worst shipping disasters took place on Barrenjoey Peninsula, during a week of stormy, southerly gales in May 1898. Lightning, hail and hurricane winds were lashing the coastline. The telegraph lines linking the lighthouse to the world crashed to the ground. The *Maitland* was a paddle steamer which ran an overnight service from Newcastle to Sydney. In the middle of the night, as the ship was struggling in mountainous seas to the east of Broken Bay, the captain decided the ship could go no further, so turned back for shelter in Broken Bay.

Suddenly, all the engines were extinguished by waves which were swamping the ship. The ship drifted onto a bombora (a rocky reef under the water) at the northern side of Broken Bay and the boat snapped in two. Twenty-one lives were lost. Some struggled onto the headland. The only ones left after the lifeline to the mainland finally gave way were the captain, two of his men and a one-year-old baby. All three were eventually winched to safety, the baby on the bosun's back. The following afternoon visibility improved and the lighthouse-keeper at Barrenjoey saw the grounded, broken-up ship. The telegraph line was quickly repaired, and the authorities at Sydney notified. The survivors were rescued. For some time, the baby was a celebrity. When she died many years later, her ashes were scattered on the site of the disaster as she had requested.

BELOW: Barrenjoey lighthouse at Palm Beach on Sydney's northern beaches in the late nineteenth century.

One of the most beautiful parts of the peninsula is the tropical rainforest oasis that lies beneath the Bilgola Plateau at Bilgola Beach. Cabbage tree palms thrive in the sheltered valley. Sensibly, motor vehicle access to the area has been discouraged with the introduction of one-way traffic systems and street closures, adding to Bilgola's sense of seclusion and other-worldliness. Newport and Mona Vale are the two southernmost beaches on the Barrenjoey Peninsula. On the western side of these suburbs, and other suburbs on the peninsula such as Clareville and Avalon, there are beautiful views of Pittwater and Ku-ring-gai Chase National Park to the west.

A reserve set aside to preserve a very large, fine specimen of *Angophora costata* can be seen in Angophora Reserve, Avalon, off Palmgrove Road. The large *Angophora* there is believed to be the oldest and largest in the world. The reserve and Hudson Park next to it are included on the Australian Heritage Commission's Register of the National Estate. It is hard to believe when walking around the reserve on the bush track that late–twentieth-century suburbia is so close at hand.

An interesting, car-free way of seeing the Barrenjoey Peninsula is to take the fifteen-minute flight by seaplane from the Sydney Harbour Seaplanes' base at Lyne Park, Rose Bay, to Pittwater, and lunch at one of the good local restaurants there, such as Jonah's, the Beach Road Restaurant or the Cottage Point Inn.

Brookvale is now the main retail and industrial area of the northern beaches. One of the first district shopping centres, Warringah Mall, was built there in 1961, and this in turn made suburbanisation more attractive—remoteness was a less significant consideration when all the goods and services that could be had in the city were conveniently placed at your doorstep. Brookvale Oval, home of the Manly-Warringah rugby league team, known as the 'Sea Eagles', which is fiercely supported by locals, was once the site of one of the first homes in the area, Brookvale House. The owners gave it to the community as a park for children in 1911.

The earliest part of the northern beaches to be settled was Manly, and for many years it was Sydney's most famous beach-side suburb, overtaken only by Bondi from the middle of this century, when motor vehicles were more common and access to Bondi was made easier than it had been in the days of the old trams. Manly and much of the land on the northern beaches was granted to settlers by Governor Macquarie, as was land elsewhere in the Sydney environs, but the infertile land and its remoteness made it unsuitable for agriculture. The Wentworth family had large land-holdings at Manly and further north on the Barrenjoey Peninsula.

In 1852, William Gilbert Smith, who had arrived in Sydney in 1827 visited Manly. He was attracted to Manly's physical beauty and saw its potential as a holiday resort and as a residential location. He bought 120 acres (50 hectares) of land which he added to, built a home at Fairlight which he called Fairlight House, and decided to try to create an antipodean version of Brighton, the British ideal of a beach resort in the middle of the nineteenth century. Smith had chosen his site well. Manly's natural beauty was exceptional, with an unusual topographical combination of both harbourside and ocean beaches, and a narrow peninsula which ends at North Head.

Smith had to make Manly accessible to Sydney (the journey by land then was circuitous and much longer than it is today). He did this by building a pier into the harbour and starting a ferry service in 1854. Over the road from the pier on the corner of the Corso stood the Pier Hotel, where the Hotel Manly now stands. The Corso, named after the famous Roman street, was at first a narrow track along which shops and houses were built up over the years. There are still a few remnants of earlier Edwardian, Victorian and Art Nouveau architecture at Manly, although the architectural ethos of the 1960s was as unkind to Manly as it was to many other parts of Sydney. As well as laying out the Corso, Smith also built the East and West esplanades along Manly Cove and the promenades along Manly Beach, called North Steyne and South Steyne.

By the 1870s, Manly was a popular resort for day-trippers (though the price of the ferry fare made it less accessible to members of the working class)[22] and also as a holiday resort in the summer months. Manly's refreshing sea breezes were a pleasant antidote to the heat, dust and humidity of a Sydney summer when the 'Brickfielder' still dumped dust over the city. Hotels and boarding houses catered to fashionable visitors. One of the earliest remaining buildings in Manly is the original Far West Children's Home (1875), on the corner of South Steyne and Victoria Parade. Today, its modern successors, the Royal Far West Children's Health Scheme headquarters and the Royal Far West School, are located in Wentworth Street, Manly.

As time went on, Manly became a fashionable permanent address for many well-to-do Sydney people, including politicians William Dalley and Robert Abbott. Manly became a municipality. The water supply became more regular when the municipal council built the Manly Reservoir in the 1890s. In 1930, sewerage problems were alleviated for Manly and much of the lower North Shore—in the short term at least—with the construction of the ocean outfall at North Head. Gradually, the gracious old estates were subdivided and Manly became a commuter suburb for a wider cross-section of people. Gilbert Smith bequeathed many of the land-holdings he had not subdivided for public parks. As with many other parts of Sydney, there was a great deal of speculative subdivision of the Manly area between 1900 and 1930, fed by the construction of the Spit Bridge, which made the area more accessible by car. The 1920s saw a boom in the number of flats built in the Manly area.

By the 1920s, Manly was a reasonably well built-up suburb. In 1921, before the flat-building boom really took off, the only part of Sydney with more flats as a percentage of total housing was North Sydney with 21 per cent; Manly had 19 per cent in 1921 but this figure rose to 30 per cent in 1933.[23]

In 1930, Manly Council established the Manly Art Gallery, which was the second public art gallery in Sydney after the Art Gallery of New South Wales. It is dedicated to the acquisition, collection and preservation of works of art which are of significance to the Manly region.[24] At the time the museum was created, there was no other suburban public gallery in Australia. Artists such as A. Dattilo Rubbo and Margaret Preston helped build the collection by giving examples of their own work to the museum. The greatest strength of the collection

435

ABOVE: This engraving from the *Illustrated Sydney News* (16 December 1865) shows people enjoying Christmas, antipodean-style, at Manly Cove in the mid-nineteenth century.

is its early modern paintings, many of which were created in Sydney. One of the greatest financial benefactors to the museum was Lady Askin, wife of former premier Sir Robin Askin (Askin later changed his first name to Robert), who represented the seat of Manly in the Legislative Assembly. An interesting feature of the museum is its collection of old swimming costumes and beach and surfing memorabilia, on permanent loan from David Jones Australia.

From 1838, swimming in the sea was legally forbidden, as it was considered both dangerous and indecent. The law was unpopular, and often breached, but it still stood until 1903. In the previous year, a Manly resident and owner of the local newspaper, William Gocher, informed his readers and anyone else who cared to know that he proposed to go surfing at midday on 2 October 1902. He was not arrested until his third attempt, and his case was taken to court. The following year in the late spring, surfing was legalised as long as neck-to-knee costumes were worn. Manly's new role as a surfing beach could now begin, and development along the ocean front followed this new physical activity. The 1920s saw surfing and the nurturing of suntans become popular leisure activities in Australia and elsewhere. This was the first decade when the blond, Adonis-like surf lifesaver became a cultural ideal in Sydney and Australia. The South Steyne Surf Lifesaving Club was built in the 1930s and awarded the Sulman Prize for Architecture. Manly could continue to live up to its reputation of being 'Seven miles from Sydney and a thousand miles from care'.

In 1931, an old wharf (no longer needed after the construction of the Spit Bridge and easier road transport to the city) was converted into the Manly Fun Pier. In the 1980s, the pier was refurbished and came to life once again, after a fashion at least. For many decades this century, Manly has been a sociological melting pot where bodgies, widgies and, later, rockers, mods, cools and surfies would hang out and play, and gang up on each other in a manner redolent of the larrikins of previous years.[25] Rockers and their elder brothers and sisters, the bodgies, wore tight black jeans and striped T-shirts or sweaters, and leather jackets if they could afford them. The rockers' chief rivals were the surfies, who did not wear jeans and were considered 'square'. The 'cools' (who were referred to by this title by others rather than by themselves) were more middle class and lived on the North Shore. The boys wore corduroy trousers and suede shoes, and the girls were conservatively dressed and well groomed. Their social life centred more on parties and balls than at Manly Pier, and their preferred music was jazz.

On the other side of Manly Cove is Under Water World, home of performing seals and dolphins which caters to a slightly younger audience than the rockers, cools et al. who used

436

BELOW: A view of The Esplanade and the Manly ferry wharf taken from Dalley's Tower in the late nineteenth century.

to hang out at Manly Pier. It has recently been bought by a property developer and its future is uncertain. Further along is the stuccoed Manly Pavilion, built in the 1930s Spanish style, with titled fish and shell motifs. It is one of Sydney's more significant harbourside buildings, as most of the other dressing pavilions in Sydney are on the ocean beaches.

Up on the hill near North Head looms St Patrick's College. The 60 acres (24 hectares) of land was granted to the Catholic Church in 1879 and the college for priests was opened in 1889. The location was thought ideal as a seminary as it was isolated from the general population. Now the college has gone, and the building has been leased by the Catholic Church to a hotel management school. The church plans, together with Lend Lease, to develop part of the land. The scale and nature of the development have been called into question, particularly by the local council. It wants land-use principles for the whole of the North Head peninsula to be determined simultaneously. Local residents are also opposed to the development, and it has been discovered that the land forms one of the few remaining viable habitats in Sydney for the long-nosed bandicoot. The National Parks and Wildlife Service, which occupies parkland at North Head, is monitoring the local bandicoot population. In 1996, sightings of bandicoots fleeing the land as it was being cleared were reported in the local press.

437

Just below the college lies the idyllically secluded and preserved Shelly Beach. One of the best walks in the Manly area is from Manly Cove, down the Corso and along Manly Beach, then around to Shelly Beach to Le Kiosk restaurant. Shelly Beach is also a very good picnic spot. At the end of North Head, wedged between the Sydney Harbour National Park which takes up most of the headland, is the military reserve which houses the School of Artillery and army barracks. On the eastern fringe of the park is the North Head Water Pollution Control Plant, which gauges the water quality of Sydney's northern beaches.

In 1988, Warringah Council created a coastal walk which extends all the way from Queenscliff Bridge at Manly Lagoon to Palm Beach.

The Anzac Bridge at
Glebe under
construction in 1994, as
viewed from Annandale.
The Harbour Bridge
in the background is
almost dwarfed by the
new bridge, which
replaced the old Glebe
Island Bridge at
Blackwattle Bay.

438

ABOVE: Palm Beach and the Barrenjoey Peninsula, with Barrenjoey Lighthouse visible on the peninsula and the beach pool at the beach's southern end in the foreground. *(Marcus Clinton)*

ABOVE: Henrietta Villa, built by Captain John Piper in what is now Point Piper, was demolished to make way for the small Woollahra House. Elizabeth Heneretta Villa, *1820, Richard Read Jnr (Image Library, State Library of NSW)*
BELOW: The town of Parramatta seen from the Governor's Domain, 1822. Government House is on the left in the middle ground. Parramatta, New South Wales, *1824, Joseph Lycett (Rex Nan Kivell Collection, National Library of Australia)*

ABOVE: Alexander Riley's Burwood Villa (1822), fringed by the natural bushland which then covered much of western Sydney. *Burwood Villa, New South Wales, the property of Alexander Riley Esqre., 1825, Joseph Lycett (Rex Nan Kivell Collection, National Library of Australia)*

BELOW: John and Elizabeth Macarthur's Elizabeth Farm near Parramatta. It is the oldest surviving building in Australia. *The residence of John McArthur Esqre, near Parramatta, New South Wales, 1825, Joseph Lycett (Rex Nan Kivell Collection, National Library of Australia)*

ABOVE: Aerial view of The Spit near Mosman, Middle Harbour. Until the Spit Bridge was built in 1924, the upper North Shore was isolated from the rest of Sydney and only accessible by an extremely circuitous route or, in the case of Manly, by ferry from Circular Quay.

BELOW: When the First Fleet sailed into Botany Bay in 1788, Arthur Phillip's expectations of a suitable site for settlement were not met. There was no ready freshwater supply and the wide bay must have seemed rather inhospitable to the colonists after the verdant abundance they were expecting. First Fleet in Botany Bay, *1788, Charles Gore (Image Library, State Library of NSW)*

CHAPTER SEVENTEEN

THE WESTERN SUBURBS

THE WEST OF SYDNEY is much vaster than any other region. It is also the most populous. Its boundaries, broadly speaking, run from Pyrmont along the Parramatta River to Parramatta, then further west to the foot of the Blue Mountains, south to Liverpool and Campbelltown, and then in an eastward arc to Marrickville. As Sydney has sprawled westward, mostly since 1945, Parramatta is close to being the geographic and demographic centre of Sydney.

After the south and north of Sydney had been substantially urbanised by 1961, there was nowhere else to go but westward. The rocky sandstone Hornsby and Woronora plateaux set the limit to growth closer to the coast. Bit by bit, rural and semi-rural land has been engulfed and swallowed up by suburban subdivisions. In the 1960s, Campbelltown, Camden and Penrith were country towns. Now, they are part of Sydney's conurbation.

Sydney's west is so huge that the region is more easily subdivided into three sections: the inner- and middle-western suburbs and the outer west, known as Western Sydney. Broadly speaking, the Inner West covers the municipalities of Drummoyne, Hunters Hill, Leichhardt and Marrickville. The Middle West covers Burwood, Ashfield, Canterbury, Concord, Ryde and Strathfield. Western Sydney covers Auburn, Holroyd, Parramatta, Baulkham Hills, Blacktown, Penrith, Campbelltown, Liverpool, Fairfield, Wollondilly and Camden. In 1996, Western Sydney comprised almost 40 per cent of Sydney's population. Most of the population growth in Sydney in recent decades has been in Western Sydney. This growth has been a result of the pursuit of the great Australian dream of home ownership.

Only in recent years have the environmental consequences of Sydney's westward sprawl on the land and Sydney's air quality been understood. But there is more than the environment at stake. Another critical issue is to ensure that employment opportunities and public infrastructure follow the westward flow of population. Building roads, public transport, and health and education services of the same quality as in other parts of Sydney is an important task. Often, state and federal governments' longevity depends on how well they are seen to be acting in the interests of swinging voters in the western suburbs' marginal electorates. Unemployment in Western Sydney is well above Sydney's average. Despite this relative economic adversity, however, Western Sydney is like a city within a city, with all the variations and subtleties of any large centre of population. A sense of local pride and regional ownership of Western Sydney is increasingly evident.

On the other hand, compared to the growth in Western Sydney, the population of the Inner West and Middle West has been stable, and sometimes even in decline. But the demographics of the Inner West and Middle West have also been undergoing significant change. The western suburbs of Sydney are home for many of Sydney's residents of a non–English background and recently arrived immigrants.[1] Fairfield, Auburn, Marrickville and Canterbury–Bankstown could now be considered some of the main centres of multicultural Sydney—and Australia.

440

Much of the Inner and Middle West was heavily timbered country at the time of European settlement, and, like the North Shore, some of the first exploitation of the land was timber cutting. Areas such as Ashfield, Burwood, Leichhardt, Canterbury, Drummoyne, Strathfield and Marrickville had large and dense stands of forest where blackbutt (*Eucalyptus pilularis*), forest red gum (*Eucalyptus tetricornis*), *Angophora costata*, turpentine (*Syncarpia glomulifera*), ironbark (*Eucalyptus paniculata*) and grey gum (*Eucalyptus punctata*) grew. None of this remains, apart from some isolated tree specimens in public parks and reserves. Along the more coastal flats and easterly headlands of the Parramatta River, the country would have looked more like the rest of the coastal Sydney sandstone country.

Further to the west, from Auburn onwards, the land became scrubbier and the trees more widely spaced as the average rainfall declined, with paperbarks and tea-trees becoming more dominant. Grey box and forest red gum (*Eucalyptus tetricornis*) would have been more common. Along the upper reaches of the Parramatta River were areas of mangroves and saltmarsh, although land reclamation programs eliminated many of these from the 1920s to the 1970s.[2] Many wetlands around Canada Bay, Exile Bay at Homebush and Yaralla Bay, among others, were used as rubbish tips, upon which parks were eventually built. Only fringes of mangrove vegetation can be seen here today. Much of the estuarine land around Homebush Bay and Silverwater will eventually form part of Millennium Park.

From Parramatta westward to the Hawkesbury–Nepean River, south to Camden and Campbelltown and north to Windsor lies the typical woodland of the outer Cumberland Plain. This is the driest part of the Sydney region, and rainfall in many areas here is less than 800 millimetres per annum. Here, the grey box and the forest red gum thrived.

There is now little of the Cumberland Plain that remains in its natural state. This has implications for the pollution of the Hawkesbury–Nepean River and its tributaries, as well as the preservation of Sydney's biodiversity. One of the focal points for the controversy about Sydney's continuing sprawl along the Cumberland Plain is the old Australian Defence Industries site at St Marys, which covers about 1600 hectares. This land was used to manufacture and store ammunition during World War II. It lies along South Creek, a tributary of the Hawkesbury River.

The Department of Urban Affairs and Planning has set the framework for future development of this site. A key consideration is preserving the important remnants of native vegetation of the Cumberland Plain that Western Sydney has almost completely gobbled up. Kangaroos and emus still thrive in this bushland oasis which is surrounded by Sydney suburbia. Another important issue is making sure that future development does not worsen the level of pollution in South Creek and the Hawkesbury–Nepean River.

Lend Lease has become a joint venturer with federal government–owned Australian Defence Industries, and proposals to build 10 000 houses there have attracted attention from local and state governments. The local residents and their representative councils are wary of the scale of proposed redevelopment. They are fearful of the pressure a large increase in population would have on the transport network and the level of unemployment. The local residents' action groups are pushing for the entire 1600 hectares to be set aside as parkland. The state government has set a framework for development of the site which will provide for about 700 hectares of open space. Of all Sydney's prospective residential redevelopment sites, this is the one with the greatest capacity to be a flashpoint between the interests of environmentalists and developers.

The west of Sydney is not yet as blessed with national parks or open spaces as the coastal areas are, although a serious attempt was made to rectify this by the Wran government, which set aside land near Campbelltown for the Mt Annan Botanic Garden and Arboretum, and land at Homebush Bay for Bicentennial Park, to be enhanced by the addition of much more nearby land into part of the large 400-hectare Millennium Park along the Parramatta River. The opportunity afforded to resolve this imbalance at the ADI site is considerable.

The forests of Western Sydney were gradually cleared to make way for the estates of Sydney's early well-off settlers, who were often retired officers and soldiers of the marines, or emancipist convicts and their children. Early grantees were George Johnston, famous for his role in the Rum Rebellion, who was granted land now covered by Annandale, and Simeon Lord, who was granted land at Dobroyd Point, now part of Haberfield. Surgeon John Harris, who lived on his land in Ultimo, was also granted a large amount of land along the southern shore of the Parramatta River which included much of what is now Five Dock and Drummoyne. Captain Rowley, another member of the Rum Corps, was given a grant of 750 acres (300 hectares) which he called Burwood Farm. This land and Burwood House were later sold to Alexander Riley, a prosperous landowner of early Sydney. Riley also owned rural land at Raby, near present-day Campbelltown. Surveyor General Thomas Alt was granted land at Ashfield. The land was later bought and added to by Joseph Underwood, brother of James. Joseph built a large house called Ashfield Park in the 1820s. Ashfield was conveniently situated on the junction of the Liverpool and Parramatta roads. By 1838, allotments for the village of Ashfield were laid out, and the first residential subdivisions of the Underwood estate were made in 1859. Thomas Hyndes was an early landowner at Enfield, where he built a home on the Cooks River and St Thomas's Church, Enfield.

To reward Major George Druitt, the man who had acted as engineer for the building of the Parramatta and Liverpool roads in Sydney, 1000 acres (400 hectares) of land was granted to him in an area which was called Mt Druitt. Another early large land-holder was former surgeon William Redfern, who called his 800-acre (320-hectare) land grant Campbell Fields, where the town of Campbelltown later developed. Governor Macquarie called the area Airds, after his wife's family estate.

In 1811, Parramatta Road was a 15-mile (24-kilometre) long road which had been built but not sealed. Many of the old towns established by Macquarie were located in what is now Sydney's west: Liverpool at the head of the Georges River; Windsor, Wilberforce and Richmond, all on the Hawkesbury River; and Pitt Town and Castlereagh on the Nepean River. Campbelltown could be considered as the last of the Macquarie towns, founded in the 1820s. Much of Sydney's west was opened up to settlement during the Macquarie era. He built and improved roads and bridges, such as the Windsor, Parramatta and Liverpool roads, all of which opened up the fertile rural country in three directions.

Liverpool, the first Macquarie town, lies on the Georges River, to the southwest of Sydney, which was the gateway to the fertile rural country of Appin, Camden, and further south to Illawarra and the Southern Highlands. With the new roads came a growth in the size of these townships. By 1819, Liverpool was a small township with about thirty houses. St Luke's Church, designed by Francis Greenway, is one of the most historic buildings there. Another historic landmark is the Liverpool Technical College (1830).

Penrith, on the Nepean River, was an important staging post for coaches on their route from Sydney over the Blue Mountains. One of the early grantees in the area was Irish political prisoner, the Reverend Henry Fulton. Prospect Hill was named by Watkin Tench because of the vista it gave to the Blue Mountains, then called the Carmarthen Hills. The settlement of Prospect was one of the earliest in the colony, dating from 1791. In the late twentieth century, the area is most famous for the water reservoir that was originally built in 1888. An early landowner was William Lawson, one of the first men to cross the Blue Mountains in 1813. The site of Lawson's forty-room mansion, now demolished, is in part of the grounds that contain the reservoir.

Immediately to the west of Prospect is Blacktown, one of the areas of Sydney undergoing the greatest population growth, where Macquarie established a settlement for Aborigines that was called Blacks' Town, on the site where the suburb of Plumpton now lies. The Native Institution, relocated to Blacktown from Parramatta in 1823, had closed by 1825 and, by 1850, Blacks' Town was deserted. The area was semi-rural until the 1960s.

Homebush and Burwood were staging posts on the journey to and from Parramatta. Inevitably, public hotels (pubs), post offices and general stores were built along these roads, and separate villages gradually developed. At Burwood, a convict stockade was built in the early years of the nineteenth century as this was close to the middle of the journey between Parramatta and the town of Sydney. The stockade stood on the present-day site of St Luke's Oval.

Bushrangers roamed the west of Sydney in the late eighteenth and early nineteenth centuries. Burwood House was raided by bushrangers in 1826. The culprits were later caught and executed. By 1830, however, most of the bushrangers had moved to more remote parts of the interior.

One man who was a victim of bushranging activity was Robert Wardell, barrister and publisher (with William Wentworth) of the *Australian*. He owned 2500 acres (1000 hectares) of land around Petersham, much of which was heavily timbered. On a journey of inspection around his property, he found a humpy near his boundary on the Cooks River, in which three escaped convicts were camping. One of them, John Jenkins, who had deserted a road gang on the Georges River, shot Wardell dead. The three men were eventually hanged. When Jenkins was asked in the court if there was any reason he should not be sentenced to hang, a court reporter wrote:

> Jenkins said he had a good deal to say, and throwing himself into a threatening and unbecoming attitude, remarked that he had not had a fair trial, a b_____y old woman had been palmed upon him for Counsel; he did not care a b_____r for dying or a d__m for any one in Court; and that he would as soon shoot every b____y b_____r in Court.[3]

443

From the 1830s to 1860s, many of the early land grants were subdivided into smaller blocks and sold off. Small villages developed, especially around railway stations when the Sydney to Parramatta railway was opened in 1855. There were stations at Newtown, Ashfield, Burwood and Homebush. Some prosperous Sydneysiders built homes in these newly opened-up areas along the railway line, often on large blocks of land. Slowly, industry developed along the railway lines and the Parramatta River. By the middle of the nineteenth century, there were brickworks at Burwood and Croydon, a steam mill, and a soap and candle manufacturer in Ashfield.

The pace of industrialisation intensified. Land was flatter and therefore easier to build on, and also cheaper than it was elsewhere. One example of heavier industry was the Australian Gas Light Company works at Mortlake on the Parramatta River. This gasworks, which was located on 100 acres (40 hectares) of land, burnt enormous amounts of coal. It closed down in 1976 with the introduction of natural gas to Sydney. The gasworks has subsequently been used as the main reticulation system for the delivery of natural gas. The site is now being remediated, and will be rezoned for predominantly residential development, with open foreshore access.

By 1947, the process of industrialisation along the Parramatta River was well entrenched. More than 90 per cent of the foreshore in the Auburn municipality and 39 per cent of the foreshore of Concord were industrialised. In the Inner West, the proportion of industrial land was also very high: at Balmain, and at Glebe and Annandale along the shores of Blackwattle Bay, it was around 69 per cent.[4]

From the 1870s, transport became an even more important influence in the growth and development of the west of Sydney. More railway stations were added on the Parramatta line, such as Croydon in 1875 and Strathfield in 1885. In the 1890s, Strathfield became the main railway junction between the western and northern railway lines. Large Victorian homes were built near these new railway stations, particularly at Strathfield, and many of them are still standing today. The tramway system acted as a feeder service for the railway line. Access to trams and trains in the era before motor cars made suburban subdivision, and thus population growth, feasible. Transport and the subsequent suburban development had an influence on increasing the importance of the small towns that had grown up along the railway line, and which had also become the terminus for tramlines.

444 In the early years of the twentieth century, the concept of the garden suburb, originally developed in Britain, spread to Sydney. The underlying idea was that new areas should be designed so that close and cohesive communities could be developed. This would be done with careful and meticulous planning. Housing (which was always low density), well-kept gardens and public spaces should be organised in an orderly way. Open areas and streets should be landscaped, and there would be neatly clipped nature strips in front of houses. Each area would be subdivided as a distinct suburban entity, with the subtle aim of self-containment. Often these areas were laid out with both curved and straight streets, directed towards enhancing the sylvan character of these enclaves.

One of the garden suburbs created in this period was Haberfield, which was conceived and largely built between 1904 and 1914. Today, it is preserved as an area of distinctive Federation architecture. Richard Stanton, the developer, went on to design Rosebery, with its mixed residential and industrial uses. J. Spencer-Stansfield was the architect of Haberfield. Covenants were imposed on future development in the suburb to restrict further construction in weatherboard (a cheaper material and therefore considered less desirable). Many of the decorative motifs were Australian, as befitted the Federation era. Haberfield was not, however, the ideal model of the garden suburb: the layout was rectilinear and there was not much planned open space, but it did aspire to the ideal of homogeneous, planned and orderly self-containment. Some of the architectural purity has faded away: there was an unfortunate tendency, in some cases, to replace old stained-glass, timber-framed windows with modern aluminium ones, but recent awareness of heritage issues will reduce the threat to the architectural character of the suburb.

In 1904, the Appian Way at Burwood, one of Sydney's more interesting and unusual property developments, was created by the Hoskins family, who lived locally. The Hoskins family built forty houses in the Federation style before they sold off the subdivided land, laid the street out with ornamental trees and created a central communal recreational area. Cricket, tennis and rugby were the major recreational sports in these genteel parts of the west.

At the end of the day, however, the concept of the garden suburb was infrequently realised. At the same time as Haberfield was being built, part of Dame Eadith Walker's large Yaralla estate at Concord West was being subdivided and sold off. This is a much more typical example of Sydney's suburban growth in the inter-war period. The original owner of the estate was Isaac Nichols, an emancipist who was Sydney's first postmaster. He called his 50-acre (20-hectare) grant Yaralla, which was an Aboriginal word for 'camp'.

The old Yaralla House can still be seen from the Parramatta River. It was designed by Edmund Blacket in the Italianate style and, for many years, was one of Sydney's best and largest homes. The Concord Repatriation General Hospital was originally established as a military hospital during World War II. It stands in 40 acres (16 hectares) of grounds of the old Yaralla estate, between Yaralla House, built on the peninsula between Majors Bay and Yaralla Bay, and the Thomas Walker Convalescent Hospital for Women (1893), built further to the northwest at Rocky Point with money provided in Thomas Walker's will. Since 1939, Yarralla House has been the Dame Eadith Walker Convalescent Hospital. It is administered by the Royal Prince Alfred Hospital.

445

The allotments of the Yaralla estate were larger than typical Victorian subdivisions. There was enough land for the gardens to surround each house. Later, in the early 1920s, more of the Yaralla Estate was subdivided. This was the era of the suburban, California-style bungalow, and there were plenty of these built at Concord as well as other parts of the inner- and middle-western suburbs. Between 1921 and 1933 the population of Concord grew to reflect the influence of all this building activity, doubling to 24 000. Row upon row of dark liver-brick bungalows were built with heavily featured red-tiled roofs, neatly bounded from their neighbours with picket fences.

Most of the suburban developments of the early twentieth century—and later—were built and designed by builders with limited aesthetic sensibilities, much to the (sometimes haughty and high-handed) dismay of the architectural profession, whose services were infrequently retained. As disapproving as some people were of this suburbanisation, it was a very popular move. Many people fled the Victorian terrace housing of the inner city, and the threat of bubonic plague, typhoid, polio and diphtheria, to live in this new, often unsewered suburban environment, which did, however, offer a safer and more healthy way of life. There were no larrikin pushes here, as there were in many crowded and deteriorating inner-city neighbourhoods. Fresh air, a garden and a casual outdoor life were becoming, along with home ownership, part of the working-class, urban Australian dream.

Many changes were wrought in the Inner and Middle West in the 1920s. This residential boom was assisted by the accelerated pace of industrialisation and employment opportunities created with the opening of the Chullora railway workshop and other industries in the Canterbury–Bankstown, Villawood and Homebush areas. There was more cheap land available in the west, and in the postwar boom period, many industries which wanted to expand could not do so unless they relocated. The County of Cumberland Planning Scheme of the late 1940s approved of, and tried to encourage, relocation of industry to the outer suburbs, and because of cost and topography, this usually meant the west. Jobs could move out to where the population was growing. By 1961, Bankstown had the second-highest number of residents who were employed in the manufacturing industry.[5] This all changed from the 1970s, when the number of industrial jobs started their inexorable decline in Sydney, and in Australia generally.

The growth of Sydney's west from 1947 onwards was staggering. The population of Bankstown more than doubled between 1947 and 1954, as did that of Auburn. Fairfield's population grew by more than 200 per cent in that same period and has continued to grow. In 1947, the population of Fairfield was 16 000; in 1961, it was 80 000; and in 1991, it was 175 000. Other areas with very high and sustained population growth are Liverpool and Penrith. The guiding hand of government was a strong influence on some of the patterns of settlement from the time the Cumberland Planning Scheme was brought into effect. Later, in 1968, the State Planning Authority identified Mt Druitt, Blacktown and Penrith as new areas for development. At the time, Blacktown and Penrith existed as towns serving semi-rural populations. The civic centre of Mt Druitt was built from scratch, as a result of the State Planning Authority's scheme.

Often the provision of government services such as schools and hospitals has lagged behind suburbanisation. The opening of Westmead Hospital and the relocation of hospital beds in the west during Laurie Brereton's term as minister for health in the 1980s were politically controversial examples of bringing community services to the population.

The University of Western Sydney (UWS) is another example of relocating infrastructure to where it is needed. The form and structure of the UWS is a good indication of how big the area known as Western Sydney is. It was established in 1989 and is Australia's first 'federated' university with three members, or components: UWS Nepean, the largest, with campuses at Parramatta and Penrith; UWS Macarthur, with campuses at Campbelltown and Bankstown; and UWS Hawkesbury, with campuses at Richmond and Blacktown.

Like Sydney's other inner suburbs, the inner-western suburbs of Sydney have undergone many transitions and changes since 1788. Their proximity to the early settlement of Sydney made them attractive areas for the rich and powerful to build gracious country estates. In the second half of the nineteenth century, easy access to Sydney's port facilities made the Inner West an attractive area to locate industries. Industries, in turn, resulted in a new wave of industrial workers looking for employment, and the converse was also true: some industries were attracted to the Inner West because of the availability of labour there.

From the early twentieth century, the exodus of many people to the outer suburbs, accelerated the process of urban decay. Then, with the wave of postwar immigration, non–English-speaking people, unable to afford their own homes, and more accustomed to a

446

more closely settled existence, moved into these areas which often offered low rents and attractive opportunities for people who wanted to open small businesses.

A visit to any of these suburbs provides an interesting view of history and the march of progress in urban improvement and gentrification. Run-down relics of the past—workers' cottages, terrace houses, seedy-looking pubs and often disused factories (many of which have been redeveloped into medium-density town houses)—can be viewed together with the more preserved items of historical interest, such as grand houses and villas which have been restored by their present owners or by local groups. There is some ugly redevelopment, particularly dating back to the 1960s and early 1970s, which almost destroyed the character of some of these neighbourhoods, but the vibrant street life, as well as the architectural, physical and social diversity, makes many parts of the Inner West some of Sydney's more interesting neighbourhoods.

'Glebe' is an old English word used to describe parcels of land owned by the Church. In the early years of European settlement, Glebe was such a place. The land was granted to the Church of England in the early nineteenth century. Although densely wooded, it had a pleasing, northeastern aspect to the town of Sydney. Glebe has the largest number of 1860s and 1870s cottages and terraces in Australia. It is also socially diverse. There are pockets of students and migrants, as well as a growing number of more affluent residents who are attracted to the convenience of the inner city.

A stroll along Glebe Point Road gives an interesting slice of inner-city life. There is a wide array of fine restaurants—one of the biggest in any area of Sydney—colourful cafés, antique and other speciality shops, architectural restoration centres, a very large health food shop, delicatessens and fine bookshops. This diversity means that Glebe still has a quirky, bohemian, slightly anarchic ambience missing in other parts of the Inner West and inner-city suburbs. This is partly because of its proximity to the University of Sydney and its convenience as a place for students to live—although the escalating land prices and rising rents are making this area less affordable. The Harold Park Hotel was, for many years, one of Sydney's most popular venues for poetry readings and literary evenings. Literary readings have given way to regular comedy nights, and there are proposals to redevelop the site for medium-density housing.

In 1789, Richard Johnson, the first clergyman in the colony, received a land grant of 160 hectares, 3 kilometres west of Sydney Cove, in an area of rough, hilly and densely forested land, which must have looked as though it was suitable for very little. Timber was cut there, and the foreshore areas were frequented by fishermen who scoured the coves along the harbour frontage. Otherwise, the land that is now covered by the suburb of Glebe was unused and seemingly unusable.

The Church of England did very little with its land for nearly thirty years, so it remained unoccupied. In 1828, the church had established a corporation, the charter of which was to acquire and dispose of lands. Funds raised would be spent on the construction of roads, schools and churches to serve the expanding population. Thus, in 1828, the Glebe lands were subdivided and sold, with the exception of two lots, Bishopsthorpe (the area now bounded by Derwent, Westmoreland and Mount Vernon streets), which was set aside for the residence of the bishop, and an area running down to the harbour which was given to the trustees of St Phillip's Church.

Soon after the subdivisions, wealthy landowners began to commission the building of grand residences in the Glebe area. It was easily accessible to the city, but sufficiently distant from its baser elements—such as convicts—who lived in the town itself.

St John's Church on the corner of St Johns Road and Glebe Point Road was designed by Edmund Blacket, a resident of Glebe for nineteen years. It was built from stone quarried at Pyrmont, and opened its doors in December 1870.

One early Glebe mansion that is still standing is Toxteth House, which is the main building within St Scholastica's school in Avenue Road. Toxteth House was designed by the eminent architect John Verge for George Allen, and was completed in 1834. Allen came to Sydney in 1816 with his mother and sisters and brothers, following the arrest of their stepfather for tax evasion. He carried a letter of introduction to Governor Macquarie, who arranged for Allen to work for the Crown solicitor. In 1822, Allen completed his legal training, becoming the first solicitor to serve his whole five years of articles in Sydney. He developed a thriving legal practice in Elizabeth Street, became chairman of the Australian Gas Light Company, and served on the Council of Education. Allen's initial Elizabeth Street practice was the forerunner to Allen, Allen and Hemsley, which is one of the oldest, and still one of the pre-eminent Sydney law firms.

Toxteth House was designed in the Regency style. It is two storeys high, with a single-storey verandah which has fluted pillars. Perhaps its most lavish feature was its grounds. Part of what was once the orchard is now covered by Harold Park Paceway.

When George died in 1877, his son, George Wigram Allen, added considerable embellishments to the house in the Victorian style, including a third storey, a tower and a ballroom. George Wigram Allen followed his father into the law firm and was a prominent member of the community. He became minister of justice and speaker of the Legislative Assembly. Allen also became the first mayor of the independent Municipality of Glebe, which was created in 1859. He retained this position for eighteen consecutive terms.

In 1904, Toxteth House was purchased by the Catholic Church and passed to the Sisters of the Order of the Good Samaritans, who had been displaced from their convent in Pitt Street because of the construction of Central Railway. The sisters established an educational complex there called St Scholastica's.

What was once the gatehouse to the Toxteth Estate, called the Lodge, is a fine example of Gothic Revival architecture. It was built in about 1877 and stands on the corner of Avenue and Toxteth roads. Mansfield, who was also responsible for designing the Royal Prince Alfred Hospital and was the founder of the Royal Australian Institute of Architects, married George

Wigram Allen's daughter and lived at the Lodge.

Nearby is Tranby, at 13 Mansfield Street. This post-Regency–style house was, at one time, a hostel for the University of Sydney, and later home to the Reverend John Hope. In 1958, it was presented to the Aborigines Co-operative of the Australian Board of Missions, and it is used as a training centre for Aboriginal students.

Another of John Verge's houses in Glebe to have survived (partially) is Lyndhurst, a Georgian mansion built between 1833 and 1836. Lyndhurst is located in Darghan Street, in eastern Glebe. It was built for Dr James Bowman, a leading member of Sydney's coterie of exclusives. Bowman was the chief surgeon in the colony, and the inspector of hospitals. He married into the Macarthur family.

Unlike Toxteth House, Lyndhurst did not remain a family home for a significant amount of time. By 1847, it had become the site of an Anglican school, then a Catholic school in 1852 and, later still, a laundry, an ice-cream factory and a block of flats. It has regained some of its dignity. The land, which once stretched to Blackwattle Bay, was taken over by the Department of Main Roads, who planned to use it for the northwestern expressway, but the house was saved at the last minute and restored.

The battle for Lyndhurst was an early flashpoint in the resident action movement of the early 1970s. A green ban was imposed by the Builders' Labourers Federation, which was then under the control of Jack Mundey. Unfortunately, the house's once fine vista towards the city has long since been built out. It is occupied by the Historic Houses Trust.

The Abbey in Bridge Road was designed as a Presbyterian church by Thomas Rowe in 1876. Designed in the Victorian Gothic style, the church was originally located on Parramatta Road, but it was relocated in 1927 to the relatively quieter spot it occupies today. Hamilton, the house that had previously stood on the site, was incorporated into the church hall, and Reussdale became the church manse. In 1977, the former church became a restaurant. Reussdale stands beside it, in a state of decay.

From its beginnings as a grand suburb for the wealthy members of Sydney society, the character of Glebe began to evolve. By the 1830s, cottages, workshops and small factories were reaching Glebe Point Road, and starting to encroach on the grander residences. The St Phillip's land was subdivided in 1842 into thirty-two 1-acre (0.4-hectare) lots and let out on 28-year leases, with low rent, but with the land conditional upon the lessee building a house or houses of a substantial nature. A number of workmen's cottages were built, and Glebe became the point of destination for the many people who wanted to leave the poorly serviced, unhygienic city conditions; Glebe, along with Balmain, Newtown, Redfern and Paddington, was one of Sydney's most populous suburbs between 1841 and 1891. It was not as heavily industrialised as other suburbs in the Inner West such as Balmain and Leichhardt. Most of the local industry was concentrated around Blackwattle Bay.

In 1856, the Bishopsthorpe area was subdivided and allotments leased out as 99-year leases. The other former Glebe area, St Phillip's, was by then run-down. It was close to the slaughterhouses at Blackwattle Bay and was considered an unpleasant and unhealthy place to

449

ABOVE: Men queueing for the dole at Harold Park during the Great Depression of the 1930s.

450

live. A look today at the architecture of the two areas shows quite clearly the differences in character.

When the original St Phillip's leases expired in 1870, the timber huts were cleared and the land was offered for lease again, for fifty years. Developers erected cottages which they advertised as being suitable for tradesmen and mechanics. These houses, which were designed in long, narrow allotments with narrow lanes at the rear, now constitute a significant part of the Glebe landscape.

The area soon went into a state of decline. Increasing competition from the new commercial district along Broadway resulted in the closure of many shops and hotels on Glebe Point Road. By the 1930s, social problems caused by the Depression and the rise of street gangs hastened the decline, though tenants were still attracted by the cheap, fixed rents. The population remained predominantly working class and Australian-born until the postwar period.

By the 1960s, students from the University of Sydney and migrants, predominantly from southern Europe, began to move in. Some of Glebe's traditional working-class population was displaced by the demolition of a number of old houses built to make way for the construction of apartment blocks. This devastated many parts of Glebe.

The Glebe Estate is a Commonwealth-sponsored and funded urban regeneration project of the early 1970s. It covers the area bounded by St Johns Road, Wentworth Park Road, Cowper Street, Arundel Street and Ross Street. The Glebe Estate had previously been earmarked for future resumption as part of a proposed expressway. The regeneration project was undertaken by the Whitlam government. Its owner, the Anglican Church, had originally intended to sell it, but when redevelopment plans were rejected, it prevailed on the government to restore the houses and adapt them for low-cost accommodation.

The conversion of the Glebe Estate to low-cost housing was a victory for the residents' groups. The houses are painted in the heritage colours of cream, stone, crimson, dark brown and deep green. The urban renewal of the Glebe Estate was a prototype for what would later be built at Woolloomooloo by the Housing Commission. One of Sydney's Bicentennial parks was built at Glebe, at the edge of Rozelle Bay on land once used for industry.

Annandale is largely undeveloped, in the sense that 95 per cent of the Victorian housing still stands—a much higher proportion than that which remains at nearby Glebe or Balmain. Most of it is late Victorian, built between 1880 and 1910. Annandale was originally known as Johnston's Bush, after George Johnston, the military leader of the Rum Rebellion, who was granted 140 acres (57 hectares) between 1793 and 1794. Like other men of note in the colony in its founding years, such as Captain John Piper, William Balmain, landowner John Jamison and surgeon and pastoralist D'Arcy Wentworth, he lived with a female convict. They stayed together until Johnston's death in 1823 and had six children. Their union was formalised in 1814 by the Reverend Samuel Marsden, the notorious 'flogging parson'.

Johnston named his land-holding after Annan, his Scottish birthplace. In 1799, he began building a comfortable home. By the time the estate was completed, it was well set up, with its own bakery, butcher, vineyard, stores and slaughterhouse. It was approached from a set of gates on Parramatta Road, along an avenue of Norfolk Island pines which are believed to have been the first planted in Australia. Johnston had been lieutenant governor of Norfolk Island in 1796, where he had developed a fondness for the trees. Annandale House was demolished in 1905, but the gatehouse still stands in Johnston Street within the grounds of the primary school.

The estate was subdivided from 1876, much later than many other parts of the Inner West. Unlike Glebe and Balmain, it was not situated so close to the harbour and port facilities, so there was little industrial activity there. The suburb is well planned, which distinguishes it from other suburbs around the industrial inner harbour, many of which grew in a more organic, less organised way. Annandale is sunny, as it slopes northward down towards Rozelle Bay. It has numerous straight, wide streets such as Johnston Street, the main street which runs from Parramatta Road to Rozelle Bay. These wide streets give the suburb an air of Victorian middle-class gentility and refinement which is lacking in many other parts of Victorian inner Sydney—but this refinement comes at the expense of a loss of some inner-city bustle. The land between Parramatta Road, Johnston Street, Booth Street and Nelson Street was sold to property developer John Young, an important figure in Annandale's (and Sydney's) development.

Young came to Sydney in 1870, having been a successful architect in London, where he had helped with the design of the Crystal Palace. Upon his arrival, he decided that property development would be more profitable than practising architecture. He was the building contractor for the Department of Lands Building in Bridge Street, the General Post Office in Martin Place and St Mary's Cathedral. Young's company was keen to see the Annandale area developed and held a competition for the best plan for their new suburb. The winning outline came from architect and surveyor Ferdinand Reuss, who envisaged wide and regular streets.

Johnston Street was to be the finest street, and Annandale, a model suburb. John Young built the landmark 'witches' houses' at the northern end of Johnston Street in the 1880s. Some were built for his three daughters. Young also owned the Abbey at number 272. It is said he built the Abbey to try to induce his wife back to Sydney, after they had become estranged and she had moved to London. Sadly, she died before he could persuade her. The first of the witches' houses, Kenilworth, at 260 Johnston Street, was once leased by Young to Sir Henry Parkes at a very cheap rent, when Parkes became bankrupt and ill in the 1890s. Parkes died there in 1896. Some said sceptically that Young's choice of a tenant was a canny move for a property developer to make—it added a greater tone of respectability to the neighbourhood.

While the middle classes resided around the Johnston Street area, workers were taking advantage of continued subdivision and cheap land prices around Johnstons Creek in the valley between Annandale and Glebe, which meant Young's dreams of an entirely grand, middle-class suburb were not to be.

Like other parts of the inner city built in the nineteenth century, many people left Annandale and moved further out in the first half of the twentieth century. From the 1960s, people began to take more of an interest and renovated old properties.

Balmain sits on a chunky peninsula that juts out into the southwestern end of the harbour, opposite Millers Point. The peninsula was the boundary between the traditional areas occupied by the Gadigal Aboriginal group, who lived to the east, and the Wangal group, who lived to the west. Birchgrove lies on the western side of the Balmain peninsula, separated from Balmain by Snails Bay. The more industrial and historically more working-class parts of Balmain lie on the eastern side of the peninsula. Balmain's location on a peninsula gives the suburb an air of relative isolation and remoteness, despite its industrial character and the density of recent property developments. There are four ferry wharves in this suburb which is almost surrounded by the harbour: Yurulbin Point, Elliott Street, Thames Street in Mort Bay, and the Darling Street Wharf.

Balmain is named after the original grantee of land in the area, William Balmain, who was a surgeon on the First Fleet. He was a foe of John Macarthur and the other men of the Rum Corps. Balmain was granted 550 acres (220 hectares) on the peninsula to the west of Cockle

Bay (Darling Harbour) in 1800, although he had little to do with the area. He must have thought the grant was valueless, as the following year he sold the land for 5 shillings to his friend John Gilchrist, and returned to England.

In the earliest days of settlement, the peninsula had been used as a kangaroo trapping ground where the sporting men of the colony would gather to drive kangaroo mobs from the plain (where Leichhardt and Lilyfield are now) down to the point. This use of the land was not to continue. Gilchrist subdivided and sold his land between 1825 and 1831. By then, the land was becoming attractive to shipbuilding firms, as the distances by water to Millers Point and Sydney Cove were short. This usage set the direction of Balmain's development. In 1840, a ferry service between Balmain and Millers Point was established. It was from this time that the place became a popular and fashionable residential area, which it would continue to be until the suburb became industrialised from the 1870s onwards. In 1877, the popular local appetite for swimming in the harbour was severely tested when a shark bit off a boy's leg in the water near the Darling Street ferry wharf.[6] He did not survive the attack.

Private Whitfield was the original grantee of 30 acres (12 hectares) now known as Birchgrove. He did not make great use of his land, and it passed through several hands before being acquired by John Birch, the paymaster of Macquarie's 73rd Regiment, in 1810. Birch built Birch Grove House. This was demolished in 1967. The former Long Nose Point (now known as Yurulbin Point), at the end of Louisa Road, marks the boundary between the harbour and the Parramatta River.

Along Birchgrove Road, there are a number of houses dating from between 1840 and 1870, showing touches of Gothic style. St John's the Evangelist was built in 1882, designed by E. H. Buchanan (who also designed Balmain Town Hall). Originally intended as a school and church, the building has had several additions made to it. The lion's head fountain in the courtyard came from the first Bank of New South Wales in Macquarie Place.

One of Balmain's first important industrialists was a man called Thomas Rowntree, and he is remembered by the Rowntree Monument, which can be found in a small plot facing Rowntree Street. Rowntree came to Australia from England when gold was discovered, and he settled in Balmain in 1851. He was mayor of Balmain for two years, and he built Northumberland House at 87 Darling Street and Woodleigh in Stack Street, a house which was designed by Edmund Blacket. The grounds of Northumberland House have been subdivided, although the original residence remains.

Rowntree established a major ship-repairing business with Thomas Sutcliffe Mort, who soon took over the dry dock and developed it into an engineering business. Mort's business ventures changed the entire character of Balmain. By 1892, the population was solidly industrial and blue collar. For many years, Mort's Dock was the biggest private employer in Sydney. It closed in 1958, about a decade before containerisation of the port facilities in Sydney changed the nature of maritime industry forever. Typical occupations of the residents of Balmain included builders, engineers, carpenters and boilermakers. Industry was heavily concentrated along the harbour foreshore of Balmain.

453

In the 1890s, another large industrial complex, Lever Brothers, manufacturer of Sunlight soap, was established nearby at White Bay. Colgate-Palmolive, another soap maker, was also based on the Balmain peninsula. The Colgate-Palmolive factory site is being redeveloped into luxury medium-density housing.

Balmain's long-term connection with Sydney's industrial workforce meant that it was an important incubator of the trade union movement and the Labor Party. Many of the early stalwarts of the inner-city branches of the Labor Party in suburbs such as Balmain were Irish Catholics, and the Irish Catholic connection with the Labor Party in New South Wales continues to this day. Political meetings were held, and differences thrashed out in the pubs close to Mort's Dock and other employers. Opposing factions of the Labor Party have long fought for political supremacy in Balmain and other suburbs of the Inner West.

Grander Balmain residences were built despite the industrialisation. The manager of Mort's Dock, James Franki, built Montrose overlooking Mort Bay. It is still standing in Thames Street, Balmain. The eminent architect, Edmund Blacket, moved to Balmain in 1871, and he designed Glendenning, at 393 Darling Street. Blacket later moved to Alderley, in Booth Street, which was incorporated into the Balmain Hospital complex. Another early house is Hampton Villa in Grafton Street. Built in the late 1840s, Parkes once lived there. Ewenton, which faces Ewenton Park in East Balmain, was built by Robert Blake in 1854, and was later sold by him to Ewen Wallace Cameron, one of Mort's associates. Cameron added another wing to the house in 1872, and the two different periods of construction are clearly visible.

The prime residential property at Balmain and Birchgrove is located at Louisa and Wharf roads. Many of the houses have steep drops to the water, as many of the residential areas of the peninsula are well elevated. One old Balmain pub, the Sir William Wallace Hotel, built in 1878, has valiantly resisted gentrification, unlike others such as the Mort Bay Hotel. Balmain's memorials to the building frenzy that culminated in the centenary celebrations of European settlement are the courthouse and library on the corner of Darling and Montague streets.

In the 1960s, the area was 'rediscovered' and the new residents formed community groups who fought for the preservation of items of historical interest, and for access to foreshore land. Old boarding houses were renovated during the 1970s and 1980s, and turned into mansions. Workshops which had some connection with industry or the harbour, such as sailmakers and wharf workshops, are losing their links with the past and becoming advertising agencies and photographic studios.

Most of Balmain and Birchgrove's links with the industrial past have been severed, although there are some exceptions, such as the Caltex Terminal and the boat yard. Much of the old industrial land has been sold for medium- to high-density residential development, often of a dubious quality. The tiny, narrow streets were not designed for the motor car and intensive medium-density development of land formerly used for industry.

Like other parts of the Inner West, Balmain has an abundant supply of good restaurants, pubs, cafés, antique shops and bookshops. The main shopping area is along Darling Street. Two of Balmain's sporting institutions are the recently restored Dawn Fraser Swimming Pool

RIGHT: Glebe Island container terminal with the Harbour Bridge in the background. Containerisation of the wharves transformed Sydney's port facilities in the 1970s.

455

on the Parramatta River, and the Balmain ('Tigers') Leagues Club, home of the local rugby league football team. The pool is much older than Dawn Fraser, the three-time Olympic gold medal–winning swimmer, who has lived most of her life at Balmain and is still one of the area's more famous local identities. Birchgrove Park at the end of the peninsula has one of the best-located sporting fields and tennis courts in Sydney.

Further towards the city, White Bay houses a container terminal, a bulk wheat terminal and a coal loader. On the eastern side of the bay is Glebe Island, no longer the separate, 13-hectare island covered in thick scrub it once was. The island was named because of its proximity to the Glebe, the land owned by the Church of England, and was barely touched before the 1850s when it was chosen as an ideal site for an abattoir. Edmund Blacket drew up the plans for the project and work was commenced in 1853. A shortage of workers during the goldrush era hampered its progress. Another major problem for the site was the transportation of stock. The original intention was that the animals would be transported by punt to the island, but this was not very practical, so Abattoir Road was built connecting the island to the mainland at Balmain.

This did not solve the problems. Residents of the area grew increasingly irritated by the constant noise of stampeding sheep and cattle, and demanded that the abattoir be closed.

A public inquiry was held and concluded that the project had been a complete failure. A series of sweeping improvements were made, and the abattoir continued to run, despite the protests of the residents. It was not until 1915 that the abattoir was moved further away to Homebush Bay.

From the 1920s, Glebe Island was used as a base for grain handling, and from 1942 to 1945, it was used as the landing and re-embarking base for American troops, who were transferred from their anchored ships to the island by harbour ferries. None of the island's original buildings remains, and the only reminder of even a small part of its history is a small plaque commemorating the arrival of the American troops in 1942. Glebe Island's port facilities were containerised in the 1970s.

The first bridge connecting Pyrmont to Glebe Island was of timber construction, built during the 1850s and known as Blackbutts Bridge. This was replaced in 1903 by a more substantial structure, the Glebe Island Bridge, a four-lane bridge with an electric swing span. With the Pyrmont Bridge, it formed the transport access to the north and west of the city. The bridge was built of wrought iron, supported on stone and concrete pillars. It was a significant engineering achievement of the day, but completely inadequate for the late twentieth century. A new, very imposing and starkly beautiful bridge, renamed the Anzac Bridge, replaced it in 1995.

One of the most remarkable collections of buildings can be found on the Parramatta River at Rozelle, to the immediate west of Balmain. Formerly known as Callan Park, and later as Rozelle Hospital, it is now the campus for the Sydney College of the Arts or Kirkbride, and is administered by the University of Sydney. The new name for the building commemorates one of the more understanding and humane nineteenth-century practitioners in the emerging medical science of psychiatry. Callan Park was for many years dedicated to looking after the insane and mentally ill, including shell-shock victims from World War II. It was designed by James Barnet and opened in 1885. The complex consists of a series of pavilions which divided patients according to their sex and degree of mental illness. The gardens were laid out by Charles Moore, the director of the Royal Botanic Gardens. There is pressure to redevelop some of the grounds for accommodation for the aged. This is proving to be a lively political issue. Many Sydneysiders are concerned that prime harbour-foreshore land is being sold and redeveloped, even though the aim of providing aged accommodation is a worthy one.

Leichhardt is named after the German explorer Ludwig Leichhardt, who disappeared without a trace while journeying across northern Australia. Before then, it was known as Piperston because one of the first land grants there was made in 1811 to Captain John Piper. When Piper ran into financial difficulties, he sold his land-holding, which covered today's suburb, to Walter Beames and others. One of the bigger landmarks in the area for many years was the Colonial Regency house built by barrister James Foster. His estate, called Elswick, stood near present-day Thornley Street. Another later owner of Elswick was one of Sydney's first solicitors, James Norton, after whom Leichhardt's Norton Street was named.

For many years, Leichhardt was a rural retreat. This idyll, however, was not to last. The mid– to late–nineteenth-century population boom of Sydney meant that Leichhardt, like so many other present-day inner-city suburbs, was carved up and subdivided. The Municipality of Leichhardt, proclaimed in 1871, covered 1300 acres (520 hectares). Along Norton Street, on the corner of Marion Street, are two fine pieces of late–nineteenth-century architecture built at the time of the boom in the area: the Town Hall and the Leichhardt Primary School.

The development of the municipality was closely related to the development of transport networks. Horse-drawn buses serviced Leichhardt to an extent, but were not sufficient to cope with an increasing population and, by 1884, a steam tramway was completed, running along Norton Street to Short Street. The tram extended as far as Darley Street by 1887.

The greater accessibility afforded by the extension of the tramway system enhanced subdivision sales in Leichhardt. Until early in the 1900s the environment in this growing suburb was marred by malodorous mangrove and mud flats at the mouth of Iron Cove and Long Cove creeks. Iron Cove Bay was a dumping ground for waste, including sewerage from Leichhardt and surrounding areas. A number of proposals for reclamation of the flats were put forward, until finally work commenced on the Hawthorne Canal in 1904, which was built along the old course of Long Cove Creek. This canal divides Leichhardt from Haberfield.

457

For the first half of the twentieth century, Leichhardt's fortunes waned along with those of other inner-city suburbs. Properties were resumed to allow for the extension of the goods railway line from Glebe Island that cut across the western border of the suburb. In turn, the goods railway attracted more industry to the area. During the Depression of the 1930s, many houses were left to fall into decline. By the 1950s, an increasing number of people, particularly immigrants, began to acquire property in the area, which was not only cheap but conveniently located close to jobs, transport and the city centre. These factors also played a part in the period of residential and commercial upsurge in the area during the 1970s, as did a growing consciousness of the architectural value of the old houses.

As well as being a rapidly gentrifying inner-city suburb, Leichhardt is a commercial and, to a declining degree, residential centre of the Italian community in Sydney. The leading Italian language newspaper, *La Fiamma*, has been published there since 1947. The newspaper was established by the Italian Capuchin order of priests as a means of trying to arrest the support of communism in the Italian community. Many good Italian restaurants, cafés and delicatessens, and other food supply shops are to be found there, both in Norton Street and Parramatta Road. The fashionability of Leichhardt as an area for restaurants is putting pressure on rents, and some longer-term tenants are moving out.

The Italian community has been part of the Leichhardt landscape since the late nineteenth century. Many of the early immigrants established small retail businesses such as fruit and vegetable shops, fish shops or cabinet and woodworking businesses. Among the most famous of the craftsmen who lived in the Leichhardt municipal area were the Melocco brothers, emigrants from the northern Italian region of Friuli. They became famous throughout Sydney for their mosaic, marble and terrazzo tile work. By 1933, there were 400 Italian-born people

ABOVE: Members of Sydney's Italian community in the early 1960s. Leichhardt still holds a strongly Italian influence.

458

in the Leichhardt area.[7] As a result of the postwar boom in immigration, this number had increased to more than 4500 by 1961.[8] Since that time, Leichhardt has been the closest Sydney has to a 'Little Italy', although the proportion of the population actually born in Italy has never been greater than 25 per cent. The well-known Italian social sporting club Apia was founded in Norton Street, Leichhardt, in 1961. By 1996, burdened with crippling debt, it had closed. The Italian flavour of Leichhardt has, in the past fifteen years, become more affluent. Leichhardt continues to develop into an area of the Inner West with some of the most interesting commercial infrastructure, which makes the area lively at all hours of the day and night. The proliferation of restaurants and nightlife led to the opening in 1998 of a new multiplex cinema in Norton Street.

Because wholesale redevelopment has not taken place in Leichhardt, a number of its oldest and most prominent buildings remain, so that the history of the suburb can be seen through its architectural styles. The main buildings—the Police Station, the Post Office and the Town Hall—date, like many other public buildings in the inner-city suburbs, from the 1880s, reflecting the flourishing prosperity of the area in that era. Many of the former factories around the area have been converted to residential use.

Leichhardt Council, responsible for Leichhardt, Annandale, Glebe, Balmain and Rozelle, was long dominated by various factions of the Labor Party. From the late 1960s, the advent of local middle-class residents' action groups challenged the long reign of the local Labor Party machine, which in those days was usually in favour of property developments and relatively indifferent to heritage and conservation issues. Its traditional blue-collar support base was disintegrating with the decline of industry in the Inner West. Residents' action groups wanted to preserve local heritage and restrict the redevelopment of industrial sites for medium- and high-density housing. They also wanted to restrict the construction of expressways through local neighbourhoods. Some of these newer residents adopted some dubious old political practices such as stacking of Labor Party branches. Politics became very dirty. The local council elections of 1977 and 1980 were hotly contested. In a dramatic meeting in the Balmain Town Hall, the local membership branch books disappeared during a conveniently timed blackout. The low point in the factional battle was the vicious bashing of Peter Baldwin, a member of the left wing of the Labor Party who had detected irregularities with local branch membership before the local council election in 1980. Leichhardt Council is now administered by a more politically diverse range of people. One of the most fascinating pieces of documentary television in recent years, 'Rats in the Ranks', focused on the machinations and ruminations within Leichhardt Council.

Ryde was the third settlement in Australia, conveniently located almost halfway along the Parramatta River between Parramatta and Sydney, to the west of the Lane Cove River. Originally the area was known as the Field of Mars, a large grant of common land of 2500 hectares set aside in 1804. This common ran from the Lane Cove River towards Pennant Hills. Gradually, the land was deforested and used for grazing. By 1900, after agitation from local residents, some of the common land was sold off.

The area known as Putney was once known as Kissing Point—probably a reference to the shallowness of the Parramatta River at that point, which meant that oceangoing vessels started to 'kiss' (a nautical term for 'touch') the river bottom. To the west of Kissing Point, the deep-water channel of the river peters out and the water becomes shallower. This meant that heavy cargo on large ships had to be reshipped on smaller boats to travel further west. A commercial centre developed around Church Street, where the Ryde Bridge crosses the river. It was in the Ryde area that the first beer brewery was established by James Squire on land he was granted in 1795. Squire grew barley, built a malt house on his land and experimented with growing hops. He operated his business until his death in 1822. Squire befriended Bennelong, and gave him sanctuary in his final years. Bennelong lived in a humpy in Squire's garden.

The land around Ryde was used for orcharding until the subdivisions of the late nineteenth century, which were a result of the new railway link between Hornsby and Sydney. The popular variety of green apple, the Granny Smith, first grew at Ryde as a result of a freak accident of nature in Maria Smith's orchard in the 1860s. Apple seeds self-seeded and were cross-pollinated to form the green apple variety named after the orchardist. The apples became a commercial success as they had an unusually long shelf life and were excellent-tasting, both raw and cooked. An interesting vestige of Ryde's former days as an orcharding district is the location of the Ryde School of Horticulture and the many plant nurseries which still operate in the area.

The Gladesville and Iron Cove bridges, built in the 1880s, greatly improved access to the city. In 1889, the northern train line from Sydney to Newcastle passed through Strathfield and Ryde, and Ryde (now West Ryde) railway station was built. This stepped up the pace of subdivision. The whole area of Ryde soon became so large and populous that the area was divided in 1954, into West Ryde and Ryde (or Top Ryde). It was here that the first district shopping centre in Sydney was built in 1957. Gladesville Hospital (1837) forms the southeastern boundary between the Ryde district and Hunters Hill.

There are still some old buildings at Ryde, such as the Ryde Police Station (1837) on the corner of Belmore Street and Victoria Road. The Field of Mars Refuge Centre lies in the valley of the Lane Cove River, and covers an area once part of the Field of Mars Common. It is this relatively central location in the northwestern area of Sydney which has made Ryde a favourable place to establish Macquarie University and the large Macquarie shopping centre. Many light- and high-technology–based industries have been established in this area over the past thirty years.

Hunters Hill is Sydney's oldest and most beautiful garden suburb. It is a residential enclave within twenty minutes of the city proper, created long before any town planners developed theories as to what garden suburbia should look like. Hunters Hill and Woolwich lie on a long and narrow peninsula which juts into and forms the westerly meeting point of the Lane Cove and Parramatta rivers. It is one of the smallest municipalities of Sydney, both in terms of size and population. The seclusion of the area is heightened by the expressway and Fig Tree and Tarban Creek bridges. These lead to the large intersection of Victoria Road and Burns Bay Road. Tarban Creek Bridge is one of the most modern of Sydney's bridges. It was not built until 1965. These improvements to the roads came at some cost to the area. Streets were destroyed and one of the oldest and most beautiful houses, St Malo, was demolished

Aborigines of the Kameraigal tribe lived in the rock caves on the Hunters Hill shoreline. The last one to live in the area, called Black Lucy, died in the late 1920s. The Hunters Hill community had built her a two-room house.[9] In the 1830s, the Tarban Creek Asylum for the Insane, designed by Mortimer Lewis, was established. It was the forerunner of the existing Gladesville Hospital, which was reached from Drummoyne by a punt running from the end of Victoria Road across the Parramatta River to Bedlam Point. The medical superintendent of the hospital from 1848, Dr Francis Campbell, was a resident of Hunters Hill and the first psychiatrist in Australia. From the time of Campbell's administration, Tarban Creek Asylum

ABOVE: Gladesville and Hunters Hill during construction of the Gladesville and Fig Tree bridges in the 1960s.

was used to treat and cure people, rather than just to lock them away. Those who were congenitally retarded with no hope of treatment and cure were sent to Parramatta Hospital for the Insane, the former Female Factory. The original buildings at the Tarban Creek Asylum (later renamed Gladesville Hospital) were designed by one-time Colonial Architect Mortimer Lewis, in the Greek Revival style. The hospital was decommissioned in 1995 and some of the land is now being redeveloped into medium-density town houses.

The presence of the asylum, together with the convict settlement at nearby Cockatoo Island (from which bushranger Captain Thunderbolt escaped), made Hunters Hill a relatively dangerous place to live.[10] The Field of Mars Common was another area that provided refuge to roaming outlaws. The development of a permanent community at Hunters Hill was delayed until the arrival of the Joubert brothers in 1847.

Some of the earliest landowners there were Mary Reiby and John Clarke, but they did not make the area their permanent home. Clarke bought land at the eastern end of the peninsula, known as Woolwich. Reiby built two cottages in 1835 (later incorporated into Fig Tree House) on a 60-acre (24-hectare) grant. She also grew fruit on her land. Reiby could find no buyers when she tried to sell it in 1838, so it was rented until 1847 when it was sold to the person who would be called the father of Hunters Hill, Didier Numa Joubert. He set to work, with the assistance of skilled Italian stonemasons, and created a small village with a French atmosphere. Didier Joubert built and lived in St Malo next to Fig Tree House. The Joubert family went on to build at least fifteen houses, including Passy, in the classical French style, which was occupied by Sydney's first consul general. Didier's son Numa ran a ferry service to Sydney until 1906, when the business was sold to the Sydney Harbour Ferry Company. Numa built the tower on Fig Tree House, which stands just near Fig Tree Bridge, and was once used as the base for his ferrying operations.

Jules Joubert, Didier's younger brother, also settled there. He had a varied, adventurous and peripatetic career, but still found time to build on the peninsula, and boast about it in his memoirs to the extent that he made no reference at all to his elder brother Didier.[11] It was the strong French connection with the Joubert family that induced the Marist Brothers, a French religious order of the Catholic Church, to buy land in the area and set up a school and a seminary which later grew into St Joseph's College, one of Sydney's Greater Public Schools for boys.

Two other French settlers in the area were the Count de Milhau and Leonard Bordier. De Milhau was in exile as a result of choosing the wrong side in the French Revolution of 1848. He came to Australia with Leonard Bordier. Bordier imported four prefabricated timber houses in 1855, which were assembled in Ferry Street by German tradesmen, who had accompanied the houses on the journey over. The ferry wharf at the bottom of Ferry Street was built shortly after the houses. The only one of these houses remaining is The Chalet at 1 Yerton Avenue.[12]

Charles Jeanneret, another early settler, was not French, but was born in Australia of Huguenot ancestry. His parents were English. Jeanneret lived in one of de Milhau's wooden houses, next door to his parents-in-law. He had a very long (thirty-year) career building stone houses at Hunters Hill, and concentrated his building activities on the southern side of the peninsula. His earlier houses were built in sandstone blocks and, later, in brick. Many members of the Jeanneret family settled in the area, and built and lived in many other Hunters Hill houses. They often married people from other long-term Hunters Hill families.

The Hunters Hill municipality was incorporated in 1861. Jules Joubert was the first mayor, and de Milhau and Jeanneret sat on the council. The legacy of these early plantings still gives Hunters Hill its sylvan character, possibly more than any other area of Sydney other than the upper North Shore. By 1900, Hunters Hill was a close community with a wide range of housing from large mansions and villas to small workmen's cottages, many of which were built to house the stonemasons and other artisans who worked locally.

Some of the early residents were Italian. These included Angelo Tornaghi, a renowned clockmaker, and John Cuneo, who built the first hotel in the suburb in 1861. Tornaghi bought 30 acres (12 hectares) of land on the peninsula and lived in Hunters Hill for more than forty years until his death in 1906. Many Irish people also settled in the area. One of the earliest policies of the council was to encourage the planting of street trees.

463

Another Irish family of Hunters Hill was the FitzGeralds. The FitzGerald family are long-term residents of Hunters Hill who married into other local families, and who have stayed in the area for more than a century. Robert D. FitzGerald arrived from Tralee, Ireland, and was appointed deputy surveyor. He wrote an authoritative book on Australian native orchids in collaboration with lithographer James Stopps, another local resident. FitzGerald's grandson was the poet, also called Robert D. FitzGerald, who lived in Hunters Hill all his life until his death in 1987. His wife, Marjorie, grew up in Hunters Hill and was related to another local family, the Piguenits, who lived at Saintonge in 24 Avenue Road. W. C. Piguenit was a well-known landscape artist of the nineteenth century. Fifth-generation members of the FitzGerald family still live at Hunters Hill today. Other families who have lived continuously at Hunters Hill include members of the Cuneo family.[13]

A recent development built along starkly different lines to what has gone before is Sid Londish's Pulpit Point Estate, on the site of the former Mobil oil refinery. In the middle of the nineteenth century, this area served as recreational 'pleasure gardens', operated by Charles Jeanneret. The development bears no relationship to the rest of the peninsula, and is more reminiscent of a gated community in Florida or southern California. The 'dress circle' of the estate is populated with houses of starkly different architectural styles, including a house designed by Harry Seidler. There is an avenue of *faux* French mansions lower down, and a marina and communal swimming pool. It is quite unlike anything else in Sydney, but it may, in certain respects be a model, good or otherwise, for medium-density redevelopment on former industrial sites along the Parramatta River.

Hunters Hill Town Hall is one of Sydney's oldest, and there are still so many fine works of nineteenth-century architecture in the suburb that the entire area is classified by the National Trust—excluding, one can only imagine, the recent development on Pulpit Point. The Heritage

Commission also classified it as a Conservation Area.

One of the earliest battles to preserve open parkland in the 1970s took place at Hunters Hill. The Battlers for Kellys Bush were a group of thirteen women who formed one of the earliest residents' action groups in Sydney. They persuaded the Builders' Labourers' Federation (BLF) to impose a green ban on Kellys Bush in 1971. The final act in the fight for Kellys Bush was the purchase of the land by the state government, which turned it into a reserve. Hunters Hill is now well supplied with open parkland; apart from Kellys Bush there is also the reserve at Clarkes Point, Woolwich, which was bought by the council and converted into public land. Altogether, there are 60 hectares of parkland at Hunters Hill.

Hunters Hill and Woolwich did not manage to escape the presence of industry. This was to be expected as the end of the peninsula is so close to Cockatoo Island and the Balmain peninsula. The industries in the area were mostly on the southeastern side of the peninsula, near Margaret Street and Nelson Parade. They included Mort's Dry Dock, built in 1902, some shipbuilding yards nearby, a tin-smelting business which lasted until 1967, and chemical factories near Nelson Parade. They have now gone. The only presence of heavy industry was the Mobil oil storage depot, which was demolished in 1988. The dry dock, which was cut into the sandstone on Clarkes Point, was the largest dry dock in Australia when it was built in 1902. Until recently, the dock was used by the army. Near Clarkes Point is the popular Woolwich Pier Hotel.

The construction of the expressway on Burns Bay Road had a substantial effect on Hunters Hill. Whole streets were lost, as were many houses and cottages in Church Street. The area was also threatened with inappropriate development in the 1960s. The Hunters Hill Trust was formed in 1968 to meet the threat to the integrity of the suburb, becoming one of the largest civic trusts in Australia. It soon substantially controlled the council. Sadly, this has not ensured that the late–twentieth-century development is of the same consistently high quality as that of the century before.

In 1988, the state government determined that Parramatta should be given the important task of being Sydney's second central business district. This was a big promotion: in 1949, Parramatta was just one of twenty district centres in the Cumberland Planning Scheme. Curiously enough, Parramatta's role as the alternative CBD in Sydney has historical resonance, as it was the second site for settlement chosen soon after the arrival of the First Fleet in 1788.

Just as the first roads and train lines ran to and from the city of Sydney, so, too, new transport routes, both road and rail, will be designed to lead to and from Parramatta. Access in all directions will be improved. The proposed orbital (ring) road in Sydney's west, planned to link the Pacific Highway with the Great Western and Hume highways, will consolidate Parramatta's new central significance in the Sydney region. Regional centres that will form part of Parramatta's satellite network include Liverpool, Penrith–Castlereagh and Hornsby.

Parramatta provides one of the best contrasts there is between the old and new in the Sydney region. Cultural facilities have been established in the Parramatta area. One of the greatest of these is the Parramatta Riverside Theatres for the performing arts which were built as a Bicentennial project. Local, state and international arts groups of all kinds perform there—drama, ballet, and popular and classical music. The two main performing groups based at Parramatta are the New South Wales Ballet and the Parramatta Theatre Company. Retailing is also big business in the Parramatta region.

Westfield Parramatta is Sydney's largest underground shopping mall, and one of the largest in the southern hemisphere. Just as it is in the United States, spending a day at a shopping mall is the central social experience for many Sydneysiders, the closest thing there is to a neighbourhood meeting place. In 1991, Parramatta provided almost as many jobs as North Sydney, particularly in the areas of health and community services, manufacturing and property and business services.[14]

The first visit by the colonists to the west of Sydney took place soon after the First Fleet landed. In February 1788, Phillip and his party travelled west. They spent the first night at Homebush Bay and travelled inland as far as present-day Concord. This first journey took them up a tributary of the Parramatta River, the Duck River. The next trip in April took them up to the end of the tidal section of the Parramatta River, where Parramatta stands today, 16 miles (25 kilometres) from the camp at Sydney Cove. The area was initially (until 1791) called Rose Hill in honour of George Rose, who had probably been responsible for Phillip's selection as governor of the new colony. The country there looked promising: the trees were large and well spaced, and the land was level to gently undulating. Phillip and his men travelled inland as far as Prospect Hill. Phillip set up a settlement at Parramatta, and this was done in early November 1788.

Governor Phillip's first task was to clear the land of timber, a necessary precursor for building work and agriculture. In 1790, Watkin Tench wrote wryly about the main street of the town, commenting that it was to be 'a mile long, and of such breadth as will make Pall Mall and Portland Place hide their diminished heads'. Lieutenant Dawes planned and laid out the town and the main streets in 1791. Wattle-and-daub convict huts 24 feet long and 12 feet wide (approximately 8 metres by 3 metres) were built along the streets. Each hut was planned to contain ten convicts. Enough space between these huts was set aside for convicts to grow vegetables, which they could sell if they wished. By 1790, 200 acres (80 hectares) had been cleared, and much of this was under cultivation. Inducing the convicts to work the soil deep enough was difficult. They were told to dig sixteen rods per day, and many of these rods were just scratched over.

Accommodation for the women and families was around the corner in Church Street. The first public buildings were a storehouse, barracks for soldiers and the governor's early wattle-and-daub house, which stood at the end of George Street. In June 1791, the name of the settlement was changed to Parramatta, an Aboriginal word meaning 'plenty of eels', an indication of the location on that part of the Parramatta River where the tidal influence from the harbour diminished. Freshwater eels would go no further down the Parramatta River than Parramatta. Thus, the local rugby league team are known as the 'Eels'.

Parramatta's population grew quickly. So great were the hopes for Parramatta that, by the following year, a rudimentary town hall was built and a market was established so that the convicts could sell whatever they produced in their gardens. James Ruse, who had served his term by August 1789, was one of the first grantees of land and indeed the first emancipist settler in the Parramatta area. A convict from Cornwall, he was first given $1\frac{1}{2}$ acres (0.6 hectares), with the promise of a 30-acre (12-hectare) land grant if he succeeded at farming. He did succeed—possibly because he dug the soil more slowly and more deeply and he never dug more than eight or nine rods a day.[15] The first harvest was gathered in November 1789, all of which was kept for seed.[16] Consequently, Ruse was granted more land in March 1791, which he worked without convict labour.

He called his land Experiment Farm. Just as he was the first emancipist male to have served his sentence in the new colony, so was his wife, Elizabeth, the first emancipist female to have done so. By 1791, Ruse had built a brick cottage close to where the Experiment Farm Cottage stands today. This later cottage was built by the man who bought Experiment Farm from Ruse in 1793. Today the farm is in Ruse Street, Harris Park. Ruse went on to work better, more productive land along the Hawkesbury River.

John Harris arrived in Sydney as a surgeon, and he was sent to Parramatta to look after the convicts there soon after his arrival in 1790. He received a land grant of 300 acres (120 hectares) and bought Experiment Farm, where he built a cottage in 1798. Harris sided with Governor King in opposing the illegal trade in rum, and thus fell from favour with many of his fellow officers. In 1802, probably on a flimsy pretext in an effort to get rid of him, Harris was charged with the military offence of ungentlemanly conduct, because he reported private conversations with his fellow officers to Governor King. The next year, he was charged again for disclosing how two of his fellow officers had voted in a court martial. The charge was defeated on the technicality that the date of the alleged offence was misstated as being on the nineteenth *ultimo* (meaning the previous month), rather than the nineteenth *instant* (meaning the present month). Harris later named the estate which was granted to him in 1804 on the western side of Cockle Bay 'Ultimo'.

Ironically, Harris later joined forces with his fellow officers during Bligh's governorship as he thoroughly disapproved of Bligh's autocratic leadership style. Harris was appointed as a magistrate by Acting Governor George Johnston, but later fell out with the rebel government as he criticised John Macarthur, the *de facto* leader, who was also his close neighbour in Harris Park at Elizabeth Farm. The antagonism between the two men must have been uncomfortable to deal with. Elizabeth Farm is a mere 500 metres from Harris's Experiment Farm Cottage. Harris was one of the first directors of the Bank of New South Wales and died a wealthy man in 1838 with considerable land-holdings as far west as Bathurst.

Macarthur was granted 100 acres (40 hectares) of land on the Elizabeth Farm site in 1793. The house on Elizabeth Farm is the oldest building in Australia. Macarthur extended his land-holdings in the area and by 1816 he owned 850 acres (340 hectares) extending as far as the Duck River. This covered the area where Rose Hill, the racecourse of the same name, and the industrial suburb of Camellia lie. It was to Elizabeth Farm that Macarthur and his wife Elizabeth first brought merino sheep. Another early resident of the Parramatta area was the Reverend Samuel Marsden, who lived north of the river and presided over St John's Church. Marsden, whose father was a blacksmith, was taken up by an evangelical group within the Church of England which 'sponsored the education for the ministry of promising but ill-connected youths'.[17] Humanitarian and politician William Wilberforce recommended him for the position of assistant to the chaplain of New South Wales in 1793, and he arrived in Sydney in 1794. While guarding his mostly convict flock at Parramatta, he developed another sort of flock which was more profitable, and one which he had more success at managing: sheep. Marsden soon became one of the largest landowners and woolgrowers in the Parramatta area. His role as magistrate made him unpopular with convicts, who nicknamed him the 'flogging parson'. Even Thomas Bigge thought his style as magistrate was 'stamped with severity'. His curatorial obligations made him responsible for the wellbeing of the inmates of the 'Female Factory' and the orphanage at Parramatta. Marsden had rocky relationships with Macarthur and Macquarie, whose lenient attitude towards emancipists he strongly disapproved of. Marsden is buried in the grounds of St John's Church, Parramatta.

Like many other parts of the colony, Parramatta was much improved during Lachlan Macquarie's term in office. Streets were laid out and (rather unimaginatively and repetitively) named Macquarie, Pitt, George, Church and Marsden streets. More permanent buildings were constructed in an orderly manner. In 1813, the first fair in the colony was held there. This fair was the precursor to the Royal Easter Show. There was also an annual banquet to which the local Aborigines were invited. At these banquets, Aborigines held corroborees on the site of the present corner of Macquarie and Marsden streets.

Macquarie made several improvements and extensions to St John's Church, all of which, apart from the twin towers, were later rebuilt in the 1850s. He built a hospital, now demolished, and a soldiers' barracks called the Lancer Barracks, most of which still remains. Macquarie also built the Female Factory at Rydalmere, where female convicts were put to work spinning and weaving woollen cloth, as well as the local commissariat stores.

The Female Factory was a euphemistic term to describe the women's gaol. Before the factory was built, convict women lived in a room on the first floor of the gaol, until the space became so overcrowded that they had to find whatever lodging they could elsewhere.

The factory was designed by Francis Greenway and built in 1819 to house 300 women on 4 acres (1.6 hectares) of land at Rydalmere. Those who could not be reformed by the system had their hair shorn off, a form of disgrace in a world where one's relative physical charms were often a passport to survival. Many of the women were sent to the factory when they incon-veniently became pregnant while on assigned service. Male settlers were allowed to use the factory as a matrimonial agency. Some would visit and inspect the inmates with a view to finding prospective marriage partners. Those selected would be given tickets-of-leave, but they often decided to leave the men who selected them as soon as they possibly could.

The factory soon became overcrowded. The inmates revolted in 1827 and again in 1843, when the population there had risen to 1200 following extensions in the late 1830s. The extensions were not popular: the new cells were designed for solitary confinement, a punishment meted out to women who were convicted of offences within the colony. After criticism from the Home Office of this form of punishment, windows were added to the cells, making them more bearable. With the abolition of transportation by 1847, the reason for the factory's existence had ceased to exist. Women were discharged or given tickets-of-leave, and only the infirm stayed on. The building then became an institution for the insane.

One magnificent building which used to be a landmark at Rydalmere was Subiaco, designed by John Verge and built in 1836 for Hannibal Macarthur, John Macarthur's nephew. It stood on 140 acres (56 hectares) of land on the northern side of the Parramatta River, opposite Elizabeth Farm. The design of the front of the house was said to have used the Petit Trianon in Versailles as inspiration.[18] In 1848, the house and land were bought by Catholic Archbishop Polding and a Benedictine monastery was established there. The nuns moved on to West Pennant Hills in 1957 and, in 1961, the house was tragically demolished to make way for a factory car park. As architect Professor Leslie Wilkinson wrote at the time: 'Historically and architecturally, Subiaco cried out for preservation; it is in good condition and exhibits craftsmanship in stone, cedar and plaster of a high order.'[19]

The township of Parramatta extended along Church Street to the other side of the river in the nineteenth century. Parramatta could boast many inns as it stood on the road to other parts of the colony, such as Windsor and Richmond, and the Great Northern Road to the Hunter River. From 1840 onwards, much of the remaining Crown land was sold off, and land-holdings were subdivided from the 1850s. By 1852, Parramatta had settled into a period of decline with the dismantling of the convict system. Although the houses and cottages with their vineyards, orchards and gardens were very pretty, Parramatta in those days did not have 'the air of a thriving place'. Rents on houses were half what they were closer to the city.[20]

The impetus for subdivision was accelerated from 1855 with the opening of the railway to Sydney. Parramatta was incorporated as a municipality in 1862. Experiment Farm was sold off in smaller lots through the 1870s and 1880s. Elizabeth Farm was sold by the Macarthurs in 1881 and subdivided in 1883. The Town Hall was built in the same year. In 1938, Parramatta was declared a city.

Between 1921 and 1991, the population of Parramatta grew from 14 500 to 133 000. Much of the population growth occurred between 1947 and 1961, and the population has been relatively stable since the early 1970s. From the time of Parramatta's selection as one of the district centres under the Cumberland Scheme in the early 1960s, it became a bustling modern retail centre. Industry also developed in the surrounding areas at Rydalmere, South Granville and Ermington, and elsewhere along the Parramatta River. Ermington had been a semi-rural area until the 1920s, and Rydalmere was created by a subdivision of an old vineyard estate in 1886. Gregory Blaxland and Hannibal Macarthur were previous occupants of the estate. Victoria Road which runs from Rozelle to Parramatta was built in 1890. Before that, Kissing Point Road had connected this area with Ryde.

Parramatta Park is part of what was once known as the Governor's Domain. It used to extend as far as Baulkham Hills and Toongabbie. Grains were grown there along the Parramatta River on the land called 'Government Farm'. Macquarie extended the Domain by buying back land which had previously been granted, and improved and enlarged Government House, first built in 1799. Some of the land was cleared, but much of it remained in its native state.

Government House at Parramatta is the oldest public building on the Australian mainland. From the time it was completed, Government House was used to a greater extent—it was more comfortable than Government House in Bridge Street—until the construction of the new Government House in the Botanic Gardens. After the new Government House had been completed in Sydney, Old Government House at Parramatta became dilapidated. It was uninhabitable by 1855, and eventually leased to The King's School. The last governor to occupy Old Government House at Parramatta was Sir Charles FitzRoy, whose wife was killed in the grounds in a tragic riding accident in 1847. Parts of the Governor's Domain were sold off from 1859, including the land upon which the suburbs of Westmead and Toongabbie lie. The land which was sold was used as orchards for many years, until rising land values, following the construction of a railway station at Westmead in 1883, made subdivision possible. One of the largest hospital complexes in Australia, Westmead Hospital (established in 1978), covers much of what was once part of the Governor's Domain.

One of the most remarkable exercises in readapting a heritage site to modern use in Sydney has been the restoration and conversion of the Female Orphan School complex, the first building in Australia created for charitable purposes. Since 1998, the 22 hectares of land has become the Parramatta campus of the University of Western Sydney, Nepean. The site has had a long institutional history. After the orphanage closed, from 1888 until the mid-1980s it was the Rydalmere Psychiatric Hospital. There are many significant buildings there, including some built by early–twentieth-century Government Architect Walter Liberty Vernon.

469

To the north and west of Parramatta lie the suburbs of Rouse Hill, Castle Hill and Baulkham Hills. Until recent years, like so much of Western Sydney, these areas were semi-rural. This is changing, and the density of settlement is increasing. The Rouse Hill area has been earmarked by the government as a residential development area and transformation of the area is proceeding, albeit at a slower pace than was originally anticipated. The Rouse Hill area will, once the plans come to pass, become a vast, 70 000-lot suburban district the same size as Canberra. Other areas of the west of Sydney that are undergoing similar development pressure are Blacktown and Liverpool.

A government farm was established at Castle Hill in 1801 by Governor King. Many Irish convicts were sent to work clearing land and building the settlement. They often considered themselves to be oppressed political prisoners (unlike the rest of the convicts) and persecuted because of their nationality. In 1804, many of these Irish convicts rose up against their oppressors in an ill-organised rebellion known as the battle of Vinegar Hill. It started in Castle Hill and was supposed to spread south to Parramatta, from where the rebels would march to Sydney. The temptation to consume a keg of rum was, however, irresistible. One of the rebels, emboldened by drink, set fire to a building and soon Castle Hill was ablaze. The response of the authorities was swift and effective. Led by George Johnston, soldiers travelled overnight to Parramatta then sought the rebels. The soldiers soon surrounded the rebels and they surrendered after a *mêlée* at Vinegar Hill. One of the leaders, Phillip Cunningham, was hanged at the government store at Parramatta. The other leaders were court-martialled, and most of them were hanged in various public places and their corpses left to rot as an example to others. The rest of the corps of rebels were sent to work at the Coal River (Newcastle) as punishment.

470

Since the mid-1980s, Homebush Bay has been the site of Sydney's greatest building works ever to be undertaken both by state government and private enterprise. Homebush Bay contains the Bicentennial Park (1988), the Sydney International Aquatic Centre (1994), the Sydney Showground (1998), Stadium Australia (1999) and most of the venues for the 2000 Olympics.

Two of the first European property owners in the Homebush area were D'Arcy Wentworth, father of William Charles Wentworth, and John Blaxland, who was one of the earlier free settlers in the colony. At the time Blaxland arrived, he was a gentleman and man of means. His brother Gregory crossed the Blue Mountains with William Lawson and William Charles Wentworth in 1813. Both Blaxland brothers profited greatly from their relatively elevated social and economic position. John Blaxland and D'Arcy Wentworth received their land grants in Homebush from Governor King in 1806.

At the time of Wentworth's grant of land on the western side of Homebush Bay, Wentworth was working as a surgeon in Parramatta. D'Arcy Wentworth started one of the first horse-racing studs in Australia there and, after his son's appointment as president of the Sydney Turf Club, race meetings were held on the Wentworth land at Homebush until the completion of Randwick racecourse in 1860.

D'Arcy Wentworth named his property Home Bush. In fact, this was one of the first recorded usages of the word 'bush' to describe the Australian countryside, an expression which has stuck and broadened to include the Australian landscape generally. To British minds, the word 'country' would have connoted tame and closely settled agricultural land where intensive farming and grazing were practised. This environment was starkly dissimilar to the terrain in this foreign and sometimes inhospitable land. One of the later occupants of Home Bush (by then known as Homebush) was Louisa Meredith, who lived there with her husband in the early 1840s. She painted a vivid picture of the area. By then, the homestead was dilapidated, but it was enclosed by verandas to keep out the heat and had a pretty view north across bushland to the Parramatta River. Louisa Meredith vividly described her one-time home:

> Homebush was a fair specimen of a New South Wales settler's residence, possessing many Colonial peculiarities. The house stood on the highest ground of the estate, and for some hundreds of acres all around not a native tree or even a stump was visible, so completely had the land been cleared, though not worth cultivation. This desert barrenness was relieved close to the house, by three magnificent Norfolk Island pines … and the then broken and ruined fruit trees of what had been two very large orchards …
>
> A curving road, nearly half a mile long, and some twenty yards wide, with a good rail fence on either side, led from the entrance gate, on the public road, to the house, and this, being unadorned by a single tree, was, according to a Colonial stretch of courtesy, termed the 'Avenue'; much to my mystification … During nearly the whole time of our residence here the public road near us was infested by a gang of bush-rangers, or rather footpads, who committed many robberies on persons travelling past.
>
> Another unpleasant class of neighbours were the native dogs, or dingoes, evidently a species of wolf, or perhaps the connecting link between wolf and dog. These creatures were very numerous around us, and their howling or yelling at night in the neighbouring forests had a most dismal, unearthly kind of tone …
>
> One portion of our land at Homebush consisted of salt-water marshes, covered in high tides, and producing immense quantities of a species of samphire … A tree which we called the mangrove, grew very luxuriantly on the brink of the salt water all along the embankments … In the too-completely cleared space around Homebush these belts of green trees skirting the water were of great value … Twice a day the Parramatta steamer puffed in sight, as she passed the mouth of the wide creek down which we looked towards the estuary. And with a telescope, on a Sunday morning, we could plainly see the carriages and pedestrians going to the new church at Kissing Point … on a still night [we could hear] the drums beat at the Parramatta Barracks … Some of the vineyards and orange-groves near us were extensive and very beautiful. The large orange-trees, gay with their golden fruit and exquisitely fragrant bridal-blossoms, are among the noblest of the acclimatised products here, and, with the many other exotics common in every garden in Sydney, were quite a delight to see …[21]

Blaxland called his grant Newington. It lay to the west of Wentworth's Home Bush, along the southern side of the Parramatta River, and extended to the Duck River and Parramatta Road. It was named after the village in Kent in which Blaxland was born. Blaxland built an elegant Colonial mansion on the grant in 1832. The building became the core of the Methodist Newington School which relocated to Stanmore in 1880. In the early 1960s, it was used as a hospital for aged women. In 1961, the County of Cumberland gave it the highest possible classification of historical building.[22] It shared this classification with Hyde Park Barracks and the Rum Hospital in Macquarie Street, Elizabeth Bay House and Vaucluse House. The Regency-style mansion lies within the grounds of the Silverwater Prison. The western portion of the Blaxland estate was subdivided after the 1860s when the Blaxlands sold the land. The eastern portion was acquired by the federal government for defence purposes and was for many years the location of the Royal Australian Navy Armaments Depot (RANAD).

Since 1998, the new Sydney Showground at Homebush Bay has been the location for the annual Royal Easter Show. This is really a case of the Easter Show moving (almost) full circle back to where it started at Westmead in 1824. After moving to Prince Alfred Park near Central Railway Station in the nineteenth century, the Easter Show was held at the showground at Moore Park between 1882 and 1997.

The Easter Show is the big annual event where Sydneysiders rub shoulders with people from rural Australia. For many years, particularly during boom times in the wool industry, it was the highlight of the social calendar for country people. The original focus of the show was agricultural, and it still is. Prize cattle, sheep and livestock are judged, and showjumping and other equestrian events are held. One of the highlights of the show is the display of agricultural produce from the various regions of New South Wales. Massive district exhibits of produce—fruit and vegetables, jams, pickles, grains and wool—are shown. Prizes are awarded for the best exhibits.

There is something for everyone at the show. There is a sideshow alley and a pavilion for selling the traditional 'showbags', which are full of sweets and promotional material. The animal nursery displays pets of all types and sizes, both regular and exotic, and various registered breeds are judged for awards of excellence. There is also a display of farmyard animals that attracts young city children. There are arts and craft exhibitions and wood-chopping competitions where men swing their axes with great momentum through dense, hardwood eucalypt timber. The woodchopping competitions began in the days when the huge forests of timber in rural Australia were felled by axe. Perhaps the best spectacle of the show is the Grand Parade, where hundreds of livestock that have won prizes are put on display in the main arena in a parade adroitly choreographed by the ringmaster.

The first version of the Royal Agricultural Society (RAS), which organises the Easter Show, was formed in 1822 by leading pastoralists such as Samuel Marsden, John Jamison, William Cox (who built the road between Sydney and Bathurst), explorers and pastoralists John Oxley and Gregory Blaxland, and Judge Barron Field. Although John Macarthur did not play any role in the founding of the Royal Agricultural Society, his son William was later president of the RAS.

Jules Joubert, long-time secretary of the RAS and one of the early settlers at Hunters Hill, advocated its relocation from Parramatta to Sydney at a spot then called the Cleveland Paddock, now known as Prince Alfred Park, and a change of the date from October to coincide with Easter. The first Easter Show was held in 1869 and nearly 40 000 people attended. Joubert also organised the Intercolonial Exhibition of 1870 at Prince Alfred Park which 185 000 people attended. He later lobbied for the staging of the International Exhibition of 1879–80 in the Garden Palace. This was not such a financial success: although attendances were very high, the exhibition lost more than £100 000. During his term as secretary of the RAS, Joubert's policy of encouraging overseas companies to exhibit their manufactured goods was questioned by his colleagues in the society. They considered that the role of the RAS should be more exclusively directed to promoting Australian products.

The society grew tired of paying the high annual rental to the City Council for the use of Prince Alfred Park and persuaded the government to give it 40 acres (16 hectares) of land which was part of the Moore Park Common at a nominal rent. At the time of the grant, the common was a rocky, swampy and sandy patch of land, covered with low, scrubby bushland. This land-holding was later added to, and eventually covered 28 hectares.

From 1893, Queen Victoria consented to the prefix 'Royal' being added to the Agricultural Society, and thus to the Easter Show. The new, Homebush headquarters of the Royal Easter Show is 5 hectares larger, with 22 000 square metres of exhibition space linked by inter-connecting halls, unlike at Moore Park. A railway link from the city to Homebush Bay just next to the Showground has been built, so that the Show is only fifteen minutes from the city.

The Homebush Bay area (including the land once covered by Blaxland's Newington), environmentally speaking, is a paradoxical contrast between environmental degradation and uniqueness. The burdensome legacy of the heavy industry that was located in Homebush Bay from the late nineteenth century until the 1980s is the soil degradation of some parts of the area and the dangerously polluted sediments in the bay itself. Despite this heavy industry and pollution, however, the relatively low-density usage of the land, compared to acre upon acre of all-consuming suburban sprawl, has meant that many natural habitats have survived.

A significant amount of land in the Homebush Bay area is reclaimed, often with infill which is itself contaminated with toxins. For decades, domestic, commercial and industrial wastes were dumped in the area. The process of capping and containing toxic waste has been undertaken to make the area safe.

There are many aspects of environmental uniqueness. The Homebush Bay area lies at the eastern end of the Cumberland Plain and the Newington eucalyptus forest is the last remaining stand of its type on Wianamatta shale soil. The Newington land that was used as the Royal Australian Navy Armaments Depot (RANAD) will form part of the proposed Silverwater Nature Reserve.

The Olympic Village will house 15 000 athletes and officials, and is located on the eastern fringe of the old Newington estate. After the Olympics, the housing will be sold off and the area will become a new residential suburb. The construction of this village is already environmentally sensitive as it is close to wetlands at Haslams Creek and the proposed Silverwater Nature Reserve. The wetlands to the immediate west of the village on Haslams Creek are the home of the shy and protected migratory bird, Latham's snipe, which is easily disturbed.

Homebush Bay also contains some of the most significant remaining estuarine wetlands on the Parramatta River. Much of the eucalyptus forest and the wetlands are listed on the

474

ABOVE: Industry along a mangrove-lined section of the Parramatta River in the 1970s. The mangrove's importance in the health and ecology of the estuarine environment is now well recognised and it is no longer ripped out as a matter of course. The mangrove habitat and wetlands at Homebush Bay are now protected as part of the Bicentennial Park.
BELOW: Aerial view of Homebush Bay before its redevelopment for the year 2000 Olympics. The former brickpit site can be seen at the centre. Much remediation and decontamination work has been carried out at the Homebush site, in order to live up to the promise of a 'green' Olympics in Sydney.

Register of the National Estate.[23] The green and gold bell frog, which is a recognised endangered species, lives in the brick pit which will also become part of a new, post-Olympic Millennium Park. The brick pit is a 500-metre–wide hole in the ground from which clay has been extracted down to the sandstone rock, which was in turn quarried.

Bicentennial Park is one of the largest parks in Sydney's west. There, 60 hectares of wetland and 40 hectares of parkland have been preserved and set aside for public use. The area gives an intriguing glimpse of how this part of Sydney would once have looked. There are mangroves with their large network of roots protruding from the water, salt marshes and a waterbird refuge. A wooden pathway leads through the mangroves where 140 species of birds can be seen. As well as walking and bird-watching, there is a playground and an 8-kilometre bicycle track.

The state abattoirs used to be located on 850 acres of land, part of which is covered by the awe-inspiring Stadium Australia, one of the most graceful yet impressive structures ever to be built in Sydney. The Moreton Bay figs the cattle used to stand under while awaiting their fate in the abattoirs have been preserved and will be relocated to provide shade for arriving spectators. The stadium is the largest ever built for the Olympics, with a capacity of 110 000 people. The opening and closing events, the track and field events, the soccer finals and the finishing point of the Olympic marathon will all be held there. After the Olympics, the stadium will become one of Sydney's key venues for sports, especially football, and large-scale performances. The offices for the abattoirs were built on the site of the old Wentworth homestead, and are being preserved.

Other Olympic sites in Homebush Bay are: the Sydney International Aquatic Centre and warm-up area, Sydney International Athletic Centre and warm-up area, State Sports Centre, Tennis Centre, and Multi-Use Indoor Arena. Other Olympic sites around Sydney are: the rowing facility on the Penrith Lakes, the Equestrian Centre at Horsley Park to the west of Homebush, and Darling Harbour, which will be the secondary Olympic site where the weightlifting, judo and boxing will be held.

After 2000, the next stage of development at Homebush Bay will be the construction of the Millennium Park. Like Centennial Park, it will probably evolve rather than be completely built by a certain date. Some of its area will be a conservation zone. The National Parks and Wildlife Service may administer those parts of the park which are in a more natural state, and another authority may look after the recreational and sporting facilities. Bicentennial Park will be included within Millennium Park. There is a further proposal to use a bridge over the Parramatta River to integrate parkland at Meadowbank near Ryde, now under the administration of Ryde Council, in the same way that parklands and reserves were aggregated in the 1970s to create the Sydney Harbour National Park. The new Millennium Park will do a great deal to redress the imbalance in open space between the eastern, harbour-side areas of Sydney and Sydney's west. It can only be hoped that the state government has the determination to proceed with this project after the expenditure that will have been incurred in preparing Sydney for the Olympics.

ABOVE: Fishing along the Upper Georges River near Picnic Point.

Chapter Eighteen

SOUTH SYDNEY, THE SOUTH AND SOUTHEAST

THE SUBURBS OF SYDNEY which stretch from Randwick and Coogee all the way down the coast to Cronulla cover a diverse area, from the inner-city suburbs and industrial areas of South Sydney, such as Redfern, Newtown, Alexandria, Mascot and Botany, the southeastern suburbs of Randwick, Coogee, Kensington and Maroubra, and the residential southern suburbs south of the Cooks River.

The different components of southern Sydney are often divided by the area's waterways: the wide, northern side of Botany Bay is the southern boundary of both the southeastern suburbs and South Sydney. The southern suburbs proper begin south of the Cooks River. The upper reaches of the Georges River beyond the junction of the Woronora River mark the beginning of Sydney's west. Port Hacking is the southeasternmost point of the Sydney region. Beyond this lies the Royal National Park, the Woronora Plateau and the Illawarra.

For those arriving by aeroplane, southern Sydney is the gateway to the city, as Sydney Airport lies on the northern shores of Botany Bay. Not far from the airport is La Perouse, for many years one of Sydney's largest indigenous communities. On the southern side of the bay is Kurnell, now almost as famous for its large oil refinery as it is for being the site of Captain Cook's first landing place in Australia.

Port Hacking is a more spectacular estuary than Botany Bay, with its undulating landscape and abundance of bays and coves. Port Hacking is the outlet for the Hacking River, which rises on the Woronora Plateau, much of which lies within the National Park. The northern side of Port Hacking is a boat-owner's paradise, and home to many keen sailors, particularly in waterfront suburbs such as Yowie Bay, Lilli Pilli and Gymea Bay.

Cronulla, Sydney's best-known southern beach-side suburb, lies on the northern side of

Port Hacking. Cronulla Beach is long, stretching all the way up to the Kurnell Peninsula. The Botany Bay National Park covers much of this neck of land. Cronulla is one of the busiest parts of Sydney's south. The surf attracts thousands of train commuters there on hot summer days—it is one of the few beaches connected by rail to other parts of Sydney.

The sand dunes of Cronulla, famous as they are, have been decimated over the course of the twentieth century. In the 1920s, the sand dunes were tall enough to serve as the location for a movie set in the Palestinian desert, *Forty Thousand Horsemen*, starring Australian early cinema legend Chips Rafferty. In the intervening years, the sandhills have served as part of the raw materials used in the building industry and are sadly just a shadow of their former majestic selves.

Sydney's south covers a wide geographic area and a wide cross-section of Sydney's heterogeneous community, from the affluent boating enthusiasts who live in waterfront homes around Port Hacking and on the lower reaches of the Georges River, to the industrial workers of Botany, Mascot, Waterloo and Alexandria, the surfers of Cronulla, Coogee and Maroubra, and recently arrived immigrants who are concentrated in the Rockdale area. Generally, the pattern is the same for all parts of Sydney: those who can afford it usually prefer to live closer to the water. The main district centres for the south are Hurstville and Miranda. Altogether, there are seven municipal council areas: Botany, Hurstville, Kogarah, Randwick, Rockdale, South Sydney and Sutherland. The total population of these municipalities is more than 600 000.

The south was for a long time, until the beginning of the twentieth century, the most forgotten part of Sydney. It was here that much of Sydney's early industry was located, as were other institutions where distance from the city was an important consideration. In the earlier years of European settlement in Sydney, Simeon Lord based his woollen factory on the northern shore of Botany Bay where the Lachlan Swamp ran into the sea. Another early, originally government-operated mill was built on the Lachlan Swamp (which originated in the middle of present-day Centennial Park), closer to Sydney and near where Todman Avenue, Kensington, is.

Another example of use of the area's 'remoteness' is Prince Henry Hospital, which was originally built on Little Bay to quarantine patients suffering from smallpox, and later typhoid, leprosy and tuberculosis patients. The Botany Cemetery, Long Bay Gaol, the old sewage outfall at Malabar (which caused a great deal of water pollution on Sydney's beaches until the late 1980s) and the Anzac Rifle Range at Malabar—all are land uses which serve as reminders of the area's formerly remote status. As with so many other parts of Sydney, it was the development of cheap public transport from the mid-1880s—first the tram, then the railway or bus—which made possible southern Sydney's evolution as a residential area and a pleasant place to live.

Although industry has long been present in this part of Sydney, the area of the Cooks River was, until the mid-nineteenth century, a retreat. In the 1830s, merchant and businessman Alexander Brodie Spark commissioned architect John Verge to build a villa on the southern side of the Cooks River, which he named Tempe House. It still stands near the Cooks River Bridge on the Princes Highway at Arncliffe. Verge also designed Tusculum at Potts Point for Spark, but Tempe was always Spark's principal home. For many years, Tempe House was occupied by the Sisters of the Good Samaritan, who used it to provide accommodation for 'fallen women'. It is now owned by Qantas.

When Captain James Cook sailed into Botany Bay in 1770, he and his party were struck by the abundance of marine life in the estuary, and initially named it Sting-Ray Bay. Soon afterwards, however, impressed by the large numbers of plant species collected around the bay, Cook and Joseph Banks renamed it Botany Bay. Specimens of the plants found there can be seen in the Royal Botanic Gardens in Sydney.

The Aborigines who witnessed the arrival of the *Endeavour* at first chose not to acknowledge the newcomers. When a rowboat carrying Cook, Banks and his assistant, Daniel Solander, came close to shore, the Aborigines ran off into the woods. Later, a 'village' of about eight huts was seen by the men of the *Endeavour*. Again, the people in the huts pretended that no one was watching them. Then, as the Englishmen were trying to land, the Aborigines objected and shaped to throw their spears. A musket was fired at the legs of one of the men, who ran off. Rather than deterring further resistance, this act of violence caused the Aborigines to hurl their spears at the boat. This unhappy incident meant that the Aborigines continued, quite sensibly, to disappear whenever these new arrivals approached them.

On a journey through the surrounding bush, it was reported that the countryside was:

> agreeably variegated with wood and lawn, the trees being straight and tall, and without underwood. The country might be cultivated without cutting down one of them. The grass grows in large tufts … and there is plenty of it … [Banks and Solander] went up the country, where they found the soil to be a deep black mould, which appeared to be calculated for the production of any type of grain. They saw some of the finest meadows that were ever beheld, and met with a few rocky places, the stone of which is sandy, and seemed to be admirably adapted for building … the captain went up the country on the north side of the bay, which he found to resemble the moory grounds of England; but the land was thinly covered with plants about sixteen inches high … The name of Botany Bay was given this place from the large number of plants collected by Messrs Banks and Solander.[1]

Not only was there ground fit for cultivation in the eyes of the first European visitors to Botany Bay, there was also abundant bird life, including quail, cockatoos and parrots, waterbirds such as ducks and pelicans, and a plentiful supply of fish, oysters and mussels. The *Endeavour* stayed and explored around Botany Bay for ten days, between late April and early May 1770. It must have been a good, wet season.

The expectations of the First Fleet as to what Botany Bay would look like and be able to provide were quickly dashed in early 1788. Instead of a fertile haven, they found poor, intermittently sandy and swampy country, and little fresh water. The fleet sailed further north to the next inlet, Port Jackson.

Botany Bay, however, did not remain unvisited by Europeans for long. Two French ships, under the command of Jean François de Galaup, Comte de La Pérouse, also arrived in late January 1788. The French sailed into Botany Bay to recuperate, having been the victims of an attack in Samoa, and there they camped for about six weeks (until 10 March) in the area now known as La Perouse and on the adjacent beach (now known as Frenchmans Bay).

While there, there was fairly regular contact between the French and the British, and there seems to have been an informal agreement between the two camps that any British convicts who escaped from Sydney Cove and managed to find their way to Botany Bay would be given a day's supply of food and sent back to the British settlement. To maintain contact, a route was established between Sydney Cove and Botany Bay, and this can probably lay claim to being the oldest track in Australia: Frenchmans Road, in what is now Randwick, may follow part of the route along the ridges to the south of the small penal camp to Botany Bay.

After the repaired ships left Botany Bay on 10 March, they were never heard of again until the shipwrecks were found in the Solomon Islands in 1826. The story of La Pérouse's voyage and visit to Botany Bay is recounted in the La Pérouse Museum at Botany Bay. This was the Bicentennial gift from France to the people of Australia.

After the French left, the area around Botany Bay remained largely unused, and the colony of Sydney spread westward to Parramatta and towards the east, rather than towards the more rugged and less accessible south. George Bass navigated Botany Bay and the Cooks River up to Bankstown soon after his arrival in Sydney in 1795, but little settlement took place. The lack of arable soil and the distance from Sydney did not make the south an attractive place for settlement at a time when food production was a top priority.

Bass and Flinders explored the coast south of Port Jackson in a small sailing boat in 1796, and camped overnight at the site of present-day Cronulla, at the mouth of Port Hacking. It took a long time for the area to become settled: Port Hacking, being shallower with shifting sand bars, was not sufficiently navigable, so that access by ferry or steamboat was difficult. The development of the area had to wait for the railway at the end of the nineteenth century.

South Sydney is one of the most industrial areas in Sydney, built up from the late nineteenth century. A reminder of South Sydney's industrial past is the Alexandra Canal, built in the 1890s as an inbound waterway from Alexandria to Botany Bay at a time when tanneries, foundries, soap making factories and woollen mills were located in the middle of the corridor that runs from Darling Harbour and the wharves of Pyrmont southward to Botany Bay. At the end of this corridor is Sydney's main port at Botany, built in the 1970s.

The Alexandra Canal is still one of Sydney's most polluted waterways, although recently steps have been taken to remediate it. Many Sydneysiders still recall the stench from the old blood-and-bone factory on Botany Road, which was then the main route from the city to Kingsford Smith (Sydney) Airport in the 1960s. With the construction of the port at Botany and the longer-term presence of Sydney's only airport, the industrial corridor is one of the city's most important zones for warehousing and freight distribution. The area of South Sydney includes the suburbs of Waterloo, Alexandria, Zetland, Beaconsfield, Mascot, Botany, Redfern and Newtown (although Newtown could also be considered as part of the Inner West).

The character of many of the old industrial suburbs is changing. As industry is moving out of the area, many of the old industrial sites have been, and will continue to be, redeveloped into medium- and higher-density housing. Good examples of this are at Green Park, Alexandria and parts of Redfern. In 1999, the railway that is being built from Central Station to Sydney Airport will stop at Green Park.

The suburb will be attractive for people seeking good transport links to the city and the rest of Sydney's railway network. Like the development by the CityWest Development Corporation at Pyrmont and Ultimo, Green Park is the result of heavy government planning directed towards establishing inner-city areas of medium-density housing on former industrial land. The state government established a South Sydney Development Corporation with the aim of promoting the development of South Sydney. The aim is to increase the population of South Sydney by 25 000 by 2008.

Redfern is named after Surgeon William Redfern, who was granted 100 acres (40 hectares) of land bounded by present-day Cleveland, Regent, Redfern and Elizabeth streets, where the suburb named after him lies. Since the 1890s, the suburb has been, like nearby Waterloo and Woolloomooloo, synonymous with poverty and low socio-economic status. In the late nineteenth and early twentieth centuries, the only alternative for many people living in the area who were unable to find work was to catch, kill and sell rabbits. People who did this were called 'rabbit-ohs'. Rabbit meat has, since the rabbit plague of the late nineteenth century, been considered an inferior meat in Australia because it was so cheap—landowners would willingly permit people onto their property if they were going to reduce the incidence of these pests that devoured their grazing pastures. In the minds of some people, particularly those who can remember the economically lean years of the Depression, rabbit meat still bears the stigma of being inferior to lamb and beef.

One group of people living in South Sydney who sold rabbit meat were the members of the South Sydney Rugby Union Club and later the South Sydney Rugby League Club. These footballers hawked rabbit meat in the streets of Redfern and South Sydney. That is why the team is known as the 'Rabbit-ohs'. Since 1959, the rabbit has become a permanent mascot, featured on the football jerseys of the team members. Redfern and South Sydney Rugby League still have strong local community connections. The other local, A-grade rugby league team in the Redfern area is the Aboriginal Redfern All Blacks.

Many Syrians and people of Arabic descent established businesses in Redfern from the end of the nineteenth century, such as George Dan, Stanton and Aziz Melick, and Anthony and

Simon Coorey. There is still a high concentration of residents of Arabic descent, as the shops and restaurants near the corner of Cleveland and Elizabeth streets indicate. In the past fifteen years, there has been a large proliferation of wholesale outlets for clothing and shoe manufacturers along Redfern Street and Regent Street. The process of inner-city revival and regeneration has not passed Redfern by, and property prices now reflect this trend.

To the east of Redfern's land grant, John Baptist ran a nursery. When Baptist's land was subdivided, the streets were given botanical names to commemorate the land's former use, such as Zamia, Boronia and Telopea streets. Prince Alfred Park in Redfern was, for more than half a century, the site of Sydney's main railway terminus. When Central Station was completed, Eveleigh Station was renamed Redfern Station. The Eveleigh Railway Workshops consume much of the land that formed part of Redfern's original grant, and are one of the most architecturally interesting nineteenth-century industrial complexes in Sydney. The Eveleigh railway yards are one of the largest intact railway workshops in the world.

For many years, since the demise of the old steam trains, the future use of the land was unclear. The Australian Technology Park (ATP) now covers 14 hectares of land at Eveleigh. The ATP is jointly owned by the University of Sydney, New South Wales University and the University of Technology. The aim of the park is to provide a link between education, research and industry. It was funded by the federal government's Better Cities Program in 1991. The old New Engine Workshop is the National Innovation Centre. The old Craven Brothers crane is still housed within the centre, as a reminder of its former industrial use.

The Eveleigh workshops act as the buffer between Redfern and Alexandria on the eastern side and Newtown, Darlington and Erskineville to the west. All three of these latter suburbs share King Street as a main arterial road to the city. From the early years of the colony, King Street was the main route to the Cooks River. South of Newtown, King Street becomes the Princes Highway, which continues down the south coast as far as Melbourne.

In the first part of the nineteenth century, the land around Newtown was used for farming, and soon a village sprang up. The major impetus for Newtown's growth in the mid-nineteenth century was the railway line that ran through the suburb from 1855. The first public school opened at Newtown in 1863 and, in 1874, the Edmund Blacket–designed St Stephen's Church was completed. This is one of Blacket's finest works. In the nearby cemetery is a mass grave for those whose lives were lost when the *Dunbar* sank off Watsons Bay. Newtown's location close to the University of Sydney and Royal Prince Alfred Hospital means that the area is a popular place for students and nurses, although rising property prices are putting the rents in Newtown beyond the means of many students.

In the past fifteen years, King Street, one of the longest ribbon retail precincts in Sydney, has been undergoing the same sort of change as Oxford Street did from the early 1970s. Intermingled with the smarter shops and restaurants are the older-style and more idiosyncratic businesses. King Street, Newtown, is one of the longest strip shopping centres in Sydney. Like Oxford Street, King Street has attracted commercial activity catering to the gay market, and is Sydney's second gay precinct.

ABOVE: Redfern Railway Station, now the site of Prince Alfred Park and once Sydney's main railway terminus, c. 1890.

483

Sydney Park, opened to the public in the late 1980s, gives local residents access to green space that was missing before and this adds to the amenity of the area and, with it, rising land values. Newtown was less architecturally interfered with in the 1960s than was Glebe, and this adds to its charm. In another ten years, its working-class roots may have almost disappeared. The survival of much imposing civic and domestic Victorian architecture provides a good framework for urban renewal and increasing popularity as a suburb lived in by owner-occupiers.

Randwick, Waverley, Clovelly and Coogee are the older southeastern residential suburbs. These areas, like much of the Inner West, were settled by the wealthy as a retreat from the city. Their first recorded uses by white settlers were as hunting grounds, where kangaroos were the main prey. Access roads were mostly built by timber cutters who supplied the growing city with the stately red gums which grew around Coogee and Randwick. Access to Randwick along the sandhills of Moore Park and the steep route up Alison Road was dusty in warm weather and muddy when it rained.

In the late nineteenth century, Coogee became a fashionable seaside resort. Its attractions included the Coogee Aquarium (1887) and the amusement pier, which was built in 1928 and jutted almost 200 metres into the sea. It broke up in stormy weather in 1933. Taking a tram trip (from 1884) to Coogee on Sunday was a popular pastime. The advent of trams made the area more accessible as a commuter suburb, as well as a popular recreational spot. Arthur Streeton's work *Coogee Bay* shows vividly how picturesque Coogee was in the late nineteenth century. There are still some isolated examples of Victorian mansions and villas. Most of them did not survive the flat-building boom of the 1960s, and the earlier boom of the 1920s. One famous Coogee institution is Wylie's Baths, originally built in 1907 on the cliff face and hewn out of the sandstone rock at the southern end of the beach. Another pool at Coogee caters exclusively to women. Like other beachside suburbs close to the city, Coogee has undergone a property boom. The once down-at-heel area boasts many fine restaurants and shops. Coogee is also home of one of Sydney's most popular hotel music venues, Selina's in the Coogee Bay Hotel.

At Coogee, evidence of one of Sydney's most ghoulish and notorious murders came to light on 25 April 1935, Anzac Day, at the Coogee Baths in Dolphin Street when a large, 4.5-metre tiger shark vomited up a tattooed human arm.[2] The shark had been caught in the waters off Coogee eight days before by a commercial fisherman, who handed it over to his brother, the proprietor of the baths. After the arm was gingerly removed from the pool by a policeman, the body was identified (because of the distinctive tattoo of two boxers) as James Smith, a boxer and small-time criminal. The arm had been hacked off crudely after the person had been killed. Police targeted Patrick Brady as the chief suspect. Brady was a small-time criminal who was connected to respectable boat builder and North Shore resident, Reginald Holmes. When the police inquiries moved on to Holmes, Holmes tried to take his life in a dramatic scene while speeding on his boat around Sydney Harbour. His brother wrestled him down after leaping from a police launch to apprehend him. When questioned by the police, Holmes claimed that the victim, Smith, and Brady had been blackmailing him. Holmes, by then the key witness, was then found shot dead in his car at Millers Point. His assassin was waterfront worker Jack Strong. At his trial, Brady was not convicted as the judge directed the jury there was insufficient evidence. The next link the police pursued was that between Strong and Albert Stannard, a prosperous businessman and proprietor of a harbour-launch company. The charges against Stannard did not stick and he was also acquitted.

The motive for the murders and the reason for the involvement of the various actors in the mystery were never explained. Rumours abounded of drug importing, insurance fraud and police corruption (or a heady mixture of all of these). The most likely connection seems to be to a ring of people who sank boats for insurance purposes. Twenty years after the event in the baths, criminologist Alex Castles obtained access to the police records. It turned out that Smith, the original shark victim, was a police informant. Police had evidence that Smith and Holmes were involved in the suspected insurance-fraud ring. Smith also said that he had done runs to pick up smuggled goods such as cigarettes off the coast. The conspirators had fallen

485

ABOVE: Cooling off in the water at Coogee Beach (c. 1890), before swimming in the ocean became legal in the early twentieth century.

out (as they so often do), and Smith had been blackmailing the respectable, middle-class Holmes about his illegal activities, thus the motive for this murder. It did not, however, explain why Holmes was killed, or what Stannard's role in the bizarre saga was.

Sydney's biggest racecourse is at Randwick. The site was first selected by Governor Bourke and surveyed and laid out by Mortimer Lewis, the Colonial Architect, in 1833. At first the racecourse was used only occasionally, but the growing popularity and demand for horseracing in the 1860s was to be an important reason that the tramway—first horse-drawn, then electric—was extended there. This attracted people who worked in the racing industry— jockeys, trainers, blacksmiths and farriers—into the area. One of the biggest horse sales in Australia each year is at the Newmarket stables at Randwick, owned and managed by the Inglis family. For many, a trip to the races at Randwick, especially during the spring and autumn carnivals, is one of Sydney's most fun and colourful pastimes.

Kensington is another suburb that has long been connected with the horseracing industry. For many years, a rival racecourse to Randwick's operated at Kensington where the University of New South Wales stands. Another important sporting activity in the Kensington–Eastlakes area is golf, which has, since 1882, been played at the Australian Golf Club. Kensington,

Rosebery and other nearby suburbs became residential areas in the inter-war period, with the dominant architectural mode being the liver-brick bungalow. This was more than half a century after Randwick first became a residential area.

Randwick's development owes much to early landowner, Simeon Pearce. It was named after his home town in England. Pearce arrived in the depression of the 1840s as a young man with £1 in his pocket. He later became a surveyor with the Commissioner for Lands in Sydney. This allowed him to roam over Sydney and its environs, selecting for himself good portions of speculative land. He chose Randwick as a place to live and as the base for his commercial activities. He made a fortune in land speculation through the 1850s. He also set up market gardens there, which prospered during the gold rush when demand rose dramatically due to increased immigration.

Pearce became good friends with Bishop Barker, and persuaded him to move his residence to Randwick from Camperdown, on the site where St Paul's College now stands at Sydney University. The Bishop's presence in the area added an extra lustre to the area. The bishop built St Jude's Church and Cemetery in the 1860s and lived in a large house on the corner of Carrington and Alison roads. St Jude's was designed by Edmund Blacket. Randwick was the first municipality to be incorporated, and the first council there was elected in 1859.

The Destitute Children's Asylum, which later became the Prince of Wales Hospital, was built in 1856 on a 60-acre (27-hectare) grant in Avoca Street, Randwick. It was also designed by Edmund Blacket. The building is still being used as administrative offices for the large hospital complex, which includes a general hospital, the Royal Women's Hospital and the Sydney Children's Hospital, as well as a private hospital. There was, in the second half of the nineteenth century, a diverse social mix within the Randwick area. Affluent gentlefolk were attracted to the sea breezes and distance from the city, while skilled tradesmen were employed in the construction of the large mansions and villas in the area. Struggling immigrants lived at Irishtown or 'Struggletown', near the corner of St Pauls and Perouse roads just to the east of the asylum, and small-scale market gardeners also lived in the area.

The tram finally came to Randwick in 1886. Local aldermen had tried to lobby the government for a railway from the 1870s, but the political strength of the rural lobby in urging the extension of the rural railway system meant the railway was unaffordable. When the tramline was built, there was a predictable boom in subdivision and building in the Randwick area. A vivid illustration of the pattern of suburbanisation is the pattern in which public schools opened in the area: Randwick's was in 1885, Coogee's in 1895 and Maroubra's in 1904. By 1896, the population in the Randwick municipality (which included the area from Randwick south to La Perouse) had grown to nearly 8000 residents, reached 19 000 by 1910 and then increased by 90 per cent to 36 000 in the four years to 1914. Between 700 and 800 houses were built every year in the period between the arrival of the tram and World War I.

Nor did the building boom of the 1920s pass Randwick by. By 1925, the population was 66 000. Sadly, the next housing boom in the 1960s and 1970s claimed as its victim much of the fine nineteenth-century architecture in the area. Randwick was becoming a densely populated suburb with the added advantage of being close to Sydney's second university, the University of New South Wales, which was founded in 1949. Blocks of flats proliferated on the site where proud Victorian villas and mansions once stood. A walk down St Marks Road and Dutruc Street shows the wide variety of architectural styles in the area.

The suburb of Maroubra was not settled until the early twentieth century. It remained isolated for much longer than nearby Randwick and Coogee; the tram did not reach Maroubra until 1921. For many years in the early twentieth century, the beach was occupied by weekend campers. That far out of town, it was possible to live an idyllic life away from the prying eyes of neighbours and governments. One group of campers was known as the Sunshine Club, a group of young men who squatted on the beach during World War II. Whenever the beach was visited by members of the Manpower Commission, set up with the task of organising labour for the war effort, members of the club would head for the surf and avoid calls to enlist.[3] The area and other parts of the southeastern suburbs, such as Yarra Bay, were popular secluded havens for two-up schools. At Maroubra, two-up was played on the site of the Anzac Rifle Range. However, inter-war residential subdivision was slowly engulfing the sandhills of Maroubra and other undeveloped portions of the southeast. Unemployed men were put to work digging and relocating the sand dunes so that subdivision would be easier. The many rows of liver-brick bungalows in the area are the result of this building activity.

A smallpox epidemic in the early 1880s led the government to select Little Bay as a good spot for isolating Sydney's smallpox, diphtheria, whooping cough and typhoid patients. It was a safe distance away from the population so that further contagion could be prevented. The hospital was at first nothing but a series of canvas tents, but it was on this site that the Coast Hospital—from 1934 called the Royal Prince Henry Hospital—was built. A section of it was also used as a leper colony. Coincidentally, the site of this was very close to that of the 'Blacks' Hospital', which was nothing but a cave with an overhanging rock at Little Bay. In the late 1780s, sick Aborigines, stricken with smallpox, stayed in the cave and those who were well enough picked up the food which was laid out for them at the entrance. A great number of Aborigines died there, and accounts describe passers-by seeing numbers of skulls and bones scattered around.

Another use to which the Maroubra–Little Bay area was put was as the location of an institution called the State Reformatory for Women, for those who were classified as inebriates. The reformatory operated from 1907. Later, a state penitentiary for men, now known as Long Bay Gaol, was established. Since 1969, the women's gaol has been located at Mulawa Training and Detention Centre, Silverwater.

In the Depression of the 1930s, the unemployed around La Perouse were allowed to shelter in a gully on land owned by the NSW Golf Club called 'Happy Valley'. The valley was relatively sheltered from wintry southerly winds blowing off Botany Bay. There were other shantytowns nearby on Yarra Bay called 'Frog Hollow' and 'Hill 60'. A strong community spirit developed within the shantytowns. Notices to quit Happy Valley were issued in 1938,

ABOVE: Shanty houses at Happy Valley, La Perouse, during the 1930s Great Depression.

488

yet some residents defiantly chose to stay on. The population at the time was about 800. The camp was vacated before the outbreak of World War II. The other two camps were occupied until the late 1950s, often by postwar immigrants.[4]

The northern headland of Botany Bay was reserved from the 1820s for government uses. A customs post was erected at La Perouse, which still stands in the Botany Bay National Park very close to the La Pérouse Museum. The post was intended to prevent smuggling, and it was used until the 1890s. Fear of invasion resulted in the construction of a battery on Bare Island in 1885. The fort was manned regularly and, in 1915, was taken over by the local militia. Since the 1880s, an Aboriginal community has been resident at La Perouse. Nearby Yarra Bay was a pleasure ground in the early years of the twentieth century. There were sports fields, including a cricket ground, and refreshment rooms. Fishermen could camp overnight in huts on the beach. The popularity of this resort declined, like so many others, during the Depression years.

One of the earliest attempts to build government housing took place at Daceyville, named after a local politician, J. R. Dacey. The Housing Board bought sandy and barren land near Kingsford. Between 1912 and 1920, 300 houses were built by the Public Works Department.

The houses borrowed from the style of both the English cottage and the Californian bungalow, with a few Australian Federation touches as well. The director of the Royal Botanic Gardens landscaped the streets and the public areas. Another unusual housing scheme used to exist at Matraville. Volunteers combined during World War I and the years immediately afterwards, to build the Matraville Soldiers Garden Village, on 72 acres (30 hectares) of land developed as a housing estate for injured war veterans. By 1921, sixty cottages had been built. The estate was demolished during Sir Robert Askin's term as premier and the area is used for medium-density housing.

One early activity in the southeastern suburbs that can still be seen in a fragmentary form is market gardening. Although the land appeared sandy and barren, it did have extremely fertile soil around the swampy areas, and an extensive, permanent water supply. From the 1830s, this area was an important area for growing Sydney's vegetables. Many of the market gardeners were Chinese. Market gardening in the Botany area was flourishing by the 1880s. There are still vegetable plots in the area today, in an area near the Botany Cemetery on the edge of Yarra Bay, and further south at West Botany Street, Arncliffe.

489

The issue of air traffic and aircraft noise in the southeastern suburbs and elsewhere has been one of the liveliest political issues in Sydney since the late 1980s when the decision to build a third runway was taken by the federal and state governments. The runway opened in 1994. Most of it lies on reclaimed land that juts into Botany Bay. Suburbs in which the noise was not to increase, according to noise and environment studies relied on during the planning process, *were* adversely affected, and residents were furious. The methodology used to predict areas to be affected by the runway was found to be defective.

When the new runway opened, the old east–west runway was closed, and this created a new 'spaghetti'-type flight pattern which sprayed aircraft noise in many new directions in many safe Labor and marginal federal parliamentary seats. Some of the suburbs which benefited from the closure of the east–west runway were in marginal Labor-held seats, so the political nature of processes by which the flight paths were determined was highlighted. Many other affected suburbs were either safe Labor seats or blue-ribbon Liberal Party seats, the most conspicuous of them being the electorate of Bennelong, represented by then prominent shadow minister, and later leader of the opposition and Liberal prime minister, John Howard.

Noise levels were so high in some areas such as Sydenham, Marrickville and Leichhardt that the government offered to insulate thousands of houses, schools, hospitals and other buildings so that the impact of the noise could be reduced. Local residents, led by their local councils, blockaded the airport on many occasions bringing air traffic in and out of Sydney to a state of chaos. John Howard pledged that the east–west runway would be reopened if he won the next federal election. The Labor Party's political support collapsed in many parts of Sydney affected by the third runway.

490

ABOVE: A row of family vaults at Botany cemetery, with the oil refinery in the background.

There was a vicious electoral backlash against the federal Labor government in 1996, although both the federal Labor government and the Liberal–National Party coalition then in power in New South Wales had strongly advocated the third runway at the time the decision was made to build it. The Liberal government has changed the flight paths and new areas previously unaffected are sharing the burden of aircraft noise. The issue continues to dog federal politics: a Liberal member resigned from the party in protest at the new flight paths in 1997.

The issue of whether a new airport will be built further out on the outskirts of Sydney still has not been resolved. Neither of Australia's two major airlines, Qantas and Ansett, is enthusiastic about the idea. The two main candidates have been Badgerys Creek and the Holsworthy Air Base southwest of Liverpool.

Badgerys Creek is now at the margin of Sydney's urban sprawl, and therefore becoming increasingly unacceptable as a 'green field' airport site, particularly for the local residents there. An airport at Holsworthy would cause possible pollution of two of Sydney's largest water reservoirs at Warragamba Dam and Prospect Reservoir. There are other apparently insurmountable environmental issues. The need for a second airport will probably remain in the 'too hard' basket for many years to come. One alternative is to locate a second airport outside the Sydney Basin and create efficient access to the city by means of a high-speed train.

Another sensitive political issue in the suburbs around Botany Bay is the level of water pollution brought about by the construction of the port facilities and the third runway. The pollution in the bay and the rivers that flow into it is caused by the discharge of ballast water from inbound cargo ships, and the raw sewage and industrial waste that flows down the Georges and Cooks rivers and Alexandra Canal. This pollution has killed off many of the sea grasses that once grew in the bay, and were havens and breeding grounds for fish, especially on the southern side of the bay. The construction of the third runway meant that 60 million tonnes of sand was dredged from the bay's floor, causing further erosion of the nearby beaches. The once valuable oyster-farming industry is a local victim of pollution.

Thomas Holt was the first person to attempt oyster cultivation in the southern Sydney area. He unsuccessfully tried to use French oyster-farming methods that were not suitable in the warmer, shallower water of the area around Gwawley Bay. The oysters cooked in their shells, or were covered and suffocated in silt. Oyster lovers also pillaged whatever remained. Early in the twentieth century, others succeeded in oyster farming where Holt had failed using methods more appropriate to Sydney's warmer waters.

The once significant and valuable oyster industry in the southern suburbs has been destroyed by the combined forces of a deadly parasite and water pollution. In the 1970s, 43 000 bags of oysters were produced each year in the Georges and Woronora rivers. Pollution has killed the industry in the past decade. Commercial fishing has been banned in the Cooks River and part of the Georges River. Only a concerted effort by local councils in the area and the state government will be able to turn back the tide of pollution of the waterways of Sydney's south. Local councils are concerned that too much attention is being focused on Sydney's most famous waterway, Sydney Harbour, at the expense of these waterways.

Pollution, environmental degradation and urban growth have led to Botany and other nearby suburbs of Sydney being very different places than they once were. For example, in the 1840s, Botany was best known as a recreation and resort area. One of the best known attractions was the Sir Joseph Banks Hotel, originally built on 30 hectares of land at what was called Banks Meadow, now Banksmeadow. Invalids went to stay at the hotel to recover from their illnesses. Steeplechases were held in the grounds, and an animal menagerie, then the biggest in the Sydney area, was another drawcard. In the Victorian period, the hotel buildings were added to. The area became even more popular when the tramway was extended from Redfern in 1882. The old buildings are now sadly run-down and ripe for medium-density residential development.

Brighton-le-Sands on the western side of Botany Bay was intended to have the resort-like quality its name suggested. New Brighton, as it was originally called, was first developed in the 1880s by Thomas Saywell. A resort for the working classes was built, with a hotel, swimming baths and parkland. People would travel from the railway station at Rockdale by tram to the beach. When the hotel lost its liquor licence in the 1890s, the building became the first home for Scots College, later relocated to Bellevue Hill. Now, the suburb lies just south of the busy airport, with the skyline of the city in the background.

It has managed to retain a resort-like quality despite being so close to the airport. One of the most architecturally imposing hotels, the Novotel Brighton Beach, was built on the corner of Bay Street and the Grand Parade during the 1980s, and this has added to the holiday-like flavour of the suburb.

Further to the south and southwest of Brighton-le-Sands are pleasant waterside and residential suburbs, such as Sans Souci, Kogarah and Blakehurst. Many parts of the southern suburbs were originally densely timbered, and timber getting was one of the first industries in the Kogarah and nearby Blakehurst areas. Early resort hotels in Sans Souci and Sandringham were augmented by a pleasure garden at Tom Uglys Point from the 1860s, and resort estates were subdivided along the whole shoreline. The St George area, around Hurstville and Kogarah between the Cooks and Georges rivers, is the name adopted by local building society St George. It started its corporate life in 1937 providing finance for home builders. In the postwar era, the building society boomed, along with the local population and the local construction industry. By the 1970s, it was the largest building society in Sydney. It is now a fully fledged bank, and has absorbed other once large building societies. Its corporate headquarters are still in Kogarah.

Sydney took a long time to spread south of the Georges River. In 1814, Gregory Blaxland was granted 1000 acres (400 hectares) on the southern side of Botany Bay, but, like many grantees of remote land, he never took up residence there, and sold his land two years later to John Connell, a Sydney merchant.

In 1815, James Birnie was granted 700 acres (280 hectares) on the western edge of the Kurnell peninsula, which he named Alpha Farm (although this came to be called Halpha Farm due to the error of a semi-literate clerk). Both Birnie and Connell were based in the town of Sydney itself. Their lands were used as bases of timber-getting operations, and they considered their estates as rural retreats. Connell's son, John, took an active interest in rural life and lived at Kurnell working the land. Kurnell's historic manor, Fernleigh, was built by the Connell family in the 1860s.

Land grants around the area were made to others, but few grantees chose to settle there. It was not until a leading nineteenth-century businessman, Thomas Holt, took an interest in the area that any kind of serious 'pioneering' along the southern shore took place. Holt arrived in Australia in 1842 from Yorkshire and became one of Sydney's leading men of commerce in the nineteenth century. He worked variously as a wool buyer, cattle grower and grazier in what would later become Queensland, and was a close business associate of Thomas Sutcliffe Mort. Together, Holt and Mort founded the Australian Mutual Provident Society (AMP).

The land that Holt owned was a sizeable piece of property: it ran from the shores of Botany Bay in the north to Port Hacking in the south; and from the Pacific Ocean in the east, to an 11-mile (18-kilometre) frontage on the Georges and Woronora rivers in the west. In the late

ABOVE: Aerial of Brighton-le-Sands at Botany Bay, looking south to Lady Robinsons Beach and the Georges River.

1850s, Holt converted Rocky Point House into a home which he renamed Sans Souci—the name of the suburb on the northern side of the Georges River near the Captain Cook Bridge. The house was converted into a hotel in the 1860s.

Holt's attempts to make productive use of his land failed. The area was not fit for grazing either cattle or sheep—the grasses lacked the nutrients necessary for the feeding and breeding of large stock. He also cut a large amount of the timber on his land, including stands of blackbutt, red gum and swamp mahogany, which were floated downstream to the building site of Sutherland House or sold to the timber industry in Sydney.

Holt, while residing at a large estate called The Warren on Cooks River at present-day Tempe, became interested in the unsettled thousands of acres he owned nearby. In his later years, he built the even grander Sutherland House at present-day Sylvania in the 1880s. It stood on the southern shore of the Georges River, on a beach to the east of Tom Uglys Bridge. The Holt family occupied the house and enormous garden, and leased smaller, 500-acre (200-hectare) blocks of land to farmers. Sutherland House was intended to be the seat of residence for the Holt family on the Sutherland estate for many generations, but it was unfortunately destroyed in 1918, in suspicious circumstances.

494

ABOVE: Two families of the unemployed pose in front of their home in Cook Park, Brighton-le-Sands, during the Great Depression of the 1930s. Unemployment in Australia was higher than in Britain or the United States, and hardship much more keenly felt.

In the depression of the 1890s, the Holt family leased the whole estate, except for the 700 acres (280 hectares) on which Sutherland House stood, to the Holt-Sutherland Estate Land Company Ltd. As well as seeking the coal-mining lease, the syndicate wanted to irrigate the land. Again, the venture failed. The tenant farmers were unable to put the land to profitable use. A special Act of Parliament was needed to free up the land and convert it to freehold. The land could then be subdivided. Some of it was sold off in the first half of the twentieth century, and used for orcharding and poultry farming. A great deal of the land, however, had still not been subdivided by 1953.[5]

In the 1870s, the inland southern suburbs of Sydney effectively terminated at St Peters, just south of Newtown. Settlement from there on was spread out along a series of villages, such as Canterbury, Tempe and Hurstville.

In 1873, a group of businessmen formed a consortium to build a southern railway to serve the dual purposes of making land subdivision profitable and make transport of coal and dairy products from Wollongong to Sydney easier. It was proposed that the railway extend as far as the Shoalhaven River. This idea created a frenzy of land speculation. It was not unusual in those days for politicians to play a real-life version of the board game Monopoly by buying large tracts of land which could (through clever political manoeuvring) rise sharply in value in the event that the railway passed through their land or, even better, if a railway station was built on it. Politicians Henry Parkes and John Sutherland (after whom the suburb Sutherland was named) did this, buying more than 4000 acres (1600 hectares) at Jamberoo. The then secretary of public works, Francis Wright, had a building company which bought a large area of land at Hurstville where a railway station was eventually located.

Thomas Holt also encouraged the railway venture, and subdivided some of his land at Lady Robinsons Beach and Rocky Point, both areas lying right next to the proposed railway. Many other speculators followed suit buying up land slightly further west. One of emancipist Samuel Terry's descendants bought land on present-day Connells Point and Kyle Bay. In the late 1870s and early 1880s, speculating on the proposed route of the Illawarra railway was one of the hottest deals in town.

The government refused to pay Holt the money (£15 000) he demanded for the land which the railway was to have taken from Rocky Point on the northern side of the Georges River; another railway crossing was chosen at Como. By 1886, the Illawarra railway had reached Sutherland, 26 kilometres south of Sydney. Sutherland also lies on the Princes Highway. That year, there were only four permanent buildings there: the new railway station, a station-master's residence, a railway-keeper's cottage and a general store. By the Centenary year of 1888, the railway extended as far as Wollongong.

The first industry in Sutherland was timber cutting, as the area was extremely heavily wooded. Farms were established once the land had been cleared, and a small township grew around the railway station from the late nineteenth century. The Shire of Sutherland was created in 1906, at a time when there were only 1600 residents. From the early twentieth century, the original farming areas were subdivided and the commuters moved east from Sutherland to new suburbs such as Sylvania, Miranda, Caringbah, Gymea and Cronulla.

In 1879, the national park was dedicated. It has been designated 'Royal' since 1954. This park is the second oldest national park in the world, after Yellowstone National Park in the United States. The Royal National Park covers an area of more than 16 000 hectares and can be reached by ferry from Bundeena or by car from Audley. In 1994, 95 per cent of the park was destroyed in a fierce bushfire, but much of it is regenerating.

Although most native bushland is able to regenerate after fires, a problem for the Royal National Park and other parks around Sydney is their frequency. Many native plants take about fifteen years to reproduce. If fires occur more frequently than this, some species are unable to regenerate, thus threatening survival of some plant species within the parks' ecosystems.

The issue of how much native bushland should be cleared to prevent bushfires is a lively political debate. Until the fires of 1994, many people argued that clearing the bushland and creating fire tracks was environmentally irresponsible, as it would necessarily involve destruction of native habitats. In some instances, preventative measures were not taken, and this worsened the damage sustained in the 1994 bushfires.

In the first half of the twentieth century, the southern suburbs were a haven for holiday-makers and residents alike. People could take the Princes Highway to Tom Uglys Point. From 1910, access was easier when a tramway connected Tom Uglys Point to Kogarah. From the point, a punt ran across the Georges River to Sylvania. The punt, used to transport larger loads bound for market, was operated by rope until a steam ferry was introduced in the 1880s. Tom Uglys Bridge was not completed until 1929. (The bridge was expanded in 1987.) In 1966, another bridge, the Captain Cook Bridge connecting Sans Souci with Taren Point to the east of Tom Uglys Bridge, was also built.

Until Tom Uglys Bridge was built, the lack of easy access to the southern side of the Georges River set a limit to growth of the area. After World War I, soldier settlers and others were given plots of land for orcharding and poultry farming. At the end of the war, much of the shire was farmland, with a large amount of native bush and mangrove swamps. By 1947, the presence of the bridge and the pressure on land values created by the housing boom meant that many larger plots south of the Georges River were subdivided. In the postwar period from 1947 to 1961, the Municipality of Sutherland was the fastest-growing area of Sydney. The population increased by nearly 300 per cent from 29 000 to 112 000.

Sylvania is situated 22 kilometres south of Sydney on the southern side of the Georges River. The name is thought to have evolved from its sylvan setting, which must have impressed the early settlers. Sylvania was also a part of Thomas Holt's estate, a fact commemorated by the naming of Holt Street, which runs into Sylvania Waters, an area reclaimed from the shallow parts of Gwawley Bay. Sylvania Waters was developed by L. J. Hooker during the 1960s as the Sylvania Waters Estate, where most of the blocks have water frontages offering swimming and boating facilities. It is this part of the southern suburbs which is among the most affluent, with properties sold for increasingly high prices.

Sylvania Waters lies in Gwawley Bay, the site of Thomas Holt's failed attempt at oyster farming. Nearly 300 acres (120 hectares) of mangrove swampland around the bay has been reclaimed into a waterside suburb. The bay is one of the few privately owned waterways in New South Wales. A concrete wall was built on piles to contain the land. Sand from the Cronulla sandhills was used as landfill. Much land was kept as open recreational space, and the size of the lots were relatively large. Most of the development was done by speculative builders. It is unlikely that a major land reclamation scheme such as Sylvania Waters would satisfy environmental standards today.

Sylvania Waters is regarded by many as a boat-owners' paradise. The area was made famous, for a brief period, with a television series called 'Sylvania Waters', featuring a real-life family, the Donahers. In the 1970s, the book and the movie *Puberty Blues*, written by Gabrielle Carey and Kathy Lette, made the local high schools and the Cronulla male-dominated teenage surf culture—where boys were surfers and the girls just watched—famous, if not notorious.

ABOVE: Oyster leases on the Georges River in 1990. The once-flourishing local oyster farming industry has been decimated by water pollution and commercial fishing has also been banned along some sections of the Georges River.

A trip to the Sylvania shopping centre gives an interesting glimpse at the contrast between inner-city and suburban life in an area where there is relatively little social and ethnic diversity. It looks like many of Sydney's shopping centres used to in the 1960s, and represents an interesting form of retail time-travel back to previous decades. Just next to the shopping centre, on the other hand, is a very 1990s state-of-the-art gymnasium and fitness centre, a testament to how important the goal of physical fitness is in beachside Sydney.

Cronulla is located 26 kilometres south of Sydney, just north of the entrance to Port Hacking, in the Shire of Sutherland. The name 'Cronulla' is derived from an Aboriginal word meaning 'the place of pink sea-shells'. The Dharawal Aborigines who lived in the area referred to the entrance to Port Hacking as 'Deeban'. When Bass and Flinders camped overnight at a northern cove near the entrance to Port Hacking in March 1796, their efforts to fish were hampered by the presence of sharks, who were not at all timid. They rose to the surface of the water to look at the men in the tiny *Tom Thumb*.

In 1840, Cronulla Beach was named Kurranulla by surveyor Robert Dixon, and was not changed to 'Cronulla' until 1908. The area became a popular picnic place in 1885 when the railway line to Sutherland made Cronulla accessible. In 1895, the whole area was subdivided and offered for sale at £10 an acre.

Following this, the beach suburb became extremely popular as a holiday town. Beach houses were rented for the school holidays, and hotels such as the Cecil Hotel were established. By 1891, it had its own official post office, and there was a school there by 1910. In 1939, the suburb was itself linked to Sydney by rail.

The south of Sydney possesses some of Sydney's prettiest scenery, and is a great location for avid boating, fishing and surfing enthusiasts, although surfers grumble about the pollution on Cronulla Beach. To a jaundiced former resident of the southern beaches of Sydney, the area suffers badly from having been 'attacked by philistines'. The natural beauty of the area has been and is still being whittled away by man's depredations on the landscape. Much of the rich bird life and natural landscape has disappeared forever, as have the crabs, prawns and sea horses which thrived, along with the oyster leases.[6]

CONCLUSION

SINCE THE MID-1990s, Australia has undergone another one of its remarkable economic booms. This time, the focus has been more heavily concentrated in Sydney than at any other period in living history. Sometimes, it even appears that the Sydney region is shearing off, economically at least, from the rest of Australia, in some new form of highly energised regionalism. Sydney is the city that has most clearly benefited from Australia's globalisation over the past twenty years, and is experiencing a sense of optimism—not all of which can be attributed to pre-Olympics euphoria.

Examples tell only part of the story. In January 1999, the average cost of a home was 40 per cent greater than in the second-largest (and second-most expensive) city, Melbourne. Most of the employment growth over the past four years has been in New South Wales, and in Sydney, in particular. While that is wonderful for Sydney's residents (especially if they are also property owners), it does raise some questions about how the Australian political, social and economic landscape is evolving. Governments and individuals must be both sensitive and responsive to the less positive implications of this heavily regionalised growth.

Just as Sydney has been lucky, other parts of Australia have been less so. Which part of Australia one resides in clearly determines, in a manner it never has before, what a person's prospects are. Regions that depend on the production and export of commodities, especially rural areas, have been far less blessed by fate in recent years—and even decades—than cities such as Sydney. This is a painful change for that sizeable rural sector of the community that long believed that the rest of the nation rode on its back. It is not only the rural regions that have experienced the sharp sting of economic contraction. For example, Adelaide, the South Australian capital which depended until the middle of the twentieth century on the pastoral industry and traditional manufacturing industries for its economic wellbeing, has experienced economic stagnation with a corresponding decline in population.

Sydney, on the other hand, has experienced a huge surge in employment in the construction, financial, information technology, telecommunications and other knowledge-based services and industries. A telling illustration of this is the fact that Sydney and Singapore are two of the areas in the Asia–Pacific region with the highest usage of the Internet. One in four Sydneysiders is a regular user of the Internet, a similar figure to that of the United States.[1]

The disjunction and dissonance between regions across Australia also applies within Sydney itself. The enclaves of high employment in the lower and upper North Shore and eastern suburbs are counterbalanced by the arc of relative disadvantage which extends through many parts of Sydney's west and southwest.

Determining what approach to take towards those who have slipped out of the affluent 'mainstream' will play a large role in forming the future shape of Australia's national consciousness (and conscience). Poverty and social disadvantage should not be blithely accepted as the inevitable result of progress. This perpetuates the weaknesses within a system which has for too long relied on welfare as the primary tool for smoothing out unfair outcomes. High welfare dependence renders the victims of progress impotent and incapable of developing the very qualities they most need: a sense of optimism and self-reliance. Raising levels of literacy and training is a critical part of the solution, and is one of the more urgent tasks facing state and federal governments. It is a confounding and frustrating fact that some sectors of the economy, most notably the information technology industries, are experiencing labour shortages, while unemployment levels in some areas are approaching 20 per cent.

Providing safe communities is another important ingredient in smoothing out the social and economic imbalances, both within Sydney and throughout Australia. When high-crime areas coincide with high-unemployment areas, the benefits of patchy economic growth seem even more unfair. It is even worse when these two factors are present in neighbourhoods with high levels of ethnic and racial diversity. This, unfortunately, seems to be an emerging picture within metropolitan Sydney itself. Yet raising the issue of high crime rates, particularly within non–English-speaking communities, is a politically charged minefield. Anyone who even mentions the topic is accused of racism, even if they also sincerely assert that one of the most successful achievements within Australian society in the past fifty years has been the development of a multi-racial society.

Perhaps, at a time when the Sydney region has been enjoying such a surge in economic activity, it is time to revive the idea promoted early in the twentieth century of a 'Greater Sydney Movement'. The planning and future of Sydney, at both a tangible and an intangible level, should not be left to a sometimes apparently ill-coordinated cluster of state government departments—the Roads and Traffic Authority, the Department of Transport, the Department of Urban Affairs and Planning, and an almost dizzying plethora of forty-one local councils, to name just a few. There should be a way of looking at this great city in its entirety, rather than as a maze of fiefdoms, each with its own agenda and set of priorities.

An important part of achieving this goal is for more people to become engaged in debate as to how Sydneysiders themselves can help make this great city an even better place in which to live and work. Only by becoming involved can the city's residents ensure that the nature of the growth and development of Sydney is as good as our city and its people deserve.

REFERENCES

CHAPTER ONE

1. 1991 Census. This is for the Sydney statistical region. If the outlying areas of the Central Coast, the Blue Mountains and the Hawkesbury are excluded, the population of Sydney is just more than 3.2 million.
2. For information on the geological development of Australia and the Sydney area, see *Australia: Evolution of a Continent*, BMR Palaeogeographic Group, AGPS, 1992; *The Greening of Gondwana: The 400 Million Year Story of Australia's Plants*, Mary E. White, Reed Australia, Sydney, 1993.
3. Louisa (Mrs Charles) Meredith, *Notes and Sketches of New South Wales during a residence in the colony from 1839 to 1844*, John Murray, London, 1844, p. 49.
4. John White, *Journal of a Voyage to New South Wales*, London, 1790, pp. 177–8.
5. James O'Hara, *The History of New South Wales*, printed for J. Hatchard (London : J. Brettell), 1817, p. 54.
6. White, op. cit., p. 182.
7. James J. Auchmuty (ed.), *The Voyage of Governor Phillip to Botany Bay*, Angus & Robertson, Sydney, in assoc. with the Royal Australian Historical Society, Sydney, 1970.
8. Watkin Tench, *A Narrative of the Expedition to Botany Bay*, printed for J. Debrett, London, 1789, p. 129.
9. Watkin Tench, *A Complete Account of the Settlement at Port Jackson, in New South Wales*, G. Nicol & J. Sewell, London, 1793, p. 107.
10. Bureau of Meteorology, *Climate of Australia*, October 1989, p. 9.
11. Sydney Parkinson, *A Journal of a Voyage to the South Seas in His Majesty's Ship the* Endeavour, printed for Charles Dilly et al., London, 1784, p. 134.
12. Arthur Bowes Smyth, extract from diary, 31 October 1831, extracted from Bernard Smith, *European Vision and the South Pacific*, 2nd edn, Oxford University Press, Melbourne, 1989.
13. Meredith, op. cit., p. 56.
14. James Inglis, *Our Australian Cousins: 'Maori'*, Macmillan & Co, London, 1880.
15. R. Horvath, G. Harrison & R. Dowling, *Sydney: A Social Atlas*, Sydney University Press, Sydney, 1989.
16. Australian Bureau of Statistics, 1991.
17. Peter Cunningham, *Two Years in New South Wales: Comprising sketches of the actual state of society etc.*, 3rd edn, Henry Colburn, London, 1828.
18. See Frank Crowley, *A Documentary History of Australia*, vol. 3 (Colonial Australia), Thomas Nelson, Melbourne, 1973–1980, pp. 288–9.
19. For a fuller analysis of this phenomenon, see Elaine Thompson, *Fair Enough: Egalitarianism in Australia*, UNSW Press, Sydney, 1994, esp. ch. 8.
20. Deborah Hart, *John Olsen*, Craftsman House, c. 1991, p. 93.
21. Australian Bureau of Statistics, *Census Characteristics of New South Wales: 1991 Census*, p. 70.

CHAPTER TWO

1. J. C. Beaglehole (ed.), *The Journals of Captain James Cook on His Voyages of Discovery*, vol. 1, University Press, Cambridge, in assoc. with the Hakluyt Society, 1968–69, p. 399.
2. V. J. Attenbrow, A Case Study from the Upper Mangrove Creek Catchment, NSW, Australia (in press), esp. table 39(9.4), p. 127.

3. D. J. Mulvaney & J. P. White (eds), *Australians to 1788*, Australians: A Historical Library, Fairfax, Syme & Weldon and Associates, Sydney, 1987, chs 5 & 17.

4. James L. Kohen, *Aboriginal Environmental Impacts*, UNSW Press, Sydney, 1995, p. 40.

5. John Hunter, *An Historical Journal of the Transactions at Port Jackson and Norfolk Island*, printed for John Stockdale, London, 1793, p. 77.

6. V. J. Attenbrow, 'Port Jackson Archaeological Project', in *Aboriginal Studies*, no. 2, 1991, p. 40.

7. Norman B. Tindale, *Aboriginal Tribes of Australia: Their Terrain, Environmental Controls, Distribution, Limits and Proper Names*, Australian National University Press, Canberra, 1974, p. 127.

8. See Wild, Stephen 'A musical interlude', in D. J. Mulvaney & J. P. White (eds), *Australians to 1788*, Australians: A Historical Library, Fairfax, Syme & Weldon and Associates, Sydney, 1987, esp. p. 345.

9. Peter Turbet, *The Aborigines of the Sydney District before 1788*, Kangaroo Press, Sydney, 1989, p. 27.

10. Diana Plater, 'Aboriginal people and community', in S. Fitzgerald & G. Wotherspoon (eds), *Minorities: Cultural Diversity in Sydney*, State Library of New South Wales, Sydney, in assoc. with the Sydney History Group, 1995, pp. 36ff.

11. *Historical Records of Australia*, vol. 9, p. 849.

12. Turbet, Peter, op. cit., p. 21.

13. ibid., p. 24.

14. James Kohen, *The Darug and Their Neighbours: The Traditional Aboriginal Owners of the Sydney Region*, Darug Link, Sydney, in assoc. with the Blacktown and District Historical Society, 1993, p. 6.

15. Jean A. Ellis, *This is the Dreaming: Australian Aboriginal Legends*, Collins Dove, Melbourne, 1994, p. 101.

16. P. S. C. Tacon, M. Wilson & W. Chippindale, 'Birth of the rainbow serpent in Arnhem Land rock art and oral history', *Archaeol. Oceania*, 31, 1996, pp. 103–124.

17. ibid.

18. Tench, *Settlement*, p. 200.

19. ibid., p. 105.

20. ibid., pp. 193ff.

21. James L. Kohen & R. Lampert, 'Hunters and fishers in the Sydney region', in D. J. Mulvaney & J. P. White (eds), *Australians to 1788*, Australians: A Historical Library, Fairfax, Syme & Weldon and Associates, Sydney, 1987, p. 354.

22. V. J. Attenbrow & D. Steele, 'Fishing in Port Jackson, NSW: More than met the eye', *Antiquity*, vol. 69 no. 262, 1995, p. 47.

23. Tench, *Settlement*, p. 125.

24. Tench, *A Compete Account of the Settlement at Port Jackson*, in *Sydney's First Four Years*, L. F. Fitzhardinge (ed.), Library of Australian History, Sydney, in assoc. with the Royal Australian Historical Society, 1979, pp. 154–5.

25. Turbet, op. cit., pp. 14–15.

26. See Henry Reynolds, *Frontier: Aborigines, Settlers and Land*, 1987, Allen & Unwin, Sydney, 1996, pp. 182–4.

27. *Historical Records of Australia*, series 1, vol. 1, pp. 13–14.

28. Phillip to Lord Sydney, *Historical Records of New South Wales*, vol. 1, part 2, p. 129.

29. Ibid.

30. Keith Willey, *When the Sky Fell Down: The Destruction of the Tribes of the Sydney Region*, Collins, Sydney, 1979, p. 71.

31. Tench, *Settlement*, pp. 55 & 90.

32. See L. F. Fitzhardinge (ed.), *Sydney's First Four Years*, Library of Australian History, Sydney, in assoc. with the Royal Australian Historical Society, 1979, Tench's narratives annotated, p. 319, n. 8.

33. See Alan Frost, *Botany Bay Mirages: Illusions of Australia's Convict Beginnings*, Melbourne University Press, Melbourne, 1994, ch. 10; P. H. Curson, *Times of Crisis: Epidemics in Sydney, 1788–1900*, Sydney University Press, Sydney, 1985, ch. 3.

34. William Bradley, *A Voyage to New South Wales: The Journal of Lieutenant William Bradley RN of HMS Sirius, 1786–1792*, Trustees of the Public Library of New South Wales, Sydney, in assoc. with Ure Smith, 1969, pp. 181–182.

35. Jackelin Troy, 'By slow degrees we began … to understand each other', p. 49, in Ross Gibson (ed.), *Exchanges: Cross-cultural Encounters in Australia and the Pacific*, Historic Houses Trust of New South Wales, Sydney, 1996.

36. David Collins, *An Account of the English Colony in New South Wales: With Remarks on the Dispositions, Customs, Manners Etc. of the Native Inhabitants of the Country*, printed for T. Cadell Jun. and W. Davies, London, 1798, pp. 596–7.

37. Hobart to King, 30 January 1802, *Historical Records of New South Wales*, vol. 4, p. 648.

502

38. King to Earl Camden, 30 April 1805, *Historical Records of New South Wales*, vol. 5, p. 599.

39. *Sydney Gazette*, 3 June 1804.

40. Kohen, op. cit., p. 68.

41. Possibly Simeon Lord.

42. Jacques Arago, J., *Narrative of a Voyage Round the World*, London, 1823, pp. 168–177.

43. Despatch by Macquarie to Earl Bathurst, 27 March 1819, *Historical Records of Australia*, vol. 10, p. 95.

44. Kohen, op. cit., p. 69.

45. Frank Debenham, *The Voyage of Captain Bellingshausen to the Antarctic Seas 1819–21*, printed for the Hakluyt Society, London, 1945, vol. 1, pp. 162–3, vol. 2, pp. 336–7.

46. This and the following quotes taken from Minutes of Evidence before Select Committee, 3 August 1835, pp. 13ff.

47. Kohen, op. cit., pp. 74–5.

48. Plater, op. cit., p. 37; Kohen, op. cit., p. 19.

49. Report from the Select Committee on the Aborigines and the Protectorate, NSWLCVP, 1849.

50. Kohen, op. cit., pp. 76–7.

51. Meredith Wilkie, *The Survival of the Aboriginal Family in New South Wales 1788–1981: A Review of Government Policies and Administration*, Family and Children's Services Agency, Sydney, 1982.

52. See generally Kohen, op. cit., ch. 8.

53. ibid., pp. 92–8.

54. Sir Ronald Darling Wilson (National Inquiry into the Separation of Aboriginal and Torres Strait Islander Children from Their Families (Australia)), *Bringing Them Home: Report of the National Inquiry into the Separation of Aboriginal and Torres Strait Islander Children from Their Families*, Human Rights and Equal Opportunity Commission, Sydney, 1997, p. 28.

55. Alexander Irvine in reply to a Circular Letter from the Select Committee on the Aborigines and the Protectorate, NSWLCVP, 1849, p. 18.

56. *Bringing Them Home*, p. 39.

57. See Kohen, op. cit., p. 111.

58. ibid., p. 120.

59. *Bringing Them Home*, p. 32.

60. Andrew Markus, *Governing Savages*, Allen & Unwin , Sydney, 1990, pp. 178–9.

61. *Bringing Them Home*, p. 48.

62. James Miller, James, *Koori, A Will to Win: The Heroic Resistance, Survival and Triumph of Black Australia*, Angus & Robertson, Sydney, 1985, p. 170.

63. Debra Jopson, *Sydney Morning Herald*, 2 July 1996, p. 1.

64. *Bringing Them Home*, p. 36.

65. See Peter McKenzie & Ann Stephen, 'La Perouse: An urban Aboriginal community', ch. 8, in Max Kelly (ed.), *Sydney: City of Suburbs*, UNSW Press, Sydney, in assoc. with Sydney History Group, c. 1987.

66. Kohen, op. cit., p. 121.

67. For information on the La Perouse community, see McKenzie & Stephen, loc. cit.

68. Plater, op.cit., p. 41.

69. ibid., p. 44.

70. 'Four Corners', 12 May 1997.

71. Philip Cornford, 'When the money moved into Redfern', *Sydney Morning Herald*, 6 June 1995, p. 13.

CHAPTER THREE

1. David Collins, *An Account of the English Colony in New South Wales: With Remarks on the Dispositions, Customs, Manners Etc. of the Native Inhabitants of the Country*, printed for T. Cadell Jun. and W. Davies, London, 1798, p. 5.

2. George William Anderson, *A New, Authentic and Complete Collection of Voyages Round the World, Undertaken and Performed by Royal Authority* (first voyage), Alex. Hogg, London, 1784–[1786], pp. 60–61.

3. See Alan Frost, *Botany Bay Mirages: Illusions of Australia's Convict Beginnings*, Melbourne University Press, Melbourne, 1994, ch. 1.

4. For further information on the convicts, see Robert Hughes, *The Fatal Shore: A History of the Transportation of Convicts to Australia, 1787–1868*, Collins Harvill, London, 1987, pp. 71ff & ch. 6; John Cobley, *The Crimes of the First Fleet Convicts*, Angus & Robertson, Sydney, 1970; Alan Frost Alan, *Botany Bay Mirages: Illusions of Australia's Convict Beginnings*, Melbourne University Press, Melbourne, 1994.

5. Watkin Tench, *A Narrative of the Expedition to Botany Bay*, printed for J. Debrett, London, 1789, p. 47.

6. John McManners (ed.), *The Oxford Illustrated History of Christianity*, Oxford University Press, Oxford, c. 1990, p. 343.

7. Collins, op. cit., p. 13.

8. The gallows moved around considerably in the days when Sydney was the centre of the penal colony—to the corner of Park and Castlereagh Street; then to Sussex Street; then to behind where Victoria Barracks now stand; then, in 1820, back to the old George Street gaol (see below); then to the front gate of the Darlinghurst Gaol when it was built. See Joseph Fowles, *Sydney in 1848*, J. Fowles, 1848, p. 71.

9. Watkin Tench, *A Compete Account of the Settlement at Port Jackson*, in *Sydney's First Four Years*, L. F. Fitzhardinge (ed.), Library of Australian History, Sydney, in assoc. with the Royal Australian Historical Society, 1979, p. 71.

10. Shingles were made from casuarina. See James J. Auchmuty (ed.), *The Voyage of Governor Phillip to Botany Bay*, Angus & Robertson, Sydney, in assoc. with the Royal Australian Historical Society, Sydney, 1970, p. 71.

11. Watkin Tench, *A Complete Account of the Settlement at Port Jackson, in New South Wales*, G. Nicol & J. Sewell, London, 1793, p. 74.

12. Tench, ibid., p. 2.

13. Geoffrey Scott, *Sydney's Highways of History*, Georgian House, Melbourne, 1958, p. 49.

14. Tench, *Settlement*, p. 51.

15. ibid.., p. 110.

16. Collins, op. cit., pp. 137–8.

17. Collins, ibid., p. 146.

18. Although the term *emancipist* in its strict sense is used for a convict who is pardoned before the full term of sentence has been served, it is used throughout to refer also to those convicts who served their terms in full.

19. See Hughes, op. cit., pp. 177ff.

20. See George Rudé, *Protest and Punishment: The Story of the Social and Political Protesters Transported to Australia, 1788–1868*, Clarendon Press, Oxford, and Oxford University Press, New York, 1978, p. 9.

21. Collins, op. cit., pp. 129, 132.

22. D. R. Hainsworth, *The Sydney Traders: Simeon Lord and His Contemporaries, 1788–1821*, Cassell Australia, Melbourne, 1972, p. 23.

23. Frank Crowley, *A Documentary History of Australia*, vol. 1 (Colonial Australia), Thomas Nelson, Melbourne, 1973–1980, p. 87 quoting (Ensign) G. Bond, in *A Brief Account of the Colony of Port Jackson in New South Wales, its Native Inhabitants, Productions etc*, Southampton, 1803, pp. 7–9.

24. See Hainsworth, op. cit., p. 38.

25. ibid., p. 39.

26. ibid., p. 206.

27. ibid., p. 164.

28. John Turnbull, *A Voyage Round the World in the Years 1800, 1801, 1802, 1803, and 1804*, 2nd edn, A. Maxwell, London, 1813, p. 82.

29. ibid., p. 467.

30. The Trial of John Macarthur, 25 January 1808: see *Historical Records of New South Wales*, vol. 6, p. 423.

31. For a recent discussion of Foveaux's merits, see Anne-Maree Whitaker, 'Joseph Foveaux: A gentleman of high reputation', vol. 83, part 1, *JRAHS*, p. 17.

32. C. H. Bertie, *The Story of Sydney*, Shakespeare Head Press, Australia, 1933.

33. J. Ritchie, *Lachlan Macquarie: A Biography*, Melbourne University Press, Melbourne, 1986, p. 105.

34. ibid., p. 121.

35. Richard Waterhouse, *Private Pleasures, Public Leisure: A History of Australian Popular Culture since 1788*, Longman Australia, South Melbourne, 1995, p. 16.

36. Brian Elliott & Adrian Mitchell (eds), *Bards in the Wilderness: Australian Colonial Poetry to 1920*, Nelson, Melbourne, 1970, p. 29.

37. For a detailed analysis of the Bigge Report and the evidence before it, see John Ritchie, *Punishment and Profit: New South Wales Under Governor Macquarie*, 3 vols, esp. vol. 3, chs 8 & 9.

38. Ritchie, *Punishment and Profit*, p. 217.

39. See Bernard Smith, *European Vision and the South Pacific*, 2nd edn, Oxford University Press, Melbourne, 1989, pp. 159ff.

40. See *Australian Dictionary of Biography*, vol. 2, Melbourne University Press, Melbourne, pp. 378–9.

504

CHAPTER FOUR

1. G. Sherington, *Australia's Immigrants 1788–1978*, George Allen & Unwin, Sydney, 1980, p. 23.
2. Peter Cunningham, *Two Years in New South Wales*, facs. edn, vol. 2, Libraries Board of South Australia, Adelaide, 1996, p. 74.
3. Sherington, op. cit., p. 37.
4. Cunningham, op. cit., vol. 2, pp. 119ff.
5. ibid., vol. 2, p. 52.
6. Census figures 1841; see Frank Crowley, *A Documentary History of Australia*, vol. 2 (Colonial Australia), Thomas Nelson, Melbourne, 1973–1980, pp. 5–7.
7. ibid., p. 33.
8. Sherington, op. cit., p. 37.
9. ibid., p. 38.
10. See *Australian Dictionary of Biography* (Judith Iltis), vol. 1, Melbourne University Press, Melbourne, pp. 221–223.
11. J. B. Hirst, *The Strange Birth of Colonial Democracy: New South Wales 1848–1884*, Allen & Unwin, Sydney, 1988, pp. 17ff.
12. For more information, see George Rudé, *Protest and Punishment: The Story of the Social and Political Protesters Transported to Australia, 1788–1868*, Clarendon Press, Oxford, and Oxford University Press, New York, 1978, pp. 240–1.
13. Sir Henry Parkes, *Fifty Years of the Making of Australian History*, Longmans, Green, London, 1892, p. 14.
14. ibid., p. 20.
15. Clark, C. M. H., *A History of Australia*, vol. 3, Melbourne University Press, Melbourne, 1973, pp. 191–2.
16. Shirley Fitzgerald, *Sydney 1842–1992*, Hale & Iremonger, Sydney, c. 1992, pp. 42–3.
17. Genuine Botany Bay Eclogues No. 1, Australian Courtship, *Sydney Gazette*. See Crowley, op. cit., vol. 1, pp. 431–2.
18. See Crowley, op. cit., pp. 65–7.
19. Taken from p. 27, Joseph Fowles, *Sydney in 1848*, J. Fowles, 1848, p. 27.
20. Jocelyn Hackforth-Jones, *The Convict Artists*, Macmillan, South Melbourne, 1977.
21. Bernard Smith, *European Vision and the South Pacific*, 2nd edn, Oxford University Press, Melbourne, 1989, pp. 308–9.
22. For more information on the development of rugby football, see Thomas V. Hickie, *They Ran with the Ball: How Rugby Football Began in Australia*, Longman Cheshire., Melbourne, 1993.
23. For further information about the history of popular culture, see Richard Waterhouse, *Private Pleasures, Public Leisure: A History of Australian Popular Culture since 1788*, Longman Australia, South Melbourne, 1995.
24. Fowles, op. cit., dedication page to Governor FitzRoy.

CHAPTER FIVE

1. G. C. Mundy, *Our Antipodes: or, Residence and Rambles in the Australasian Colonies, with a Glimpse of the Gold Fields*, London, 1852, vol. 3, pp. 305ff.
2. J. R. Godley (ed.), *Letters from Early New Zealand by Charlotte Godley 1850–1853*, Whitcombe & Tombs, Christchurch, 1951, pp. 355–6, see Frank Crowley, *A Documentary History of Australia*, vol. 2 (Colonial Australia), Thomas Nelson, Melbourne, 1973–1980, p. 237.
3. Crowley, ibid., vol. 2, p. 248.
4. Crowley, ibid., vol. 2, p. 310.
5. John Askew, *A Voyage to Australia & New Zealand Including a Visit to Adelaide, Melbourne, Sydney, Hunter's River, Newcastle, Maitland and Auckland*, Simpkin Marshall, London, 1857, p. 185.
6. Crowley, op. cit., vol. 2, p. 224.
7. J. Askew, *A Journey to Australia & New Zealand*, quoted in Crowley, op. cit., vol. 2, p. 315.
8. Frank Fowler, *Southern Lights and Shadows*, Sampson Low, London, 1859; see Barry Groom & Warwick Wickman, *Sydney, the 1850s: The Lost Collections*, Macleay Museum, University of Sydney, 1982, p. 13.
9. Askew, op. cit., p. 202.
10. W. S. Jevons, articles published in *Sydney Morning Herald*, 6, 7, 9, 13, 16, 23, 30 No. & 7 December 1929.
11. G. Sherington, *Australia's Immigrants 1788–1978*, George Allen & Unwin, Sydney, 1980, p. 56.
12. James Inglis, *Our Australian Cousins: 'Maori'*, Macmillan & Co, London, 1880, p. 200–1.
13. ibid., p. 144.
14. Shirley Fitzgerald, *Sydney 1842–1992*, Hale & Iremonger, Sydney, c. 1992, p. 236.
15. T. A. Coghlan, *Results of the Census of the Seven Colonies of Australasia*, GPO, Sydney, 1894, p. 115.

16. F. Gerstaecker, *Narrative of a Journey Round the World, Comprising a Winter-Passage across the Andes to Chile, with a visit to the Gold Regions of California and Australia, the South Sea Islands, Java etc*, London, 1853.
17. *Sydney Morning Herald*, 17 Sep. 1879, International Exhibition Supplement, in Crowley, op. cit., vol. 3, p. 64.
18. W. S. Jevons, *A Social Survey of Australian Cities: Redfern*, 1858.
19. *Sydney Morning Herald*, International Exhibition Supplement, 17 Sep. 1879.
20. Inglis, op. cit., pp. 144–6.
21. Richard Twopeny, *Town Life in Australia*, Elliot Stock, London, 1885, pp. 89ff; see Crowley, op. cit, vol. 3, pp. 99–101.
22. Francis L. W. Adams, *Australian Essays*, W. Inglis, Melbourne, 1866.
23. John Hirst, *The Strange Birth of Colonial Democracy: New South Wales 1848–1884*, Allen & Unwin, Sydney, 1988, p. 39.
24. See further *Australian Dictionary of Biography*; A. W. Martin, *Henry Parkes: A Biography*, Melbourne University Press, Melbourne, 1980.
25. Sir Henry Parkes, *Fifty Years of the Making of Australian History*, Longmans, Green, London, 1892, pp. 8–9.
26. ibid., p. 1.
27. High school education to matriculation (university) level was fairly uncommon until after 1945.
28. Elaine Thompson, *Fair Enough: Egalitarianism in Australia*, UNSW Press, Sydney, 1994, p. 224.
29. ibid., p. 227.
30. *Australian Dictionary of Biography*, vol. 5, Melbourne University Press, p. 403. Entry written by A.W. Martin. For more information on Parkes, see Martin, op. cit., 1980.
31. *Australian Dictionary of Biography*, vol. 5, p. 405.
32. See Martin, op. cit., chs 15 & 16.
33. C. H. Bertie, *The Story of Sydney*, Shakespeare Head Press, Australia, 1933.
34. Inglis, op. cit., pp. 147–8.
35. Mark Twain, *Following the Equator: A Journey around the World*, American Pub. Co., Hartford, 1897.
36. Coghlan, op. cit., p. 170.
37. Louis Stone, *Jonah*, 2nd edn, Endeavour Press, Sydney, 1933, pp. 10 & 37.
38. Inglis, op. cit., pp. 175–6.
39. ibid., p. 176.
40. See Vance Palmer, *The Legend of the Nineties*, Melbourne University Press, Melbourne, 1963, ch. 5.
41. On the history of the nineteenth-century development of cricket and rugby in Sydney, see Thomas V. Hickie, *They Ran with the Ball: How Rugby Football Began in Australia*, Longman Cheshire., Melbourne, 1993.
42. Inglis, op. cit., pp. 174–5.
43. Keith Dunstan, *Wowsers*, Cassell Australia, Melbourne, 1968, p. 2.
44. ibid., p. 96.
45. Coghlan, op. cit., p. 16.
46. ibid., p. 25.
47. Sherington, op. cit., p. 87.
48. J. Jeffries, 'The Chinese and the seamen's strike: A lecture', in Crowley, op. cit., vol. 3, p. 98.
49. L. Kong Meng, Cheok Hong Cheong & Louis Ah Mouy (eds), *The Chinese Question in Australia, 1878–79*, pp. 28ff, in Crowley, op. cit., p. 99.
50. See further: Myra Willard, *History of the White Australia Policy*, Melbourne University Press, Melbourne, 1923, ch. 4 (quote at p. 74).
51. Crowley, op. cit., vol. 3, pp. 255–6.
52. Willard, op. cit., p. 94.
53. Parkes, op. cit., pp. 473–4.
54. ibid.
55. W. D. Borrie et al., *A White Australia: Australia's Population Problem*, Australasian Publishing: The Australian Institute of Political Science, Sydney, 1947, pp. 228–230.
56. Sherington, op. cit., p. 75.
57. ibid., p. 85.
58. F. K. Crowley (ed.), *A New History of Australia*, Heinemann, Melbourne, 1974, p. 305.

CHAPTER SIX

1. F. K. Crowley (ed.), *A New History of Australia*, Heinemann, Melbourne, 1974, p. 261.
2. For details on the Coningham/O'Haran case, see Cyril Pearl, *Wild Men of Sydney*, W. H. Allen, London, 1958, ch. 9.

3. Shirley Fitzgerald, *Sydney 1842–1992*, Hale & Iremonger, Sydney, c. 1992, p. 216.

4. Sources: C. H. Bertie, *The Story of Sydney*, Shakespeare Head Press, Australia, 1933, p. 69; Anthony Barker, *What Happened When: A Chronology of Australia from 1788*, Allen & Unwin, Sydney, 1992.

5. Pearl, op. cit., p. 114.

6. Pearl, op. cit., p. 118.

7. Crowley, *A New History of Australia*, p. 297.

8. Richard Waterhouse, *Private Pleasures, Public Leisure: A History of Australian Popular Culture since 1788*, Longman Australia, South Melbourne, 1995, p. 161.

9. ibid., pp. 160–3.

10. Crowley, *A New History of Australia*, p. 354.

11. For further information, see *Australian Dictionary of Biography*; L. F. Fitzhardinge, *That Fiery Particle, 1862–1914: A Political Biography*, vols 1 & 11, Angus & Robertson, Sydney, 1964.

12. *Round Table*, March 1919, vol. 9, no. 34, pp. 388ff.

13. Bertie, op. cit., p. 69.

14. R. Gibbons, 'The fall of the giant: Trams versus trains and buses in Sydney 1900–61, in G. Wotherspoon (ed.), *Sydney's Transport: Studies in Urban History*, Hale & Iremonger, Sydney, in assoc. with the Sydney History Group, 1983.

15. Fitzgerald, op. cit., p. 236.

16. M. T. Daly, *Sydney Boom, Sydney Bust: The City and Its Property Market*, George Allen & Unwin, Sydney, 1982.

17. Denis Winston, *Sydney's Great Experiment: The Progress of the Cumberland County Plan*, Angus & Robertson, Sydney, 1957.

18. L. Hovenden, 'The impact of the motor vehicle', in G. Wotherspoon (ed.), *Sydney's Transport: Studies in Urban History*, op. cit., p. 148.

19. ibid., p. 152.

20. Peter Kirkpatrick, *The Sea Coast of Bohemia: Literary Life in Sydney's Roaring Twenties*, University of Queensland Press, St Lucia, 1992, pp. 271ff.

21. For a full description of Sydney's bohemian life in the early twentieth century, see Kirkpatrick, op. cit.

22. Annette Bain, 'Brighter days', in Jill Roe (ed.), *Twentieth Century Sydney: Studies in Urban and Social History*, Hale & Iremonger, Sydney, in assoc. with the Sydney History Group, 1980, p. 41.

23. Kenneth Slessor, *Darlinghurst Nights*, Angus & Robertson, Sydney, 1981, p. 19.

24. Frank Crowley, *A Documentary History of Australia*, vol. 4, Thomas Nelson, Melbourne, 1973–1980, p. 411.

25. Heather Radi, in ch. 9 of Crowley, *A New History of Australia*, op. cit., p. 359.

26. Max Kelly, 'Pleasure and profit: The Eastern Suburbs come of age 1919–29', in Roe, op. cit., p. 3.

27. ibid.

28. See further Rosemary Broomham, 'Promoting the dream: The politics of housing in New South Wales between the wars', *National Trust Quarterly*, no. 83, April 1997.

29. Radi, op. cit., p. 360.

30. Keith Dunstan, *Wowsers*, Cassell Australia, Melbourne, 1968, pp. 208ff.

31. Bertie, op. cit., p. 70.

32. Nairn Bede, *The Big Fella: Jack Lang and the Australian Labor Party 1891–1949*, Melbourne University Press, Melbourne, 1986, p. 197.

33. ibid., p. 206.

34. 1 November, 1930.

35. Wendy Lowenstein, Wendy, *Weevils in the Flour: An Oral Record of the 1930s Depression in Australia*, Scribe, Fitzroy, 1998, p. 210

36. ibid., p. 241.

37. Radi, op. cit., p. 416.

38. Lowenstein, op. cit., p. 15.

39. For a more detailed account of the conflict in the Pacific which affected Australia, see G. C. Bolton in ch. 10 of Crowley, *A New History of Australia*, op. cit., pp. 465ff.

CHAPTER SEVEN

1. Commonwealth Parliamentary debates, House of Representatives, 2 August 1945, pp. 4911–12, in Frank Crowley, *A Documentary History of Australia*, vol. 5, Thomas Nelson, Melbourne, 1973–1980, p. 126.

2. G. Sherington, *Australia's Immigrants 1788–1978*, George Allen & Unwin, Sydney, 1980, p.134.

3. ibid., p.142.
4. For a closer look at the history of Greek migration to Sydney, see L. Janiszewski & E. Alexakis, 'That bastard Ulysses: An insight into the early Greek presence 1910–1940', in Shirley Fitzgerald & Garry Wotherspoon (eds), *Minorities: Cultural Diversity in Sydney*, State :Library of NSW Press, Sydney, in assoc. with the Sydney History Group. 1995, ch. 1.
5. Anastasios Tamis, *An Illustrated History of the Greeks in Australia*, Dardalis Archives of the Greek Community, Latrobe University, Melbourne, 1997, pp. 83–4.
6. Sherington, op. cit., p. 146.
7. Ethnic Affairs Commission of NSW, *The People of New South Wales: Statistics from the 1996 Census*, Sydney, p. 3.
8. Patrick White, *The Vivisector*, Vintage, p. 460.
9. Carolyn Allport, in Jill Roe (ed.), *Twentieth Century Sydney: Studies in Urban and Social History*, Hale & Iremonger, Sydney, in assoc. with the Sydney History Group, 1980, p. 48.
10. Peter Spearitt & Christina DeMarco, *Planning Sydney's Future*, commissioned by NSW Department of Planning, Allen & Unwin, 1988, pp. 22 & 39.
11. Stella Lees & June Senyard, *The 1950s: How Australia Became a Modern Society, and Everyone Got a House and Car*, Hyland House, Melbourne, 1987, p. 29.
12. Denis Winston, *Sydney's Great Experiment: The Progress of the Cumberland County Plan*, Angus & Robertson, Sydney, 1957, p. 56.
13. ibid., p. 60.
14. State Planning Authority of NSW, *Sydney Region: Growth and Change—Prelude to a Plan*, Sydney, 1967, p. 67.
15. Spearitt & DeMarco, op. cit., p. 55.
16. C. Allport, 'Castles of security: The New South Wales Housing Commission and home ownership 1941–61', in Max Kelly (ed.), *Sydney: City of Suburbs*, UNSW Press, in assoc. with the Sydney History Group, c. 1987, p. 103.
17. G. Aplin, 'The rise of suburban Sydney', in Kelly, ibid., p. 193.
18. Richard Cardew, 'Flats in Sydney: The Thirty Per Cent Solution?', in Roe, op cit., p. 79.
19. Spearitt & DeMarco, op. cit., p. 44.
20. Australian Bureau of Statistics, *Sydney: A Social Atlas*, 1989, p. 82.
21. Richard Apperly, Robert Irving & Peter Reynolds, *A Pictorial Guide to Identifying Australian Architecture: Styles and Terms from 1788 to the Present*, Angus & Robertson, Sydney, 1989, p. 217.
22. R. Gibbons, 'The fall of the giant: Trams versus trains and buses in Sydney 1900–61, in G. Wotherspoon (ed.), *Sydney's Transport: Studies in Urban History*, Hale & Iremonger, Sydney, in assoc. with the Sydney History Group, 1983, p. 170.
23. Gibbons, ibid., p. 173.
24. Aplin, op. cit., p. 193.
25. State Planning Authority of New South Wales, op cit., p. 29.
26. ibid, p. 10.
27. ibid, p. 31.
28. ibid, p. 42.
29. Paul Ashton, *The Accidental City: Planning Sydney since 1788*, Hale & Iremonger, Sydney, 1995, pp. 92–4.
30. M. T. Daly, *Sydney Boom, Sydney Bust: The City and Its Property Market*, George Allen & Unwin, Sydney, 1982, pp. 13 & 62.
31. ibid., p. 46.
32. Richard Waterhouse, *Private Pleasures, Public Leisure: A History of Australian Popular Culture since 1788*, Longman Australia, South Melbourne, 1995, p. 200.
33. Lees & Senyard, op. cit., p. 18.
34. ibid., p. 46.
35. Interview with Leo Schofield, 9 April 1997.
36. ibid.
37. For a detailed analysis of the Sydney Push, please refer to Anne Coombs, *Sex and Anarchy: The Life and Death of the Sydney Push*, Viking, Ringwood, 1996.

CHAPTER EIGHT

1. LBJ are the initials of the then US President Lyndon Baines Johnson.
2. See Elaine Thompson, *Fair Enough: Egalitarianism in Australia*, UNSW Press, Sydney, 1994, pp. 178–83.
3. For a closer look at the boom and bust of the late 1960s and 1970s, see M. T. Daly, *Sydney Boom, Sydney Bust: The City and Its Property Market*, George Allen & Unwin, Sydney, 1982.

4. Peter Spearitt & Christina DeMarco, *Planning Sydney's Future*, commissioned by NSW Department of Planning, Allen & Unwin, 1988, p. 52.

5. Interview with N. K. Wran.

6. Geraldine O'Brien, 'Circular Quay plans get go-ahead', *Sydney Morning Herald*, 2 September 1994, p. 5.

7. Geraldine O'Brien, 'Quay plan ignites fresh controversy', *Sydney Morning Herald*, 1 June 1994, p. 9.

8. *Sydney Morning Herald*, 1 June 1994, p. 14.

9. Geraldine O'Brien, 'Quay plan ignites fresh controversy', *Sydney Morning Herald*, 1 June 1994, p. 9.

10. Spearitt & DeMarco, op. cit., p. 43.

11. For a fuller description of the council's Living City strategy, see the Council of the City Sydney's brochure.

12. Paola Totaro, 'More people are calling the CBD home', *Sydney Morning Herald*, p. 2.

13. Sarah McCarthy, The Rise and Development of the City Residential Market in Sydney, Oct 1993, Grad. Dip. in Urban Estate Management, UTS, Sydney.

14. Max Kelly (ed.), *Sydney: City of Suburbs*, UNSW Press, in assoc. with the Sydney History Group, c. 1987, p. 200.

15. Statement by Immigration Minister A. R. Downer in Frank Crowley, *A Documentary History of Australia*, vol. 5, Thomas Nelson, Melbourne, 1973–1980, p. 375.

16. ibid., p. 375.

17. G. Sherington, *Australia's Immigrants 1788–1978*, George Allen & Unwin, Sydney, 1980, p. 156.

18. ibid., p. 160.

19. Source: Ethnic Affairs Commission of New South Wales, *The People of New South Wales: Statistics from the 1996 Census*, Sydney.

20. Thompson, op. cit., p. 233.

CHAPTER NINE

1. John Thomas Bigge, *Report of the Commissioner of Inquiry into the State of the Colony of New South Wales*, June 1822, pp. 27 & 53.

2. *Historical Records of Australia*, vol. 9, p. 719.

3. Eliza Walker, 'Old Sydney in the 1840s' *JRAHS*, vol. 16, p. 293.

4. Sir James Fairfax, 'Some recollections of old Sydney' (1919), *JRAHS*, 5, p. 6.

5. Louisa (Mrs Charles) Meredith, *Notes and Sketches of New South Wales during a residence in the colony from 1839 to 1844*, John Murray, London, 1844, p. 36.

6. Walker, op. cit., p. 300.

7. For further information, see Grace Karskens, *The Rocks: Life in Early Sydney*, Melbourne University Press, Melbourne, 1997.

8. S. Fitzgerald & C. Keating, *Millers Point: The Urban Village*, Hale & Iremonger, Sydney, 1991, p. 66.

9. ibid., p. 104.

10. Stephen Davies, 'The price of Walsh Bay', *National Trust Quarterly*, no. 84, July 1997, p. 7.

11. M. Dupain & H. Morton, *Georgian Architecture in Australia: With Some Examples of the post-Georgian Period*, Ure Smith, Sydney, 1963.

CHAPTER TEN

1. For a good glimpse of what Sydney Cove looked like in the early nineteenth century, start this walk at the stone map of Sydney Cove at the southern end of Circular Quay West, near Alfred Street.

2. Anne Robertson, *Treasures of the State Library of New South Wales: The Australiana Collection*, Collins Australia, Sydney, in assoc. with the State Library of New South Wales, 1988, p. 21.

3. *The Australian*, 15 July 1841.

4. J. C. Byrne, *Twelve Years Wanderings in the British Colonies from 1835 to 1847*, in David Latta, *Lost Glories: A Memorial to Forgotten Australian Buildings*, Angus & Robertson, Sydney, 1986.

5. Latta, ibid., p. 72.

6. Lachlan Macquarie, Diary entry, September 1820, Mitchell Library, State Library of New South Wales.

7. John Askew, *A Voyage to Australia & New Zealand Including a Visit to Adelaide, Melbourne, Sydney, Hunter's River, Newcastle, Maitland and Auckland* (1857), in Frank Crowley, *A Documentary History of Australia* (Colonial Australia), vol. 2, Thomas Nelson, Melbourne, 1973–1980, p. 315.

8. Bernard & Kate Smith, *The Architectural Character of Glebe Sydney*, Sydney University Press, 1973, pp. 33–5.

9. P. Bridges & D. McDonald, *James Barnet: Colonial Architect*, Hale & Iremonger, Sydney, c. 1988, pp. 58ff.

10. Ronald Strahan, *Rare and Curious Specimens: An Illustrated History of the Australian Museum*, Australian Museum, Sydney, 1979, p. 35.
11. G. C. Mundy, *Our Antipodes, or, Residence and rambles in the Australian colonies*, vol. 1, 1852, pp. 72–3.
12. *Historical Records of New South Wales*, vol. 6, p. 305.
13. See vol. 9, *Historical Records of Australia*, pp. 734ff, 883 ff.
14. Louisa (Mrs Charles) Meredith, *Notes and Sketches of New South Wales during a residence in the colony from 1839 to 1844*, John Murray, London, 1844, pp. 39ff.
15. P. C. Peck, *Recollections of Sydney* (London : 1850), pp.64ff, in Crowley, op. cit., pp. 157–8.
16. Askew, op. cit., p. 206.
17. For more detailed information on the Royal Botanic Gardens, see Lionel Gilbert, *The Royal Botanic Gardens, Sydney: A History 1816–1985*, Oxford University Press, Melbourne, 1986.
18. Elizabeth Windschuttle, *Taste and Science: The Women of the Macleay Family, 1790–1850*, Historic Houses Trust of New South Wales, Glebe, 1988, pp. 66ff.
19. Helena Scott's letter to Edward Ramsay, 22 October 1862 in Marion Ord (ed.), *Historical Drawings of Native Flowers*, Craftsman House, Sydney, 1988, p. 13.
20. *Sydney Morning Herald*, 23 September 1882.
21. Gilbert, op. cit., p. 108.
22. Gilbert, op. cit., p. 111.
23. N. Gould, *Town and Bush: Stray Notes on Australia*, Routledge, London, 1896, pp. 144ff.
24. Gilbert, op. cit., p. 138.
25. For further information on the Opera House, see Philip Drew, *Sydney Opera House: Jørn Utzon*, Phaidon Press, London, 1995; Commonwealth Dept of Environment, Sports and Territories and the NSW Dept Urban Affairs and Planning, *Sydney Opera House in Its Harbour Setting: Nomination of Sydney Opera House in Its Harbour Setting for Inscription on the World Heritage List by the Government of Australia 1996*, Historic Houses Trust of New South Wales, Glebe, 1996.

CHAPTER ELEVEN

1. Morton Herman, *The Architecture of Victorian Sydney*, Angus & Robertson, Sydney, 1956, p. 7.
2. Kenneth Slessor, 'A Portrait of Sydney', in *Bread and Wine: Selected Prose of Kenneth Slessor*, Angus & Robertson, 1970, p. 8.
3. Herman, op. cit., front paper.
4. City model in Town Hall Offices, City of Sydney, August 1996.
5. Eliza Walker, Eliza Walker, 'Old Sydney in the 1840s', *JRAHS*, vol. 16, p. 315.
6. Slessor, 'The Lane', op. cit., pp. 25–6.
7. *Sydney Morning Herald*, 6 May 1996, p. 16.
8. Michael Christie, *The Sydney Markets 1788–1988*, Sydney Market Authority, Flemington, 1988.
9. Greta Gerathy, 'Sydney Municipality in the 1880s', *JRAHS*, vol. 58, part 1, p. 23.
10. Fitzgerald, S., *Sydney 1842–1992*, (1992), Hale and Iremonger, p. 94.
11. P. Bridges & D. McDonald, *James Barnet: Colonial Architect*, Hale & Iremonger, Sydney, c. 1988.
12. Slessor, 'Portrait of Sydney, op. cit., p. 10.
13. Isadore Brodsky, *The Streets of Sydney*, Old Sydney Free Press, Sydney, 1962.
14. Georgie Swift interview, January 1997.
15. Barbara Salisbury, *The Strand Arcade: A History*, Hale & Iremonger, Sydney, 1990, p. 16.
16. ibid., p. 82.
17. Suzanne D. Rutland, 'The golden age of Sydney's Jewry', in S. Fitzgerald & G. Wotherspoon (eds), *Minorities: Cultural Diversity in Sydney*, State Library of New South Wales, Sydney, in assoc. with the Sydney History Group, 1995, pp. 103 ff.
18. S. Edgar & B. Nairn, *Australian Dictionary of Biography*, vol. 6, p. 82.

CHAPTER TWELVE

1. 'A brief account of the colony of Port Jackson … with an interesting account of the Murder of Mr Clode' by Ensign Bond (1803), Mitchell Library, State Library of New South Wales.
2. Helen Pitt, 'Sydney's alien nation', *Sydney Morning Herald*, 5 June 1996, p. 17.
3. Interview with Henry Tsang, May 1997.

4. Paola Totaro, *Sydney Morning Herald*, 26 July 1995, p. 2.
5. Committee on Treadwheel Labour Report in *Sydney Gazette*, 13 December 1825.
6. C. H. Bertie, *The Story of Sydney*, Shakespeare Head Press, Australia, 1933, pp. 64–65.
7. Shirley Fitzgerald, *Sydney 1842–1992*, Hale & Iremonger, Sydney, c. 1992, p. 208.
8. Helen Proudfoot, 'Sydney changes scale', in Lenore Coltheart, *Significant Sites: History and Public Works in New South Wales*, Hale & Iremonger, Sydney, c. 1989, p. 66.
9. Proudfoot, ibid., p. 62.
10. Proudfoot, ibid., p. 74.
11. P. R. Stephenson, *The History and Description of Sydney Harbour*, Reed, Sydney, 1980, p. 205.

CHAPTER THIRTEEN

1. Kenneth Slessor, 'A Portrait of Sydney', in *Bread and Wine: Selected Prose of Kenneth Slessor*, Angus & Robertson, 1970, pp. 5–6.
2. David Collins, *An Account of the English Colony in New South Wales: With Remarks on the Dispositions, Customs, Manners Etc. of the Native Inhabitants of the Country*, printed for T. Cadell Jun. and W. Davies, London, 1798, pp. 11–12.
3. NSW National Parks and Wildlife Service, *Sydney Harbour National Park: Draft Plan of Management*, Sydney, 1996, p. 2.
4. ibid., p. 12.
5. ibid., p. 65.
6. Graeme Andrews, *The Ferries of Sydney*, Reed, Sydney, 1994, p. 156.
7. ibid., p. 91.
8. Source: Sydney Ferries Public Relations Officer Chris Fullagar, 20 Sept 1996.
9. Collins, op. cit., p. 13.
10. J. S. Kerr, *Fort Denison: An Investigation for the Maritime Services Boards of NSW*, National Trust of New South Wales, Sydney, 1986, p. 12; see also *Fort Denison Draft Conservation Plan*, NSW National Parks and Wildlife Service, October 1995, for historical information on Fort Denison.
11. NSW National Parks and Wildlife Service, *Draft Plan of Management*, pp. 13–14.
12. Bonyhady, Tim, 'Streeton's shriek', *Sydney Morning Herald*, 29 April 1995, Spectrum 8A.
13. ibid.
14. On the history of the resumption of harbour foreshore, see Robin Tranter, 'People's realm: A Sydney Harbour battle', *History (JRAHS)*, no. 43, October 1995, p. 4.
15. Sources: interview with Peter Doyle, 24 June 1997; Peter Doyle, *King Tide: My Life*, William Heinemann Australia, Port Melbourne, 1996.
16. Victor Coppleson, *Shark Attack*, Angus & Robertson, Sydney, 1958, p. 62.
17. ibid., p. 73.
18. Bruce Stannard, *The Blue-Water Bushmen: The Colourful Story of Autsralia's Best and Boldest Boatmen*, Angus & Robertson, Sydney, 1981, p. 32.
19. *Sydney Gazette*, 15 Feb. 1826.

CHAPTER FOURTEEN

1. James Inglis, *Our Australian Cousins: 'Maori'*, Macmillan & Co, London, 1880, p. 142.
2. Shirley Fitzgerald, *Sydney 1842–1992*, Hale & Iremonger, Sydney, c. 1992, p. 211.
3. Phil Wilkins, 'Street wise marshall a real tough customer', *Sydney Morning Herald*, 20 Oct. 1992, p. 44.
4. George Farwell, *Requiem for Woolloomooloo*, Hodder & Stoughton, Sydney, 1971, p. 154.
5. M. T. Daly, *Sydney Boom, Sydney Bust: The City and Its Property Market*, George Allen & Unwin, Sydney, 1982.
6. Fitzgerald, op. cit., p. 296.
7. For more information, see *Final Report of the Royal Commission into the New South Wales Police Service*, vol. 1, ch. 3, Royal Commission into the New South Wales Police Service, Sydney, May 1997.
8. For detailed information on the Nielsen case, *see* Phillip Cornford, 'Juanita's lament', *Sydney Morning Herald*, 1 July 1995, Spectrum section, p. 1.
9. William C. Foster, *Sir Thomas Livingston Mitchell and His World, 1792–1855*, Institution of Surveyors (NSW), Sydney, 1985.
10. Daniel Thomas, article in *Good Weekend*, *Sydney Morning Herald*, 26 June 1993.

11. ibid., p. 32.

12. H. C. Brewster & V. Luther, *King's Cross Calling* (Mastercraft Print & Publishing Co., Sydney)., 1945 (?).

13. Max Kelly, *Faces of the Street: William Street, Sydney 1916*, Doak Press, Paddington, 1982, p. 25.

14. Kelly, ibid., p. 25.

15. Brewster & Luther, ibid., p. 77.

16. Eric Russell, *Woollahra: A History in Pictures*, John Ferguson : Woollahra Municipal Council, Sydney, 1980, p. 100.

17. Mark Seymour, 'Writing minority history: Sources for Italians', in S. Fitzgerald & G. Wotherspoon (eds), *Minorities: Cultural Diversity in Sydney*, State Library of New South Wales, Sydney, in assoc. with the Sydney History Group, 1995, pp. 162–8.

18. For a detailed history on the development of the Sydney gay subculture, please refer to Garry Wotherspoon, *City of the Plain: History of a Gay Sub-Culture*, Hale & Iremonger, Sydney, 1991.

CHAPTER FIFTEEN

1. L. G. Norman, *Historical Notes on Paddington*, Council of the City of Sydney, Sydney, 1961.

2. Max Kelly, *Faces of the Street: William Street, Sydney 1916*, Doak Press, Paddington, 1982, p. 42.

3. Max Kelly, *Paddock Full of Houses: Paddington, 1840–1890*, Doak Press, Paddington, 1978, p. 23.

4. ibid., p. 185.

5. Peter Spearritt, *Sydney since the Twenties*, Hale & Iremonger, Sydney, 1978, p. 24.

6. G. Nesta Griffiths, *Some Houses and People of New South Wales*, Ure Smith, Sydney, 1949, p. 152.

7. ibid., p. 165.

8. Gilbert Mant, *The Big Show*, Horwitz, North Sydney, 1972, pp. 56 & 61.

9. Frank Crowley, *A Documentary History of Australia*, vol. 4, Thomas Nelson, Melbourne, 1973–1980, p. 177.

10. ibid., pp. 177–8.

CHAPTER SIXTEEN

1. Doug Benson & Jocelyn Howell, *Taken for Granted: The Bushland of Sydney and Its Suburbs*, Kangaroo Press, Sydney, in assoc. with the Royal Botanic Gardens, 1990, p. 17.

2. David Collins, *An Account of the English Colony in New South Wales: With Remarks on the Dispositions, Customs, Manners Etc. of the Native Inhabitants of the Country*, printed for T. Cadell Jun. and W. Davies, London, 1798, p. 353.

3. D. R. Hainsworth, *The Sydney Traders: Simeon Lord and His Contemporaries*, Melbourne University Press, Melbourne, 1981, p. 15.

4. Peter Cunningham, *Two Years in New South Wales: Comprising sketches of the actual state of society etc.*, 3rd edn, Henry Colburn, London, 1828, vol. 2, letter XXII.

5. G. Nesta Griffiths, *Some Houses and People of New South Wales*, Ure Smith, Sydney, 1949, p. 107, quoting Governors Despatches in Mitchell Library, 6 August 1832.

6. Gavin Souter, *Mosman: A History*, Melbourne University Press, Melbourne, 1994, pp. 38–41.

7. Peter Spearritt, *Sydney since the Twenties*, Hale & Iremonger, Sydney, 1978, p. 41.

8. Souter, ibid., pp. 285–7.

9. Ronald Strahan, *Beauty and the Beasts: A History of Taronga Zoo, Western Plains Zoo and Their Antecedents*, Zoological Parks Board of New South Wales in assoc. with Surrey Beatty & Sons, Sydney, 1991, pp. 49 ff.

10. Albie Thoms, *Bohemians in the Bush: The Artists' Camps of Mosman* (exhibition catalogue), Art Gallery of New South Wales, Sydney, 1991, p. 39.

11. ibid., p. 45.

12. Ann Galbally & Anne Gray, *Letters from Smike: The Letters of Arthur Streeton, 1890–1943*, Oxford University Press, Melbourne, 1989, p. 187.

13. Jill Roe, 'Three visions of Sydney Heads from Balmoral Beach', in Jill Roe (ed.), *Twentieth Century Sydney: Studies in Urban and Social History*, Hale & Iremonger, Sydney, in assoc. with the Sydney History Group, 1980, p. 91.

14. ibid., p. 102, quoting article in *The Star* by George Arundale.

15. Robert Freestone, 'The garden suburb: The great level of social reform', in Max Kelly (ed.), *Sydney: City of Suburbs*, UNSW Press, Sydney, in assoc. with Sydney History Group, c. 1987, p. 61.

16. L. G. Thorne, *North Shore, Sydney: From 1788 to Today*, Angus & Robertson, Sydney, 1970, p. 168.

17. Joan Lawrence, *Pittwater Paradise*, Kingsclear Books, Crows Nest, c. 1994, pp. 40–1.

18. Jervis Sparks, *Tales from Barranjoey* [sic], J. Sparks, Palm Beach, 1992, p. 181.

19. ibid., pp. 125–128.

20. See further: Sparks, ibid.
21. ibid., p. 67.
22. Paul Ashton, 'Inventing Manly 1853–1890', in Kelly, op. cit., p. 154.
23. Spearritt, op. cit., p. 71.
24. Costin-Nielsen, History of the Manly Art Gallery and Museum, unpublished.
25. Spearritt, op. cit., p. 237.

CHAPTER SEVENTEEN

1. Sources: Australian Bureau of Statistics, *Sydney: A Social Atlas*, Australian Bureau of Statistics, Canberra, 1991 Census; Ethnic Affairs Commission of New South Wales, *The People of New South Wales: Statistics from the 1996 Census*, Sydney, 1991 Census.
2. Doug Benson & Jocelyn Howell, *Taken for Granted: The Bushland of Sydney and Its Suburbs*, Kangaroo Press, Sydney, in assoc. with the Royal Botanic Gardens, 1990, p. 56. This work is of incalculable assistance generally in trying to build a picture of the Sydney region before European settlement.
3. *The Australian*, 11 November 1834.
4. Spearritt, *Sydney since the Twenties*, p. 196.
5. Freestone, Robert, 'The great lever of social reform: The garden suburb 1900–1930', in Max Kelly (ed.), *Sydney: City of Suburbs*, UNSW Press, Sydney, in assoc. with Sydney History Group, c. 1987, p. 62.
6. Peter Spearritt, *Sydney since the Twenties*, Hale & Iremonger, Sydney, 1978, p. 125.
7. Herman, Morton, *The Blackets: An Era of Australian Architecture*, Angus & Robertson, Sydney, 1963, pp. 164–5.
8. ibid., p. 165.
9. Max Solling & Peter Reynolds, *Leichhardt: On the Margins of the City*, Allen & Unwin, Sydney, 1997, p. 224.
10. ibid., p. 226.
11. Hunter's Hill Trust, *Heritage of Hunter's Hill*, Hunter's Hill Trust, Hunter's Hill, 1982, p. 1.
12. Sherry, Beverley, *Hunters Hill: Australia's Oldest Garden Suburb*, David Ell Press, Sydney, 1989, p. 35. This book gives a very good account of the development of Hunters Hill.
13. ibid., p. 3.
14. ibid.
15. Conversation with Rosaleen Tidswell, November 1996. FitzGerald is also the writer's great-uncle.
16. Sources: *Regional Economic Indicators, Parramatta*, vol. 2, issue 2, May 1998, Western Sydney Research Institute, p. 4; *Building a Better Future: Cities for the 21st Century*, NSW Department of Planning, Sydney, 1995, p. 131.
17. Watkin Tench, *A Complete Account of the Settlement at Port Jackson, in New South Wales*, G. Nicol & J. Sewell, London, 1793, p. 197.
18. James Jervis, *The Story of Parramatta and District*, Shakespeare Head Press, Sydney, 1933, p. 12.
19. A. Yarwood, *Australian Dictionary of Biography*, vol. 2, p. 208.
20. W. G. Verge, *John Verge, An Early Australian Architect: His Ledger and His Clients*, Wentworth, Sydney, 1962, pp. 73–4.
21. *Sydney Morning Herald*, 30 May 1961.
22. G. C. Mundy, *Our Antipodes: or, Residence and Rambles in the Australasian Colonies, with a Glimpse of the Gold Fields*, London, 1852, vol. 1, pp. 141–2.
23. Louisa (Mrs Charles) Meredith, *Notes and Sketches of New South Wales during a residence in the colony from 1839 to 1844*, John Murray, London, 1844, pp. 129–33, 153, 155ff.
24. Cumberland County Council, *Historic Buildings: Parramatta*, Cumberland County Council, Parramatta, 1961, p. 32.

CHAPTER EIGHTEEN

1. Cook's First Voyage in George William Anderson, *A New, Authentic and Complete Collection of Voyages Round the World, Undertaken and Performed by Royal Authority* (first voyage), Alex. Hogg, London, 1784–[1786], pp. 60–61.
2. R. Hall, 'Murky waters: The real story of the shark arm murders, *Good Weekend Magazine, Sydney Morning Herald*, 15 July 1995, p. 22; see also A. Castles, *The Shark Arm Murders*, Wakefield Press, Sydney, 1995.
3. Randwick Municipal Council, *Randwick: A Social History*, New South Wales University Press, Sydney, in assoc. with Randwick Municipal Council, 1985, p. 140.
4. Frances Pollon (ed.), *The Book of Sydney Suburbs*, Angus & Robertson, Sydney, 1988, p. 150.
5. D. F. Salt, *Gateway to the South: An Intimate Insight into the Origins of the Sutherland Shire: First Stop Sylvania!*, D. F. Salt, Sutherland, 1987, p. 36.
6. ibid., p. 117.

BIBLIOGRAPHY

Books

Adams, Francis L. W. *Australian Essays*. W. Inglis, Melbourne, 1866.

Aird, W. V. *The Water Supply, Sewerage, and Drainage of Sydney*, Halstead Press, Sydney, 1961.

Albiston, Jordie. *Botany Bay Document: A Poetic History of the Women of Botany Bay*. Black Pepper, North Fitzroy Vic., 1996.

Amery, L. S. *The Empire in the New Era: Speeches Delivered during an Empire Tour 1927–1928*. Edward Arnold & Co., London, 1928.

Ancher, Edward A. *Mosman's Bay: The Romance of an Old Whaling Station*. Wentworth Press, Sydney, in assoc. with Mosman Historical Society, 1976 (first published in 1909).

Anderson, George William. *A New, Authentic and Complete Collection of Voyages Round the World, Undertaken and Performed by Royal Authority* (First Voyage). Alex. Hogg, London, 1784.

Andrews, Graeme. *Port Jackson 200: An Affectionate Look at Sydney Harbour*. Reed, Sydney, 1986.

Andrews, Graeme. *The Ferries of Sydney*. Reed, Sydney, 1994.

Aplin, Graeme & Storey, John. *Waterfront Sydney 1860–1920*. George Allen & Unwin, Sydney, 1984.

Aplin, G. (ed.). *A Difficult Infant: Sydney before Macquarie*, NSW University Press, Sydney, 1988.

Apperly, R., Irving, R. & Reynolds, P. *A Pictorial Guide to Identifying Australian Architecture: Styles and Terms from 1788 to Present*. Angus & Robertson, Sydney, 1989.

Arago, Jacques. *Narrative of a Voyage round the World*. London, 1823.

Arndell, R. M. *Pioneers of Portland Head*. 2nd edn, R. S. Arndell, Epping, 1984.

Ashton, Paul. *Waving the Waratah: Bicentenary New South Wales*. New South Wales Bicentennial Council, Sydney, 1989.

Ashton, Paul. *The Accidental City: Planning Sydney since 1788*. Hale & Iremonger, Sydney, 1993.

Ashton, Paul & Blackmore, Kate. *Centennial Park: A History*, NSW University Press, Sydney, 1988.

Attenbrow, V. J. A Case Study from the Upper Mangrove Creek Catchment, NSW, Australia (in press), esp. table 39(9.4), p. 127.

Attenbrow, V. J. & Steele, D. 'Fishing in Port Jackson, NSW: More than met the eye'. *Antiquity*, vol. 69, no. 262, 1995, p. 47.

Auchmuty, J. J. (ed.). *The Voyage of Governor Phillip to Botany Bay*. Angus & Robertson, Sydney, in assoc. with the Royal Australian Historical Society, 1970.

Australian Dictionary of Biography (vols 1–13). Melbourne University Press, Melbourne.

Baglin, Douglass & Austin, Yvonne. *Sandstone Sydney*. Rigby, Adelaide, 1976.

Baker, H. C. *Historic Buildings: Parramatta*, Cumberland County Council, Parramatta, 1961.

Barker, Anthony. *What Happened When?: A Chronology of Australia from 1788*. Allen & Unwin, Sydney, 1992.

Barnard, Marjorie. *Sydney: The Story of a City*. Melbourne University Press, Melbourne, 1956.

Barrington, George. *The History of New South Wales etc*. Printed for M. Jones, London, 1802.

Beaglehole, J. C. (ed.). *The Journals of Captain James Cook on His Voyages of Discovery* (vol. 1). University Press, Cambridge, in assoc. with the Hakluyt Society, 1968–69.

Beasley, Margo. *The Town Hall: A Social History*. City of Sydney, in assoc. with Hale & Iremonger, Sydney, 1998.

Beatty, Bill. *Tales of Old Australia*. Lifetime Distributors, Australia, 1994.

Benson, D. & Howell, J., *Taken for Granted: The Bushland of Sydney and Its Suburbs*, Kangaroo Press, Sydney, in assoc. with the Royal Botanic Gardens, 1990.

Berndt, Ronald M. & Catherine H. *The World of the First Australians: Aboriginal Traditional Life, Past and Present*. Aboriginal Studies Press for the Australian Institute of Aboriginal Studies, Canberra, 1988.

Bertie, C. H. *The Story of Sydney*. Shakespeare Head Press, Sydney, 1933.

Bertie, C. H. *Old Colonial By-Ways*. Ure Smith, Sydney, in assoc. with the National Trust of Australia (NSW), 1974.

Bertie, C. H. *Stories of Old Sydney*. Angus & Robertson, Sydney, 1912(?).

Bertie, C. H. *The Expansion of Sydney: A March of Progress, 1840–1914*. James R. Tyrrell, Sydney, 1914.

Bertie, C. H. *The Street Names of Early Sydney and Some Street History* (undated, no publisher stated).

Bigge, John Thomas. *Report of the Commissioner of Inquiry into the State of the Colony of New South Wales*. London, 1822.

Bigge, John Thomas. *Report of the Commissioner of Inquiry, on the State of Agriculture and Trade in the Colony of New South Wales* (reprint). Libraries Board of South Australia, Adelaide, 1966.

Birch, Alan & Macmillan, David. *The Sydney Scene 1788–1960*. Melbourne University Press, Melbourne, 1962.

Blainey, Geoffrey. *A Land Half Won*. Macmillan, South Melbourne, 1980.

Blainey, Geoffrey. *The Tyranny of Distance: How Distance Shaped Australia's History*. Pan Macmillan, Sydney, 1991.

Bolton, Geoffrey. *The Oxford History of Australia: The Middle Way, 1942–1995* (vol. 5). Oxford University Press, Melbourne, 1996.

Borrie, W. D. et al. *A White Australia: Australia's Population Problem*, Australasian Publishing Co., Sydney, 1947.

Bowd, B. T. (ed.). *The History of the Waverley Municipal District*. Waverley Municipal Council, Sydney, 1959.

Boyd, Robin. *Australia's Home: Its Origins, Builders and Occupiers*. Melbourne University Press, Melbourne, 1991.

Boyd, Robin. *The Australian Ugliness*. F. W. Cheshire, Melbourne, 1960.

Bradley, William. *A Voyage to New South Wales: The Journal of Lieutenant William Bradley RN of* Sirius*, 1786–1792* (facsimile edition). Trustees of the Public Library of New South Wales, Sydney, in assoc. with Ure Smith, 1969.

Brett, Judith. *Robert Menzies' Forgotten People*. Macmillan Australia, Sydney, 1992.

Brewster, H. C. & Luther, V. *King's Cross Calling*. H. C. Brewster, Sydney (no date).

Bridges, Peter & McDonald, Don. *James Barnet: Colonial Architect*. Hale & Iremonger, Sydney, c. 1988.

Broadbent, James. *The Australian Colonial House: Architecture and Society in New South Wales, 1788–1842*. Horden House, in assoc. with the Historic Houses Trust of New South Wales, Sydney, 1997.

Broadbent, James, Evans, Ian & Lucas, Clive. *The Golden Decade of Australian Architecture: The Work of John Verge*. David Ell Press, Sydney, 1978.

Brodsky, Isadore. *The Streets of Sydney*. Old Sydney Free Press, Sydney, 1962.

Brodsky, Isadore. *Sydney Takes the Stage*. Old Sydney Free Press, Sydney, 1963.

Brodsky, Isadore. *Heart of the Rocks of Old Sydney*. Old Sydney Free Press, Sydney, 1965.

Brodsky, Isadore. *Sydney's Little World of Woolloomooloo*. Old Sydney Free Press, Sydney, 1966.

Broome, R. *Aboriginal Australians: Black Response to White Dominance, 1788–1980*. Allen & Unwin, Sydney, 1982.

Buddee, Eric C. *Birthplace of the Nation: A History of the Rocks*. Pioneer Productions, Toongabbie, 1986.

Burgmann, Verity & Lee, Jenny (eds). *A Most Valuable Acquisition: A People's History of Australia since 1788*, McPhee Gribble/Penguin Books, Melbourne, 1988.

Butler, Kevin, Cameron, Kate & Percival, Bob. *The Myth of Terra Nullius: Invasion and Resistance—The Early Years*. Board of Studies NSW, Sydney, 1995.

Caiger, George (ed.). *A Coast Chronicle: The History of the Prince Henry Hospital*. Halstead Press, Sydney, 1963.

Caley, George. *Reflections on the Colony of New South Wales*. Lansdowne Press, Melbourne, 1966.

Campbell, Eric. *The Rallying Point: My Story of the New Guard*. Melbourne University Press, London, 1965.

Campion, Edmund. *A Place in the City*. Penguin Books, Melbourne, 1994.

Cannon, Michael. *Life in the Cities* (Australia in the Victorian Age, vol. 3). Thomas Nelson, Melbourne, 1975.

Carter, Paul. *The Calling to Come*. Historic Houses Trust of New South Wales, Sydney, 1996.

Cassidy, Elaine et al. (eds). *Impressions of Woollahra: Past and Present*. Allen & Unwin, Sydney, 1988.

Castles, A. *The Shark Arm Murders: The Thrilling Story of a Tiger Shark and a Tattooed Arm*. Wakefield Press, Kent Town, South Australia, 1995.

Cathcart, Michael (abridged by). *Manning Clark's History of Australia*. Melbourne University Press, Melbourne, 1993.

Child, John. *Trees of the Sydney Region*. Cheshire-Lansdowne, Melbourne, 1968.

Christie, Michael. *The Sydney Markets*. Sydney Market Authority, Flemington, 1988.

Christmas, Linda. *The Ribbon and the Ragged Square: An Australian Journey*. Penguin Books, Harmondsworth, 1986.

CityWest Development Corporation. *Doors Were Always Open: Recollections of Pyrmont and Ultimo*. Sydney, 1997.

Clark, C. M. H. (ed.). *Select Documents in Australian History 1851–1900*. Angus & Robertson, Sydney, 1962.

Clark, C. M. H. (ed.). *Select Documents in Australian History 1788–1850*. Angus & Robertson, Sydney, 1965.

Clark, C. M. H. *A History of Australia* (vols 1–6). Melbourne University Press, Sydney, 1962.

Clark, J. H. *Field Sports of the Native Inhabitants of New South Wales*. Edward Orme (J. F. Dove), London, 1813.

Clune, Frank. *Saga of Sydney: The Birth, Growth and Maturity of the Mother City of Australia*. Halstead Press, Sydney, 1961.

Clune, Frank. *Serenade to Sydney: Some Historical Landmarks*. Angus & Robertson, Sydney, 1967.

Cobley, John. *Sydney Cove, 1788*. Hodder & Stoughton, Sydney, 1962.

Cobley, John. *Sydney Cove 1789–1790*. Angus & Roberston, Sydney, 1963.

Cobley, John. *Sydney Cove 1791–1792*. Angus & Roberston, Sydney, 1965.

Cobley, John. *The Crimes of the First Fleet Convicts*. Angus & Robertson, Sydney, 1970.

Coghlan, T. A. *Statistics of the Seven Colonies of Australasia, 1861 to 1987*. Government Printer, Sydney, 1898.

Coghlan, T. A. *Statistical Account of the Seven Colonies of Australasia*. Charles Potter, Sydney, 1894.

Cohen, Eve. *Paddington: Something Old, Something New*. E. Cohen, Sydney, 1989.

Coleman, Peter (ed.). *Australian Civilisation: A Symposium*. F. W. Cheshire, Melbourne, 1962.

Collins, David. *An Account of the English Colony in New South Wales: With Remarks on the Dispositions, Customs, Manners etc. of the Native Inhabitants of the Country*. T. Cadell Jun. & W. Davies, London, 1798.

515

Coltheart, Lenore & Fraser, Don (eds). *Landmarks in Public Works: Engineers and Their Works in New South Wales, 1884–1914*. Hale & Iremonger, Sydney, 1987.

Coltheart, Lenore. *Significant Sites: History and Public Works in New South Wales*. Hale & Iremonger, Sydney, c. 1989.

Coombs, Anne. *Sex and Anarchy: The Life and Death of the Sydney Push*. Viking, Melbourne, 1996.

Corbyn, Charles Adam. *Sydney Revels of Bacchus, Cupid and Momus*. Ure Smith, Sydney, 1970.

Craven, Ian (ed.). *Australian Popular Culture*. Cambridge University Press, Cambridge, 1994.

Cronin, Leonard. *Key Guide to Australian Mammals*. Reed, Sydney, 1991.

Crowley, F. K. *A Documentary History of Australia* (vols 1–5). Thomas Nelson, Melbourne, 1973–1980.

Crowley, F. K. *A New History of Australia*. William Heinemann, Melbourne, 1974.

Cunningham, Peter. *Two Years in New South Wales: A Series of Letters* (vols 1 & 2). Henry Colburn, London, 1827.

Curson, P. H. *Times of Crisis: Epidemics in Sydney, 1788–1900*. Sydney University Press, Sydney, 1985.

Daly, M. T. *Sydney Boom, Sydney Bust: The City and Its Property Market*. George Allen & Unwin, Sydney, 1982.

D'Apulget, Lou. *Yachting in Australia: From Colonial Skiffs to America's Cup Defence*. Collins, Sydney, 1986.

Dark, J. O. (principal author). *Trees and Shrubs for Eastern Australia* (rev. edn). New South Wales University Press, Sydney, 1986.

Davidson, Jim (ed.). *The Sydney–Melbourne Book*. Allen & Unwin, Sydney, 1986.

Davies, Simon. *The Islands of Sydney Harbour*. Hale & Iremonger, Sydney, 1984.

Davison, Graeme & McConville, Chris. *A Heritage Handbook*. Allen & Unwin, Sydney, 1991.

Day, David. *Claiming a Continent: A History of Australia*. Angus & Robertson, Sydney, 1996.

De Vries-Evans, Susanna. *Historic Sydney as Seen by its Early Artists*. Angus & Robertson, Sydney, 1983.

Debenham, Frank. *The Voyage of Captain Bellingshausen to the Antarctic Seas 1819–21*. Printed for the Hakluyt Society, London, 1945.

DeMarco, Christine, Riera, Brian & Spearritt, Peter. *Aird's Guide to Sydney*. Airds Books, Melbourne, 1991.

Dennis, C. J. *The Songs of a Sentimental Bloke*. Angus & Robertson, Sydney, 1916.

Department of Environment, Sports and Territories & NSW Department of Urban Affairs and Planning. *Sydney Opera House in its Harbour Setting: Nomination of Sydney Opera House in its Harbour Setting for Inscription on the World Heritage List by the Government of Australia 1996*. Historic Houses Trust of New South Wales, Sydney, 1996.

Digby, Everard (ed.). *Australian Men of Mark*. Charles F. Maxwell, Sydney, 1889(?).

Dirks, Jo. *Sydney Downtown*. Kangaroo Press, Sydney, 1993.

Docker, John. *The Nervous Nineties: Australian Cultural Life in the 1890s*. Oxford University Press, Melbourne, 1991.

Doyle, Peter. *King Tide: My Life*. William Heinemann Australia, Port Melbourne, 1996.

Drew, Philip. *Sydney Opera House: Jørn Utzon*. Phaidon Press, London, 1995.

Drewe, Robert et al. *Bondi*. James Fraser Publishing, Surry Hills, 1984.

Dunstan, Keith. *Wowsers*. Cassell Australia, Melbourne, 1968.

Dunstan, Keith. *The Perfect Cup: The Story of Coffee*. David Ell Press, Sydney, 1989.

Dupain, Max & Morton, Herman. *Georgian Architecture in Australia*. Ure Smith, Sydney, 1963.

Dysart, Dinah & Proudfoot, Helen. *Lindesay: A Biography of the House*. National Trust of Australia, Sydney, 1984.

Eakin, Robin. *Aunts up the Cross*. Macmillan, South Melbourne, 1980.

Emmett, Peter. *Fleeting Encounters: Pictures and Chronicles of the First Fleet*. Historic Houses Trust, Sydney, 1995.

Eldershaw, M. Barnard. *The Life and Times of Captain John Piper*, Ure Smith, Sydney, in assoc. with the National Trust of Australia (NSW), 1973.

Elliott, Brian & Mitchell, Adrian (eds). *Bards in the Wilderness: Australian Colonial Poetry to 1920*. Nelson, Melbourne, 1970.

Ellis, Jean A. *From the Dreamtime: Australian Aboriginal Legends*. HarperCollins, Melbourne, c. 1991.

Ellis, Jean A. *This is the Dreaming: Australian Aboriginal Legends*, CollinsDove, Melbourne, 1994.

Ellis, M. H. *John Macarthur*. Angus & Robertson, Sydney, 1955.

Ellis, M. H. *Francis Greenway: His Life and Times*. Angus & Robertson, Sydney, 1959.

Ellyard, D. & Wraxworthy, R. *The Proud Arch: The Story of the Sydney Harbour Bridge*, Bay Books, Sydney, 1982.

Ellyard, David. *Droughts and Flooding Rains: The Weather of Australia*. Angus & Robertson, Sydney, 1994.

Evans, Ian. *The Australian Home*, Flannel Flower Press, Sydney, 1983.

Evatt, H. V. *Rum Rebellion: A Study of the Overthrow of Governor Bligh by John Macarthur and the New South Wales Corp*. Angus & Robertson, Sydney, 1938.

Fahey, Warren. *When Mabel Laid the Table: The Folklore of Eating and Drinking in Australia*. State Library of NSW Press, Sydney, 1992.

Fairley, Alan. *A Field Guide to Sydney Bushland*. Rigby, Adelaide, 1976.

Fairley, Alan. *Sydney's Best Bushland Walks*. Envirobooks, Sydney, 1993.

Farwell, George, *Requiem for Woolloomooloo*, Hodder & Stoughton, Sydney, 1971.

516

Fitzgerald, Ross & Hearn, Mark. *Bligh, Macarthur and the Rum Rebellion*. Kangaroo Press, Sydney, 1988.

Fitzgerald, Shirley & Keating, Christopher. *Millers Point, the Urban Village*. Hale & Iremonger, Sydney, 1991.

Fitzgerald, Shirley & Wotherspoon, Garry (eds). *Minorities: Cultural Diversity in Sydney*. State Library of NSW Press, Sydney, 1995.

Fitzgerald, Shirley. *Rising Damp: Sydney 1870–90*. Oxford University Press, Melbourne, 1987.

Fitzgerald, Shirley. *Sydney 1842–1992*. Hale & Iremonger, Sydney, 1992.

Fitzhardinge, L. F. *That Fiery Particle, 1862–1914: A Political Biography* (vol. 1). Angus & Robertson, Sydney, 1964.

Fitzhardinge, L. F. (ed.). *Sydney's First Four Years*. Library of Australian History, Sydney, in assoc. with the Royal Australian Historical Society, 1979.

Fitzsimmons, Portia. *Eastern Suburbs Album*. Atrand, Sydney, 1985.

Flannery, Tim. *The Future Eaters: An Ecological History of the Australasian Lands and People*. Reed Books, Sydney, 1994.

Flood, Josephine, *Archaeology of the Dreamtime: The Story of Prehistoric Australia and its People*, Collins Australia, Sydney, 1989.

Flower, Cedric. *The Antipodes Observed: Artists of Australia, 1788–1850*. Sun Books, Melbourne, 1975.

Foster, A. G. *Early Sydney*. Tyrrell's, Sydney, 1920.

Fowler, F. *Southern Lights and Shadows*. Sampson Low, London, 1859.

Fowles, Joseph. *Sydney in 1848*. Ure Smith, Sydney, 1962 (facsimile edition).

Freeland, J. M. *Architecture in Australia: A History*. F.W. Cheshire, Melbourne, 1968.

Freeland, J. M. *Architect Extraordinary: The Life and Work of J. Horbury Hunt, 1838–1904*. Cassell Australia, Melbourne, 1970.

Freudenberg, Graham. *Cause for Power: The Official History of the New South Wales Branch of the Australian Labor Party*. Pluto Press, Sydney, 1991.

Frost, Alan. *Botany Bay Mirages: Illusions of Australia's Convict Beginnings*. Melbourne University Press, Melbourne, 1994.

Froude, J. A. *Oceana: or, England and Her Colonies*. Longmans, Green & Co., London, 1886.

Gerstaecker, F. *Narrative of a Journey round the World, Comprising a Winter-Passage across the Andes to Chile, with a Visit to the Gold Regions of California and Australia, the South Sea Islands, Java etc*. London, 1853.

Gamble, A. & Souter, N. *Around the Quay: Sketches of Sydney Cove and The Rocks*. Craftsman's Press, Sydney, 1989.

Gibson, Ross (ed.). *Exchanges: Cross-Cultural Encounters in Australia and the Pacific*. Historic Houses Trust of New South Wales, Sydney, 1996.

Giese, Diana. *Beyond Chinatown: Changing Perspectives on the Top End Chinese Experience*. National Library of Australia, Canberra, 1995.

Gilbert, Lionel. *The Royal Botanic Gardens, Sydney: A History 1816–1985*. Oxford University Press, Melbourne, 1986.

Gill, Lydia. *My Town: Sydney in the 1930s*. State Library of NSW Press, Sydney, 1993.

Gould, N. *Town and Bush: Stray Notes on Australia*. Routledge, London, 1896.

Grant, Jacqueline. *Jonah's: A History from 1928*. Jacqueline Grant, Sydney, 1995.

Gray, Robert & Smith, Vivian (eds). *Sydney's Poems: A Selection on the Occasion of the City's One Hundred and Fiftieth Anniversary 1842–1992*. Primavera Press, Sydney, 1992.

Greenwood, Gordon (ed.). *Australia: A Social and Political History*. Angus & Robertson, Sydney, 1955.

Groom, Barry & Wickman, Warren. *Sydney, the 1850s: The Lost Collections*. Macleay Museum, University of Sydney, Sydney, 1982.

Hackforth-Jones, Jocelyn, *The Convict Artists*, Macmillan, South Melbourne, 1977.

Hainsworth, D. R. *The Sydney Traders: Simeon Lord and His Contemporaries, 1788–1821*. Cassell Australia, Melbourne, 1972.

Hall, Humphrey & Cripps, Alfred J. *The Romance of the Sydney Stage*. Currency Press, Sydney, in assoc. with the National Library of Australia, 1996.

Hardy, Bobbie. *Early Hawkesbury Settlers*. Kangaroo Press, Sydney, 1985.

Hart, Deborah. *John Olsen*. Craftsman House, Sydney, 1991.

Haskell, John. *Sydney Architecture*. University of NSW Press, Sydney, 1997.

Henderson, Gerard. *Menzies' Child: The Liberal Party of Australia 1944–1994*. Allen & Unwin, Sydney, 1994.

Herman, Morton. *The Early Australian Architects and Their Work*. Angus & Robertson, Sydney, 1954.

Herman, Morton. *The Architecture of Victorian Sydney*. Angus & Robertson, Sydney, 1956.

Herman, Morton. *The Blackets: An Era of Australian Architecture*. Angus & Robertson, Sydney, 1963.

Hickie, Thomas. *They Ran with the Ball: How Rugby Football Began in Australia*. Longman Cheshire, Melbourne 1993.

Hillier, Rob. *A Place Called Paddington*. Ure Smith, Sydney, 1970.

Hindwood, K. A. & McGill, A. R. *The Birds of Sydney*. Royal Zoological Society of NSW, Sydney, 1958.

Hirst, John. *The Strange Birth of Colonial Democracy: New South Wales 1848–1884*. Allen & Unwin, Sydney, 1988.

Historical Records of Australia. Library Committee of the Commonwealth Parliament, Sydney, 1914–1925.

Historical Records of New South Wales. Government Printer, Sydney, 1982–1901.

Hoorn, Jeanette. *The Lycett Album: Drawings of Aborigines and Australian Scenery*. National Library of Australia, Canberra, 1990.

Horne, Donald. *The Lucky Country*. 4th edn, Penguin Books, Melbourne, 1971.

Horvath, Ronald, Harrison, Grahame & Dowling, Robyn. *Sydney: A Social Atlas*. Sydney University Press, Sydney, 1989.

Howard, R. *The Story of Sydney's George Street*. View Productions, Sydney, 1984.

Howie, Ann C. (ed.). *Who's Who in Australia*. Information Australia, Melbourne, 1990.

Hubble, Ava. *The Strange Case of Eugene Goossens and Other Tales from the Opera House*. Collins, Sydney, 1988.

Hughes, Robert. *The Fatal Shore: A History of the Transportation of Convicts to Australia, 1787–1868*. Collins Harvill, London, 1987.

Hughes, Robert. *The Art of Australia*. Penguin, Melbourne, 1970.

Huie, Jacqueline. *Untourist Sydney: An Insider's Guide to the Best Places to Stay, Things to See, Do, Eat and Buy*. UnTourist Co., Sydney, 1995.

Hunter, John. *An Historical Journal of the Transactions at Port Jackson and Norfolk Island*. Printed for John Stockdale, London, 1793.

Hunter's Hill Trust. *Heritage of Hunter's Hill*. Hunter's Hill Trust, Sydney, 1969.

Ingleton, Geoffrey C. *True Patriots All, or, News from Early Australia as Told in a Collection of Broadsides*. Angus & Robertson, Sydney, 1952.

Inglis, James. *Our Australian Cousins*. Macmillan & Co., London, 1880.

Irvin, Eric. *Sydney as It Might Have Been: Dreams that Died on the Drawing Board*. Alpha Books, Sydney, 1974.

Irving, Robert, Kinstler, John & Dupain, Max. *Fine Houses of Sydney*. Methuen Australia, Sydney, 1982.

Jahn, Graham. *A Guide to Sydney Architecture*. Watermark Press, Sydney, 1997.

Jennings, Guy & Jennings, Joan. *My Holiday and Other Early Travels from Manly to Palm Beach 1861*. Aramo, Sydney, 1991.

Jervis, James. *The Cradle City of Australia: A History of Parramatta, 1788–1961*. Halstead Press, Sydney, 1961.

Jervis, James. *The Story of Parramatta and District*. Shakespeare Head Press, Sydney, 1933.

Jose, Arthur W. *The Romantic Nineties*. Angus & Robertson, Sydney, 1933.

Jupp, J. (ed.). *Ethnic Politics in Australia*. Allen & Unwin, Sydney, 1984.

Jupp, J. (ed.). *The Australian People: An Encyclopaedia of the Nation, Its People and Their Origins*, Angus & Robertson, Sydney, 1988.

Karskens, Grace. *The Rocks: Life in Early Sydney*. Melbourne University Press, Melbourne, 1997.

Keating, Christopher. *Surry Hills: The City's Backyard*. Hale & Iremonger, Sydney, 1991.

Kelly, Max (ed.). *Nineteenth-Century Sydney*. Sydney University Press, Sydney, 1978.

Kelly, Max. *Paddock Full of Houses: Paddington 1840–1890*. Doak Press, Sydney, 1978.

Kelly, Max (ed.). *Sydney: City of Suburbs*. NSW University Press, Sydney, 1987.

Kelly, Max. *Plague Sydney 1900*. Doak Press, Sydney, 1981.

Kelly, Max. *Anchored in a Small Cove: A History and Archaeology of The Rocks*, Sydney Cove Authority, Sydney, 1997.

Kelly, P. *The End of Certainty: The Story of the 1980s*. Allen & Unwin, Sydney, 1992.

Kennedy, Brian & Kennedy, Barbara. *Sydney and Suburbs: A History and Description*. Reed, Sydney, 1982.

Kerr, J. S. *Cockatoo Island: Penal and Institutional Remains*. National Trust of Australia (NSW), Sydney, 1984.

Kerr, J. S. *Fort Denison: An Investigation for the Maritime Services Board of NSW*. National Trust of Australia (NSW), Sydney, 1986.

Kerr, Jill and Broadbent, James. *Gothick Taste in the Colony of New South Wales*. David Ell Press, Sydney, 1980.

Kerr, Joan & Falkus, Hugh. *From Sydney Cove to Duntroon: A Family Album of Early Life in Australia*. Victor Gollancz, London, 1982.

Kingsmill, John. *Australia Street: A Boy's-Eye View of the 1920s and 1930s*. Hale & Iremonger, Sydney, 1991.

Kingston, Beverley. *The Oxford History of Australia: Glad, Confident Morning 1869–1900*. Oxford University Press, Melbourne, 1988.

Kirkpatrick, Peter. *The Sea Coast of Bohemia: Literary Life in Sydney's Roaring Twenties*. University of Queensland Press, Brisbane, 1992.

Kohen, James. *The Darug and Their Neighbours*, Blacktown and District Historical Society, Blacktown, 1993.

Kohen, James. *Aboriginal Environmental Impacts*. University of NSW Press, Sydney, 1995.

Kukathas, Chandran (ed.). *Multicultural Citizens: The Philosophy of Politics and Identity*. The Centre for Independent Studies, Australia, 1993.

Landman, Peta & Bogle, Michael. *Sydney Museums Guide*. Kingsclear Books, Sydney, 1992.

Lang, J. T. *I Remember*. Invincible Press, Australia, 1956.

Lang, J. T. *The Great Bust: The Depression of the Thirties*. McNamara's Books, Australia, 1962.

Lang, John Dunmore. *An Historical and Statistical Account of New South Wales*. vols 1 & 2, Sampson Low, Marston, Low & Searle, London, 1875.

Latta, David. *Lost Glories*. Angus & Robertson, Sydney, 1986.

Lawrence, Joan. *Pictorial Memories of St George, Rockdale, Kogarah and Hurstville*, Kingsclear Books, Sydney, 1986.

Lawrence, Joan. *Pittwater Paradise*. Kingsclear Books, Sydney, 1994.

Lees, Stella & Senyard, June. *The 1950s: How Australia Became a Modern Society and Everyone Got a House and Car*. Hyland House, Melbourne, 1987.

Lester Tropman & Assoc. *Masterplan and Plan of Management for Macquarie Place, 1990*. Lester Tropman & Associates, Sydney, 1990.

Lindsay, Norman. *Bohemians of the Bulletin*. Angus & Robertson, Sydney, 1965.

Lowenstein, Wendy. *Weevils in the Flour: An Oral Record of the 1930s Depression in Australia*. Hyland House, Melbourne, 1979.

Lynch, W. B. & Larcombe, F. A. *Randwick 1859–1959*. Oswald Ziegler Publications, Sydney, 1959.

Macintyre, Stuart. *The Oxford History of Australia: The Succeeding Age 1901–1942*. Oxford University Press, Australia, 1986.

Mackaness, George. *Blue Bloods of Botany Bay*. Collins, Sydney, 1953.

Mackaness, George. *The Life of Vice-Admiral William Bligh*. Angus & Robertson, Sydney, 1931.

Mant, Gilbert. *The Big Show*. Horwitz Publications, Sydney, 1972.

Markus, Andrew. *Governing Savages*. Allen & Unwin, Sydney, 1990.

Martin, A. W. *Henry Parkes: A Biography*, Melbourne University Press, Melbourne, 1980.

Martin, A. W. *Robert Menzies: A Life.* vol. 1, Melbourne University Press, Melbourne, 1993.

Martin, G. (ed.). *The Founding of Australia: The Argument about Australia's Origins*. Hale & Iremonger, Sydney, 1978.

Matthews, Phillip. *Ku-ring-gai: Living with Trees*. Currawong Press, Sydney, 1978.

McCarter, Jim. *These People Lived*. The Worker Newspaper, Brisbane, 1944.

McCormick, Tim. *First Views of Australia 1788–1825*. David Ell Press, Sydney, 1987.

McGill, Jeff, Fowler, Verlie & Richardson, Keith. *Campbelltown's Streets & Suburbs*. Campbelltown and Airds Historical Society, Campbelltown, 1995.

McGrath, Sandra. *Brett Whiteley*. Bay Books, Sydney, 1979.

McKenna, A. & Thompson, J. *Family Bush Walks in and around Sydney*. Lothian Books, Australia, 1992.

Meader, Chrys, Cashman, Richard & Carolan, Anne. *Marrickville: People and Places*. Hale & Iremonger, Sydney, 1994.

Meredith, Louisa (Mrs Charles). *Notes and Sketches of New South Wales during a Residence in the Colony from 1839 to 1844*. John Murray, London, 1844.

Messent, David. *The Rocks: Sydney's Birthplace*. David Messent Photography, Sydney, 1995.

Miller, James. *Koori: A Will to Win*. Angus & Robertson, Sydney, 1985.

Moore, David (text by Rodney Hall). *Sydney Harbour*. Chapter and Verse, in assoc. with State Library of New South Wales Press, Sydney, 1993.

Moore, Ivy. *Glimpses of Old Sydney and NSW*. Dey, Sydney, 1945.

Moorehead, Alan. *The Fatal Impact: The Invasion of the South Pacific 1767–1840*. Hamish Hamilton, London, 1966.

Morris, Jan. *Sydney*. Viking/Penguin Books, London, 1992.

Morton-Evans, Michael. *The Australian Book of Lists*. Simon & Schuster, Sydney, 1994.

Mourot, Suzanne. *This Was Sydney: A Pictorial History from 1788 to the Present Time*. Ure Smith, Sydney, 1969.

Mudie, James. *The Felonry of New South Wales*. Whaley & Co., London, 1837.

Mulvaney, D. J. & White, J. P. (eds). *Australians to 1788* (Australian: A Historical Library). Fairfax, Syme & Weldon, Sydney, 1987.

Mundy, G. C. *Our Antipodes: or, Residence and Rambles in the Australasian Colonies, with a Glimpse of the Gold Fields*. vols 1–3, Richard Bentley, London, 1852.

Murphy, Brian. *The Other Australia: Experiences of Migration*. Cambridge University Press, Melbourne, 1993.

Murray, Alec. *Alec Murray's Album: Personalities of Australia*. Ure Smith, Sydney, 1948 (?).

Murray, Les. *Collected Poems*. William Heinemann Australia, Australia, 1994.

Museum of Sydney. *Sydney Vistas: Panoramic Views 1799–1995*. Historic Houses Trust, Sydney, 1995.

Nagarajan, Vijay. *Australian Law through 200 Years*. Kangaroo Press, Sydney, 1989.

Nairn, Bede. *The 'Big Fella': Jack Lang and the Australian Labor Party 1891–1949*. Melbourne University Press, Melbourne, 1986.

Nashar, Beryl. *Geology of the Sydney Basin*. Jacaranda Press, Australia, 1967.

Nesta Griffiths, G. *Some Homes and People of NSW*, Ure Smith, Sydney, 1949.

Nesta Griffiths, G. *Point Piper Past and Present*. Ure Smith, Sydney, 1970.

Neville, Richard. *A Rage for Curiosity: Visualising Australia 1788–1830*. State Library of NSW Press, Sydney, 1997.

New South Wales Environment Centre. *Aspects of Sydney Harbour: Vaucluse and Watsons Bay*. Sydney, 1965.

O'Brien, John. *On Darlinghurst Hill*. Ure Smith, Sydney, 1952.

O'Brien, Lesley. *Mary MacKillop Unveiled*. CollinsDove, Melbourne, 1994.

O'Callaghan, Judith (ed.). *The Australian Dream: Design of the Fifties*. Powerhouse Publishing, Sydney, 1993.

O'Hara, James. *The History of New South Wales*. Printed for J. Hatchard, London, 1817.

Palmer, Vance. *The Legend of the Nineties*. Melbourne University Press, Melbourne, 1963.

519

Park, Ruth. *The Companion Guide to Sydney*. Collins, Sydney, 1973.

Parkes, Henry. *Fifty Years of the Making of Australian History*. Longman, Green & Co., London, 1892.

Parkinson, Sydney. *Journal of a Voyage to the South Seas in His Majesty's Ship, the Endeavour*, Printed for Charles Dilly … and James Phillips, London, 1784.

Paterson, Andrew Barton. *The Collected Verse of A. B. Paterson*. Angus & Roberston, Sydney, 1921.

Pearce, Barry. *William Dobell, 1899–1970: The Painter's Progress*. Art Gallery of New South Wales, Sydney, 1977.

Pearce, Barry. *Brett Whiteley Art & Life*. Art Gallery of New South Wales, Sydney, 1995.

Pearce, Barry & Slutzkin, Linda. *Bohemians in the Bush: The Artists' Camps of Mosman*. Art Gallery of New South Wales, Sydney, 1991.

Pearl, Cyril. *Brilliant Dan Deniehy: A Forgotten Genius*. Thomas Nelson, Australia, 1972.

Pearl, Cyril. *Wild Men of Sydney*. W. H. Allen, London, 1958.

Pearson, Margaret Mary. *Tales of Rowe Street*. Angus & Robertson, Sydney, 1947.

Phelan, Nancy. *Mosman Impressions*. Mosman Municipal Council, Sydney, 1993.

Phillips, V. *Watson's Bay Sketchbook*. Rigby, Adelaide, 1973.

Plater, D. *Other Boundaries: Inner City Aboriginal Stories*. Leichhardt Council, Sydney, 1993.

Plimer, Elizabeth & Errey, Ellen. *A House Re-Born: The Story of William Swann of Elizabeth Farm House, Parramatta*. E. M. Plimer, Sydney, 1991.

Pollon, Frances (ed.). *The Book of Sydney Suburbs*. Cornstalk Publishing, Sydney, 1996.

Porter, Peter (ed.). *The Oxford Book of Modern Australian Verse*, Oxford University Press, Australia, 1996.

Porter, Peter. *Sydney*. Time Life Books, Amsterdam, 1980.

Pringle, John Douglas. *Australian Accent*. Chatto & Windus, London, 1958.

Protos, Alec. *The Road to Botany Bay: The Story of Frenchman's Road, Randwick, through the Journals of La Pérouse and the First Fleet Writers*. Randwick and District Historical Society, Sydney, 1988.

Proudfoot, Peter. *Seaport Sydney*. University of NSW Press, Sydney, 1996.

Rade, Heather & Spearritt, Peter. *Jack Lang*, Hale & Iremonger, Sydney, 1977.

Randwick Council. *Randwick: A Social History*. University of NSW Press, Sydney, 1985.

Reece, R.H.W. *Aborigines and Colonists: Aborigines and Colonial Society in New South Wales in the 1830s and 1840s*. University of Sydney Press, Sydney, 1974.

Reed, A.W. *Myths & Legends of Australia*. A. H. & A. W. Reed, New Zealand, 1965.

Rees, Lloyd. *Lloyd Rees: An Artist Remembers*. Craftsman House, Sydney, 1987.

Reynolds, Henry. *Dispossession: Black Australians and White Invaders*. Allen & Unwin, Sydney, 1989.

Reynolds, Henry. *The Other Side of the Frontier*. Penguin Books, Melbourne, 1981.

Reynolds, Henry. *Frontier*. Allen & Unwin, Sydney, 1987.

Reynolds, Henry. *The Law of the Land*. Penguin Books, Melbourne, 1987.

Reynolds, Henry. *The Whispering in Our Hearts*. Allen & Unwin, Sydney, 1998.

Rich, E. *Goat Island Archaeological Survey and Assessment of Aboriginal Sites*. Maritime Services Board of NSW, Sydney, 1985.

Ritchie, J. *Lachlan Macquarie*. Melbourne University Press, Melbourne, 1986.

Ritchie, John (ed.). *The Evidence to the Bigge Reports*. vols 1 & 2, William Heinemann, Australia, 1971.

Ritchie, John. *Punishment and Profit*. vols 1 & 2, William Heinemann, Australia, 1970.

Robertson, Anne. *Treasures of the State Library of New South Wales: The Australiana Collections*. Collins, Sydney, 1988.

Roddewig, Richard. *Green Bans: The Birth of Australian Environmental Politics*. Allan, Osmun & Co., Sydney, 1978.

Roe, Jill (ed.). *Twentieth Century Sydney: Studies in Urban and Social History*. Hale & Iremonger, Sydney, 1980.

Roberts, Kenneth. *Captain of the Push: When a Larrikin Chief Ruled The Rocks*. Lansdowne Press, Melbourne, 1963.

Rowse, Tim. *After Mabo: Interpreting Indigenous Traditions*. Melbourne University Press, Melbourne.

Rudé, George. *Protest & Punishment*. Oxford University Press, Oxford, 1978.

Ruhen, Olaf & White, Unk. *The Rocks Sydney*. Rigby, Adelaide, 1966.

Russell, Eric. *Victorian and Edwardian Sydney from Old Photographs*. John Ferguson, Sydney, 1975.

Russell, Eric, *Woollahra: A History in Pictures*, John Ferguson, Sydney, 1980.

Russell, Eric. *The Opposite Shore: North Sydney and Its People*. John Ferguson, Sydney, 1990.

Rutledge, Helen. *My Grandfather's House: Recollections of an Australian Family*. Doubleday, Sydney, 1986.

Salisbury, Barbara. *The Strand Arcade*. Hale & Iremonger, Sydney, 1990.

Salt, D. F. *Gateway to the South: An Intimate Insight into the Origins of the Sutherland Shire: First Stop Sylvania!*. Daphne Salt, Sutherland, 1987.

Schedvin, C. B. *Australia and the Great Depression*. Sydney University Press, Sydney, 1970.

Scott, Geoffrey. *Sydney's Highways of History*. Georgian House, Melbourne, 1958.

Serle, Geoffrey. *The Creative Spirit in Australia: A Cultural History*. William Heinemann, Australia, 1973.

Sharpe, Alan. *Manly to Palm Beach*. Atrand, Sydney, 1983.

Shaw, A.G.L. *Convicts and the Colonies: A Study of Penal Transportation from Great Britain and Ireland to Australia and Other Parts of the Empire*. Melbourne University Press, Melbourne, 1977.

Sherington, G. *Australia's Immigrants*. Allen & Unwin, Sydney, 1990.

Sherry, Beverley. *Hunters Hill: Australia's Oldest Garden Suburb*. David Ell Press, Sydney, 1989.

Simpson, Margaret. *Old Sydney Buildings: A Social History*. Kangaroo Press, Sydney, 1995.

Sinclair, Keith. *A History of New Zealand* (rev. edn). Penguin Books, Auckland, 1988.

Slessor, Kenneth. *Poems*. Angus & Robertson, Sydney, 1944.

Slessor, Kenneth. *Bread and Wine*. Angus & Robertson, Sydney, 1970.

Slessor, Kenneth & Reilly, Virgil. *Darlinghurst Nights*. Angus & Robertson, Sydney, 1971.

Smith, Arthur Stanley. *Neddy: An Autobiography with Tom Noble*. Kerr Publishing, Sydney, 1993.

Smith, Bernard. *European Vision and the South Pacific*. Harper & Row, Sydney, 1984.

Smith, Bernard & Smith, Kate. *The Architectural Character of Glebe*. Sydney University Press, Sydney, 1973.

Smith, Keith Vincent. *King Bungaree*. Kangaroo Press, Sydney, 1992.

Smith, M. P. *Sydney Opera House: How It Was Built and Why It Is So*. Collins, Sydney, 1984.

Smith, Ure & Stevens, Bertram. *Domestic Architecture in Australia*. Ure Smith, Sydney, 1919.

Solling, Max & Reynolds, Peter. *Leichhardt: On the Margins of the City*. Allen & Unwin, 1997.

Souter, G. & Molnar, G. *Sydney Observed*. Angus & Robertson, Sydney, 1968.

Souter, Gavin. *Mosman: A History*. Melbourne University Press, Melbourne, 1994.

Sparks, Jervis. *Tales from Barranjoey*. Jervis Sparks, Palm Beach, 1992.

Spearritt, Peter, *Sydney since the Twenties*, Hale & Iremonger, Sydney, 1978.

Spearritt, P. *The Sydney Harbour Bridge*. George Allen & Unwin, Sydney, 1982.

Spearritt, Peter & DeMarco, Christina. *Planning Sydney's Future*. Allen & Unwin, Sydney, 1988.

Spence, Peter. *Sydney by Public Transport* (3rd edn). Gary Allen, Sydney, 1989.

Stanbury, Peter (ed.). *10,000 Years of Sydney Life*. University of Sydney, Sydney, 1980.

Stannard, Bruce. *Blue-Water Bushmen*. Angus & Robertson, Sydney, 1981.

Steege, Joan (ed.). *Palm Beach 1788–1988*. Palm Beach Association, Sydney, 1984.

Steketee, Mike & Cockburn, Milton. *Wran: An Unauthorised Biography*. Allen & Unwin, Sydney, 1986.

Stephens, Bertram. *The Charm of Sydney*. Angus & Robertson, Sydney.

Stephens, Tony & O'Neill, Annette. *Larrikin Days*. Macarthur Press, Sydney, 1983.

Stephensen, P. R. *The History and Description of Sydney Harbour*. Rigby, Adelaide, 1966.

Stewart, Douglas. *A Man of Sydney: An Appreciation of Kenneth Slessor*. Thomas Nelson, Australia, 1977.

Stockdale, John. *The Voyage of Governor Phillip to Botany Bay*. John Stockdale, London, 1889.

Stone, Louis. *Jonah*. Endeavour Press, Sydney, 1911.

Strahan, Ronald. *Rare and Curious Specimens*. Australian Museum, Sydney, 1979.

Strahan, Ronald. *Beauty and the Beasts*. Zoological Parks Board, 1991.

Struckmeyer, H. I. M. & Totterdell, J. M. (eds). *Australia: Evolution of a Continent*. Australian Government Publishing Service, Canberra, 1992.

Stuart, Geoff. *Secrets in Stone*. Brandname Properties, Sydney, 1993.

Suburbs. Kangaroo Press, Sydney, 1990.

Sudjic, Deyan. *The 100 Mile City*. Flamingo/HarperCollins, London, 1993.

Sydney (Eyewitness Travel Guide), Dorling Kindersley, London, 1996.

Tamis, Anastasios. *An Illustrated History of the Greeks in Australia*. Latrobe University, Melbourne, 1997.

Taylor, Griffith. *Sydneyside Scenery*. Angus & Robertson, Sydney, 1958.

Tench, W. *A Narrative of the Expedition to Botany Bay*. Printed for J. Debrett, London, 1789.

Tench, W. *A Complete Account of the Settlement at Port Jackson, in New South Wales*. G. Nicol & J. Sewell, London, 1793.

Thompson, Elaine. *Fair Enough: Egalitarianism in Australia*. University of NSW Press, Sydney, 1993.

Thorne, Les G. *North Shore Sydney: From 1788 to Today* (2nd edn). Angus & Robertson, Sydney, 1970.

Townsend, Helen. *Baby Boomers: Growing up in Australia in the 1940s, 50s and 60s*. Simon & Schuster, Sydney, 1988.

Troy, Jackelin. 'By slow degrees we began … to understand each other', *Exchanges: Cross-cultural Encounters in Australia and the Pacific*. Historic Houses Trust of New South Wales, 1996, p. 49.

Troy, P. (ed.). *Australian Cities, Issues, Strategies and Policies for Urban Australia in the 1990s*. Cambridge University Press, 1995.

Turbet, Peter. *The Aborigines of the Sydney District before 1788*. Kangaroo Press, Sydney, 1989.

Turnbull, John. *A Voyage round the World in the Years 1800, 1801, 1802, 1803, and 1804* (2nd edn). A. Maxwell, London, 1813.

Turner, Ian. *Sydney's Burning*. Heinemann, Melbourne, 1967.

Turner, R. & Rodger, R. *In the Shadow of a Gaol*. Platypus Pacific Film and Television, Sydney, 1990 (video).

Twain, Mark. *Following the Equator: A Journey around the World*. American Publishing Co., Hartford, 1897.

Twopeny, Richard. *Town Life in Australia*. Penguin, Melbourne, 1976.

Underwood, A. J. & Chapman, M. G. *Seashores: A Beachcomber's Guide*, NSW University Press, Sydney, 1993.

Tyrrell, James R. *Old Books, Old Friends, Old Sydney*. Angus & Robertson, Sydney, 1952.

Vaux, James Hardy. *Memoirs of James Hardy Vaux*. Hunt & Clarke, London 1827.

Verge, W.G. *John Verge: His Ledger and His Clients*. Wentworth Books, Sydney, 1962.

Vialoux, A. & Reeves, C. M. *Leichhardt, Its History and Progress*. Sydney, 1921.

Walker, J. *Two Hundred Years in Retrospect: Kurnell-Sutherland 1770–1970* (2nd edn). Sydney, 1970.

Ward, Russell. *Australia since the Coming of Man*. Mead & Beckett Publishing, Sydney, 1987.

Ward, Russell. *The Australian Legend*. Oxford University Press, Melbourne, 1958.

Warne, Catherine. *Lower North Shore*. Atrand, Sydney, 1984.

Waterhouse, Richard. *Private Pleasures, Public Leisure*. Longman Australia, Melbourne, 1995.

Watling, Thomas. *Letters from an Exile at Botany Bay to his Aunt at Dumfries*.

Watson, J. A. (ed.). *Beyond Architecture: Marion Mahony and Walter Burley Griffin*. Powerhouse Museum, Sydney, 1998.

Waverley Municipal Council. *Waverley: A Celebration of Waverley' 125th Year*. Waverley Municipal Council, Sydney, 1984.

Webber, Peter. *The Design of Sydney*. Law Book Company, Sydney, 1988.

Wentworth, W. C. *A Statistical Account of the British Settlements in Australasia*. vols 1 & 2, Shackell and Arrowsmith, London, 1824.

White, John. *Journal of a Voyage to New South Wales*. J. Debrett, London, 1840.

White, Mary E. *After the Greening*. Kangaroo Press, Sydney, 1994.

White, Patrick. *The Vivisector*. Vintage/Random House, London, 1970.

White, Unk & Scriber, Charles. *Sydney Harbour Sketchbook*. Rigby, Australia, 1968.

Wilkie, Meredith. *The Survival of the Aboriginal Family in New South Wales 1788–1981*. Family and Children's Services Agency Aboriginal Children's Research Project, Sydney, 1982.

Willard, Myra. *History of the White Australia Policy*. Melbourne University Press, Melbourne, 1923.

Willey, Keith. *When the Sky Fell down*. Collins, Sydney, 1979.

Williams, Matthew. *Australia in the 1930s*. Trocadero Publishing, Sydney, 1985.

Willmot, Eric. *Pemulwuy: The Rainbow Warrior*. Weldon, Sydney, 1987.

Wills, Colin. *Rhymes of Sydney*. Pylon Press, Sydney, 1982.

Wilson, Edwin (ed.). *Discovering the Domain*. Hale & Iremonger, Sydney, 1986.

Wilson, Edwin. *The Wishing Tree.*, Kangaroo Press, Sydney, 1992.

Windschuttle, Elizabeth. *Taste and Science: The Macleay Women*. Historic Houses Trust, Sydney, 1988.

Winston, Denis. *Sydney's Great Experiment: The Progress of the Cumberland County Plan*. Angus & Robertson, Sydney, 1957.

Woollahra History and Heritage Society. *Watsons Bay: A Walk back in Time*. Sydney, 1987.

Wotherspoon, Garry (ed.). *Sydney's Transport: Studies in Urban History*. Hale & Iremonger, Sydney, 1983.

Wotherspoon, Garry. *City of the Plain*. Hale & Iremonger, Sydney, 1991.

Guides, Booklets and Reports

An Illustrated Guide to Sydney. Gibbs, Shallard & Co., 1882.

Art Gallery of New South Wales Handbook, Sydney, 1988.

Benson, D. H. & Howell, J. *Sydney Bushland: Two Centuries of Change*. Royal Botanic Gardens, Sydney, 1988.

Blacklock, Lorna. *Short Tours of Old Sydney*. Royal Australian Historical Society, Australia, 1965.

Bringing them Home. Report of the National Inquiry into the Separation of Aboriginal and Torres Strait Islander Children from Their Families, Human Rights and Equal Opportunity Commission, Commonwealth of Australia, Canberra, 1997.

Buhrich, Libby. *Bushwalks and Picnics around Sydney*. Sally Milner Publishing, Sydney, 1991.

Burnswoods, Jan & Fletcher, Jim. *Sydney and the Bush*. NSW Department of Education, Sydney, 1980.

Cadman's Cottage Historic Site: Plan of Management. NSW National Parks & Wildlife Service, Sydney, 1995.

Census: Characteristics of New South Wales. Australian Bureau of Statistics (cat. no. 2710.1), Canberra, 1991.

Climate of Australia. Bureau of Meteorology, Australia, 1989.

Cumberland County Council. *Central Area of Sydney* (Historic Buildings). vol. 2, Sydney, 1962.

Cumberland County Council. *Liverpool and Campbelltown* (Historic Buildings). vol. 3, Sydney, 1963.

Department of Defence. *Cockatoo Island, Sydney Harbour, New South Wales, Australia: Invitation to Register Interest to Purchase*.

Department of Planning. *Building a Better Future: Cities for the 21st Century*. Sydney, 1995.

Department of Urban Affairs and Planning. *Planning Parramatta River: Guide to the Draft Parramatta River Reaches Report*. Sydney, 1996.

Department of Urban Affairs and Planning. *Sydney as a Global City: A Discussion Paper*. Sydney, 1996.

Ethnic Affairs Commission. *The People of New South Wales: Guide to the 1991 Census.*

Flynn, Christine. *Bookshops of Sydney.* Primavera Press, Sydney, 1987.

Fox and Associates. *Homebush Bay Conservation Study.* Department of Environment and Planning, Sydney, 1986.

Historic Houses Trust of New South Wales. *A Walk around the Cross: The Villas of Woolloomooloo Hill.* Historic Houses Trust, Sydney, 1980.

Hyde Park Barracks. Angus & Robertson/State Planning Authority of NSW, Sydney, 1965.

Lawrence, Joan. *Sydney from Circular Quay.* Hale & Iremonger, Sydney, 1987.

Lawrence, Joan. *Sydney from the Rocks.* Hale & Iremonger, Sydney, 1988.

Lawrence, Joan. *Sydney Good Walks Guide.* Kingsclear Books, Sydney, 1991.

Lawrence, Joan. *Balmain, Glebe and Annandale Walks.* Hale & Iremonger, Sydney, 1992.

Lawrence, Joan. *Eastern Suburbs Walks,* Hale & Iremonger, Sydney, 1993.

Lawson, Henry. *The Flour Bin.* Talkarra Press for the Book Collectors' Society, Sydney, 1955.

Lord, Stephen & Daniel, George (eds). *Bushwalks in the Sydney Region.* vols 1 & 2, National Parks Association, Sydney, 1989.

Matthews, Anne. *Thomas Cook Travellers: Sydney & New South Wales.* AA Publishing, UK, 1993.

McDougall, Garry. *Heritage Walks in New South Wales.* Kangaroo Press, Australia, 1992.

Messent, David *Seven Days in Sydney.* David Messent Photography, Sydney, 1993.

Messent, David. *The Complete Guide to Sydney Harbour.* David Messent Photography, Sydney, 1994.

National Trust of Australia (NSW). *The Tank Stream Tour.* Sydney, 1989.

New South Wales: Its Present State and Future Prospects. D. Walter, London, 1837.

Paddington: Its History, Trade and Industries. Paddington Municipal Council, Sydney, 1910.

Paton, Neil. *Walks in the Sydney Harbour National Park.* Kangaroo Press, Sydney, 1987.

The People of New South Wales. Ethnic Affairs Commission, Sydney, 1991.

Proudfoot, Helen. *Cadman's Cottage: Sydney Cove's Oldest Building.* Proudfoot Press, Sydney, 1988.

Rayner, Michael & Grausm, Philip. *Sydney since the Opera House: An Architectural Walking Guide.* Royal Australian Institute of Architects, Sydney, 1990.

Ross, Valerie. *A Hawkesbury Story.* Library of Australian History, Sydney, 1989.

Spindler, Graham. *Walking the Lower North Shore: From North Sydney to the Lane Cove River.* Kangaroo Press, Sydney, 1989.

State Planning Authority of NSW. *Windsor and Richmond* (Historic Buildings). Sydney, 1967.

Sydney Harbour Bridge: Official Souvenir & Programme. Alfred James Kent, Sydney, 1932.

Sydney Ports Handbook. Sydney Ports Corporation, 1996.

Thorn, Julia. *Seeing Sydney by Bicycle.* Kangaroo Press, Sydney, 1990.

Walks in the City. Sydney's Engineering Heritage Committee.

Waugh, James William. *The Stranger's Guide to Sydney.* Sydney, 1861.

Yeomans, J. *A Guide to the Sydney Opera House.* Sydney, 1977.

Reports

City of Sydney Corporate Plan 1966–1999.

Department of Planning. *Sydney and Middle Harbours: Sydney Regional Environmental Plan No. 23 & Design and Management Guidelines.* Sydney, 1990.

Department of Urban Affairs and Planning. *Demographic Change in New South Wales and Its Implications.* Sydney, 1995.

Department of Urban Affairs and Planning. *State of the Region: A Review of Recent Trends and Their Strategic Planning Implications for the Sydney-Newcastle-Wollongong Greater Metropolitan Region in 1995.* Sydney, 1996.

Department of Urban Affairs and Planning. *Sydney Region Local Government Areas 1991–2021* (1995 revision). Sydney, 1995.

Environmental Performance for the Sydney Olympics (Green Games Watch 2000). Sydney, 1996.

Farrell, Denis. *Sydney: A Social Atlas* (1991 Census). Australian Bureau of Statistics, Canberra, 1993.

Heritage Council of NSW. *1995 Annual Report.* Sydney, 1995.

Myer, Andrew. *Millennium Park: Legacy of the Sydney Olympics* (Green Games Watch 2000). Sydney, 1996.

Department of Planning. *Islands Study: An Environmental Study of Fort Denison, Rodd, Clark and Goat Islands.* Sydney, 1992.

Department of Transport. *Integrated Transport Strategy for the Greater Metropolitan Region.* Sydney, 1995.

New South Wales Legislative Council. *Cockatoo Island: Report from the Board of Enquiry into the Management of Cockatoo Island NSW.* Sydney, 1858.

New South Wales Parliamentary Select Committee. *Report: The Condition of the Working Classes of the Metropolis.* Sydney, 1860.

Sydney City Council. *Accessible City: An Integrated Strategy for Central Sydney.* Sydney.

Sydney Cove Redevelopment Authority. *Annual Report 1996.* Sydney, 1996.

Sydney Cove Redevelopment Authority. *Susannah Place 1844: A Museum in the Making.* Sydney, 1993.

Sydney Cove Redevelopment Authority. *The Rocks: Sydney's Original Village.* Sydney, 1988.

Sydney Region Growth & Change: Prelude to a Plan. State Planning Authority of NSW, Sydney, 1967.

Sydney's Future: A Discussion Paper on Planning the Greater Metropolitan Region. 1993.

Sydney's Green Belt. Cumberland County Council, 1963.

Urban Australia: Trends and Prospects (Research Report No. 2). Australian Urban and Regional Development Review, Canberra, 1995.

West Rocks: Action Plan 29. City Planning & Building Department, Council of City of Sydney, 1976.

Journals, Magazines and Periodicals

The Australian

The Bulletin

Australian Town and Country Journal

Daily Telegraph

Empire

History: Magazine of the Royal Australian Historical Society

Illustrated Sydney News

Journal of the Royal Australian Historical Society

National Trust Quarterly

Sands Sydney and Suburban Directory

Smith's Weekly

South Asian Register

Sun-Herald

Sydney Gazette

Sydney Herald

Sydney Institute, The Sydney Papers

The Sydney Mail

Sydney Morning Herald

INDEX

527

528

531

533

PICTURE CREDITS

p. x—© David Moore, David Moore Photography

CHAPTER 1 p. 3—Fairfax Photo Library; p. 9—Fairfax Photo Library; p. 16—Image Library, State Library of New South Wales; p. 19—'Circular Quay', engraving, *Illustrated Sydney News*, 28 March 1874, Image Library, State Library of New South Wales.

CHAPTER 2 p. 24—'Portrait of Bennelong', engraving, c. 1800, Image Library, State Library of New South Wales; p. 44—Image Library, State Library of New South Wales; p. 45—Image Library, State Library of New South Wales; p. 49—Brendon Read/*Sydney Morning Herald*, Fairfax Photo Library; p. 52—'Eveleigh Street: Aborigines in Redfern Today', © Mark Tedeschi, Image Library, State Library of New South Wales.

CHAPTER 3 p. 57 (left)—Engraved portrait of Arthur Phillip, frontispiece to *The Voyage of Governor Phillip to Botany Bay: With an Account of the Establishment of the Colonies of Port Jackson and Norfolk Island* (1789), Image Library, State Library of New South Wales; p. 57 (right)—'Sydney Cove, Port Jackson, in the County of Cumberlnd, New South Wales, July 1788', Image Library, State Library of New South Wales; p. 62—Engraved portrait of John Macarthur, Image Library, State Library of New South Wales; p. 67—'Plan de la ville de Sydney' (1802), by C. A. Lesueur, in *Voyage de decouvertes aux Terres Australes* (1811), Image Library, State Library of New South Wales; p. 72—'Vue de la Partie Meridionale de Sydney' (1803), by C. A. Lesueur, in *Voyages de decouvertes aux Terres Australes* (1811), Image Library, State Library of New South Wales.

CHAPTER 4 p. 80—'Plan of the Town and suburbs of Sydney, August 1822', Image Library, State Library of New South Wales; p. 84—'George Street from the wharf', engraving by John Carmichael, in *Select Views of Sydney, New South Wales* (1829), Image Library, State Library of New South Wales; p. 88—Engraved portrait of Caroline Chisholm, frontispiece to Mackensie, E., *Memoirs of Mrs Caroline Chisholm* (1852), Image Library, State Library of New South Wales.

CHAPTER 5 p. 104—Charles Henry Kerry, Tyrrell Collection, National Library of Australia; p. 113—Coogee Beach, bathers and bathing machines, engraving, c. 1880, Image Library, State Library of New South Wales; p. 120 (left)—Image Library, State Library of New South Wales; p. 120 (right)—Image Library, State Library of New South Wales; p. 131 (left)—Image Library, State Library of New South Wales; p. 131 (right)—Cover of *Boomerang*, 25 February 1888, Image Library, State Library of New South Wales.

CHAPTER 6 p. 135—Image Library, State Library of New South Wales; p. 144 (top)—Image Library, State Library of New South Wales; p. 144 (bottom)—Image Library, State Library of New South Wales; p. 147—Image Library, State Library of New South Wales; p. 149—Image Library, State Library of New South Wales; p. 154 (left)—Image Library, State Library of New South Wales; p. 154 (right)—Image Library, State Library of New South Wales; p. 165—Image Library, State Library of New South Wales; p. 167 (top)—Image Library, State Library of New South Wales; p. 167 (bottom)—Image Library, State Library of New South Wales.

CHAPTER 7 p. 170—Image Library, State Library of New South Wales; p. 180—Daily Sun, Fairfax Photo Library; p. 185—Image Library, State Library of New South Wales; p. 189—ACP Publishing.

CHAPTER 8 p. 193—Roger Scott, Fairfax Photo Library; p. 198—Robert Pearce/*Herald News*, Fairfax Photo Library; p. 200—Ian Lever/Australian Tourist Commission; p. 202—S. H. Golding/*Sun-Herald*, Fairfax Photo Library; p. 210—Asian immigrants at Cabramatta, © Mark Tedeschi, Image Library, State Library of New South Wales.

CHAPTER 9 p. 218—Album: Old Sydney 1901, National Library of Australia; p. 221—Henry King, Tyrrell Collection, National Library of Australia; p. 224—C. H. Kerry, Tyrrell Collection, National Library of Australia; p. 227 (top)—Image Library, State Library of New South Wales; p. 227 (bottom)—Image Library, State Library of New South Wales; p. 234—Image Library, State Library of New South Wales; p. 241—Image Library, State Library of New South Wales; p. 247—© David Moore, David Moore Photography; p. 248—Image Library, State Library of New South Wales.·

CHAPTER 10 p. 252—N. E. Brown, Fairfax Photo Library; p. 254—Marcus Clinton; p. 257—Fairfax Photo Library; p. 260—Image Library, State Library of New South Wales; p. 277—Image Library, State Library of New South Wales.

CHAPTER 11 p. 284 (top)—Tyrrell Collection, National Library of Australia; p. 284 (bottom)—Tyrrell Collection, National Library of Australia; p. 291 (left)—C. H. Kerry, Tyrrell Collection, National Library of Australia; p. 291 (right)—Image Library, State Library of New South Wales; p. 294 (top)—Image Library, State Library of New South Wales; p. 294 (bottom)—Robert Pearce/*Sydney Morning Herald*, Fairfax Photo Library; p. 301 (left)—Fairfax Photo Library; p. 301 (right)—C. H. Kerry, Tyrrell Collection, National Library of Australia.

CHAPTER 12 p. 307—Fairfax Photo Library; p. 311—© David Moore, David Moore Photography; p. 313—C. H. Kerry, Tyrrell Collection, National Library of Australia; p. 314—C. H. Kerry, Tyrrell Collection, National Library of Australia; p. 317—Robert Pearce/*Sydney Morning Herald*, Fairfax Photo Library.

CHAPTER 13 p. 323—'Vaucluse Bay, Port Jackson, Sydney', engraving in Wallis, J., *Historical Account of the Colony of New South Wales, 1821*, Image Library, State Library of New South Wales; p. 326—Australian Tourist Commission; p. 336—C. H. Kerry, Tyrrell Collection, National Library of Australia; p. 339—'Hippocampus', engraving by T. L. Busby after a drawing by G. Perry, Image Library, State Library of New South Wales.

CHAPTER 14 p. 351—Fairfax Photo Library; p. 353—Image Library, State Library of New South Wales; p. 356—Image Library, State Library of New South Wales; p. 365—'Attempted escape of Prisoners from Darlinghurst Gaol', *Illustrated Sydney News*, 16 November 1884, Image Library, State Library of New South Wales; pp. 336–7—Oxford Street by night, engraving, c. 1880, Image Library, State Library of New South Wales; p. 369—Image Library, State Library of New South Wales.

CHAPTER 15 p. 383—Image Library, State Library of New South Wales; p. 388—Image Library, State Library of New South Wales; p. 399—Image Library, State Library of New South Wales.

CHAPTER 16 p. 402—Kylie Pickett/*Sydney Morning Herald*, Fairfax Photo Library; p. 406—Image Library, State Library of New South Wales; p. 409—C. H. Kerry, Tyrrell Collection, National Library of Australia; p. 410—Image Library, State Library of New South Wales; p. 416—Tyrrell Collection, National Library of Australia; p. 422—Tyrrell Collection, National Library of Australia; p. 432—Henry King, Tyrrell Collection, National Library of Australia; p. 435—'Christmas in Australia', engraving, *Illustrated Sydney News*, 16 December 1865, Image Library, State Library of New South Wales; p. 436—Henry King, Tyrrell Collection, National Library of Australia.

CHAPTER 17 p. 438—Robert Pearce/*Sydney Morning Herald*, Fairfax Photo Library; p. 450—Fairfax Photo Library; p. 455—Stevens/Sydney Morning Herald, Fairfax Photo Library; p. 458—Fairfax Photo Library; p. 461—Burke, Fairfax Photo Library; p. 474 (top)—Fairfax Photo Library; p. 474 (bottom)—Greg White/*Sydney Morning Herald*, Fairfax Photo Library.

CHAPTER 18 p. 476—Peter Morris/*Sydney Morning Herald*, Fairfax Photo Library; p. 483—Image Library, State Library of New South Wales; p. 485—C. H. Kerry, Tyrrell Collection, National Library of Australia; p. 488—Fairfax Photo Library; p. 490—Peter Rae/*Sydney Morning Herald*, Fairfax Photo Library; p. 493—Fairfax Photo Library; p. 494—S. J. Hood, Fairfax Photo Library; p. 497—Peter Rae/*Sydney Morning Herald*, Fairfax Photo Library.